Contents

How to Use This Book

General categories are listed in the table of contents; for more specific information on what is included in the book, use the index.

Unless otherwise noted, all shops are OPEN Monday–Saturday, CLOSED Sunday. To save space, abbreviations have been used for the days of the week and for the months.

Small shops, if in busy shopping areas, usually conform to the policies of their larger neighbors; the hours of the department stores are listed, as the only major change occurs during the Christmas shopping season, when they are all open every evening. Others conform to the eccentricities of their area of town. If unsure, call ahead.

Where a shop or restaurant accepts credit cards, the following key is used:

AE	American Express
CB	Carte Blanche
DC	Diners' Club
MC	Master Charge
V	Visa

I LOVE NEW YORK

GUIDE
New Edition

Marilyn J. Appleberg

Illustrated by
Albert Pfeiffer

COLLIER BOOKS
Macmillan Publishing Company
New York

COLLIER MACMILLAN PUBLISHERS
London

The Manhattan street map reprinted at the back of this book is reproduced with permission of the Hagstrom Map Company, Inc. Copyright Hagstrom Map Company, Inc., New York, No. 1161.

The New York City subway map, also at the back of the book, is reproduced with permission of the New York City Transit Authority, copyright New York City Transit Authority.

Macmillan Publishing Company
866 Third Avenue, New York, N.Y. 10022
Collier Macmillan Canada, Inc.

Library of Congress Cataloging-in-Publication Data
Appleberg, Marilyn J.
  I love New York guide.
  Includes index.
  1. New York (N.Y.)—Description—1981-   —Guide-
books. I. Title.
F128.18.A79 1985   917.47′10443   85-20929
ISBN 0-02-097230-X

Macmillan books are available at special discounts for bulk purchases for sales promotions, premiums, fund-raising, or educational use. For details, contact:
Special Sales Director
Macmillan Publishing Company
866 Third Avenue
New York, N.Y. 10022
Second Revised Edition 1986

10 9 8 7 6 5 4 3 2 1

Printed in the United States of America

Introduction

New York! It's the ultimate urban experience—reviled by those who hate it but revered by those who love it (a distinct majority).

More than anything else New York is a city of superlatives, a place where the best, the brightest, the biggest is the norm. That's what comes of having world-class theater, music, museums and galleries. Add to this an even longer agenda of world-renowned shops and restaurants, and you know why it's a magnet for tourists and why its natives are so fiercely proud.

But remember that New York has always been defined by its diversity, so after you have done the expected—the Met, the Modern, Mad Ave and Lincoln Center, the Empire State Building and on and off Broadway theater—then go exploring.

See a tiger in the Bronx, visit a Tibetan temple on Staten Island, sail the East River on a 70-foot yawl, have a drink beneath the clouds at Windows on the World, eat a meal in Chinatown, then cross the "border" into Little Italy for a pastry (or vice versa), walk across the Brooklyn Bridge and gaze back at the picture-postcard-perfect view of what this native New Yorker knows to be the greatest city in the world.

If I could I would take every visitor to the city by the hand and show him or her my New York—this book is the next best thing; as for natives, it was written for me and, by extension, for them. It is intended to make your relationship with New York, whether you are a visitor or a native, more than it could otherwise be—to know New York is to love New York, and this book is dedicated to that end.

Basic Information

Helpful Hints

Manhattan is an island, a mere 13.4 miles long, and at its widest, 2.3 miles. Its grid pattern layout makes getting around an easy task. Avenues run north and south, with Fifth Avenue the divider between the East and West sides of the island (the lower the house address, be it East or West, the closer it is to Fifth Avenue). Broadway, a former wagon trail, is the grand exception to the rule—it cuts diagonally through Manhattan as it moves downtown from the West to the East side. As it intersects other avenues on its way downtown, Broadway creates Columbus Circle, Times Square, Herald Square, Madison Square, and Union Square. Streets in Manhattan run east or west and ascend in numerical order as one travels north.

Downtown areas of the city, roughly below West 14 Street and East 1 Street, were settled before the grid system and follow no particular pattern. These are among the city's oldest districts and include the Financial District, the Seaport, Greenwich Village and Chinatown. A good map, a knowledgeable guide, or a fearless reliance on serendipity is recommended.

See Manhattan Address locater, page 3. NOTE: Sixth Avenue and Avenue of the Americas are used interchangably.

Weather

New York has four distinct seasons, and a visit during any one of them will have its own character. Spring and fall offer moderate temperatures; the summer average is 75°F (23°C) with fairly high humidity, and the winter temperatures often hover near 32°F (0°C). But remember that indoor temperatures are often the opposite of outdoor—very cool in summer (air conditioning) and warm in winter (central heating). Therefore layering of clothing is best; dress for comfort.

Getting Around

New York's mass-transit system is extensive and efficient. Subways offer speed but can offend the eye and ear. Buses offer a view while you are getting to your destination at a slower pace. Taxis can be expensive during rush-hour traffic jams and elusive during rainstorms, but a blessing when your feet hurt.

Caveat

First, about the city. Common sense *must* prevail regarding where you go and at what time you go there. Specifics: Secure your wallet or purse, do not flaunt cash or gold jewelry and under no circumstances play 3-card monte—a shell game with cards—it's for suckers.

Second, about the book. New York is ever-moving, ever-changing, ever-growing—that's what makes it so special. It's also what makes the city so difficult to document. Though at press time all information contained herein is correct, changes will surely take place. Phone numbers are included and it is recommended always to call ahead.

Tourist Information Centers

These are the main information sources for tourists about places, events, or travel.

New York Convention and Visitors Bureau
2 Columbus Circle at West 59 Street & Broadway. 397-8222. The bureau will answer questions, provide guides and maps in 6 languages, tickets for TV shows, discount coupons for theater tickets and a current list of the city's hotel rates and major attractions. OPEN Mon-Fri 9am-6pm; Sat, Sun & Holidays 10am-6pm.

New York State Department of Commerce
230 Park Avenue at East 46 Street, Room 866. 309-0560. Information on tour packages in the city and statewide vacation and recreational activities. These are the creators of "I ♥ New York." OPEN Mon-Fri 9am-5pm.

Times Square Information Center
207 West 43 Street. 397-8222. Information on shows, tickets, and goings-on in the theater district. OPEN Mon-Fri 9am-6pm; Sat, Sun & Holidays 10am-6pm.

Travelers Aid
207 West 43 Street. 944-0013. A nationwide service which helps robbery victims, lost persons, wayward children. Works closely with the police. OPEN Mon-Fri 8:30am-6:30pm. In summer, Sat & Sun 9:30am-3pm as well. Also at Kennedy Airport, International Arrivals Building, (1-718)656-4870. OPEN year round Mon-Fri 10am-10pm; Sat & Sun 3-10pm.

Parking

Street parking in Manhattan, if you can find a spot, is subject to a variety of restrictions, always posted. Meter street parking ranges from 20 minutes to 1 hour. Be sure to read the signs carefully: your car may be ticketed or towed away if illegally parked; both can be expensive and troublesome.
Municipal Garages
    Eighth Avenue & West 52 Street
    Leonard Street at Lafayette Street

Delancey Street at Essex Street
Park Row & Pearl Street
Washington Street & Greenwich Avenue
In addition, there are hundreds of private parking facilities in Manhattan, with costs varying according to location and time of day and week. Always check the closing times or you may be left without your car till morning.

Manhattan Address Locator

To locate avenue addresses, take the address, drop the last figure, divide by 2, add or subtract the number indicated below. The answer is the nearest numbered cross street.

To find addresses on numbered cross streets, remember—numbers increase east or west from Fifth Avenue, which runs north-south.

Ave. A, B, C & D	Add 3
1st Ave & 2nd Ave.	Add 3
3rd Ave.	Add 10
4th Ave.	Add 8
5th Ave.	
Up to 200	Add 13
Up to 400	Add 16
Up to 600	Add 18
Up to 775	Add 20
From 775 to 1286 drop last figure and subtract 18	
Up to 1500	Add 45
Above 2000	Add 24
Ave. of the Americas	Sub. 12
7th Ave.	Add 12
Above 110th St.	Add 20
8th Ave.	Add 10
9th Ave.	Add 13
10th Ave.	Add 14
Amsterdam Ave.	Add 60
Audubon Ave.	Add 165
Broadway (23 to 192 Sts.)	Subt. 30
Columbus Ave.	Add 60
Convent Ave.	Add 127
Central Park West	Divide
house number by 10 and add 60	
Edgecombe Ave.	Add 134
Ft. Washington Ave.	Add 158
Lenox Ave.	Add 110
Lexington Ave.	Add 22
Madison Ave.	Add 26
Manhattan Ave.	Add 100
Park Ave.	Add 35
Pleasant Ave.	Add 101
Riverside Drive	Divide
house number by 10 and add 72 up to 165th Street	
St. Nicholas Ave.	Add 110
Wadsworth Ave.	Add 173
West End Ave.	Add 60

Bus & Subway Information

Information and directions to anywhere by sub-

way or bus available 24 hours a day, 7 days a week. Call (1-718) 330-1234.

Buses
Fare $1. Half fare for senior citizens and handicapped at all times.
Exact change or tokens only, no bills, pennies or 50¢ pieces. Bus stops are marked with signs on red, white, and blue stanchions that display approximate time schedules and route maps. There are yellow lines on the curb. Glass-enclosed bus shelters are provided at many stops.
Board the front of the bus and deposit fare, exit in the rear. Smoking is not allowed. Animals (except Seeing Eye dogs or pets in carrying cases) are not permitted to travel on buses.
Most buses run 24 hours, 7 days a week, albeit on reduced schedules in non-peak hours and days.

Free Transfers
If you wish to transfer from an uptown or downtown bus to a crosstown bus, or vice versa, ask the bus driver for a free transfer upon boarding.

Long-Distance & Commuter Buses
George Washington Bus Terminal: 564-1114.
Greyhound: 635-0800.
Port Authority Bus Terminal: 564-8484.
Trailways: 730-7460.

Subways
Fare $1. Free return coupons for senior citizens and handicapped, good for three days.
Tokens must be purchased for entry. Token-booth operator can supply you with a free subway map and information. He can make change up to a $20.00 bill only. If you plan on using public transportation, buy a supply of tokens to save time. Buses also take subway tokens.
There is only one train class on the subway. Smoking is not allowed in the station or on the train. Animals (except Seeing Eye dogs or pets in carrying cases) are not permitted to travel on trains. Subway trains run 24 hours a day, 7 days a week, although on reduced schedules in non-peak hours and days.

Staten Island Rapid Transit
Fare $1. Train information on Staten Island 24 hours a day, 7 days a week. Call (1-718) 447-8601.

PATH (Hudson Tubes)
Fare $1. Trains to and from New Jersey. Information 24 hours a day, 7 days a week. In N.Y. 466-7649; N.J. (1-201) 963-2558.

Taxis

Taxicabs are easily available in New York City, except perhaps during peak rush hours and in the rain. Simply walk to the curb and extend your arm. Taxis are yellow; a lighted sign indicates it's available. Off-duty taxis will not stop. When you want to be sure, calling for one is best. All those listed work 7 days a week, 24 hours a day.

All City Radio Taxi: 796-1111.
Dial-a-Cab: (1-718) 743-8383.
Ding-a-Ling: 691-9191.
Minute Men: 899-5600.
Scull's Angels: 457-7777.
XYZ: 685-3333.

Railroad Information

For long-distance rail travel:
Amtrak: 736-4545.
Harlem, Hudson, New Haven (Grand Central): 532-4900.
Long Island Railroad (Penn Station): 739-4200.

Telephone Services

Emergency: Dial 911
Area Codes
Manhattan and Bronx: 212
Brooklyn, Queens & Staten Island: 1-718
Telephone Information
Manhattan & Bronx: 411
Brooklyn, Queens & Staten Island: (1-718) 555-1212.
Operator Assistance: 0
Out-of-Town: 1 + area code + 555-1212
International Calls
Many countries can now be direct dialed. Dial 0 (operator) for information concerning the code number of a particular country. Otherwise have the operator assist in placing the call.
Pay Telephones
25¢ for the first 3 minutes. Information is free.
Telegrams
(For variations on the traditional; see SHOPPING, Specialty Shops & Services: Telegrams: Unusual.)
Western Union
Mailgram, Telegram, Worldwide Cablegram: 1-800 257-2441.
RCA Global Communications
806-7000.
Recorded Services
Children's Story: 976-3636.
Dial-a-Joke: 976-3838.
Dow Jones Report: 976-4141.
Free Daily Events in the City: 755-4100.
Hayden Planetarium Sky Report: 873-0404.
Inspiration, Mrs. Norman Vincent Peale: 532-2266.
Jazz-Line: (1-718) 465-7500.
Kennedy Airport Parking Conditions: (1-718) 495-5400.
Lottery and Lotto Winners: 976-2020.
OTB Results: 976-2121.
Newsphone: 976-1111.
Parks Department Information: 472-1003.
PATH Train Service Information: 732-8920.
Ski Conditions, N.Y.S.: 755-8100.
Sportsphone: 976-1313, 976-2525.
Time: 976-1616.
Weather: 976-1212.
Horoscopes by Phone
Aries: 976-5050.
Taurus: 976-5151.
Gemini: 976-5252.
Cancer: 976-5353.
Leo: 976-5454.
Virgo: 976-5656.

Libra: 976-5757.
Scorpio: 976-5858.
Sagittarius: 976-5959.
Capricorn: 976-6060.
Aquarius: 976-6161.
Pisces: 976-6262.

New York Public Library
Telephone Reference Information Service
Will answer any ready reference question you may have. An invaluable service. Tip: Manhattan is usually busy, try the others first.
Manhattan: 340-0849. *Mon-Fri 9am-6pm; Sat 10am-6pm.*
Brooklyn: (1-718) 780-7700. *Mon-Fri 9am-5pm.*
Queens: (1-718) 990-0714. *Mon-Fri 10am-8:45pm; Sat 10am-5:15pm.*
Library on Call
(1-718) 780-7817. Answers to questions during non-library hours. In Westchester: 682-8360. *OPEN Mon-Thurs 5-10pm. Sat 10am-6pm, Sun 1-5pm.*
Homework Hotline
(1-718) 780-7766. Teachers and librarians help children answer difficult homework questions. *OPEN Mon-Thurs 5-8pm* during school year. In Westchester: 682-9759.
Grammar Hotline:
Dial REWRITE Mon-Fri 1-4pm.

Banks

All commercial banks are *OPEN Mon-Fri 9am-3pm,*. They are *CLOSED Sat & Sun and all legal holidays.* Some savings institutions are open Fri evening and Sat morning but they are the exceptions. If you intend to change a travelers check, be sure you have proper identification with you. Most banks do not exchange foreign currency—Bank Leumi, with branches throughout the city, does. *See* TRAVEL & VACATION, Travelers Checks, for addresses.

Legal Holidays

On these days banks, post offices, schools, offices and most businesses are closed. But the good news is that many special events take place. *See* ANNUAL EVENTS, Calendar for specific listings.
  New Years Day: Jan 1
  Martin Luther King's Birthday: 3rd Mon in Jan
  Lincoln's Birthday: Feb 12
  Washington's Birthday: 3rd Mon in Feb
  Memorial Day: 3rd Mon in May
  Independence Day: July 4
  Labor Day: 1st Mon in Sept
  Columbus Day: 2nd Mon in Oct
  Election Day: 1st Tues in Nov
  Veteran's Day: Nov 11
  Thanksgiving Day: 3rd Thurs in Nov
  Christmas Day: Dec 25

New York Publications

For current happenings in New York at any given time these are the best sources available at any newsstand.

The Daily News:
Daily AM and PM.
New York Magazine:
Weekly every Monday. Great for current goings-on.
The New Yorker:
Weekly every Monday.
The New York Post:
Monday-Saturday AM and PM.
The New York Times:
Daily. On Friday, *the best* for weekend events.
The Village Voice:
Weekly every Wednesday. Great source for music and nightlife info. Leans toward the cultural and political left.

Postal Services

Post Offices
General Post Office, 421 Eighth Avenue at West 33 Street. 971-7731 weekdays till 6pm; 971-7176 after 6pm, weekends and holidays. Full service. *OPEN 7:30am-8pm: limited service 24 hours, 7 days a week.* Stamps available from self-service machines 24 hours, 7 days a week. Call for location of office nearest you.
Stamps
Available at all post offices. *OPEN 8am-6pm* and at the General Post Office, 421 Eighth Avenue at West 33 Street *24 hours, 7 days a week* from self-service machines. Otherwise, stamps may be obtained from vending machines in most pharmacies, though at a premium.
Express Letters
971-7411. Guaranteed 24-hour delivery of any mail brought to one of the specially designated post offices before 5pm; to major cities only. Call for location of post office nearest to you which features the service.

Zip Codes
For zip code information call 971-7411 weekdays till 5pm; 971-7176 after 5pm, weekends and holidays. *See also* map following Index.
Manhattan Post Office Stations

Zip Code	Station	Address
10199	James A. Farley Post Ofc.	421 Eighth Ave
10002	Knickerbocker	128 East Broadway
10003	Cooper	93 Fourth Ave
10004	Bowling Green	25 Broadway
10005	Wall Street	73 Pine St
10006	Trinity	25 Broadway
10007	Church Street	90 Church St
10009	Peter Stuyvesant	432 East 14th St
10010	Madison Sq.	149 East 23rd St
10011	Old Chelsea	217 West 18th St
10012	Prince	103 Prince St
10013	Canal Street	350 Canal St
10014	Village	201 Varick St
10016	Murray Hill	115 East 34th St
10017	Grand Central	450 Lexington Ave
10018	Midtown	221 West 38th St
10019	Radio City	322 West 52nd St
10020	Rockefeller Ctr.	610 Fifth Ave
10021	Lenox Hill	217 East 70th St
10022	Franklin D. Roosevelt	909 Third Ave
10023	Ansonia	1980 Broadway
10024	Planetarium	127 West 83rd St
10025	Cathedral	215 West 104th St
10026	Morningside	232 West 116th St
10027	Manhattanville	365 West 125th St
10028	Gracie	229 East 85th St
10029	Hell Gate	153 East 110th St
10030	College	217 West 140th St
10031	Hamilton Grange	521 West 146th St
10032	Audubon	515 West 165th St
10033	Washington Bridge	555 West 180th St
10034	Inwood	90 Vermilyea Ave
10035	Triborough	167 East 124th St
10036	Times Square	340 West 42nd St
10037	Lincolnton	2266 Fifth Ave
10038	Peck Slip	1 Peck Slip
10039	Colonial Park	99 Macombs Pl
10040	Fort George	4558 Broadway
1012	Yorkville	1591 Third Ave

Hotels

Plaza Hotel

When choosing where to stay, remember Manhattan is only 13.4 miles long and 2.3 miles at its widest, so your choice of location will be more a matter of your interests and your desire for either tranquility or frenzy. In any case, in New York distance is measured by time not space.

Things to Know

· All prices are subject to change; that's why they are not quoted.
· Valuables should be deposited in the hotel safe when not in use.
· *You* keep your key when going out.
· Write the New York Convention and Visitor's Bureau, Two Columbus Circle, New York, N.Y. 10019 for their New York City Tour Package Directory listing weekend bargains at almost all the city's hotels. Or call the hotel using the 800 toll-free number listed in the entry.

Deluxe

Hotel Carlyle
35 East 76 Street. (10021) 744-1600. Superb "small" hotel, exclusive and European in manner; it's a permanent home to those who can afford the best. Impeccable service, tasteful rooms, and its location in the heart of auction and antique country is a boon to art lovers. Excellent restaurant; in the Café Carlyle, Bobby Short, a New York institution not to be missed; the Bemelmans Bar. Garage facilities. 503 rooms. 177 available to transients.

The Helmsley Palace
455 Madison Avenue at East 50 Street. (10017) 888-7000. (1-800) 221-4982. Overlooking St. Patrick's Cathedral. A 55-story glass tower atop the historic 19th-century Villard Houses, now the hotel's exquisite public rooms retaining the original fireplaces, mosaic ceilings and wood paneling. Plush period-style rooms, concierge and multilingual staff, Harry's New York Bar, private dining facilities, afternoon tea in the Gold Room, 24-hour room service. 775 rooms, 75 suites (including 4 triplexes above the 37th fl). Weekend package.

Mayfair Regent
610 Park Avenue at East 65 Street. (10021) 288-0800. (1-800) 545-4000. One of the so-called "baby grands." Quiet elegance with a continental air. Luxury service and surroundings. Spacious high-ceilinged rooms; some suites have fireplaces. Concierge; 24-hour room service; secretarial and limousine arrangements. Lovely lobby lounge for afternoon tea and next door the fine Le Cirque restaurant. Banquet room. 80 rooms; 119 suites. Weekend package.

No. 1022
1022 Lexington Avenue at East 73 St. (10021) 697-1536. New York's tiniest hotel is an 1870s town house on the Upper East Side. Three suites and a studio have the feel and look of an English country home. The pretty light-filled rooms have skylights, fireplaces, bathrooms with Jacuzzis, answer machines for messages, TV camera intercom. The ultimate in comfort and exclusivity. Daily or monthly rates. Room service is from the fine Jack's restaurant downstairs.

Park Lane Hotel
36 Central Park South. (10019) 371-4000. (1-800) 221-4982. A beautiful 46-story modern hotel whose owner Harry Helmsley is in residence, ensuring enduring good service. Breathtaking Central Park views. Elegant rooms: all the amenities, plus underground garage. Good restaurant and bar. Banquet ballroom. 640 rooms. Weekend package.

The Pierre
Fifth Avenue at 61 Street. (10021) 838-8000. (1-800) 828-1188. Built in 1930 as an exclusive hotel and newly renovated; it's a consistent best. Elegant and worldly with an excellent multilingual staff, concierge, valet service, twice daily maid service; 24-hour room service. Glorious spacious rooms, upper levels view Central Park. Café Pierre for dining and dancing. Valet parking; dogs allowed. 236 rooms.

Plaza Hotel
Fifth Avenue at 59 Street. (10019) 759-3000. (1-800) 228-3000. This grande dame has lost some of her allure but it's still a sentimental and elegant New York landmark, drawing the famous, the rich and the royal since 1907. High-ceilinged rooms—the best are the ones with Central Park views. Excellent restaurants, especially the Edwardian Room; the Palm Court for tea and violins, and the Oak Bar for drinks. 24-hour room service. 900 rooms. Weekend package.

Ritz-Carlton
112 Central Park South. (10019) 757-1900. (1-800) 223-7990. Formerly the Navarro. This "small" luxurious hotel has a sedate English country-home feel. The rooms are charming and 96 of them offer spectacular park views. Down pillows, linen sheets, Courvoisier and Kron-chocolate nightcap, nightly turn-down service, 24-hour room and valet service make this a luxurious choice. Multilingual staff serves a large discerning European clientele. On premises, the Jockey Club (the original is in DC) with its million $ art collection on its pine-paneled walls. 240 rooms. Weekend package.

St. Regis Sheraton
2 East 55 Street. (10022) 753-4500. (1-800) 325-3535. Old World landmark hotel built in 1904 by John Jacob Astor for those who could appreciate and afford the "best of everything." High-ceilinged, exquisitely decorated rooms recently refurbished. Excellent room service. Dinner and dancing, fascinating King Cole Bar with its Maxfield Parrish mural. The most elegant lobby shops in town. 520 rooms. Weekend package.

Sherry-Netherland
781 Fifth Avenue at 59 Street. (10022) 355-2800 (1-800) 223-0522. Impeccable Old World manners and finesse distinguish this 1927 hotel. Draws many Hollywood luminaries. The Cafe Bar (the Grill) is one of the city's most popular spots for lunch, cocktails, or late-night piano music. Park-filled views, fireplaces; 145 of 372 rooms available for transients.

United Nations Plaza
1 United Nations Plaza at East 44 Street & First Avenue. (10017) 355-3400 (1-800) 228-9000. A dazzling 13-story hotel perched on top of two sleek skyscraper towers. Understated elegance adding up to pure luxury. Modern decor, international ambiance (29 languages available at front desk). Health club, 24-hour tennis, swimming pool, underground garage, 24-hour room service. Good restaurant and lounge and absolutely the best city-filled views. 442 rooms; 150 apartments. Weekend package.

The Waldorf-Astoria
301 Park Avenue at East 50 Street. (10022) 355-3000. Every inch the venerable institution and now undergoing a 5-year, $100 million refurbishing. Among its permanent residents (in the Towers, floors 28-42) the Duchess of Windsor and the American representative to the UN. Every President since Hoover has slept here (the Presidential Suite, $2,000 a night). Special consideration for special situations; 30 languages available; 24-hour room service; children in parents' room free of charge. More boutiques, *boites*, and ballrooms than in some small cities. Despite its size and popularity, service still tends to be good. Now part of Hilton chain. 1,852 rooms. Weekend package.

American Stanhope
995 Fifth Avenue at 81 Street. (10028) 288-5800.

(1-800) 847-8483. Beautifully situated opposite the Metropolitan Museum of Art and Central Park. Spacious and quiet accommodations, charmingly refurbished to create an old-fashioned ambiance; American art and antique filled. A variety of personal services: baby-sitting, dog walking, free morning limo service. Charming sidewalk café for sophisticated people-watching and quite good restaurant. 296 rooms. Weekend package.

Algonquin
59 West 44 Street. (10036) 840-6800. An aging legend; magnet for literary and theatrical folk since 1902. Traditional and fascinating—and that's just the lobby. Every room has private bath, air conditioning, and color cable TV. Three dining rooms, wonderful late-night supper; (see RESTAURANTS, Late Night/24-Hour Dining: The Rose Room) and the Blue Bar, where you're *always* in good company. Civilized late checkout. 200 rooms. Weekend package.

Barbizon Plaza
106 Central Park South. (10019) 247-7000. (1-800) 223-5493. Bright and comfortable, smartly located Best Western Hotel. Park view, good restaurant, popular Library discotheque and bar; roof terrace. Garage facilities. Free bicycles on weekends in season. 805 rooms. Weekend package.

Hotel Bedford
118 East 40 Street. (10010) 697-4800. (1-800) 221-6881. Comfortable, good location popular with businesspeople and diplomats. Pleasant rooms have fully equipped kitchenettes, air conditioning, color cable TV, direct-dial phones. 200 rooms. Weekend package.

Beekman Tower
1 Mitchell Place at East 49 Street & First Avenue. (10017) 355-7300. (1-800) 223-6663. (Manhattan East Apartment Hotel Group.) Comfortable, attractively decorated apartment hotel in UN area. Kitchen facilities, air conditioning, color TV. Indoor/outdoor penthouse cocktail lounge for great views. 160 apartments. Weekend package.

Berkshire Place
21 East 52 Street. (10022) 753-5800. (1-800) 228-2121. Desirable small hotel between Fifth and Madison, personalized service. Spacious, tasteful rooms. Popular Rendez-Vous Bistro restaurant and the sunlit Atrium Bar. Small meeting rooms. 400 rooms. Weekend package.

Hotel Beverly
125 East 50 Street. (10022) 753-2700. (1-800) 223-0945. Quiet, unpretentious, congenial atmosphere. Convenient East Side location. Renovated rooms have air conditioning, color cable TV; many have fully equipped kitchenettes and terraces. Room service, laundry/valet. On-premises coffee shop and restaurant. Children free in parents' room. 300 rooms. Weekend package.

Doral Inn
Lexington Avenue at East 49 Street. (10022) 755-1200. (1-800) 223-5823. Large renewed hotel, well-located, efficient, modern. In addition to the basic amenities, there are squash courts, sauna,

game room. Bar, restaurant, 24-hour coffee shop. 583 rooms. Weekend package.

Doral Park Avenue Hotel

70 Park Avenue at East 38 Street. (10016) 687-7050. (1-800) 847-4135. Traditional elegance, meticulous service; beautiful rooms. Situated in quiet Murray Hill just below Midtown. Outdoor café, nice restaurant and bar. Meeting facilities. Airport pickup on request. 200 rooms. Weekend package.

Doral Tuscany

120 East 39 Street. (10016) 686-1600. (1-800) 847-4078. Solicitous staff, a quiet tree-lined Murray Hill block, and a Dow Jones ticker tape in the lobby make this an extremely civilized place to stay. Large, traditionally decorated rooms have color cable TV, butler's pantry with refrigerator, some exercise bikes. Business clientele. 143 rooms. Weekend package.

Dorset

30 West 54 Street. (10019) 247-7300. Quiet, discreet and comfortable choice. Museum of Modern Art neighbor located just off Fifth Avenue. All rooms air conditioned, color TV; no charge for children under age 14 in parents' room. Very attentive staff. Good restaurant and bar. 200 rooms.

Drake Swissôtel

440 Park Avenue at East 56 Street. (10022) 421-0900. (1-800) 223-5652. Newly remodeled. Casual elegance, beautifully located. Pretty rooms have refrigerators, first-run movies, telephone in bathroom; some have wraparound terraces. Lobby lounge for continental breakfast; Wellington Grill restaurant. 562 rooms. Weekend package.

Eastgate Tower

222 East 39 Street. (10016) 687-8000. (1-800) 223-6663. (Manhattan East Apartment Hotel Group.) Motor hotel with full apartment/hotel facilities located on charming plaza in Murray Hill area. Garage, restaurant, outdoor sidewalk café in summer. Good services for travelers. 192 apartments. Weekend package.

Hotel Elysée

60 East 54 Street. (10022) 753-1066. Between Madison and Park Avenues. Well-located small, nonchaotic "artsy" hotel. Individually decorated rooms. Children under age 12 free in parents' room. Friendly choice. Famed Monkey Bar for meals, drinks and late-night entertainment. 120 rooms.

Essex House

160 Central Park South. (10019). 247-0300 (1-800) 221-4862. Large, tastefully decorated, traditional New York hotel now under the banner of Japan Airlines. Central Park is its front yard and the rooms overlooking it are choice. (Suburban New Yorkers escape to here.) Convention facilities. Two restaurants, cocktail lounge, 715 rooms. Weekend package.

Golden Tulip Barbizon

140 East 63 Street. (10021) 838-5700. (1-800) 223-1020. Formerly the all women Barbizon: The classic exterior was retained, the interior now

thoroughly modern. HBO, Olympic swimming pool and health club. La Mairee Restaurant, Café Barbizon and the Rousseau Room with fireplace. 368 rooms plus 8 suites. Weekend package.

Grand Hyatt New York

Park Avenue at Grand Central Terminal. (10017) 883-1234. (1-800) 228-9000. The 30-story shell of the former Commodore Hotel sheathed in mirrored glass; the interior a modern cosmopolitan hotel adjacent to Grand Central. Favored by business people for its location. The Regency Club for special attention on 31st and 32nd floors. A 4-story atrium lobby; Crystal Fountain restaurant; Sun Garden cocktail lounge cantilevered over 42 Street. Health club facilities available: tennis, squash, racquetball, sauna. 1,407 rooms. Weekend package.

Halloran House

525 Lexington Avenue at East 49 Street. (10017) 755-4000. (1-800) 223-0939. A 1929 building completely renovated and modernized. On a more personal level than most directed to the executive trade. Concierge, room service, secretarial and babysitting services available. No charge for children under age 18 in parents' room. Three restaurants and lounges. Meeting and banquet facilities. 652 rooms. Weekend package.

Holiday Inn-57th Street

440 West 57 Street. (10019) 581-8100. (1-800) 231-0405. Far west location. Combination of both modern and traditional decor. Color TV, air conditioning, coffee shop, restaurant, cocktail bar, banquet facilities. Free indoor garage. Rooftop swimming pool in summer. 600 rooms.

Hotel Inter-Continental New York

111 East 48 Street. (10017) 755-5900. (1-800) 327-0200. The former Barclay (built in 1926) underwent a $30 million restoration, the results—a wonderful hotel, gracious and elegant, calm and comfortable. The staff is firmly committed to excellence. Concierge, 24-hour room service, laundry/valet. The recreated 1926 lobby with its Tiffany-glass skylight for afternoon tea, the Barclay Restaurant, the Barclay Terrace and Bar, and the elegant La Recolte. 784 rooms. Weekend package.

Hotel Lexington

511 Lexington Avenue at East 48 Street. (10017) 755-4400. Large older hotel being updated. All rooms air conditioned, color TV, private baths. Two coffee shops. New home of the Playboy Club, an entertainment center for cardholders and hotel guests. 800 rooms.

Loew's Summit

Lexington Avenue at East 51 Street. (10022) 752-7000. (1-800) 223-0888. Modern, slick East Side favorite. Well contained with lobby lounge/and Maude's Bar, Restaurant, shopping arcade, and garage. No charge for children under age 18 in parents' room. Complimentary health club privileges. Meeting and banquet facilities. 767 rooms. Weekend package.

Lombardy
111 East 56 Street. (10022) 753-8600. For privacy, a residential co-op hotel with room decors to appeal to a myriad of tastes. Good quiet location just off Park Avenue. Tasteful accommodations with serving pantries and refrigerators. Its restaurant is the excellent Laurent. 176 units.

Lowell
28 East 63 Street. (10021) 838-1400. This impressively located Old World hotel recently transformed by a sky's-the-limit renovation, is a lovely choice. Landmark building elegantly restored. Studios and 1 and 2 bedroom suites, some with wood-burning fireplaces; terraces; all with fully equipped kitchens. Mainly residential; some transient. 126 rooms.

Marriott Marquis
1540 Broadway at West 45 St. (10036) 398-1900. (1-800) 228-9290. Right on the Great White Way; a 50-story modern convention hotel; a major part of the rehabilitation of Times Square. This largest of Marriotts contains the world's tallest (37 stories) atrium on the 8th floor lobby level, reached by glass elevators. Also featured: a 3-story revolving restaurant and lounge on the 46th floor; a 24-hour restaurant among several others; health club and a 1,500 seat legitimate theater (it will *never* make up for the loss of the Morosco and Helen Hayes demolished for this project), meeting rooms and ballrooms galore. 1,876 rooms.

Middletowne Harley Hotel
148 East 48 Street. (10017). 755-3000. (1-800) 321-2323. Newly refurbished with an eye toward the executive or diplomat drawn to the location between Lexington and Third. Full kitchens in all rooms, suites with fireplaces. No room service, bar or restaurant. Residential feeling. 194 rooms.

Murray Hill East
149 East 39 Street. (10016) 661-2100. (1-800) 221-3037. Apartment hotel between Third and Lexington (the former Lyden), with daily, weekly or monthly rates. Pleasantly furnished studios, with or without dining areas, and one and two bedroom suites are great for family visits or corporate use. No restaurant or bar. 125 units. Weekend package.

The New York Helmsley
212 East 42 Street. 490-8900. (10017) (1-800) 221-4982. New 40-story Helmsley hotel in the UN area combines elegant European comfort (down pillows, linen towels) with New York efficiency. Top-level executive features include: fast check in and out, translation and typing facilities, underground parking, 24-hour room service and bathroom phones. Mindy's Restaurant and Harry's New York Bar. 800 rooms. Weekend package.

New York Hilton
1335 Avenue of the Americas at West 53 Street. (10019) 586-7000. Very frenetic New York army-sized 46-story hotel with interesting personal features: heated bathroom floors, for one. Big with conventions; good business and foreign traveler services. Executive Tower, the top 6 floors, for executive amenities, including a ticker tape. Café New York, open 24 hours, among many other eating and drinking places on premises. No charge for children in parents' room. 2,131 rooms. Weekend package.

New York Penta
401 Seventh Avenue at West 33 St. (10001) 736-5000. (1-800) 223-8585. Built as the New York Statler in 1919, this huge newly refurbished landmark hotel near Macy's and Madison Square Garden caters to the convention trade. Well-situated for the new Convention Center. Multilingual staff; valet parking. 1,705 rooms. Weekend package.

Novotel
226 West 52 Street. (10019). 315-0100. (1-800) 221-3185. Well-known European chain brings well-priced accommodations designed for the business traveler to New York. Convenient to the theater district, this 26-story hotel is built atop a pre-existing 4-story commercial building. The sound-proofed rooms all have individually controlled air conditioning, color cable TV with in-room first-run films. Laundry and valet service; hospitality suites. Restaurant, brasserie and wine bar on premises. 470 rooms.

Omni Park Central
870 Seventh Avenue at West 56 Street. (10019) 484-3300. (1-800) 228-2121. Formerly the New York Sheraton. Large, comfortable, no-nonsense hotel. In-room, first-run movies, a disco, bar, several restaurants, and pizza too! Good for families; two children under age 17 free in parents' room. 1,500 rooms. Weekend package.

Parker Meridien
118 West 57 Street. (10019) 245-5000. (1-800) 223-9918. New 40-story hotel French-owned and operated. Fine West Side location; smallish rooms are soundproof and there is a racquet and fitness club, glass-enclosed rooftop swimming pool; 24-hour room service. Maurice for *nouvelle cuisine* and the lovely lobby lounge for breakfast and drinks. 600 transient rooms, 100 rentals. Weekend package.

Plaza Athenée
37 East 64 Street. (10021) 734-9100. (1-800) 223-5672. The dowager Alrae Hotel underwent a $40 million renovation, under the auspices of Trusthouse Forte; renamed for its glamorous Parisienne sister. The 16-story luxury hotel's rooms are decorated with Louis XV reproductions and Directoire-style furnishings. European-trained staff; sophisticated international clientele. Handsome lounge for drinks or afternoon tea; Le Regence restaurant. 160 rooms including 34 suites; 2 duplex apts.

Plaza 50
155 East 50 Street. (10022) 751-5710. (1-800) 223-6663. Good East Side business location. Air-conditioned apartment hotel, full kitchens, color TV, some private terraces. Laundry facilities available; full hotel services. 118 rooms. Weekend package.

Regency Hotel
Park Avenue at East 61 Street. (10022) 759-4100. (1-800) 223-0888. Tasteful modern Loew's hotel with a refined European flair; quiet location.

Elegantly furnished rooms; congenial piano lounge. Fine restaurant is a power-broker's breakfast spot. 490 rooms.

Roosevelt Hotel
Madison Avenue at East 45 Street. (10017) 661-9600. (1-800) 223-1870. Very fine, newly redecorated older hotel located right in the middle of it all. Attractive, comfortable, quiet rooms. Two restaurants, a bar, coffee shop. Geared to an executive clientele. 1,100 rooms. Weekend package.

St. Moritz-on-the-Park
50 Central Park South. (10019) 755-5800. (1-800) 221-4774. Small modern rooms in a nostalgic setting, many with great views of Central Park. *Very* European sidewalk Café de la Paix, and Rumpelmeyer's for the sweet tooth or afternoon tea. 800 rooms. Weekend package.

Shelburne Murray Hill
303 Lexington Avenue at East 37 Street. (10016) 689-5200. (1-800) 223-6663. (Manhattan East Apartment Hotel Group.) Full hotel services and long-term residency available in lovely, quiet location. Billy Budd restaurant. 252 apartments. Weekend package.

Sheraton Centre
Seventh Avenue at West 52 Street. (10019) 581-1000. (1-800) 325-3535. Formerly the Americana. Large, busy, modern, and highly commercial, in the midst of it all. Conveniences include valet parking and first-run, in-room movies. Convention and business group accommodations. Four restaurants; 2 bars. 1,828 rooms. Weekend package.

Sheraton City Squire Hotel
790 Seventh Avenue at West 51 Street. (10019) 581-3300. (1-800) 325-3535. Modern comfortable rooms, air conditioning, color TV, some private terraces. Great location for theater going. Best feature, a glass-enclosed, year-round swimming pool. Valet parking, enclosed garage. 724 rooms. Weekend package.

Sheraton Russell Hotel
Park Avenue at East 37 Street. (10016) 685-7676. (1-800) 325-3535. Off the beaten track Sheraton, originally a 1920s apartment building. Quiet, comfortable rooms, some with fireplaces. Lovely, gracious small hotel with a good bar and restaurant. Free parking. 175 rooms. Weekend package.

The Surrey Hotel
20 East 76 Street. (10021) 288-3700. (1-800) 223-6663. Exclusive location, apartment hotel. Well-appointed, very large rooms. Air conditioned, color TV, room service. The fine Les Pleiades restaurant, cocktail lounge, and bar. 111 apartments.

Southgate Tower
371 Seventh Avenue at West 31 Street. (10001) 563-1800. (1-800) 223-6663. (Manhattan East Apartment Hotel Group) Newly refurbished 30-story structure opposite Madison Square Garden, near Penn Plaza. All rooms have fully equipped kitchens or serving pantries; some have terraces. Full hotel services, valet, maid and room service. Nice lobby shops. Geared to a business clientele. Parking facilities; 2 restaurants. Meeting and banquet rooms. 525 rooms. Weekend package.

Vista International
3 World Trade Center. (10048) 938-9100. This 22-story Hilton International hotel is the first major one to be built in Lower Manhattan since 1836. Sandwiched between its twin towering neighbors, it offers views of the Statue of Liberty in the Harbor to 50% of its guests, direct access to the World Trade Center concourse of shops, a shuttle bus to midtown, and on the weekends, bicycles for sightseeing. Not to mention a jogging track, rooftop swimming pool and Fitness Center. Close to Wall Street, the Seaport and other downtown attractions. Extra pampering for execs on the 20 and 21 floors. Lobby café for breakfast or tea; American Harvest Restaurant. 825 rooms; 4 duplex suites. Weekend package.

Warwick
65 West 54 Street. (10019) 247-2700. (1-800) 223-4099. Popular with TV people and clothing buyers because of its location. Large, comfortable rooms, air conditioning, color TV. Helpful staff. Good restaurant and bar. 500 rooms. Weekend package.

Westbury
East 69 Street at Madison Avenue. (10021) 535-6566. (1-800) 223-5672. Stylish yet serene, recently refurbished Trusthouse Forte Hotel with well-appointed, spacious accommodations in excellent upper East Side location. Old World luxury feel; concierge service; 24-hour room service. Convenient to the prestigious art galleries and auction houses. Banquet facilities. The wonderful Polo Restaurant. 300 rooms. Weekend package.

Windsor Harley Hotel
100 West 58 Street. (10019) 265-2100. (1-800) 221-4982. Remodeled, well located, and comfortable member of the Helmsley hotel family. Excellent service; attractive, spacious accommodations. Chinese restaurant and bar on premises. 300 rooms. Weekend package.

Moderate

Adams
2 East 86 Street. 744-1800. Semi-residential, traditionally decorated hotel with park views from the west. Every room has private bath, color TV, kitchenettes in the suites. Jascha Heifetz and Pablo Casals have slept here. 329 rooms. 174 apartments.

Blackstone
50 East 58 Street. (10022) 355-4200. Small, quiet hotel retains much of original Art Deco 1920s flavor in both style and comfort of living. European clientele. Personalized service, air conditioning, cable color TV. 180 rooms.

Century Paramount Hotel
235 West 46 Street. (10036) 764-5501. (1-800) 223-9868. A refurbished oldie tourist-class hotel. Comfortable large rooms with air conditioning, private baths, color TV. Courteous management, European clientele. Coffee shop and lounge. 650 rooms.

Chelsea Hotel

222 West 23 Street. (10011) 243-3700. A lively landmark. Home to the famous and infamous of every era since 1833. Suggested for the adventuresome and offbeat—dare I say bohemian? The rooms—large, soundproof with kitchens—are as checkered as its past—some excellent, some condemnable. 400 rooms.

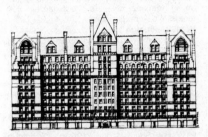

Chelsea Hotel

Hotel Edison

228 West 47 Street. (10036) 840-5000. (1-800) 223-1900. At the low end of moderate, a tourist mecca smack in the middle of the Theater District. Busy, comfortable; all the large rooms are air conditioned and have TV. Coffee shop, restaurant and a cocktail lounge. Garage facilities. 1,000 rooms.

Empire Hotel

44 West 63 Street. (10023) 265-7400. (1-800) 223-9868. Across from Lincoln Center; a simple, amiable hotel; well-managed and clean. Color TV, air conditioning, direct-dial phones, free parking. Special rates for foreign visitors, students; no charge for children under age 14 in parents' room. No room service, but on premises is the popular O'Neal's Baloon (*see* RESTAURANTS, Bars & Burgers). 600 rooms.

Gorham Hotel

136 West 55 Street. (10019) 245-1800. Small, quiet, easy hotel built in 1938. Rooms have fully equipped kitchenettes, air conditioning, color TV; personal service, on premises restaurant. Underground garage. Good value for prime location. 165 rooms.

Gramercy Park Hotel

2 Lexington Avenue at East 21 Street. (10010) 475-4320. (1-800) 221-4083. Old World hotel in a stylish and historic location. Attractive and gracious service. Air conditioning, color TV, access to New York's only private park. Newer rooms face the park; some have kitchenettes. Traditional restaurant, cocktail lounge and piano bar. 500 rooms.

Henry Hudson Hotel

353 West 57 Street. (10019) 265-6100. Large, traditional residential hotel in Coliseum area, convenient to Broadway theaters. Swimming pool, sundeck. Only 50 of the 1,000 rooms are for transients.

Howard Johnson's Motor Lodge

851 Eighth Avenue at West 51 Street. (10019) 581-4100. (1-800) 654-2000. Well known, comfortable, and modern. Near Theater District. In-room, first-run movies, cocktail lounges, restaurant. No charge for children under age 18 in parents' room. Free parking (but in-out charge). 300 rooms. Weekend package.

Kitano

66 Park Avenue at East 38 Street. (10016) 685-0022. (1-800) 223-5823. New York's only Japanese-owned-and-operated hotel presents an interesting mix of efficiency and serenity. A few authentic tatami suites with traditional tubs are available. Restaurant and ceremonial tea room. Good Murray Hill location. 90 rooms. Weekend package.

Madison Towers Hotel

22 East 38 Street. (10016) 685-3700. (1-800) 225-4340. Renovated oldie (the former Lancaster Hotel) in good Murray Hill location. Small, nicely decorated rooms; color TV; individually controlled heat and air conditioning. Draws fashion buyers, business travelers and tour groups. Whaler Bar, with woodburning fireplace in winter, for food and drink. Banquet facilities. 214 rooms. Weekend package.

Mayflower Hotel

15 Central Park West at 61 Street. (10023) 265-0060. (1-800) 223-4164. Lincoln Center vicinity facing Central Park. Newly renovated. Large rooms all have private baths and pantries; color cable TV available, room service. Conservatory restaurant and café. 577 rooms.

Milford Plaza

270 West 45 Street. (10036) 869-3600; (1-800) 221-2690. Theater District location makes this convenient for Broadway-goers; but it's a noisy choice especially on lower floors where they house the tour groups. Contemporary decor, 3-story marble atrium lobby, show biz motif. For the price packaged handiwipes instead of face cloths—a minus. Kippy's Pier 44 Restaurant on premises. 1,310 rooms. Weekend package.

Morgans

237 Madison Avenue at East 37 Street. (10016) 686-0300. In Murray Hill, the 50 year-old Executive Hotel refurbished and brought into the modern age by the creators of Studio 54 no less. The sleek, simple black and gray decor of the smallish rooms is up-to-the-minute (by famed French designer Andrée Putman) with all built-in furnishings, Brooks Brothers shirting fabric on the down comforters. Service oriented to the entertainment, fashion and corporate traveler. Some rooms with VCRs and Jacuzzis; 24-hour room and valet service; refrigerators. Restaurant and bar on premises. 154 rooms. Weekend package.

Hotel Olcott

27 West 72 Street. (10023) 877-4200. Just off Central Park West, near trendy Columbus Avenue, longtime residential hotel with some rooms for transients. Comfortable accommodations, direct dial phones, color TV available. Reserve well in advance. Good value.

River Hotel
180 Christopher Street at West St. (10014) 206-1020. Unusual location on the far western edge of Greenwich Village overlooking the Hudson River. Small rooms have platform beds, color TV, in-house movies. Night maid and concierge, 24-hour valet and limousine service. Rooftop La Grande Corniche restaurant for good food with a view (see RESTAURANTS, Rooms with a View). 48 rooms.

Ramada Inn
800 Eighth Avenue at West 48 Street. (10019) 581-7000. (1-800) 228-2828. Homey hotel, attractively furnished. Good for families (children under age 18 in same room free). Pluses: in-room first-run movies, open-air rooftop swimming pool, free parking (but in-out charge). 363 rooms. Weekend package.

Roger Smith
501 Lexington Avenue at East 47 Street. (10017) 755-1400. Comfortable, low-key older hotel undergoing renovation. Suites all have cooking facilities, some have fireplaces. No room service. Even Fido is welcome here. Free serve-yourself Continental breakfast on weekends. Late checkout. Nibbles restaurant on premises. 180 rooms.

Royalton
44 West 44 Street. (10036) 730-1344. Built in 1899, designed by architect Stanford White as a private club. Comfortable, clean and dated traditional hotel serves as a home to many Europeans and literary types. Not all rooms have private bath. Air conditioning, color TV. Coffee shop room service. 142 rooms.

Salisbury
123 West 57 Street. (10019) 246-1300. (1-800) 223-0680. In the heart of a fashionable shopping area, quiet, traditionally decorated hotel; a good bet for families. Most rooms have serving pantries with refrigerators (albeit no cooking), all have air conditioning and color TV. Children under age 12 in parents' room free. Coffee shop but no bar (evidence of ownership by the adjacent Calvary Baptist Church). Banquet and meeting facilities. Weekend package. 320 rooms.

San Carlos Hotel
150 East 50 Street. (10022) 755-1800. (1-800) 722-2012. Comfortable hotel between Lexington and Third Avenues; a good business location. Amiable staff. Most rooms have fully equipped serving pantries; all have air conditioning, color TV, direct-dial phones. Gin Ray Japanese Restaurant on premises. Garage facilities. 140 rooms.

Shoreham
33 West 55 Street. (10019) 247-6700. Comfortable, practical rooms (mostly suites) with serving pantries, air conditioning, color cable TV. Excellent location just off Fifth Avenue for restaurants, shopping. On premises restaurant is the famed La Caravelle; courteous management. European clientele. 76 rooms.

Travel Inn
515 West 42 Street. (10036) 695-7171. (1-800) 223-1900. Courteous, efficient, close to Theater Row. Popular with families and tour groups. Newly redecorated rooms. All the amenities plus out-door pool, saunas, solarium, roof-top sundeck. Great for summer stays. Memorial Day-Labor Day up to 5 kids in parents' room free of charge. Pets allowed. 250 rooms. Weekend package.

Tudor Hotel
304 East 42 Street. (10017) 986-8800. (1-800) 221-1253. Quiet, Old English-flavored hotel in UN neighborhood. Small pleasant rooms have air conditioning, color TV, direct-dial phones. Draws an international clientele. Roof garden. 600 rooms. Weekend package.

Hotel Wellington
871 Seventh Avenue at West 55 Street. (10019) 247-3900. (1-800) 652-1212. Nice hotel near Carnegie Hall, which may be why it attracts musicians. Rooms and service are good. Friendly ambiance. All rooms, though small, are air conditioned, with color TV, some with kitchenettes. On premises coffee shop, restaurant and lounge; lobby shops. 700 rooms.

Wentworth Hotel
59 West 46 Street. (10036) 719-2300. Old hotel in the process of upgrading. Comfortable: good location for theater. 350 rooms.

Wyndham
42 West 58 Street. (10019) 753-3500. Word of mouth find. Privately owned, discreetly run, well-appointed hotel caters to theatrical and movie industry clientele (Ginger Rogers is a regular). Quiet, impeccable service. Good value albeit no room service or direct-dial phones. Elevators still manned by operator, locked lobby at all times. 148 rooms.

Westpark Hotel
308 West 58 Street at Columbus Circle. (10019) 246-6440. Attractive, modest, almost-budget choice in the West Side/Coliseum area. Completely renovated rooms; some face Central Park. Color TV/radio; multilingual staff. 99 rooms. Weekend package.

Budget

Allerton House
130 East 57 Street. (10022) 753-8841. Well located for East Side shopping, convenient to all transportation. Homey and secure for women only; many are older permanent residents. Not all rooms have private bath or air conditioning. TV room, sun roof, Irish Pavillion. Restaurant. 63 rooms.

Collingwood Hotel
45 West 35 Street. (10001) 947-2500. Near Macy's Herald Square. Comfortable, clean accommodations, air conditioning, color TV, some rooms with kitchenettes, not all have private bath. 250 rooms.

Hotel Diplomat
108 West 43 Street. (10036) 921-5666. Large, renovated rooms in a family-run hotel in the Theater District. Multilingual staff. Not all rooms have private bath. 220 rooms.

Excelsior
45 West 81 Street. (10024) 362-9200. Kitchen-

ette-equipped rooms. Terrific budget choice on pretty tree-lined street Upper West Side residential street. Clean and tidy rooms. High up-park views; room service in the AM. Air conditioned, private baths, color TV. 300 rooms.

Iroquois Hotel
49 West 44 Street. (10036) 840-3080. Comfortable, family-style hotel. All rooms have private bath, color cable TV, air conditioning. Many suites with kitchenettes. Theater District location. 135 rooms.

Mansfield Hotel
12 West 44 Street. (10036) 944-6050. Just off Fifth Avenue, a simple tourist hotel located in a 1907 Stanford White building. Not all of the smallish rooms have private bath or air conditioning. Color cable TV but few other amenities. 200 rooms.

Martha Washington Hotel
30 East 30 Street. (10016) 689-1900. For women only; comfortable and secure, but quality of rooms varies greatly. Not all have private bath. Air conditioning and TV may be rented. Rooftop sundeck. 500 rooms.

Pickwick Arms
230 East 51 Street. (10022) 355-0300. Pleasant, newly refurbished; not all rooms have private bath or air conditioning. No TV. Popular with foreign tourists. A plus is the East Side Turtle Bay neighborhood. 400 rooms.

Remington
129 West 46 Street. (10036) 221-2600. A small Theater District budget hotel. 140 rooms.

Seville
Madison Avenue at East 29 Street. (10016) 532-4100. (1-800) 431-5022. An old hotel with an interior face-lift; all new furnishings and fixtures, TV, air conditioning. Complimentary Continental breakfast. Not all rooms have private bath. 500 rooms.

Stanford
43 West 32 Street. (10001) 563-1480. Modern, newly renovated hotel attracts South American clientele. Near Herald Square shopping and Madison Square Garden. Color TV in each room. 160 rooms.

Times Square Motor Hotel
255 West 43 Street. (10109) 354-7900. Busy, comfortable tourist hotel right in Times Square country. Family plan available. Not all rooms have private bath. Air conditioning; 24-hour deli on premises. Parking facilities. 800 rooms.

Wales
1295 Madison Avenue at East 92 Street. (10028) 876-6000. Well-managed, no frills, homey hotel in up and coming Carnegie Hill residential neighborhood. Large, airy, spacious rooms, many kitchenettes; some have Central Park-filled views. Not all are air conditioned. Sarabeth's Kitchen restaurant on premises. 97 rooms.

Hostels & Y's

Flushing YMCA
138-46 Northern Boulevard, Flushing, Queens.

(1-718) 961-6880. For men only. Excellent co-ed exercise facilities, two swimming pools, handball, squash. Coffee shop. 150 rooms.

International House
500 Riverside Drive nr West 122 Street. 678-5000. Summer and mid-winter vacation. Anyone in academic life can stay. Daily, weekly, monthly rates. Cafeteria, pub, dancing, gym, sun terrace, study facilities. 500 rooms.

International Student Center
38 West 88 Street. 787-7706; West 55th & Broadway, 757-8030. For men and women students all year. Rock bottom prices. Cooking facilities available at 88 Street only. Dormitory rooms only.

Manhattan College Residence Halls
4513 Manhattan College Parkway, Bronx, 548-1400, ext. 438. For men and women students. Beginning of June to mid-Aug only. 100 rooms.

McBurney YMCA
215 West 23 Street. 741-9210. For men over 18 only. Co-ed gymnasium, swimming pool, track, and sauna. 279 rooms.

92 Street Y
1395 Lexington Avenue. 427-6000, ext. 126. Dormlike rooms; weekly rates. Proof of job or study program required, as is a personal interview.

Sloan House YMCA
356 West 34 Street. 760-5859. Large co-ed residence facilities. Student discounts. Cafeteria, gift shop, checkroom, safe-deposit boxes, laundry facilities. 1,500 rooms.

Vanderbilt YMCA
224 East 47 Street. 755-2410. Great location. Co-ed residence facilities. Gym, swimming pool, sauna, excellent cafeteria. Laundry facilities. 438 rooms.

West Side YMCA
5 West 63 Street. 787-4400. Men over 18, and two floors reserved for women students only. Co-ed gymnasium, swimming pool, track, sauna, cafeteria. 536 rooms.

YWCA
30 Third Avenue nr Atlantic Avenue. Brooklyn. (1-718) 875-1190. Near the Brooklyn Academy of Music. For women over 18 who work or are students. Swimming pool; discount on classes. 150 rooms.

Hotels near the Airports

By virtue of their location these tend to be frenetic.

JFK International Airport

JFK Airport Hilton
JFK International Airport. 138-10 135 Avenue nr 138 Street, Jamaica, Queens. (11436) (1-718) 322-8700. Friendly, modern, and efficient. Provides transportation to and from terminals. 330 rooms.

Quality Inn
JFK International Airport. 175-15 Rockaway Boulevard, Jamaica, Queens. (11434) (1-718) 995-5000. (1-800) 228-5151. Transportation to

and from the airport 24 hours a day. Clean, neat, modern facilities including coffee shop, restaurant, lounge. 260 rooms.

JFK Plaza Hotel
135-30 140 Street, Jamaica, Queens. (11436) (1-718) 659-6000. (1-800) 654-2000. New hotel with modern decor and facilities. Restaurant 6am-1am; shuttle service to and from the airport terminals. 370 rooms.

Viscount Hotel-New York JFK
JFK International Airport, Van Wyck Expressway, Jamaica, Queens. (11430) (1-718) 995-9000. (1-800) 255-3050. Newly decorated modern Trusthouse Forte hotel right at the airport. Newly geared to the executive trade—meeting banquet facilities. Free airport limo; free parking; multilingual staff; secretarial services available. Health club privileges; no smoking rooms. Restaurant and lounge on premises. Children under age 18 free in parents' room. 520 rooms.

LaGuardia Airport
Holiday Inn-LaGuardia
100-15 Ditmars Boulevard. East Elmhurst, Queens. (11369) (1-718) 898-1225. Modern hotel with all conveniences Holiday Inns are noted for. Outdoor swimming pool in season. Restaurant/lounge 6:30am-10pm. A courtesy van picks up guests from their flights. 224 rooms.

King's Inn at LaGuardia Airport
87-02 23 Avenue, East Elmhurst, Queens. (11369) (1-718) 672-7900. Comfortable. Free transportation to and from your flight. Restaurant, coffee shop and nightclub on the premises. 75 rooms.

Sheraton Inn at LaGuardia Airport
90-10 Grand Central Parkway. (11370) East Elmhurst, Queens. (1-718) 446-4800. (1-800) 325-3535. Clean and modern facilities, con-

venient to the airport. Modern and quiet for comfortable stay. Shuttle service to airport. Restaurant and lounge; outdoor pool in summer. 280 rooms.

Newark International Airport
Howard Johnson's Motor Lodge
U.S. Highways 1&9. South Haynes Avenue. (07114) (1-201) 824-4000. (1-800) 654-2000. Newly renovated, comfortable motel. Restaurant and lounge till 3am, coffee shop 6am-1am. Shuttle service to the airport. Outdoor pool in summer. 340 rooms.

Something Different

A European idea crosses the sea. In lieu of a hotel, try "Bed & Breakfast" in the Big Apple. Accommodations vary—be very specific regarding your needs: no cats, dogs; quiet; no loft ladders, steps, etc.

B & B Group (New Yorkers at Home)
301 East 60 Street. (10022) 838-7015. A bed and breakfast referral service which matches travelers with hosts who have available spare rooms (sometimes whole apartments without the host at home). Over 135 listings in Manhattan, a few in Queens and Westchester. Single or double occupancy; reserve at least 2 weeks ahead; minimum stay is 2 nights. Job or bank references are required.

Urban Ventures
P.O. Box 426, New York 10024. 662-1234. The pioneer bed and breakfast people in NY. Over 300 listings in Manhattan, some in Brooklyn and Queens. Several levels of accommodation including some with private bath.

Travel & Vacation Information

Grand Central Terminal

Passports

During peak travel periods, apply at least 4 weeks in advance of scheduled departure. Some renewals can be done through the mail, call before going to the office. If you have left an inadequate amount of time before your trip, bring your airline ticket with you to the office. An emergency need for a passport after hours or on weekends requires a call to the passport duty officer in Washington. (1-202) 655-4000.

United States Passport Office
630 Fifth Avenue at 50 Street. Room 270. 541-7700 (recording); 541-7710 (questions, info). One of life's more frustrating experiences. The *only* place where you can get a passport in 24 hours. For first timers proof of US citizenship is required as well as ID with a photo or a description plus 2 photos (see below). Be prepared to wait for up to 5 hours in peak periods. Payment by personal check or money order. *OPEN Mon-Fri 8:30am-3:30pm. CLOSED Sat, Sun & holidays.*

County Clerk's Office
60 Centre Street, lower level. 374-8361. For a renewal of a passport at least 3 weeks in advance of departure—the secret is out—*there are NO LINES here.* Check the County Clerk's Office in the other boroughs; they perform the same service. Payment by personal check or money order. *OPEN Mon-Fri 9am-1pm; 2pm-3pm. CLOSED Sat, Sun & holidays.*

Passport Photographs
Two identical recent photos 2" square are needed. These can be done by any photographer as long as they fit the required specifications. For details, call 541-7700.

Acme Passport Photos
630 Fifth Avenue nr 50 St. lower shopping concourse. 247-2911. In the same building as the Passport Office. Color or black-and-white photos while you wait. *OPEN Mon-Fri 8am-5pm.*

Inoculations & Vaccinations

To ascertain what vaccinations are required for the countries you intend to visit, call United States Government International Vaccination Information located at JFK International Airport. (1-718) 995-9135.

Intermedic
777 Third Avenue nr East 48 St. 486-8974. For a low annual fee you can get an updated directory of reputable English-speaking physicians in over 200 cities around the world; info on necessary immunizations. *OPEN Mon-Fri 9am-5pm.*

International Health Care Service
New York Hospital-Cornell Medical Center, 440 East 69 Street. 472-4284. Devoted exclusively to the medical needs of international travelers. Provides worldwide health info, immunizations when required; provides post-travel tests and treatment if required. Staffed by infectious-disease specialists. Fees vary; worthwhile investment for those traveling to lesser-developed countries. Appointment required 4 to 5 weeks before departure. *OPEN Mon-Thurs 4-8pm.*

Other Important Numbers

Immigration & Naturalization Service
349-8735

U.S. Customs Service, General Information
466-5550

Currency Exchange

New York City banks do not as a policy exchange foreign currency, so it is best to arrive with some American dollars. At the JFK International Arrivals Building, second floor, there is a Foreign Exchange. 656-8444. OPEN Sun-Thurs 8am-9:30pm; Fri & Sat till 10:30pm. If you are going abroad, it's best to buy some foreign currency. You can purchase the currency at the following exchange offices:

Bank Leumi
Convenient locations throughout the city; foreign exchange department in all branches.
111 Broadway nr Wall St.
301 Third Avenue at East 23 St.
845 Third Avenue at East 52 St.
1148 Third Avenue at East 67 St.
1960 Broadway at West 66 St.
1660 Second Avenue at East 86 St.
188 Montague Street, Brooklyn.
301 East Fordham Road, Bronx.
El Al Terminal, JFK Airport.
Deak-Perera International
41 East 42 Street. 883-0400. *OPEN Mon-Fri 9am-5:30pm, Sat 10am-2pm.*
Perera Fifth Avenue
630 Fifth Avenue nr 51 St. 757-6915. *OPEN Mon-Fri 9am-5pm.*

Travelers Checks

Banks and almost all shops accept them.

American Express Travel Service
65 Broadway nr Wall St. 323-5121.
150 East 42 Street. 687-3700.
374 Park Avenue nr East 53 St. 421-8240.
125 Broad Street nr Water St. 323-4590.
822 Lexington Avenue nr East 63 St. 758-6510.
B. Altman, 355 Fifth Avenue at 34 St. 683-5367.
Bloomingdale's, 1000 Third Avenue at East 59 St., 8th fl. 705-3172.
Macy's Herald Square, Broadway & West 34 Street, balcony. 695-8075.
Abraham & Straus, 420 Fulton Street, Brooklyn. (1-718) 875-3881.
For refunds for lost or stolen American Express Travelers Checks, call (1-800) 968-8300, collect from anywhere in New York State.
Barclay's Bank of New York
19 Nassau Street nr Cedar St. 233-4200.
3 Park Avenue nr East 34 St. 689-9009.
300 Park Avenue nr East 49 St. 421-1400.
15 West 50 Street. 265-1105.
9 West 57 Street. 644-0850.
For information and refund inquiries: 233-1511.
Thomas Cook
18 East 48 Street. 921-3800. (Currency exchange, too.)
Refund information: 921-3800.

Lost Property

Railroads
Pennsylvania Station: 560-7389.
Grand Central Station: 340-2555.
New York City Subways
370 Jay Street, Brooklyn: (1-718) 625-6200.
New York City Buses
Queens, Brooklyn, Staten Island: 370 Jay St. Brooklyn. (1-718) 625-6200; (1-718) 330-4484. Manhattan, Bronx: 605 West 132 Street. 690-9543; 690-9368 or 690-9400.
Port Authority Bus Terminal
41 Street & Eighth Avenue. *Mon-Fri* 466-7000, ext 219; *Sat, Sun, holidays* 564-9523, ext 219.
Airports
JFK International Airport
Lost property would be held by the individual airline on which you traveled. If loss occurred on airport grounds or at the International Arrivals Building, call (1-718) 656-4120.
LaGuardia Airport
Lost and Found: (1-718) 476-5115. Also contact individual airline on which you traveled.
Newark International Airport
Lost and Found: (1-201) 961-2235. Also call individual airline on which you traveled.
Taxicabs
By law anything left in a taxi must be turned in to the police station closest to where you were dropped off. To report a loss, call the Taxi & Limousine Commission Lost & Found, 825-0416. Within 48 hours, if the missing article has not been recovered, call 374-5084.

Traveler's Aid

Traveler's Aid Society of New York
207 West 43 Street. 944-0013. Nationwide service helps crime victims, stranded travelers, wayward children. Works closely with the police. *OPEN Mon-Fri 8:30am-6:30pm. Memorial Day-Labor Day Sat & Sun 9:30am-3pm as well.* Also at the International Arrivals Building, Kennedy Airport. (1-718) 656-4870 *OPEN year round Mon-Fri 10am-10pm, Sat & Sun 3-10pm.*
Lost Anywhere
Contact the nearest police station. Addresses are located on page 241.
Lost Child
The Police: 911
Lost or Found Dog
ASPCA
441 East 92 Street. 876-7700. Also put up notices in shops in the area of loss with a description of pet and your phone number *only.* Ads in local neighborhood publications are also helpful.

Tourist Offices (International)

For literature and helpful travel information.

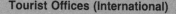

Antigua Department of Tourism & Trade
610 Fifth Avenue at 49 St. 541-4117.
Argentine National Tourist Office
12 West 56 Street. 397-1400.
Austrian National Tourist Office
545 Fifth Avenue nr 45 St. 697-0651.
Bahamas Tourist Office
10 Columbus Circle at West 59 St. 757-1611.
Barbados Tourist Board
800 Second Avenue nr East 42 St. 986-6516.
Belgian National Tourist Office
745 Fifth Avenue nr 57 St. 758-8130.
Bermuda Department of Tourism
630 Fifth Avenue nr 50 St. 397-7700.
Bonaire Dutch Antilles Tourist Information
1466 Broadway. 869-2004.
Brazilian Tourism Authority
60 East 42 Street. 286-9600.
British Tourist Authority
40 West 57 Street. 581-4700.
Bulgarian Tourist Office
161 East 86 Street. 722-1110.
Caribbean Tourism Association
20 East 46 Street. 682-0435.
Cayman Islands Department of Tourism
420 Lexington Avenue nr East 43 St. 682-5582.
Ceylon Tourist Board
609 Fifth Avenue nr 49 St. 935-0369.
Colombian Government Tourist Office
140 East 57 Street. 688-0151.
Costa Rica Tourist Board
630 Fifth Avenue nr 50 St. 245-6370.
Curaçao Tourist Board
400 Madison Avenue nr East 47 St. 751-8266.
Czechoslovakia La Tourist Bureau
10 East 40 Street. 689-9720.
Danish National Tourist Office
75 Rockefeller Plaza nr 51 St. 582-2802.
Dominican Republic Tourist Information
485 Madison Avenue nr East 52 St. 826-0750.
Eastern Caribbean Tourist Association
220 East 42 Street. 986-9370.
Ecuadorian National Tourist Office
15 East 40 Street. 684-3060.
Egyptian Government Tourist Office
630 Fifth Avenue nr 50 St. 246-6960.
Finland National Tourist Office
75 Rockefeller Plaza nr 49 St. 582-2802.
French Government Tourist Office
610 Fifth Avenue nr 49 St. 757-1125.
French West Indies Tourist Board
610 Fifth Avenue nr 49 St. 757-1125.
German National Tourist Office
747 Third Avenue nr East 46 St. 308-3300.
Ghana International
19 East 47 Street. 832-1300.
Greek National Tourist Office
645 Fifth Avenue nr 51 St. 421-5777.
Grenada Tourist Office
141 East 44 Street. 599-0301.
Haiti Government Tourist Bureau
1270 Avenue of the Americas. 757-3517.
Honduras Information Service
501 Fifth Avenue nr 42 St. 490-0766.
Hong Kong Tourist Association
548 Fifth Avenue. 869-5008.

Hungarian Travel Bureau
630 Fifth Avenue nr 50 St. 582-7412.
Icelandic National Tourist Office
75 Rockefeller Plaza nr 51 St. 582-2802.
India Government Tourist Office
30 Rockefeller Plaza nr 49 St. 586-4901.
Irish Tourist Board
590 Fifth Avenue at 48 St. 869-5500.
Israel Government Tourist Office
Empire State Building, 350 Fifth Avenue at 34 St. 560-0650.
Italian Government Tourist Office (E.N.I.T.)
630 Fifth Avenue nr 50 St. 245-4822.
Jamaica Tourist Board
866 Second Avenue nr East 46 St. 688-7650.
Japan National Tourist Organization
630 Fifth Avenue nr 50 St. 757-5640.
Kenya Tourist Office
424 Madison Avenue nr East 49 St. 486-1300.
Korea National Tourism Corporation
460 Park Avenue at East 58 St. 688-7543.
Luxembourg National Tourist Office
801 Second Avenue nr East 42 St. 370-9850.
Mexican National Tourist Council
405 Park Avenue at East 45 St. 755-7212.
Moroccan National Tourist Office
521 Fifth Avenue nr 43 St. 557-2520.
Netherlands National Tourist Office
437 Madison Avenue. 223-8141.
Norwegian National Tourist Office
75 Rockefeller Plaza nr 51 St. 582-5802.
Philippine Tourism
556 Fifth Avenue nr 45 St. 575-7915.
Polish National Tourist Office
500 Fifth Avenue nr 42 St. 391-0844.
Portuguese National Tourist Office
548 Fifth Avenue nr 45 St. 354-4403.
Commonwealth of Puerto Rico Tourism
1290 Avenue of the Americas nr West 51 St. 541-6630.
Quebec Government House
17 West 50 Street. 397-0200.
Rumanian National Tourist Office
573 Third Avenue nr East 38 St. 697-6971.
Saba Tourist Information Office
25 West 39 Street. 840-6655.
St. Eustatius Tourist Office Information
25 West 39 Street. 840-6655.
St. Maarten Tourist Information Office
25 West 39 Street. 840-6655.
Scandinavian Tourist Office
75 Rockefeller Plaza nr 51 St. 582-2802.
Soviet Union—Intourist
630 Fifth Avenue nr 50 St. 757-3884.
Spanish National Tourist Office
665 Fifth Avenue nr 53 St. 759-8822.
Swedish National Tourist Office
75 Rockefeller Plaza nr 51 St. 582-2802.
Swiss National Tourist Office
608 Fifth Avenue nr 49 St. 757-5944.
Taiwan Visitors Association
1 World Trade Center. 466-0691.
Trinidad & Tobago Tourist Board
400 Madison Avenue nr East 47 St. 838-7750.
Turkish Tourism & Information Office
821 United Nations Plaza nr East 46 St. 687-2194.

Venezuelan Government Tourist Bureau
7 East 51 Street. 355-1101.
Virgin Islands Government Tourist Office
1270 Avenue of the Americas nr West 50 St.
582-4520.
Yugoslav National Tourist Office
630 Fifth Avenue nr 50 St. 757-2801.

Domestic Auto Services

Exxon Touring Service
1251 Avenue of the Americas at West 50 Street,
ground fl. 398-2690. Will provide a marked map
while you wait, but be prepared for a line. *OPEN
Mon-Fri 8:30am-4:45pm.*

—Mail Service

Map with suggested routings can be obtained
from the following by mail. Advise destination,
time of year, and length of time to travel. Allow
several weeks for reply.
   Mobil Travel Service
   Box 25, Versailles, Kentucky 40383.
   Texaco Travel Service
   Box 1459, Houston, Texas 77001.

Animals in Transit

Animalport, ASPCA
Air Cargo Center, JFK International Airport,
Jamaica, Queens. (1-718) 656-6042. Care and
feeding of large and small animals in transit. Also
a boarding kennel for vacationers' pets. Im-
munization proof required. *OPEN 24 hours a day,
7 days a week.*

Passenger Ship Lines

*The New York Passenger Ship Terminal is on the
Hudson River at West 52 Street. Check the* New
York Times *for daily listings of arrivals and de-
partures.*

Chandris Cruises, Inc.
666 Fifth Avenue nr 53 St. 586-8370. (1-800) 223-
0848.
Cunard Line, Ltd.
555 Fifth Avenue nr 46 St. 661-7777.
Delta Lines
1 World Trade Center. 432-4700.
Eastern Steamship Lines, Inc.
1114 Avenue of the Americas. 575-0440.
Epirotiki Lines
551 Fifth Avenue. 599-1750.
Hellenic Mediterranean Lines
200 Park Avenue at East 45 Street. 697-4220.
Holland America Cruises
2 Penn Plaza nr West 31 St. 760-3880.
Home Lines Cruises, Inc.
1 World Trade Center. 775-9041.
Karageorgis Lines, Inc.
1350 Avenue of the Americas nr West 55 St.
582-3007.

K Lines-Hellenic Cruises
645 Fifth Avenue nr 51 St. 751-2435. (1-800) 223-
7880.
Japan Line New York, Ltd.
1 World Trade Center. 466-3900.
Prudential Lines
1 World Trade Center. 524-8212. (1-800) 221-
4118.
Royal Netherlands Steamship Company
5 World Trade Center. 938-9200.
Sun Line Cruises
1 Rockefeller Plaza. 397-6400. (1-800) 468-6400.

Car Hire

Drive Yourself
Avis
National Reservations & Information: (1-800)
331-1212. International: (1-800) 331-2112.
Kennedy International Airport: (1-718) 656-5266.
LaGuardia Airport: (1-718) 457-5500.
Newark Airport: (1-201) 961-4300.
Out of Town: (1-800) 228-9650.
Budget Rent-a-Car
Local Reservations & Information: 541-4222.
Kennedy International Airport: (1-718) 843-3030.
LaGuardia: (1-718) 672-8500.
Newark: (1-201) 961-2990.
Out of Town: (1-800) 228-9650.
Hertz
24-hour information and reservations domestic
and worldwide: (1-800) 654-3131.
Olins Rent-a-Car
207 West 76 Street. 580-6640.
337 East 64 Street. 580-9217.
142 East 31 Street. 580-6643.
21 East 12 Street. 580-9218.

Chauffeur-Driven
(See also SHOPPING, Specialty Shops & Services: Limousines.)
Carey Cadillac
41 East 42 Street, Suite 1710. 937-3100. Cadil-
lacs and chauffeurs. Hourly rates. *Available 24
hours a day.* AE, CB, DC, MC, V.
Cooper Classics Ltd.
132 Perry Street. 929-0094. Rent a mint-condition
vintage or new Rolls. Call in advance. *24-hour
phone service.* AE, MC, V.
Fugazy Continental Limousine Service
426-6600. Limousines and sedans with courteous
uniformed chauffeurs. *Available 24 hours a day.*
AE, DC, MC, V.
Smith Limousine
636 West 47 St. 247-0711. Cadillac limousine
only. For a lighter touch rent a white one. *OPEN 24
hours a day.* AE, MC, V.

Coach & Bus Hire

Greyhound Group Travel
630 Fifth Avenue nr 50 St. 971-6426.
Fugazy Continental Corporation
114-02 New York Boulevard, Jamaica, Queens.
(1-718) 291-3000.

Trailways Charters
230 Park Avenue. 563-9650.

Bus Stations

George Washington Bridge Bus Station
West 178 Street & Broadway. 564-1114.
Port Authority Bus Terminal
West 41 Street & Eighth Avenue. 564-8484.

Train Stations

Grand Central Station
Lexington Avenue & East 42 Street. MetroNorth Info: 532-4900.
Pennsylvania Station
West 33 Street & Seventh Avenue. Amtrak 736-4545; LIRR 739-4200.

Airports

These are the three major airports serving New York City:
JFK International Airport
Jamaica, Queens. (1-718) 656-4520.
LaGuardia Airport
Flushing, Queens. (1-718) 476-5000.
Newark International Airport
Newark, New Jersey. (1-201) 961-2000.

Airlines

The Central Airlines Ticket Office, 100 East 42 Street, 986-0888, handles all the major airlines, can arrange for tickets, answer questions.
AeroMexico
444 Madison Avenue nr East 49 St. 391-2900.
Air Canada
488 Madison Avenue nr East 51 St. 869-1900.
Air France
666 Fifth Avenue nr 52 St. 247-0100.
Air India
400 Park Avenue nr East 52 St. 751-6200.
Air Jamaica
19 East 49 Street. 688-1212.
Air New Zealand
(1-800) 262-1234.
Air Panama
630 Fifth Avenue nr 50 St. 246-4065.
Alaska Airlines
(1-800) 426-5206.
Alitalia Air Lines
666 Fifth Avenue nr 52 St. 582-8900.
American Airlines
100 East 42 Street. 431-1132.
Austrian Airlines
608 Fifth Avenue nr 49 St. 265-6350.
Avianca Airlines
6 West 49 Street. 246-5241.
British Airways
530 Fifth Avenue nr 44 St. 687-1600.

British West Indian Airlines (BWIA)
5 West 49 Street. 581-3200. 397-8800.
Capitol International Airways
230 Park Avenue nr East 47 St. 883-0750.
China Airlines
630 Fifth Avenue, Brooklyn. (1-718) 399-7870.
Continental Airlines
1 World Trade Center. 974-0028.
Czechoslovak Airlines (CSA)
545 Fifth Avenue nr 45 St. 682-5833.
Delta Airlines
400 Madison Avenue nr East 47 St. 239-0700.
Dominican Airlines
1270 Avenue of the Americas. 397-3420.
East Hampton Airlines
East Hampton Airport. (1-516) 537-0560.
Eastern Airlines
100 East 42 Street. Domestic: 986-5000; international: 661-3500.
Egyptair
720 Fifth Avenue nr 56 St. 581-5600.
El Al Israel Airlines
850 Third Avenue nr East 53 St. 486-2600.
Finnair-Finnish Airlines
580 Fifth Avenue nr 46 St. 889-7070.
Hawaiian Airlines
708 Third Avenue nr East 44 St. 355-4843.
Iberia Airlines
565 Fifth Avenue nr 45 St. 793-3300.
Icelandic Airlines
630 Fifth Avenue nr 49 St. 757-8585.
Irish International Airlines (Aer Lingus)
590 Fifth Avenue nr 48 St. 557-1110.
Japan Airlines
655 Fifth Avenue nr 52 St. 838-4400.
KLM Royal Dutch Airlines
437 Madison Avenue nr East 49 St. 759-3600.
Lan Chile Airlines
6 West 51 Street. (1-800) 225-5526.
Lufthansa Airlines
680 Fifth Avenue nr 53 St. 895-1277.
Mexicana Airlines
60 East 42 St. 687-0388.
New York Air
565-1100.
Northeastern
(1-800) 327-3788.
Northwest Orient Airlines
100 East 42 Street at USAir. 767-6868.
Olympic Airways
647 Fifth Avenue nr 52 St. 838-3600.
Ozark Airlines
100 East 42 Street. 586-3612.
Pan Am National
600 Fifth Avenue nr 49 St. 687-2600.
People Express
772-0344.
Philippine Airlines
626 Fifth Avenue nr 50 St. (1-800) 227-4600.
Piedmont Airlines
100 East 42 Street. 489-1460.
Qantas Airlines
542 Fifth Avenue nr 45 St. (1-800) 227-4500.
Republic Airlines
1 East 59 Street. 581-8851.

Royal Air Maroc
680 Fifth Avenue nr 53 St. 974-3854.
Sabena Belgian World Airlines
16 West 49 Street. 961-6200.
Scandinavian Airlines
638 Fifth Avenue nr 51 St. 657-7700.
Singapore Airlines
535 Fifth Avenue nr 44 St. (1-800) 227-3314.
Swissair
608 Fifth Avenue nr East 48 St. 990-4500.
TAP Portuguese Airways
521 Fifth Avenue nr 43 St. 944-2100.
Trans World Airlines (TWA)
624 & 630 Fifth Avenue nr 50 St. Domestic: 290-2121; international: 290-2141.
United Airlines
595 Fifth Avenue nr 48 St. 867-3000.
U.S. Air
100 East 42 Street. 736-3200.
Varig Brazilian Airlines
634 Fifth Avenue nr 51 St. 682-3100.
Viasa Venezuelan International Airways
18 East 48 Street. 486-4360.
Western Airlines
609 Fifth Avenue nr 49 St. 966-1646.
World Airways
500 Fifth Avenue at 42 St. 267-7111.
Yugoslav Airlines
630 Fifth Avenue nr 50 St. 765-4050.
Zambia Airways
370 Lexington Avenue nr East 41 St. 685-1112.

Getting to & from the Airports

Train
JFK Express
Take the train to the plane. Air-conditioned, luggage racks, good security. Stops in Manhattan: West 57 Street & Avenue of the Americas; 47-50 Streets/Rockefeller Center; West 42 Street & Avenue of the Americas; West 34 Street/Herald Square; West 4 Street/Washington Square; Chambers Street; Broadway-Nassau; Jay Street/Borough Hall, Brooklyn. At Howard Beach a bus takes you the last leg of the journey. The trip takes approx. 1 hour. From Manhattan: *Every 20 minutes 5am-midnight.* From JFK: *Every 20 minutes 5:50am-12:50am.* For info call: 878-7439.
PATH
To Newark Airport: take PATH to Newark Penn Station, then the Airlink Shuttle Bus from Bus Lane #1. Bus *every 20 minutes 7am - 11:30pm.* PATH info, call 466-7649.

Express Bus
Carey Coach
To JFK from Park Avenue at East 41 Street (opp. Grand Central Terminal) *every 20-30 minutes 5am-1am;* from Port Authority Bus Terminal, Eighth Avenue & West 41 Street, *every 20-30 minutes 7am-9:30pm.* From JFK to Grand Central Terminal *every 20-30 minutes 5:15am-midnight;* to Port Authority Bus Terminal *every 20-30 minutes 7am-9:30pm.***Travel Time 45 mins-1 hr. Call 632-0500 for info.**To LaGuardia from Park

Avenue & East 41 Street *every 15 minutes from 6am-11:45pm;* from Port Authority *every.15 minutes 7am-9:30pm.* From LaGuardia to Grand Central Terminal *every 15 minutes 6:50-12:35am;* to Port Authority *every 15 minutes 8:05-10:05pm.***Travel Time 30-55 minutes.**
Olympia Trails
Departs World Trade Center, the former East Side Airlines Terminal and Grand Central Terminal to Newark Airport *every 20-30 minutes 5am-midnight;* from Newark *every 20-30 minutes 5am-1am.***Travel Time 30-50 minutes; call 964-6233 for info.**
New Jersey Transit
Port Authority Bus Terminal, Eighth Avenue at West 41 Street to and from Newark International Airport *every 15 minutes 5am-1am; every 30 minutes 1am-5am.***Travel Time 30-40 minutes; for info call 762-5100; (1-201) 782-5100.**

Mini Bus or Van
Abbey Midtown
To JFK and LaGuardia from major midtown hotels *every hour on the hour 7am-6:30pm.* From JFK *6:30am-11pm;* from LaGuardia *8am-midnight.***Travel Time 45 minutes-1 hour. Call 361-8280 for details.**
Fugazy Share-A-Ride
938-9111, ext 7274. From the Vista International Hotel to JFK and LaGuardia Airports *every hour 8am-6pm.*
Newark Airport-New York City Mini Bus
To Newark Airport from major midtown hotels on call *every hour 7am-6:30pm;* from the airport to midtown, *every hour 8am-midnight.***Travel Time 30-40 minutes. Call 361-9092 for info.**

By Air
Note: Some carriers such as TWA offer free helicopter service to First and Business class fliers; check with them.

New York Helicopter
(1-800) 645-3494. Wide body 9 or 14 passenger Dauphin jet copters. Reserve 1 day in advance. From East River at East 34 Street to LaGuardia (6 minutes) to JFK (another 9 minutes), and direct to Newark (10 minutes). Every 40-50 minutes 7am-9pm. From World Trade Battery Park Heliport, West Street at the Hudson River to all 3 airports, Mon-Fri only, 7am-11am & 3-7pm.

Bus/Subway
This the most economical way but can be slow, hot and crowded.

To JFK take the E or F Train to Kew Gardens/Union Turnpike then the Green Lines Q-10 bus to the Airport; also, the A train from the West Side, Lower Manhattan and Brooklyn to Howard Beach and there pick up the Airport Bus.
From JFK, take the Triboro Coach Q-33 bus from Airport Main Terminal to the 74 Street Station, Jackson Heights, Queens. Connects to the E, N, F, GG & #7 subway lines. Buses run every 15 minutes till midnight, then every 40 minutes till 5am. Call 335-1000 for bus info.

Sightseeing

Brooklyn Bridge

For more sightseeing opportunities see also AN-NUAL EVENTS and HISTORIC NEW YORK.

Viewpoints

A view from the top is one of the best ways to acquaint yourself with New York City.

Brooklyn Bridge
City Hall Park in Manhattan to Cadman Plaza West, in Brooklyn Heights. There was no bridge in the world that had an elevated promenade when John Roebling planned the one for his bridge in 1869. This boardwalk for the exclusive use of pedestrians (and now, of course, bicycles) was to afford uninterrupted views in every direction. When the bridge was opened in 1883, 150,300 pedestrians paid one penny each to walk the one-mile-plus across the Great East River Bridge, as it was then called. It's free now and the view is considerably different than one hundred years ago—but it is no less magnificent. *Don't miss this walk,* even if you only go to the first tower. If you do walk across to Brooklyn, head over to the Brooklyn Heights Esplanade for another famous view. (*See also* HISTORIC NEW YORK, Bridges.)
Brooklyn Heights Esplanade (Promenade)
From Remsen to Orange Streets Brooklyn. The esplanade provides the most celebrated skyline view of the city, from across the East River. (*See*

also RESTAURANTS, Rooms with a View: The River Café.)
Empire State Building
350 Fifth Avenue at 34 Street. 736-3100. The third tallest building in the world; 102 stories (1,250 ft). There are 2 observation decks—one on the 86th fl and one, glass-enclosed, on the 102nd. Visibility 50 miles on a clear day; it's a 360° view. *OPEN 7 days 9:30am-midnight.* Last ticket sold 11:45pm. (*See also* HISTORIC NEW YORK, Modern Architecture.) Admission charge; discount for children under 12.
Rainbow Room
30 Rockefeller Plaza. (*See* NIGHTLIFE, Dinner/Dancing.)
RCA Building
30 Rockefeller Plaza nr 49 Street. 489-2947. The tallest of the Rockefeller Plaza complex, standing 70 stories high (850 ft). On a clear day there's a 50-mile view in all directions. Rain checks given if visibility is less than 2 miles. Observation roof *OPEN 7 days April-Oct 10am-8:45pm; till 7pm rest of the year.* Admission charge; children under 6 free; discount for children 6-12 and senior citizens. Reservations required for groups of 18 or more.
Riverside Church
West 120 Street & Riverside Drive. 222-5900. The enclosed observation platform, 392 ft high, affords a lovely view of the Manhattan skyline. *OPEN Mon-Sat 11am-3pm, Sun 12:30pm-4pm.*

Nominal admission charge; children under 6 not admitted.

Statue of Liberty
Liberty Island. 269-5755. Lady Liberty is undergoing a much-needed restoration before her 100th birthday. A metal scaffold will encase her familiar form until the rededication on that date. Her torch has been removed and a new one is being created by French craftsmen imported to America for the task. The island and the Statue will not be open again until July 4, 1986.

Statue of Liberty

Top of the Sixes
666 Fifth Avenue. (See RESTAURANTS; Rooms with a View.)

Williamsburgh Savings Bank Tower
1 Hanson Place at Ashland Place, Brooklyn. (Halsey, McCormick & Helmer, 1929.) (1-718) 636-7334. A skyscraper grew in Brooklyn—the only one. The 26th-fl outdoor observation deck of this handsome building provides wonderful Manhattan and Brooklyn views. *OPEN only Mon 10am-2pm.* FREE

Windows on the World
World Trade Center, North Tower (#1). (See RESTAURANTS; Rooms with a View.)

World Trade Center, Observation Deck
South Tower (#2). 466-7377. The world's second-tallest building (1,377 ft). Enclosed observation deck on the 107th fl. Outdoor observation deck on the 110th fl (¼ mile high!) is the world's highest. *OPEN (outdoors, wind and weather permitting) 7 days 9:30am-9:30pm. CLOSED Christmas Day, New Year's Eve.* Admission charge. Children under 6 free. Discount for children 6-12 and senior citizens. Call 938-0032 for

dining and viewing packages. Call 466-7397 for group rates.

New York Tours

By Coach
A great variety of escorted coach tours are offered in comfortable air-conditioned buses. Commentaries are given en route.

Crossroads Sightseeing
701 Seventh Avenue at West 47 Street. 581-2828. Half- or full-day guided tours of Manhattan covering all the well-known highlights.

Gray Line of New York
900 Eighth Avenue at West 54 Street. 397-2600. A choice of different tours uptown, downtown, and out-of-town. From 2 hours to all day.

Harlem Spirituals
Departs from Short Line, 166 West 46 Street. 275-1408. Fascinating bus tours that focus on the past and present of the 5½ square miles of New York known as Harlem. *Sun, 9am:* a 4-hour tour of Black Harlem, from 110 to 162 Streets. Visit with the gospel-singing congregation of the First Corinthian Baptist Church. *Fri & Sat at 7:30pm:* the tour includes a soul-food feast at Sylvia's (*see* RESTAURANTS, Soul & Creole) and a visit to the famed Small's Paradise for some hot jazz. Call for reservations.

Manhattan Sightseeing Bus Tours
150 West 49 Street. 869-5005. A choice of 10 different part-day or full-day tours. Reserve a week in advance for the all-day excursion.

New York Big Apple Tours
162 West 56 Street. 582-6339. Primarily for foreign tourists. Tours in French, German, Italian and Spanish. Call for further details.

Penny Sightseeing Company
303 West 42 Street. Room 503. 246-4220. A 4½-hour tour through Harlem by bus. *Mar-Oct. Mon & Thurs 10am, Sat 11am.* Reservations are necessary.

Short Line American Sightseeing International
168 West 46 Street. 354-5122. "Vista cruiser" glass-roof coaches make the views even more dramatic. Ten tours daily with commentary.

Specialized Tours

Adventure on a Shoestring, Inc.
300 West 53 Street. 265-2663. Off-the-beaten-path views of New York life and people. As popular with natives as with visitors.

Art Tours of New York
63 East 82 Street. 772-3888. Grads with arts degrees guide you through the cultural side of New York. Galleries, museums, music and theater—often behind the scenes. Groups or individuals; from a half day to a week.

Backstage on Broadway
228 West 47 Street. 575-8065. Go behind the scenes of a Broadway show—onstage and back-

stage. Escorted by a professional actor. Groups or individuals.

Brooklyn Brownstone Tours
130 St. Edwards Street, Brooklyn. (1-718) 875-9084. (6-9pm). With native son, Louis Singer, tour Brooklyn areas rich in brownstone architecture: Park Slope, Bedford Village, Stuyvesant Heights, Fort Greene, Cobble Hill, Boerum Hill and Brooklyn Heights. See the interior of at least 3 houses, churches or private clubs.

Gallery Passport
1170 Broadway nr West 27 Street. 288-3578. Unique tours of museums, galleries, historic sights for groups of 10 or more. Multilingual guides available.

Harlem Your Way! Tours Unlimited
129 West 130 Street. 866-6997; 690-1687. Harlem-based group shows you the soul of *the* Black American community: the food, the gospel music, the brownstones, the nightlife, the cultural institutions. Customized walk, bike or limo tours conducted by knowledgeable Harlemites. Call for details.

Hungry Pedalers
771 West End Avenue, New York, N.Y. 10025. 222-2243. City bike tours highlight the historic and gastronomic delights of areas such as Brighton Beach and Atlantic Avenue, Brooklyn, Harlem, and Little Italy. Call or write for schedule. *Every other weekend July-Oct.*

Inside New York
203 East 72 Street. 861-0709. An inside view of New York as fashion capital—from Seventh Avenue to SoHo to the Lower East Side. Fashion shows, luncheon, shopping at discount.

Metropolitan Historic Structures Association
Dyckman House, 4881 Broadway at West 204 St. 304-9422. Tours of historic house museums and designated landmarks, including churches, graveyards, college campuses, theaters throughout the five boroughs. Tailored to the interests of your group. Year round; call or write for info.

Passkey Associates
425 Park Avenue. 688-6926. Custom-designed, multilingual programs, events and activities for conventions, corporate meetings, or travel groups.

Planner's New York Tours
Unusual tours of rarely visited areas of Central Manhattan, Brooklyn, Harlem, Bronx, Queens and Lower Manhattan in a glass-roofed bus. Guides are graduate students in urban planning. Emphasis on history and architecture. For groups. 3½ hours. Call 772-5605.

Rothschild Fine Arts
205 West End Avenue. 873-9142. Expensive but worth it for those serious about art. A husband and wife, knowledgeable experts, escort you to galleries, artists' studios, and museums in chauffeured limo. Tour custom-tailored to your special art interests.

Tours de Force
121 West 72 Street. 595-0267. The creative life of New York: art, theater, fashion. Visits to galleries and artists' studios, meet the performers after the show.

Your Way
P.O. Box 1232, New York, N.Y. 10022. '(1-516) 883-4560. Custom-designed tourist arrangements. Escorted or self-directed itineraries planned.

Young Visitors
145 West 88 Street. 595-8100. Imaginative tours for children and student groups. Emphasis on the history and ethnic flavor of the particular area chosen.

Walking Tours

Classical America
P.O. Box 821, Times Square Station, New York, N.Y. 10036. 753-4376. A national club that sponsors tours focusing on the architecture, sculpture and garden design in the classical style, i.e. Beaux Arts, American Renaissance, neo-classicism. Stanford White and Charles McKim birthday tours. Lectures during the winter. Tours: *Spring & Fall, Sat & Sun afternoons.*

Discover New York Tours
Municipal Art Society, 457 Madison Avenue at East 51 Street. 935-3960. Three-hour knowledgeably guided walks covering the architecture, history and current goings-on in New York Cityscaping. Great way to discover New York's architectural treasures. Shine only; no reservations necessary; call for schedule. *May-Nov, Sun at 2pm.*

Friends of Cast Iron
Expertly guided tours to acquaint people with the splendid 19th-century iron-front architecture of New York. Predominantly in SoHo and TriBeCa. For info call 427-2488. Rain or shine. *Spring & fall, Sun at 2pm.*

Fulton Fish Market
South Street Seaport Museum. 669-9400. For early birds who want to see the catch. A 1 hour and 45 minute tour of the Fulton Fish Market, begun in 1823, and still going strong. Price of the tour includes, breakfast and a bowl of Manhattan (of course) clam chowder. Reserve 2 weeks in advance with full payment; call for details. *End of May-Oct every other Thurs at 6am.*

Grand Central Terminal Tour
A guided walk through New York's grand Beaux Arts beauty, sponsored by the Municipal Art Society, instrumental in the battle to preserve the station. *Year round, every Wed 12:30-1:30pm.* Meet: Main Terminal, beneath the Kodak photo ad. For info call 935-3960. FREE (*See also* HISTORIC NEW YORK, Historic Buildings & Areas: Grand Central Terminal.)

Greenwich Village Walking Tours
Guided tours of Greenwich Village, with a view of its past and present. *Year round. 7 days a week.* Groups or individuals. For details, call 226-1426 between 8am & noon.

Heritage Trail
Lower Manhattan from Civic Center to the South Street Seaport. A 3-mile do-it-yourself walking tour. Buildings, open spaces, and monuments

representing key elements in the economic, social and political evolution of New York have signposts presenting a brief history of each. Map available at Convention & Visitors Bureau or the Vista Hotel.

Holidays in New York
152 West 58 Street. 765-2515. Kay Perper's unique walking tours of Lower Manhattan, Village, SoHo, Chinatown, Little Italy. Emphasis on learning and experiencing. *Sun only.*

92 Street Y
1395 Lexington Avenue. 427-6000. Fun and fascinating—journeys to areas of historic, social and architectural importance. *Early spring-fall, Sun mornings.* Rain or shine. Call for schedule and reservations.

Sunday Walking Tours
Museum of the City of New York, Fifth Avenue & 103 Street. 534-1672. For over 25 years the Museum has sponsored leisurely-paced explorations of New York neighborhoods, highlighting social, historical and architectural details. *April-Oct, Every Sun.* Rain or shine; no reservations necessary.

Urban Park Rangers
From The Dairy, Central Park at 65 Street. 397-3156. The Rangers give tours that focus on every facet of that urban miracle, Central Park: a bird walk, a lake tour, tree i.d., historical and geological tours and more. *Year round, every Sun at 2pm.* For details, call 360-3091.

From the Air

Island Helicopters
Heliport, East 34 Street at the East River. 889-986. Expensive but unforgettable birds-eye view of the city from a sightseeing helicopter. Choice of 5-7, 10-12, 15-17, 20-22 or 35-40 minutes covering a distance of 16 to 100 miles. Costs vary per flight length. Minimum 2 people; no reservations necessary. *Remember to bring your camera.* Free parking. *Available 7 days a week 9am-5pm & 7-9pm.*

On Your Own

For those of you who prefer to make your own way. Make sure also to check the HISTORIC NEW YORK *and* ANNUAL EVENTS *chapters, for more to do on your own.*

Atriums
Foliage-bedecked, glass-topped or enclosed oases in midtown where one can sit, sometimes sip or sup and reflect—often made easy by the presence of reflecting pools and waterfalls. There's even free entertainment on occasion. Listed below are some of these very special urban spaces.

AT & T Building
Madison Avenue, East 55 & 56 Streets. *OPEN Mon-Fri 8am-10pm; Sat & Sun 10am-6pm.*

Chemcourt
277 Park Avenue at East 47 Street. The city's largest indoor green space—a 3-story, block

long greenhouse. *OPEN 7 days, 24 hours a day.*

Citicorp Market
Lexington Avenue, East 53 & 54 Streets. Seven-story high skylit atrium-agora; 27 shops and restaurants. *OPEN Mon-Fri 7am-midnight; Sat 8am-midnight; Sun 10pm-midnight.*

Galleria
East 57 Street between Park & Lexington Avenues. *OPEN Mon-Sat 8am-10pm; Sun till 6pm.*

IBM Atrium
Madison Avenue at East 57 Street. Mon-Fri a kiosk for snacks and beverages amid the bamboo trees. Also, NY Botanical Garden outlet shop. Atrium *OPEN 7 days 8am-10pm.*

Olympic Tower
Fifth Avenue at East 51 Street. Food available Mon-Fri 8am-10:30pm; Sat 9am-8pm. Atrium *OPEN 7 days 7am-midnight.*

Park Avenue Atrium
East 45 to 46 Street between Park & Lexington Avenues. *OPEN Mon-Fri 8am-6pm.*

Park Avenue Plaza
East 52 to 53 Street between Park & Madison Avenues. Cafe Marguery for snacks Mon-Fri 8am-7:30pm. Atrium *OPEN 7 days 7:30am-7pm.*

Trump Tower
Fifth Avenue & East 56 Street. Posh shopping plaza. Bistro *OPEN 7 days noon-4am.* Atrium *OPEN Mon-Sat 10am-6pm.*

Central Park: The Dairy
In the Park, at 65 Street. 397-3156. An 1870 Gothic Revival building designed as a milk dispensary for working-class mothers and their babies. Newly restored, it serves as the Park's information center with changing exhibitions, a slide show every ½ hour, free literature and maps, as well as cards and books for sale. Starting point for lectures and tours on all aspects of Central Park given by the Urban Park Rangers (*see* Walking Tours). *OPEN Feb 1-Oct 31 Tues-Thurs, Sat & Sun 11am-5pm; Fri 1-5pm; Nov 1-Jan 31 till 4pm. CLOSED Mon.*

Federal Reserve Bank
33 Liberty Street nr William Street. 791-6130. See the gold vault, currency-processing, the security area, and a brief film about the central bank. Call for reservations at least 1 week in advance. *One-hour tours, Mon-Fri 10 & 11am, 1 & 2pm.* FREE

Guinness World Records Exhibit Hall
Empire State Building, Fifth Avenue at 34 Street, concourse level. 947-2335. Memorabilia, minutiae, and videotapes of the feats chronicled in the *Guinness Book of World Records. OPEN 7 days 9:30am-6pm.* Allow 45 minutes. Admission charge; discount for children under 12, senior citizens.

Intrepid Sea-Air-Space Museum
Pier 86, West 46 Street & the Hudson River. 245-0072. Born in 1943, this well-traveled 900-foot aircraft carrier—the former U.S.S. *Intrepid*—is now a fascinating museum. In addition to the air-

craft on board, there are crew area exhibits, an audio-visual presentation, and the Hall of Honor, dedicated to America's Medal Of Honor recipients. The *Intrepid* had an illustrious 31-year career in WW II and southeast Asia; it was also the rescue ship for the *Mercury* and *Gemini* space missions. Gift shop, cafeteria. Half-price for children and seniors. Group rates (245-2533) available. *OPEN Wed-Sun 10am-5pm.*

Metropolitan Opera House Backstage
Lincoln Center, Broadway & West 64 Street. 582-3512. For 1½ hours take a fascinating tour of the scenic and costume shops, stage area and rehearsal facilities. Admission fee, lower for students. *Oct-June, Mon-Fri at 3:30pm; Sat at 10:30am.*

NBC Studio Tour
30 Rockefeller Plaza nr 49 St. 664-4000. Guided tours of the TV and radio stations located in the RCA Building. *Mon-Sat 10am-4pm.* Admission charge. Children under age 6 not admitted. Reserve for groups of 10 or more.

The New York Experience
McGraw-Hill Building, 1221 Avenue of the Americas nr West 48 St, lower plaza. 869-0345. Multimedia extravaganza: see and hear New York's past and present. *OPEN Mon-Thurs 11am-7pm, Fri & Sat till 8pm, Sun & holidays noon-8pm.* Shows every hour on the hour. Admission charge. Discount for children under age 12 and senior citizens. For group sales 869-0346. Also includes a free visit to Little Old New York, turn-of-the-century replica of how we were. *OPEN Mon-Sat from 11am; Sun from noon.*

New York Public Transit Exhibit
Schermerhorn Street & Boerum Place, Brooklyn. (1-718) 330-3060. Memorabilia covering a century of transit development. Fully restored subway cars, trolleys, fare-collection devices, models, movies, and slide show. *OPEN 7 days 9:30am-4pm. CLOSED Thanksgiving, Christmas and New Year's Day.* Token admission charge, lower for children under 17. A or F train to Jay Street/Boro Hall. (*See also* Nostalgia Special.)

New York Stock Exchange
20 Broad Street nr Wall Street. 623-5168. In front of what is now 60 Wall Street, 24 brokers met in 1792 under a buttonwood tree and agreed to a strict conduct of business, creating the New York Stock Exchange. The building that houses it dates from 1903. Exhibit hall and gallery overlooking the trading floor. Every ½ hour (till 3pm) there's a brief explanation of the hectic goings-on. Advance reservations are necessary for groups of 10 or more. *OPEN to the public Mon-Fri 9:30am-4pm.* FREE

Nostalgia Special
IND Subway, West 57 Street & Avenue of the Americas. The "B" Line. (1-718) 330-3060 or (1-718) 330-3063. Ride a genuine vintage subway train, first to the Transit Exhibit (see above), then take a 45-minute ride out to Rockaway Beach. Magnificent views of Jamaica Bay Wildlife area en route. Budget priorities may affect service. Call first. *OPEN Sat, Sun, holidays only from (approx.) Memorial Day weekend to Thanksgiving*

weekend. Admission charge; discount for those under age 18.

New York Stock Exchange

Radio City Music Hall Entertainment Center
Avenue of the Americas at West 50 Street. 757-3100. The "Showplace of the Nation" survives and thrives with spectaculars for the whole family: live shows with colorful costumes, scenery and the incomparable 36—collectively known as the Rockettes. Fascinating 1-hour long backstage tours. 541-9436. Group tours available. *See also* Rockefeller Center.

Rockefeller Center
30 Rockefeller Plaza. 489-2949. Through the concourse every 45 minutes, *Mon-Sat 9:30am-4:45pm.* One-hour guided tour includes Radio City Music Hall backstage, the observation deck of the 70-story RCA Building, and a private roof garden. Admission charge. Discount for children under 12, students, and senior citizens.

Schapiro's Winery
126 Rivington Street at Essex Street. 674-4404. It's not the Napa Valley but it is the only working winery in Manhattan, founded in 1899. Tour the wine cellars, see the presses, taste the wine. *Half-hour tours every hour 11am-4pm* (from noon in summer) *every Sun.* No reservations necessary. FREE

South Street Seaport Marketplace
At Fulton & South Streets. New York's hottest new attraction is one of the oldest areas of the city. The 19th-century seaport area has been renewed. The 11 blocks of historic buildings are squeaky clean and the tall ships have been joined by chic boutiques and a mind-boggling array of food stalls and cafés. There's plenty to do and see but many New Yorkers miss the gritty old seaport. *OPEN 7*

days. (*See also* HISTORIC NEW YORK, Historic Buildings & Areas: Schermerhorn Row *and* MUSEUMS & GALLERIES, Historic Museums: South Street Seaport Museum.) *OPEN Mon-Sat 10am-10pm; Sun noon-6pm.*

United Nations Headquarters
First Avenue bet East 42 & East 48 Streets. 754-7713. Visitors' entrance at East 46 Street. The monolithic Secretariat building, the General Assembly building, and the Dag Hammarskjöld Library make up the complex. Free tickets for meetings of the General Assembly and Councils when in session; call for info. *OPEN 7 days 9:15am-4:45pm.* Paid guided tours every 15 mins. (no children under age 5 admitted). Student discounts. Don't miss the International Gift Shop in the lower level. *See also* HISTORIC NEW YORK: Modern Architecture.

River Trips

Andrew Fletcher
South Street Seaport, Pier 16. 964-9082. Board this sidewheel excursion paddlewheel boat and see the sights of NY Harbor for 1½ hours. It's a bargain excursion and a pure delight. Sails *April-Oct Mon-Fri noon, 2, 4, 6, 7, 8pm; Sat & Sun at 10am as well.* Buy tickets at the Pilot House; call to reserve. Available for charter and private parties.

Circle Line Cruise
Circle Line Plaza, West 42 Street & the Hudson River. 563-3200. The best way to cover 35 miles of sightseeing without becoming footsore. A relaxing—and in summer, refreshing—3 hours. Narration often amusing as well as informative. Junk food available; soft drinks & beer, too. Group rates for 15 or more adults. Age twelve half price. *Late March-mid Nov, 7 days a week. Sailings every 45 minutes 9:45-5:50pm.*

Circle Line Twilight Cruise
Circle Line Plaza, West 42 Street & the Hudson River, 563-3200. A floating cocktail lounge with the world's best views. Two-hour twilight cruise, dancing to a live band. Fee includes hors d'oeuvres, open bar, tax & tips. Jacket required. *June-Aug, every Wed & Thurs at 7:30pm.* Reserve in advance. AE, DC, MC, V. (no refunds)

Ellis Island Ferry & Tour
Battery Park & South Ferry. 269-5755. A poignant reminder of New York's role as adopted home of 12 million people from other lands. The "Island of Tears" as it was called by those who for one reason or another did not make it through, was designated an immigration station in 1890. The present building dates from 1900 and is being restored as part of the Statue of Liberty Centennial Celebration; to be completed and reopened to the public in 1986. Call for update.

Hudson River Day Line
Pier 81, foot of West 41 Street. 279-5151. A 2½-hour scenic cruise up the Hudson River to Bear Mountain. Disembark there for a 4-hour stopover for swimming, boating, nature trails. Or sail for 30 min. more and disembark for a 3-hour stop at West Point (sightseeing bus tour, additional fare). Cafeteria on board. *Daily from Memorial Day weekend to mid-Sept EXCEPT Mon, Tues & Fri in June. DEPARTURE 9:30am. RETURN 6:30pm.* (*See also* Day Trips, Escorted.) Fare lower for seniors, half fare for kids under age 12. Group rates for 25 or more adults; call 279-5151. Also, for group activities at Bear Mountain call (1-914) 786-2701; at West Point, call (1-914) 446-4520.

Petrel
From Battery Park. 825-1976. Sail New York Harbor on the spectacular 70-foot yawl that JFK sailed when he was President. *Mid April-mid Oct,* during the week there is a variety of lunchtimes (1 hour, 45 mins); happy hour (1½ hrs), sunset (1½ hrs) and moonlight outings. Weekends there are 2 harbor sails during the day as well. Reservations and payment must be made well in advance (it's very popular with city-wise NYers); be forewarned they go *rain or shine* so be prepared to get wet or lose your money because there are *no refunds or date changes unless* the Captain wills it. Bar on board, you may bring food. Wear soft-soled shoes.

Pioneer
South Street Seaport, Pier 16, Fulton & South Streets. 669-9400. Sail New York Harbor for 3 hours on a 102-foot schooner built in 1885. Course depends on wind and tides. Bring food and drink, dress appropriately. Maximum 25 passengers. *May-Oct Wed-Sun noon-2pm; 7 days 3-5pm; Sat & Sun 6-9pm; Mon-Fri 6-9pm, only if not chartered.* Charters Mon-Sat 9pm-midnight only. Call ahead for reservations and payment. No radios.

Staten Island Ferry
In Manhattan: at the foot of Whitehall Street at Battery Park: 248-8097. In Staten Island: at the foot of Bay Street, St. George: (1-718) 727-2508. A 25-minute boat ride crosses Upper New York Bay. Wonderful views and it costs only a penny a minute! Snack bar on board. *Passengers & autos 24 hours a day. 7 days a week. Weekends every ½ hour, weekdays every 20 minutes.*

Statue of Liberty Ferry
(*See* Viewpoints.)

Ventura
Pier 11, on the East River, at the foot of Wall Street. Built as a millionaire's yacht in 1922, the Ventura, lovingly restored in 1975, now sails the waters of Manhattan with lunch-hour sails *Mon-Fri noon-1pm; Sat & Sun at noon, 3 & 6pm.* A deposit is required with all reservations. Also available for private & group charter. For details, call 344-5942.

World Yacht Luxury Harbor Cruises
Cruise on NY's first luxury restaurant yachts. *See* RESTAURANTS, Rooms with a View: Empress/Riveranda.

Day Trips from New York City

Escorted
Historic Hudson Tour
Carey Gray Line, 900 Eighth Avenue at West 54

Street. 765-1600. Leave at 9am for an all-day excursion. Travel by bus to Lyndhurst and West Point, have lunch, and return to New York via a scenic Hudson River boat trip. *June-Oct. Tues & Thurs only.* Call for rates.

Long Island Rail Road Tours
Penn Station, 34 Street and Eighth Avenue. *June-mid Nov.* The LIRR offers escorted combination rail, bus, and boat tours of Long Island: *Spring Flower Tour*—Planting Fields, Oyster Bay, the Vanderbilt Museum & Mansion; *Great South Bay Boat Cruise*—All-day train, bus, boat tour; *Bridgeport Ferry Tour*—150-mile land/water cruise; *Famous Homes & Garden Tour*—Sagamore Hill & Old Westbury Gardens; *Lands End*—the Hamptons & Montauk; *Island Hopping*—Greenport, Shelter Island & Sag Harbor. Also special tours, *July & Aug, Mon, Tues & Wed* (to the Hamptons). Some of these include meals. For details on each tour, call 526-7782; for train schedules, call 739-4200.

Atlantic City, N.J.
Though it's out of New York State, it deserves a mention because it's the only place on the East Coast (so far) that has legalized gambling. Besides casinos, top-name entertainers, and restaurants, there's the famed saltwater taffy. Carey Gray Line has day trips, call 397-2600.

Bear Mountain
Palisades Interstate Park, N.Y. (1-914) 786-2701. Forty-five miles from New York. At its highest point, 1,305 ft. Recreation facilities: swimming, nature trails, playing fields, skiing, museum, zoo, picnic areas. (*See also* River Trips: Hudson River Day Line.)

Boscobel Restoration
Garrison-on-Hudson, N.Y. 562-7444 or (1-914) 265-3638. A grand Federal-style mansion built in 1806 by States Morris Dyckman, a Loyalist. Located on 36 acres of formal gardens and lawns overlooking the Hudson. Elegant 19th-century furnishings include some Duncan Phyfe. A calendar of special events is available. The Christmas candlelight tour is very special. *OPEN March-Dec. Wed-Mon 10am-4pm; till 5pm in summer. CLOSED Tues, Thanksgiving & Christmas Day & all of Jan & Feb.* Admission includes 45-min tour. Lower for kids age 6-14; under 6 are free.

Brotherhood Winery
Washingtonville, N.Y. (1-914) 496-9101. Founded by monks, it's America's oldest winery. Tour the caves and learn about winemaking. Harvest time is a special treat. *OPEN early Feb-March & end of Nov weekends only, 11am-4pm. April-June & Sept-mid Nov, weekdays as well, noon-3pm. End of June-end of Sept, weekdays 10am-4pm; weekends 11am-4pm. CLOSED mid Nov-early Feb. Mid Nov-Christmas* there are mini tours only on weekends. Call for details.

FDR Home
Hyde Park, N.Y. (1-914) 229-9115. Franklin D. Roosevelt was born and reared in this large, rather plain country house built in 1826 (remodeled 1915). The museum contains a wealth of memorabilia from the Roosevelt presidency (tape-cassette tours available). In the Rose Garden, a simple slab of white Vermont marble marks the resting place of FDR and wife Eleanor. *OPEN year round 7 days 9am-5pm. CLOSED Thanksgiving, Christmas & New Year's Day.* Admission charge includes Vanderbilt Mansion (*see also* Vanderbilt Mansion). Children under age 16 and senior citizens free.

Lyndhurst
Tarrytown, N.Y. (1-914) 631-0313. A Gothic Revival castle designed in 1838 by Alexander Jackson Davis for General William Paulding, an early NYC mayor. Enlarged in 1864, then purchased by railroad tycoon Jay Gould in 1870. Opulent interiors, period furnishings, a carriage house, and the remains of one of the world's largest greenhouses. *OPEN April-Oct, Wed-Sun 10am-5pm; Nov & Dec, Sat & Sun only. CLOSED Jan-March.* Admission charge includes tour. Children under 6 free.

Old Bethpage Village
Round Swamp Road, Old Bethpage, Long Island. (1-516) 420-5280 (for directions). This outdoor historical museum is a restoration of a pre-Civil War rural Long Island village. Active village of craftsmen and a working historical 1850s farm. Site of the big Long Island Fair in Oct. Cafeteria and picnic facilities available. Nearby: Bethpage State Park. *OPEN Tues-Sun 10am-5pm; Dec-Feb till 4pm. CLOSED some winter holidays.* Admission charge, lower for children. Call (1-516) 420-5288 for group reservations.

Old Westbury Gardens
Old Westbury, Long Island (1-516) 333-0048. Several hundred acres of formal English Gardens. Beautifully furnished Georgian-style manor house built in 1909, once the property of millionaire John S. Phipps. *OPEN only May-Oct, Wed-Sun 10am-5pm. In June & July till twilight.* Admission charge: discount for children 6-12; under 6, free.

Planting Fields Arboretum
Oyster Bay, Long Island (1-516) 922-9200. A 409-acre country estate laid out into English gardens (the azalea walk is magnificent). It's a tranquil oasis, and on the grounds, Coe Hall, a 75-room Tudor-style mansion containing an eclectic collection of artifacts from all over the world. Gardens and greenhouse *OPEN year round 7 days 9am-4:30pm. CLOSED Christmas Day.* Admission charge (free weekdays Sept-May). Mansion *OPEN April-end of Sept only, Tues-Thurs 1-3:30pm.* Admission charge.

Sag Harbor, Long Island
(1-516) 725-0540; 725-0011. Charming 19th-century waterside whaling center with historic houses and buildings. A 1793 Customs House, old cemetery, and Whaling Museum.

Sleepy Hollow Restorations
(1-914) 631-8200. In the lower Hudson Valley immortalized in Washington Irving's "Legend of Sleepy Hollow." All 3 of the following are *OPEN year round 7 days. 10am-5pm.* Separate or combination admission available. Discount for chil-

dren under 14 (under 6 free) and senior citizens. Picnicking permissible at all 3 sites.

Philipsburg Manor
North Tarrytown, N.Y. Restored early-1700s Dutch-American water-powered gristmill, barn, and stone manor house. Spinning and weaving demonstrations, costumed guides.

Sunnyside
Tarrytown, N.Y. Located on 20 acres, the 19th-century estate of Washington Irving. Personal memorabilia and furnishings, including over 3,000 books!

Van Cortlandt Manor
Croton-on-Hudson, N.Y. The Revolutionary War estate of one of America's Founding Fathers. Such notables as Ben Franklin and Lafayette dined here. Original furnishings and paintings.

Vanderbilt Mansion
Hyde Park, N.Y. (1-914) 229-9115. Sumptuous 1898 Italian Renaissance residence of Frederick Vanderbilt, the Commodore's son, designed by McKim, Mead & White. Opulent furnishings and paintings from the 16th-18th centuries. *OPEN April-Oct 7 days, 10am-6pm; balance of the year 9am-5pm. CLOSED Thanksgiving, Christmas &* *New Year's Day.* Admission charge includes FDR Home. Free for children under age 16 and seniors.

Vanderbilt Museum & Planetarium
Little Neck Road, Centerport, Long Island. Planetarium: (1-516) 757-7500 (recorded info; sky show times). Museum: (1-516) 261-5656. William K. Vanderbilt's "Eagle's Nest." A 24-room Spanish Baroque mansion situated on 43 acres overlooking the harbor contains wonderful art treasures. Planetarium *OPEN Sept-June Fri, Sat & Sun; July-Aug. Tues-Sun.* Call for show times and theme, and special programs for school children. Admission charge. Discount for children over 6 and senior citizens. Museum *OPEN May-Oct Tues-Sun 10am-4pm. Sun & holidays till 5 pm.* Admission charge; discount for senior citizens.

West Point, N.Y.
U.S. Military Academy. (1-914) 938-2638. The famed military academy magnificently perched above the Hudson. Fort Putnam *OPEN mid May-Nov 7 days, 10:30-4pm.* Museum *OPEN year round 10:30am-4:15pm.* Cadet dress parades early Sept-Nov and in April-May. The Chapel and Visitors' Center *OPEN 7 days 8:30am-4pm.* (*See* also River Trips.)

Annual Events

New York Marathon runner

Calendar

The following is a list of annual events in the city that cover every area of interest. They are the great and small happenings that give the Big Apple its flavor, and many of them are FREE.

January

Legal Holidays
New Years Day, Jan 1; Martin Luther King Jr. Birthday, 3rd Mon.

Poetry Project
St. Marks Church, Second Avenue & East 10 Street. Jan. 1 from 7pm-3am. The Annual New Years Benefit for the resident Poetry Project, at this treasure of a landmark church. Over 100 poets, dancers and musicians perform. Tickets may be reserved, admission charge. Call 674-0910 for info.

Chinese New Year—"Kung Ha Fa Choy"
Early Jan-mid Feb. Based on the lunar calendar. A 10-day celebration ushered in by a barrage of fireworks and a paper-dragon dance through Chi-natown's streets. Many area restaurants have extravagant banquets for the occasion. For particulars, call 397-8222. FREE

Winter Festival
Central Park, The Great Lawn at 81 Street. Early Jan. One-day festival. Demonstrations of cross-country skiing, snow-sculpture contest, fashion shows. Herman's World of Sporting Goods supplies everything, including the snow. For exact date, call 408-0100. FREE

National Boat Show
New York Coliseum, West 59 Street at Columbus Circle. 757-5000. Mid-Jan, for approximately 10 days. All the latest pleasure craft and equipment, a cure for cabin fever. Admission charge.

Ice Capades
Madison Square Garden, 4 Penn Plaza. 564-4400. Late Jan, for approximately 2 weeks. Artistry on ice, colorful and entertaining extravaganza to delight adults and kids. Tickets can be purchased in advance.

Greater New York Auto Show
New York Coliseum, West 59 Street at Columbus Circle. 757-5000. Late Jan, for approximately 9 days. The latest-model cars. Admission charge.

Winter Antiques Show
7th Regiment Armory, Park Avenue & East 67 Street. Late Jan-early Feb. Very high-quality antique show, with dealers from all over the country. Sponsored by the East Side Settlement House; call 665-5250 for info. Admission charge.

February

NOTE: *In honor of Lincoln's and Washington's birthdays the large department stores traditionally run fantastic sales. Check the daily newspapers for particulars.*

Legal Holidays
Lincoln's Birthday, Feb 12; Washington's Birthday, 3rd Mon.

Black History Month
The entire month of Feb is devoted to a celebration of Black history and culture. Events in all the boroughs; check the newspapers and call 397-8222 for specifics.

Chinese Lantern-Day Parade
On the 15th day of the Lunar New Year. Mid-Feb (depending on the moon). Chinatown's schoolchildren parade to City Hall to present handmade paper lanterns to the mayor. Singing, dancing and Kung Fu demonstrations. Call 397-8222 for exact date. FREE

Westminster Kennel Club Dog Show
Madison Square Garden, 4 Penn Plaza. 564-4400. Mid-Feb, for 2 days. The show of shows for dog lovers. Call for exact date. Admission charge.

National Antiques Show
Madison Square Garden, 4 Penn Plaza. 564-4400. Mid-Feb, for approximately 5 days. One of the year's biggest antique and collectible shows, much quality; some junk. Call for exact date. Admission charge.

March

Empire State Building Run-Up
Start: the lobby. Finish: the 86th-floor observation

deck. Early March. An invitational run up this unique course. The prize, a model of the building *sans* steps. Sponsored by the NY Road Runners Club. For info call 860-4455.

The Armory Show
7th Regiment Armory, Park Avenue & East 67 Street. Early March, preview plus 4 days. Renowned international antiques show for the benefit of WNET, public television. For details, call 777-5218.

St. Patrick's Day Parade
Fifth Avenue from 44 to 86 Street. March 17, 11am. A spirited wearin' of the green (including the usually white line down the avenue), with marching bands and smiling politicians. "Kiss Me I'm Irish" buttons abound. For details, call 397-8222. FREE

Ringling Bros. and Barnum & Bailey Circus
Madison Square Garden, 4 Penn Plaza. 564-4400. The world-famed 3-ring circus comes to town every year, usually at the end of March, and stays until the end of May. For children of all ages. Tickets may be purchased in advance. Also, find out the date the animals parade to the Garden.

—March or April
Depending on when Easter falls.

Ukrainian Easter Egg Exhibit
Ukrainian Museum, 203 Second Avenue nr East 13 St. 228-0110. Mid-March–mid-April, Wed-Sun 1-5pm. A display of over 200 colorful Ukrainian Easter eggs—*pysanky*—decorated by the wax-resistant method in designs that are representative of various regions. The tradition stems from pagan times, and most have symbolic meanings, such as prosperity or health. Call for exact dates. Admission charge. Workshops too, mid-March till Easter.

Easter Lilies Display
Channel Gardens, Rockefeller Center. An annual Easter treat.

Annual Easter Flower Show
Macy's Herald Square, 151 West 34 Street. Palm Sunday-Easter Sunday. On the main fl and 6th fl, and in The Cellar, this huge store literally blooms. For info call 560-4495. FREE

Egg Rolling Contest
Central Park, The Great Lawn, West 81 Street. Sponsored by the Parks Department. On the Sat of Easter weekend 9am-3pm. Wooden eggs are used. For children aged 6-13. For info call 408-0204. FREE

Easter Parade
Fifth Avenue from 49 to 59 Street. Easter Sunday 11am-2:30pm. More a display of Easter finery than a parade. Major events in front of St. Patrick's Cathedral at 51 Street.

April
Coney Island Amusement Park starts its season, and it's time for the Mets and Yankee baseball teams to begin to play ball. Call 397-8222 for exact dates.

Street Entertainers
A sure sign of spring's arrival is the profusion of street performers that appear along with the daffodils. The street theater tends to be where the crowds are, always weather permitting. Here are a few of the main "stages":

Battery Park & Wall Street
Weekdays, noon.

Central Park
At the zoo entrance; the zoo plaza; the Mall nr 72 Street Daily.

Fifth Avenue
From Rockefeller Center (50 Street) to Central Park (59 Street). Daily, noon & 5pm.

Greenwich Village
Daily and weekends in Washington Square Park.

Metropolitan Museum of Art
Fifth Avenue at 82 Street. Daily.

The New York Public Library
Fifth Avenue at 42 Street. Weekdays at noon.

Theater District
Intermission: matinee and evening performances.

Broadway Show League
Heckscher Diamond in Central Park at East 62 Street. 736-9099. Mid April-July (weather permitting) Thurs at noon & 2pm. A 20-team softball league comprised of people involved in the theater. At times the cast and crew of one Broadway show plays another. FREE

Stuyvesant Park Festival
Second Avenue at East 17 Street. One Sun in mid-April. The very first of the spring season's outdoor fairs—and none too soon. A lovely park setting for buying antiques, collectibles, rare books, crafts and new merchandise too. For info call 674-5094. FREE

New York Antiquarian Book Fair
7th Regiment Armory, Park Avenue & East 67 Street. April, one weekend. First editions, manuscripts, autographs, atlases, drawings, prints, maps. Price range $25-25,000. Admission.

Spring Flower Display
The Channel Gardens, Rockefeller Plaza nr Fifth Ave. Mid-April–mid-May. A small, superb garden in the middle of Manhattan right where and when you need it.

Five Boro Bike Tour
End of April, one Sun at 8am. Starts & ends at Battery Park, Manhattan. An annual rite of spring—what the marathon is to runners, this is to pedalers. Through the 5 boroughs, covering 32 miles. Over 17,000 participants make this the world's largest bicycle event. Sponsored by Citibank and American Youth Hostels. For info call 431-7100.

May
Check the April listings for ongoing events.

Legal Holiday
Memorial Day, last Mon.

Parades
The following take place during May:
    Armed Forces Day Parade
    Brooklyn Bridge Day Parade
    Bronx Day Parade,

Greek Parade
Martin Luther King, Jr., Memorial Day
Parade
Norwegian Independence Day Parade
Call 397-8222 for exact dates and routes.

Block Fairs

From May to Oct uptown, downtown, and all around New York town, street fairs and block parties have become traditional weekend summer fare. Music, games, food, rummage, antiques, collectibles, often for the benefit of neighborhood and block beautification projects. Some of the best are included in this calendar. For a current list of each weekend's fairs and festivals check the *New York Times* Weekend section on Fri, and by all means, check notices on billboards and lampposts. FREE

Greenmarkets

In all the boroughs. May-Dec. The Council on the Environment introduced the idea and it's a gem. Farm-fresh produce and baked goods sold in inner-city neighborhood parks by farmers, dairymen, butchers and bakers from NY, NJ and PA. Union Square Park is the biggest and best every Wed & Sat 8am-late afternoon, year round. For info call 840-7355.

Brooklyn Heights Promenade Art Show

Along the East River, Remsen to Clark Streets. (1-718) 783-3077. First weekend in May, 11am-6pm. Over 100 artists, photographers and artisans with the New York skyline as backdrop. A quality show. (Also, first weekend in Oct.) FREE

Citicorp Center

The Market, East 53 Street & Lexington Avenue. 559-2330. Entertainment events and concerts, including jazz, Shakespeare, musical sing-alongs, and more. In either the Atrium or the outdoor plaza. Calendar available there. *OPEN 7 days.* FREE

Cherry Blossoms

Brooklyn Botanic Gardens, 1000 Washington Avenue, Brooklyn. (1-718) 622-4433. Early to mid-May, depending on the weather. Don't go to DC, go to Brooklyn, for one of Mother Nature's most spectacular limited engagements. A glorious display. Call for exact date. Voluntary donation.

Ninth Avenue International Festival

Ninth Avenue from West 37 to West 59 Street. Third Sunday in May. In midtown's international food market, a mile-long annual celebration of New York's ethnic diversity. There's entertainment, but the emphasis is on eating, so go hungry! FREE

Sephardic Fair

Spanish and Portuguese (Shearith Israel) Synagogue, Central Park West at 70 Street. 873-0300. One Sun in mid-May 10am-5pm. Tour the landmark home of America's oldest Jewish congregation. See prayer shawls being loomed, jewelry being crafted, potters vending wine cups, and scribes penning marriage contracts. Also, sample Sephardic delicacies. Call for exact date.

Ye Olde Village Fair

Bet Seventh Avenue South & Hudson Street, two blocks south of Sheridan Square. One Sat in mid-May noon-10pm. Come to Bedford, Barrow & Commerce—archetypal narrow Greenwich Village streets—for their crowded fun- and food-filled annual community bash. Outdoor cafe, a big band, and dancing under the stars. A kids street, too. FREE

You Gotta Have Park

Central Park. Mid-May, one weekend. A variety of park-related festivities—races, concerts, games—to reinforce the tradition of Central Park as urban oasis. Acts as a fund-raiser for the Central Park Conservancy, a nonprofit group that assists in park maintenance and renovation. For info call 315-0385. Donation requested

Ukrainian Festival

East 7 Street bet Second Ave & the Bowery. Usually the third weekend in May. *Pierogi,* polkas, and *pysanky.* Old-country music, crafts and costumes too, in the heart of New York's Ukrainian community. Call 674-1615 for exact date. FREE

Storytelling Hour

Central Park, Hans Christian Andersen Statue nr Conservatory Pond (74 Street). Storytelling from late May to Sept every Sat at 11am for one hour. Of interest to children age 3-7. The statue itself is a delight. For info, call 397-3156. FREE

Park Avenue Antiques Show

7th Regiment Armory, Park Avenue & East 67 Street. 288-0200. End of May for 1 week. Prestigious show of American and European antiques and art. For info call (1-516) 822-2372. Admission charge.

L'eggs Mini Marathon

Start: Central Park West & 66 Street. Finish: Tavern-on-the-Green. End of May. World's biggest race for women only—6.2 miles (10,000 meters). For info, call 860-4455.

—Memorial Day Weekend

Last weekend in May. The unofficial start of summer. All New York City beaches open.

Washington Square Outdoor Art Show

Fifth Avenue, Washington Square Park & environs. Memorial Day weekend and early June for 3 weekends, noon-sundown. The streets of Greenwich Village in the Washington Square area become an art gallery with 600 exhibitors. LaGuardia Place is filled with imaginative crafts, too. For exact dates, call 982-6255. *See also* September, Labor Day weekend. FREE

June

Check the April & May listings for ongoing summer events.

Parades

The following take place in June:
Salute to Israel Parade
Puerto Rican Day Parade
For exact dates, call 397-8222.

Museum Mile

Fifth Avenue from 105 to 82 Street. First Tues in June, 6-9pm. A grand open house when, for one evening, 10 of NY's prized cultural institutions are open free of charge—entertainment too. For info call 397-8222. FREE

A Little Noon Music
St. Marks Park, Second Avenue & East 10 Street. June & July every Thurs at noon. In front of the oldest site of worship in the city, a series of musical interludes: jazz, classical and pop. Intermission snacks courtesy of the 2nd Avenue Deli. Sponsored by the Third Street Music School & the 10th & Stuyvesant Streets Block Assoc. For info call 777-3240. FREE

Children's Day Fair
Staten Island Museum, 75 Stuyvesant Place, St. George, Staten Island. First Sat in June 11am-3pm. Among other activities, arts and crafts including kite-making, painting, hand-puppet decorating. Nominal fees. For info, call (1-718) 727-1135.

"Seventh Heaven"
Seventh Avenue from Flatbush Avenue to 12 Street, Park Slope, Brooklyn. First Sun in June, 10am-6pm. A 17-block neighborhood celebration in Brooklyn's landmark brownstone district. Food, crafts, entertainment, and a 5-mile run. For info, call (1-718) 789-4100.

Basically Bach
Avery Fisher Hall, Broadway & West 65 Street. 874-2424. Early June for 6 days. Tickets can be purchased in advance.

Big Apple Circus
June-Aug at various locations throughout the city. Our very own 1-ring circus thrills and delights kids of all ages. Admission charge. For info, call 369-5110.

Belmont Stakes
Belmont Park Race Track, Hempstead Turnpike & Plainfield Avenue, Elmont, Long Island. New York's thoroughbred of horseraces and a jewel in the Triple Crown. Early June. For exact date, call (1-718) 641-4700. Admission charge.

Goldman Memorial Band
Damrosch Park, West 62 Street & Amsterdam Avenue. Early June-mid Aug. Wed-Fri & Sun 8-10pm. Since 1917, popular traditional band concerts. Enduring and endearing. For info, call 867-8290. FREE

The Met in the Parks
Central Park, Great Lawn, Manhattan
Snug Harbor, Staten Island
Cunningham Park, Queens
Marine Park, Brooklyn
Prospect Park, Brooklyn
Van Cortlandt Park, Bronx
In June—free outdoor evening (8:30pm) performances in the city's parks by the Metropolitan Opera Company. Picnic and Puccini, a New York summer joy. For details, call 362-6000.

Festival of Saint Anthony of Padua
Sullivan Street bet West Houston & Spring Sts. Early June for 2 weeks. An Italian street *festa,* with music, games of chance, rides for the kids, but mostly glorious aromatic food for sale. A spring must. For exact date, call 777-2755. FREE

Lower East Side Jewish Festival
East Broadway from Rutgers to Montgomery Streets. One Sun, early-mid June. The Old World still lives on the Lower East Side albeit there is some Spanish and Chinese mixed in with the Yiddish these days. Books, baked goods, entertainment. Go, you'll enjoy. For info, call 475-6200. FREE

Music for a City Evening
The Channel Gardens, Rockefeller Plaza nr Fifth Ave; Exxon Park, 1251 Avenue of the Americas; McGraw-Hill Park, 1221 Avenue of the Americas. Mid June-mid Aug, every Tues & Thurs, 4:30-6pm. Jazz, Dixieland, and singing concerts by top-name entertainers. For exact dates and programs, call 489-3899. FREE

New York Women's Jazz Festival
Mid-June for 8 days at various locations around the city in- and outdoors, free and pay performances, a salute to women in jazz. For details, call the Universal Jazz Coalition, 505-5660.

Kool Jazz Festival New York
Approx. June 25-July 5. Hot and cool jazz in the concert halls of New York City and environs. For ticket info, call 787-2020; tickets at Ticketron.

Summer Arts Festival
Bell Plaza, Avenue of the Americas, bet West 41 & 42 Streets. End of June-end of Aug, every Tues at noon. Performances designed to showcase ethnic and cultural diversity with up and coming talent. For info, call 395-2357. FREE

Shakespeare in the Park
Delacorte Theater, Central Park. Enter from either East or West 81 Street. Late June-early Sept. Joseph Papp productions of Shakespeare in a lovely outdoor theater. Tickets distributed at 6:30pm to *very* early comers for that evening's performance. For details, 861-PAPP. FREE (although you may be asked for a contribution; better yet, be sure of a seat—become a sponsor).

July
Check the April, May, & June listings for ongoing summer events.

Legal Holiday
Independence Day, July 4.

—Independence Day (July 4th) Weekend Celebrations

Macy's Fireworks Display
On barges in the East River. Best view: FDR Drive (closed to traffic) from 14 to 51 Streets. Access East 23, 34 and 48 Streets. A cherished New York July 4 tradition. The spectacular pyrotechnics begin at 9:15pm. Call 560-4495 for details. FREE

Fourth of July Harbor Festival
OP Sail '76 started it; now there's always a nautical event as part of the July 4 celebration. For exact time and place, call 397-8222. FREE

Fourth of July in Old New York Festival
Battery Park vicinity of Lower Manhattan. Noon to early evening. Food, entertainment, patriotic ceremonies and a parade from Bowling Green to City Hall. For details, call 397-8222. FREE

American Crafts Festival
Lincoln Center, West 64 Street & Broadway. First 2 weekends in July. In a beautiful outdoor setting 400 skilled artisans are selected to display their crafts: leather, jewelry, blown and stained glass, quilts, baskets, furniture, toys, and so much more. All for sale. There's also a children's festival within the larger crafts festival. Puppets, magic, mime, clowns, singing, playing, maskmaking, and a sheep-shearing demonstration followed by spinning and weaving of the wool. For info, call 677-4627. FREE

Summerpier
South Street Seaport Museum, Pier 16 at Fulton Street. Early July-mid August Fri & Sat at 8pm. Jazz on the waterfront with lower Manhattan as the backdrop. Tickets (2 per person) given out to first comers 2 hours before the performance. Call 669-9400 for info. FREE

Summergarden
Museum of Modern Art Sculpture Garden, 14 West 54 Street. 708-9840. Early July-mid Aug, every Fri & Sat at 6pm. Music with sculpture and fountains as backdrop. Very special time and place. FREE

Department of Parks & Recreation Mobile Units
From mid-July to late Aug mobile entertainment units travel to the city's parks and playgrounds with puppet shows, music, arts, crafts, and sports supplies. For info, Manhattan, 408-0100; Bronx, (1-718) 430-1800; Queens, (1-718) 520-5900; Brooklyn, (1-718) 965-8900; Staten Island, (1-718) 390-8000. FREE

Washington Square Music Festival
Washington Square Park, at the foot of Fifth Avenue. July & Aug, Tues at 8pm. The oldest open-air concert series in New York. Chamber music in Greenwich Village outdoors and FREE. For details, call 431-1088.

Saturdays at Canarsie Pier
Canarsie, Brooklyn. July-Aug, every Sat 1-3pm. Outdoor children's entertainment. For info, call (1-718) 783-4469. FREE

Brooklyn Philharmonic
July. Six evenings of beautiful music at various outdoor Brooklyn locations. For dates and places, call (1-718) 636-4120. FREE

Chinatown Outdoor Festival
Columbus Park at Bayard & Mulberry Streets. Mid-July to Sept, Sat & Sun 4-6pm. A program of Chinese performing arts from traditional opera to modern pop. For dates, call 431-9740. FREE

Mostly Mozart Festival
Lincoln Center, Avery Fisher Hall, Broadway & West 65 Street. 874-2424. Mid-July–Aug for 6 weeks. Mozart lives! Beginning with a free outdoor afternoon concert, then mainly evening concerts in a relaxed atmosphere at bargain prices.

Festa Italiana
Our Lady of Pompeii at Carmine & Bleecker Streets. Last 2 weeks in July. A colorful *festa* in the old Greenwich Village Italian community. Call 989-6805.

August
Check the April, May, June & July listings for ongoing summer events.

St. Stephen's Day Parade (Hungarian Parade)
For exact date and route call 397-8222.

New York Philharmonic Park Concerts
Central Park, Great Lawn, Manhattan
Snug Harbor, Staten Island
Cunningham Park, Queens
Prospect Park, Brooklyn
Van Cortlandt Park, Bronx
One of New York's special summer treats. Concerts under the stars, the first of the season usually accompanied by a fireworks display. A different program each week in Aug. Good picnic time and place. For details, call 755-4100 or 877-2011. FREE

Governor's Cup Race
Battery Park City Esplanade. Late Aug. A 16-mile sailing race in NY Bay to the Verrazano Narrows Bridge and back to Pier A. Best viewing: Manhattan: the esplanade, Battery Park; Brooklyn: Shore Road (Belt Parkway), 69 Street Pier to Bay 8 Street; Staten Island: Von Briesen Park in Fort Wadsworth, Edgewater Street Rosewater.

Greenwich Village Jazz Festival
End of Aug for 11 days. The kick-off is a free concert in Washington Square Park, then a club-hopping marathon to see some greats. Films, lectures, too. Reservations advised. Buy a festival pass in advance for discounts and freebies. Call 242-1785 for info.

Lincoln Center Out-of-Doors
Lincoln Center Plaza, Broadway & West 65 Street. Mid-Aug to Labor Day daily 11am-8pm. The annual 3-week al-fresco smorgasbord of music, dance and theater. For details, call 877-1800. FREE

Harlem Week
At various sites in the community. Sponsored by the Uptown Chamber of Commerce. Mid-Aug for 1 week, Harlem struts its stuff in the largest Black and Hispanic festival in the world. Indoor and outdoor activities for every age. Salutes the Black community's past, present, and future. Culminates with Harlem Day. Call 427-7200. FREE

September
Theaters, the New York City and Metropolitan Opera Companies, and the New York Philharmonic launch their new seasons. In general, New York cultural life begins anew.

Legal Holiday
Labor Day, 1st Mon.

Parades
Labor Day Parade
Steuben Day (German) Parade
For details call 397-8222.

—Labor Day Weekend
The unofficial end of summer. Check the newspapers for special events marking this last weekend hurrah of summer.

Labor Day Street Fair
West 42 Street, Ninth to Tenth Avenues.

Labor Day Mon, noon-7pm. Performances, booths, music, and food for all in celebration of the pride of work and workers. For info call District 1199, 582-1890.

Washington Square Outdoor Art Exhibit
Fifth Avenue, from 14th to Houston Street, University & LaGuardia Places & the vicinity of Washington Square Park. The streets of Greenwich Village in the Washington Square area become an al fresco art gallery. Labor Day weekend and the 2 following weekends, noon to dusk. For info, call 982-6255. FREE

West Indian American Day Carnival & Parade
Labor Day weekend. A colorful, spirited Caribbean carnival modeled after the harvest carnival of Trinidad & Tobago fills the streets. Begins with an outdoor entertainment extravaganza Fri eve (entrance fee) and culminates Mon 9am-11pm, Eastern Parkway & Utica Avenue, Brooklyn, with a Mardi Gras-style parade of floats, elaborate costumes, and West Indian music. For details, call (1-718) 773-4052. FREE

West Indian Day Festival "Kiddie Carnival"
Brooklyn Museum (parking lot), 200 Eastern Parkway, Brooklyn. Labor Day weekend, Sat & Sun, 10am-4pm. The kids get into the fun, too. They get an opportunity to design and create their own costumes for this colorful ethnic festival. For info, call (1-718) 783-4469. FREE

New York Dance Festival
Delacorte Theater, Central Park at 81 Street. 535-5630. Early Sept for 1 week. An end-of-summer city dance tradition in the open air—from classical to avant-garde, and much in between. Tickets distributed first-come basis at 6:15pm for 8pm performance. FREE

One World Festival
St. Vartan's Armenian Cathedral, 630 Second Avenue at East 35 St. Early Sept (a week after Labor Day) for 1 weekend. Sat noon-11pm, Sun noon-7pm. At least 30 nationalities are represented in this display of international entertainment, food, antiques and crafts on the streets surrounding the cathedral. For kids, puppet shows, roller skating, face-painting, carnival games and entertainment. For exact date, call 686-0710. FREE

TAMA Fair
Third Avenue from East 14 to East 34 Street. Early Sept on the 1st Sun after Labor Day. 11am-dusk. Food, crafts, antiques, general merchandise, junk, art, rides, and games take the place of cars on 1 mile of the avenue. For details, call 674-5094. FREE

New York Is Book Country
Fifth Avenue, 48 to 57 Street. Third Sun in Sept 11am-5pm. For book lovers: the avenue contains the country's largest concentration of book stores. On the streets: kiosks representing major publishers. Previews of new books, authors and live entertainment, book-binding demonstrations. Bring the kids. FREE

Edgar Allan Poe Festival
West 84 Street from West End Avenue to Riverside Drive. One Sat in mid-Sept, 11am-6pm. Honors famed poet who lived at No. 255 when he wrote "The Raven." Readings, music, food, palmist, and astrologers. For details, call 799-4285 or 877-2699. FREE

Steuben Day Parade (German)
Mid-Sept. For exact date, call 397-8222.

Feast of San Gennaro
Mulberry Street from Houston to Worth Street, Little Italy. Mid- to late Sept for 11 days, noon to midnight. Eating and gaming are the major activities at the oldest, grandest and largest *festa* of them all. In honor of the patron saint of Naples, it begins with the Triumphant March from *Aida*. For exact dates, call 226-9546. FREE

Flatbush Frolic
Cortelyou Road bet Coney Island Avenue & East 17 Street. One Sun in mid-Sept, noon-6pm. A community celebration with an old-fashioned, small-town flavor. Ethnic food, entertainment, arts and crafts. For exact date, call 469-8990. FREE

Atlantic Antic
Atlantic Avenue bet Fourth Avenue & the East River, Brooklyn Heights. One Sun late Sept for 1 Sun 10am-6pm. A community festival 12 blocks long to celebrate downtown Brooklyn. Food, entertainment, lots to do and see. Parade at 11:30am. For exact date, call (1-718) 875-8993. FREE

Third Avenue Festival
Third Avenue bet East 68 & East 90 Streets. Mid-Sept, one Sun 11am-dusk. Arts and crafts, antiques, exotic food, entertainment. Fun for all. FREE

New York Film Festival
Alice Tully Hall, Broadway & West 65 Street. 362-1911. From third week in Sept for 2 weeks. A fine film festival since 1963. Afternoon and evening screenings. Tickets can be bought in advance.

Fifth Avenue Mile
82 to 62 Streets on Fifth Avenue. Late Sept, one Sat at 3:15pm. The world's fastest runners on New York's most chic avenue. Over 100,000 spectators line the course for this brief but exhilarating, elite event. For info, call 860-4455.

Once Upon a Sunday
Museum of Modern Art, 11 West 53 Street. One Sun in late Sept 11am-3:30pm. Cartoons, films, stories, games, and refreshments on this day the museum sets aside for kids. Admission charge. Discount for children 6-12, under age 6 free. For info, call 708-9400.

Mayor's Cup
Battery Park, Fireboat House, Pier A. Last Sat in Sept at 10am. An annual NY Harbor schooner race sponsored by the South Street Seaport Museum to commemorate a sailing tradition (19th-century fishing schooners raced back to port with their catch; first in received the best prices). Rain or shine. For info, call 669-9400, and for passage on the spectator boat, *Martha's Vineyard,* call 669-9416.

October

Hockey (NY Rangers) and basketball (NY Knicks) seasons begin at Madison Square Garden. For details, call 564-4400.

Legal Holiday
Columbus Day, 2nd Mon.

Parades
The following take place in October:
Columbus Day Parade
Pulaski Day Parade
Early to mid-Oct. For exact dates and routes, call 397-8222.

Brooklyn Heights Promenade Art Show
Along the East River, Remsen to Clark Streets. First weekend in Oct. *See* May for details.

Harvest Festival
Jacques Marchais Center of Tibetan Art, 338 Lighthouse Avenue, Staten Island. Mid-Oct for 1 weekend, noon-6pm. A Tibetan festival in and around this lovely replica of a Tibetan monastery. For details, call (1-718) 987-3478.

Old Home Day
Richmondtown Restoration, 441 Clarke Avenue nr Arthur Kill Road, Staten Island. Third Sun in Oct 10am-5pm. All the period houses are open for this fall festival. Crafts demonstrations in each building, homemade foods and gifts, square dancing. Admission charge. For info, call (1-718) 351-1611.

Fall Antiques Show at the Pier
West 54 Street & the Hudson River, Pier 90. End of Oct, preview plus 4 days. The foremost American antiques show in the country, a bonanza for Americana collectors. Benefits the Museum of American Folk Art. Parking available. For info, call 777-5218 or 581-2676.

New York City Marathon
Starting point: Staten Island side of the Verrazano Narrows Bridge at 10:45am. Finish line: Tavern-on-the-Green, West Drive in Central Park. Manhattan, at 12:53pm. Last Sun in Oct. See how they run: 17,000-plus men, women, *and* kids cover a 26-mile course through all 5 boroughs. Come and cheer them on. For exact date call 860-4455.

Houdini Pilgrimage
Machpelah Cemetery, Glendale, Queens. The afternoon of October 31, Harry Houdini, master magician, died on Halloween. Led by the Society of American Magicians, there is an annual visit to his grave for a dignified wand-breaking ceremony at the exact moment that he died.

Annual Village Halloween Parade
Start: Houston Street & Sixth Avenue to West 10 Street down Fifth Avenue to gala balloon-filled finish at Washington Square Arch. Oct 31 at 6pm. Join in or just watch the spooky spectacle. For kids, ghouls, and goblins of all ages. The annual procession features generally bizarre costumes and wonderful live music. Eerie vignettes are highlighted along the way. FREE

November

Legal Holidays
Veteran's Day, Nov 11.
Thanksgiving Day, 3rd Thurs.

National Horse Show
Madison Square Garden, 4 Penn Plaza. 546-4400. Early Nov for approximately 6 days. A good show for serious horse enthusiasts. Call for details. Admission charge.

Christmas Star Show
Hayden Planetarium, Central Park West & 81 Street. Late Nov-early Jan. A fascinating special holiday-season. Planetarium show conjuring up the sky over Bethlehem at the time of Christ's birth. For info, call 873-8828. Admission charge.

Lord & Taylor's Christmas Windows
424 Fifth Avenue at 39 Street. From the Tues before Thanksgiving to Jan 1. Lavish, animated scenes on a Christmas-holiday theme fill this store's Fifth Avenue windows to the delight of all. For info, call 391-3344. FREE

Radio City Music Hall
Avenue of the Americas at West 50 Street. 246-4600. Late Nov-early Jan. Christmas Spectacular-huge entertainment extravaganza featuring the world-famed Rockettes. Highlight: traditional Nativity Pageant. Buy advance tickets.

Macy's Thanksgiving Parade
South from West 77 Street & Central Park West to Columbus Circle, down Broadway to the reviewing stand at Macy's Herald Square (West 34 Street). Thanksgiving Day (3rd Thurs in Nov) at 9:15am, see the grandest parade of them all. The biggest stars are the gigantic balloons (inflation the night before on CPW is a gas), although big-name live entertainers are there, too. Santa's official arrival in town. Dress warmly. Call Macy's Special Events hotline, 560-4495. FREE

Origami Holiday Tree
American Museum of Natural History, 79 Street & Central Park West. From Thanksgiving to the 12th day of Christmas, the museum displays a 25-foot tree decorated with 4,000 origami decorations. Workshops are given in this art of Japanese paper-folding in conjunction with the exhibition. For info, call 873-1300.

Macy's Santa Land & Marionette Show
Macy's Herald Square, West 34 Street & Broadway. From the day after Thanksgiving to Dec 24, Santa is in residence here to greet and be photographed with youngsters. There is a delightful 20-minute marionette show hourly from 10:30am to 4:30pm. For info, call 695-4400.

December

There are fairs, festivals, musical programs, Messiah's galore throughout the city during the holiday season. Check the newspapers for specifics.

Legal Holiday
Christmas Day, Dec 25.

Christmas in Richmondtown
Richmondtown Restoration, 441 Clarke Avenue nr Arthur Kill Rd, Staten Island. First or second Sun in Dec 10am-4pm. The restoration buildings are all open and specially decorated in period fashion for Christmas as it was celebrated in the 18th and 19th centuries. Costumed guides, parlor games, popcorn stringing, homemade foods and items for sale. For info, call (1-718) 351-1611. FREE

The Christmas Revels
Symphony Space, Broadway at West 95 Street. 864-5400. Early Dec. Celebration of the winter solstice. A variety of fascinating groups. Five performances. Reserve in advance. Admission charge.

Carousel & Holiday Display
Lever House Lobby, 390 Park Avenue at East 53 Street. Early Dec-Jan 2, an animated carousel and colorful display to delight youngsters. For details, call 688-6000. FREE

Tree-Lighting Ceremony
Rockefeller Center, Fifth Avenue bet 50 & 51 Streets. One weekday in early Dec, 4:30pm. Lights on a mammoth Christmas tree are lit, accompanied by caroling and figure-skating demonstrations. A stirring sight and it's FREE. For exact date, call 489-4300.

WBAI Holiday Crafts Fair
Ferris Booth Hall, Columbia University, West 115 Street & Broadway. For 3 weekends preceding Christmas. More than 4,000 artisans from 35 states partake in the annual holiday crafts fair for the benefit of independent radio station WBAI. Excellent for Christmas shopping. Homemade food and drink; entertainment too. Admission charge, half price for kids under age 10. For exact dates, call 279-0707.

Metropolitan Museum Christmas Tree
Metropolitan Museum of Art, Fifth Avenue & 82 Street. 879-5500. In the medieval Sculpture Hall a 20-foot Baroque tree decorated with 18th-century cherubs and angels and an elaborate nativity scene.

Nutcracker Ballet
Lincoln Center, New York State Theater, Broadway & West 65 Street. 870-5500. Early Dec-early Jan. Tchaikovsky's Christmas gift to us all and a New York tradition. The magical ballet performed by the famed New York City Ballet, ably assisted by children, 8-13, from the School of American Ballet. Very popular, so purchase tickets early.

Annual Children's Christmas Party
Museum of the City of New York, Fifth Avenue & 104 Street. 534-1672. Second Mon in Dec, 2-5pm. Everything a child's party should have: music, movies, games, refreshments and Santa. Best for age 3 and up, accompanied by a parent. Reserve in advance. Admission charge.

American Crafts Holiday Festival
NYU Loeb Student Center, LaGuardia Place at Washington Square South. Second and 3rd weekends in Dec. Over 200 displays of jewelry, musical instruments, furniture, clothing, stained and blown glass, and more. Great place to Christmas-shop. And for the kids, handcrafted toys, entertainment, demonstrations, and wholesome food. Admission charge applicable to purchase. Children under 12 free. For info, call 677-4627.

Fifth Avenue Holiday Festival
Fifth Avenue bet 34 & 57 Streets. Two Sundays before Christmas 11am-3pm. The avenue, closed to traffic, becomes a Christmas shopping and entertainment mall. Participatory activities for kids. For details, call 736-7900. FREE

"'Twas the Night Before Christmas"
Church of the Intercession, West 155 Street & Broadway. 283-6200. On the Sun before Christmas at 4pm, a procession of carolers visits the Trinity Cemetery grave of Clement Clarke Moore, who wrote "A Visit from St. Nicholas," to sing and lay a wreath.

Chanukah Celebration
92nd Street YM-YWHA, 1395 Lexington Avenue. 427-6000. First night of Chanukah: candle-lighting ceremony, children's storytelling, puppet and magic shows, holiday play, music, and refreshments. FREE

Messiah Sing-In
Lincoln Center, Avery Fisher Hall, 874-2424. One week before Christmas, one evening at 7:30pm. Twenty-one guest conductors lead—you and 3,000 others—the chorus in a run-through and performance of Handel's *Messiah*. Loud, enthusiastic, joyful, thrilling! Bring the score or purchase one in the lobby. No experience necessary. Admission charge.

A Christmas Carol
South Street Seaport Museum, Trans-Lux Theater, 210 Front Street. 669-9400. The annual reading by Zoe Caldwell, Ann Jackson and Eli Wallach of Dickens' famed Christmas tale. Call for tickets; half price for children.

Kwanzaa
Dec 26-Jan 1. A 7-day citywide holiday tribute to the cultural roots of Afro-Americans. Check the newspapers for specific events.

—New Year's Eve

Times Square. Every Dec 31 since 1904 a 6-foot illuminated ball (now an apple), has moved down what is the rest of the year a flagpole atop the Times Tower (now 1 Times Square Building). It takes the last 59 seconds of the old year to descend, and at midnight the new year is illuminated at the pole's base. Thousands gather to see it happen in Times Square; the less hardy watch on television. For details, call 397-8222. (The Tower, and this tradition, may be lost in the Times Square Redevelopment Project.) FREE

New Year Run
Start and Finish: Tavern on the Green, Central Park at West 67 Street. At midnight more than 3,000 men and women have a run around Central Park. Many are costumed. Prizes for the best costumed and fastest runners; champagne for all who run. Registration fee. For details, call 860-4455.

Fireworks
Fireworks greet the New Year in Central Park at midnight. Best viewing: Bethesda Fountain, 72 Street; Central Park West & West 96 Street; Tavern on the Green, West 67 Street & Central Park West and Fifth Avenue at 90 Street. Also, Prospect Park, Grand Army Plaza, Brooklyn, fireworks accompanied by music, hot cider and cookies. Festivities begin at 11:30pm. For info, call 397-3111. FREE

Historic New York

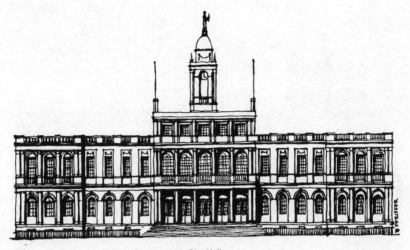

City Hall

New York City: the Boroughs

The Bronx
The only one of the five boroughs connected to the American mainland—all of the others are islands or part of Long Island. In 1874 the western portion of the Bronx became part of the city and in 1895 the eastern part followed suit. Named for founder Jonas Bronck, but famed for its Yankees, its zoo, and its cheer.

Brooklyn
One in seven Americans is said to have roots here. Established as a town in 1658 and as a city in 1834, by 1860 it was America's third largest city. It was consolidated into Greater New York City in 1898. Breukelen—as it was called in Dutch— covers 70 square miles at the southwest end of Long Island. Probably the best-known borough after Manhattan: its colorful image no doubt stems from having spawned Mario Lanza, Mae West, the former Brooklyn Dodgers, Woody Allen and Nathan's hotdogs.

Manhattan
The smallest of the five boroughs, the island is a mere 13.4 miles long and 2.3 miles at its widest point. Manhattan functions as the city's, and to a great extent the world's, nerve center in the areas of finance, art, fashion, and theater.

Queens
Queens is the largest borough, comprising almost one-third of the city's land mass, 114.7 square miles. Named for Catherine de Braganza, wife of Charles II, it is the gateway to New York City for anyone arriving by plane at either Kennedy International or LaGuardia Airport.

Staten Island
The third-largest borough in area, it is the least densely populated, although that is changing rapidly as a result of the construction of the Verrazano Bridge, which joins the Island to Brooklyn. Still just a famed ferry ride away from Manhattan, Staten Island is historically rich (*see* HISTORIC NEW YORK, Historic Buildings & Areas, Staten Island) and is blessed with large areas of untouched natural beauty. (*See also* PARKS & GARDENS.)

Historic Buildings & Areas

This list covers New York's most historic buildings, monuments and houses, as well as notable structures and districts. Historic sites open to the public under city or federal government auspices are subject to changes in budget allocations, which can affect days and times of access. Always call before visiting one unless you are in the vicinity. For convenience, the listings in this section are by borough.

Manhattan
Abigail Adams Smith Museum
421 East 61 Street nr First Ave. 838-6878. An elegant Federal-style carriage house built in 1799 and converted into a residence in 1826; furnished in the late-18th- and early-19th-century styles; a charming Colonial-style garden. Restored by the Colonial Dames of America. *OPEN Mon-Fri 10am-4pm, June & July, Wed 5:30-8pm as well. CLOSED legal holidays.* Admission charge in-

cludes free tour. Lower for senior citizens; children under 12 accompanied by adult, free.

Abigail Adams Smith Museum

Amster Yard
211-215 East 49 Street bet Second & Third Aves. An irregularly shaped courtyard originally (1870) made up of small workshops and houses. Converted in 1945 by designer James Amster into a charming commercial enclave with Old World overtones.

Ansonia Hotel
2109 Broadway bet West 73 & West 74 Sts. (Graves & Duboy.) An exuberant architectural masterpiece finished in 1904. Heavily constructed to be fireproof, this apartment hotel turned out to be virtually soundproof, drawing the likes of Enrico Caruso, Ezio Pinza, Igor Stravinsky, Lily Pons, and Arturo Toscanini.

Ansonia Hotel

Arsenal
Central Park, Fifth Avenue at 64 Street. (Martin E. Thompson, 1848.) Pre-dating the park itself, the Arsenal was built to house the state's cache of artillery and ammunition. Troops were quartered here during the Civil War. Now the home of the Department of Parks and Recreation.

Audubon Terrace Historic District
Riverside Drive to Broadway bet West 155 & West 156 Sts. Originally part of the estate belonging to ornithologist J. J. Audubon. Now a cultural and historic section comprised of 4 small museums and the National Institute of Arts and Letters (*see* MUSEUMS & GALLERIES).

Beekman Place
East 49 to 51 Streets, east of First Avenue. A retreat from Manhattan's bustle so near yet so far. This quiet enclave is one of New York's nearly hidden special places.

Bouwerie Lane Theater
330 Bowery at Bond Street (Henry Engelbert, 1874.) Originally the Bond Street Savings Bank. French Second Empire in cast iron, no less.

Bowery
Third Avenue from Cooper Square (East 7 Street) to Canal Street. From Dutch farm *(bouwerie)* to entertainment center to derelicts' Skid Row—remnants of all these incarnations survive amid the commercial kitchen-equipment stores and the cash-and-carry discount lighting-fixture and lamp emporiums.

Broadway
Synonymous with legitimate theater in New York, though that district is just a small part of what is the city's longest street. It runs from the Battery, at the tip of Manhattan, up into Yonkers. *See also* Times Square.

Carnegie Hall
154 West 57 Street at Seventh Avenue. 247-7459. (William B. Tuthill.) Built under the direction of steel magnate Andrew Carnegie, the Hall made its debut May 5, 1891, with a concert conducted by Tchaikovsky. Not only has it survived the competition of Lincoln Center, but it thrives still. Consult newspapers for current performances.

Cast-Iron District
Broadway & West Broadway from Canal to Duane Streets. Many of New York's commercial buildings in the 1850s and '60s were constructed in cast iron—elaborate yet inexpensive and the forerunner of today's skyscraper, with a supporting core and curtain walls. This area, combined with SoHo to the north, constitutes the largest concentration of cast-iron architecture in the world. Friends of Cast-Iron Architecture sponsor tours of this area. Call 427-2488.

Castle Clinton National Monument
Battery Park. 344-7220. (John McComb, Jr., 1807–11.) Originally West Battery, an island defense post. Given to the city in 1823, it became successively Castle Garden (the concert hall where P. T. Barnum presented Jenny Lind in 1850), the Emigrant Landing Depot, and then, until 1941, the city's Aquarium. Restored, it's now a National Historic Monument. Tours on request. *OPEN Mon-Fri 9am-5pm; Memorial Day-Labor Day, Wed-Sun only. CLOSED Jan-March.* FREE

Centre Market Place
Bet Broome & Grand Streets. Gun-sellers clustered here because of the proximity to the old police headquarters. Several survive. Note the John Jovino Co. sign at No. 5.

Chamber of Commerce of the State of NY

65 Liberty Street at Liberty Place. An ornate Beaux Arts landmark building dating from 1901.

Chamber of Commerce

Charlton-King-Vandam Historic District

9-43, 20-42 Charlton Street; 1-49, 16-54 King Street; 9-29 Vandam Street; 43-51 MacDougal Street. The city's largest concentration of Federal-style houses, on a site that belonged first to Aaron Burr and later to John Jacob Astor.

Chelsea Historic District

West 20 & West 22 Streets, Ninth to Tenth Avenue. Comprised mainly of land from the estate of Clement Clark Moore (author of "A Visit from St. Nicholas"). This area, developed in the 1830s and containing lovely Greek Revival and Italianate residences, is making a fashionable comeback. As bodegas give way to boutiques, reactions are mixed.

Chelsea Hotel

222 West 23 Street bet Seventh & Eighth Aves. 243-3700. (Hubert, Pirsson & Co.) A literary landmark built in 1884 as a cooperative apartment house. It became a hotel in 1905. Among its former residents: Thomas Wolfe, Dylan Thomas, Mark Twain, and O. Henry. (*See also* HOTELS, Moderate)

Chinatown

Centered roughly within the boundaries of Canal, Worth & Mulberry Streets, the Bowery & Chatham Square. A feast for the senses; New York's colorful and bustling Chinese enclave, with streets of restaurants serving every type of Chinese food imaginable, from Cantonese to Fookinese. Note the pagoda telephone booths on the streets.

City Hall

City Hall Park, bet Broadway & Park Row. 566-5200. (Mangin and McComb, 1802–11.) Federal-period architecture enriched by French Renaissance detailing. New York City's seat of government since 1811. The Governor's rooms containing original 19th-century furnishings are *OPEN Mon-Fri 9am-4pm*. Free tours bet 10am & 3pm. Groups by appointment; call 566-8681. FREE

William Clark House

51 Market Street bet Monroe & Madison Sts. A superb four-story Federal house built in 1824.

Colonnade Row (La Grange Terrace)

428-434 Lafayette Street bet East 4 St & Astor Pl. (Attributed to Alexander Jackson Davis, 1833.) Some of the best examples of Greek Revival town houses. Only four of the original nine survive and they're more than just a little bit shabby. At one time home to New York's elite: the Astors, the Delanos, the Vanderbilts. Across from Joe Papp's Public Theater.

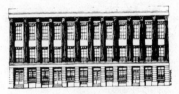

Colonnade Row

Dakota Apartments

1 West 72 Street at Central Park West. (Henry J. Hardenbergh, 1884.) New York's first luxury apartment house, built for Singer Sewing Machine heir Edward Clark, amidst run-down farms and shanties. It was thought to be as remote as "Dakotas in Indian territory" but became, and remains, a prestigious address. Present-day tenants include Lauren Bacall and Leonard Bernstein. John Lennon lived and died here. Yoko and son, Sean, are still in residence.

Diamond Center

West 47 Street bet Fifth Ave & Ave of the Americas. Contrary to popular mythology, this is the only street in America that comes close to being paved with gold and diamonds. Shop after shop offers a dazzling assortment of jewelry, but almost as fascinating is the constant action among dealers, mainly Hasidic Jews, buying and selling 80% of all the diamonds in the country. A bustling area.

Dakota Apartments

Dyckman House
4881 Broadway at West 204 St. 304-9422. Built in 1725/1783, this is the only 18th-century Dutch farmhouse remaining in Manhattan. Restored and furnished with Dutch and English Colonial antiques and household items. Now it serves as a museum of Dutch New York and the headquarters of the Metropolitan Historic Structures Association. Lovely informal garden. *OPEN Tues-Sun 11am-4pm.* FREE. Group tours by appointment.

Ellis Island
New York Harbor, southwest of Manhattan's tip. Entry point for more than 11 million immigrants beginning in 1892 (till 1954). The enormous Registry Hall, the Baggage Room and the Ticket Office are among those rooms to be restored as part of the Statue of Liberty's centennial celebration. To reopen to the public in 1986. A poignant place. *See also* SIGHTSEEING, River Trips: Ellis Island Ferry & Tour.

English Terrace Row
20-38 West 10 Street bet Fifth Ave & Ave of the Americas. (James Renwick, Jr., 1856–58.) Modeled after England's row houses, abandoning the high Dutch stoop. On a lovely Greenwich Village street.

Federal Hall National Memorial
26 Wall Street at Nassau St. (Town & Davis, 1834–1842.) 264-8711. This Greek Revival building occupies the site of New York's original city hall (1699), which later (1788) served as the new country's Federal Hall, where George Washington took the presidential oath in 1789. The present building served as a customs house and later as the Sub-Treasury. Now a National Historic site housing mementos of colonial and early Federal New York, including Washington's inaugural suit. *OPEN Mon-Fri 9am-5pm.* Classical concerts, in summer, Wed at 12:30pm. FREE

Fire Watchtower
Marcus Garvey Park, Madison Avenue & East 122 Street. A cast-iron octagonal structure built in 1856. The last remaining fire tower in the city.

Fire Watchtower

Flatiron Building
175 Fifth Avenue at East 23 Street. (D. H. Burn-

ham & Co.) Built in 1902 and originally known as the Fuller Building; its obvious nickname stuck. At 286 ft, it was one of New York's first steel skeleton skyscrapers. It was designed in an Italian Renaissance manner and covered by a limestone skin. The shiplike structure, which appears to sail up the avenue, was the most popular subject of picture postcards at the turn of the century. At the time the phrase "23 Skiddoo" originated at its prow. Police were assigned this spot to chase men who stopped to gaze at the upturned skirts of ladies at this the windiest corner in the city.

General Grant National Memorial
Riverside Drive & West 122 Street. 666-1640. (John H. Duncan, 1897.) Where Ulysses S. Grant and his wife are entombed. Photographic exhibits of his life as general and president plus a collection of Civil War artifacts. Mosaic benches ringing the monument, done by neighborhood youths, are controversial to those who do not recognize urban folk art. Hope for their survival. *OPEN Wed-Sun 9am-5pm. CLOSED holidays.* FREE

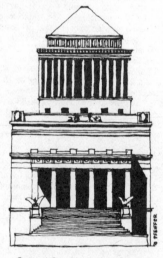

General Grant National Memorial
(Grant's Tomb)

General Post Office
West 31 to West 33 Street from Eighth to Ninth Avenue. 971-5331. (McKim, Mead & White, 1913.) A Corinthian-columned façade that bears the well-known, overblown, and often untrue inscription "Neither snow, nor rain, nor heat, nor gloom of night stays these couriers from the swift completion of their appointed rounds." Tours available. Write Post Master, New York Post Office, J.A.F. Building, Room 3217, N.Y. N.Y. 10199, giving dates and number of people. No children under age 12.

Governor's House
Governor's Island. Andes & Barry Roads. A true Georgian-style building, built ca. 1708, that housed the British colonial governors.

Governor's Island
New York Harbor, south of Manhattan's tip. In 1652 it was set aside as the Dutch governor's estate (*see* Governor's House), but it is best known as a military fortification from the 1790s. In 1966 the Coast Guard took command of it. Recently designated a National Historic Landmark. *OPEN to the public only two days a year, mid-May & mid-Sept, noon-4pm.* Call 668-7255 for details.

Gracie Mansion (mayors' residence)
In Carl Schurz Park, East 88 Street & East End Avenue. A Federal-style country villa built in 1799 by wealthy merchant Archibald Gracie. The 18th- and 19th-century furnishings have provided a graceful residence for New York's mayors since 1942. Tours of public rooms, the garden and the private quarters (*except* the mayor's bedroom). *OPEN by appointment only April-Oct, Wed only 10am-4pm.* Admission charge at door; lower for school-age children and senior citizens. No school groups below 3rd grade. Write well in advance: Tour Program, Gracie Mansion, East 88 St. & East End Ave, New York, N.Y. 10028. For info call 570-4747.

Gracie Mansion

Grand Central Terminal
East 42 Street & Vanderbilt Avenue. (Warren & Wetmore, Reed & Stem, 1913.) Over 500 trains a day are accommodated by this massive Beaux Arts structure, completed in 1913. Its cathedral-like main concourse, 75 ft wide by 240 ft long, with a 116-ft-high vaulted ceiling, is traversed by a half-million people a day. Free guided tour every Wed at 12:30pm. *See* page 23.

Greenwich Village
Approximately west of University Place from East 14 to Spring Street. The largest designated historic district in New York City. Historically rich; traditional home of artists and writers. The area and its residents run from the offbeat to the upbeat. Its winding streets offer a wealth of architectural treasures, charming bistros and trendy boutiques. Meander. *See also* Charlton-King-Vandam Historic District, English Terrace Row, Grove Court, Isaacs-Hendricks House, Jefferson Market Library, MacDougal Alley, MacDougal Street, Milligan Place/Patchin Place, Narrowest House, St. Luke's Place, Washington Mews, Washington Square North.

Grove Court
South side of Grove Street bet Bedford & Hudson Sts. (View through gates bet 10 & 12 Grove St.) Built in 1854 as laborers' quarters, this charming secluded mews in Greenwich Village was then known as "Mixed Ale Alley."

Hall of Fame for Great Americans
West 181 Street & University Avenue, Bronx. 220-6312. (McKim, Mead & White, 1901, 1914.) A classical columned pavilion housing bronze busts of famous American men and women who have achieved excellence in the arts, humanities, science, or government. *OPEN Mon-Sat 9am-5pm.* FREE

Hamilton Grange National Memorial
287 Convent Avenue nr West 141 St. 283-5154. Founding Father and first Secretary of the Treasury Alexander Hamilton's "country" retreat, designed by John McComb, Jr. Built in 1801, it's one of the few Federal-period mansions remaining in Manhattan. Furnished with fine Federal period pieces. *OPEN Wed-Sun 9am-5pm.* FREE

Harlem
North of West 110 Street to West 155 Street, west of Fifth Avenue to Broadway. A small 18th-century farm community that grew up to be the largest black community in America. Vestiges of a proud past—elegant row houses, fine commercial structures, excellent churches—exist within a blighted present. Interesting and enlightening. Take one of the bus or walking tours and see for yourself. *See* SIGHTSEEING, New York Tours: Harlem Spirituals, Harlem Your Way *and* Penny Sightseeing.

Harlem Courthouse
170 East 121 Street at Sylvan Place. (Thom & Wilson, 1893.) A richly decorated brick-and-stone courthouse now a landmark.

Harlem Courthouse

Haughwout Building
488 Broadway at Broome Street. (J. P. Gaynor, 1857.) This Palladio-inspired cast-iron building houses what was the first practical safety elevator in the world, by Otis.

Isaacs-Hendricks House
77 Bedford Street at Commerce Street. Built in 1799, it's the oldest surviving house in Greenwich Village, but only the side and rear retain the original clapboard structure. Adjacent is the Narrowest House.

Haughwout Building

Jefferson Market Library
425 Avenue of the Americas at West 10 Street. 243-4334. (Vaux & Withers, 1877; renovated interiors. Giorgio Cavaglieri, 1967.) Originally a courthouse built on the site of an old market, this extraordinary building is a Victorian Gothic celebration. Saved by Greenwich Villagers to become a branch of the New York Public Library. Don't miss a look at the adjacent community garden. *OPEN winter: Mon, Tues & Fri 10am-6pm; Wed & Thurs noon-8pm; Sat 10am-5pm. Summer: Mon, Thurs & Fri noon-6pm; Tues from 10am; Wed noon-8pm; Sat 11am-6pm.*

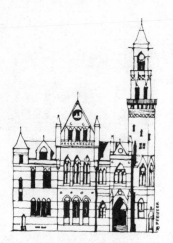

Jefferson Market Library

Little Italy
Houston south to Canal Streets, and Lafayette Street east to the Bowery. New York's old Italian community settled between 1880 and 1924 thrives still. Good Italian restaurants, outdoor *cafès*, colorful street *feste*, music, and atmosphere.

Mulberry is main street. The Feast of San Gennaro is the biggest, *see* ANNUAL EVENTS, Sept.

Lower East Side
Below Houston Street east of the Bowery to the East River. Historically the area that absorbed the masses of Jewish immigrants who flooded these shores in the 1880s and '90s, becoming the world's largest Jewish community. The pushcarts are gone, but it's still a bargain hunter's paradise (principally, Orchard Street) and home to New York's newest immigrants—the Puerto Ricans who call their turf *Loiseida*.

MacDougal Alley
MacDougal Street bet West 8 St & Washington Sq No. A charming cul-de-sac, adjacent to Greenwich Village's busiest thoroughfare, 8th Street.

MacDougal Street
Bet West 3 & Bleecker Streets. Ever-changing, busy Greenwich Village street reflects shifts in fashion, food, and music. Between colorful and bizarre. People-watch at a café—Reggio or Café Figaro are best.

Merchants' Exchange (Citibank)
55 Wall Street bet William & Hanover Sts. (Isaiah Rogers, 1836–1842. Remodeled, McKim, Mead & White, 1907.) First a merchants' exchange, then the Customs House (1863–99), this massive double-colonnaded (second set of columns added 1907) building has housed a bank since 1907.

Milligan Place/Patchin Place
Avenue of the Americas (west side) bet West 10 & 11 Streets; West 10 Street (north side) bet Greenwich Ave and Ave of the Americas. Two peaceful cul-de-sacs built originally as boardinghouses for the Basque employees of a nearby hotel. Writers Theodore Dreiser and e. e. cummings have been residents of Patchin Place.

Mooney House
18 Bowery at Pell St. In Chinatown, Manhattan's oldest surviving row house. It was built between the British evacuation (1783) and Washington's inauguration (1789) by merchant Edward Mooney, who had been a breeder of racehorses. Restored in 1971.

Morris-Jumel Mansion
Roger Morris Park, Edgecombe Avenue at West 160 St. 923-8008. Georgian Colonial mansion, built in 1765 (remodeled 1810) as the Morris family's summer residence. Served briefly as Washington's headquarters in 1776. Contains magnificent Georgian, Federal, and French Empire-style furnishings, silver, and china. Lovely herb and rose garden. Third floor museum area for changing exhibits. *OPEN Tues-Sun 10am-4pm. CLOSED Christmas & New Year's Day.* Small admission charge. Special programs are offered, including jazz and classical concerts.

Municipal Building
Centre Street at Chambers Street. (McKim, Mead & White, 1914.) Straddling a city street, this is an imposing, almost imperial civic skyscraper. Each year thousands of couples get married in a civil chapel on the 2nd floor of this building. (The ceremony takes 66 seconds and costs $5.) Atop the exterior, Adolph A. Weinman's *Civic Fame.*

Narrowest House

75½ Bedford Street bet Morton & Commerce Sts. Built in 1873. Only 9½ ft wide, spanning a onetime carriageway, it was home to poet Edna St. Vincent Millay in 1923. Adjacent to the oldest house in Greenwich Village, Isaacs-Hendricks House, #77.

New York Public Library, Main Branch

Fifth Avenue at 42 Street. 340-0849. (Carrère & Hastings, 1911.) A magnificent Beaux Arts building, it houses one of the world's most extensive libraries, the result of a merger in 1895 of three large private libraries—Astor, Tilden, and Lenox. The 5.5 million books are mainly for reference, and it's completely FREE. Half-hour free tours from main lobby Mon, Tues & Wed 11am-2pm. *See also* MUSEUMS & GALLERIES: Libraries.

New York Yacht Club

37 West 44 Street bet Fifth Ave & Ave of the Americas. (Warren & Wetmore, 1899.) Built on land donated by member J. P. Morgan. Beaux Arts with three bay windows fashioned after the stern of 18th-century sailing ships. Home of the America's Cup until it went to Australia in 1983.

Old Merchant's House

29 East 4 Street bet Lafayette St & the Bowery. 777-1089. (Attributed to Minard Lafever.) A true treasure. A completely intact 4-story Greek Reviv-

Old Merchant's House

al house built in 1832. The property of wealthy merchant and hardware importer Seabury Tredwell from 1835. It retains most of its original fittings and furniture, as well as clothing belonging to Tredwell's daughter Gertrude, who lived here until she died in 1933 at age 93. *OPEN only Sun 1-4pm.* Group tours weekdays by appointment. Admission charge. Special rates for senior citizens and students.

Old New York City Courthouse

52 Chambers Street bet Broadway & Centre Sts backing City Hall. (John Kellum, 1872.) A stately Italianate edifice better known as the "Tweed Courthouse" as a result of nine years of construc-

tion costing $8-12 million, most of which lined the pockets of "Boss" William Tweed and his ring. Now houses the Municipal Archives.

Patchin Place

(*See* Milligan Place.)

Pearl Street

In the Financial District. In Dutch colonial times, the street was the original shoreline of the East River, and so named for the mother-of-pearl oyster shells scattered along the beach.

Players Club

16 Gramercy Park South bet Irving Pl & Park Ave So. 475-6116. Built in 1845, it was remodeled by Stanford White in 1888 when famed actor Edwin Booth bought it to serve as an actors' club. Staid Gramercy Park residents were aghast. *OPEN by appointment only.*

The Plaza Hotel

Fifth Avenue & 59 Street. (Henry J. Hardenbergh, 1907.) This 18-story French Renaissance building by the same architect as the Dakota is more than an architectural landmark. Its exhuberant style, its fortunate situation on a spacious plaza across from Central Park, and its legendary past make it a sentimental favorite. Ernest Hemingway is reported to have recommended to Scott Fitzgerald that he leave his liver to Princeton but his heart to the Plaza; quite understandable. *See also* HOTELS, Deluxe.

The Players

Police Headquarters (former)

240 Centre Street bet Grand & Broome Sts. (Hoppin & Koen, 1909.) A Beaux Arts beauty of a bygone era. The police moved in 1973. Plans for its use included cultural center, or community facility. Alas, it will soon become luxury co-op residences.

Public Baths, City of New York
East 23 Street nr FDR Drive. (Arnold W. Brunner and William Martin Aiken, 1906.) A public bath worthy of ancient Rome.

Public Baths

Public Theater
425 Lafayette Street bet East 4 Street & Astor Place. (Alexander Saeltzer, 1849. Additions, Griffith Thomas, 1859, and Thomas Sent, 1881.) Originally New York's first free library—the Astor—it is now home to the creative genius of Joseph Papp. Seven theaters are housed within; it's downtown's Lincoln Center for Off Broadway (where "Hair" and "Chorus Line" were born), film, jazz and more.

Puck Building
295 Lafayette Street bet Houston & Mulberry Sts. (Albert Wagner, 1885.) Since 1983, it is a condo complex devoted to art and design but this brick Romanesque Revival building once housed the world's largest concentration of lithographers and printers. From 1887–1916 it was home to the satirical weekly, *Puck*. The two gold-leafed Pucks, three stories up, remain to remind.

Renwick Triangle
Nos. 112-128 East Tenth Street, 23-35 Stuyvesant Street. Attributed to James Renwick, Jr. architect of St. Patrick's and Grace Churches. Built in 1861, they stand much as they were when completed and form a handsome, historic enclave in the bustling East Village.

Riverside-West 105th Street Historic District
Riverside Drive bet West 105 & 106 Streets. 1899–1902 enclave of French Beaux Arts town houses overlooking the river.

St. Luke's Place
Bet Seventh Avenue So. & Hudson Street. (1852–53.) In Greenwich Village, a handsome block of brick and brownstone row houses, No. 6 was home of colorful New York Mayor Jimmy Walker.

St. Marks Historic District
East 10 & Stuyvesant Streets bet Second & Third Aves. This East Village oasis contains three of the earliest Federal buildings standing in Manhattan—St. Marks Church-in-the-Bowery (1799), the Stuyvesant-Fish House (1804) and #44 Stuyvesant Street (1795), all traceable back to Dutch governor Peter Stuyvesant, on whose farmland the district rests. Stuyvesant Street, the only true east-west street in Manhattan, was the driveway to the governor's mansion. (*See also* St. Marks Church, Renwick Triangle *and* Stuyvesant-Fish House.)

St. Marks Place
East 8 Street from Third Avenue to Tompkins Square Park. 1830s Greek Revival row houses went psychedelic, forming the main street of the 1960s hippie phenomenon. Now a punk haven and the East Village's main street.

Sara Delano Roosevelt Memorial House
47 East 65 Street. In 1910 Mrs. Roosevelt commissioned an architect to build twin town houses—one (No. 49) for her son and his future wife and one for herself. FDR lived there until he became governor of New York in 1928; his mother lived at No. 47 until her death in 1941.

Schermerhorn Row
2-18 Fulton, 91-92 South, 159-171 John, 189-195 Front Streets. Dating from the early 19th century, these Georgian-Federal and Greek Revival buildings were originally warehouses and counting-houses in the bustling seaport. Now a part of the South Street Seaport Museum project to evoke the area's rich history. The 12 buildings have been sanitized and now house commercial tenants. Facing cobbled Fulton Street, they are the rich architectural legacy of a time long gone. (*See also* MUSEUMS & GALLERIES, Historic Museums: South Street Seaport Museum.

Seventh Regiment Armory
Park Avenue bet East 66 & East 67 Streets. (Charles W. Clinton, 1880.) A Victorian incarnation of a medieval fortress. Outstanding: a great drill hall 187 by 290 ft and the Veterans' Room and library decorated under the direction of Louis Comfort Tiffany. Site of the prestigious Winter Antiques Show, every Jan; *see* ANNUAL EVENTS, Calendar.

72nd Street Subway Kiosk
In the middle of Broadway at West 72 Street. (Heins & La Farge.) One of the last remaining street-level architectural artifacts of the original IRT subway line built in 1904. Now a city landmark.

Shubert Alley
From West 44 to West 45 Streets bet Seventh & Eighth Aves. A short private alley where many an actor cooled his heels awaiting the verdict of J. J. and Lee Shubert, theatrical impresarios. Now houses a theatrical memorabilia gift shop.

Singer Building (Paul Building)
561 Broadway bet Spring and Prince Streets. Ernest Flagg in 1907 designed this as office and loft space for the Singer Sewing Machine Co. Highly innovative use of cast iron, terra-cotta paneling, and plate glass.

Sniffen Court Historic District
150-158 East 36 Street bet Third & Lexington Aves. A charming 19th-century Murray Hill mews of ten Romanesque Revival brick carriage houses.

SoHo
An acronym meaning South of Houston Street, the term covers New York's art-colony neighborhood. Bounded by West Broadway, Canal, Lafayette, and Houston Streets. Rich in galleries, restaurants, trendy boutiques, and cast-iron architecture.

"Striver's Row"

West 138-139 Streets bet Adam Clayton Powell & Frederick Douglass Blvds. In 1891 builder David H. King commissioned several leading architects of the day—James Brown Lord, Bruce Price and Clarence S. Luce, and McKim, Mead & White. The results, the King Model Houses, a harmonious grouping of row houses and apartments. Originally built to house well-to-do white residents, in the '20s and '30s they became home to successful Blacks and known as "Strivers Row."

Stuyvesant-Fish House

21 Stuyvesant Street bet Second & Third Aves. A Federal house built in 1804 by Dutch Governor Peter Stuyvesant's great-grandson as a wedding gift to his daughter. Now home to Longacre Press. City, state and National Landmark.

Stuyvesant-Fish House

Surrogate's Court Hall of Records

31 Chambers Street at Centre Street. (John R. Thomas, Horgan & Slattery, 1899-1907.) An impressive civic monument; its central hall is one of the finest Beaux Arts rooms this side of the Paris Opera House.

Surrogate's Court

Sutton Place

East of First Avenue from East 49 to East 59 Street. A prestigious area of elegant town houses and cooperative apartment houses, overlooking the East River.

Theodore Roosevelt Birthplace

28 East 20 Street bet Broadway & Park Ave So. 260-1616. Where Roosevelt was born in 1858. The original 1848 building was destroyed and this replica was built in 1923. Fascinating collection of "Teddy" memorabilia in five Victorian period rooms. *OPEN 7 days in summer 9am-5pm, balance of year Wed-Sun 9am-5pm, last tour at 4:30pm. CLOSED Thanksgiving, Christmas & New Year's Day. Also, the Wed after a Mon holiday.* Small admission charge, children and senior citizens free Sept-May. Sat 2pm free concerts.

Theodore Roosevelt Birthplace

Times Square

From West 42 to West 47 Streets at the intersection of Broadway & Seventh Avenue. Named for the Times Tower, which is no longer there. The area is synonymous with theater, bright lights, honky-tonk, and tourists. For better or worse (the worst: between Broadway & Eighth Ave) it's a hub of this city. Now scheduled for a huge redevelopment which is stirring debate. Is no life really better than low life?

Triangle Fire Plaque

Washington Place & Greene Street. On the building which housed the Triangle Shirtwaist Co., where a tragic fire on March 25, 1911 claimed the lives of 146 young women. The tragedy led to improved safety conditions in factories.

TriBeCa

Below Canal Street, west of Broadway. Translation—the triangle below Canal. It's the city's newest neighborhood. In reality it's the old Washington Market commercial district that's become residential and trendy.

Union Club
101 East 69 Street at Park Avenue. (Delano & Aldrich, 1932.) Oldest private club in New York.

U.S. Custom House
Bowling Green. (Cass Gilbert, 1907.) In the luxurious Beaux Arts style: 4 massive limestone sculptures representing the four continents are an integral part of the façade. Inside, a huge oval rotunda with 1937 WPA murals by Reginald Marsh. Vacant since 1971, when Customs moved to the World Trade Center. Possible future use: as a Holocaust Museum, though some think it too exuberant for such a somber theme.

U.S. Custom House

Villard House
451-455 Madison Avenue bet East 50 & East 51 Sts. (McKim, Mead & White, 1884.) 24 East 51 Street (Babb, Cook & Willard, 1866.) 29½ East 50 Street (McKim, Mead & White, 1909.) Italian Renaissance buildings modeled after Rome's Palazzo della Cancelleria, built by newspaper owner Henry Villard. They have variously seen service as home to the New York Catholic Archdiocese and to Random House Publishing Co. Now the entrance and public rooms of the appropriately named Helmsley Palace Hotel. (*See* HOTELS, Deluxe.) Also, houses the Urban Center, (*See* MUSEUMS & GALLERIES, General Art Museums.)

Villard Houses

Wall Street
In 1653 the northern frontier of the city was here— a Dutch wall of thick wooden planks for protection against attack. Completely dismantled by the

English in 1699, but the name remained. Now the world-renowned center of high finance.

Washington Mews
University Place to Fifth Avenue bet East 8 St & Washington Sq No. A 19th-century Greenwich Village mews lined with converted stables on the north side.

Washington Square North
Nos. 1-13, 21-26 Washington Square North bet Fifth Ave & University Pl. (Town & Davis, ca. 1831.) Made famous by Henry James's *Washington Square*. "The Row," when built, housed New York's socially prominent. No. 8 was once the mayor's official residence.

Washington Square North

Woolworth Building
233 Broadway bet Park Pl & Barclay St. (Cass Gilbert, 1913.) One of NY's most dramatic commercial buildings, this neo-Gothic tower rises 792 ft in the air and is the jewel of the downtown skyline. It was the world's tallest till 1930. Fittingly dubbed a "cathedral of commerce." Don't miss the lobby. In the ceiling's carved figures you'll see representations of the architect holding a model of the building and of F. W. Woolworth himself, counting his 5s & 10s. (He paid $13 million *in cash* to have it built.) Given landmark status in 1983.

Yorkville
East 75 to East 88 Street from Lexington to York Avenue. A *klein Deutschland*—little Germany— within Manhattan's chic Upper East Side. The boundaries are loose, but the main street is East 86 Street.

Brooklyn

Albemarle Terrace
East of 21 Street bet Church Ave & Albemarle Rd, Brooklyn. Landmark Georgian Revival row houses in a charming cul-de-sac.

Brooklyn Heights
Roughly bet Cadman Plaza West & the East River (the Esplanade) & Atlantic Avenue & Poplar Street, Brooklyn. Called *Ihpetonga*—"high, sandy bank"—by the Canarsie Indians. Fifty blocks of rich 19th-century architecture overlooking the East River. The breathtaking vista of Lower Manhattan's skyline from the Esplanade is a must see.

Grace Court Alley
East of Hicks Street nr Joralemon St, Brooklyn Heights. A charming mews, formerly a stable alley for Remsen Street's mansions.

Grand Army Plaza

At the intersection of Flatbush Avenue, Prospect Park West, Eastern Parkway & Vanderbilt Avenue, Brooklyn. (Frederick Law Olmsted and Calvert Vaux, 1870.) The Plaza is designed in the spirit of L'Etoile in Paris. The Soldiers' and Sailors' Memorial Arch (1892) honors the Union effort in the Civil War.

Grand Army Plaza

Jennie Jerome House

197 Amity Street, Brooklyn. Birthplace of Jennie Jerome (Jan 9, 1854), wife of Lord Randolph Churchill, mother of Winston.

Lefferts Homestead

In Prospect Park, Flatbush Avenue at Empire Boulevard, Brooklyn. (1-718) 965-6586. An English "Dutch Colonial" farmhouse, built in 1783. Transferred to the park in 1918, it's now a museum with period furnishings. *OPEN Wed-Sun, 1-4pm.* FREE

Litchfield Villa

In Prospect Park, Prospect Park West bet 4 & 5 Sts, Brooklyn. (Alexander Jackson Davis, 1857.) A romantic Italianate villa built for wealthy lawyer Edwin C. Litchfield. Now serves as the Department of Parks and Recreation Brooklyn headquarters.

Litchfield Villa

Middagh Street

Bet Willow & Hicks Sts, Brooklyn Heights. One of the Heights' earliest streets, ca. 1817. Many of the remaining houses are of wood. No. 24 (1824) on the southeast corner of Willow is a wooden Federal house in exquisite condition.

Montague Terrace

1-13 Montague Terrace bet Remsen & Montague Sts, Brooklyn Heights. An English-style terrace row beautifully preserved. Author Thomas Wolfe lived at No. 5.

Park Slope Historic District

Grand Army Plaza to Bartel-Pritchard Square along Prospect Park West. Brooklyn's "Gold Coast," a residential area containing 1,900 structures of architectural interest dating from the 1860s to World War II.

Sheepshead Bay

Emmons Avenue from Knapp Street to Shore Boulevard, Brooklyn. A small fishing port with boats coming and going and fine fish restaurants. Nice for a weekend early-evening outing.

Van Nuyse House (Coe House)

1128 East 34 Street bet Flatbush Ave & Ave J, Brooklyn. Parts of this Dutch house date back to 1744. Completed by Johannes Van Nuyse in 1806.

Van Nuyse-Magaw House

1041 East 22 Street bet Aves I & J, Brooklyn. A Dutch Colonial house built ca. 1800. Moved to its present site in 1916.

Willow Place

43-49 Willow Place, Brooklyn Heights. Built in 1846, this is Brooklyn's last surviving colonnade row. An imitation of the "classy" row on Lafayette Place in Manhattan.

Wyckoff-Bennett House

1669 East 22 Street at Kings Highway, Brooklyn. Built ca. 1766, this is considered the finest example of Dutch Colonial architecture in Brooklyn. Two glass windowpanes are etched with the name and rank of two Hessian soldiers quartered there during the Revolution. A fourth-generation Bennett still lives there.

Bronx

Bartow-Pell Mansion

Shore Road, Pelham Bay Park, Bronx. 885-1461. A Greek Revival country house built ca. 1836. Filled with period furnishings. Beautiful sunken gardens, a breathtaking view of Long Island Sound. *OPEN: Wed, Sat & Sun, noon-4pm.* Small admission charge. Children under 12 accompanied by adult free.

City Island

A narrow 230-acre island with a salty New England flavor, right here in New York, specifically, the Bronx. For good fishing and fish-eating. Marinas for boating enthusiasts. Difficult to reach without a car.

Lorillard Snuff Mill

New York Botanical Garden, Bronx Park. Built on the Bronx River in 1840 by the Lorillard tobacco family as a mill to grind snuff, this fieldstone building now serves as a public snack bar in summer.

Poe Cottage

Grand Concourse at East Kingsbridge Road, Bronx. 881-8900. Built in 1816, it was the home of

Edgar Allan Poe and his consumptive wife, Virginia, from 1846 to 1849, and the place where he wrote "Annabelle Lee" and "The Bells." *OPEN Wed-Fri & Sun 1-5pm. Sat 10am-4pm.* Small admission charge. Children under 12 accompanied by adult free.

Valentine-Varian House (Bronx County Historical Society Museum)
3266 Bainbridge Avenue bet Van Cortlandt Ave & East 208 St., Bronx. 881-8900. A 2-story fieldstone farmhouse, dating from 1775, that now serves as a museum of local history. *OPEN Sat 10am-4pm. Sun 1-5pm.* Small admission charge; children under 12, free. Group visits by appointment.

Van Cortlandt Mansion
Van Cortlandt Park, Broadway north of West 242 Street, Bronx 543-3344. A Georgian-style fieldstone manor house built in 1748. Washington's headquarters at various times during the American Revolution (yes, he slept here too). The interior is a treasure house of colonial artifacts and furnishings. *OPEN Tues-Sat 10am-4:30pm. Sun 2-4:30pm.* Small admission, lower for seniors; children free with adult. Groups by appointment.

Queens

Bowne House
37-01 Bowne Street bet 37 & 38 Aves, Flushing, Queens. (1-718) 359-0528. Quaker John Bowne's home, Queens's oldest building, built in 1661. Used as a clandestine meeting place for the then-forbidden Society of Friends. Contains Colonial furnishings. Guided tours (last one 4:10pm). *OPEN Tues, Sat, Sun 2:30-4:30pm.* Admission charge. Children under 12 accompanied by adult, free. *See also* Kingsland Homestead which is nearby.

Hunter's Point Historic District
45 Avenue bet 21 & 23 Sts, Long Island City, Queens. A complete block of well-preserved row houses dating from the 1870s.

King Manor
King Park, Jamaica Avenue between 150 & 153 Streets, Jamaica, Queens. (1-718) 523-1653. Home of Rufus King, Federalist statesman, member of the Continental Congress, senator, and unsuccessful candidate for president. Its oldest section dates back to 1730. Period rooms. *OPEN Thurs 1-4pm.* Small admission charge, children under age 6 free.

Kingsland Homestead
Weeping Beech Park, 143-35 37 Avenue & Parson's Boulevard, Flushing, Queens. (1-718) 939-0647. Location of Queens Historical Society, this farmhouse built in 1774 by a wealthy Quaker farmer is an interesting mix of Dutch and English architectural traditions. Moved from its original location, it's now a museum containing period rooms plus changing exhibits. *OPEN Tues, Sat, Sun 2:30-4:30pm.* Contribution suggested. *See also* Bowne House which is nearby.

Lent Homestead
78-03 19 Road at 78 Street, Astoria, Queens. A well-preserved simple Dutch Colonial farmhouse built in 1729. It still retains its original stonework.

Cornelius Van Wyck House
37-04 Douglaston Parkway at Alston Place, Douglaston, Queens. A 1735 Dutch farmhouse built by Revolutionary War patriot Cornelius Van Wyck. A landmark, but unfortunately renovated.

Weeping Beech Tree
37 Avenue bet Parsons Blvd & Bowne St, Flushing, Queens. A shoot from a rare Belgian tree was purchased by Samuel Parsons, a Flushing nurseryman, in 1847. It became the first tree ever designated a New York City landmark. It is over 60 ft high, with 85-ft spread and a trunk circumference of 14 ft. *See* Kingsland Homestead, also in the park.

Weeping Beech Tree

Staten Island

Alice Austen House (Clear Comfort)
2 Hylan Boulevard, Rosebank, Staten Island. (1-718) 816-4506. Built ca. 1691 by a Dutch merchant, it was bought in 1844 by wealthy John Austen, whose granddaughter Alice was a pioneer in the field of photography. Her legacy: 3,000 glass-plate negatives of pictures taken between 1880 and 1930. Prints from those plates are on view, so too Victorian furnishings, and the view of the harbor is spectacular. Special events year round. Call for schedule or join and receive the newsletter. *OPEN only Sat & Sun 10 am-4pm.* Small donation.

Conference House (Billopp House)
7455 Hylan Boulevard, Tottenville, Staten Island. (1-718) 984-2086. This 1680 manor house was built by British naval Captain Christopher Billopp and was the site of the only Revolutionary War conference: rebels Ben Franklin, John Adams, and Edward Rutledge turned down British offers of clemency in return for a cease-fire. *OPEN Wed-Sun 1-5pm.* Small admission charge; children under 12 accompanied by adult, free.

Gardiner-Tyler Residence
27 Tyler Street bet Clove Rd & Broadway intersection, West Brighton, Staten Island. A grand mansion built in 1835. Home of Julia Gardiner Tyler, widow of President John Tyler, from 1868 to 1874.

Housman House
308 St. John Avenue at Watchogue Road, Westerleigh, Staten Island. The original small, one-room stone section of this farmhouse was built in

1730. In 1760 the clapboard addition was attached.

Kreuzer-Pelton House
1262 Richmond Terrace nr Pelton Pl, Livingston, Staten Island. Three distinct architectural periods are visible in the construction—the 1722 stone cottage, a shingled addition from 1770, and the 2-story back section, 1836.

Neville House
806 Richmond Terrace bet Clinton Ave & Tysen St, Livingston, Staten Island. One of the few remaining pre-Revolutionary War homes in New York. John Neville, a retired sea captain, had visited the Caribbean: his 1770 house reflects what he saw. Later a saloon, the Old Stone Jug.

Poillon House
4515 Hylan Boulevard bet Hales Ave & Woods of Arden Rd, Annadale, Staten Island. Built in 1720, though there are remnants of a 1696 structure in the basement. Noted landscape architect Frederick Law Olmsted lived here and made extensive changes in the structure in 1848.

Richmondtown Restoration
Arthur Kill & Richmond Roads, Richmondtown, Staten Island. (1-718) 351-1611. Originally known as Cocclestown when founded in 1685 by Dutch, French, Walloon, and English settlers, Richmondtown is now the site of an ambitious plan to restore and reconstruct approximately 31 buildings of major historical interest covering the years 1690–1890. Costumed interpreters and crafts people, such as a tinsmith, a potter, and a basketmaker create the atmosphere of a small working period village. *OPEN Wed-Fri 10am-5pm; Sat, Sun & Mon holidays 1-5pm.* Admission charge. Group tours are available. The following are a part of Richmondtown Restoration

> **Billiou-Stillwell-Perine House**
> The original one-room fieldstone farmhouse, built in 1662, is Staten Island's oldest home. Additions date from 1680, 1790, and 1830.

> **Lake-Tysen House**
> This Dutch Colonial wooden farmhouse was built in 1740 by Joseph Guyon, a French Huguenot descendant.

> **Treasure House**
> The clapboard part dates from 1700, the stone cellar and north wing from 1770. Its name is derived from the discovery in 1850 of $7,000 in British coin, presumed secreted during the American Revolution.

> **Voorlezer's House**
> Built in 1695, this is the oldest known elementary school building in the US; it was also used for religious services. A *voorlezer* was a layman who taught school to the Dutch children; he lived on the premises as well.

Scott-Edwards House
752 Delafield Avenue bet Clove Rd & Raymond Pl, West New Brighton, Staten Island. A 1730 Dutch farmhouse remodeled in 1849. In the 1840s was home of Supreme Court Justice Ogden Edwards.

Snug Harbor Cultural Center
Richmond Terrace from Tysen Street to Kissel Avenue, Livingston, Staten Island. (1-718) 448-2500. Five magnificent Greek Revival buildings built in the 1830s–1840s as a home for "aged, decrepit and worn-out sailors" by wealthy Captain Robert Randall. In all, 26 buildings in an 80-acre park, it now serves as a performing and visual arts facility with a maritime historic heritage. Soon to be the new home of the Staten Island Institute of Arts & Sciences. *OPEN 7 days 9am-5pm.* FREE. In summer paid tours Sun 2pm, from main gate; call for info.

Statues & Monuments

Abingdon Square Memorial
Abingdon Square. (Philip Martigny, 1921.) Memorial to World War I dead features the "doughboy."

Alice In Wonderland
Central Park, 76 Street nr Fifth Avenue. (José de Creeft, 1959.) A bronze statue created for children to enjoy by climbing and crawling—and so they do. The artist admits to pressure from his daughter to take the job.

Alma Mater
Low Library, Columbia University. (Daniel Chester French, 1903.) This 8-ft-tall bronze lady has presided over graduations and riots.

Hans Christian Andersen
Central Park, Conservatory Pond. (Georg John Lober, 1956.) This bronze statue, a gift from Danish and American school children, provides the natural place for the reading of Andersen's fairy tales (*see* KIDS' NEW YORK, Children's Entertainment: Storytelling). The 2-ft-tall "Ugly Duckling" was once stolen but later returned.

Angel of the Waters (Bethesda Fountain)
Esplanade, Central Park nr West 72 Street. (Emma Stebbins, 1873.) The bronze lady of the fountain usually watches over some interesting city rites—like Frisbee throwing. The cherubs represent temperance, purity, health and peace.

Angel of the Waters
(Bethesda Fountain)

Armillary Sphere
Flushing Meadows-Corona Park, Queens. (Paul Manship, 1964.) Bronze group on granite base, commissioned for 1964–65 World's Fair.

Atlas Bearing the Heavens
International Building, Rockefeller Center, Fifth Avenue nr 51 Street. (Lee Lawrie, 1937.) The 15-ft-tall bronze figure resides on a 9-ft pedestal. It was picketed at its installation for Atlas' reputed resemblance to Fascist dictator Mussolini.

Balto
Central Park, nr Fifth Avenue & 66 Street. (Frederick George Richard Roth, 1925.) Schoolchildren's money helped erect this bronze statue of the sled dog that led the team of huskies that carried serum through a blizzard to Nome, Alaska, during a 1925 diphtheria epidemic.

Henry Ward Beecher
Fulton Street bet Court & Joralemon Streets, Brooklyn. (John Quincy Adams Ward, 1891.) A fine bronze work of an abolitionist by an abolitionist.

James Gordon Bennett Memorial
Herald Square. (Antonin Jean Carles, 1940.) Bronze figure and clock once graced the top of Bennett's *New York Herald* building. Check the owl; his eyes blink 18 times a minute.

Simón Bolívar
Central Park South at Avenue of the Americas. (Sally James Farnham, 1921.) The South American liberator on horseback in bronze on a polished-granite pedestal.

Edwin Booth in the Character of Hamlet
Gramercy Park. (Edmond T. Quinn, 1918.) Booth, America's leading Shakespearean actor of his time, lived at 16 Gramercy Park South from 1888 until his death in 1906.

William Cullen Bryant
Bryant Park. (Herbert Adams, 1911.) Bronze statue of the famed poet and journalist.

Central Park Mall (aka Literary Walk)
　Robert Burns,
　Bronze, Sir John Steell, 1880.
　Fitz-Greene Halleck,
　Bronze, James Wilson Alexander MacDonald, 1877.
　Victor Herbert,
　Bronze, Edmond T. Quinn, 1927.
　Samuel F. B. Morse,
　Bronze, Byron M. Pickett, 1871.
　Sir Walter Scott,
　Bronze, Sir John Steell, 1871.
　William Shakespeare,
　Bronze, John Quincy Adams Ward, 1870. (The sculptor was paid $20,000 for this work.)

Civic Virtue
Richard S. Newcomb Square, Queens. (Frederick William MacMonnies, 1922.) This male (as opposed to the usual female) embodiment of virtue was banished from City Hall Park in 1941 by women protesters.

Cleopatra's Needle
In Central Park behind the Metropolitan Museum. Dating from 1600 BC, this obelisk was a gift from Egypt in 1880. Pollution is taking its toll where time had not.

George M. Cohan
Broadway & West 46 Street. (George Lober, 1959.) The famed song-and-dance man in bronze, permanently giving his "regards to Broadway."

Christopher Columbus
Columbus Circle. (Gaetano Russo, 1892.) White marble statue atop a 77-ft granite column honoring Columbus (one of four in the city), erected on the 400th anniversary of America's discovery.

Peter Cooper
Cooper Square, Bowery at East 7 Street. (Augustus Saint-Gaudens, 1897.) Philanthropist Cooper in bronze sits proudly in front of Cooper nion, the free institution he founded to teach practical arts and sciences.

Dear America
Adjacent to 55 Water Street. (Peter Wormser, William Fellows.) New York's Vietnam Veterans Memorial, unveiled May 6, 1985, 10 years after the war ended, is a translucent glass-block wall, 16 feet high and 70 feet long, inscribed with excerpts of letters to and from those who served— some of whom came home, others did not. It is a poignant tribute.

Delacorte Musical Clock
Central Park Zoo. (Andrea Spadini, 1965.) Almost as popular as the zoo's live residents, these bronze ones do a dance every hour to the tune of one of 32 nursery tunes.

Abraham de Peyster
Bowling Green. (George Edwin Bissell, 1896.) Bronze statue of prosperous colonial merchant de Peyster stands where an ill-fated one of George III once stood.

Father Duffy Memorial
Duffy Square, Broadway bet West 46 & West 47 Streets. (Charles Keck, 1937.) A bronze statue with a polished granite base and cross whose subject is straight out of Damon Runyon. Duffy, whose parish was tawdry Times Square of the '20s, was chaplain to the Fighting 69th in WWI.

Eagles and Prey
Central Park Mall. (Kristin Fratin, 1850.) One of the earliest pieces to grace the park.

The Falconer
Central Park, 72 Street Transverse. (George G. Simonds, 1872.) The graceful 10-foot bronze statue back after a 25-year absence.

Firemen's Memorial
Riverside Drive at West 100 Street. (Attilio Piccirilli, 1913.) Representations of Duty and Courage in tribute to the men, and a bronze plaque in tribute to the horses, of the Fire Department.

Benjamin Franklin
Park Row at Nassau & Spruce Streets. (Ernst Plassmann, 1872.) In Franklin's left hand is a copy of his paper the *Pennsylvania Gazette*.

Giuseppe Garibaldi
Washington Square Park. (Giovanni Turini, 1888.) A tribute from Italian Americans to Garibaldi's victorious efforts to unite Italy.

"Golden Boy"
AT&T Building, 550 Madison Avenue. (Evelyn Beatrice Longman, 1916.) Bronze and gold-leaf corporate symbol moved from its former perch

atop the old Lower Manhattan AT&T headquarters to the lobby of new uptown digs. His real name, *Genius of Electricity*.

Horace Greeley
City Hall Park. (John Quincy Adams Ward, 1916.) Bronze statue of famed editor and unsuccessful presidential candidate. Seated in an armchair, Greeley holds a copy of the *Tribune*—not surprisingly, since he owned it.

Nathan Hale
City Hall Park. (Frederick MacMonnies, 1893.) An imaginary portrait in bronze of a very real hero who was executed by the British as a spy in 1776.

Alexander Hamilton
Central Park, East Drive at 83 Street. (Carl Conrads, 1880.) This granite statue of the famed Federalist was presented to the city by Hamilton's son John C. Hamilton.

Alexander Lyman Holley
Washington Square Park. (John Quincy Adams Ward, 1889.) Bronze bust of inventor and engineer Holley is reputed to be one of the prolific sculptor's best public works.

Hudson Memorial Column
Henry Hudson Parkway & West 227 Street. Bronx. (Karl Bitter, 1909–39.) Commissioned to commemorate the 300th anniversary of Hudson's discovery of the river that bears his name.

Indian Hunter
Central Park Mall. (John Quincy Adams Ward, 1869.) This bronze group, initially cast in plaster, was done from sketches made during a visit to the West.

Washington Irving
Terrace Garden, Prospect Park, Brooklyn. (James Wilson Alexander MacDonald, 1871.) A bronze bust of "the father of American literature."

Joan of Arc
Riverside Drive at West 93 Street. (Anna Vaughn Hyatt Huntington, 1915.) Bronze statue on granite pedestal contains fragments of stone from the tower where Joan was imprisoned in Rouen and from Rheims Cathedral.

John F. Kennedy Memorial
Within Grand Army Plaza, Brooklyn. (Neil Estern, 1965.) This bronze bust is New York's only official memorial to the late President.

Lafayette
Union Square. (Frédéric August Bartholdi, 1876.) Inscription: "As soon as I heard of American independence my heart was enlisted."

Lafayette and Washington
Morningside Park. (Frédéric August Bartholdi, 1890.) The allies in independence by the famed French sculptor.

Abraham Lincoln
Garden Terrace, Prospect Park, Brooklyn. (Henry Kirke Brown, 1869.) Abe's right hand points to a manuscript now missing.

Lions
New York Public Library, Fifth Avenue & 41 Street. (Edward Clark Potter, 1911.) The closest thing New York has to a mascot—a matched pair, no less. Dubbed Patience and Fortitude by Mayor Fiorello LaGuardia, they are dear to the hearts of all New Yorkers.

Maine Memorial Fountain
Columbus Circle. (Attilio Piccirilli, 1913.) A dramatic bronze-and-marble memorial to those who perished on the battleship *Maine*, 1898. Recently refurbished.

Manhattan & Brooklyn
Brooklyn Museum, Eastern Parkway, Brooklyn. (Daniel Chester French, 1916.) Symbolic representations of the two boroughs. Their original site, the Brooklyn end of the Manhattan Bridge.

Thomas Moore
Terrace Garden, Prospect Park, Brooklyn. (John G. Draddy, 1879.) Erin's beloved poet in bronze.

Mother Goose
Central Park, East Drive off 72 Street. (Frederick G. R. Roth, 1938.) This 8-ft granite embodiment of Mother and her goose stands on the site of the old Central Park Casino.

107th Infantry
Fifth Avenue at 67 Street. (Karl M. Illava, 1927.) The sculptor, an alumnus of the 107th in World War I, is depicted in this bronze work.

Peace
United Nations Gardens. (Antun Augustinčić, 1954.) This bronze statue was presented to the United Nations by the government of Yugoslavia.

Prison Ship Martyrs' Monument
Fort Greene Park, Brooklyn. (McKim, Mead & White, 1908.) The world's tallest Doric column, 148 ft 8 in. A memorial to American patriots who died on British prison ships anchored in the bay during the Revolution.

Prometheus
Lower Plaza, Rockefeller Center. (Paul Manship, 1934.) The fire-giver in bronze with gold-leaf covering set in a fountain-pool 18 feet high oversees ice skaters in winter, alfresco diners in summer.

Pulitzer Memorial—Fountain of Abundance
Grand Army Plaza, Fifth Avenue bet West 58 & West 59 Streets. (Karl Bitter, 1916.) This was the sculptor's last work. It became a legendary part of the roaring 20s when Scott and Zelda Fitzgerald went wading in the fountain.

Rocket Thrower
Flushing Meadows-Corona Park, Flushing, Queens. (Donald DeLue, 1964.) This bronze work was commissioned for the 1964 World's Fair as a permanent fixture for the park.

Roosevelt Memorial
American Museum of Natural History, Central Park West at 79 Street. (James Earle Fraser, 1940.) This bronze group, 16 ft tall, is one of the largest and best equestrian statues in the world.

General José de San Martín
Central Park South at Avenue of the Americas. (Luis J. Daumas, 1951.) Argentina's liberator on horseback. A gift from the city of Buenos Aires.

Sculpture Garden
Brooklyn Museum, Eastern Parkway at Washington Avenue, Brooklyn. (1-718) 638-5000. An outdoor garden display of architectural ornamentation and sculpture salvaged from demolition sites in the city.

Seventh Regiment Memorial
Central Park, West Drive nr West 67 St. (John

Quincy Adams Ward, 1873.) In memory of the 58 members of this New York State regiment who died in the Civil War.

William Henry Seward
Madison Square Park. (Randolph Rogers, 1876.) Secretary of State Seward's head on President Lincoln's body, done previously by the sculptor in Philadelphia.

William Tecumseh Sherman
Grand Army Plaza, Fifth Avenue at 59 Street. (Augustus Saint-Gaudens, 1903.) A graceful bronze equestrian group in tribute to Civil War General Sherman. Exhibited first at the 1900 Paris Exposition.

Soldiers' and Sailors' Monument
Riverside Drive at West 89 Street. A white marble monument built in 1902 to commemorate the Civil War dead.

Statue of Liberty National Monument
Liberty Island, New York Harbor. Probably the most famous statue in the world, *Liberty Enlightening the World*, sculpted by Frédéric Auguste Bartholdi, is better known as the Statue of Liberty. The proud lady stands 152 ft high atop a 150-foot base. A gift from France to the US in 1886, she has become a symbolic representation of freedom. Undergoing a long overdue restoration. (*See also* SIGHTSEEING, Viewpoints.)

Still Hunt
Central Park, East Drive at 76 Street. (Edward Kerneys, 1907.) Crouched bronze panther on natural rock—*very* realistic.

Straus Memorial
Broadway at West 106 Street. (Henry Augustus Lukeman, 1915.) In memory: Ida Straus chose to stay with husband Isador, and both perished on the maiden voyage of the *Titanic*.

Peter Stuyvesant
Stuyvesant Square. (Gertrude Vanderbilt Whitney, 1941.) A bronze statue of New York's Dutch governor, peg-legged Peter Stuyvesant. He's buried in nearby St. Marks Church. (*See* Churches & Synagogues.)

Swords into Plowshares
North Gardens, United Nations. (Evgeniy Vuchetich, 1959.) This 9-ft-tall bronze statue was a gift from the USSR.

Tempest
Central Park nr Delacorte Theater. (Milton Hebald, 1973.) Dedicated to Joseph Papp, the very alive theatrical genius who among other joys presents free Shakespeare in the Park. This statue violates an 1876 law prohibiting commemorative statues until 5 years after the subject or dedicatee's death. No one has complained.

Albert Bertil Thorvalsden, Self-Portrait
Central Park, off East 96 Street. (Donated by Denmark, 1894.) The great Neoclassical sculptor. Made from the original, it was donated by the Danes in recognition of Thorvalsden's influence on early American sculpture.

Untermeyer Fountain (Dancing Girls)
Central Park, Conservatory Gardens. (Walter Schott, 1947.) Beautifully sculpted spirited maidens; the stone base is from Untermeyer's home.

Giuseppi Verdi
Verdi Square, Broadway & West 73 Street. (Pasquale Civiletti, 1906.) Carrara marble statue of the great Italian composer.

Giovanni da Verrazano
Battery Park. (Ettore Ximenes, 1909.) Erected by proud Italian Americans honoring this man who is thought to have sighted New York Harbor pre-Henry Hudson.

George Washington
Union Square Park. (Henry Kirke Brown, with John Quincy Adams Ward, 1856.) A beautiful bronze equestrian statue.

George Washington
Steps of Federal Hall, Wall & Broad Streets. (John Quincy Adams Ward, 1833.) On the site of Washington's inauguration. The statue's pedestal is said to contain a stone from the spot where he stood on that day.

Washington Arch
Foot of Fifth Avenue, Washington Square Park. (McKim, Mead & White, 1892.) First erected in wood in 1889 for the centennial celebration of Washington's inauguration. Pianist Paderewski gave a benefit concert to raise money for a permanent one.

Washington Arch

Daniel Webster
Central Park nr 72 St. (Thomas Ball, 1876.) Bronze statue of the famed American statesman, with his memorable words "Liberty and union, now and forever, one and inseparable."

Churches & Synagogues

There are more than 2,250 churches and 600 synagogues in New York City. The following are the most historic or architecturally interesting.

Anshe Chesed (Old Congregation) (Jewish)
172-176 Norfolk Street bet Stanton & East Houston Sts. (Alexander Saeltzer, 1849.) The city's oldest and, at one time, largest synagogue. Today, sadly, it is a mess. The congregation has long since moved uptown.

Bialystoker Synagogue
7 Willet Street bet Grand & Broome Sts. A freestanding Federal building (1826), originally a rural Methodist Church. Since 1908, a place of worship for Lower East Side Jews.

Bialystoker Synagogue

Brighton Heights Reformed Church
320 St. Mark's Place at Fort Place, Staten Island. A lovely white wood-framed church built in 1866.

Brotherhood Synagogue (originally Friends' Meeting House)
28 Gramercy Park South bet Irving Pl & Third Ave. Built in 1859, and remodeled as a synagogue in 1975. Now a landmark.

Cathedral of St. John the Divine (Episcopal)
Amsterdam Avenue at West 112 Street. 678-6922. Begun in 1892, the work continued until 1941 and has now resumed—in the medieval manner, each stone is being hand-cut. This massive eclectic cathedral will be the world's largest when completed. Tours available. *OPEN 7 days, 7am-5pm.* Don't miss the lovely Biblical Garden (*see* PARKS & GARDENS, Gardens).

Central Synagogue (Reform Jewish)
652 Lexington Avenue at East 55 St. (Henry Fernbach.) A Moorish Revival edifice. Since 1872, the city's oldest synagogue in continuous use. Its Eternal Light, kindled in 1872, replaced by electricity in 1946, still burns.

Christ Church (Episcopal)
Henry Hudson Parkway at West 252 Street, Riverdale, Bronx. (Richard M. Upjohn, 1866.) A small, picturesque parish church.

Church of the Ascension (Episcopal)
36-38 Fifth Avenue at 10 St. (Richard Upjohn, 1841. Interior remodeled McKim, Mead & White, 1889.) New York's first Gothic Revival church. Beautiful altar mural and stained glass by John La Farge.

Church of the Holy Apostles (Episcopal)
300 Ninth Avenue at West 28 St. (Minard Lafever, 1848. Transepts: Richard Upjohn & Son, 1858.) A handsome spire crowns this gem of a church. Stained-glass windows by William Jay Bolton.

Central Synagogue

Church of the Intercession (Episcopal)
Broadway at West 155 Street. 283-6200. (Cram, Goodhue & Ferguson, 1914.) Beautifully situated (in rural Trinity Cemetery—*see* Graveyards) large English Gothic country church. Altar inlaid with hundreds of stones from the Holy Land and other areas of early Christianity. *Sun services 8am-3pm.*

Church of St. Andrew (Episcopal)
4 Arthur Kill Road at Old Mill Road, Richmondtown, Staten Island. (William H. Mersereau, 1872.) As if transplanted, a picturesque random-fieldstone English parish church with graveyard, in a lovely setting.

Church of St. Ignatius Loyola (Roman Catholic)
980 Park Avenue at East 84 St. (Ditmas & Schickel, 1898.) The lower church was dedicated initially to St. Laurence O'Toole, and the main altar was later dedicated to St. Ignatius Loyola, founder of the Jesuits. A reflection of the parish's changing character.

Church of St. Ignatius Loyola

Church of St. Mary the Virgin (Episcopal)
145 West 46 Street bet Ave of the Americas &
Broadway. This Theater District church is very
high Episcopal—incense and all.

Church of St. Vincent Ferrer (Roman Catholic)
869 Lexington Avenue at East 66 St. (Bertram
Grosvenor Goodhue, 1923.) Goodhue himself re-
garded this as one of his best. It has a magnificent
rose window.

Civic Center Synagogue (Shaare Zedek)
49 White Street bet Church St & Broadway. (William N. Breger Assocs, 1967.) An incongruous
marble swirl tucked between two tenements.

Congregation B'nai Jeshurun (Jewish)
257 West 88 Street bet Broadway & West End
Ave. (Henry B. Herts & Walter Schneider, 1918.)
An exotic Byzantine edifice.

Congregation Chasam Sofer (Jewish)
8-10 Clinton Street bet Stanton & East Houston
Sts. Dating from 1853, it's the city's second-oldest
surviving synagogue.

Congregation K'hal Adath Jeshurun (Jewish)
14 Eldridge Street bet Forsyth & Canal Sts. (Her-
ter Brothers, 1887.) Ornate Lower East Side synagogue now being restored after years of disuse.

Congregation Shearith Israel (Jewish)
99 Central Park West at West 70 St. (Brunner &
Tryon, 1897.) Home of North America's oldest
Jewish congregation. The Sephardic (of Spanish
and Portuguese origins) synagogue contains
religious articles from 3 centuries. Site of an annual Sephardic Fair; *see* ANNUAL EVENTS,
May. (*See also* Graveyards.)

Fifth Avenue Synagogue
5 East 62 Street bet Fifth & Madison Aves. (Per-
cival Goodman, 1959.) Limestone temple with
stained-glass windows that can be appreciated
only after dark when the interior lights come on.

First Moravian Church
154 Lexington Avenue at East 30 St. Small, lovely
brick church, built ca. 1845.

First Presbyterian Church
48 Fifth Avenue at West 11 & West 12 Sts.
(Joseph C. Wells, 1846.) Gothic Revival church
with a lovely cast-iron-and-wood fence.

First Reformed Church of College Point
14 Avenue at 119 Street, Queens. A beautiful
wooden country church built in 1872.

First Warsaw Congregation (Jewish)
58-60 Rivington Street bet Eldridge & Allen Sts.
Built in 1903, originally Congregation Adath
Jeshurun of Jassy. Lovely, but sadly it has been
vandalized.

Flatbush Dutch Reformed Church
890 Flatbush Avenue at Church Ave, Brooklyn.
Built 1793–1798, the third church on the site, it's
an elegant Federal-style building. The steeple has
its original bell (imported from Holland), which
tolled the death of President Washington and continues to do so on the demise of a Chief Executive.

Flatlands Dutch Reformed Church
3931 Kings Highway bet Flatbush Ave & East 40
St, Brooklyn. A beautifully situated white-painted
clapboard church built in 1848. Dutifully visited by
British soldiers during the American Revolution

while the church's congregation prayed in Dutch
for their expulsion.

Flatbush Dutch Reformed Church

Friends' Meeting House
137-16 Northern Boulevard bet Main & Union Sts,
Flushing, Queens. (1-718) 358-9636. It is the oldest house of worship standing in the city. Used
continuously since 1694, except for 1776–83
when the British used it successively as prison,
storehouse, and hospital. In the rear, separate
doors for men and women. The Quakers of Flushing were pioneers in demands for religious freedom. *OPEN 1st & 3rd Sun of every month 2-4pm.*

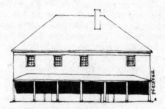

Friends' Meeting House

Friends' Meeting House & Seminary
221 East 15 Street & Rutherford Place. (Charles
T. Bunting, 1860.) Quaker conservative.

Grace Church & Rectory (Episcopal)
800 Broadway at East 10 St. (James Renwick, Jr.,
1846.) This is Renwick's magnificent example of
Gothic Revival architecture pre-dating his later
masterpiece, St. Patrick's Cathedral. Its serene
English garden was landscaped by Vaux & Company.

Grace Episcopal Church
155-03 Jamaica Avenue bet 155 St & Parsons
Blvd, Jamaica, Queens. The congregation was

founded in 1702. This, the third church on this site, is a rugged Gothic Revival edifice. Statesman, and four-time New York Senator Rufus King is buried in the charming churchyard which dates from 1734.

Sullivan Sts. (McKim, Mead & White, 1892.) This Neo-Italian-Renaissance-style church and campanile are very much a part of the Greenwich Village skyline.

Grace Church

John Street United Methodist Church
44 John Street bet Nassau & William Sts. This church dates from 1841, but the first Methodist church was on this site in 1766, making it America's oldest Methodist congregation.

John Street United Methodist Church

Judson Memorial Baptist Church
55 Washington Square South bet Thompson &

Judson Memorial Baptist Church

The Little Church Around the Corner (Church of the Transfiguration) (Episcopal)
1 East 29 Street bet Fifth & Madison Aves. Built 1849–1861. In 1870, a local pastor refused funeral services for an actor and suggested the "little church around the corner." Its name and its popularity with theater people are now tradition. The stained-glass windows are dedicated to past actors. Beautifully landscaped.

Marble Collegiate Church (Reformed)
272 Fifth Avenue at 29 St. (S. A. Warner, 1854.) Limestone Gothic Revival. Noted most for one of its former pastors, Dr. Norman Vincent Peale, and one of its former parishioners, Richard Nixon.

Mariners' Temple (Baptist)
12 Oliver Street at Henry St. (Minard Lafever, 1842.) Originally it was a Baptist seamen's church; historically it is noted as a haven for immigrants of all nations. This church, reflecting the area's changing character, now conducts services in both Spanish and Chinese.

New Lots Reformed Church
620 New Lots Avenue at Schenck Ave, Brooklyn. Built in 1824 of wood, it stands virtually unaltered. Records show that the Dutch farmers of New Lots built it for $35 in out-of-pocket expenses.

New Utrecht Reformed Church
18 Avenue bet 83 & 84 Sts, Brooklyn. The fieldstone for this Georgian Gothic edifice came from the original 1699 church on this spot, demolished to build this one in 1828. The windows are of Victorian milk glass.

Old St. Patrick's Cathedral (Roman Catholic)
260-264 Mulberry Street bet Prince & East Houston Sts. (Joseph Mangin, 1815.) New York's original Roman Catholic cathedral, replaced by up-

town St. Patrick's (1879) after a disastrous fire. It was restored in 1868 but demoted to a parish church. (*See also* Graveyards.)

Marble Collegiate Church

Our Lady of Lebanon Roman Catholic Church
Remsen & Henry Streets, Brooklyn Heights. (Richard Upjohn, 1846.) Originally Congregational Church of the Pilgrims: a fragment of Plymouth Rock projects from one of its walls. The west and south doors are salvage from the ill-fated liner *Normandie*.
Plymouth Church of the Pilgrims
Orange Street bet Henry & Hicks Sts, Brooklyn Heights. (1-718) 624-4743. Abolitionist Henry Ward Beecher's church from 1847 to 1887. Pew 89 is where Abraham Lincoln once worshiped. A piece of Plymouth Rock is preserved in its arcade. *Tours Sun following 11am services.*
Reformed Dutch Church of Newtown
85-15 Broadway at Corona Ave, Elmhurst, Queens. Dating from 1831, it is one of the oldest wooden churches in the city.
Riverdale Presbyterian Church
4765 Henry Hudson Parkway West at West 249 St, Bronx. (James Renwick, Jr., 1863.) A charming Gothic Revival building. Very much the English parish church.
Riverside Church (Interdenominational)
490 Riverside Drive at West 122 St. 222-5900. (Allen & Collens and Henry C. Pelton, 1930.) The church, endowed by John D. Rockefeller, Jr., occupies a prominent site along the Hudson. The tower of this steel-framed structure, 392 ft high, serves as an office building and houses the world's largest carillon and bell. (*See also* SIGHTSEEING, Viewpoints.)
Roman Catholic Church of the Transfiguration
25 Mott Street at Pell St. This unpretentious little

Georgian-style house of worship was built in 1801 by English Lutherans.
St. Ann's Church
Clinton Street at Livingston St, Brooklyn Heights. (James Renwick, Jr., 1869.) Renwick produced here Brooklyn's only example of "Venetian" Gothic architecture, denoted by the façade's varying colors and textures of stone.
St. Ann's Church (Episcopal)
295 St. Ann's Avenue bet East 139 & East 141 Sts, Bronx. Gouverneur Morris, Jr., built this fieldstone church on his estate for family worship. Consecrated in 1841, it's the earliest church building surviving in the Bronx. The cemetery and crypts contain many members of the Morris family. (Gouverneur Morris, Sr., drafted the final version of the Constitution.)
St. Augustine's Chapel (Episcopal)
290 Henry Street bet Montgomery & Jackson Sts. An 1828 Georgian fieldstone building, originally All Saints' Free Church.
St. Bartholomew's Church (Episcopal)
Park Avenue bet East 50 & East 51 Sts. (Bertram Grosvenor Goodhue, 1919.) This congregation followed New York's inexorable movement uptown with locations at Great Jones Street, then 44 Street, and finally a Byzantine splendor with terraced gardens, in the midst of Park Avenue's skyscrapers. The Romanesque porch, from the former building, is by McKim, Mead & White, 1902. As of this writing, preservationists are fighting to prevent the landmark community house and garden from becoming a skyscraper. Say a prayer.

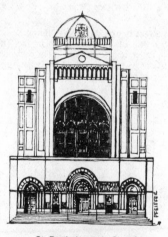

St. Bartholomew's Church

St. Benedict's Church (Roman Catholic)
342 West 53 Street bet Eighth & Ninth Ave. This congregation for black Catholics was founded in 1883. It was moved in the 1890s to this Italianate building.

St. Clement's Church (Episcopal)
423 West 46 Street bet Ninth & Tenth Aves. Picturesque parish church built ca. 1870. Perhaps reflecting its Theater District location, dance and dramatic presentations are often offered here.

St. George's Episcopal Church
Rutherford Place at East 16 Street off Stuyvesant Square. (Blesch & Eidlitz, 1856.) Romanesque brownstone known as "Morgan's Church" after tough church elder, financier J. P. Morgan.

St. George's Ukrainian Catholic Church
East 7 Street & Hall Place. New (1977) religious centerpiece of old Ukrainian neighborhood.

St. James Church (Roman Catholic)
32 James Street bet St. James Pl & Madison St. (Attributed to Minard Lafever, 1837.) Greek Revival in Connecticut brownstone, a cheap and easy-to-carve material that unfortunately weathers poorly. The community is raising money for structural repairs.

St. James Church

St. Jean Baptiste Church (Roman Catholic)
Lexington Avenue at East 76 Street. (Nicholas Serracino, 1913.) A single patron, the story goes, named Thomas Fortune Ryan, endowed this building when the little church on the site offered him standing-room-only one Sunday. The original congregation was French Canadian.

St. John the Baptist Church (Roman Catholic)
211 West 30 Street bet Seventh & Eighth Aves. (Napoleon Le Brun, 1872.) A single-spired brownstone church with lovely white marble interior.

St. John's Episcopal Church
1331 Bay Street at New Lane, Rosebank, Staten Island. (Arthur D. Gilman, 1871.) A lovely rose-colored Victorian Gothic church.

St. Joseph's Roman Catholic Church
365 Avenue of the Americas at Washington Pl. (John Doran, 1834.) An imposing Greek Revival "temple" in Greenwich Village.

St. Luke-in-the-Fields Church (Episcopal)
485 Hudson Street bet Barrow & Christopher Sts. (James N. Wells, 1822.) This area was rural to parishioners living at Manhattan's tip, hence the name of what was then a charming country parish church. A tragic fire devastated it in 1981. Restoration is underway.

St. Luke-in-the-Fields Church

St. Mark's Church-in-the-Bowery (Episcopal)
East 10 Street & Second Avenue. 674-6377. Built on the 1601 site of Dutch governor Peter Stuyvesant's family chapel. Originally a stark Georgian structure (1799) it served as the first parish in Manhattan independent of Trinity Church. The Greek Revival steeple was completed in 1836; the Italianate portico was added in 1854. Beautifully restored following a devastating fire in 1978, it's an historical, architectural and cultural treasure, where Isadora Duncan danced and Edna St. Vincent Millay and Robert Frost read their works, Danspace and the Poetry Project continues the tradition. A National Historic Landmark and centerpiece of the St. Mark's Historic District.

St. Mark's Church-in-the-Bowery

St. Patrick's Cathedral (Roman Catholic)
Fifth Avenue & 50 Street. 753-2261. (James Ren-

wick, Jr., 1858-1879.) A Renwick masterpiece. The cathedral, a mix of English and French Gothic, took 21 years to complete. The seat of New York's Catholic Archdiocese. *OPEN 7 days 7am-9pm. Mass daily at 7, 7:30, 8, 8:30am & noon & 12:30pm.*

St. Patrick's Roman Catholic Church
53 St. Patrick's Place bet Center St & Clarke Ave, Richmondtown, Staten Island. A white-painted brick church built in 1862.

St. Patrick's Cathedral

St. Paul's Chapel (Episcopal)
Columbia University, Amsterdam Avenue bet West 116 & West 117 Sts. (Howells & Stokes, 1907.) Considered one of the best of Columbia's buildings. The 24 windows in the dome are decorated with the coats of arms of old New York families associated with city and university history.

St. Paul's Chapel (Episcopal)
Broadway & Fulton Street. 285-0874. (Archibald Thomas McBean, 1764-1766. Tower, steeple, porch, James Crommelin Lawrence, 1794.) This Georgian-style church is New York's oldest surviving public building. Distinguished worshipers included George Washington, Governor George Clinton, Lafayette and Cornwallis. Surrounded by its peaceful old cemetery (*see also* Graveyards). *OPEN 7 days 8am-4pm.* Musical program every Thurs afternoon at 12:10pm.

St. Peter's Church (Episcopal)
344 West 20 Street bet Eighth & Ninth Aves. (James W. Smith, 1836-1838.) Based on designs by Clement Clarke Moore, this Chelsea church is one of the earliest examples of an English Gothic parish church that was to become so popular in years to follow.

St. Peter's Church (Episcopal)
2500 Westchester Avenue nr St. Peter's Ave,

Bronx. Picturesque 1855 Gothic Revival church.

St. Paul's Chapel

St. Peter's Church (Roman Catholic)
22 Barclay Street at Church St. (John R. Haggerty and Thomas Thomas, 1838.) An impressive granite Greek Revival edifice. Its first incarnation on this site in 1786 was only the second Roman Catholic church to be built in the city.

St. Peter's Church

St. Peter's Church (Lutheran)
East 54 Street & Lexington Avenue. (Hugh Stubbins & Assocs., 1977.) The old church building came down to make way for the Citicorp complex, and a new, ultra-modern one, on the same site, nests within the skyscraper's shadow. Still renowned for its Sunday jazz vespers.

St. Stephen's Church (Roman Catholic)
149 East 28 Street. (James Renwick, Jr., 1854.)

Romanesque Revival in brownstone. Interior mural by Constantino Brumidi.

St. Teresa's Roman Catholic Church
16-18 Rutgers Street at Henry St. Built in 1841, originally the First Presbyterian Church of New York. It now conducts services in English, Spanish and Chinese.

St. Thomas' Church (Episcopal)
1 West 53 Street at Fifth Ave. (Cram, Goodhue & Ferguson, 1914.) Richly detailed French Gothic church; many feel it's New York's most beautiful. Popular with the city's fashionable rich for weddings; its "Bride's Door" ornamentation contains both a lover's knot *and* a dollar sign. The stonemason's commentary went unnoticed for 3 years.

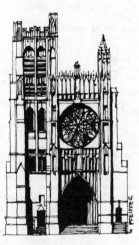

St. Thomas' Church

Sea and Land Church
61 Henry Street at Market St. A Georgian-Federal church with Gothic windows, built in 1817. Now the First Chinese Presbyterian Church.

Serbian Orthodox Cathedral of St. Sava
15 West 25 Street bet Fifth Ave & Ave of the Americas. (Richard Upjohn, 1855.) Originally Trinity Chapel, part of Trinity Parish, this brownstone church is now a Croation sanctuary.

Temple Emanu-El (Reform Jewish)
1 East 65 Street at Fifth Avenue. 744-1400. (Robert D. Kohn, Charles Butler, and Clarence Stein, 1929.) New York's "fashionable" synagogue. Founded by wealthy German Jews. Built in the Byzantine-Romanesque style, it is the largest synagogue in America, with a capacity of 2,500. *OPEN 7 days 10am-5pm. Services Fri 5:15pm & Sat 10:30am.*

Trinity Church (Episcopal)
Broadway & Wall Street. 285-0872. (Richard Upjohn, 1846.) This church was founded by royal charter of England's King William III. The first two churches on the site were destroyed. The 280-foot spire of the present Gothic Revival edifice made it New York's tallest until the turn of the century; its old cemetery is a green oasis in summertime. Church *OPEN Mon-Fri 7am-6pm, Sat & Sun till 4pm.* Exhibit Room *OPEN Mon-Fri 10:30am-4pm.* FREE. (*See also* Graveyards.)

Village Community Church
143 West 13 Street bet Ave of the Americas & Seventh Ave. (Samuel Thompson, 1846.) An excellent Greek Revival structure that now stands empty. A synagogue and church used to share these quarters, but unfortunately the ecumenical spirit did not last. Now part of a residential coop complex.

Woodrow United Methodist Church
1109 Woodrow Road nr Rossville Ave, Woodrow, Staten Island. Built in 1842. It is pure Greek Revival, except for the added tower and belfry.

Woodrow United Methodist Church

Graveyards

In the 18th and early 19th centuries, New Yorkers buried their dead in churchyards or in nearby cemeteries. Of some 90 burial grounds, only a bare few remain, especially within the confines of "the City." After 1830, one needed a special permit for burial south of Canal Street, and after 1852 burial within Manhattan was completely prohibited. Trinity Cemetery is still active, but interment is aboveground in crypts. (According to the sales brochure, those with a view are extremely expensive.)

Cornell Graveyard
Adjacent to 1463 Greenport Road, Far Rockaway, Queens. A tiny 18th-century burial plot of Richard Cornell and his descendants, the first white settlers, in what was then the Indian Rockaways.

First Shearith Israel Graveyard
55 St. James Place bet Oliver & James Sts. 1683-

1828. Dating from their arrival in 1654, the Congregation Beth Shearith is the oldest Jewish congregation in America. This is the earliest surviving burial ground of these Spanish and Portuguese Jews. (*See also* Second *and* Third Cemetery of the Spanish & Portuguese Synagogue.) Consecrated in 1656; the oldest gravestone is dated 1683. The English translation on one of the tombstones reads:

> Here lies buried,
> The unmarried man Walter J. Judah
> Old in wisdom, tender in years.

Green-Wood Cemetery
Main Gate: Fifth Avenue & 25 Street, Brooklyn. (Gates: Richard Upjohn, 1861-1865.) (1-718) 768-7300. Breaking with the traditional forms of interment—churchyards, family plots or compact enclosures—this cemetery's 478 acres were opened in 1840. Beautifully landscaped and encompassing Brooklyn's highest point, 216 ft above sea level; the natural setting and view are unsurpassed. Magnificent Gothic Revival mausoleums and monuments decorate many of the 500,000 graves, including those of Currier and Ives, Peter Cooper, Samuel Morse, Horace Greeley, DeWitt Clinton, "Boss" Tweed, and Lola Montez. *OPEN 7 days 8am-4pm.* For info regarding 3-hour Sun walking tours of the cemetery in the spring and fall, call (1-718) 439-8828.

Green-Wood Cemetery

Lawrence Family Graveyard
20 Road & 35 Street, Steinway, Queens. The private burial ground of a distinguished Queens family. The earliest grave is dated 1703, the rest span two and one half centuries of family history. The Lawrences were related to George Washington.

Lawrence Memorial Park
216 Street & 42 Avenue, Bayside, Queens. A second Lawrence family graveyard begun in 1832 contains the remains of a New York City mayor and Stock Exchange president, as well as an Indian named Mocassin, given the first name Lawrence and buried with the family.

New York City Marble Cemetery
52-74 East 2 Street bet First & Second Aves. In this marble cemetery, opened in 1832, there are markers and headstones which can be seen

through a handsome iron fence. Members of the Kips, Roosevelt, and Fish families are buried here.

New York Marble Cemetery
Entrance on Second Avenue bet East 2 & East 3 Sts (west side). Opened in 1830, giving 156 prominent New Yorkers an opportunity for burial in what was then a fashionable area. Among them the Scribners, the Hoyts, the Varicks, and the Beekmans. Tablets on the brick wall served as the only markers. Only slightly visible through a fence on the avenue.

Old St. Patrick's Cemetery
Mulberry Street bet Prince & East Houston Sts. In Little Italy. A 9-ft brick wall hides most of the churchyard from view; the earliest graves date from 1804. The crypt beneath the church holds the remains of two early bishops of the Catholic Church, as well as those of early Irish settlers in this country.

Old West Farms Soldier Cemetery
East 180 Street at Bryant Ave, Bronx. Veterans of the War of 1812, the Civil War, the Spanish-American War and World War I are buried here.

St. Mark's-in-the-Bowery East & West Yards
East 10 Street & Second Avenue. Though the graveyard was covered over by cobblestones, it is still a peaceful, historically rich spot. Some memorial tablets and markers are still visible on this former site of Peter Stuyvesant's country chapel. Stuyvesant himself is buried here.

St. Paul's Churchyard
Broadway & Fulton Street. Though not as old as Trinity's graveyard, St. Paul's yard offers a pleasant, albeit somber, spot to reflect upon the past within the shadow of the present—the World Trade Center towers. *OPEN 7 days 8am-3:30pm.*

Second Cemetery of the Spanish & Portuguese Synagogue Shearith Israel
72-76 West 11 Street bet Fifth Ave & Ave of the Americas. 1805-1829. Burials began here in 1805, but the large cemetery was reduced by the laying out of West 11 Street in 1830. The displaced graves were moved to West 21 Street.

Sleight Family Graveyard
Arthur Kill Road at Rossville Ave, Rossville, Staten Island. 1750-1850. Also known as the Rossville or Blazing Star Burial Ground. Many of the island's early settlers are buried here, in what was originally a family plot.

Third Cemetery of the Spanish & Portuguese Synagogue
West 21 Street bet Ave of the Americas & Seventh Ave. The northernmost burial ground of the Congregation Shearith Israel; consecrated in 1829.

Trinity Cemetery
Riverside Drive to Amsterdam Avenue, West 153 to West 155 Street. 368-1600. Founded 1842. Once part of the farm belonging to naturalist J. J. Audubon, who is buried here, it became the rural burial place of Wall Street's Trinity Church and is still active offering aboveground (crypt) resting places. Clement Clarke Moore, author of "A Visit from St. Nicholas," is also buried here. His grave is visited every Christmas by carolers (*see also* AN-

NUAL EVENTS, December). *OPEN 7 days 8am-8pm.*

Trinity Church Graveyard
Broadway & Wall Street. 602-0800. In this historic graveyard, Manhattan's earliest, the oldest stone is dated 1681, pre-dating the church itself. Two tombstones of note: those of Alexander Hamilton and inventor Robert Fulton. Also of note is the Martyr's Monument honoring the men who died imprisoned at the old Sugarhouse during the American Revolution and who are interred here. At the north end a faded stone reads:
> Hark from tombs a doleful sound
> Mine ears attend the cry
> Ye living men come view the ground
> Where you must shortly lie

OPEN Mon-Fri 7am-5pm; Sat & Sun till 3pm.

Vanderbilt Mausoleum
Moravian Cemetery, Todt Hill Road, New Dorp, Staten Island. (Richard Morris Hunt, 1866. Landscaped by Frederick Law Olmsted.) Burial site of Cornelius Vanderbilt and family.

Van Pelt-Rezeau Cemetery
Tysen Court, Richmondtown, Staten Island. Ca. 1780. A homestead burial plot containing five generations of the Van Pelt-Rezeau families.

Woodlawn Cemetery
Entrance Jerome Avenue north of Bainbridge Avenue, Bronx. 920-0500. Elaborate tombs, in some cases replicas of European chapels and monuments, fill this 400-acre Gilded Age cemetery, founded 1863. Among the distinguished buried here: Mayor Fiorello LaGuardia, Bat Masterson, the Woolworths, Jay Gould, Joseph Pulitzer, Damon Runyon. It's also a bird sanctuary. Map available at office. *OPEN 7 days, 9am-4:30pm.*

Modern Architecture

Almost everything's up-to-date in New York City—here are some of the best and/or most interesting examples.

A T & T Building
550 Madison Avenue at East 56 Street. (Philip Johnson, John Burgee, Architects, 1984) This monumental corporate statement is, per square foot, the most expensive office building *ever* constructed. Its 36 stories, climbing 660 feet (equivalent to 60 stories), of pinky beige stoney creek granite is topped by a much ballyhooed Classical pediment. Enormous archways, worthy of ancient imperial Rome, lead to a 6-story-high public arcade, where "Golden Boy," which formerly topped their downtown headquarters, greets you. Plaza *OPEN Mon-Fri 8am-10pm; Sat & Sun 10am-6pm.*

Burlington House
1345 Avenue of the Americas at West 54 St. A 50-story tower. The spacious plaza features two unique spherical fountains.

CBS Building
51 West 52 Street. (Eero Saarinen & Assocs., 1965.) A freestanding concrete-framed tower, called "Black Rock" by some.

A T & T Building

Chase Manhattan Bank & Plaza
1 Chase Manhattan Plaza bet Nassau & William Sts. (Skidmore, Owings & Merrill, 1960.) One of Lower Manhattan's first aluminum-and-glass high rises on one of the first "name it after yourself" plazas that tells you nothing of where it is located.

Chanin Building
122 East 42 Street at Lexington Ave. (Sloan & Robertson, 1929.) Like nearby Chrysler Building, an Art Deco winner. Wonderful bas-relief façade.

Chrysler Building
405 Lexington Avenue at East 42 St. (William Van Alen, 1930.) One of the first skyscrapers with stainless steel on its outside including the gargoyles modeled after car-hood ornaments. For a few months before the Empire State Building's completion, it was the world's tallest, 1,048 ft to the top of its Art Deco spire. The elevators and lobby are Art Deco jewels. Don't miss taking a *good* look at them.

Cinema I & Cinema II
1001 Third Avenue bet East 59 & East 60 Sts. (Abraham W. Geller & Assocs., 1962.) One of the first "piggy-back" sets of cinemas—known as art houses then.

Citicorp Center
Lexington Avenue bet East 53 & East 54 Sts. (Hugh Stubbins & Assocs., 1977.) Though its unique silhouette stems from a summit sun collector that never came to pass, its addition to the city's skyline is a welcome respite from the flattop boxes of the '50s and '60s. Its satiny silver veneer is another eye-catcher. An interesting array of shops and restaurants, and a sunlit-atrium public space for relaxing and enjoying free entertainment events comprise the Citicorp Market, a modern agora on its first 3 floors. Atrium *OPEN Mon-*

Fri 7am-midnight; Sat 8am-midnight; Sun 10am-midnight.

Daily News Building
220 East 42 Street bet Second and Third Aves. (Howells & Hood, 1930.) Art Deco ornamentation graces the street floor's interior and exterior. In the lobby, a huge revolving globe.

88 Pine Street
Bet Water & Front Sts. (I. M. Pei & Assocs., 1974.) Elegant aluminum-and-glass structure.

Empire State Building
350 Fifth Avenue at 34 St. (Shreve, Lamb & Harmon, 1931.) Though at 1,250 feet it's no longer the world's tallest, it remains the enduring symbol of this city and state, its romantic image enhanced by the colored lights on its majestic peak changing for seasonal and ceremonial occasions. Examples: red & green at Christmas; red, white & blue for July 4; blue & white when the Yankees win *big;* and, of course, red on Valentine's Day. (*See also* SIGHTSEEING, Viewpoints.)

Equitable Building
120 Broadway at Cedar St. (Ernest R. Graham, 1915.) An unrelenting mass whose sheer volume was responsible for the first zoning law in 1916.

Ford Foundation Building
320 East 42 Street bet First & Second Aves. (Kevin Roche, John Dinkeloo & Assocs., 1967.) Brick and glass with a tree-filled, 130-ft-high interior enclosed central garden, the first real atrium in the city, albeit not truly for the public. Unique.

Galleria
117 East 57 Street bet Park & Lexington Aves. (David Kenneth Specter, Philip Birnbaum, 1975.) Mixed-use extravaganza. A skylit public gallery through to 58 Street with offices, luxury apartments, and a private health club atop. Millionaire Stewart Mott its most famous non-resident. Atrium *OPEN Mon-Sat 8am-10pm; Sun till 6pm.*

General Motors Building
767 Fifth Avenue bet East 58 & East 59 Sts. (Edward Durell Stone, Emery Roth & Sons, 1968.) Down came the Savoy Plaza Hotel in 1966 and up came this 50-story white Georgian marble tower.

Grace Building
41 West 42 Street at Avenue of the Americas. (Skidmore, Owings & Merrill, 1974.) A swooping glass structure.

Guggenheim Museum
Fifth Avenue bet East 88 & East 89 Sts. (Frank Lloyd Wright, 1959.) The master was Wright. Go for the building as much as for the art. (*See also* MUSEUMS & GALLERIES, General Art Museums.)

IBM
590 Madison Avenue at East 57 Street. (Edward Larrabee Barnes, 1982.) A sleek, 43-story green-granite and glass tower, its entry set back under 40 cantilevered floors. The huge bamboo tree-filled glass shed is a tranquil public plaza for sitting or sipping; it also provides entry to Bonwit Teller, houses a New York Botanical Garden outlet shop and the IBM Product Center. Adjacent to the Atrium, the IBM Gallery of Science & Art (*see MUSEUMS & GALLERIES, Science Museums*). Atrium Plaza *OPEN 7 days 8am-10pm.*

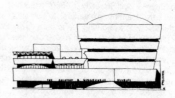

Guggenheim Museum

Kips Bay Branch, New York Public Library
446 Third Avenue at East 31 St. (Giorgio Cavaglieri, 1971.) A public building with style and books.

Kips Bay Plaza
East 30 to East 33 Street, First to Second Avenue. (I. M. Pei & Assocs. & S. J. Kessler, 1960 & 1965.) New York's first exposed-concrete apartment buildings.

Lescaze House
211 East 48 Street bet Second & Third Aves. (William Lescaze, 1934.) Office and house of the architect combined in this pioneer example of modern town-house architecture.

Lever House
390 Park Avenue bet East 53 & East 54 Sts. (Skidmore, Owings & Merrill, 1952.) One of the first metal-and-glass-walled structures. *Very* avant garde at its time. Recently designated a landmark to the dismay of its owners who would have preferred to raze it in favor of a taller (read more profitable) building.

Lincoln Center for the Performing Arts
West 62 to West 66 Street, Columbus to Amsterdam Avenue. 877-1800. Architecturally, the whole is greater than the sum of its parts. Most impressive at night. Note the Met's lobby murals by Chagall. Culturally, unsurpassed for variety and integrity. One-hour paid tours of major buildings. Admission lower for seniors, students and children under age 13. *OPEN 7 days 10am-5pm. CLOSED Christmas & New Year's Day.*

Madison Square Garden Center
West 31 to West 33 Street, Seventh to Eighth Avenue. (Charles Luckman Assocs., 1968.) An entertainment-and-office complex composed of the 20,000-seat Garden, the 1,000-seat Felt Forum, as well as a 500-seat cinema, a bowling center, and an office building, on the site of the former and sorely missed old Penn Station.

Marine Midland Building
140 Broadway at Cedar St. (Skidmore, Owings & Merrill, 1967.) A sleek, elegant skyscraper rising 52 orderly stories above an attractive plaza.

McGraw-Hill Building (former)
330 West 42 Street bet Eighth & Ninth Aves. (Raymond Hood, Godley & Fouilhoux, 1931.) International-style masterpiece in sea-green terra cotta with Art Deco details at street level.

Paul Mellon House
125 East 70 Street bet Park & Lexington Aves.

One of Manhattan's most recent (1965) millionaire's town houses.

Mobil Building

150 East 42 Street bet Lexington and Third Aves. (Harrison & Abramovitz.) This 1955 stainless-steel skyscraper was the first in the world to be fully air conditioned.

NYC Department of Cultural Affairs

2 Columbus Circle bet Broadway & Eighth Aves. (Edward Durell Stone, 1965.) A Huntington Hartford conceit that has always looked vacant. Now put to good use: home of the NYC Convention & Visitors Bureau and the City Gallery. (*See* MUSEUM & GALLERIES, General Art Museums.)

919 Third Avenue

Entrances on East 55 & East 56 Streets. What's most interesting about this brown glass office structure is the little red brick 1890 building that seems to stand as its sentry on the corner of East 55 Street—P. J. Clark's Tavern, famed watering hole and holdout against Tishman Realty. (*See* RESTAURANTS, Bars & Burgers.)

Olympic Tower

645 Fifth Avenue at 51 St. (Skidmore, Owings & Merrill, 1976.) A multipurpose building. Shops, offices, apartments—with a ground-level landscaped public arcade that's no longer a secret. Arcade *OPEN 7 days 7am-midnight.*

127 John Street

At Water Street. (Emery Roth & Sons, 1969; lobby & plaza, Corchia deHarak Assocs.) Whimsical urban design tips its hat to the pedestrian. Canvas-and-pipe structures to sit and climb on; a 45-by-50-ft digital timepiece involves you on the Water Street side.

100 William Street

At John Street. (Davis, Brody & Assocs., 1973.) Elegant natural slate building.

One United Nations Plaza

First Avenue at East 44 Street. (Kevin Roche, John Dinkeloo & Assocs., 1976.) Elegant aluminum-and-glass combo of offices and the sleek UN Plaza Hotel (*see* HOTELS, Deluxe). Much style.

Pan Am Building

200 Park Avenue at East 46 St. (Emery Roth & Sons, Pietro Belluschi and Walther Gropius, 1963.) Perched in the midst of the Grand Central complex, it was controversial for its size and its site, but now very much a part of the city skyline.

Philip Morris

Park Avenue bet East 41 & 42 Streets. (Ulrich Franzen & Assocs., 1983.) This 26-story gray granite corporate facility is the first to use its building bonus (public amenity in exchange for extra bulk) as a cultural facility. Its appealing pedestrian space is a 42-ft-high enclosed sculpture court—an extension of the Whitney Museum of Modern Art (*see* MUSEUMS & GALLERIES, General Art Museums.) Also notable: the offices are elegantly appointed with such energy-wise features as ceiling fans and windows that actually *open!*

Police Headquarters

Bet Park Row, Pearl, Henry & New Streets. (Gruzen & Partners, M. Paul Friedberg & Assocs.,

1973.) Brick and concrete plazas and terraces—civic design at its best. There's an 1890 paddy wagon on display in the lobby.

Radio City Music Hall

Avenue of the Americas at West 50 Street. 246-4600. Part of the Rockefeller Center complex, this 1932 theater, dubbed the nation's showplace, can seat 6,000. Its interior is magnificence on a grand scale, from the world's largest chandeliers in a 50-ft-high foyer to the 32-ft-high organ pipes. Fine Art Deco details. (There is a tour available page 25.)

River House

435 East 52 Street at Sutton Place. (Bottomly, Wagner & White, 1931.) Then and now, classic residential building for the *very* rich. Private yacht mooring was displaced by FDR Drive.

Rockefeller Center

West 48 to West 51 Street, Fifth Avenue to Avenue of the Americas. A building complex of harmony and grace, built mainly between 1931 and 1940. Functionalism and elegance combined. Underground passages/shopping arcades, soaring towers each an individual yet very much a part of the whole, a plaza of gardens, skaters, cafés, and something its builders seemed very much to have in mind—people. For tours *see* page 25.

Roosevelt Island

East River, parallel to East 50 to East 86 Streets. Earlier, Welfare Island, where the city's poor and chronically ill were housed. Now the site of a new community. Getting there is more than half the fun via an aerial tramway from Second Avenue and East 60 Street.

Seagram Building

375 Park Avenue bet East 52 & East 53 Sts. (Ludwig Mies van der Rohe and Philip Johnson, Kahn & Jacobs, 1958.) A bronze-and-glass tribute to modernity by the master.

77 Water Street

Bet Old Slip, Gouverneur Lane & Front Street. (Emery Roth & Sons, 1970.) In the Seaport area, a sleek building whose arcade of pools and bridges involves and invites the pedestrian at street level.

747 Third Avenue

At East 47 Street. (Emery Roth & Co., 1972.) Interesting here is not so much the building as the *Streetscape.* Designer Pamela Waters (1971) brings humor and functionalism together in her treatment of sidewalk seats, trash bins, and telephone booths.

666 Fifth Avenue

Bet West 52 & West 53 Streets. (Carson & Lundin, 1967.) Embossed aluminum-coated skyscraper. Isamu Noguchi waterfall in the arcade. Top of the Sixes on 39 offers city-filled views, *see* RESTAURANTS, Rooms with a View.

Time-Life Building

1271 Avenue of the Americas at West 50 Street. (Harrison & Abramovitz, 1960.) This one began the Sixth Avenue building boom. More of the same includes the Exxon (at 1251), McGraw-Hill (at 1221), and Celanese (at 1211) buildings. Part of the Rockefeller Center complex in a geographic sense only.

Trump Tower
725 Fifth Avenue at 56 St. (Swanke, Hayden, Connell & Partners, 1983.) A 68-story bronze glass mixed-use megastructure famed for the cost of its condos (90% above $1 million—albeit all with views in three directions) and the pricey pride of shops housed in its ritzy, glitzy 80,000-square-foot skylight capped, peach marble (chosen for its complexion flattering qualities) and brass atrium. Manhattan's first vertical shopping mall features a dazzling albeit overdone environment—a waterwall, live piano music and liveried doormen. For snacks ddl Bistro. Atrium OPEN Mon-Sat 10am-6pm.

Tudor City
East 40 to East 43 Street, First to Second Avenues. (Fred F. French Co., 1925-28; H. Douglas Ives.) Twelve buildings containing 3,000 apartments form the crux of a private "city" on a perch above First Avenue.

Turtle Bay Gardens
226-246 East 49 Street. 227-247 East 48 Street bet Second & Third Aves. In 1920 the 4-story Italianate houses on two blocks came to share a common garden on a cooperative basis. All living rooms face the gardens, kitchens are on the street side. Counted among its present-day residents is a frequently sighted Katharine Hepburn.

Union Carbide Building
270 Park Avenue bet East 47 & East 48 Sts. (Skidmore, Owings & Merrill, 1960.) A gray-glass-and-black-steel tower.

United Nations Headquarters
First Avenue bet East 42 & East 48 Sts. Visitors' entrance at East 45 Street. (International Committee of Architects, Wallace K. Harrison, Chairman, 1947-1953.) 754-7765. These buildings became the UN's permanent headquarters in 1952. The monolithic Secretariat Building, the General Assembly Building, and the Dag Hammarskjöld Library (1963) make up the complex. Flags of the 138 member nations fly in alphabetical order. OPEN 7 days, paid tours 9:15am-4:45pm (no children under age 5). Reserve for groups of 15 or more; call 754-4440; for foreign language tours, call 754-7539. A small number of free tickets are available for Assembly and Council sessions.

Washington Square Village, Nos. 1&2
West 3 to Bleecker Street, West Broadway to Mercer Street. (S. J. Kessler, 1956-1958.) Large and colorful, but very un-Greenwich Village. Zoning restrictions followed to prevent a repetition.

Waterside Plaza
FDR Drive bet East 25 & East 30 Sts. (Davis Brody & Assocs., 1974.) An effort to utilize the waterfront for living. Handsome buildings (1,600 apartments) surrounded by shopping and pedestrian plazas and an adjacent marina. A bit isolated.

World Trade Center
West, Washington, Barclay, West Broadway, Vesey, Church & Liberty Streets. (Minoru Yamasaki & Assoc. and Emery Roth & Sons, 1962-1977.) It seems that all downtown roads lead to these twin 110-story monoliths that now dominate the New York skyline. New city folklore: Philippe

Petit's tightrope walk between the towers, and George Willig's climb up the outside. For an unsurpassed view of the Apple and more, go to the Observation Deck (see page 22) or to the spectacular restaurant on the 107th floor, (see RESTAURANTS, Rooms with a View).

Outdoor Sculpture

Locations of some changing exhibits:
Wave Hill
Entrance Independence Avenue & West 249 Street, Bronx.
Hammarskjöld Plaza
866 Second Avenue at East 47 Street.
Waterside Plaza
East River Drive at 23 Street.
Robert Moses Plaza
Fordham University at Lincoln Center, Columbus Avenue at West 62 Street.

Alamo
Cooper Square at Astor Place. (Bernard J. Rosenthal, 1967.) This was one of the first "sculpture in environment" pieces to stand in a public place. Cube revolves on its axis when pushed. Graffiti is a constant problem.

Bust of Sylvette
100 Bleecker Street. (Pablo Picasso, adapted by sculptor Carl Nesjar, 1968.) In Greenwich Village. Concrete with black basalt pebbles. It is 36 ft high, 20 ft long, 12½ in thick, and weighs 60 tons. It is New York's only public Picasso.

Cube
140 Broadway. (Isamu Noguchi, 1973.) Brilliant red steel covered in sheet aluminum, 28 ft tall. Because it's an enclosed mass, a building permit had to be issued to allow its construction.

Cubed Curve
Time-Life Building, 1271 Avenue of the Americas. (William Crovello, 1971.) Hollow-steel sculpture, 12 ft high and 8 ft wide, painted blue.

Delacorte Fountain
Roosevelt Island. An artificial geyser reaching a maximum height of 250 ft.

5 in One
Police Plaza at the Municipal Building. (Bernard Rosenthal, 1974.) The interlocking disks represent the city's five boroughs. Symbolically, they are made of a weathering steel.

Group of Four Trees
Chase Manhattan Plaza. (Jean Dubuffet, 1972.) A steel framework covered in fiberglass and plastic resin, painted with polyurethane. The prefabricated sections were made in France and assembled here. Dubuffet's first outdoor sculpture in the US.

Le Guichet (The Ticket Window)
Library & Museum of the Performing Arts, Lincoln Center. (Alexander Calder, 1972.) Blackened steel stabile created for a public space.

Helix
Plaza, 77 Water Street. (Rudolph de Harak, 1969.) A stainless-steel-and-marble contemporary version of an ornamental spiral.

Martin Luther King, Jr., Memorial
Martin Luther King High School, Amsterdam Avenue at West 66 St. (William Tarr, 1974.) In weathering steel, a personal yet powerful tribute to the slain Black leader.

Night Presence IV
Park Avenue at East 92 Street. (Louise Nevelson, 1972.) In steel, 22 ft high, weighing 4½ tons; from a 1944 model; a gift from the artist to the city.

Peace Form One
Ralph Bunche Park. First Avenue at East 43 Street. (Daniel La Rue Johnson, 1980.) A 50-foot stainless-steel obelisk dedicated to late Nobel Peace Prize laureate and UN Undersecretary Ralph J. Bunche.

Queen Elizabeth I Memorial
Orient Overseas Building Plaza, 88 Pine Street. (Yu Yu Yang, 1974.) Two unjoined stainless-steel units, and a pedestal of Italian marble as a plaque, serve as a commemorative to the late great ocean liner.

Reclining Figure
Lincoln Center, Reflecting Pool. (Henry Moore, 1965.) A bronze sculpture in two sections in a pool. The largest piece ever created by Moore.

Rejected Skin
77 Water Street. (William Tarr, 1971.) Rejected aluminum from the building's construction, compacted, make up this put-on sculpture. The touch of red is from a junked ambulance.

Seuil Configuration
Fifth Avenue at 79 Street. (Jean Arp, 1972.) Up for interpretation by park visitors, its stainless-steel construction reflects its surroundings.

Shadows and Flags
Louise Nevelson Plaza, junction of William & Liberty Streets. (Louise Nevelson, 1979.) On round columns, 7 black-painted steel vertical sculptures.

Single Form
Secretariat Building, United Nations. (Barbara Hepworth, 1964.) A powerful bronze piece, 21 ft high, weighing 5 tons. In memory of the late Dag Hammarskjöld.

Sun Triangle
McGraw-Hill Building, 1221 Avenue of the Americas. (Athelstan Spilhaus, 1973.) Various parts of this mirror-polished stainless-steel modern sundial point to the noon sun on the winter and summer solstice and on the spring and fall equinox.

Taxi
Chemical Bank, 277 Park Avenue at East 48 Street. (J. Seward Johnson, Jr., 1983.) A most realistic "dashing Dan."

(212) 127-1972 Telephone Booth
127 John Street. (Albert Wilson, 1972.) This steel cutout is a totally original and functional piece of public sculpture.

Two-Piece Reclining Figure
Central Park Duck Pond nr Fifth Ave & 59 St. The latest addition to the city's roster of public art is a bronze by Henry Moore that floats on an anchored raft. It was donated in gratitude by George Ablah, who loaned 25 Moore sculptures to the city—all of which were returned unscathed.

Unisphere
Flushing Meadows-Corona Park, Flushing, Queens. (Peter Muller-Munk, Inc., 1964.) The symbol of the 1964 World's Fair in stainless steel.

Outdoor Artwork

Many buildings, especially in Lower Manhattan, have become "canvas" for talented city artists. Standouts are Richard Haas's trompe l'oeil murals which never fail to amuse or delight.

Barney's
West 17 Street at Seventh Avenue. Only the first floor windows are fake.

Central Park Health Bar
Sheep Meadow at 69 Street. Imaginary latticework light as the food sold.

Con Edison Substation
Peck Slip & South Street. Bridging the gap. Probably Haas's best mural to date.

Mulberry Street
Bet Hester & Grand Streets. Two storefronts that are not.

114 Prince Street
In SoHo, two real windows are among the 53 painted ones. Note the cat.

Schools

Charles E. Merrill Hall, NYU Graduate School of Business Administration
Church & Thames Streets. (Skidmore, Owings & Merrill, 1975.) In the financial district, a spare, businesslike monolith fitting its purpose.

City University Graduate Center
33 West 42 Street bet Fifth Ave & Ave of the Americas. Former concert hall, Aeolian Hall, 1912, put to good, practical use by CUNY. Remodeled in 1970 by Carl J. Petrilli & Assocs. An elegant pedestrian arcade cuts through to 43 Street.

Columbia University
From West 114 to West 120 Street bet Broadway & Amsterdam Avenue. (Original design and buildings, McKim, Mead & White, 1897.) The university's growth beyond what the original architectural plan called for led to much deviation but ultimately a happy coexistence between old and new. Best of the old, Low Memorial Library (1897); best of the new, Sherman Fairchild Center for the Life Sciences (1977).

Cooper Union Foundation Building
Cooper Square at East 7 Street bet Lafayette St & the Bowery. (Frederick A. Peterson, 1859; interior reconstructed, John Hejduk, 1975.) Endowed by Peter Cooper, it's one of the earliest free institutions of education in America (1859). Its emphasis was on trades and useful arts to afford students a livelihood. The Great Hall is where Abraham Lincoln delivered his famous "right makes might" speech in 1860. A thriving institution still tuition-free.

Fashion Institute of Technology
From West 26 to West 28 Streets, Seventh to Eighth Avenues. This city campus, having taken 20 years to complete, reflects the architectural styles of several seasons.

Cooper Union Foundation Building

Hunter College
Park Avenue bet East 68 & East 69 Streets. (Shreve, Lamb & Harmon, Harrison & Fouilhoux, Associated Architects, 1940.) Still too new-looking for the grand-dowager appearance of that area of Park Avenue.

Low Memorial Library, Columbia University

New School for Social Research
66 West 12 Street bet Fifth Avenue & Avenue of the Americas. (Joseph Urban, 1930.) Formed by Europe's refugee intelligentsia in the 1930s, it is no longer an exile in academic or architectural terms. The school has become an integral part of Greenwich Village and New York City life.

New York University
Most of the area on all sides of Washington Square Park belong to the university, forming a hodgepodge of architectural styles. The restored buildings are more successful than many of their thoroughly modern neighbors and Bobst Library casts an unfortunate shadow on Washington Square Park. Though the park itself is public property, it serves as unofficial campus; site of outdoor graduation ceremonies.

Yeshiva University
Amsterdam Avenue from West 183 to West 187 Street. (Main Building, Charles B. Meyers Assocs., 1928.) A grab bag of architectural tricks and treats, with the Main Building remaining the visual highpoint.

Bridges

New York has 65 bridges connecting its boroughs and islands to each other and to beyond the city and state limits. Listed are a few of the major ones.

Brooklyn Bridge
City Hall Park, Manhattan, to Cadman Plaza, Brooklyn. (John A. & Washington Roebling, 1867-1883.) This 1,595-ft suspension bridge (the world's longest when built) of grace and beauty is a 100-year-old monument to the builder's ingenuity and imagination. (*See also* SIGHTSEEING, Viewpoints.)

George Washington Bridge
Hudson River at West 178 Street to Fort Lee, N.J. (O. H. Ammann & Cass Gilbert, 1931.) New York's only bridge link to New Jersey—one pure 3,500-ft line spanning the Hudson.

Manhattan Bridge
Bet Canal Street & the Bowery in Manhattan to Flatbush Avenue Extension in Brooklyn. (O. F. Nichols, 1909.) Entered through a regal Beaux Arts colonnade by Carrère and Hastings, the bridge spans 1,470 ft.

Queensborough Bridge
From East 59 & East 60 Street, Manhattan, to Queens Plaza. (Gustav Lindenthal, engineer, Palmer & Hornbostel, architects, 1909.) An ornate cantilevered bridge spanning 1,182 ft.

Triborough Bridge
(O. H. Ammann, engineer, Aymar Embury II, architect, 1936.) More accurately a series of interconnecting bridges from Queens to Wards Island and from Manhattan and the Bronx to Randalls Island, crossing the East and Harlem rivers and the Bronx Kill.

Verrazano Narrows Bridge
Fort Hamilton & 92 Street, Brooklyn, to Lily Pond Road, Fort Wadsworth, Staten Island. (O. H. Ammann, 1964.) The world's second longest suspension bridge, 4,260 ft, links Brooklyn to Staten Island. Named for Giovanni da Verrazano, the first European to sight New York Harbor, 1524.

Williamsburg Bridge
From Delancey & Clinton Street in Manhattan to Washington Plaza in Brooklyn. (Leffert L. Buck, 1903.) This 1,600 ft span replaced the Brooklyn Bridge as the world's longest and had a telling effect on the Brooklyn side, as the bridge allowed Lower East Side immigrants easy access to a new promised land—Brooklyn.

Haunted New York

Listed below are sites in New York City where lively spirits are reported to dwell.

428 West 44 Street
This former residence of actress June Havoc was the scene of several séances conducted to find the source of mysterious tapping sounds. At least two spirits were allegedly "contacted."

Morris-Jumel Mansion
Edgecombe Avenue & West 160 Street. Washington's headquarters during the Battle of Harlem Heights in 1776 and later home of French merchant Stephen Jumel and wife. Schoolchildren and their teachers have seen a woman's form and, on another occasion, the ghost of a soldier.

Morris-Jumel Mansion

Old Merchant's House
29 East 4 Street nr the Bowery. This house, once owned by wealthy merchant Seabury Tredwell, is reputed to be haunted by a lovely young woman in 19th-century dress. She is assumed to be Tredwell's daughter, Gertrude, who became a spinster recluse following a romance thwarted by her father. A white aura has been reported above the third floor fireplace.

St. Mark's-in-the-Bowery
East 10 Street at Second Avenue. The shimmering image of a woman and a tapping sound attributed to Peter Stuyvesant's peg leg have given people pause.

12 Gay Street
A well-dressed ghost in evening clothes appeared here one night, presumably looking for old friend Jimmy Walker, the colorful mayor of New York who once owned the house.

Museums & Galleries

Metropolitan Museum of Art
Fifth Avenue Entrance

Annual Art Events

Washington Square Outdoor Art Show
See ANNUAL EVENTS, Calendar, Memorial Day
Weekend (last weekend in May) *and* Labor Day
Weekend (first weekend in September).
Museum Mile
Upper Fifth Avenue bet 104 & 82 Streets. The first
Tues in June, 6-9pm. A celebration of the un-
matched cultural riches of this part of the city. The
avenue is closed to traffic; there's music, mime,
dance and performances and best of all, the 10
museums along the Mile (El Museo del Barrio,
Museum of the City of New York, International
Center of Photography, Jewish Museum, Cooper-
Hewitt Museum of Decorative Arts & Design,
National Academy of Design, Solomon R. Guggenheim Museum, YIVO Institute for Jewish Research, Goethe House New York, Metropolitan
Museum of Art) are open to the public free of
charge. For details call 722-1313.
41 Union Square/Open Studios
41 Union Square West. The first weekend in Oct,
10am-5pm, this building which houses over 80
artists in an area of the city with a rich artistic
heritage hosts an Open House. Professional
artists of every discipline open their working studios. Browse, buy or simply chat with the artists.

Art Tours

Tours which offer an opportunity to visit galleries,
museums, artists' studios and lofts in parts of the
city are available year round; for a selection of
some of these *see* SIGHTSEEING, New York
Tours, Specialized.

Museums

*Each of the larger museums has a shop where
you can purchase adaptations, reproductions,
books, posters, and postcards. Suggested contribution means just that. If you cannot afford what
is posted, then don't be embarrassed to give less.*

General Art Museums
See also HISTORIC NEW YORK *for landmark
buildings and mansions that now house col-
lections of art and period furnishings.*
African-American Institute
833 United Nations Plaza, First Avenue & East 47
Street. 949-5666. Traditional and contemporary
African arts and crafts presented in rotating exhibits. Group tours by appointment. *OPEN Mon-
Fri 9am-5pm, Sat 11am-5pm. CLOSED Sun.*
FREE
American Crafts Museum II
International Paper Plaza, 77 West 45 Street.
391-6770. America's only museum devoted solely to crafts. A unique permanent collection recording American craft activity from 1900 to the
present, plus changing exhibitions in metal, wood,
glass, and fiber. *OPEN Tues-Sat 10am-5pm, Sun
11am-5pm. CLOSED Mon.* Admission charge;
discount for children under 16, students, and
senior citizens.
**American Academy & Institute of Arts &
Letters**
Broadway & West 155 Street. Entrance Audubon
Terrace. 368-5900. Three exhibits a year of American sculpture, painting, and architecture. Call for
schedule. *OPEN only March-June, Nov-Dec,
Tues-Sun 1-4pm. CLOSED holidays.* FREE
Asia House Gallery
725 Park Avenue at East 70 St. 288-6400.

Fascinating aspects of traditional Asian art are highlighted in several exhibitions each year. On permanent view are objects from the Mr. & Mrs. John D. Rockefeller III collection. Film, dance and musical programs. Reference library. Membership available. *OPEN Tues-Sat 11am-6pm; Sun noon-5pm. CLOSED Mon. Early July-early Sept OPEN Mon-Thurs & Sat & Sun. CLOSED Fri.* Admission charge.

Bronx Museum of the Arts
1040 Grand Concourse nr East 165 Street, Bronx. 681-6000. Newly housed in the former Young Israel Synagogue. Changing exhibitions of contemporary painting, sculpture, graphic arts and photography. *OPEN Sat-Thurs 10am-4:30pm. Sun 11-4:30pm. CLOSED Fri.* Suggested contribution.

Brooklyn Museum
188 Eastern Parkway at Washington Ave, Brooklyn. (1-718) 638-5000. An outstanding museum begun in 1823 (the building's cornerstone was laid by Lafayette) covering a wide range of interests: Egyptian, Classical, Middle Eastern, Oriental, American, and European art, Oceanic and New World cultures, prints and drawings, period rooms from 1675, a sculpture garden with 19th-century architectural ornaments (*see* PARKS & GARDENS, Gardens) and more. An active community department presents a wide range of special events and activities. Call for current roster. Painting and sculpture classes; membership available. Wonderful gift shop. *OPEN Mon, Wed-Fri 10-5; Sat 11-6; Sun 1-6; CLOSED Tues.* Suggested contribution. Free for seniors, children under age 12 and members.

Center for African Art
54 East 68 Street. 861-1200. In a town house setting, a new museum devoted exclusively to the broad geographic, cultural and temporal range of African art. *OPEN Tues-Sat 10am-5pm; Sun noon-6pm. CLOSED Mon.* Admission charge; half price for seniors and children.

Center for Inter-American Relations
680 Park Avenue at East 68 St. 249-8950. Exhibits from South and Central America, the Caribbean, and Canada, ranging from pre-Columbian to contemporary painting, sculpture, photography and decorative arts. *OPEN Tues-Sun noon-6pm.* Suggested contribution.

China House Gallery
China Institute of America, 125 East 65 Street. 744-8181. Twice a year, exhibits of classical Chinese art. Exhibitions: *mid March-mid May & end Oct-Jan. OPEN Mon-Fri 10am-5pm. Sat 11am-5pm. Sun 2-5pm. CLOSED holidays.* Contribution.

City Gallery
2 Columbus Circle at West 59 St, 2nd fl. 974-1150. Operated by the City of New York Department of Cultural Affairs, dedicated to exhibiting art that is an expression of the city's diverse communities and its cultural vitality. Curated by non-profit arts organizations throughout New York City's five boroughs. *OPEN Mon-Fri. CLOSED Sat & Sun & all holidays.* FREE

Cloisters
Fort Tryon Park. 923-3700. One of NY's artistic and spiritual treasures, beautifully situated above the Hudson River. Medieval art and architecture comprise this branch of the Metropolitan Museum of Art which opened in 1938. Parts of five cloisters from medieval monasteries provide a unique environment in which to see the Unicorn Tapestries, illuminated manuscripts, and the Chalice of Antioch. Recorded medieval music sets the mood. Live concerts are offered in spring and fall; call for details. Free public tours Tues, Wed & Thurs at 3pm; group tours by appointment. Gift shop. *OPEN Tues-Sun 9:30am-5:15pm. CLOSED Mon.* Suggested contribution.

Cooper-Hewitt Museum (The Smithsonian Institution National Museum of Design)
2 East 91 Street. 860-6868. The restored 64-room Andrew Carnegie Mansion houses the most important collection of design and decorative arts in the world. Outstanding examples of ceramics, textiles, prints, glass, metalwork, book papers, and wallpapers. The drawings and prints collection is America's largest. The Library spans 3,000 years of design. Workshops, seminars, lectures, performances. *OPEN Tues 10am-9pm. Wed-Sat 10am-5pm. Sun noon-5pm. CLOSED Mon.* Admission charge; children under age 12 free. Tues after 5pm free for everyone.

The Dog Museum of America
51 Madison Avenue nr East 27 St. Lobby. 696-8350. Four shows yearly of art and sculpture depicting man's (and woman's) best friend—the

Brooklyn Museum

dog. Established by the American Kennel Club, it's the first museum of its kind. *OPEN Mon-Fri 10am-4pm.* Admission charge.

Frick Collection
1 East 70 Street. 288-0700. Henry Clay Frick's residence (built 1913-14) houses masterpieces of 14th- to 19th-century European paintings, exquisite 18th-century French and Italian Renaissance furniture, Oriental porcelain, and Limoges enamel. Chamber music concert and lecture programs. Don't miss this jewel of a museum. Call for schedule. *OPEN Tues-Sat 10am-6pm. Sun 1-6pm. CLOSED Mon & holidays.* Admission charge; discount for children and senior citizens. Children under age 10 not admitted; ages 10-16 must be accompanied by an adult.

Goethe House New York
1014 Fifth Avenue at 83 St. 744-8310. On Museum Mile, housed in a 1907 Beaux Arts town house. New York arm of Munich, Germany-based Institute to promote German culture. Exhibitions of German artists, film programs, lectures, library. *OPEN Tues & Thurs 11am-7pm; Wed-Sat noon-5pm. CLOSED Mon.* FREE

Grey Art Gallery & Study Center
New York University, 33 Washington Place. 598-7603. Each year, six special changing exhibitions of art or photography, either contemporary or historical. *OPEN Tues & Thurs 10am-6:30pm. Wed 10am-8:30pm. Fri 10am-5pm. Sat 1-5pm. CLOSED Sun & Mon.* FREE

Guggenheim Museum
1071 Fifth Avenue at 88 St. 360-3500. The building (designed by Frank Lloyd Wright, it still stirs controversy) provides a unique setting for modern art. Impressionist to present-day. Eight-12 shows a year. The world's largest Vasily Kandinsky collection. Taped tours available; films, lectures, performances. Cafe, outdoors in summer. *OPEN Tues 11am-8pm; Wed-Sun & holidays till 5pm. CLOSED Mon.* Admission charge; lower for students, senior citizens; children under 7 free. Tues 5-8pm free for everyone.

Hispanic Society of America
Audubon Terrace, Broadway at West 155 Street. 926-2234. The culture of Spanish and Portuguese peoples as seen through paintings, sculpture, and the decorative arts from prehistoric times to the present. Important reference library. *OPEN Tues-Sat 10am-4pm. Sun 1-4pm. CLOSED Mon & holidays.* FREE

International Center of Photography (ICP)
1130 Fifth Avenue at 94 St. 860-1777. Located in a landmark building; devoted exclusively to the field of photography. Works by important 20th-century photographers including W. Eugene Smith, Henri Cartier-Bresson, and Ernst Haas comprise the permanent collection. There are also changing exhibitions, conservation programs, archives, resource library, workshops, seminars, courses. Membership available. Museum shop. *OPEN Tues noon-8pm; Wed-Fri till 5pm; Sat & Sun 11am-6pm. CLOSED Mon.* (Call for update.) Admission charge. Discount for children age 8-16; senior citizens and children under age 8 free. Tues eve free for all.

Jacques Marchais Center of Tibetan Art
338 Lighthouse Avenue off Richmond Road, Lighthouse Hill, Staten Island. (1-718) 987-3478. A major collection of Tibetan art housed in a replica of a Tibetan temple surrounded by lovely gardens. *OPEN April-end of Nov, Sat & Sun 1-5pm.* Small admission charge; lower for children under 12.

Jamaica Arts Center
161-04 Jamaica Avenue at 161 St, Jamaica, Queens. (1-718) 658-7400. Ten changing exhibits of print, photography, and arts and crafts. Workshops, lectures, performances. Call for schedules. *Gallery OPEN Tues-Sat 10:30am-5pm. CLOSED Sun & Mon.* FREE

Japan House Gallery
333 East 47 Street. 832-1155. The only museum in America devoted exclusively to Japanese art. Three loan exhibitions a year of Japanese art (ancient as well as contemporary) as well as No robes and masks, swords and packaging. *OPEN during exhibitions Mon-Thurs 11am-5pm. Fri till 7:30pm.* Suggested contribution.

Jewish Museum
1109 Fifth Avenue at 92 St. 860-1888. One of the largest and most beautiful collections of Judaica in America includes ceremonial objects, paintings, sculpture. Seven major exhibitions a year. New: the National Jewish Archive of Broadcasting. *OPEN Mon, Wed & Thurs noon-5:30pm; Tues till 8pm; Fri till 3pm (till 5pm in summer); Sun 11am-6pm. CLOSED Sat & major Jewish holidays.* Admission charge; lower for senior citizens and children.

Metropolitan Museum of Art
Fifth Avenue at 82 St. 879-5000. One of the world's great museums. Five thousand years of art magnificently displayed. Comprehensive collections of Greek and Roman art; the most extensive display of Egyptian treasures and the largest collection of Islamic art in the world, and major collections of Far Eastern, European, and American art. Don't miss the Temple of Dendur in its impressive setting, the Sackler Wing and the spectacular New American Wing, which houses the finest, most comprehensive collection of American art and artifacts. The eye-catcher: a 70-ft-high glass-roofed garden court housing large-scale decorative arts and the living room of a Frank Lloyd Wright house (1912-14). Also special: the serene Astor Court and the sunlit atrium housing the Lehman Collection. The best of all possible gift shops. Lovely restaurant/cafeteria/bar. Membership available. Concerts, lectures, films. *OPEN Tues 9:30am-8:45pm; Wed-Sat till 5:15pm. Sun 9:30am-5:15pm. CLOSED Mon.* Suggested contribution.

Museum of American Folk Art
125 West 55 Street. 581-2474. In its temporary new home, a 19th-century building, once the carriage house of John D. Rockefeller. American folk art, textiles, paintings, sculpture from colonial times to the present in changing exhibitions based on a theme. *OPEN Tues 10:30am-8pm; Wed-Sun till 5:30pm. CLOSED Mon.* Admission charge; lower for children and senior citizens. Children under 12 free. Tues 5-8pm free for everyone.

El Museo del Barrio
1230 Fifth Avenue at 104 St. 831-7272. The culture and heritage of the Puerto Ricans through artifacts, photographs, and paintings. *OPEN Tues-Fri 10:30am-4pm. Sat & Sun 11am-4pm. CLOSED Mon.* FREE

Museum of Modern Art
11 West 53 Street. 708-9500. Opened in 1929, this museum developed into the greatest repository of modern art in the world, covering the movement from the 1880s to the present. The handsome new MoMA has more than double the gallery space. Escalators in a glass-enclosed atrium now carry the public to six floors of galleries. On display are over 100,000 works of art: paintings & sculpture, architecture & design, drawings, prints & illustrated books, photography, film & video. As the first museum to recognize film as an art form, it has documented the development of motion pictures for nearly 50 years; two film theaters, six screenings daily. The new Philip Johnson Gallery: devoted to a permanent exhibition of architectural drawings and models. The Sculpture Garden remains one of NY's great spaces; two new restaurants—the Garden Cafe and the Member's Dining Room—overlook it. The 2-story Museum Store for gifts, art books and design objects, many of which are represented in the museum's collections. Gallery talks, weekdays 12:30pm; Thurs at 5:30 & 7pm. Membership available. *OPEN Thurs 11am-9pm; Fri-Tues till 6pm. CLOSED Wed.* Admission charge; lower for students, children under age 16 and seniors over 65. Thurs 5-9pm pay-as-you-wish.

National Academy of Design
1083 Fifth Avenue at 89 St. 369-4880. Founded in 1825 as a drawing society and school. Exhibits devoted to America's art heritage. Extensive holdings of 19th- and 20th-century paintings, prints, drawings, photography and sculpture. Library and resource center for serious research, all in a Beaux Arts mansion. *OPEN Tues noon-8pm; Wed-Sun noon-5pm. CLOSED Mon.* FREE

New Museum of Contemporary Art
583 Broadway nr Houston St. 219-1222. Founded in 1977, this experimental center for art and ideas is now located in the landmark Astor Building. It's the city's only museum concerned exclusively with contemporary art, showing emerging artists or lesser-known works of established artists. Library, archives, auditorium. *OPEN Wed noon-8pm; Thurs & Fri till 6pm; Sat 10am-6pm; Sun noon-5pm. CLOSED Mon & Tues.* Admission charge; lower for students. Free for all Wed 5-8pm.

Nicholas Roerich Museum
319 West 107 Street. 864-7752. In a former town house, artist Nicholas Roerich's expedition to the Himalayas, Tibet, and India, 1923–28, is the subject of his paintings. Every month a new exhibition of a contemporary artist. Lectures and recitals. Membership available. *OPEN Sun-Fri 2-5pm. CLOSED Sat & holidays.* FREE

Queens Museum
New York City Building, Flushing Meadows-Corona Park, Flushing, Queens. (1-718) 592-5555. A detailed (18,000 sq ft) scale model of New York City's 5 boroughs that includes *every* building is fascinating; plus changing art and sculpture exhibitions. *OPEN Tues-Sat 10am-5pm; Sun in winter noon-4pm, in summer 1-5pm. CLOSED Mon.* Suggested contribution.

Society of Illustrators
128 East 63 Street. 838-2560. Every 3 weeks there is a new exhibition of illustrations. *OPEN Mon & Wed-Fri 10am-5pm; Tues till 9pm. CLOSED Aug.* FREE

Studio Museum in Harlem
144 West 125 Street. 864-4500. Exhibitions of the works of established and emerging black artists from America, the Caribbean, and Africa. *OPEN Tues, Wed & Fri 10am-5pm; Thurs till 8pm; Sat & Sun 1-6pm. CLOSED Mon.* Small admission charge; half price for children.

Ukrainian Museum
203 Second Avenue nr East 13 St. 228-0110. Rich and colorful displays of Ukrainian folk art from the 19th and 20th centuries. Programs, workshops, and lectures available. *OPEN only Wed. Sat. Sun 1-5pm.* Admission charge; discount for children and senior citizens.

Urban Center
Municipal Art Society, 457 Madison Avenue at East 51 Street. 935-3960. Housed in the historic Villard Houses (1884). Exhibitions reflect urban development: past, present and future. Home of the Municipal Art Society's programs and a public forum for the liveable city. Galleries: downstairs & 2nd floor. Wed at 12:30pm *Club Mid,* free lunchtime talks; bring food, coffee and tea are free. *OPEN Mon-Sat 11-5. CLOSED Sun.* (See also SIGHTSEEING, New York Tours, Walking Tours: The Municipal Art Society.)

Whitney Museum of American Art
945 Madison Avenue at East 75 St. 570-3676. Works by 20th-century American artists comprise the bulk of the permanent collection. Special exhibitions are of major events in photography, folk or contemporary art. Sculpture garden and cafeteria. *OPEN Tues 1-8pm. Wed-Sat 11am-5pm. Sun & holidays noon-6pm. CLOSED Mon.* Admission charge; lower for children under 12 and senior citizens. Tues eve 6-8pm free for everyone.

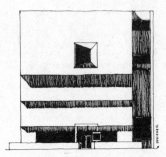

Whitney Museum of American Art

Whitney Museum of American Art at Philip Morris
120 Park Avenue at East 42 St. 878-2550. A wonderful respite from midtown's maddening crowds. A 42-foot-high sculpture space for outstanding examples of 20th-century sculpture, many of the pieces too big for the uptown Whitney. On permanent view are works by Oldenberg, Nevelson, Lichtenstein, Calder and Bourgeois. Also, in the gallery six shows a year covering all aspects of American art. Gallery tours Mon, Wed & Sat at 12:30pm; Sculpture Court tour Wed 1pm. Espresso bar. Gallery *OPEN Mon, Wed, Fri & Sat 11am-6pm; Thurs till 7:30pm.* Sculpture Court *OPEN Mon-Sat 7:30am-9:30pm; Sun 11am-7pm.* FREE

Art-&-Science Museums
Brooklyn Children's Museum
(*See* KIDS' NEW YORK.)
IBM Gallery of Science & Art
Madison Avenue at East 56 St. 407-6100. This new large (13,000 sq. ft.) exhibition space brings high quality science and art exhibits to New York that otherwise might not be seen here. Exhibitions throughout the year change periodically. Guided tours are conducted during the day. Relax in the wonderful atrium afterward. For group visits call 407-6209. *OPEN Tues-Fri 11am-6pm; Sat 10am-5pm. CLOSED Mon.* FREE
Manhattan Children's Museum
(*See* KIDS' NEW YORK.)
Staten Island Children's Museum
(*See* KIDS' NEW YORK.)
Staten Island Institute of Art & Science
75 Stuyvesant Place nr Wall St, St. George, Staten Island. (1-718) 727-1135. A museum of art, science and history founded in 1881. Records the natural history of Staten Island with its collection ranging from anthropology to zoology. Paintings, prints, sculpture, textiles. Under its auspices: the Davis Wildlife Refuge and High Rock Park Conservation Center (*see* PARKS & GARDENS, Nature & Wildlife Preserves). Archives & Library for researchers by appointment only. Programs for school children. Membership available. *OPEN Tues-Sat 10am-5pm; Sun 2-5pm. CLOSED Mon & major holidays.* FREE

Science Museums
American Museum of Natural History
Central Park West at 79 Street. 873-1300 or 873-4225. A wonder-filled place. The evolution of life on earth; huge dinosaur skeletons, lifelike animals shown in their natural habitat, and various world cultures depicted through their artifacts, clothing, sculpture, and crafts. Also a spectacular collection of some of the world's largest and best-known gems. Good gift shop. *OPEN Sun, Mon, Tues & Thurs 10am-5:45pm; Wed, Fri, & Sat till 9pm. CLOSED Thanksgiving & Christmas Day.* Suggested contribution. Free Fri & Sat 5-9pm.
Hall of Science
Flushing Meadows-Corona Park, 111 Street & 48 Avenue, Flushing, Queens. (1-718) 699-0005.

The only museum in New York City devoted exclusively to science and technology; done with imagination and ingenuity. Reopening March 1986 after extensive redesign. Lectures and workshops. *OPEN Tues-Fri 10am-4pm; Sat till 5pm; Sun 11am-5pm. CLOSED Mon, Thanksgiving, Christmas & New Year's Day.* Admission charge; lower for children, students, senior citizens.

American Museum of Natural History

Hayden Planetarium
Central Park West at 81 Street. 873-8828. Sky shows in a 75-foot dome theater *Mon-Fri 1:30 & 3:30pm; Sat 11am, noon, 1, 2, 3, 4, 5pm; Sun 1, 2, 3, 4, 5pm.* Extra shows during holiday season. Also, exhibits relating to astronomy and navigation, a 360° slide presentation, and a reference library. Admission charge (includes entry into the American Museum of Natural History), lower for children under age 12, students, and senior citizens. *Special:* Laserium, a cosmic laser-light show with either rock or classical music *Fri & Sat at 7:30pm; 9 & 10:30pm.* Admission charge.
Museum of Holography
11 Mercer Street nr Canal Street. 925-0526. The only museum of its kind in the world. Laser light used to make three-dimensional images called holograms. Individual artists, plus historic prototypes. Thurs lectures. *OPEN Wed & Fri-Sun noon-6pm, Thurs till 9pm. CLOSED Mon & Tues.* Admission charge; lower for children under 12 and senior citizens.

Historic Museums
American Museum of Immigration
In the Statue of Liberty National Monument, Liberty Island. 732-1236. CLOSED during the restoration work on the statue. To reopen July 1986. Work in progress may be viewed. Reached by ferry from Battery Park. *OPEN Wed-Sun 10am-4pm.* Last boat returns 5:15pm. For update call 269-5755.
American Museum of the Moving Image
34-31 35 Street, Astoria, Queens, (1-718) 784-4742. The lot where Paramount Pictures made movies in 1915 is functioning once more as a movie studio thanks to the Astoria Motion Picture & Television Foundation. They are also building

the first museum in the U.S. devoted to the art, technology, and history of moving image media. It will contain a state-of-the-art 200-seat theater as well as permanent and changing interactive exhibits. (To be completed spring 1987.) For now, there are exhibitions, screenings, and lectures for 20 weeks every spring and again every fall (ranging from film retrospectives to avant-garde video) at the Kaufman Astoria Studio and the Zukor Theater. Call and get on their mailing list. (There's a jitney that takes you there from East 62 Street & Third Ave.)

American Numismatic Society
Audubon Terrace, Broadway nr West 155 St. 234-3130. Two exhibit halls show a portion of the world's largest collection solely devoted to numismatics. Strongest aspect is ancient coins. Appointments can be made for special interests; excellent library. *OPEN Tues-Sat 9am-4:30pm. Sun 1-4pm.* FREE

Aunt Len's Doll and Toy Museum
6 Hamilton Terrace bet St. Nicholas & Convent Aves. 926-4172, 281-4143. In a Harlem brownstone, a feast for eye and heart. Over 5,000 dolls, accessories, miniatures, and toys. *OPEN Tues-Sun by appointment only.* Admission charge.

Bible House
1865 Broadway nr West 61 St. 581-7400. Exhibits of rare and historic Bibles; fragments of the Dead Sea Scrolls, two leaves from the Gutenberg Bible, Helen Keller's braille Bible. *OPEN Mon-Fri 9:30am-4:30pm. CLOSED holidays.* FREE

Black Fashion Museum
155 West 126 Street. 666-1320. Devoted to notable contributions by Blacks—many were slaves—to the evolution of American fashion. E.g.: a line-for-line copy of Mary Todd Lincoln's inaugural dress—made by a former slave. Exhibits change every 6 months. *OPEN 7 days noon-8pm by appointment only.* Suggested contribution.

Brooklyn Historical Society
128 Pierrepont Street nr Clinton St, Brooklyn. (1-718) 624-0890. Formerly the Long Island Historical Society. One of the largest collections of documentation pertaining to the history of Brooklyn and the rest of Long Island. Small changing exhibits. *OPEN Tues-Sat 9am-5pm. CLOSED Sun & Mon.* FREE. Nominal charge for use of the library.

City Island Historical Nautical Museum
190 Fordham Street nr King Ave, City Island, Bronx. 885-1292. City Island life from early 1700s to the present through historical and nautical memorabilia, art, and artifacts. *OPEN only Sun 2-4pm. CLOSED major holidays.* Groups by appointment. Suggested contribution.

Con Edison Energy Museum
145 East 14 Street. 460-6244. Push-button exhibits depict the stages of electrical development from 1878 arc lamp to the present. *OPEN Tues-Sat 10am-4pm. CLOSED Sun & Mon.* FREE

Fashion Institute Gallery
Fashion Institute of Technology, Shirley Goodman Resource Center & Design Laboratory, 227 West 27 Street. 760-7709. Located in the Garment District off "Fashion Avenue," the textile collection contains more than 3 million indexed swatches, 1¼ million costumes and accessories from the 18th century to the present. Fascinating fashion-theme exhibitions (past shows have highlighted the fashion duds for Snoopy, fabulous Fortuny). Monthly fashion-industry related exhibitions upstairs; one major show yearly downstairs. Library of related books and periodicals. *OPEN Tues 10am-9pm; Wed-Sat till 5pm. CLOSED Sun & Mon.* FREE

Firefighting Museum
Home Insurance Co., 59 Maiden Lane nr Williams St., 15th fl. 530-6800. Outstanding collection of firefighting memorabilia and related historical records. *OPEN Mon-Fri 10am-4pm.* Groups by appointment only. FREE

Forbes Magazine Galleries
Forbes Building, 62 Fifth Avenue at 12 Street, main fl. 620-2389. An eclectic mini-museum displaying the Forbes family collectibles. Toys, including 12,000 toy soldiers and hundreds of toy boats, trophies, Fabergé treasures, 19th-century Franco-Prussian War paintings, and a gallery devoted to American historical manuscripts and autographs, including letters from Abraham Lincoln; his stove pipe hat is here too. *OPEN Tues-Sat 10am-4pm. (Thurs is reserved for group tours and advance reservations.) CLOSED Sun, Mon & holidays.* FREE

Fraunces Tavern Museum
54 Pearl Street at Broad St. 425-1778. The site of the original tavern of Samuel Fraunces where George Washington bade farewell to his officers in 1783. Reconstructed in 1927. A present-day archeological dig beneath its basement rafters has unearthed remnants of New York's Dutch past. The museum, housed in five 18th- and 19th-century buildings, is operated by the Sons of the Revolution. Revolutionary War artifacts and memorabilia; American decorative arts, prints and paintings are displayed. Throughout the year there are lectures, performances, concerts and celebrations. On premises also, a restaurant for traditional fare. *See* RESTAURANTS, American. *OPEN Mon-Fri 10am-4pm. CLOSED Sat & Sun.* FREE

Museum of the Borough of Brooklyn at Brooklyn
Bedford Avenue & Avenue H, Brooklyn. Room 2147, Boylan Hall. (1-718) 780-5152. The visual and cultural history of Brooklyn through thematic exhibitions of paintings, sculpture, drawings, graphics, and photographs. Two exhibits a year Oct-Dec; April-early June. *OPEN Mon-Wed 11:30am-5pm; Thurs till 8pm; Sat & Sun noon-4pm. CLOSED Sat.* FREE

Museum of Broadcasting
1 East 53 Street. 752-7684. Public archive of radio and television broadcasting. An American cultural treasure chest on video and audio tape 1920s to present. The MB Theater seats 63 in front of a 12-foot screen for major exhibitions and retrospectives. The 40-seat Videotheque screens the

most asked for programs on a regular basis—lots of Lucy here. Or select a program and view it in one of the console booths. There is also a rare script library, broadcasting books and periodicals. Great fun and extremely popular—so get there early. *OPEN Tues noon-8pm; Wed-Sat till 5pm. CLOSED Sun & Mon & holidays.* Suggested admission.

Fraunces Tavern Museum

Museum of the American Indian
Broadway at West 155 Street. 283-2420. The world's largest and best collection of ethnology and archeology relating to the Indians of North, South, Central America and the West Indies. (NOTE: We may lose this museum to larger quarters in Texas!) *OPEN Tues-Sat 10am-5pm; Sun 1-5pm. CLOSED Mon.* Admission charge; lower for students and senior citizens.

Museum of the City of New York
1220 Fifth Avenue nr 103 St. 534-1672. Founded in 1923. The life and history of New York City dating back to the Indians and the Dutch seen through costumes, furniture, silver, paintings, decorative arts, ship models, toy gallery, and period rooms. Free concerts and tours on Sun. Special exhibitions. Wonderful walking tours, *see* SIGHTSEEING, New York Tours, Walking Tours. For special children's programs *see* KIDS' NEW YORK, Museums for Children. *OPEN Tues-Sat 10am-5pm; Sun & holidays 1-5pm. CLOSED Mon.* FREE

New York Historical Society
170 Central Park West at 77 St. 873-3400. The oldest museum in New York State and the second oldest in America. Devoted to American history, and New York in particular. Paintings, prints, folk art and period rooms all elegantly displayed. A library of 600,000 volumes and an impressive collection of 18th-century New York newspapers; over 1 million maps, advertising ephemera, prints, photos, lithos, architectural drawings. Changing exhibitions drawn from the collections. *OPEN Tues-Fri 11am-5pm, Sat 10am-5pm, Sun 1-5pm. CLOSED Mon.* Admission charge; lower for children.

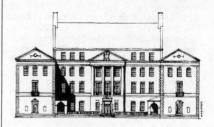

Museum of the City of New York

Police Academy Museum
235 East 20 Street, 2nd fl. 477-9753. World's largest collection of police memorabilia depicting the history of New York City's finest plus related historical items. *OPEN Mon-Fri 9am-5pm.* FREE

South Street Seaport Museum
207 Front Street. 669-9400. A nautical museum within and without walls in an 11-block area that reflects New York's historic and vital past as a busy 19th-century seaport. Restored ships and buildings, shops selling models and charts, a printing museum, and a multiscreen 50-minute film, "South Street Venture" (211 Front St). Many special concerts and events take place during spring and summer. Call for details. *OPEN year round 7 days 10am-7pm.* Entry to the district is free; admission charge to the ships, walking tours, films and exhibitions. Start at the Visitor's Center, 14 Fulton Street, or the Seaport Gallery, 215 Water Street. Discount for children under 12 and students; children under 6 and senior citizens free. (*See also* SIGHTSEEING, On Your Own: South Street Seaport Marketplace.)

Store Front Museum, Paul Robeson Theater
162-02 Liberty Avenue, Jamaica, Queens. (1-718) 523-5199. Black history and culture through exhibitions, workshops, and weekend theater performances. *OPEN Tues-Fri 9:30am-4:30pm.* FREE

Theater Museum
Minskoff Theater Arcade, 1515 Broadway bet West 44 & 45 St. 944-7161. The Theater Collection of the Museum of the City of New York has a home of its own and, appropriately enough, it's in the Theater District; it's a treat for the theater buff. Every 9 months there is a new large-scale mixed-media presentation of theater history. Memorabilia, costumes, video tapes, taped interviews with Broadway luminaries. *OPEN Wed-Sat 1-5pm; Sun 1-5pm. CLOSED Mon & Tues.* Nominal suggested admission, half price for seniors and under age 12.

Yeshiva University Museum
2520 Amsterdam Avenue nr West 185 St. 960-5390. Exhibitions that reflect Jewish historical and cultural experience. Paintings, photographs, ceremonial objects, architectural models of synagogues dating from ancient to modern times. *OPEN Mon-Thurs 11am-5pm; Sun noon-6pm. CLOSED Sat & all Jewish holidays.* Admission charge, lower for children and senior citizens.

Libraries

In New York City's 5 boroughs, there are 82 branch & research libraries. The Main Branch of the Library system is the world's largest research library.

Pierpont Morgan Library
33 East 36 Street bet Madison & Park Aves. 685-0610. (McKim, Mead & White, 1906.) A Renaissance palazzo that belonged to a prince of finance. The exterior stonework was done without cement. The opulent interior is rich, not only in furnishings and paintings, but in medieval and Renaissance manuscripts, drawings, and books as well. *OPEN Tues-Sat 10:30am-5pm; Sun 1-5pm. CLOSED Mon, Sun in July, all of Aug.* Suggested contribution.

New York Public Library
Fifth Avenue & 42 Street. A national historic landmark that covers 2 city blocks. A.k.a. the Central Research Library, it opened to the public May 24, 1911. It is quite simply one of the greatest research institutions in the world containing 6 million books, 12 million manuscripts, 2.8 million pictures. Don't miss: the newly restored splendid Gottesman Hall with its ornate carved oak paneling *(OPEN Mon-Sat 10:30am-6pm.);* the DeWitt Wallace Periodicals Room, an elegant public room with 13 new murals by trompe l'oeil master Richard Haas and most of all the Main Reading Room, for silence and solace. It's 297 feet long, 78 feet deep and contains the original chairs, tables and bronze reading lamps. *(OPEN Mon, Tues & Wed 10am-6pm; Thurs-Sat till 6pm.)* One-hour free tours of the Library Mon, Tues, Wed at 11am & 2pm leave from Astor Hall just inside the Main Entrance on Fifth Avenue. Tour and exhibit information, 930-0717.

New York Public Library

Schomburg Center
515 Lenox Avenue nr West 135 Street. 862-4000. A component of the Public Library's Research Library. This internationally renowned cultural facility, located in the heart of Harlem, began with the donated holdings of Arthur Schomburg, an Afro-Puerto Rican. Now, the world's largest collection of documentation of Black history and culture includes 20,000 reels of microfilm of news clippings; over 1,000 rare books, 60,000 photographs, 15,000 hours of taped oral history; 10,000 records; 300 videotapes; 200 films. A permanent display of African and Afro-American art and artifacts. On 135 Street, an outdoor sculpture garden,

on 136 Street an outdoor amphitheater. *OPEN winter Mon-Wed noon-8pm; Thurs 10am-6pm; in summer Mon & Wed noon-8pm, Tues-Fri 10am-6pm.* FREE

YIVO Institute for Jewish Research
Fifth Avenue at 86 Street. 535-6700. Established in 1925 in Vilna, Lithuania, this academic research center for Eastern European Jewry and Jewish culture contains more than 22 million documents, 100,000 photographs, 300,000 books. *OPEN Mon-Fri 9:30am-5:30pm.* FREE

Galleries

IMPORTANT NOTE: *The "art scene" slows during June, July, and August. Gallery hours and weeks may be shorter, and in many cases Never in August is the case. In general, call for summer hours.*

Uptown Galleries
These are located primarily on and off Madison Avenue, East 86 Street south to 57 Street.

Aaron Berman Gallery
50 West 57 Street, 14th fl. 757-7630. Modern contemporary art. *OPEN Tues-Sat 10am-5pm. Mon by appointment only.*

Aberbach Fine Art
988 Madison Avenue at East 77 St. 988-1100. Modern Masters including Botero and Dario Morales. *OPEN Tues-Fri 10am-5:30pm; Sat 11am-5:30pm. CLOSED July & Aug.*

A.C.A. Galleries
21 East 67 Street. 628-2440. Early 20th-century and contemporary American works of art. *OPEN Tues-Sat 10am-5:30pm.*

Acquavella Galleries, Inc.
18 East 79 Street. 734-6300. Impressionist, Post-Impressionist: Monet, Picasso, Miró, Pisarro. Downstairs for contemporary paintings: Guston, Gottlieb, Lichtenstein. *OPEN Mon-Sat 10am-5pm.*

Alexander Gallery
996 Madison Avenue nr East 77 St. 472-1636. Specializes in Hudson River landscapes. *OPEN year round Mon-Sat 9:30am-5:30pm.*

Alonzo Gallery, Inc.
30 West 57 Street, 4th fl. 586-2500. Long-time gallery. Contemporary abstract landscapes, still-life paintings, drawings, prints, sculpture, photographs. *OPEN Tues-Sat 11am-6pm.*

David Anderson Gallery
521 West 57 Street, 8th fl. 586-4200. Contemporary international paintings, sculpture, and graphics. *By appointment only.*

Arras Gallery East
Trump Tower, 725 Fifth Avenue at 56 St, Level A. 751-0080. Contemporary painting, tapestry, sculpture, graphics and photography. *OPEN Tues-Sat 9:30am-5:30pm.*

Babcock Galleries
20 East 67 Street. 535-9355. American works of art of the 19th and 20th centuries. Contemporary paintings, drawings, and sculpture. *By appointment only.*

J. N. Bartfield Galleries
45 West 57 Street, 2nd fl. 753-1830. Antique books, American Western art, 19th-century European art. *OPEN Mon-Fri 10am-5pm; Sat 10am-4pm.*

William Beadleston, Inc.
60 East 91 Street. 348-7234. Impressionist, Post-Impressionist, and 20th-century paintings and sculpture. *OPEN Mon-Fri 10am-5pm. CLOSED Mon in July & Aug.*

Berry-Hill Galleries, Inc.
743 Fifth Avenue nr 57 St, 2nd fl. 371-6777. American and European painting and sculpture from the 19th and 20th centuries. *OPEN Mon-Fri 9:30am-5pm; Sat 10am-4pm.*

Blum Helman Gallery, Inc.
20 West 57 Street, 2nd fl. 245-2888. Recent American painting and sculpture. *OPEN Tues-Sat 10am-6pm.*

Grace Borgenicht
1018 Madison Avenue nr East 79 St, 4th fl. 535-8040. Twentieth-century American art. *OPEN Tues-Fri 10am-5:30pm; Sat 11am-5:30pm.*

Borghi & Company
50 East 50 Street. 838-2147. Nineteenth-century art. *OPEN Mon-Fri 10am-6pm; Sat 11am-5pm.*

Brewster Gallery
41 West 57 Street, 6th fl. 980-1975. Twentieth-century modern art, especially Carrington, Calder, McCormick. Largest dealers in Miró, Chagall. Publisher of Francisco Zuñiga. *OPEN Tues-Sat 10:30am-5:30pm.*

Carus Gallery, Inc.
872 Madison Avenue at East 71 St, 2nd fl. 879-4660. German Expressionists. Constructivists. Russian avant-garde watercolors, drawings, and prints. *OPEN Tues-Sat 11am-5pm. CLOSED July; Aug by appointment only.*

Chapellier Galleries, Inc.
815 Park Avenue at East 75 St, apt. 5A. 988-8430. Works by American painters. *By appointment only.*

Cordier & Ekstrom
417 East 75 Street, 1st fl. 988-8857. Contemporary art, painting, and sculpture. *OPEN Tues-Sat 10am-5:30pm.*

Andrew Crispo Gallery
41 East 57 Street, 2nd fl. 758-9190. Nineteenth- and 20th-century American painting. *OPEN Tues-Fri 11:30am-4:30pm; Sat 10:30am-5:30pm.*

Eugenia Cucalon Gallery
145 East 72 Street, 2nd fl. 472-8741. Conceptual art: Dada, Man Ray, Oppenheimer, as well as contemporary Latin American artists. *OPEN Tues-Sat noon-6pm.*

Davis & Langdale Company
746 Madison Avenue nr East 65 St, 2nd fl. 861-2811. Eighteenth-, 19th- and 20th-century American and English paintings, watercolors, and drawings. *OPEN Tues-Sat 10am-5pm, June-Sept Mon-Fri.*

Maxwell Davidson Gallery
43 East 78 Street. 734-6702. Fine 19th- and 20th-century paintings, drawings, and sculpture. *OPEN Tues-Sat 10am-6pm.*

Davlyn Gallery
975 Madison Avenue nr East 76 St. 879-2075. Twentieth-century masters. *OPEN year round Tues-Sat 10:30am-5:30pm.*

Marisa Del Re Gallery, Inc.
41 East 57 Street, 4th fl. 688-1843. Postwar American original art: Calder, Christo, Motherwell. *OPEN Tues-Fri 10am-5:30pm; Sat 11am-5:30pm.*

Tibor de Nagy Gallery, Inc.
41 West 57 Street, 7th fl. 421-3780. Contemporary art, both abstract and representational. *OPEN Tues-Sat 10am-5:30pm.*

Sid Deutsch Gallery
43 East 80 Street, 2nd fl. 861-4429. Twentieth-century American and European art. *OPEN Tues-Sat 10am-6pm.*

Terry Dintenfass, Inc.
50 West 57 Street, 10th fl. 581-2268. Twentieth-century painting and sculpture. *OPEN Tues-Sat 10am-5:30pm.*

Theodore B. Donson, Ltd.
24 West 57 Street, 3rd fl. 245-7007. Fine Old Masters and modern prints. Author of an excellent book on prints. Collection includes Rembrandt, Dürer, Toulouse-Lautrec, Matisse, Renoir, Whistler. *OPEN year round Tues-Sat 10am-6pm.*

Paul Drey Gallery
11 East 57 Street, 4th fl. 753-2551. Old Masters paintings, drawings, sculpture, and works of art. *By appointment only.*

Robert Elkon Gallery
1063 Madison Avenue nr East 80 Street, 2nd fl. 535-3940. Contemporary painting and sculpture, 20th-century masters. *OPEN Tues-Sat 10am-5:45pm.*

André Emmerich Gallery, Inc.
41 East 57 Street, 5th & 9th fls. 752-0124. Contemporary American and European art, pre-Columbian and ancient art. Painters include Al Held, Hans Hofmann, Morris Louis, David Hockney, Helen Frankenthaler, Kenneth Noland. Sculptors include Anthony Caro, Beverly Pepper, Sylvia Stone. *OPEN Tues-Sat 10am-5:30pm; July & Aug by appointment only.*

Richard L. Feigen & Company, Inc.
113 East 79 Street. 628-0700. Fifteenth- to 20th-century masters. *By appointment only.*

David Findlay Galleries, Inc.
984 Madison Avenue nr East 77 St. 249-2909. Nineteenth- and 20th-century European paintings. Sculpture as well. *OPEN Tues-Sat 10am-5pm.*

Wally Findlay
17 East 57 Street. 421-5390. Impressionist, Post-Impressionist, contemporary art of the French school. Mass appeal. *OPEN year round Mon-Sat 9:30am-5:30pm.*

Fischbach
24 West 57 Street, 8th fl. 759-2345. Twentieth-century American paintings, drawings. *OPEN Tues-Sat 10am-5:30pm.*

Forum Gallery
1018 Madison Avenue nr East 78 St, 5th fl. 772-7666. Contemporary figurative American paint-

ings and sculpture. *OPEN Tues-Sat 10am-5:30pm. In summer Mon-Fri.*

Xavier Fourcade, Inc.
36 East 75 Street. 535-3980. Twentieth-century European and American painting and sculpture. *OPEN Tues-Fri 10am-5:30pm; Sat 10am-5pm.*

Allan Frumkin Gallery
50 West 57 Street, 2nd fl. 757-6655. Contemporary paintings, Realism, West Coast artists, ceramics, sculpture. *OPEN Tues-Fri 10am-6pm; Sat noon-5:30pm. June-Aug, Mon-Fri.*

Galerie St. Etienne, Inc.
24 East 57 Street, 8th fl. 245-6734. Private dealer. Nineteenth- and 20th-century Austrian and German art; 19th- and 20th-century Naive art; Grandma Moses. *OPEN Tues-Sat 11am-5pm.*

Getler/Pall/Saper
50 West 57 Street, 7th fl. 581-2724. Contemporary paintings, drawings and prints by Richard Carboni, Squeak Carnwath, Lance Kiland, Stephanie Rose, T. L. Solien, Steven Sorman. *OPEN Tues-Sat 10am-5:30pm.*

Gimpel & Weitzenhoffer, Ltd.
1040 Madison Avenue at East 79 St. 628-1897. Twentieth-century American and European paintings and sculpture. *OPEN Tues-Sat 9:30am-5:30pm. June-Aug Mon-Fri.*

James Goodman Gallery
1020 Madison Avenue nr East 79 St, 4th fl. 772-2288. Twentieth-century American and European paintings, drawings, watercolors, sculpture. *OPEN Mon-Sat 10am-5pm.*

Graham Gallery
1014 Madison Avenue nr East 78 St. 535-5767. Primarily 19th- and early 20th-century American art and Western painting and sculpture. On 3rd floor, modern gallery features a series of contemporary artists. *OPEN Tues-Sat 10am-5pm; June-Aug. Mon-Fri.*

Grand Central Art Galleries, Inc.
24 West 57 Street, 2nd fl. 867-3344. Late-19th-century American masters; 20th-century representational American art. *OPEN Mon-Fri 10am-6pm; Sun till 5pm.*

Gruenebaum Gallery
38 East 57 Street, 3rd fl. 838-8245. Contemporary American art. *OPEN Tues-Sat 9:30am-5:30pm. CLOSED Aug.*

Stephen Hahn, Inc.
9 East 79 Street. 570-0020. Private dealer. French paintings of the 19th and 20th centuries. *By appointment only.*

Hamilton Gallery of Contemporary Art
20 West 57 Street, 6th fl. 598-0195. Contemporary paintings and sculpture. *OPEN Tues-Sat 10am-5:30pm.*

Hammer Galleries
33 West 57 Street. 644-4400. Nineteenth- and 20th-century European and American paintings. Graphics on 3rd floor, Leroy Neiman. *OPEN Mon-Fri 9:30am-5:30pm; Sat 10am-5pm.*

Lillian Heidenberg Gallery, Ltd.
50 West 57 Street, 8th fl. 586-3808. Twentieth-century modern master and contemporary painting, sculpture, and graphics. *OPEN Tues-Fri*

10am-5:30pm; Sat 11am-5:30pm. July-Aug Mon-Fri.

Hirschl & Adler Galleries, Inc.
21 East 70 Street. 535-8810. Top-quality 18th-, 19th-, and 20th-century American and European painting, sculpture, and drawings. Contemporary art and print departments too. *OPEN Tues-Fri 9:30am-5:30pm; Sat 9:30am-5pm.*

Leonard Hutton Galleries
33 East 74 Street, 2nd fl. 249-9700. Specializes in German Expressionists and Russian avant-garde works of art. *OPEN Mon-Fri 10am-5:30pm. Sat 10am-5pm. Aug by appointment only.*

Incurable Collector, Inc.
42 East 57 Street. 755-0140. English sporting, marine, and landscape paintings from the 18th and 19th centuries. Also, English Regency furniture. *OPEN Mon-Fri 9:30am-5:30pm; Sat 10am-4pm.*

Iolas-Jackson
52 East 57 Street, 755-6778. Contemporary paintings and sculpture. *OPEN Tues-Fri 10am-5:30pm; Sat 11am-5pm. CLOSED July & Aug.*

Sidney Janis Gallery
110 West 57 Street, 6th fl. 586-0110. Three generations of modern art from Cubism to Pop to Minimal painting. *OPEN Mon-Sat 10am-5pm.*

Jaro Art Galleries, Inc.
955 Madison Avenue nr East 75 St. 734-5475. Specializes in Yugoslavian Naives. *OPEN Mon-Sat 10am-6pm.*

Julie: Artisan's Gallery
687 Madison Avenue nr East 62 St. 688-2345. Fanciful wearable arts and crafts. All one of a kind. First gallery to show clothing as an art form created by contemporary craft people. *OPEN Mon-Sat 11am-6pm.*

Kennedy Galleries, Inc.
40 West 57 Street, 5th fl. 541-9600. American paintings, sculpture, and graphics of the 18th, 19th, and 20th centuries plus European fine prints. *OPEN Tues-Sat 9:30am-5:30pm. In summer Mon-Sat by appointment only.*

Coe Kerr Gallery
49 East 82 Street. 628-1340. Nineteenth- and 20th-century American paintings, including the Wyeths. *OPEN year round Mon-Fri 9am-5pm.*

Knoedler & Co.
19 East 70 Street. 794-0550. Old Masters, 19th- and 20th-century European and American paintings and sculpture. *OPEN Tues-Fri 9:30am-5pm; Sat 10am-5pm. June-Aug Mon-Fri.*

Kolodny
1001 Madison Avenue nr East 77 St. 472-9132. American and European paintings: 19th- to early-20th-century landscapes, genre, still lifes, portraits and seascapes. *OPEN Mon-Sat 11am-5pm. In summer, Tues-Fri.*

Kornblee Gallery
20 West 57 Street, 8th fl. 586-1178. Contemporary paintings and sculpture. *OPEN Tues-Fri 10am-5:30pm; Sat 11am-5pm. CLOSED Aug.*

Kraushaar Galleries
724 Fifth Avenue nr 57th St, 7th fl. 307-5730. Paintings, drawings, and sculpture by 20th-

century American artists, especially members of the Eight: Glackens, Sloan, Henri, etc. *OPEN Tues-Sat 9:30am-5:30pm. In summer Mon-Fri till 5pm.*

La Boetle, Inc.
9 East 82 Street, 3rd fl. 535-4865. Expressionists, Surrealists, Constructivists, Art of the Bauhaus, and Dada. *OPEN Tues-Sat 10am-5:30pm.*

Lefebre Gallery
47 East 77 Street, 2nd fl. 744-3384. Mainly European contemporary paintings and sculpture. *OPEN Tues-Sat 10am-5:30pm. CLOSED July & Aug.*

Marlborough Gallery, Inc.
40 West 57 Street, 2nd fl. 541-4900. Twentieth-century contemporary paintings, sculpture, photographs, graphics. *OPEN Mon-Sat 10am-5:30pm.*

James Maroney, Inc.
129a East 74 Street. 879-2252. Private dealer. Nineteenth- and early 20th-century American paintings and watercolors *By appointment only.*

Barbara Mathes Gallery
851 Madison Avenue nr East 70 St, 2nd fl. 249-3600. Nineteenth- and 20th-century American art: Avery, Cornell, deKooning, Dine, Francis, Lichtenstein, Motherwell, Rothko, Stella, Hockney, Balthus, Gottlieb. *OPEN Tues-Sat 9:30am-5:30pm. June & July Mon-Fri; CLOSED Aug.*

Pierre Matisse Gallery Corporation
41 East 57 Street, 4th fl. 355-6269. Contemporary paintings and sculpture, including Miró. *OPEN Tues-Sat 10am-5pm. CLOSED July & Aug.*

Midtown Galleries, Inc.
11 East 57 Street, 3rd fl. 758-1900. Contemporary American artists represented. *OPEN Tues-Sat 10am-5:30pm.*

Eduard Nakhamkin Fine Arts
1070 Madison Avenue nr East 81 St. 734-0271.*Also, 599 Broadway at Houston St. Contemporary Russian art-in-exile. Prints, graphics, oils, sculpture. *OPEN Mon-Sat 10am-6pm; Sun noon-5pm. *Mon-Fri 10am-6pm; Sat & Sun by appointment.*

Newhouse Galleries, Inc.
19 East 66 Street. 879-2700. Dutch 17th-, Italian 15th-, and American 18th- and 19th-century paintings. Large and very good operation. Strong in Old Masters. *OPEN year round Mon-Fri 9:30am-5pm.*

Odyssia Gallery
730 Fifth Avenue at 57 St, 3rd fl. 517-9112. Contemporary American and European paintings: William Allan, Ellen Lanyon, Robert Birmelin. *By appointment only.*

Pace Gallery of New York, Inc.
32 East 57 Street, 2nd fl. 421-3292. Twentieth-century painting, sculpture, and graphics. Dine, Nevelson, Schnabel, Calder, Samaris, Dubuffet. *OPEN Tues-Fri 9:30am-5:30pm; Sat 10am-6pm.*

William Pall Gallery
63 East 57 Street, 4th fl. 860-3400. Nineteenth- and 20th-century European and American art. *OPEN by appointment only.*

Marilyn Pearl Gallery
38 East 57 Street, 6th fl. 838-6310. Both contem-

porary American masters and lesser-known artists. Exhibits change monthly. *OPEN Tues-Sat 10am-5:30pm. CLOSED Aug.*

Peris Galleries
1016 Madison Avenue nr East 78 St. 472-3200. Paintings and sculpture by 20th-century masters: Calder, Picasso, Braque, Chagall, Dufy. *OPEN Tues-Sat 10am-5pm. June & July Mon-Fri; Aug by appointment only.*

Elinor Poindexter
831-2520. Private dealer. Contemporary painting and sculpture, primarily American. *By appointment only.*

Rolly-Michaux
943 Madison Avenue nr East 75 St. 535-1460. Contemporary art of Miró, Pel, Delaunay, Calder, Moore. *OPEN Tues-Sat 10:30am-5:30pm. In summer 11am-5pm.*

Alex Rosenberg Gallery—Transworld Art
20 West 57 Street, 7th fl. 757-2700. Contemporary American art: paintings, sculpture, photography. Eclectic exhibits. *OPEN Mon-Sat 10am-5pm.*

Rosenberg & Stiebel, Inc.
32 East 57 Street, 5th fl. 753-4368. Fine paintings, drawings, works of art, and French furniture. *OPEN year round Mon-Fri 10am-5pm.*

Rothschild Fine Arts
205 West End Avenue nr West 70 St. 873-9142. Private dealer. Buys and sells Impressionist, Post-Impressionist, modern, and contemporary art. *By appointment only.*

Serge Sabarsky Gallery, Inc.
987 Madison Avenue nr East 76 St. 628-6281. Twentieth-century German and Austrian Expressionists: Beckmann, Grosz, Feininger, Dix, Schiele, Klimt, Klee. *OPEN Tues-Sat noon-6pm. In summer till 5pm.*

A.M. Sachs Gallery
29 West 57 Street, 3rd fl. 421-8686. Contemporary painting and sculpture, John Ferren, Stephen Pace, Craig McPherson. *OPEN Tues-Sat 10am-5:30pm. July Mon-Fri; Aug by appointment only.*

Saidenberg Gallery, Inc.
1018 Madison Avenue nr East 78 St, 3rd fl. 288-3387. Twentieth-century European and American paintings, sculpture, and graphic art. Specialists in Picasso, Klee, Leger. *OPEN Tues-Fri 10am-5pm; Sat 1-5pm. CLOSED Aug.*

Salander-O'Reilly Galleries, Inc.
22 East 80 Street. 879-6606. Nineteenth- to 20th-century American modernist paintings: Hudson River, American Impressionists, Ashcan School, Precisionist, New York School. Also, contemporary painters. *OPEN Mon-Sat 10am-5:30pm.*

Schaeffer Galleries, Inc.
983 Park Avenue nr East 83 St, 2nd fl. 535-6410, -6411. Old Masters paintings and drawings of the 17th, 18th, and 19th centuries. *OPEN year round Mon-Fri 10am-5pm.*

H. Shickman Gallery
1000 Park Avenue nr East 84 St. 249-3800. Fine Old Masters paintings and drawings, 19th-century French paintings. *OPEN Mon-Sat 10am-6pm.*

Robert Schoelkopf Gallery, Ltd.
50 West 57 Street, 12A. 765-3540. Late 19th- and 20th-century American painting, sculpture and drawings. *OPEN Tues-Sat 10am-5pm.*

Schweitzer Gallery
958 Madison Avenue nr East 75 St, 2nd fl. 535-5430. European and American paintings from the Old Masters to the 20th century. *OPEN year round Mon-Fri 10am-5:30pm.*

Shepherd Gallery, Assoc.
21 East 84 Street. 861-4050. Nineteenth-century European art. *OPEN Tues-Sat 11am-6pm. CLOSED mid Aug-Labor Day.*

Sanford & Patricia Smith Gallery
1045 Madison Avenue at East 79 St. 744-6171. Nineteenth- and 20th-century American and Western bronzes, American antiques, marine paintings and sculpture. *OPEN Mon-Sat 11am-6pm.*

Holly Solomon
742 Fifth Avenue at 56 St. 757-7777. Contemporary art with an emphasis on narrative and decorative patterns. *OPEN Mon-Sat 10:30am-6pm.*

Solomon & Company Fine Art
959 Madison Avenue nr East 75 St. 737-8200. Twentieth-century American and European painting and sculpture. *OPEN Mon-Sat 11am-5pm.*

Soufer
1015 Madison Avenue nr East 79 St. 628-3225. Twentieth-century European and American painting, watercolors, and sculpture. *OPEN Tues-Sat 10:30am-5:30pm.*

Ira Spanierman, Inc.
50 East 78 Street. 879-7085. Nineteenth- and 20th-century American art. *OPEN Tues-Sat 9:30am-5:30pm. Mid June-mid Sept Mon-Fri.*

Spectrum Fine Art Ltd.
30 West 57 Street, 3rd fl. 246-2525. Specializing in sports-related art. Bellows, Riggs, Wilder. *OPEN Mon-Fri 9:30am-5:30pm.*

Spencer A. Samuels & Company, Ltd.
13 East 76 Street. 988-4556. Specializing in 14th-to 20th-century paintings, drawings and sculpture. Many Great Masters: Rembrandt and Tiepolo. *By appointment only.*

Sportsman's Edge, Ltd.
136 East 74 Street. 249-5010. Contemporary sporting and wildlife art; original oils, watercolors, sculpture and prints. *OPEN Mon-Sat 10am-6pm.*

Staempfli Gallery, Inc.
47 East 77 Street, 2nd fl. 535-1919. Contemporary American and European painting and sculpture. *OPEN Tues-Sat 10am-5:30pm. In summer, Mon-Fri.*

Allan Stone Gallery
48 East 86 Street, 2nd fl. 988-6870. Twentieth-century masters and contemporary art with an emphasis on Abstract Expressionism. *OPEN Tues-Fri 10am-6pm; Sat 10am-5pm. CLOSED July & Aug.*

Tatistcheff & Company, Inc.
50 West 57 Street, 8th fl. 664-0907. New American Realist and figurative paintings and works on paper. *OPEN Tues-Sat 10am-6pm.*

E.V. Thaw & Company, Inc.
726 Park Avenue at East 70 St. 535-6333. Large private dealer; master paintings and drawings of all periods. *By appointment only.*

Jack Tilton Gallery
24 West 57 Street, 3rd fl. 247-7480. Betty Parson's former director; continues her tradition of introducing unknown artists. Contemporary sculpture, painting, drawing. *OPEN Tues-Sat 10am-5:30pm. CLOSED Aug.*

Touchstone Gallery
118 East 64 Street. 826-6111. Contemporary painting and sculpture by young American artists. *OPEN Tues-Sat 10am-5:30pm.*

Vasarely Center
1015 Madison Avenue nr East 78 St, ground & 4th fls. 744-2332. Exhibits and sells works by Victor Vasarely. *OPEN Sun-Fri 10:30am-5:30pm.*

Viridian Gallery
24 West 57 Street, 8th fl. 245-2882. Contemporary art, painting, sculpture, graphics. *OPEN Tues-Sat 10am-5:30pm.*

Felix Vercel Galerie
710 Madison Avenue nr East 63 St. 832-9590. School of Paris and commercial contemporary art with some Old Masters sculpture too. *OPEN Tues-Sat 10am-6pm. CLOSED Aug.*

Hans Weissenberg
688-8430. Dutch, Flemish, and Italian 17th-century paintings. *By appointment only.*

Washburn Gallery, Inc.
42 East 57 Street, 4th fl. 753-0546. Also downtown at 113 Greene Street nr Prince St. 966-3151. American abstract paintings, 1930s & 1940s; sculpture, drawings. *OPEN Tues-Sat 10:30am-5pm. In summer Mon-Fri.*

Weintraub Gallery
992 Madison Avenue nr East 77 St. 879-1195. Nineteenth- and 20th-century European paintings, sculpture and graphics. *OPEN Tues-Sat 10am-5pm. In summer Mon-Fri.*

Wildenstein & Co., Inc.
19 East 64 Street. 879-0500. The world's foremost selection of old and modern paintings and objects of art. *OPEN year round Mon-Fri 10am-5pm.*

Willard Gallery, Inc.
29 East 72 Street, 2nd fl. 744-2925. Painting and sculpture, chiefly contemporary American. *OPEN Tues-Sat 10am-6pm. CLOSED Aug.*

Zabriskie Gallery
724 Fifth Avenue at 56 St, 12th fl. 307-7430. Contemporary and earlier American painting and sculpture. Some European. *OPEN Mon-Sat 10am-5:30pm.*

André Zarre
41 East 57 Street, 4th fl. 752-0498. Specializes only in 20th-century American artists; paintings, sculpture, and works on paper. *OPEN Tues-Sat 10am-5:30pm.*

SoHo Galleries

Pam Adler Gallery
578 Broadway nr Prince St, upstairs. 980-9696. Contemporary American artists; painting and sculpture. *OPEN Tues-Sat 10am-5:30pm. Call for summer hours.*

Mary Boone
417 West Broadway nr Spring St. 431-1818. Con-

temporary paintings and drawings. *OPEN Tues-Sat 10am-6pm. July & Aug by appointment only.*

Blue Moon Gallery
808 Broadway nr East 11 St. 475-4681. Modern European paintings, sculpture, drawing, and prints. Specializes in Leger, Picasso and Surrealism. *By appointment only.*

Susan Caldwell, Inc.
383 West Broadway nr Spring St, 2nd fl. 966-6500. Contemporary painting, sculpture and drawings. Private dealer. *By appointment only Tues-Sat 10am-6pm.*

Leo Castelli Gallery
420 West Broadway nr Spring St, 2nd fl. 431-5160. Top gallery for contemporary paintings, drawings, and sculpture: Artschwager, Johns, Kelly, Lichtenstein, Oldenburg, Rauschenberg, Rosenquist, Stella, Warhol, among others. *OPEN Tues-Sat 10am-6pm.*

Cayman Gallery
381 West Broadway nr Broome St, 2nd fl. 966-6699. Owned by the Historical Society of the Friends of Puerto Rico. Dedicated to the advancement of Hispanic culture. Exhibitions, films, library. *OPEN Tues-Sat 11am-6pm.*

Paula Cooper Gallery
155 Wooster Street nr Houston St. 674-0766. Contemporary and advanced American abstract art. *OPEN Tues-Sat 10am-6pm.*

Charles Cowles
420 West Broadway nr Prince St. 925-3500. Contemporary paintings, photography and sculpture. *OPEN Tues-Sat 10am-6pm.*

Elements
90 Hudson Street nr Worth St. 226-5910. Contemporary ceramics, wood, wall hangings. *OPEN Tues-Sat 11am-5:30pm. CLOSED Aug.*

Rose Esman Gallery
121 Spring Street at Greene St. 219-3044. Contemporary painting and sculpture and Russian Revolutionary, 1912-25. *OPEN Tues-Sat 10am-6pm. CLOSED Aug.*

Ronald Feldman Fine Arts
31 Mercer Street nr Grand St. 226-3232. Nineteenth- and 20th-century American and European art. *OPEN Tues-Sat 10am-6pm; Mon by appointment. July & Aug by appointment.*

14 Sculptors Gallery
164 Mercer Street nr Houston St. 966-5790. Artist-run gallery exhibits advanced contemporary sculpture in all media. *OPEN Tues-Sun 11am-6pm. CLOSED mid-July-Aug.*

Heller Gallery
71 Greene Street nr Spring St. 966-5948. Contemporary glass sculpture. *OPEN Mon-Sat 11am-6pm; Sun noon-5pm.*

Nancy Hoffman
429 West Broadway nr Prince St. 966-6676. Good contemporary art, including works by Don Eddy, Juan Gonzalez, Jack Tworkov, Fumio Yoshimura, Don Nice, Joseph Raffael, Paul Sarkisian, David Parrish and Carolyn Brady. *OPEN Tues-Sat 10am-6pm.*

Max Hutchinson Gallery
138 Greene Street nr Houston St. 966-3066.

Sculpture and painting in all media by American artists. *OPEN Tues-Sat 10am-6pm. CLOSED Aug.*

Jack Gallery
138 Prince Street nr West Broadway. 966-4235. Contemporary paintings and sculpture. *OPEN year round Mon-Fri 10am-6pm; Sat 11am-6pm; Sun noon-6pm.*

Phyllis Kind
136 Greene Street nr Houston St. 925-1200. Contemporary American art and Naive artists. *OPEN Tues-Sat 10am-6pm. Aug by appointment only.*

Monique Knowlton Gallery
153 Mercer Street nr Houston St. 431-8807. Young contemporary American artists. *OPEN Tues-Sat 10am-6pm.*

Chuck Levitan Gallery
42 Grand Street at West Broadway. 966-2782. Contemporary American art, paintings, and sculpture: Kate Millet, Will Barnet, Marisol. *OPEN Tues-Sat 1:30-5pm. CLOSED July & Aug.*

Louis K. Meisel
141 Prince Street nr West Broadway. 677-1340. Photorealist art by Audrey Flack, Charles Bell, Hilo Chen, Ron Kleemann. Abstract trompe l'oeil paintings by James Harvard and Jack Lemback. Pop art by Mel Ramos. Also Theodoros Stamas, Abstract Expressionist. *OPEN Tues-Sat 10am-6pm. CLOSED Aug.*

Elise Meyer, Inc.
410 West Broadway nr Spring St. 925-3527. Contemporary European and young British artists. Also contemporary sculpture and paintings by American artists. *OPEN Tues-Sat 10am- 6pm.*

Alexander F. Milliken, Inc.
98 Prince Street nr Greene St, 3rd fl. 966-7800. Contemporary painting and sculpture: Wendell Castle, Steve Hawley, Mary Ann Currier, Steven Lorber, Ed Hendricks, Lois Polansky. A very good eye for less familiar artists as well. *OPEN Tues-Sat 10am-6pm.*

O.K. Harris
383 West Broadway nr Broome St. 431-3600. Largest art gallery in the world. Presents 4-5 one-man shows every 3 weeks. Specializes in contemporary painting, sculpture, photography, and mixed media. Very good place to "discover" new artists. *OPEN Tues-Sat 10am-6pm. CLOSED mid-July-Labor Day.*

Pinder Gallery
127 Greene Street nr Houston St. 533-4881. Cooperative gallery representing contemporary American painters and sculptors. *OPEN Tues-Sat 11am-5:30pm; call for Sun hours.*

Pleiades Gallery
164 Mercer Street nr Houston St. 226-9093. Contemporary American art in mixed media. *OPEN Tues-Sun 11am-6pm.*

Sonnabend Gallery
420 West Broadway nr Prince St, 3rd fl. 966-6160. Contemporary and avant-garde paintings and sculpture: vintage and contemporary photographs. Videotapes and films by artists at Castelli, 142 Greene Street. *OPEN Tues-Sat 10am-6pm. CLOSED July-Aug.*

Sperone Westwater Fischer, Inc.
142 Greene Street nr Houston St, 2nd fl. 431-

3685. European and American contemporary art. *OPEN Tues-Sat 10am-6pm. July & Aug, by appointment only.*

Edward Thorp
103 Prince Street at Greene St, 2nd fl. 431-6880. Contemporary American painting and sculpture. *OPEN Tues-Sat 10am-6pm. CLOSED Aug.*

22 Wooster Gallery
22 Wooster Street nr Grand St. 431-6445. Contemporary American painting, sculpture, photography. *OPEN Tues-Sun noon-6pm.*

Jordan Volpe Gallery
457 West Broadway nr Prince St. 533-3900. Very fine, documented original American paintings. Mission furniture and American art pottery. *CLOSED Sun & Mon.*

Ward-Nasse, Inc.
178 Prince Street nr Thompson St. 925-6951. A cooperative art gallery with a very large membership. Varied styles in contemporary painting and sculpture. *OPEN Tues-Sat 11am-5:30pm; Sun 1-4pm.*

John Weber Gallery
142 Greene Street nr Houston St, 3rd fl. 966-6115. European and contemporary artists, emphasis on minimalist and nonfigurative work. *OPEN Tues-Sat 10am-6pm.*

Vorpal SoHo
465 West Broadway nr Houston St. 777-3939. Largest collection of prints by M. C. Escher in the world. Work of Jesse Allen, Gary Smith, Yvan Kustura. *OPEN year round Mon-Wed 10am-6pm; Thurs-Sat 10am-9pm.*

East Village Galleries
This area, in reality part of the old Lower East Side, has recently experienced a "gallery boom." Avante-garde art now exists amid the Polish bars, Ukrainian restaurants and Hispanic bodegas; over 30 new galleries have opened in one year. These galleries, below 14 Street and east—well east—of Second Avenue are well worth a visit. But, if you want chic, go south to SoHo and West to TriBeCa; if not for chic, go here for the energy of it all and pray it never becomes homogenized.Below is a list of East Village galleries that draw collectors, including Europeans, and the trendy, looking for art buys and finds.

Area X
200 East 10 Street. 477-1177. *OPEN Tues-Sat noon-6pm; Sun 1-6pm.*

Avenue B
167 Avenue B at East 10 St. 473-4600. *OPEN Wed-Sun 1-7pm.*

B-Side
543 East 6 Street. 477-6792. *OPEN Wed-Sun 1-6pm.*

Beulah Land
162 Avenue A at East 10 St. 473-9310. A gallery/bar. *OPEN 7 days 8pm-4am.*

Cash/Newhouse
170 Avenue B at East 10 St. 673-9366. *OPEN Wed-Sun 1-6pm.*

Civilian Warfare
155 Avenue B nr East 10 St. 475-7498. *OPEN Wed-Sun noon-6pm.*

Facchetti-Burk
328 East 11 Street. 477-3385. *OPEN Wed-Fri 11am-6pm; Fri Sat & Sun 1-6pm.*

Garet
204 East 10 Street. 475-8701. *OPEN Tues-Sat. 11am-6pm; Sun 1-6pm.*

Gracie Mansion Gallery
167 Avenue A nr East 10 St. 477-7331. *OPEN Wed-Sun 1-6pm.*

International with Monument
111 East 7 Street. 420-0517. *OPEN Tues-Sat noon-6pm.*

Mo David
436 East 9 Street. 533-2050. *OPEN Wed-Sun 1-6pm.*

Nature Morte
204 East 10 Street. 420-9544. *OPEN Wed-Sun noon-6:30pm.*

Pat Hearn
735 East 9 Street. 598-4282. *OPEN Wed-Sun 1-6pm.*

Piezo Electric
437 East 6 Street. 505-6243. *OPEN Wed-Sun 1-6pm.*

P.P.O.W.
216 East 10 Street. 477-4084. *OPEN Wed-Sun noon-6pm.*

Sensory Evolution
443 East 6 Street. 505-9144. *OPEN Wed-Sun 1-6pm.*

Sharpe
175 Avenue B at East 11 St. 777-4622. *OPEN Tues-Sun 1-6pm.*

Vox Populi
511 East 6 Street. 477-2279. *OPEN Tues-Sun noon-6pm.*

Wolff
513 East 6 Street. 460-5844. *OPEN Wed-Sun noon-6pm.*

Eastern Art
Asian Gallery
1049 Madison Avenue nr East 80 St. 734-1379. Chinese, Indian, Korean, Japanese, Tibetan, Nepalese, and Southeast Asian art. *OPEN Mon-Sat 10am-6pm.*

Jacques Carcanagues, Inc.
119 Spring Street nr Greene St. 431-3116. Ethnographic items from Afghanistan, Central America, Guatemala, India, Thailand, Indonesia, Japan, Korea, the Philippines, and more. *OPEN year round Tues-Sat 11am-6pm.*

Frank Caro Gallery
41 East 57 Street, 2nd fl. 753-2166. Ancient art of China, India, and Southeast Asia. *OPEN Tues-Sat 9am-4:30pm.*

Ralph M. Chait Galleries, Inc.
12 East 56 Street. 758-0937. Top-quality Chinese works of art, porcelain, pottery from the Neolithic period to 1800. *OPEN Mon-Sat 10am-5:30pm.*

Chinese Gallery of Art
15 East 71 Street. 535-1730. Porcelain, ceramic sculpture, and paintings from the early 6th century, Ming Dynasty, to the 18th century. *By appointment only.*

De Havenon, Inc.
160 East 65 Street, 29th fl. 249-9572. Primitive

African and Oceanic art. *By appointment only.*

Eastern Arts
365 Bleecker Street at Charles St. 929-7460. Mainly Indonesian, also, Oceanic art of the Asmat and of the Sepik River. Kashmiri and Balinese jewelry. *OPEN 7 days noon-7pm.*

E & J Frankel, Ltd.
1020 Madison nr East 78 St. 879-5733. Specializes in Oriental art from China: Shang Dynasty-1840s porcelains and jade; from Japan, all-periods screen paintings and furnishings. *OPEN Mon-Sat 10am-5:30pm.*

Glass Gallery
315 Central Park West at West 91 St, apt. 8W. 787-4704. Japanese prints and contemporary European graphics. American paintings. *OPEN Wed-Sat 1-6pm & by appointment.*

Hamsa Gallery, Ltd.
169 East 78 Street, 2nd fl. 288-2832. Oriental and Indian art, and handicrafts. *By appointment only.*

Charles D. Kelekian
667 Madison Avenue nr East 61 St, 10th fl. 517-3816. Est. 1893. Specializing in Egyptian, Greek, and Near East Islamic art. *By appointment only.*

Navin Kumar
967 Madison Avenue nr East 75 St. 734-4075. Indian, Tibetan, Islamic, and Nepalese art. *OPEN Mon-Sat 10am-6pm.*

Pace Primitive of New York, Inc.
32 East 57 Street, 10th fl. 421-3688. Antique African art and artifacts. *OPEN Tues-Fri 9:30am-5:30pm. Sat 10am-6pm.*

F. Rolin & Company, Inc.
1025 Madison Avenue nr East 84 St. 879-0077. Primitive art. The best in New York. *By appointment only.*

Ronin Gallery
605 Madison Avenue nr East 57 Street, 2nd fl. 688-0188. Large selection of 17th- to 20th-century Japanese woodblock prints. *OPEN Mon-Sat 10am-6pm.*

Segy Gallery of African Art
50 West 57 Street, 12th fl. 355-3859. Authentic ancient ceremonial, religious, magical fetishes, masks and statues from Africa. *OPEN Mon-Fri 11am-4:30pm; Sat 2-5pm.*

Merton D. Simpson
1063 Madison Avenue nr East 80 Street, 3rd fl. 988-6290. Mainly African, also Oceanic, and American Indian Art. *OPEN Tues-Sat 11am-6pm.*

Tribal Arts Gallery
84 East 10 Street. 982-4556. West and Central African sculpture (inexpensive): masks, head-pieces, ancestor figures, fetishes, guardian figures. *OPEN Wed-Sat noon-6pm.*

Ed Waldman Collection, Inc.
231 East 58 Street. 838-2140. Indian art temple hangings to miniatures, sculptures, bronzes, weaving from Thailand, China, Japan, and Southeast Asia, 14th century to contemporary. *OPEN Mon-Sat 9:30am-6pm.*

Weisbrod & Dy Ltd.
906 Madison Avenue nr East 72 Street. 734-6350. Museum-quality Oriental works of art: porcelain, jade, bronzes. *OPEN Mon-Sat 10am-5pm.*

Doris Wiener Gallery
772-8631. Southeast Asian art, Indian art from BC to 18th century; Indian paintings, sculpture. *By appointment only.*

William H. Wolff
22 East 76 Street. 988-7411. Far Eastern art, sculpture in bronze and stone. *OPEN Mon-Sat 10am-5pm.*

Prints & Posters

A Clean, Well-Lighted Place
363 Bleecker Street nr Charles St. 255-3656. Contemporary prints, including works by Will Barnet, Thom DeJong, Hockney, Motherwell. *OPEN Tues-Sat noon-7pm; Sun 1-5pm.*

AFI Gallery
145 West 55 Street. 246-8019. Master prints, tapestries, drawings: Chagall, Braque, Calder, Cocteau, Fini, Miró, Picasso. *By appointment only.*

Brooke Alexander, Inc.
59 Wooster nr Broome St. 2nd fl. 925-4338. Contemporary American and European paintings, drawings and sculpture, and contemporary American prints. Publisher of prints by Bartlett, Beal, Haas, Katz, Motherwell, Pearlstein, Welliver. *OPEN Tues-Fri 10am-6pm; Sat 10am-5:30pm.*

Associated American Artists (A.A.A.)
20 West 57 Street, 6th fl. 399-5510. America's largest print dealer. Both old and new. Original etchings, lithographs, woodcuts, and serigraphs, from the 15th to 20th century. Publisher of prints by Appel, Hirsch, Klabunde, Lucioni, Soyer, Wunderlich. *OPEN Mon-Sat 10am-6pm.*

Aldis Browne Fine Arts, Ltd.
16 East 78 Street. 772-6222. Specializes in classic prints of the 19th and 20th centuries and related unique works. *Call for hours.*

Castelli Graphics
4 East 77 Street, 2nd fl. 288-3202. Publisher of prints by Artschwager, Johns, Lichtenstein, Oldenburg, Stella, and Warhol as well as limited-edition photographic photofolios and books. *OPEN Tues-Sat 10am-6pm.*

Circle Gallery-SoHo
435 West Broadway nr Prince St. 226-7880. Also, 468 West Broadway. 677-5100. Owns over 20 galleries in the US, all specializing in moderately priced graphics with mass appeal, including works by Erte and Peter Max. *OPEN Tues-Fri 10am-6pm; Sat from 11am.*

Fitch-Febvrel Gallery
5 East 57 Street, 12th fl. 688-8522. Nineteenth- and 20th-century fine prints. *OPEN Tues-Sat 11am-5:30pm. Aug by appointment only.*

Lucien Goldschmidt, Inc.
1117 Madison Avenue nr East 84 St. 879-0070. Continental European drawings, prints, illustrated books. *OPEN Mon-Fri 10am-6pm; Sat till 5pm.*

Martin Gordon, Inc.
1000 Park Avenue at East 84 St. 249-7350. Prints by 19th- and 20th-century masters. *By appointment only.*

Isselbacher Gallery
41 East 78 Street. 472-1766. Late 19th- and 20th-

century prints, woodcuts, etchings: Chagall, Lautrec, Matisse, Miró, Renoir, Picasso. *OPEN Tues-Sat 10:30am-5:30pm.*

Japan Gallery
1210 Lexington Avenue nr East 82 St. 288-2241. Specializes in Japanese woodblock prints from the 18th century to the present. *OPEN Tues-Sat 10:30am-6:30pm.*

Jane Kahan Gallery
922 Madison Avenue at East 73 Street, 2nd fl. 744-1490. Large collection of Chagall prints; also Agam, Appel, Calder, Hundertwasser, Kand, Lindner, Masson, Matta, Miró, Picasso, Tobiasse, Vasarely, Bolotowsky. *OPEN Mon-Sat 10am-5:30pm.*

Kathryn Markel Fine Arts, Inc.
50 West 57 Street, 7th fl. 581-1909. Contemporary art on paper, collages, paintings, watercolors and artists' books. *OPEN Tues-Sat 10am-5:30pm.*

Multiple Impressions, Ltd.
17 Greenwich Avenue nr Christopher St. 255-5301. Contemporary American and European original graphics: Kozo, Masson, Friedlaender, Altman, Schippert. Several one-man shows a year. *OPEN Mon-Sat 11:30am-7:30pm; Sun 12:30-6:30pm.*

Multiples/Marian Goodman Gallery
24 West 57 Street, 4th fl. 977-7160. Publisher of prints by Arakawa, Richard Artschwager, Jennifer Bartlett, Ed Baynard, Larry Bell, Lichtenstein, Oldenburg, Denis Oppenheim, Rauschenberg, Jasper Johns, Sol Lewitt, Mimmo Paladino, Rosenquist, Ruscha, Warhol, Wegman, Wesselmann. Paintings, drawings, sculpture. *OPEN Mon-Sat 10am-6pm.*

Old Print Shop
150 Lexington Avenue at East 30 Street. 683-3950. Original old prints of Audubon, Currier & Ives, 18th-century maps, marines and some American paintings. *OPEN Mon-Sat 9am-5pm.*

Pace Editions
32 East 57 Street, 3rd fl. 421-3237. Contemporary prints: Jim Dine, Louise Nevelson, Al Held; also, Master prints: Matisse, Picasso, Avery. *OPEN Tues-Fri 9:30am-5:30pm; Sat 10am-6pm. In summer, Mon-Fri.*

Reiss-Cohen, Inc.
628-2496. Major graphics of the 19th and 20th centuries: Braque, Bonnard, Chagall, Kandinsky, Lautrec, Leger, Miró, Matisse, Picasso, Renoir, Rouault. *By appointment only.*

William H. Schab Gallery, Inc.
11 East 57 Street, 5th fl. 758-0327. Old Master and modern prints, lithographs, woodcuts, engravings, etchings: Dürer, Rembrandt, Goya, Old Masters drawings: Tiepolo, Tintoretto. *OPEN Mon-Sat 9am-5:30pm.*

Sindin Galleries
1035 Madison Avenue at East 79 St. 288-7902. Twentieth-century master graphics, drawings, etchings, and sculpture: Zuñiga, Chagall, Miró, Picasso. *OPEN Tues-Sat 10am-5:30pm.*

Suzuki Graphics, Inc.
38 East 57 Street, 11th fl. 752-1853. Contempo

rary Japanese-American prints, watercolors, and oils: Uchima, Giobbi, Ida, Kemble, and others. Exhibitions 5-6 times a year. *OPEN Tues-Sat 11am-5:30pm. Aug by appointment.*

David Tunick, Inc.
12 East 81 Street. 570-0090. Fine Old Masters and modern prints: Rembrandt, Lautrec, Dürer, Tiepolo, Bruegel, Canaletto; 19th-century prints: Bonnard, Goya, Cézanne, Degas, Delacroix, Géricault, Manet, Lautrec, Pissarro; 20th century: Picasso, Matisse, Braque, Whistler, Bellows, Villon. *OPEN Mon-Fri 10am-5pm. Appointment advisable.*

Weyhe Gallery
794 Lexington Avenue nr East 61 St. 838-5478. Fine prints, drawings, and sculpture of American artists of 1920s, 1930s, 1940s: Kent, Lozowick, Ganso, Gag, Dwight, Matulka, Maurer. *OPEN Tues-Sat 9:30am-5pm.*

Photography

Castelli Graphics, Marlborough and Zabriskie also show photography.

Floating Foundation of Photography
Pier 40 South, West Street at West Houston on the Hudson River. 242-3177. Nonprofit foundation (located on a barge) dedicated to the use of photography as an art form and as a means of communicative interaction. Lectures, workshops and cooperative programs. *OPEN Thurs-Sun 12:30-6pm. Wed by appointment.*

Freidus Ordover Gallery
70 Greene Street nr Spring St. 925-0113. Contemporary American photography, sculpture and painting. *OPEN Tues-Sat 10am-6pm.*

International Center of Photography
See General Art Museums.

Light
724 Fifth Avenue nr 56 St, 9th fl. 582-6552. Contemporary and 19th-century vintage photography: Paul Strand of the 1920s to young photographers of today. Changing exhibits each month. *OPEN Tues-Fri 10am-6pm; Sat 11am-5pm.*

Robert Miller
724 Fifth Avenue nr 56 St, 11th fl. 246-1625. Contemporary American art, plus 19th- and 20th-century photography. *OPEN Tues-Sat 10am-5:30pm. CLOSED Aug.*

Marcuse Pfeifer
825 Madison Avenue nr East 69 St, 2nd fl. 737-2055. Exhibits solely photographic art: Lilo Raymond, Peter Hujar, Joan Myers, David Hanson. *OPEN Tues-Sat 10am-5:30pm.*

Neikrug
224 East 68 Street. 288-7741. Town house setting for contemporary and vintage photographs including daguerrotypes. Appraisals. *OPEN Wed-Sat 1-6pm or by appointment.*

Prakapas Gallery
19 East 71 Street, 2nd fl. 737-6066. Photographic-print art from vintage 19th-century works to vintage modernist work. Exhibitions of never-before-shown photographs. *OPEN Tues-Sat noon-5pm.*

Witkin Gallery, Inc.
415 West Broadway nr Prince St., 4th fl. 925-5510. Photographic prints and books, including out-of-print photo literature. Vintage and contemporary prints: André Kertész, Steiglitz, Ansel Adams, Imogene Cunningham, Evelyn Hofer, Edward Weston, Joel Meyerowitz, George Tice, Jerry Uelsman. *OPEN Tues-Fri 11am-6pm; Sat noon-5pm.*

Daniel Wolf
30 West 57 Street, 4th fl. 586-8432. Nineteenth- and 20th-century photography: Cameron, Watkins, Baldus, Fenton, Thompson, Marcia Dalby, Jed Devine, Harold Edgerton, Andreas Feininger, William Garnett, Michael Geiger, Frank Gohlke, Sheila Metzner, Barbara Morgan, Joel Sternfeld. *OPEN Mon-Sat 11am-6pm.*

Alternative Exhibition Spaces

Devoted to assisting new or neglected artists and art forms; they are mainly nonprofit, multiple-discipline centers long on vision and usually short on funds.

Alternative Museum
17 White Street nr Church St. 966-4444. In TriBeCa, exhibitions in all media by American and other world cultures; emphasis on artists outside the mainstream. A major presenter of world music: non-Western, classical, folk, to experimental. Poetry, too. Artist-founded and -operated. *OPEN Wed-Sat 11am-6pm. CLOSED Sun-Tues.*

The Drawing Center
137 Greene Street nr Prince St. 982-5266. Nonprofit institution dedicated to the study and exhibition of works on paper. Shows of promising and well-known artists; historical and theme exhibitions. Lectures, films, symposiums, twice yearly conservation workshops. *OPEN Tues & Thurs-Sat 11am-6pm; Wed till 8pm. CLOSED Sun & Mon.*

Global Village
454 Broome Street nr Mercer St. 966-7526. Begun in 1969, it is *the* center for documentary video in New York. Workshops, internships, production. Large tape library. Weekly video and film screenings in spring and fall. Call for info, or get on their mailing list.

Henry Street Settlement
466 Grand Street at Pitt St. 598-0400. Long-time (since 1888) social service institution houses arts and performance spaces to serve the Lower East Side community. Theaters, galleries and classrooms for the performing and visual arts. Gallery noon-6pm. Performances at 7:30pm. Building *OPEN 7 days.*

Institute for Art & Urban Resources
46-01 21 Street, Long Island City, Queens. (1-718) 784-2084. Exhibition center in the areas of architecture, photography, music, fashion, video and film. Group shows and special projects by contemporary artists, at P.S. 1. *OPEN Thurs-Sun 1-6pm.* FREE

The Kitchen
59 Wooster Street nr Broome St, 2nd fl. 925-3615. Since 1971, innovative experimental dance, music, video (very strong) and performance and visual arts center. Membership available. Admission charge.

P.S. 1
46-01 21 Street, Long Island City, Queens. (1-718) 784-2084. Large art, dance and performance space located in an 1888 former public school. Run by the Institute for Art & Urban Resources. It houses 33 studios, an auditorium and a large exhibition space gallery for art, sculpture, video. *OPEN Tues-Sun 1-6pm. CLOSED Mon.* Small donation for exhibitions.

P.S. 122
150 First Avenue at East 9 St. 477-5288. Lower East Side showcase for new dance, music, film, theater, poetry and performance art. Gallery *OPEN Tues-Sun 1-5pm. CLOSED Mon.* Admission charge for events.

Parks & Gardens

Enid Haupt Conservatory, NY Botanical Garden

Vast or vest-pocket, parks and gardens in a city like New York have an incalculable value. When canyons of steel and glass have to cease or go around small or large outposts of "country," a modern miracle is wrought. The effect of greenery and open space in New York on the mind and spirit cannot be overstated.

Parks

Caveat: *It is highly recommended that you confine your park visits to daylight hours unless a specific special event is scheduled.*

General

New York City has 37,309 acres of parkland: 5,885 in the Bronx, 5,950 in Brooklyn, 2,623 in Manhattan, 16,728 in Queens, 6,123 on Staten Island.

For recorded information pertaining to the city's parks, call 472-1003; for free cultural events available on any given day in New York's five boroughs, call 755-4100. In addition, a cultural calendar is published monthly. Send a stamped self-addressed envelope to Parks Information Service, 830 Fifth Avenue, Room 2, New York, N.Y. 10021.

For further information on the city's parks, call the individual borough office:
Brooklyn: (1-718) 965-8900
Bronx: 430-1800
Manhattan: 408-0100
Queens: (1-718) 520-5900
Staten Island: (1-718) 390-8000

Central Park Conservancy
830 Fifth Avenue, New York, N.Y. 10021. 315-0385. A private non-profit citizen's group dedicated to the physical restoration of Central Park, as well as improved maintenance and security. Write for info.

Greensward Foundation
Box 610, Lenox Hill P.O., New York, N.Y. 10021. An independent organization comprised of the Friends of Central, Carl Schurz, and Prospect Parks, dedicated to the care and restoration of historic trees and monuments within these parks. Walking tours, bicycle tours, and lectures are some of what's offered.

Urban Park Rangers
Trained in the history, design, geology, wildlife and botany of the city's parks, they offer FREE walks and talks to encourage better use of them; also, to remind New Yorkers of the origins of the city's open spaces. For information on their fascinating and educational programs call the appropriate number:
Brooklyn Parks: (1-718) 856-4210
Bronx (except Crotona) Parks: 548-7880
Crotona Park: 589-0096
Manhattan Parks: 397-3091
Queens Parks: (1-718) 699-4204
Staten Island Parks: (1-718) 442-1304

Manhattan
Battery Park
State Street & Battery Place. At the southern tip of Manhattan, 21 acres extending from Bowling Green to the junction of the Hudson and East rivers. Its name resulted from a row of guns along its old shoreline. Castle Clinton, then known as

West Battery, was erected offshore on a pile of rock for the occasion of the War of 1812 (though nary a shot was ever fired). Landfill later joined it to the mainland, and Castle Clinton now sits squarely in what has become Battery Park. (*See also* HISTORIC NEW YORK, Historic Buildings & Areas.) Greenery, sea breezes, and great vistas draw mainly bankers and brokers at noon on good weather days. Departure point of the Staten Island Ferry, the Statue of Liberty Ferry, and the *Petrel* (*see* SIGHTSEEING, River Trips).

Battery Park Esplanade

Enter West & Liberty Streets. This 1.2 mile linear park that runs along the perimeter of the Battery Park landfill is the city's newest. Old-fashioned lampposts, shade trees and benches facing unimpeded Hudson River views make this an inviting spot.

Bowling Green

At the foot of Broadway. The city's first public park (1732). Colonial gentlemen used to "bowl" here, paying the annual sum of one peppercorn for the privilege. Its simple iron fence was erected in 1771 to protect the statue of George III which stood there. It failed. The day the Declaration of Independence reached New York, July 9, 1776, the statue was pulled down and apart along with some royal ornamentation on the fence.

Bryant Park

Sixth Avenue, West 40 to West 42 Street behind the New York Public Library. In 1822 these 9 acres were set aside as a potter's field, but in 1853 New York's version of London's Crystal Palace was erected on the site; it burned down 5 years later. In 1884 the park was named for William Cullen Bryant, poet and journalist. Now Midtown Manhattan's only public square will undergo a major renovation in hopes of driving out the drug dealers who have appropriated it in recent years. A huge Conservatory-style restaurant seating 1,000 is part of the proposed redesign.

Carl Schurz Park

East 84 to East 89 Street, East End Avenue to East River. The site of Gracie Mansion (1799); now the official residence of New York City's mayor (*see* HISTORIC NEW YORK, Historic Buildings & Areas). The park, located in Yorkville, the city's German area, is named after Carl Schurz, prominent 19th-century German immigrant, once senator and Secretary of the Interior.

Central Park

59 to 110 Street, Fifth Avenue to Central Park West, America's premiere urban park, an 843-acre oasis, 2½ miles long, ½ mile wide, right in the middle of Manhattan. Journalist-poet William Cullen Bryant and others saw the need to preserve some country space near the inner city, and in 1858 Frederick Law Olmsted and Calvert Vaux submitted the best plan for how it should be done. The results, a skillfull blend of man-made elements: lakes and ponds, hills and dales, secluded glens, wide meadows, a bird sanctuary, bridle paths, rambles, and nature trails. Though large enough to offer serene pockets, in recent years it's become more of a stage for New York's diverse interests, elements and behavior than a respite

from them. Over 16 million people visit and use the park annually. Rowing, jogging, horseback riding, bicycling, ice and roller skating, model-boat sailing, and tennis as well as Shakespeare, classical and rock concerts, and opera are just some of what is offered. (*See* ANNUAL EVENTS, summer months.)

Strawberry Fields is the new name of a triangular shaped area at West 72 Street and Central Park West–in honor of John Lennon.

Tavern-on-the-Green, originally a sheepfold, now offers elegant surroundings and food (*see* RESTAURANTS, Rooms with a View). The refreshment stand at the Boathouse serves more traditional park snacks. Also try the Health Bar at Sheep Meadow (69 Street) or the Ice Cream Café & Deli at Conservatory Pond (76 Street). The Park Drive is closed to motor traffic from Fri 7pm till Mon 6am; on legal holidays from 7pm the night before till 6am the morning after, year round. In addition, from May to Oct the prohibition extends to Mon-Fri 10am-3pm and Mon-Thurs 7–10pm (exception: entry West 59 & Avenue of the Americas and exit West 72 & Fifth Avenue, closed only 7-10pm).

NOTE: *The first 2 digits of the number plate of each lamppost in the park indicates the nearest cross street, so you'll never be lost. But if you lose (or find) anything in the park call the Dairy,* 397-3156. (*See also* SIGHTSEEING, On Your Own: Central Park, The Dairy.)

City Hall Park

Broadway, Park Row & Chambers Street. Formerly known as the City Common (ca. 1700), it now serves as City Hall's front yard. Schoolchildren with picnics and office workers with sun visors populate the park in fine weather.

Fort Tryon Park

Riverside Drive to Broadway, West 192 to Dyckman Street. A Rockefeller family gift to the City of New York, 62 acres of wooded hills and dales overlooking the Hudson River. It was formerly the site of C. K. G. Billings' estate. Its beautiful flower gardens and terracing make you feel miles away from the city. Fort Tryon, on the site of Fort Washington, the last holdout against the British invasion of Manhattan (it fell, Nov 16, 1776) caps a hill 250 ft above the river. The Cloisters (*see* MUSEUMS & GALLERIES, General Art Museums), located in the park, has a garden with 230 varieties of herbs and plants known before 1520. Parking facilities and a cafeteria.

Gramercy Park

Lexington Avenue, East 20 to East 21 Street. The land, originally a swamp, was bought in 1831 by Samuel B. Ruggles, one of the city's first real-estate developers. After it was drained, a private park was created for the exclusive use of those who would buy the surrounding lots. Sixty-six of the city's fashionable elite did just that and golden keys were provided for them to use the park, which was surrounded by an 8-ft fence. Though no longer golden, keys are still used by residents only. It's New York's only surviving private square.

Greenacre Park

East 51 Street bet Second & Third Avenues. A

1971 addition to the city's roster of parks. Donated by Mrs. Jean Mauzi, daughter of John D. Rockefeller, Jr., this vest-pocket park provides an oasis of cool, calm visual beauty. Very popular with brown-baggers at lunchtime.

Highbridge Park
West 155 to Dyckman Street, from Edgecombe & Amsterdam Avenues to the Harlem River Drive. Steeply sloped and very rugged terrain at West 174 Street, High Bridge (originally Aqueduct Bridge) is the oldest remaining bridge connecting Manhattan to the mainland. Originally it carried Croton River water to Manhattan. The Water Tower, built in 1872 to support a 47,000-gallon tank, now houses a carillon which plays from the tower's belfry. There is an imaginative Adventure Playground for children, a large outdoor public swimming pool and spectacular views of the Harlem River Valley.

Inwood Hill Park
Dyckman Street to the Harlem River, from Seaman to Payson Avenue. Algonquin Indians once dwelled in caves on this site; Henry Hudson likely came ashore here (1609), and during the American Revolution British and Hessian troops were quartered here. It's located in a particularly rich historic district, with Dyckman House (1783) nearby (see HISTORIC NEW YORK, Historic Buildings & Areas.) The nearly 200-acre park, rugged, hilly and wooded, contains the largest trees and oldest geological formations in Manhattan and is one of the city's truly unspoiled spots.

Madison Square Park
East 23 to East 26 Street bet Fifth & Madison Avenues. At various times in its history the area was a potter's field, the site of the city's first baseball games (1845), a luxurious residential area, and the site of the original Madison Square Garden (designed by Stanford White, who was shot dead on its roof garden by a jealous husband). The park is now primarily used by office workers from the nearby insurance companies.

Marcus Garvey Memorial Park (formerly Mount Morris Park)
120 to 124 Street at Fifth Avenue. Squarely in the path of Fifth Avenue as it pushed northward in 1835 lay a 70-foot-high rocky eminence unsuitable to build on. Since no public place for "ornamentation and beauty" had yet been laid out in Harlem, the city acquired the property for just such a purpose. Its height and location made it a natural place to put a fire watchtower, and there it still stands (at 122 Street), the last remaining one, built in 1855 of cast iron (see HISTORIC NEW YORK, Historic Buildings & Areas). The watchman would strike the bell if a fire was sighted, alerting other towers and the volunteer fire companies.

Morningside Park
West 110 to West 123 Street, from Morningside Drive to Manhattan & Morningside Avenues. Planned by Olmsted and Vaux (Central Park's architects). Located in the Morningside Heights area, it follows the crest of the hills above Harlem. Nearby is the Cathedral of St. John the Divine (see HISTORIC NEW YORK, Churches & Synagogues). Restoration is long overdue and the park is, sadly, unsafe at any hour.

Paley Park (Samuel Paley Plaza)
3 East 53 Street bet Fifth & Madison Avenues. As unlikely an oasis as one can find in the heart of Manhattan. This vest-pocket park refreshes with just the sight and sound of its 20-ft recycling waterfall. There is a snack stand for hotdogs, coffee, and soft drinks and plenty of places to sit in the shade of 17 locust trees. OPEN Mon-Sat May 1-Nov 1 8am-7pm; Nov-April 8am-6pm. CLOSED Sun & all of Jan & Feb.

Randalls Island
At the junction of the East & Harlem Rivers. Accessible via the Triborough Bridge. The stadium is the site of pop concerts in the summer and rugby games in spring. (See SPORTS, Rugby.)

Riverside Park
West 72 to West 159 Street bet Riverside Drive & the Hudson River. In the tradition of English landscaping, Frederick Law Olmsted in 1873 met the challenge of this sloping terrain to provide a playground with a view for Upper West Siders. The site of several important monuments including Soldiers' and Sailors' Monument and Grant's Tomb (see HISTORIC NEW YORK, Statues & Monuments). A great spot for summer picnics, strolls, and jogging.

Stuyvesant Square
Second Avenue East 15 to East 17 Street. This square, split by the avenue, was a gift of Peter Stuyvesant, governor of Nieuw Amsterdam. It comprised the core of fashionable New York in the late 19th century and has recently undergone a multimillion-dollar restoration. On its west side, St. George's Church (1848) and the Quaker Friends Meeting House (1860). (See HISTORIC NEW YORK, Churches & Synagogues.)

Tompkins Square
East 7 to East 10 Street, Avenue A to Avenue B. Sixteen acres of what was originally laid out as a drill ground. In the '60s, the East Village became, for a brief but memorable time, haven and mecca to hippies and "flower children." The area and park are now returned to the ethnic minorities who populate the area, predominantly Ukrainians and Puerto Ricans. Slated for a huge restoration project.

Union Square
East 14 to East 17 Street bet Broadway & Park Avenue So. Once fashionable, the garden center of this square was fenced and locked à la Gramercy Park. It became a commercial area with some of the city's finer shops in residence, Tiffany's among them, but soon became renowned as the scene of large, ofttimes unruly political gatherings—New York's Hyde Park of soapbox oratory. This former center of radicalism now sits amid a budget shopping enclave at the crossroads of a busy intersection. Its western and northern edges are the site of a Farmer's Market every Wed & Sat. Efforts to reclaim the 3.6 acre park from unsavory elements include a $7 million restoration.

Wards Island
Connected to Manhattan by a footbridge at East

102 Street & FDR Drive. Farm of the Ward family in the 1780s. A lovely, very rural park coexists on this island with Manhattan State Hospital.

Washington Square Park
At the foot of Fifth Avenue from MacDougal Street to University Place, West 4 Street to Waverly Place. A marshy area that was favored by duck hunters, then a potter's field, and next the site of hanging gallows. In 1828 it became a public park, precipitating the growth of a fashionable residential area. Now, it is the emotional if not geographical heart of Greenwich Village. All the diverse elements within the area's boundaries can be found in the park.

The central fountain and recent redesign efforts give it a definite European flavor. Interesting children's play areas and always-in-use chess tables. The city's most diligent Frisbee throwers, skilled roller-dancers, dog walkers, guitar strummers, folk singers, magicians and drug sellers share the turf with New York University students whose informal campus it has become (the scene of graduation ceremonies in June). A *very* lively example of a city park.

Brooklyn

Dyker Beach Park
Shore Parkway, east of the Verrazano Bridge. A 216.7-acre park adjacent to the Fort Hamilton Military Reservation. Beautiful views of Gravesend Bay and the Verrazano Narrows Bridge. Fine expanses of lawn, sea breezes, and good fishing.

Fort Greene Park
Myrtle & DeKalb Avenues, St. Edward & Washington Park Avenues. Formerly City (of Brooklyn) Park, designed in 1860 by the team of Frederick Law Olmsted and Calvert Vaux. From the hill, the view of Brooklyn and the harbor is spectacular. In the center stands Prison Ship Martyrs' Monument, designed in 1908 by Stanford White (see HISTORIC NEW YORK, Statues & Monuments).

Marine Park
Rockaway Inlet bet Gerritsen & Flatbush Avenues inland to Fillmore Avenue bet Burnet & East 32 Street. This is the second-largest park in New York City, covering 1,822 acres.

Prospect Park
Flatbush, Ocean & Parkside Avenues, Prospect Park West, Prospect Park Southwest. Olmsted and Vaux's ode to Brooklyn (1866-74), covering 526 acres, has remained very much as they conceived it: broad meadows, gardens, terraces, and landscaped walks. Now in the midst of a 20-year, $200 million renovation to undo years of neglect of the park's formal structures. The main entrance to the park is Grand Army Plaza, planned in the spirit of L'Etoile in Paris, with its Neo-Roman Soldiers' and Sailors' Arch, a Civil War memorial to the Union Army. Prominent among its attractions: the Zoo, small-scaled and manageable (a cafeteria too); the Palladian-style Boathouse (1905); the Croquet Shelter, a fine classical structure designed by Stanford White; the Camperdown Elm, near the boathouse, designed by nature; and the Lefferts Homestead (1783) (see HISTORIC NEW

YORK, Historic Buildings & Areas). Activities in the park include riding, ice skating, row boating, and concerts. Nearby are the Brooklyn Botanic Gardens (see Gardens), the Main Branch of the Brooklyn Public Library, and the Brooklyn Museum (see MUSEUMS & GALLERIES, General Art Museums).

Bronx
Many of what are now Bronx parks were once the private estates of prominent families.

Bronx Park
Bronx Park East & Brady Avenue. This park's 721 acres contain the New York Botanical Garden. Patterned after England's Kew Gardens, it occupies 240 acres in the park's northern extremity. Some wild and beautiful land is contained within its boundaries, including a virgin hemlock forest and the Bronx River Gorge. Another 252 acres are reserved for the animal inhabitants of the New York Zoological Park (The Bronx Zoo), opened 1899. Over 3,500 animals live in indoor and outdoor settings as close to their natural habitat as possible. Parking and cafeteria facilities. (See Zoos & Aquariums.)

Crotona Park
Fulton Avenue & East 175 Street. Selected as a park site in 1883. Formerly the estate of the Bathgate family, it was named after the ancient Greek city of Croton. The Play Center contains a bathhouse and pool dating back to the 1930s. The 147-acre park is undergoing renovation and has its own Urban Park Ranger program. Call 589-0096 for info.

Pelham Bay Park
East of Bruckner Boulevard & Middletown Road. The largest (2,118 acres) and one of the more versatile of New York City parks. Some relics of the past include Rice Memorial Stadium (1916) and the Bartow-Pell Mansion (1675) (see HISTORIC NEW YORK, Historic Buildings & Areas). In addition there's an archery range; bridle paths; the Police Department's firing range; two golf courses (see SPORTS, Municipal Golf Courses); Orchard Beach, with bathhouse and cafeteria (see Beaches); as well as some natural wildlife-preserve areas.

Van Cortlandt Park
West 242 Street to city line bet Broadway & Jerome Avenue. August Van Cortlandt, city clerk when the British occupied New York in 1776, is said to have hidden the municipal records in the family vault. It and the Van Cortlandt family mansion occupy a corner in the eastern end of the park (see HISTORIC NEW YORK, Historic Buildings & Areas). Activities include skiing in winter on artificially produced snow and, in summer, swimming and tennis. (See SPORTS.)

Queens
Alley Pond Park
Grand Central Parkway, Northern Boulevard at 233 Street, Bayside. The "alley" was a row of 18th-century commercial buildings, including a gristmill and a general store. A nearby lake was then named Alley Pond. The buildings are long

gone, but the parkland retains the name—800 acres of highlands, ponds, marsh, trees and an amazing array of wildlife. On the northern boundary, the Alley Pond Environmental Center.

Astoria Park
Bet 19 Street & the East River from Hoyt Avenue to Ditmars Boulevard, Astoria. Picnickers can get a great view of the Manhattan skyline. The Astoria Play Center and Swimming Pool, and tennis too.

Cunningham Park
193 to 210 Street, Long Island Expressway to Grand Central Parkway, Bayside. This large park offers a myriad of events and activities. In the summer months there are concerts by the New York Philharmonic plus opera and jazz. Volleyball courts, softball fields, tennis (indoor and outdoor), boccie courts, and picnic grounds.

Flushing Meadows-Corona Park
Union Turnpike from 111 Street & Grand Central Parkway to the Van Wyck Extension, Flushing. This 1,275-acre park has had a Cinderella history. Originally a swamp, then a garbage dump, the area was chosen as the site for the 1939-40 New York World's Fair. From 1946 to 1949 the United Nations General Assembly met here, and in 1964 it was again the site of the New York World's Fair. It has now become a complete recreation and entertainment park: tennis, golf, swimming, roller skating, boating, bicycling, ice skating (see SPORTS), the Queens Museum (see MUSEUMS & GALLERIES), the Queens Botanical Garden, Queens Zoo & Children's Farm (see PARKS & GARDENS), the Hall of Science, and an antique carousel. Note the Unisphere, symbol of the 1964-65 World's Fair.

Staten Island

Clove Lakes Park
1150 Clove Road nr Victory Blvd, Sunnyside. A popular picturesque park covering 69 acres. Among its unexpected delights: a brook, a waterfall, and a small lake providing picnickers with bucolic settings. For the more active there are facilities for ice skating, horseback riding, football, softball, jogging, bicycle riding, and fishing (see SPORTS). Roller-skating classes are also held May-June, Sat am. In summer New York Philharmonic and Metropolitan Opera concerts (see ANNUAL EVENTS, June & Aug).

La Tourette Park
Forest Hill & Richmond Hill Roads. Richmondtown. This 511-acre park features a beautiful golf course and clubhouse as well as bridle paths (see SPORTS) and lovely picnic areas.

Silver Lake Park
Hart Boulevard & Revere Street, Silver Lake. Children's play areas, a golf course, and a wide variety of recreational activities, including tennis, Ping-Pong, rowing, on 206 acres (see SPORTS).

Von Briesen Park
Bay Street & Wadsworth Avenue, Fort Wadsworth. A meticulously groomed city park. Its elevated harbor-front location provides a stunning aerial view of Lower Manhattan, both bays, and Brooklyn too. A good picnic spot.

Willowbrook Park
Victory Boulevard & Richmond Avenue, Bull's Head. There are ample picnic facilities in this lovely 105-acre park. A lake with fishing for children, athletic fields, an archery range, and horseshoe pitches (see SPORTS).

Botanical Gardens

Biblical Garden
Cathedral of St. John the Divine, West 112 Street & Amsterdam Avenue. 678-6888. On the grounds of the world's largest Gothic cathedral, a 1/4-acre garden where only plants mentioned in the Bible are grown. In summer, guided tours of the garden Sat 11am-2pm. OPEN 7 days sunrise to sunset. FREE

Brooklyn Botanical Garden
1000 Washington Avenue nr Empire Boulevard, Brooklyn. (1-718) 622-4433. Founded in 1910 on the site of a city dump; 50 acres of land heavily planted with the greatest variety of trees and bushes. The largest and one of the finest displays of Japanese flowering cherry trees in America as well as an unparalleled exhibition of bonsai trees. There are beautifully designed and serene Japanese Gardens, a wonderful display of magnolias in the spring, a medicinal herb harden, the Fragrance Garden, a unique garden for the blind, one of the country's largest public rose collections, a Shakespeare Garden with 80 plants cited in the Bard's works and a local flora section: a 25-acre sampling of the ecology within 100-mile radius of the city. OPEN year round, May-Aug, Tues-Fri 8am-6pm; weekends & holidays, 10am-6pm; Sept-April till 4:30pm. CLOSED Mon. FREE The Conservatory OPEN weekdays 10am-4pm; weekends and holidays 11am-4pm; nominal admission on weekends & holidays. Japanese Gardens OPEN early April-late Oct; nominal admission.

Channel Gardens
Rockefeller Center, enter Fifth Avenue bet West 49 & West 50 Streets. A gently sloped and fountained space whose name is derived from its position between the French (La Maison Francaise) and English pavilions (The British Empire Building). Its beauty is usually a reflection of the season; especially dazzling are the Easter lilies in April. The scene of concerts and musical performances in summer (see ANNUAL EVENTS, June). FREE

Conservatory Gardens
Central Park at Fifth Avenue & 105 Street. Established in the late 1930s, 4 acres of English perennial gardens firmly, albeit almost secretly, ensconced in Central Park. These harmoniously designed gardens form an oasis within an oasis. Opening onto the main lawn is the handsome wrought-iron Vanderbilt Gate. Popular spot for wedding portraits. OPEN 7 days 7:30am-4:30pm. FREE

Jefferson Market Garden
Greenwich Avenue at West 9 Street. Determined

Greenwich Villagers planted this formal English garden on the site of the old Women's House of Detention. The fence is an unfortunate necessity but it is OPEN to the public Sat & Sun 1-5pm. FREE

New York Botanical Garden
Bronx Park bet Bedford Park Blvd & Mosholu Parkway, Bronx. 220-8777 (recorded) for directions, 220-8700. This 250-acre garden, founded in 1891, was patterned after the Royal Botanical Gardens at Kew, England. The rose garden has 700 bushes of 400 different varieties: there is a magnolia dell, an azalea glen, a pine grove, a rock garden and much more. The Museum Building houses an exhibit hall devoted to ecological and environmental studies, as well as a large botanical library, auditorium and the Herbarium with dried plant specimens. The recently restored Enid Haupt Conservatory, a 90-ft central rotunda with 10 connecting greenhouses, is a glass wonderland housing exotic desert plants, a medieval herb garden, a topiary garden and more. A restored 1840 Snuff Mill now serves as a snack bar during the summer. Garden OPEN year round 7 days 9am-8pm. FREE, but there is a parking fee. The Conservatory OPEN Tues-Sun 10am-4pm; admission charge; lower for children and senior citizens.

Peace Garden
Main public entrance United Nations, First Avenue at East 45 Street. Adjacent to the UN Headquarters, 12 acres of formal rose plantings overlooking the East River. Hybrid tea roses or prolific floribunda. Japanese cherry blossoms in May. OPEN 7 days 9:30am-4:45pm. FREE

Queens Botanical Garden
43-50 Main Street, east end of Flushing Meadows-Corona Park, Flushing. Queens. (1-718) 886-3800. Thirty-nine acres of flora. Completely outdoors, so visits are very much a seasonal matter. In September 10,000 chrysanthemums are in bloom, in April 250,000 tulips put in an appearance. There is also a specialty garden to attract birds and a labeled vegetable garden. OPEN year round 7 days 9am-dusk. FREE

St. John's in the Village
Waverly Place & West 11 Street. Enter garden through the church office, 224 Waverly Place. A lovely peaceful garden. OPEN after Sunday services and weekdays 9am-5pm.

Shakespeare Garden
Central Park, south of Delacorte Theater nr West 80 Street. There has been a Shakespeare Garden in the park since 1880. This one dates from 1936. Seeds and cuttings from the same mulberry and hawthorne trees Shakespeare himself once tended in his own Stratford-on-Avon garden formed the basis of the garden. Now tended by volunteers, Shakespearean blossoms and Elizabethan herbs bloom once more. Pools, a bust of the Bard and annual flowers provide a peaceful setting. If you wish to volunteer, call 879-2555 in the evening.

Beaches

Manhattan is the only one of the five boroughs that does not have a beach. Though much sun bathing goes on in Manhattan during summer, it is usually done on the rooftops, affectionately known as a "tar beach," and on the river piers. The other four boroughs are blessed with miles and miles of beaches, all easily accessible by bus, subway, or car. City beaches are officially open from Memorial Day weekend to Labor Day, sunrise to midnight, with swimming allowed 10am-6:30pm, when lifeguards are on duty.

Brighton Beach
Brighton 15th Street to Ocean Parkway, Brooklyn. This is actually the "beginning" of the beach that due west becomes Coney Island. At this end you'll find locals: mothers with children, older retired folks, and Russian émigrés who have come to this shore, now referred to as "Little Odessa." The boardwalk has nothing but benches, so bring your lunch or buy it at a local deli on your way. As either warning or blessing: it has none of the honky-tonk atmosphere of Coney Island. The best entertainment here: the people; and it's only a short subway ride from Manhattan.

Coney Island Beach
From Ocean Parkway to West 37 Street, Brooklyn. Originally called Rabbit Island after its only inhabitants, Coney Island, from the Dutch Konijn Eiland, began its resort days in the 1830s. At that time elegant hotels drew the elite. It evolved into a more popular entertainment area with the coming of the first roller coaster in 1884. A mere shadow of its former selves, it still has a fine 3.2-mile-long sandy beach and a boardwalk over 2 miles long with everything you would expect to find at a beach resort, from cotton candy to shooting galleries. Hot summer days have drawn as many as a million people to Coney Island, which makes it a bit difficult, on weekends especially, to find a place in the sun without stepping on someone else's blanket. Still a must for Brooklyn color: Nathan's on Surf & Stillwell Avenues.

Great Kills Park
Hylan Boulevard & Hopkins Avenue, Great Kills, Staten Island. (1-718) 351-8700. The beach is part of Gateway National Recreation Area.

Manhattan Beach
Ocean Avenue bet Oriental Boulevard & MacKenzie Street, Brooklyn. (1-718) 965-6589. This small beach, only 3/10 of a mile long, draws a very young crowd. There are changing rooms available. Adjacent to the beach is a park with barbecue facilities as well as handball, tennis and basketball.

Orchard Beach
Shore Road & City Island Road, Bronx. Popular beach on the East Shore of Pelham Bay Park fronts onto Long Island Sound. Cafeteria and changing rooms.

Jacob Riis Park
Beach 149 to Beach 169 Street, Queens. (1-718) 474-4600. Operated by the National Park Service.

There is a boardwalk for strolling and a mile-long sandy beach. Other facilities include handball, paddle tennis, shuffleboard. There are ample parking facilities as well as lockers and refreshments.

Rockaway Beach
Beach First Street to Beach 109 Street, Beach 126 Street to Beach 149 Street, Queens. Nearly 10 miles of glorious sandy beach and 7 miles of boardwalk fronting on the Atlantic form the core of this recreational area.

South Beach
Fort Wadsworth to Miller Field, New Dorp, Staten Island. On 638 acres. A 7,500-ft-long boardwalk, fishing, swimming, shuffleboard and entertainment. Dressing rooms and parking facilities.

Wolf's Pond Park
Holton to Cornelia Avenue on Raritan Bay, Prince's Bay, Staten Island. Not only salt-water swimming, but a wooded area and a lake offer fishing and rustic picnic settings.

Long Island Beaches
The Long Island Tourism Commission can provide any information needed on Long Island beaches. Call (1-516) 234-4959.

Jones Beach State Park
Wantagh, Long Island (1-516) 785-1600. On Long Island's south shore, 6½ miles of gorgeous sand beach fronting the Atlantic Ocean. One of the most beautiful and complete state parks. Parking facilities, cafeterias, boardwalk, dancing, theater, miniature golf, fishing, bay, pool or ocean swimming. Buses from Port Authority Bus Terminal and the Long Island Rail Road's train-bus service provide direct access. *OPEN Memorial Day-Labor Day.*

Zoos & Aquariums

(*For Children's Zoos, see* KIDS' NEW YORK.) *All animals in Central Park, Prospect Park and Queens zoos are given names. Though the selection process is informal, there are some traditions. Hippopotamus babies in Central Park were always named for Shakespearean characters.*

Bronx Zoo
Fordham Road & Bronx River Parkway, Bronx. 367-1010 (recorded); 220-5100. An extensive 264-acre zoological park (the world's largest urban zoo) opened in 1899. Always considered one of the world's best zoos, in recent years it's become even better. Though the older buildings still house animals in indoor cages and exhibits, the real excitement comes from seeing the animals roam in simulated natural habitats, in some cases only a moat away from visitors. African Plains and Lion Island are special treats. The Skyfari ride (April-Oct) affords an aerial view. Not to be missed: the World of Birds, a tropical rain forest home, complete with storms, for over 100 species, and the World of Darkness, nocturnal animals awake in an artifically reversed night for

day. Wild Asia, seen from the *Bengali Express,* a slow-moving monorail, offers Asian elephants and Siberian tigers living as if in the Asian heartland. (Wild Asia closes for winter, check for dates and times.) Children's Zoo; Camel and Elephant rides (May-Oct). Zoo *OPEN 7 days year round, 10am-5pm, in summer, weekends & holidays till 5:30pm.* Admission charge *Fri-Mon;* discount for children under 12. FREE Tues, Wed, Thurs. Senior citizens free all times. Parking fee; membership available. Friends of the Zoo (FOZ), 220-5141, offers free guided tours to the public Sat & Sun, by appointment.

Central Park Zoo
Central Park nr East 64 Street & Fifth Avenue. The animals have new homes and the old (America's oldest) zoo has been demolished. A more modern, more humane habitat will take its place in 1987; it will be under the auspices of the well-respected New York Zoological Society. There won't be any tigers, lions, gorillas or elephants but, take heart, the sea lions will be in their same old spot.

New York Aquarium
Surf Avenue & West 8 Street, Coney Island, Brooklyn. (1-718) 266-8500. Scores of sea creatures reside within view of the ocean at Coney Island. Outdoor pools are reserved for seals, dolphins, penguins, sea lions, and turtles. Feeding time is fun time here. Over 200 varieties of fish fill the indoor tanks, including electric eels and sharks. From late April to mid-Oct the dolphins and whales star in a 20-minute show, and there is a 10-minute sea lion training session. *OPEN Mon-Wed, Fri-Sun 10am-5pm; Thurs till 1:45pm. June 15-Labor Day Sat & Sun till 6pm.* Admission charge; lower for children under 12; senior citizens free after 2pm weekdays. Parking fee. Restaurant, picnic facilities and gift shop.

Prospect Park Zoo
Empire Boulevard & Flatbush Avenue, Brooklyn. (1-718) 965-6587. Though an old-fashioned zoo, it still affords close-up views of camels, lions, and tigers within the city limits. Note the murals that decorate the buildings, depicting scenes from Rudyard Kipling's *Jungle Books.* Cafeteria and rest rooms available. *OPEN year round 7 days 11am-4:30pm.* FREE

Queens Zoo & Children's Farm
Flushing Meadows-Corona Park, 111 Street at 54 Avenue, Flushing, Queens. (1-718) 699-7239. A large but not heavily populated zoo. The 47-acre farm provides the most entertainment, especially for the kids. *OPEN year round 7 days 10am-3:45pm.* FREE. (*See also* KIDS' NEW YORK.)

Staten Island Zoological Park
Barrett Park, 614 Broadway nr Forrest Avenue, West Brighton, Staten Island. (1-718) 442-3100. This small and highly unusual zoo has on exhibit all 32 species of rattlesnake. It's the largest collection in the world and, what's more, all fangs are still intact. In addition to the rattlers, there are scorpions, Madagascan cockroaches, alligators, crocodiles and snapping turtles, along with the more usual zoo residents. Free parking. *OPEN year*

round 7 days 10am-4:45pm. CLOSED Thanksgiving, Christmas, New Year's Day. Admission charge; children under 6 and senior citizens free. Wed FREE for all.

Nature Trails & Wildlife Preserves

Davis Wildlife Refuge
Travis Avenue off Richmond Avenue, Travis, Staten Island. These 260 acres of dry and wet land attract many rarely seen birds. Trail guides are available from the Staten Island Institute of Arts and Sciences. Call (1-718) 727-1135 *Mon-Fri in the am.* FREE

Gateway National Recreation Area
Office: Floyd Bennett Field, Building 69, Brooklyn. (1-718) 630-0253. The first national park within an urban setting. The area consists of 26,000 acres of land divided into four units: Staten Island (1-718) (351-8700) includes the Great Kills Park beaches; Jamaica Bay, Queens (1-718) (474-3799), includes the Jamaica Bay Wildlife Refuge; Breezy Point, Queens (1-718) (474-4600), includes Jacob Riis Park and Beach; and Sandy Hook, N.J. (1-201) (872-0115). There is a variety of free programs and happenings. Call for info. FREE

High Rock Park Conservation Center
200 Nevada Avenue nr Richmond Rd & Rockland Avenue, Egbertville, Staten Island. (1-718) 987-6233. Ninety-two acres of natural hardwood forest that is being preserved as an environmental education center. Ongoing programs, workshops and tours year round. Great bird-watching area, best in April. *OPEN year round 7 days 9am-5pm.* FREE

Hunter Island Marine Zoology & Geology Sanctuary
Pelham Bay Park, north end of Orchard Beach, Bronx. A wooded rocky area of geological interest, plus dry marshy and underwater areas. Beautiful, popular with picnickers. FREE

Inwood Park
West 207 Street & Seaman Avenue. Three nature trails totaling 1 mile. Tree identification signs, trailside displays and Indian Caves. FREE

Jamaica Bay Wildlife Refuge
Cross Bay Boulevard bet Howard Beach & Broad Channel, Jamaica, Queens. (1-718) 474-0613. The preserve's 2,868 acres of wetlands and uplands, carved out of Jamaica Bay's 16,000 acres, is reserved for nature walks and bird-watching. One trail, 1¾ miles long, runs around the West Pond. Over 300 species of land and water fowl have been sighted, including ibis, egret and eagles (best watching: May). Weekend exhibits, slide presentations, guided walks. Visitors' Center *OPEN year round 7 days 8am-6pm (till 7pm in summer). CLOSED Christmas & New Year's Day.* Permit necessary from Visitors' Center. FREE

Pell Wildlife Refuge
Pelham Bay Park, Hutchinson River Parkway & Bartow Avenue, Bronx. Along the shoreline, a swampy and a wooded area. Popular spot for bird-watching. FREE

Staten Island Greenbelt
From Clove Lakes Park to La Tourette Park, through High Rock Park. (1-718) 987-6233. A circular marked trail 13¹⁄₁₀ miles. Hardwood forest and glacial kettles, ponds formed by the last of the great glaciers. Of much geological interest.

Wave Hill Center for Environmental Studies
Main entrance West 249 Street & Independence Avenue, Riverdale, Bronx. 549-2055. The former 28-acre estate of conservation-minded financier George Perkins and at various times home to Theodore Roosevelt, Mark Twain, Arturo Toscanini, and the United Kingdom's Ambassador to the UN. Perkins' descendants gave it to the city in 1960 to be used as a nonprofit center for the study of environmental sciences. It commands a magnificent view of the Hudson and the Palisades and there are nature trails, including a 1½-mile marked trail, greenhouses, exquisite herb, wildflower and aquatic gardens. Site of an annual sculpture show May-Sept. Workshops, concerts, slide lectures, special events. *OPEN Sept-June 7 days 10am-4:30pm; July & Aug Mon, Tues & Thurs-Sat till 5:30pm; Wed till dusk; Sun till 7pm. CLOSED Christmas & New Year's Day.* FREE except Sat & Sun. Memberships available. Lower for senior citizens; children under age 14 free.

Bird-Watching

(See also Nature Trails & Wildlife Preserves.)

Rare Bird Alert
832-6523. A recorded service available *24 hours a day, 7 days a week,* listing up-to-the-minute info on rare and interesting birds that have been sighted in the area.

American Museum of Natural History
Central Park West at 77 Street. 873-1300. Visits to Central Park, which is on one of the main bird migratory lines, for watching during the times of heaviest movement. Call for info.

Brooklyn Botanical Garden
1000 Washington Avenue nr Crown Street, Brooklyn. (1-718) 622-4433, Education Dept. A course offered in both spring and fall for fledgling bird-watchers. The Garden is in the flyway of the Atlantic migration. For details, call *Mon-Fri 9am-4:30pm.*

High Rock Park
200 Nevada Avenue, Staten Island, New York 10306. (1-718) 987-6233. This great bird-watching area has special programs, walks and workshops. Get on their mailing list; call or write.

Linnaean Society of New York
15 West 77 Street, New York, N.Y. 10024. Active group founded in 1878, for amateurs and professionals. Open to all with interest in ornithology. There are meetings held at the American Museum of Natural History, local and long-distance field trips, a monthly newsletter. Write for more info.

National Audubon Society
950 Third Avenue at East 57 Street. 832-3200.
Information on birding anywhere in the world.
Sponsors some bird walks in Central Park. *OPEN
Mon-Fri 9am-5pm.*

New York Botanical Garden
Bronx Park, Bronx Park East & Brady Avenue.
220-8747. Spring and fall, a course given on different species of birds that can be seen in and
around New York City. Guided field trips, mainly

for beginners. Call for details *Mon-Thurs 9am-
9pm; Fri till 5pm. Sat & Sun 9am-2pm.*

Queens County Bird Club
Queens Botanical Garden, 43-50 Main Street at
Dalia Street, Flushing, Queens. (1-718) 939-
6224. An active club offers single or family
membership. There are monthly meetings
(3rd Wed, except July & Aug) and field trips
all year (except July). New birders always welcome.

Kids' New York

Alice in Wonderland Statue, Central Park

Seeing New York

Here are some fun things to do with kids in the city. For more of the traditional attractions also see SIGHTSEEING; HISTORIC NEW YORK; *and* ANNUAL EVENTS, *for parades, fairs and festivals—many of which are* FREE.

Belvedere Castle
Central Park, West 79 Street, south of the Great Lawn. 772-0210. The newly restored castle is now the Central Park Learning Center, as well as a station for the National Weather Service. In the Discovery Chamber learn about the park through activities and games. Programs for summer camp groups available Wed-Fri. Gift shop with books and natural history items. *OPEN Nov1-Feb 28 Mon-Thurs, Sat & Sun 11am-4pm; Fri 1-4pm. March 1-Oct 31 till 5pm. CLOSED Mon.*

Carousel Pavilion
Central Park at 64 Street. 879-0244. A lovely antique merry-go-round. *OPEN year round (weather permitting) Mon-Fri 10:30am-4:45pm; Sat & Sun 10:30am-5:45pm; Jan weekends only.* Minimal charge.

Circle Line Cruise
Circle Line Plaza, West 42 Street & the Hudson River. 563-3200. Three-hour circumnavigation of Manhattan Island. Tour guide narrates. Snack Bar on board. *Late March-mid Nov 7 days a week.*

Sailings every 45 minutes 9:45am-5:50pm. Call for schedule. Half price for children under 12.

Empire State Building
350 Fifth Avenue at 34 Street. 736-3100. The 86th-fl observation deck has an outside terrace for a broader view. The 102nd fl is enclosed. *OPEN 7 days 9:30am-midnight (last ticket sold 11:30pm).* Admission charge; discount for children 5-11 (under age 5 free). Combine with a visit to the Guinness World Records Exhibit *(see below).*

Federal Reserve Bank
33 Liberty Street nr William Street. 791-6130. For ages 15 and up: 1-hour educational tour of the central banking operation, including the gold vault. Call for reservations at least a week in advance. *One-hour tours, Mon-Fri 10 & 11am, 1 & 2pm.* FREE

Guinness World Records Exhibit Hall
Empire State Building, 350 Fifth Avenue at 34 Street, concourse level. 947-2335. Displays, models, film clips of record breakers: the world's smallest book, largest guitar, etc. Allow 45 minutes to see it all. *OPEN 7 days 9:30am-6pm.* Admission charge; discount for children 5-11; under age 5 free. Group rates available.

Hudson River Day Line
Pier 81, foot of West 41 Street. 279-5151. A 2½-hour scenic cruise up the Hudson River to Bear Mountain. Disembark there for 4 hours. Swimming, boating, nature trails. Or sail for 30 minutes

more and disembark for 3 hours at West Point. Cafeteria on board. *Daily Memorial Day weekend to mid-Sept* (except Mon, Tues & Fri in June). Departure 9:30am. Return 6:30pm. Discount for children under 12.

Model Yachts
Central Park, Conservatory Water nr 74 Street & Fifth Avenue. Sail your own model boat or watch most Saturdays 10am-4pm, as the Central Park Model Yacht Club races radio-controlled sailboats. For schedule, call 249-3772. FREE

The New York Experience
McGraw-Hill Building, 1221 Avenue of the Americas nr West 48 Street, lower plaza. 869-0345. One-hour multi-media show simulates life in New York. Covers history of city from 1600s to present. Then walk through a re-creation of Old New York. *OPEN 7 days Mon-Thurs 11am-7pm, Fri & Sat till 8pm, Sun noon-8pm. Shows start on the hour.* Admission charge; discount for children under 12.

New York Public Transit Exhibit
Entrance: Schermerhorn Street & Boerum Place, Brooklyn. (1-718) 330-3060. No-longer-used station turned museum. Vintage subway cars from the early 1900s, movies and memorabilia. *OPEN 7 days 9:30am-4pm. CLOSED Thanksgiving, Christmas & New Year's Day.* Token admission charge; lower for children under 17.

The New York Times
229 West 43 Street. 556-1310. For student groups only. Tour newsroom, composing rooms, and pressroom. Reservation required. FREE

Police Academy Museum Tour
235 East 20 Street. 477-9753. A detective talks and answers questions about the antique and contemporary police paraphernalia there. Not recommended for children under 12. For school groups, tour of academy operations is sometimes available. Museum and academy tours by reservation only. *OPEN Mon-Fri 9am-3pm.*

Post Office
Eighth Avenue at West 33 Street. 971-5331. For children over 12. See mail being processed in the world's largest post office. Write the Post Master, Room 3217, New York Post Office, J.A.F. Building, New York, N.Y. 10199, two weeks in advance. For children under age 12, arrangements are made to tour a local post office. FREE

Roosevelt Island Tramway
Second Avenue at East 60 Street. 832-4555. A brief (4-min) but exciting ride in an aerial car, 200 ft up, to Roosevelt Island in the East River. *Every 15 mins. on the quarter hour Sun-Thurs 6am-2am. Fri & Sat 6am-3:30am.* Subway tokens required; children under 6, free.

Rowing
Loeb Boathouse. Central Park at East 72 Street. 288-7281. Spend a lovely day on Central Park Lake. Rent an aluminum rowboat. *Mid-June to early Sept, 7 days 9am-5pm.* Limit 4 people to a boat and one must be 16 or older. Hourly fee plus a refundable deposit. Call 861-6800.

Staten Island Ferry
In Manhattan: at the foot of Whitehall Street at Battery Park; 248-8097. In Staten Island: at the foot of Bay Street, St. George; (1-718) 727-2508. A 25-minute boat ride across Upper New York Bay. Wonderful views, a snack bar on board, and it costs only a penny a minute. *24 hours a day, 7 days a week. Weekends, every half hour; weekdays every 20 minutes.*

Statue of Liberty
Battery Park South Ferry. 269-5755. The Lady is undergoing a much needed restoration in honor of her 100th birthday. During work in progress the island and Statue are closed to the public and will not reopen until July 4, 1986. We look forward to it with excitement.

Museums for Children

Also included are general museums with special attractions for children.

American Museum of Natural History
Central Park West at West 79 St. 873-1300 or 873-4225. A vast complex of exhibit halls, most of which are of interest to children. *SPECIAL:* "Discovery Room" open year round (except one month in summer) involves learning through use of discovered touchable items in a box. For over age 5 accompanied by adult; tickets given out on first-come basis at 1st fl information desk. "Natural Science Center" where children learn about plants, animals and rocks found in New York City. Newest feature: "Naturemax Theatre" showing movies "To Fly" and "Living Planet" on a 4-story-high screen daily from 10:30am. Museum *OPEN Sun, Mon, Tues & Thurs 10am-5:45pm; Wed, Fri & Sat 10am-9pm. CLOSED Thanksgiving & Christmas Day.* Suggested contribution.

Aunt Len's Doll & Toy Museum
6 Hamilton Terrace bet St. Nicholas & Convent Aves. 926-4172, 281-4143. Four delightful rooms in a Harlem brownstone house a collection of over 5,000 antique dolls, dollhouses and accessories, miniatures and toys. There is also a Play and Learn Room at 19 Hamilton Terrace. *OPEN Tues-Sun by appointment only.* Admission charge; half price for children.

Brooklyn Children's Museum
145 Brooklyn Avenue at St. Mark's Avenue. Brooklyn. (1-718) 735-4400. Established in 1899 as the world's first museum for children. An environment geared to learning through discovery. Children are involved in participatory activities, crafts handling and operating museum displays. There are films, workshops and more than 50,000 objects to involve and inform the child. *OPEN Mon & Wed-Fri 1-5pm; Sat & Sun 10am-5pm. CLOSED Tues.* FREE

Brooklyn Museum
188 Eastern Parkway, Brooklyn. (1-718) 638-5000. *SPECIAL:* "What's Up?" Sat & Sun 2-3pm. For children in first to sixth grades. Learn about a different one of the museum's collections at each class through storytelling and art making with simple materials. Puppet shows Wed, Thurs & Fri 11am & 1pm. No reservation necessary: simply arrive 15 min. before start. For ages 6-12 FREE.

Museum *OPEN Wed-Sat 10am-5pm; Sun noon-5pm; Holidays 1-5pm. CLOSED Mon & Tues.* Suggested contribution.

Manhattan Children's Museum
314 West 54 Street. 765-5904. Offers a kids'-eye view with the focus on nature, culture and perception. A colorful place to have fun and learn about the world around them. Special Sat workshops, among many other unique programs. For 6-16. Call for specifics. *OPEN Wed-Sun 1-5pm.* Call in advance for school groups. Admission charge; lower for children.

Chinese Museum
8 Mott Street nr Chatham Sq. 964-1542. Chinese antiques, coins, musical instruments, temple artifacts. An 18-ft-long Chinese dragon. *OPEN 7 days 10am-2pm.* Admission charge.

Energy Museum
145 East 14 Street. 460-6244. Hands-on exhibits depicting the age of electricity—past, present, and future. Fun, educational and nostalgic. *OPEN Tues-Sat 10am-4pm. CLOSED Sun & Mon.* FREE

Forbes Magazine Galleries
62 Fifth Avenue at 12 St. 620-2389. A gallery of Forbes family collectibles including 12,000 toy soldiers and hundreds of toy boats. It's a treat. *OPEN Tues-Sat 10am-4pm. (Thurs is reserved for group tours and advance reservations.) CLOSED Sun, Mon & holidays.* FREE

Hall of Science
Flushing Meadows-Corona Park, 111 Street & 48 Avenue, Flushing, Queens. (1-718) 699-0005. Originally part of the 1964 New York World's Fair, it is now the only museum in the city devoted exclusively to science and technology. Reopening March 1986, after extensive redesign. Most exhibits are participatory or audio-visual presentations. *SPECIAL:* Stellarium and Planetarium Shows *Sat & Sun 1pm.* Admission charge. Children under 5 not admitted. Museum *OPEN Tues-Fri 10am-4pm; Sat till 5pm; Sun 11am-5pm. CLOSED Mon, Thanksgiving, Christmas, New Year's Day.* Admission charge.

Hayden Planetarium
Central Park West at 81 Street. 873-8828 for show times. 873-1300, ext. 206 for further information. A fascinating place to learn and have fun. Exhibits, many of them participatory (touch one of the world's largest meteorites, and step on scales to see what you weigh on different planets) demonstrate the workings of the universe in practical terms. *SPECIAL:* Sky Show, where the universe is projected on a huge dome, accompanied by narration: 7 days usually every hour on the hour, but call ahead. Laser Show with rock music for older children: Fri & Sat at 7:30, 9 and 10:30pm. Also courses for children age 10 and older, such as "Stars, Black Holes and Galaxies." *OPEN 7 days noon till 5pm. CLOSED Thanksgiving & Christmas Day.*

Intrepid Sea-Air-Space Museum
Pier 86, West 46 Street & the Hudson River. 245-0072. This 900—foot aircraft carrier—the former U.S.S. *Intrepid* is now a fascinating museum. On board are vintage aircraft as well as luner landing modules. Crew area exhibits, an audio-visual presentation and lots of hands-on exhibits to involve the kids (note: some of this may be intimidating for the very young or impressionable). Cafeteria on board. *OPEN Nov-April, Wed-Sun 10am-5pm; May-Oct till 7pm.* Admission charge; half price for children under age 12.

Museum of Broadcasting
1 East 53 Street. 752-7684. Fifty years of radio and television broadcasting are preserved here. Select tapes of historic moments or memorable entertainment programs. Interesting and fun. Exhibits and special programs. Very popular, get there early. *OPEN Tues noon-8pm; Wed-Sat till 5pm. CLOSED Sun, Mon & holidays.* Suggested contribution.

Museum of the American Indian
Broadway at West 155 Street. 283-2420. The world's largest collection of Indian artifacts, such as totem poles, drums, masks and warbonnets. Occasional crafts demonstrations. *OPEN Tues-Sat 10am-5pm; Sun 1-5pm. CLOSED Mon.* Admission charge, lower for children under 12.

Museum of the City of New York
1220 Fifth Avenue nr 103 St. 534-1672. A relaxed museum depicting New York's past through rich and colorful exhibits. *SPECIAL:* "Please Touch" Sat 2:40 daily for school groups by reservation. Re-creation of a Dutch household. Costumed narrator, demonstrations of all objects, which are then handled by the children. On selected Sundays, a children's introduction to the arts, with performances and participation in folk music, opera, art of the clown, etc. Puppet Show Oct-May Sat 1:30pm for ages 3 and up. Admission charge. *OPEN Tues-Sat 10am-5pm. Sun & holidays 1-5pm. CLOSED Mon.* FREE

Museum of Holography
11 Mercer Street nr Canal St. 925-0526. Focused laser beams become 3-D images that float in space. Exhibit changes periodically. A film explains the process. *OPEN Wed-Sun noon-6pm; CLOSED Mon, Tues, Thurs & some holidays.* Admission charge; discount for children under 12.

New York Historical Society
170 Central Park West nr West 77 St. 873-3400. Period rooms, antique toys, dolls, carriages, fire trucks, a replica of Noah's Ark and more. Call ahead for information. *OPEN Tues-Sun 11am-5pm. CLOSED Mon.* Contribution suggested.

Queens Museum
New York City Building, Flushing Meadows-Corona Park, Flushing, Queens. (1-718) 592-5555. Contains an 18,000-sq.-ft. scale model of New York City that is constantly updated. Light changes simulate day into night. *SPECIAL:* Arts and Crafts classes every Sat for children 5-14. There are also changing exhibits, some of which have interest for children. *OPEN Tues-Sat 10am-5pm; Sun in summer 1-5pm; Sun in winter noon-4pm. CLOSED Mon, Thanksgiving, Christmas & New Year's Day.* Contribution suggested.

Richmondtown Restoration
441 Clarke Avenue nr Arthur Kill Rd, Staten Is-

land. (1-718) 351-1611. A charming re-creation of Richmondtown as it was 200 years ago. The buildings and authentic restorations feature demonstrations of spinning, weaving, leathercraft and more. Lovely grounds for strolling, feeding the ducks. Snack bar. There are some special events during the year (*see also* ANNUAL EVENTS, Oct, Dec). *OPEN year round, Wed, Thurs, Fri 10am-5pm; Sat, Sun & Mon holidays 1-5pm. CLOSED Mon.*

South Street Seaport Museum
207 Front Street. 669-9400. The tall sailing ships are at Pier 16. Newest feature: a dramatic multi-screen movie about the history of the seaport called "South Street Venture" shown 7 days from 11am. Other special activities are often scheduled in the area as well, especially in summer. Call for details and current events. *OPEN year round 7 days 10am-7pm. CLOSED Thanksgiving, Christmas & New Year's Day.* Start at the Visitors Center, 14 Fulton Street n of the Seaport Gallery, 215 Water Street. Admission charge to board boats and for movie only. Discount for children under age 12; under 6 free.

Staten Island Children's Museum
15 Beach Street nr Bay St. Stapleton. Staten Island (moving to Sailor's Snug Harbor, Staten Island, late 1985). (1-718) 273-2060. Museum with changing thematic participatory exhibits put together with consulting artists and educators. Sample themes include the human body, visual perception. Special events every Sat & Sun at 2pm. *OPEN year round: Mon-Fri 1pm-5pm. Sat 11am-5pm, Sun noon-5pm. CLOSED Mon during the summer.*

Young People's Programs
Metropolitan Museum of Art, Fifth Avenue at 82 Street, ground fl. 879-5500. Geared to children 5-12. Art through self-expression. Involves the child in workshops, demonstrations, slide presentations, film programs, talks, and visits to the permanent collection. Introduces a child to art. *Call for specific Tues eve., Sat & Sun schedules (July & Aug Tues-Fri, daytime programs only).* Museum *OPEN Tues 9:30am-8:45pm; Wed-Sat till 5:15pm; Sun 9:30am-5:15pm. CLOSED Mon, Christmas, New Year's Day.* Suggested contribution.

Zoos & Animal Preserves

Bronx Zoo
Fordham Road & Bronx River Parkway, Bronx. 367-1010 (recorded); 220-5100. One of the world's largest zoological parks. Features animals in natural habitat settings. Upon entering, obtain a map and plan itinerary. Skyfari Train Tour (*OPEN April-Oct,*) affords good views of most areas of the park. Zoo *OPEN year round 7 days 10am-5pm; in summer, weekends & holidays till 5:30pm.* Admission charge Fri-Mon; discount for children under 12. Free Tues, Wed, Thurs. Friends of the Zoo (FOZ), 220-5141, offers free guided tours *Mon-Fri 9am-5pm.*

Bronx Zoo Children's Zoo
Fordham Road & Bronx River Parkway, Bronx. 367-1010 (recorded); 220-5100. Within this large renowned zoological park there is a unique Children's Zoo. Exhibits put them in the animals' places: burrowing like a prairie dog, perching like a bird, climbing a child-sized "spider's web." In addition there are domestic animals to pet, an infirmary for sick animals, a chick hatchery, pony cart, camel and elephant rides. Child-high signs (aimed at 3rd graders with a 200 word vocabulary) with explanations and questions are designed to make the child think. Fun and informative. *OPEN mid April-Oct, 7 days 10am-4:30pm. Small additional charge; no adult admitted without a child.*

Central Park Lehman Children's Zoo
Central Park, enter Fifth Avenue & 64 Street. 360-8288. North of the main zoo is this haven for small children. Farm animals in a charming setting. Lobby exhibit of reptiles. *OPEN year round 7 days 10am-5pm (last entry 4:30pm).* Minimal admission charge. No adult admitted without a child.

Central Park Zoo
Central Park nr Fifth Avenue & 64 Street. 360-8213. Except for the sea lion pool, the zoo is closed for an indefinite period of time for renovation. The Children's Zoo (above) remains open for the duration.

Queens County Farm Museum
73-50 Little Neck Parkway, Floral Park, Queens. (1-718) 468-4355. On 47 acres of city-owned land: a 17th-century farm house; sheep, geese, ducks, a donkey and chickens; fruit trees, greenhouses and a potting shed. School tours Mon-Wed. Special events including fireside concerts; call for schedule. *OPEN in summer Sat & Sun 11am-4pm; in winter Sat.* FREE

Great Adventure
Exit 7A on New Jersey Turnpike, Jackson, N.J. (1-201) 928-2000. A park where you go on safari in your own car. See antelopes, elephants, rhinos, vultures, baboons. Keep your windows closed and enjoy the view. *OPEN April to early May weekends 10am-10pm; OPEN 7 days early May to Oct 10am-midnight. CLOSED end Oct-early April.* Admission charge; children under 4, free.

Jamaica Bay Wildlife Refuge
Cross Bay Boulevard bet Howard Beach & Broad Channel. Queens. (1-718) 474-0613. A wonderful place for a close-to-nature walk. There are 2 trails and picnic tables; no bicycle paths. Over 300 species of wildlife sighted, including water fowl, predatory birds, songbirds. Visitors' Center *OPEN year round 7 days 8am-6pm, till 7pm in summer. CLOSED Christmas & New Year's Day.* FREE, but permit is necessary from Visitors' Center.

Long Island Game Farm
Long Island Expressway Exit 70, Manorville, Long Island. (1-516) 878-6644. Touch and feed domestic animals, some deer and llamas, all in a lovely, friendly atmosphere. *OPEN 7 days early April-Oct 9am-6pm.* Admission charge; discount for children 2-11.

New York Aquarium
Surf Avenue & West 8 Street, Coney Island,

Brooklyn. (1-718) 266-8500. Fantastic sea creatures in colorful setting, both indoor and outdoor
exhibits. Late April-mid Oct there is a whale and
dolphin show, a sea lion training session, and a
slide show in the theater. Touch Tank: touch live
marine creatures. *OPEN Mon-Wed; Fri-Sun
10am-5pm; Thurs till 1:45pm. June 15-Labor Day
Sat till 6pm & Sun till 7pm.* Admission charge;
lower for children 2-12; under age 2, free.
Prospect Park Zoo
Empire Boulevard & Flatbush Avenue, Brooklyn.
(1-718) 965-6560. Built in 1934, this is a relatively
small, but complete zoo. The Farmyard Children's
Zoo: *OPEN late June-Labor Day 10am-4pm.* Children get acquainted with small farm animals.
Pony cart and saddle pony rides too. Zoo *OPEN
year round 7 days 11am-4:30pm.* FREE
Queens Zoo & Children's Farm
Flushing Meadows-Corona Park, 111 Street at 54
Avenue, Flushing, Queens. (1-718) 699-7239.
The 18-acre zoo features mainly North American
animals—bison, deer, wolves, black bears. The
farm offers an opportunity to view and feed typical
barnyard animals. Pony cart rides too. *OPEN year
round 7 days 10am-3:45pm.* FREE
Barett Park, Staten Island Zoological Park
614 Broadway nr Forest Ave, West Brighton,
Staten Island. (1-718) 442-3100. Besides housing
the world's largest collection of rattlesnakes, there
are reptiles of every kind, bats, birds, big cats and
an otter pool. A charming children's zoo features
lectures, demonstrations and saddle pony rides.
*OPEN year round 7 days 10am-4:45pm.
CLOSED Thanksgiving, Christmas & New Year's
Day.* Admission charge; discount for children 6-
12; under age 6, free. Wed FREE for all.

Amusement Parks

Astroland Park
Coney Island, West 10 Street & Surf Avenue,
Brooklyn. (1-718) 372-0275. Kiddie rides and ma-
jor attractions for adults, including the roller coast-
er, the Cyclone—the granddad of them all.
Weather permitting *OPEN Palm Sun-mid June,
weekends only; mid June-weekend after Labor
Day, noon-midnight (later on weekends); until
mid-Oct weekends only. CLOSED mid Oct-mid-
April.* Admission FREE; cost per ride.
Rockaway's Playland
Rockaway Boulevard bet Beach 97 & 98 Sts.
Rockaway, Queens. (1-718) 945-7000. For adults
there is a pay-one-price-for-unlimited-rides policy; for kiddies there are 10-ride or 30-ride books
available. Weather permitting *OPEN weekends
only early March-late May starting at noon.
Memorial Day-week after Labor Day, noon-
midnight. Check for additional weekends in Sept.
CLOSED Oct-March.*

Playgrounds

The Parks and Recreation Department has 55

*playgrounds throughout the 5 boroughs with su-
pervised free play activities for kids 8-13. Beg. of
June-Aug. For location nearest you, call your
borough office:* Brooklyn, (1-718) 965-8900;
Bronx, 430-1800; Manhattan, 408-0100; Queens,
(1-718) 520-5900; Staten Island, (1-718) 390-
8000.
*Adventure playgrounds reflect recent trends in
innovative equipment and design for children's
play areas. The following are in Central Park:*

Adventure Playground
West 68 Street & Central Park West.
Estée Lauder Adventure Playground
East 71 Street & Fifth Avenue.
New Adventure Playground
Central Park West bet West 85 & West 86 Sts.
Sand Playground
East 85 Street & Fifth Avenue.
*In addition to those in Central Park, the following
are interesting play areas:*
Abingdon Square Park & Playground
Hudson, Bank & Bleecker Streets, Greenwich Vil-
lage.
Carl Schurz Playground
East End Avenue at East 84 Street.
Playground
Second Avenue at East 19 Street.
Playground
West 45 to West 46 Street, bet Ninth & Tenth
Aves.
Playground
Central Park West at 100 Street.
Playground
Lenox Avenue at West 139 Street.
St. Catherine's Park
First Avenue bet East 67 & East 68 Sts.
Stephen Wise Towers Play Area
West 90 to West 91 Street, Columbus to Amster-
dam Avenue.
Washington Square Park
At the foot of Fifth Avenue, Greenwich Village.

Learning

Arts & Crafts
*Many of the children's museums offer crafts
classes for children.*

Children's Art Carnival
62 Hamilton Terrace, Brooklyn. (1-718) 234-
4093. An after-school creative arts program for
children 8-14; workshops include ceramics,
sculpture, pottery, sewing, 3-D construction and
more. Call for details. FREE
92 Street YM-YWHA
1395 Lexington Avenue. 427-6000. For preschoolers 17 months to 5 years and for children
6-12, adventures in arts and crafts, including
ceramic sculpture and pottery.
YWCA
610 Lexington Avenue nr East 53 St. 755-4500. A
sampling of what's offered: ceramics workshop
(ages 8-12), découpage (13-16), stained glass
(13-16), woodworking (13-16).

Saturday Family Workshops
Belvedere Castle, Central Park, West 79 Street, south of the Great Lawn. 772-0210. Everything from meeting baby animals to planting herb gardens. Free for ages 5-11 and their families. *Year round every Sat 1-2:30pm.* Reservations are a must!

Computers
Children's Computer School
21 West 86 Street, suite 1010. 580-1335. One teacher for every 6 youngsters; each child has the use of a computer. Five 8-year-olds learn numbers, letters, play fun but educational games; 8-15 learn to program BASIC. Call for schedule.

Cooking
Hotel Inter-Continental
111 East 48 Street. 755-5900. "Cooking for Kids" teaches children 7-14 to cook in two-hour Sat sessions. Instruction from professional chefs.

Dance
Neubert Ballet Institute
Carnegie Hall, 881 Seventh Avenue nr West 57 St, Studio 805. 685-7754. Ages 3½-20. A unique institution nurtures talent from childhood to culmination as adult performing artists. The 80 courses offer a full range; two divisions, professional and educational. Training ground for the world-famed Children's Ballet Theater.
YWCA
610 Lexington Avenue nr East 53 St. 755-4500. Classes in modern, tap and ballet. Designed to develop coordination. Individual and group performances display newly acquired skills. For boys and girls 5-12. A program for teens as well.

Drama
Acting by Children Productions
320 East 49 Street. 832-6635. For children 6-18, workshops in voice training, dance, movement and acting techniques lead to performances for an audience. *Sat only.*
"Of, By and For" Children's Theater
For children 8-18. Workshops in dance, music, acting and general theater activities. Wed 5-7pm, Sat 2-7pm, year round. Performances are given as well in all 5 boroughs. Call 783-4469 for details. FREE.
Preparatory Center of Performing Arts
Brooklyn College, 154 Gershwin Hall, Brooklyn. (1-718) 780-4112. Professionally geared workshop classes in theater and dance techniques. Private lessons in music. For children 7-17. Also Dalcroze rhythm and movement (pre-instrumental and dance) for children 3-6.
Weist-Barron School of Television
35 West 45 Street. 840-7025. New York's oldest school specializing in acting for TV commercials and soap opera. A complete division for children and teens, 5-19.

Fencing
YWCA
610 Lexington Avenue nr East 53 St. 755-4500. ext. 63. Balance and grace are enhanced by acquiring basic fencing skills. For ages 9-13.
Fencers Club
154 West 71 Street. 874-9800. Founded in 1883. Membership is available to kids approximately 8 years old, depending on height. Olympic-level coaches on staff. *Evenings only.*

Gymnastics
Alzerrecas
1 East 28 Street. 683-1703. Daily 1-hour classes for toddlers, preschoolers and up. Children grouped according to ability. Initial class free.
Gymboree
684 Broadway. 505-2259. Call for info on this interesting play activity program for parents and children, 3 months to 4 years. Sessions promote self-esteem, confidence and stimulation.
Kounovsky Fitness Center
25 West 56 Street. 246-6415. Instruction on the balance beam, plus floor exercises, for girls 6-10. *Sat only.*
Manhattan Gymnastic Center
405 East 73 Street. 737-2016. Parents and toddlers together, for ages 6 months and older. Pre-gym for 4-5-year-olds; gymnastics for ages 5-16.
New York School for Circus Arts
1 East 104 Street. 369-5110. Beginner and intermediate classes based in acrobatics and balance skills for ages 8-16.
92 Street YM-YWHA
1395 Lexington Avenue. 427-6000. Wee Wizards: children aged 24-40 months engage in climbing and running, to develop confidence and coordination; instructor- and parent-supervised. Tumbling Tots: 17 months-5 years, gymnastics to develop coordination and a sense of movement; instructor- and parent-supervised.
Suzy Prudden Studios, Ltd.
2291 Broadway at West 82 Street. 595-7100. Pre-gymnastics for tots and infants aged 3 months-5 years, as well as gymnastics for boys and girls 6-16. Classed according to age, ability, and sex. *Mon-Sat by appointment only.*
YWCA
610 Lexington Avenue nr East 53 St. 755-4500. Excellent gymnastics program. Pre-school gymnastics (ages 4-5), novice (5-6 and 7-12) and 3-level beginner classes (5-6 and 7-12). Clinic, workshop, and competing/performing team.

—Gymnastics Day Camp
West Side YMCA
5 West 63 Street. Offers a gymnastics day camp for boys 8-12 years, girls 8-14. For info, call 787-4400.
YWCA
610 Lexington Avenue nr East 53 St. 755-4500. An intensive program for serious young gymnasts ages 8-12. Classes limited to 30.

Ice Skating
Ice Studio
1034 Lexington Avenue nr East 73 St. 535-0304. Instruction—private and group, primarily for kids 4 and up. *OPEN 7 days.*

Riverdale Ice Skating Center
5746 Broadway nr West 236 St, Bronx. 884-2700. Private or group (max. 12 kids), with lessons starting at age 3.
Sky Rink
450 West 33 Street, 16th fl. 695-6555. Sky-high Olympic-size indoor rink open year round. Private instruction by appointment only.

Music
Dalcroze School of Music
161 East 73 Street. 879-0316. Rhythm classes for preschoolers, singing, sight-reading, and keyboard improvisation for ages 5 and older.
Hebrew Arts School
129 West 67 Street. 362-8060. Instruction in all orchestral instruments, plus guitar, recorder and piano; classes in musical theory. Art and dance as well. For ages 6-17.
92 Street YM-YWHA
1395 Lexington Avenue. 427-6000. This Y has a good music department for instrument or vocal instruction, both group and private. There's a pre-instrumental course for 3-year-olds.
Third Street Music School Settlement
233 East 11 Street. 777-3240. Founded in 1894. Instruction begins with arts for the very young (age 2½); nursery-age children take Suzuki violin or piano, or creative dance; for older children and adults there is a wide variety of programs including individual and group lessons in all instruments.
YWCA
610 Lexington Avenue nr East 53 St. 755-4500. Flute and guitar lessons for children 5-12, plus a teen program offering classes in basic music theory, songwriting, guitar, piano and singing.
YWCA
610 Lexington Avenue nr East 53 St. 755-4500. Kids Chorus, an eight-week program of Rock to Bach, culminating in a performance for friends and family. Ages 8-12.

Painting & Drawing
Art Students' League
215 West 57 Street. 247-4510. Saturday classes in figure and still life for children 10-16.
Children's Art Carnival
62 Hamilton Terrace, Brooklyn. (1-718) 234-4093. A communications arts program is offered in the early evening and/or Sat afternoons for ages 14-18. Training for a career in the arts: graphic design, silkscreen and more. Call for information. FREE

Riding
Claremont Riding Academy
175 West 89 Street. 724-5100. For children 8-15. Mon-Sat group and private classes are offered in a small indoor ring and Central Park.
Van Cortlandt Stables
Broadway & West 254 St, Bronx. 543-4433. Private or semiprivate lessons for ages 8-12, group lessons thereafter. Also offers summer camp program. Outdoor ring.

Running
New York Road Runners Club
9 East 89 Street. 860-4455. Urban running program includes sessions in every borough and weekly races in Manhattan and the Bronx. For children 10-14. Bandit Division for age 14 and older.

Self-defense
YWCA
610 Lexington Avenue nr East 53 St. 755-4500. Provides full range of courses in judo and karate for ages 7-14. Separate program for older teens and adults.

Swimming
—Toddlers-5 Years
Aerobics West Fitness Club
131 West 86 Street. 787-3356. Infants, toddlers and older children learn to swim by playing games.
92 Street YM-YWHA
1395 Lexington Avenue. 427-6000. A swim program for toddlers 18 months to 5 years.
YWCA
610 Lexington Avenue nr East 53 St. 755-4500. Classes in basic swimming skills for water babies aged 2½-4; sprites 3-5, as well as various skill levels for ages 5-12. Infants accepted with note from doctor.

—Various Age & Skill Levels
These two Y's also have swim programs for kids at various levels. Call for details.
McBurney YMCA
215 West 23 Street. 741-9221.
West Side Y
5 West 63 Street. 787-4400.

Tennis
East Side Tennis
177 East 84 Street. 472-9114. Private or group tennis lessons are offered, starting at age 6.
Midtown Tennis Club
341 Eighth Avenue at West 27 St. 989-8572. Private or group lessons for children 5 and older.

Children's Clothes

All of the major department stores in Manhattan have large departments for children's clothing. Unless otherwise stated, all shops are open Mon-Sat.

Boutiques
Au Chat Botté
888 Madison Avenue nr East 72 St. 772-7402; 1055 Lexington Avenue nr East 75 St. 988-3482. Stylish yet practical French, Italian and British shoes and clothes for newborn to age 14.
Benetton 012
1162 Madison Avenue nr East 86 St. 879-7690. Scaled down, albeit expensive, versions of Ben-

etton sweaters, tees, pants , for children 2-16.
OPEN 7 days.

Bloomin Babies
844 Lexington Avenue at East 64 St. 744-9362. A
charming shop; sells imported children's clothing,
infant to size 6.

Botticellino
Trump Tower, 725 Fifth Avenue at 56 St, 3rd level
(shoes) 308-6402; 4th level (apparel) 319-5118.
Sophisticated Italian separates and shoes for the
sophisticated boy and girl.

Cerutti
807 Madison Avenue nr East 68 St. 737-7540.
Popular shop for expensive European and American fashions, including one-of-a-kind. Casual,
school and dress-up for infants, toddlers, girls to
size 14, boys to size 16.

Chocolate Soup
946 Madison Avenue nr East 74 St. 861-2210. A
fascinating small store for colorful clothes and
accessories, many of which are handcrafted imports. Good value. *OPEN 7 days.*

Curds & Whey for Children, Inc.
1461 Third Avenue nr East 83 St. 628-2677. Busy
shop carries a wide selection of everything one
might need for a child, from cribs and carriages to
toys, to clothing—domestic and imported—up to
size 10; shoes too. *OPEN 7 days.*

Fusen Usagi
927 Madison Avenue nr East 73 St. 772-6180.
Sophisticated outerwear, underwear and shoes.
All from Japan, mostly. in nontraditional black,
white and grays. Infant and toddler sizes only.

Glad Rags
1007 Madison Avenue nr East 77 St. 988-1880.
The basics for children from underwear to outerwear infant to size 18.

K.I.D.S.
Saks Fifth Avenue, 611 Fifth Avenue at 50 St.
753-4000. Their own shop on 8. Designer labels
for girls and boys, including Ralph Lauren, Yves
Saint-Laurent and Calvin Klein. Toys too.

Kids 'R' Us
8973 Bay Parkway, Brooklyn. (1-718) 373-0880.
Famous-brand American clothing, including
Health-Tex and OshKosh at discount prices.
Girls, sizes newborn-14. Boys, to size 20. *OPEN 7
days.*

Kidz at Bendelz
Bendel, 10 West 57 Street, ground fl. 247-1100. A
Bendel's first: snappy colorful, all natural-fiber
classic clothes for new born-size 6. Also, toys to
encourage creativity. Stylish of course.

Le Monde des Enfants
870 Madison Avenue nr East 70 St. 772-1990. A
Parisienne offshoot specializes in French cotton
knits both sporty and dressy. Girls, sizes 2-16,
boys, to 7.

Little Bits
1186 Madison Avenue nr East 86 St. 722-6139.
Lovely, offbeat handmade clothing for kids, infant
to size 14, at good prices.

Little Senli
30 Rockefeller Plaza. 307-5352; 672 Lexington
Avenue nr East 56 St. 308-1682. Cheerful, fanci-

ful clothing for newborn to 6X as well as baby gifts
and nursery accessories. Helpful staff.

Once Upon a Kid
147 East 72 Street. 734-1427. Colorful togs and
toys for tots. Infant to 6X; wide price range. Also,
inexpensive party and gift items.

Pat-Rick Shop
930 Madison Avenue nr East 73 St. 288-1444.
Owned by French children's wear manufacturer
Petit Bateau, this shop stocks a very up-to-date
selection of underwear, playclothes, and party-
clothes, mostly in sizes six months to eight years.

Peter Elliot's Whimsy
1335 Third Avenue nr East 76 St. 861-4200.
Clothes, infants and up to age 10, by the likes of
Lilac Bush, Jean Le Bourget, New Man. Stuffed
toys, clown mobiles. A fun environment for the
kids. *OPEN 7 days.*

Pinch Penny Pick-a-Pocket
1242 Madison Avenue nr East 89 St. 831-3819.
Hand-crafted clothing as well as French and
American designer duds for children, birth
through boys, size 5 and girls, preteen.

Skooteroo
141 Waverly Place nr Avenue of the Americas.
255-5821. Stylish unique Japanese imports for
newborn to size 5.

Shooting Star
213 Sixth Avenue nr Prince St. 741-7810. Durable
yet stylish natural-fiber clothing for boys and girls
1-7; exclusive designs by George Hudǎcko, Ulf
Lundqvist; hats by Patricia Hemphill, and handmade sweaters. Also, Victorian rattles, picture
frames, and lockets. Special: The Hair Parlor, for
childrens' cuts and styling. *OPEN Tues-Sun.*

Slithy Toves
49 West 72 Street. 799-6688. Distinctive shop for
American, imported, and handmade clothing, for
infant to size 10.

Small Change
1021 Lexington Avenue nr East 73 St. 772-6455.
Infants and children to size 10. Whimsical and
imaginative clothes; some stuffed toys and
accessories.

Space Kiddets
46 East 21 Street. 420-9878. Charming kids
clothes newborn to size 8 for both boys and girls.

Spring Flowers
1710 First Avenue nr East 88 St. 876-0469. Dressy and casual European imports in infant to teen
sizes. Also carries various school uniforms in
sizes 4-14.

Stone Free Kids
124 West 72 Street. 362-8903. Lovely shop specializes in natural-fiber, mainly European, some
American, children's clothing. Some one-of-a-
kind handmade things as well at expensive prices.

Tim's
878 Lexington Avenue nr East 71 St. 535-2262.
Specializes in boys' sportswear separates including Polo and Jeff Banks. Size 2 to teen sizes.

Wendy's
456 West Broadway nr Prince St. 533-2306. Newborn to children size 10. American and European
sophisticated handknits and basic clothing.

Wicker Garden's Baby
1318 Madison Avenue nr East 93 St. 348-1166.
Clothes for infants and toddlers; ready-made or
custom delicate crib and carriage linens.

Wicker Garden's Children
1325 Madison Avenue nr East 93 St. 410-7001.
Spacious, beautifully decorated shop for boys and
girls clothing up to size 10; shoes, including baby's
first pair, sneakers or party shoes up to size 3
(expert fitters). Accessories for the girls including
hats and satin undies.

West Side Kids
498 Amsterdam Avenue at West 84 St. 496-7282.
Used and imported kids clothes.

-Camp Clothing
The Camp Shop
41 West 54 Street. 505-0980. Customers are
seated while salespeople bring out merchandise
for approval. Clothing (including 200 camp uniforms), shoes and gear are stocked. Free name-
tagging *before* the seasonal rush.

Ideal Department Store
1814 Flatbush Avenue, Brooklyn. (1-718) 252-
5090. Clothes, footwear and equipment at discount prices. Features Boy Scout and Girl Scout
supplies.

Melnikoff's Department Store
1594 York Avenue nr East 84 St. 288-2419. Specialists in camping gear and clothes for boys and
girls. Prices are discount. Local delivery, name-
taping and advice are free.

—Discount Clothes
A&G Infants' & Children's Wear
261 Broome Street nr Orchard St. 966-3775.
Name-brand merchandise from layettes to size 14
at up to 25% off list prices. *OPEN Sun-Fri.
CLOSED Sat.*

Nathan Borlam's
157 Havemeyer Street nr South 2 St, Brooklyn.
(1-718) 387-2983. Many mothers say it's well
worth the trip. Up to 50% discount on children's
clothes up to juniors. *OPEN Sun-Thurs & Fri am.
CLOSED Fri afternoon, Sat.*

Goldman & Ostrow
315 Grand Street nr Allen St. 925-9151. Good
spot for name-brand and some imported infants'
and children's wear at 20% discount. Sizes newborn to 14. *OPEN 7 days.*

Greenstone's
2750 Nostrand Avenue nr Ave N, Brooklyn. (1-
718) 252-4173. A specialty shop for children. Imports and the best domestic brands; custom-
made too. Complete wardrobes for toddlers and
boys and girls through size 14 at 20% discount.

Sidney & Sari Klein, Inc.
155 Orchard Street nr Rivington St. 475-9470.
Inexpensive casual children's clothing. *OPEN 7
days.*

Klein's of Monticello
105 Orchard Street nr Delancey St. 966-1453.
Well-discounted high-fashion European and
American clothing for kids. Oshkosh, Petit
Bateau, Jean Le Bourget. Sizes 18 months-14.
OPEN Sun-Fri. CLOSED Sat.

M. Kreinen & Company, Inc.
301 Grand Street nr Allen St. 925-0239. Large
selection of better children's clothes, at good
prices. *OPEN Sun-Fri. CLOSED Sat.*

Lasky Brothers
85 Orchard Street nr Broome St. 226-9520.
Baby's first shoes and discontinued styles of well-
known brands for boys and girls. *OPEN Sun-Fri.
CLOSED Sat.*

Rice & Breskin
323 Grand Street nr Orchard St. 925-5515. Vast
inventory of famous-name infants' and children's
wear at 20% discount. *OPEN Sun-Fri. CLOSED
Sat.*

—Resale Clothes
Best Dressed Kids
2741A Broadway at West 105 St. 222-3740. Spacious shop for previously-owned kids clothes, all
neatly arranged. Infants through size 14. Helpful
service; play area for the kids.

Frugal Frog
1707 Second Avenue nr East 88 St. 876-5178. In
close quarters, inexpensive used clothing for kids,
infants through age 13. New things too at discount
prices.

Once Upon a Time
171 East 92 Street. 831-7619. High-quality used
clothing in a shop started by two grandmas.

Replay
664 West 204 Street. 942-4142. Used clothing,
toys, books, shoes, outerwear and small furnishings. Lists larger items free on bulletin board.
OPEN Tues-Sat.

Second Generation
98 Pineapple Walk nr Henry St. Brooklyn Heights.
(1-718) 643-9270. Large and lively shop with a
great selection of infant through size 16 used
clothes. Also, books and new toys and children's
furnishings.

Second Act
1046 Madison Avenue nr East 79 St, 2nd fl 988-
2440. Well-known shop with a large selection of
inexpensive used clothing for both boys and girls.
Toys, books and sporting goods too. Bulletin
board lists larger items.

Thrifty Threads for Kids
2082 East 13 Street nr Ave U, Brooklyn. (1-718)
336-8037. Used clothing, toys, carriages, cribs,
books. *OPEN Tues-Sat.*

Children's Specialty Shopping

*Again, unless otherwise stated, all shops are
OPEN Mon-Sat. Call for hours.*

Bikes
*Most of the larger toy stores also carry a good
selection of bicycles.*

Broadway Bicycle
9 West 61 Street. 265-1033. Large selection of
famous name bikes in all sizes. Convenient to
Central Park. Also rents, stores, makes repairs.
OPEN 7 days.

Morris' Toyland
1896 Third Avenue nr East 105 St. 876-0740.
Long-established shop offers an extensive line of
bicycles for children of every age. Low prices, all
merchandise guaranteed. *OPEN 7 days.*

Stuyvesant Bicycle and Toy, Inc.
349 West 14 Street. 254-5200. Best-made American children's bikes at discount prices. Rentals
too. *OPEN 7 days.*

Books

*B. Dalton, 666 Fifth Avenue at East 52 Street large
childrens' book departments. (See also SHOP-
PING, Specialty Shops & Services: Books.)*

Barnes & Noble Sales Annex
Fifth Avenue & 18 St. 807-0099. Quite a good
stock of current and backlist children's books at
discount prices. *OPEN 7 days.*

Books of Wonder
464 Hudson Street at Barrow St. 989-3270. The
largest collection of children's fantasy books in the
city. Very special are the 19th- and early-20th-
century picture books. *OPEN 7 days.*

Corner Bookstore
1313 Madison Avenue at East 93 St. 831-3554.
Half for adults and half for kids. Children's account
cards.

Eeyore's Books for Children
1066 Madison Avenue at East 81 St. 988-3404;
2252 Broadway at West 81 St. 362-0634. The
city's only store completely devoted to children's
books; baby books through young adult. Special
events including story hours (during the school
year) on Sun at 12:30pm on the East Side and
11am on the West Side. Put your name on their
mailing list. *OPEN 7 days.*

—Comic Books

Supersnipe Comics
1617 Second Avenue nr East 84 St. 879-9628.
Has a stock of over 300,000 current and back-
issue comic books. Rare as well. *OPEN Mon-Wed
& Fri from 12:30; Sat from noon.*

Diapers

General Diaper Service
For all 5 boroughs, call 417-1002. Home delivery
of 100% cotton diapers with bacteria inhibitor. Gift
certificates available. *OPEN Mon-Fri 9am-5pm.*

Dolls & Dollhouses

A Small World
1820 Flatbush Avenue, Brooklyn. (1-718) 338-
8411. Over 75 different dollhouses in stock.
They'll also custom-build houses and they carry
everything necessary for do-it-yourself building,
wiring and decorating. Call about their dollhouse
school where they show you how.

Dollhouse Antics, Inc.
1308 Madison Avenue nr East 93 St. 876-2288. A
dollhouse shop geared to both children and collectors. Complete line of accessories and furnishings.

dollsandreams
1421 Lexington Avenue nr East 93 St. 876-2434.
Lovely shop carries no commercial toys. Unique

imported or handmade toys, stuffed animals,
dolls, art supplies and books.

Manhattan Doll Hospital and Toy Shop
176 Ninth Avenue nr West 21 St. 989-5220; 4245
Broadway nr West 181 St. 928-4000. Downtown
shop: large selection of dolls, dollhouses, including lovely antique dolls for show and sale. Uptown
shop: toys, dolls, dollhouses, miniatures. Expert
repairs of antique, cloth-body, and some rubber
dolls. *OPEN Sun-Fri; CLOSED Sat.*

New York Doll Hospital
787 Lexington Avenue nr East 61 St, upstairs.
838-7527. Repairs on all kinds of dolls (no batter-
ies, please) with a reputation for care and concern
since 1900. Also buys sells and appraises antique
dolls.

Furniture

*The following department stores have a complete
selection of juvenile furniture: Alexander's, B. Altman & Co., Gimbels, and Gimbels East, and Saks
Fifth Avenue.*

Albee Baby Carriage Company, Inc.
715 Amsterdam Avenue nr West 95 St. 662-5740.
Wide selection of well-priced infant and toddler
furniture and accessories, including twin carriages. Complete layette, toys too.

Ben's for Kids
1380 Third Avenue nr East 79 St. 794-2330. A
large, very helpful, very friendly store for infant
furniture and accessories, carriages, strollers.
Some clothing for newborns to age 4.

Children's Room
318 East 45 Street. 687-3868. Scandinavian furniture for children: desks, bunk beds, modular systems, in high-tech designs.

Lederman R., Inc.
112 Rivington Street nr Essex St. 254-9646. Cribs
and bedding for kids, plus carriages, rocking
chairs, rocking horses, at discount prices. Bikes.

Lewis of London
215 East 51 Street. 688-3669; 72-17 Austin
Street, Queens. (1-718) 544-8003. Exclusive imported furniture, carriages and accessories.
Unique designs, large selection. Layette and infant clothing department, too.

Schneider's
20 Avenue A nr East 2 St. 228-3540. Nursery
through teen-age needs. Complete line of furniture, toys, carriages too, at very good prices.

Wicker Garden's Baby
1318 Madison Avenue nr East 93 St., 2nd fl. 348-
1166. Antique wicker baby furnishings and beautiful infant wear—from layette to toddler size 4.
Handcrafted accessories and toys.

—Furniture Rentals

*The following rent children's furniture and
accessories. Perfect for short stays at
Grandmother's house.*

Ben's for Kids
1380 Third Avenue nr East 79 St. 794-2330.
Rents full-sized cribs and high chairs. No charge
for pickup or delivery in Manhattan.

Curds & Whey for Children, Inc.
1461 Third Avenue nr East 83 St. 628-2677. Rent Portacribs, playpens, strollers.

Keefe & Keefe, Inc.
429 East 75 Street. 988-8800. Rent cribs, carriages, high chairs, in Manhattan only.

Wee Care Juvenile Products
168 East 91 Street. 876-4310. Rents everything from cribs to car seats.

Hairdressers

Barbershop for Boys & Girls
FAO Schwarz, Fifth Avenue at 58 Street, 3rd fl. 644-9400. This barbershop in the famed toy store specializes in first haircuts.

Hair Parlor
Shooting Star, 213 Sixth Avenue nr Prince St. 741-7810. Kathy Hess specializes in childrens' hair: shampoo, cut and blow-dry styling. In a charming shop. *OPEN Tues-Sun.*

Kenneth for Kids
Macy's Herald Square, Seventh Avenue & West 34 Street. 594-1717. The famed hairstylist's salon for children only. Boys and girls aged 2-14. TV, balloons, candy. Appointment necessary.

Michael's Children's Haircutting Salon
1263 Madison Avenue nr East 90 St. 289-9612. Specializes in European haircuts for boys and girls aged 1-12. Special seats, lollipop inducements.

Hobbies

Polk's Model Craft Hobbies, Inc.
314 Fifth Avenue nr 32 St. 279-9034. Five floors of model car, plane and boat kits, as well as toys, plastic miniatures, trains, racing sets and accessories, radio remote-control airplanes, cars, boats, tanks, architectural models and kits, science equipment, personal computers and more. Quite a place. *OPEN 7 days.*

Kites

Go Fly a Kite
1201 Lexington Avenue nr East 82 St. 472-2623. *153 East 53 Street. 308-1666. Your spirits will soar upon entering this shop completely devoted to kites: every color, shape, material and price. *OPEN 7 days.*

Kosher Baby Food

Curds & Whey for Children, Inc.
1461 Third Avenue nr East 83 St. 628-2677. Manischewitz: jars of strained or chopped chicken, beef, or veal.

Magic, Jokes & Tricks

Flosso-Hornmann Magic Company
304 West 34 Street, upstairs. 279-6079. Oldest shop of its kind in America, founded in 1865. Magic museum and demonstrations on Sat for kids. Call ahead for times.

School Supplies
Inexpensive supplies can be found at Woolworth and Lamston stores.

Stuffed Animals
The Azuma shops, located throughout the city, carry a good selection of small, charming, in-expensive stuffed animals. Many card and gift shops also carry some, though choices are usually limited to the popular characters, Snoopy and Raggedy Ann and Andy. (See also Toys.)

Grassy Point Woods
266 West 23 Street. 924-7611. Features a large selection of imported and domestic stuffed animals of every shape and size, some other toys.

If It's Furry
203 West 79 Street. 877-8129. Features imported animals, including an amazing anteater. Also carries T shirts and toys. Will gift-wrap.

Toys

Childcraft Center
155 East 23 Street. 674-4754; 150 East 58 Street. 753-3196. Imported quality educational products. Best known for their hardwood blocks, wooden tables and chairs. Over 3,000 items include building toys, dramatic play toys, musical instruments, science kits, games, puzzles, art materials, teaching aids, and books. From birth to age 15.

FAO Schwarz
745 Fifth Avenue at 58 St. 644-9400; also 5 World Trade Center (concourse level). 775-1850. Though it has stores nationwide, this large, world-famed toy emporium has lost none of its exclusivity. Features much that is opulent for the affluent: life-sized stuffed animals and miniaturized powered autos. The standards too, kites, dolls, games and toys on 3 floors. A must-visit. AE, DC, MC, V.

Geppetto's Toys
South Street Seaport Market. 608-1239. Two floors of old-fashioned no-battery toys. Dolls, Steiff stuffed animals, toy cars and, of course, wooden Pinnochios and other stringed friends. *OPEN 7 days.*

Gingerbread House
9 Christopher Street nr Greenwich Ave. 741-9101. A lovely Greenwich Village toy store for good selection of unusual imported and handmade toys as well as the traditional in crib, play pen and preschool toys. *OPEN 7 days.*

Last Wound Up
290 Columbus Avenue nr West 74 St. 787-3388. Specializes in whimsical wind-up toys, such as a walking camel, a chicken that lays eggs and a flip-over mouse. Also music boxes and some battery-operated toys. *OPEN 7 days.*

Laughing Giraffe
1065 Lexington Avenue nr East 75 St. 570-9528. Owned by two teachers; it shows. An intelligent, well-thought-out shop for toys, books, games. No "Don't Touch" signs here. Baby-gift registry too.

Mary Arnold Toys
962 Lexington Avenue nr East 70 St. 744-8510. Toys, stuffed animals, dolls and houses, arts and crafts supplies and books for all ages. A child can leave a "wish list" for special-occasion days. They also carry paper goods and helium balloons.

Penny Whistle
1281 Madison Avenue nr East 91 St. 369-3808; also 448 Columbus Avenue nr West 81 St. 873-9090. A pioneer concept in toy stores, where children are encouraged to touch and play. Emphasis is on high play value and unusual design. Prices

start as low as 20¢ and go way up. Excellent service, including gift-wrap and delivery.

Silent Sky
176 West Houston Street at Sixth Ave. 924-6381. Physical science toys—kites, boomerangs, periscopes and such are the specialty here. Sat during the school year they hold environmental workshops for ages 7-12. *OPEN Tues-Sun.*

Star Magic
743 Broadway nr East 8 St. 228-7770. A wonderful array of all things space-y. Star charts, moon maps, toy space ships, books, postcards and freeze-dried ice cream for would-be astronauts.

Toy Park
112 East 86 Street. 427-6611. A block-long store carrying brand name toys for all ages, including a very large game department. They will gift-wrap, take phone orders and deliver. *OPEN 7 days.*

—Discount Toys

Hershey's Stationers
48 Clinton Street nr Rivington St. 423-6391. For 55 years, toys and games, stuffed animals, sporting goods and stationery too. All at discount prices. *OPEN Sun-Fri. CLOSED Sat.*

Orchard Toy & Stationery Company
185 Orchard Street nr Houston St. 777-5133. Excellent stock of Kenner, Parker Brothers, Mattel, Play Skool, Fisher Price and more brand names at 20% off. *OPEN Mon-Fri & Sun 9am-6pm.*

Toys 'R' Us
2875 Flatbush Avenue nr Kings Plaza, Brooklyn. (1-718) 258-2061; also 8973 Bay Parkway, Brooklyn. (1-718) 372-4646. Very well-stocked supermarket for discount toys and games. *OPEN 7 days.*

—Recycled Toys

Play It Again
171 East 92 Street. 876-5888. Recycled toys, games, books, puzzles, bicycles, dolls, stuffed animals, as well as cribs and play pens. Everything in working order. It makes sense.

The Toy Chest
226 East 83 Street. 988-4320. Resale toys and games, high chairs, carriages, car seats.

Trains

Madison Hardware Company
105 East 23 Street. 777-1110. Authorized Lionel representative for sales and repairs of all their trains and equipment.

Red Caboose
16 West 45 Street, 4th fl. 575-0155. Extensive collection of trains and equipment at discount prices.

Children's Entertainment

A recorded listing of FREE cultural events and entertainment available in the five boroughs on any given day can be had 24 hours a day, 7 days a week. Call 755-4100.
Most branches of the New York Public Library present special programs, many of which, especially on weekends, are of interest to children. Every branch has available a FREE calendar of these special activities; pick up one for current information. The New York Times and New York Daily News on Friday and the New York Post on Saturday are good sources for happenings of special interest to kids. Also check New York magazine as well as The Village Voice.

Alice May's Puppets
Origami Center, 31 Union Square West at East 16 St. 255-0469. *Nov-May Sun at 2pm.* Puppet shows for age 3 up. Admission charge. Reservations necessary.

Barnes & Noble Sales Annex
Fifth Avenue at 18 Street. 675-5500. *Performances in the basement every weekend.* Puppet shows, musicals, plays and magic shows. FREE. Call for information.

Belevedere Castle
Central Park, West 79 Street, south of the Great Lawn. 772-0210. Imaginative participatory performances, dance concerts, magic shows, storytelling, musicals. For all ages. *Year round, every Sun, at 2 & 3pm.* No registration required.

Big Apple Circus
1 East 104 Street. 369-5110. This one-ring circus performs in Manhattan from June to Sept. There's a general admission charge and worth every penny. For info on location schedule and other performance possibilities, call the New York School for Circus Arts at the above number.

Citicorp Center
The Market, East 53 Street & Lexington Avenue. 559-4259. Saturday is Kids' Day, with free entertainment at 11:30am in the Atrium.

Courtyard Playhouse
39 Grove Street, west of Sheridan Square & Seventh Avenue South. 765-9540. *Performances Sat & Sun from the weekend after Labor Day to the end of June at 1:30pm & 3pm, daily, during Christmas school holidays.* Admission charge. Reservations necessary.

FAO Schwarz
Fifth Avenue at 58 Street. 644-9400. A variety of entertainment on weekdays, from clowns and puppet demonstrations to turtle races. Storytelling every *Thurs at 2:30pm.* FREE

First All Children's Theater
37 West 65 Street bet Columbus Avenue & Central Park West. 873-6400. *Late Oct-May, weekends.* Performances for ages 3 and up. Admission charge. Reservations necessary.

Fourth Wall Theater
79 East 4 Street. 254-5060. *Oct-June Fri-Sun at 8pm.* "Garbage of Eden." *Sat & Sun at 3:30pm,* "Toto and The Wizard of Wall Street." For age 5 to teen. Admission charge. Reservations necessary. Also *Tues at 7:30pm,* "Music Live!", New York's largest onstage rock band for 13 and up. Admission charge. Reservations necessary.

Floating Hospital Puppet Playhouse
Pier 15 at Fulton Street & the East River. 943-6535. *Performances weekly.* Music theater for the whole family. Admission charge. Reservations necessary.

Lea Wallace Puppets
First Moravian Church, 154 Lexington Avenue at East 30 St. 254-9074. Puppet shows for kids aged

3-10 *Sat 2pm*. Children participate, then make simple constructions on the show's theme. Admission charge. Reservations suggested.

Magic Towne House
1026 Third Avenue nr East 61 St. 752-1165. *Sat, Sun & school holidays year round* at 1, 2:30 & 4pm. Hour-long magic shows. Admission charge. Reservations necessary.

Museum of the City of New York
1220 Fifth Avenue nr 103 St. 534-1672. A different puppet show each week *early Oct-April, Sat 1:30pm* for ages 4 and up. Admission charge. No reservations necessary.

New Federal Theater
Henry Street Settlement, 466 Grand Street nr Delancey St. 598-0400. Family theater for kids and their parents performed weekends *Oct-mid April*. Minimal admission charge. No reservations necessary.

Off-Center Theater Company
436 West 18 Street bet Ninth & Tenth Aves. 929-8299. *Sept-May, Tues, Wed, Thurs & Sun*. Updated versions of classical fairy tales. Audience participation. Admission charge. Reservations recommended.

Onstage Children Company
413 West 46 Street bet Ninth & Tenth Aves. 246-9872. Four productions a year. *Mid Sept-May, Sat only 1:30pm & 3pm*. For ages 5 and up. Admission charge. Group rates available. Reservations necessary.

Penny Bridge Players
Undercroft of the Assumption Church, 59 Cranberry Street. Brooklyn Heights. (1-718) 855-6346. Children's fairy tales performed on weekends—*matinee hours*. Admission charge.

Penny Jones & Company Puppets
Greenwich House Music School, 46 Barrow Street nr Seventh Ave So. 924-4589. Performances *Oct-April. Sat & Sun 3:30pm* for children aged 3-8. Admission charge. Reservations necessary.

Richard Morse Mime Theater
385 Broadway. 219-0310. Weekend performances during the school year. *SPECIAL: Christmas vacation show, "The Juggler of Notre Dame," daily Dec 21-31 at 8pm*. Admission charge. Reservations suggested.

Something Different
1488 First Avenue nr East 77 St. 570-6666. This nightclub is regularly surrendered to child performers from stage and screen who entertain their peers. Suitable refreshments available. Minimum and cover. *Sat at 7pm & Sun at 5:30pm*.

Storytelling
Hans Christian Andersen Statue, Central Park nr Conservatory Water (the Model Boat Pond) at 74 St. The perfect setting for storytelling—*every Sat late May to late Sept. 11am-noon*. Fun for children age 4 and over. FREE

Swedish Cottage Marionette Theater
Enter Central Park, 81 Street & Central Park West. 988-9093. Performances *Oct-late May. Sat & Sun 11am, 1 & 3pm*. Admission charge. Reservations necessary.

Theater in a Trunk
276 West 43 Street. 921-7785. Traveling theater, *Sept-June, Mon-Fri;* schools, hospitals, community centers. For children 8-18. Skits and songs on a theme, entertainment with a light-handed message. Call for more info on this interesting and innovative group.

Thirteenth Street Theater
50 West 13 Street bet Fifth & Sixth Aves. 675-6677. *Sat & Sun year round, 1 & 3pm. 1-hour performances*. Admission charge. Reservations necessary.

Parties

For party supplies and favors, see SHOPPING, Specialty: Paper Products.

Party Entertainment to Hire
New York's parks and plazas are used as impromptu stages during the summer by aspiring actors, mimes, magicians, fire-eaters, jugglers, oompah and steel-drum bands. Any of them would be interested in entertaining indoors for a change.

Abbott Road Puppets
57 East 96 Street. 410-6071. Puppet show to entertain and, afterward, puppet-making to involve the kids. Educational and folk themes. Ages 3-11.

Jennifer the Magician
(1-201) 861-5715. Magic and comedy for kids in New York or New Jersey. She also holds a 1-day magic class for children at the Lexington Avenue YWCA.

Michael Shall
724-5556. Will teach origami to a max. of 20 kids age 6 and up for 1½ hours. He's a master at it. Each child gets an instruction kit and a creation as a party favor. Gives private lessons too.

Sandy Landsman
586-6300. A delightful clown who plays the guitar and involves the kids creatively in songs, games, and stories. Puppets and balloon sculpture too.

Princess Pricilla
586-6300. Will perform for children 1 year and up, with puppets, balloons, music and more.

Princess Sondra
244-0265. This princess is really a magic teacher and performer who enchants with her tricks and balloon sculpture too.

Roger Riddle
582-4240. A captivating entertainer delights the children with his vivid imagination.

Jeremy Sage
586-6300. Professional actor presents an unstructured, improvisational show, including an "incompetent" magic act. Challenges the kids imagination. For age 3 and up.

Larry Weeks
773-2135. This clown-magician is a professional, complete with live trained rabbit. In addition, he does juggling, balancing, balloon animals and puppets to keep the kids amused.

Bob Yorburg
730-1188. Big Bob's bag of tricks includes sleight of hand, mime, balloon animals and a live rabbit, all involving the kids.

Party Planners

Mary Arnold Toys
962 Lexington Avenue nr East 70 St. 744-8510. This shop will help plan your party by engaging the entertainment, be it clown, magician, or mime.

birthdaybakers . . . partymakers, inc.
Linda Kaye, 195 East 76 Street. 288-7112. Creative party-planning services, including custom-designed invitations, themes, entertainment, props and special-order cakes. Party gift certificates available.

Wenslo Company
663 Fifth Avenue. 757-6454. Parties based on a concept. Fantasy becomes reality when a favorite fairy tale or nursery rhyme is brought to life via well-researched locales or decorations; specially designed invitations, appropriate foods, actors, and costumes for all. Past party themes: Robin Hood, Alice in Wonderland. Like most fantasies, expensive.

Special-Activity Parties

American Stanhope Hotel
995 Fifth Avenue at 81 St. 288-5800. Two plush party rooms are available for 20 or 30 kiddies. Party consists of pizza or hot dogs, soda and birthday cake. Entertainment can be arranged by them.

birthdaybakers . . . partymakers, inc.
Linda Kaye, 288-7112. A chef, with everything needed for birthday child and up to 12 guests to bake a birthday cake, comes to your house. Chef hats, aprons and cooking diplomas, in addition to special invitations. Involves the child in the party plan. For ages 5 and up. Reserve 3 weeks in advance.

Richard Morse Mime Theater
385 Broadway. 219-0310. Bring your party to the theater. See the show and afterward the cast will sing "Happy Birthday" and chat with the kids. Minimum of 10 children; you bring the fixings, they supply table and chairs.

Mostly Magic
55 Carmine Street nr Seventh Ave. So. 924-1472. Magic club available on weekends. Price includes balloon party favors, cake, ice cream, unlimited soft drinks and an hour-long performance by a professional magician.

Museum of the City of New York
1220 Fifth Avenue nr 103 St. 534-1672. Birthday parties arranged for 10-15 kids aged 6-12. Includes a partial tour of the museum and a supervised private party in a re-created Dutch Colonial household with "please touch" demonstration. Ice cream, candy, punch, birthday cake and decorations, games and prizes. Birthday parents are invited. *Available Tues-Fri 3-4:30pm.*

Movies at Home

Charard Motion Pictures, Inc.
2110 East 24 Street, Brooklyn. (1-718) 891-4339. Available: 16mm cartoons, several on one reel; or full-length animated films, e.g., *Gay Puree, Gulliver's Travels.* Projector rentals as well.

Cinema Services
2130 Broadway. 580-2447. 16mm features, shorts and cartoons. Also rents projectors and screens.

Select Film Library
115 West 31 Street. 594-4450. Available: 16mm cartoons, full-length animations, including Disney films. Projector rentals as well.

For Parents

General

Children's Story
976-3636. A different story every day: fables, fairy tales, excerpts from the classics.

Directory of Public High Schools
Bureau of Educational and Vocational Guidance, 110 Livingston Street, Room 418, Brooklyn, N.Y. 11210. There are over 100 high schools in New York. Find out the specifics, including special or optional programs available.

Early Childhood Resource and Information Center
New York Public Library, 66 Leroy Street nr Seventh Ave So. 929-0815. An early-childhood center with workshops, parents' learning groups and a family room. Stocked with books for adults who work with children from birth to age 5. And you don't have to hush!

Elisabeth Bing Center for Parents
164 West 79 Street. 362-5304. Pre- and post-natal exercise classes. Workshops for parents and babies. Lamaze instruction.

Homework Hotline
(1-718) 780-7766. A teacher or librarian will help elementary, junior-high and high-school students (and their parents) find the solution to a difficult homework problem. *AVAILABLE Mon-Thurs 5-8pm.*

92 Street Y Parenting Center
1395 Lexington Avenue. 427-6000. Because parenting isn't easy, the center offers a variety of services, including workshops, classes and lectures with other parents and professionals.

Parents League of New York, Inc.
115 East 82 Street. 737-7385. A good source of info and services for the parent and child on such things as schools, safety and baby-sitters. Yearly fee and membership.

Parents' Press
212 West 79 Street, Suite 2 E. 874-4991. An informative and entertaining publication for parents and their children. Complimentary copies available at some McDonald's locations, children's toy and clothes shops. Otherwise by subscription.

Volunteer Services for Children
867-2220. At 8 community centers in Manhattan, volunteers tutor 1 child in reading, 1 eve a week during the school year.

Baby Care

Always personally interview a prospective baby nurse and thoroughly check out her references. A few agencies are listed below.

Anne Andrews Employment Agency
38 East 57 Street. 753-1244.
Avalon Nurses' Registry
30 East 60 Street. 371-7222.
Baby Sitters Guild
60 East 42 Street. 682-0227. *9am-9pm, 7 days a week.*
Fox Agency
30 East 60 Street. 753-2686.
London Employment Agency, Inc.
767 Lexington Avenue. 755-5064.
Park Avenue Home Employment Agency
118 East 59 Street. 753-5950.

Baby-Sitters

Avalon Nurses' Agency
30 East 60 Street. 371-7222.
Barnard College Babysitting Service
606 West 120 Street. 280-2035.
Cornell Nursing School Babysitting Service
420 East 70 Street. 472-8393.
Lenox Hill Senior Citizens Service Center
343 East 70 Street. 744-5905.
Lynn Employment Agency
2067 Broadway nr West 70 St. 874-6130.
New York University
21 Washington Place. 598-2971.
Part-Time Child Care
19 East 69 Street. 879-4343.

Day Camps (Summer)

Many of the city parks run a free play group for children 4-12 during July and August, Mon-Fri 9:30am-3:30pm. Activities and entertainment, including magicians and clowns. Call the appropriate borough office of the Parks and Recreation Department for information.

Information
   Advisory Council on Camps
   8 West 40 Street, New York, N.Y. 10018. 869-8290. 826-7133.
   New York City Bureau for Day Camp & Recreation
   377 Broadway, 5th fl. New York, N.Y. 10013. 566-7763.

Nursery Schools & Kindergartens

—Public Nursery School Programs
   Agency of Child Development. 553-6422, -6424, -6425. Information on public nursery schools in the 5 boroughs.

—Private Nursery Schools
Listed below are just a few of many in the city.

Barnard College Toddler Center
606 West 120 Street. 666-6415.

Central Park Kindergarten
1 West 89 Street. 724-8488.
Community Nursery School & Kindergarten
28 East 35 Street. 683-4988.
Congregation B'nai Jeshurun Day School
270 West 89 Street. 787-7600.
Ethical Culture Schools
33 Central Park West. 874-5200.
Friends Seminary
222 East 16 Street. 477-9500.
Jack and Jill School
St. George's Church. 209 East 16 Street. 475-0855.
Le Jardin à l'Ouest Play Group
164 West 83 Street. 362-2658.
Little Red Schoolhouse
196 Bleecker Street. 477-5316.
Morningside Montessori School
251 West 100 Street. 666-9071.
Multimedia Pre-school
40 Sutton Place. 593-1041.
New York Hospital Nursery School
435 East 70 Street. 472-6859.
New York Philanthropic League
150 West 85 Street. 873-4581. For handicapped children only.
Program for Gifted Children
Hunter College. 860-1131 for recording on procedure. Program for nursery through grade 12 for children who have been tested and accepted. Fee for testing.
Riverside Church Nursery-Kindergarten Weekday School
490 Riverside Drive. 749-7000, ext 136, 137.
Stephen Wise Free Synagogue Nursery School
30 West 68 Street. 877-4050.
Temple Emanu-El Nursery School & Kindergarten
1 East 65 Street. 744-1400.
Union Seminary Day Care Center
527 Riverside Drive. 663-5930.
Westside YMCA Co-op Nursery School
5 West 63 Street. 787-4400.
YM & YWHA Nursery School
92 Street & Lexington Avenue. 427-6000.
YWCA-YMCA Day Care
422 Ninth Avenue. 564-1300.

Scouts

Girl Scouts Council of Greater New York
335 East 46 Street. 687-8383. Call for information about becoming a Girl Scout in one of New York's 5 boroughs.
Girl Scout Retail Shop
830 Third Avenue nr East 50 St. 751-6495. Everything to do with Girl Scouting: uniforms, badges, camping equipment and publications.
Boy Scouts
345 Hudson Street nr King St. 242-1100. Call for information about becoming a Boy Scout in one of New York's 5 boroughs.

Sports

The Yankees

General Information

For information regarding a park or activity, call the appropriate borough office of the Parks and Recreation Department:
Brooklyn: (1-718) 965-8900
Bronx: 430-1800
Manhattan: 408-0100
Queens: (1-718) 520-5900
Staten Island: (1-718) 390-8000
For recorded information on goings-on in the city parks: 472-1003.

Sports Stadiums

Byrne Meadowlands Sports Complex
East Rutherford, New Jersey.
New York Cosmos (soccer) (1-201) 935-3900
New York Giants (football) (1-201) 935-8111
New York Jets (football) 421-6600
Fitzgerald Gymnasium (Queens College)
Kissena Boulevard & 65 Avenue. Flushing, Queens. (1-718) 520-7212.
John J. Downing Memorial Stadium
Randalls Island. 860-1828.
Madison Square Garden
West 33 Street & Seventh Avenue. 564-4400.
Shea Stadium
Roosevelt Avenue & 126 Street. Flushing, Queens. New York Mets (baseball) (1-718) 507-8499.

West Side Tennis Club
1 Tennis Place. Forest Hills, Queens. (1-718) 268-2300.
Yankee Stadium
West 161 Street & River Avenue. Bronx. 293-6000.

Annual Sporting Events

See also ANNUAL EVENTS, Calendar.
Madison Square Garden: 563-8000
Volvo Grand Prix Masters Tennis: Jan.
Millrose Wanamaker Track: Jan/Feb.
Golden Gloves Boxing: Jan/Feb/Mar.
Westminster Kennel Show: Feb.
USA Indoor Track & Field Championships: Feb.
National Invitational Basketball Tournament: Mar.
International Horse Show: Oct/Nov.
Flushing Meadows Park, National Tennis Center: (1-718) 592-8000
US Open Tennis Championship: early Sept.

Ticket Agent

Mackey's, Inc.
1501 Broadway, Suite 1814. 840-2800. Well-established ticket agent for all sports events. Credit card charges on the phone. AE, DC, MC, V.
OPEN Mon-Sat 8am-8pm; Sun 9am-5pm.

Sports Activities

Archery
Comanche Bowman Club
160 72 Street, Brooklyn. (1-718) 745-9271. Private club for archery enthusiasts. Schedules archery tournaments and group events.
Safari Archery
86-15 Lefferts Boulevard, Brooklyn. (1-718) 441-8883; 649-5708. Range and pro shop. Professional instruction. Rentals.

—**Municipal Archery Ranges**

Outdoor archery ranges in the city's parks are open March-October. Broadhead arrows are prohibited by the Parks Department. Call for info.

Baseball
New York City has 2 professional baseball teams: the Yankees play at Yankee Stadium, Bronx (293-6000) and the Mets at Shea Stadium, Flushing, Queens (1-718) 507-8499. The baseball season begins around the first week in April and continues through mid-October. Call the stadiums for specific game or ticket information or check the local papers.

—**Municipal Baseball Diamonds**

There are hundreds of municipal baseball facilities in the city. A permit is required for use of a field. Call 397-3114, -3115 for details. For use of ballfields in Central Park, call 408-0213.

The following League Clubs will be able to give you information on current events and exhibition games of the major teams in the city.

American League of Professional Baseball Clubs
350 Park Avenue. 371-7600.
National League of Professional Baseball Clubs
350 Park Avenue. 371-7300.

Basketball

New York's professional basketball team is the New York Knickerbockers. Home court for the "Knicks" is Madison Square Garden (563-8000). The season starts in October and can run into June. The Garden is also the scene of a heavy college basketball schedule starting in Jan, including the National Invitational Tournament. The many college courts also provide action. Although the Nets have moved to New Jersey they still have a New York following. You can see their games at the Byrne Meadowlands Arena, East Rutherford, New Jersey. (1-201) 935-3900.

—Municipal Basketball Courts

Call the Parks Department for the outdoor or indoor basketball court nearest to you.

—Exhibition Basketball Games

Harlem Globetrotters
Madison Square Garden. 563-8000. A New York legend. Fun, frolic and comedy on a grand scale. Usually in Feb.
Harlem Wizards
757-6300. Exhibition team similar in style to the Harlem Globetrotters' comedy antics. Just as spunky, still unspoiled.

Bicycling

Central Park is closed to vehicular traffic on weekends, which permits the cyclist an exhaust-free course for pedaling. In addition there are 91.1 miles of Bikeways in New York City (every borough but Staten Island) including Broadway, West 59-23 Streets; Fifth Avenue, 23 Street-Waverly Place; Sixth Avenue, West 8-59 Streets; Brooklyn Bridge, Centre Street-Cadman Plaza East. Call the Department of Transportation for more information on existing bike lanes: 566-1517.
NOTE: The Metropolitan Transportation Authority prohibits carrying bicycles on subways, buses and the Metro-North commuter railroads.

—Bicycle Tours

Country Cycling Tours
140 West 83 Street. 874-5151. For carless city-dweller bikers. Whisks riders and bikes into the country for weekend or 4-10 day tours.
Hungry Pedalers
See SIGHTSEEING, Specialized Tours.
Transportation Alternatives
Bicycle lobbying group organizes free bike trips around the metropolitan area. Write for info: 2121 Broadway, New York, N.Y. 10023 or call 255-0971.

—Bicycle Rental & Instruction

Bicycles Metro
1311 Lexington Avenue at East 88 St. 427-4450. Three-speed and 10-speed rentals; repairs, parts and sales.
Bicycles Plus
1400 Third Avenue nr East 79 St. 794-2929. Also 204 East 85 Street. 794-2201. Three-speed bike rentals.
Broadway Bicycle
663 Amsterdam Avenue at West 92 St. 866-7600. Near Central Park—3-speed and 10-speed rentals; no deposit with "good" ID.
Dixon's Bicycle Shop
792 Union Street, Brooklyn. (1-718) 636-0067. Nearby to Prospect Park.
Pedal Pusher Bicycles
328 East 66 Street. 879-0740. Expert private lessons by appointment. Rentals of 3- and 10-speed bikes. Repairs; a full line of accessories for the bike and the biker. (Everything but bike sales.) *CLOSED Tues.*

Boating

Clove Lakes Park
Victory Boulevard & Clove Road, Staten Island. (1-718) 816-0324. Rent an aluminum rowboat. Must be over 16 with proof of age. Deposit required. *OPEN April-mid Oct, 7 days, 9am-6pm.*
Loeb Boathouse
Central Park, nr East 74 Street. 288-7281. Rent a boat for rowing. Must be over 16 years of age, with proof. Rather large deposit required. *OPEN April-Oct 7 days 9am-6pm.*
Pelham Bay Park
Hunter Island Lagoon, Bronx. 430-1890. The only regatta course in New York City for both canoeing and rowing. Competitions held by private rowing clubs during spring and summer. Call for details.

Boccie

There are 100 boccie courts in the city. Just a few are listed.
Annual Boccie Tournament: the 3rd weekend in August, Thompson Street Playground, at Spring Street. For details, call 661-5190.

Brooklyn

Bushwick Park
Knickerbocker & Irving Avenues. 2 boccie courts.
Byrne Memorial Park
3 Street & 4th Avenue. 2 boccie courts.
McCarren Park
Driggs Avenue & Lorimer Street. 4 boccie courts.
Playground
Shore Parkway & 17 Avenue. 2 boccie courts.

Manhattan

Culliver Park
East River & 125 Street. 8 boccie courts.
East River Park
At Broome Street. 3 boccie courts.
Highbridge Park
West 173 Street. 2 boccie courts.
Playground
Houston Street & First Avenue. 5 boccie courts.
Randalls Island
Sunken Meadow Park. 4 boccie courts.

Thompson Street Playground
95 Thompson Street at Spring Street. 2 boccie courts.

Wards Island
Recreation Area. 4 boccie courts.

Queens

Cunningham Park
196 Street & Union Turnpike, Flushing. 1 boccie court.

Flushing Meadows-Corona Park
2 boccie courts.

Highland Park
Lower Elton Street & Jamaica Avenue, Cypress Hills. 2 boccie courts.

Triborough Playground
66 East Hoyt Avenue, Long Island City. 2 boccie courts.

Staten Island

DeMatti Playground
Tompkins Avenue & Chestnut Street. 1 boccie court.

Stapleton Houses Playground
Tompkins Street & Tompkins Avenue, Stapleton. 1 boccie court.

Bowling

Fiesta Lanes
2826 Westchester Avenue, Bronx. 824-2600. Call for league or open bowling times, mainly during the day. *OPEN 7 days 9am-midnight.*

Madison Square Garden Bowling Center
4 Penn Plaza, West 31-West 33 Street at Seventh Avenue. 563-8160. Complete pro shop: resident pro. 48 lanes. Snack bar. *OPEN 7 days.* League bowling *4:30-10:30pm.* Open bowling *9:30am-4:30pm.*

Whitestone Lanes
30-05 Whitestone Parkway at Linden Place, Flushing, Queens. (1-718) 353-6300. Open bowling, 48 lanes. Snack bar on premises. *OPEN 7 days, 24 hours.*

—Bowling Instruction

National Bowling Recreation Arena, Inc.
270 Eighth Avenue nr West 23 St, 2nd fl. 242-7675. Instruction Sat. Call in advance to reserve.

Boxing

Major boxing events are held at Madison Square Garden. Children under 14 are not admitted. Call 563-8000 for details.

Gleason's Gym
252 West 30 Street, 2nd fl 947-3744. Well known for rigorous training and workout facilities. Will supply everything for the boxer, including a sparring partner. Come in just to watch; it's all from another time. Lessons for pros and amateurs. Nominal admission charge. *OPEN 7 days 10:30am-7:30pm.*

Gramercy Gym
116 East 14 Street. 473-8732. In business 50 years: 2 rings available for professional (serious) boxers. Sparring partners, equipment, lockers and Damon Runyon humor provided. *OPEN Mon-Fri 4-8pm.*

—Boxing Equipment
The best and the oldest wholesaler of equipment

to professional boxers and rings is Everlast. Call the Everlast Co. for nearest retail outlet. 993-0100.

Cricket

Below is a listing of some municipal cricket pitches in the city.

Flushing Meadows-Corona Park
Northeast of amphitheater. 1 cricket pitch.

Marine Park
Avenue U & Stuart Street, Brooklyn. 4 cricket pitches.

Red Hook Recreation Area Stadium
Bay & Columbia Streets, Brooklyn. 1 cricket pitch.

Van Cortlandt Park
Broadway & West 250 Street, Bronx. 10 cricket pitches.

Walker Park
Delafield Place, Bard & Davis Avenues, Staten Island. 1 cricket pitch.

Croquet

To play croquet on a municipal green you must obtain a permit. Season runs from April to October. Call 360-8204 for information.

New York Croquet Club
502 Park Avenue. 688-5495. An athletic and social club that uses the Croquet Green in Central Park's Sheep Meadow nr 69 Street. Permit for use of the green is purchased by the club. Club dues cover equipment and permit costs. National Croquet Championships in Sept and Tournaments in April.

Diving (Skin or Scuba)

Aqua Lung School of New York
1089 Second Avenue. 582-2800. Taught by Fran Gaar, TV's "Sea Hunt" diving adviser; 12 professional assistants. P.A.D.I. W-M#1; N.A.U.I.#6609. Semi-private classes, certifications. Pool at First Avenue & 88 Street.

Central Skindivers Discount Center
160-09 Jamaica Avenue, Jamaica, Queens. (1-718) 739-5772. (1-516) 826-8888. Diving on Long Island; class and private lessons.

Kings County Divers Corporation
3040 Avenue U, Brooklyn. (1-718) 648-4232. Scuba diving classes taught at indoor pools. Equipment, rental, sales and service.

Professional Dive Trips, Inc.
2417 Shore Parkway, Brooklyn. (1-718) 332-9574. Taught by diving expert Bill Reddan. Private group or semi-private lessons. Wreck trips, night dives, underwater photography, lobstering.

Scuba at the Exchange
Information hotline (1-718) 855-6761 for basic scuba lessons at convenient locations in Manhattan and Brooklyn.

Scuba World
167 West 72 Street, 2nd fl. 496-2220. Instructions, equipment rental, repair, sales. Travel too.

Fencing

—Fencing Instruction

Fencers Club, Inc.
174 West 71 Street. 977-4150; 874-9800 (eve-

nings). Est. 1880, it's America's oldest fencing club. Professional fencing championship competitors. For men and women all levels, all ages, group and individual. Call for appointment.

Santelli Salle D'Armes
40 West 27 Street. 683-2823. Expert instruction and outfitting.

McBurney YMCA
215 West 23 Street. 741-9216. For adults and teens, fencing taught by a pro. Free to members.

Fishing

In order to fresh-water fish in New York City, you must get a New York State fresh-water fishing license, for ages 16-70. You can obtain an application from tackle stores or the Department of Environmental Conservation, 488-2770. Salt water requires a line and reel only.
Check the Sports section on Friday of the Daily News *for what is "running" that particular week. Surf-casting can be done year round from any beach in the city without a license.*

—Municipal Park Fishing

Central Park
72 Street Lake. Filled with carp, catfish, bullheads. Harlem Meer, 110 Street: carp, catfish.

Kissena Park Lake
Rose Avenue & 160 Street, Flushing, Queens. Catfish.

Prospect Park Lake
Brooklyn. Designated areas. Catfish, carp.

Van Cortlandt Park
West 242 Street, east of Broadway. Catfish, bullheads.

Wolf's Pond
Wolf's Pond Park, Staten Island. Catfish, carp.

—Fishing Boats

City Island: *Miss City Island* 824-4234; *North Star* 822-0945; *Ebb Tide* 938-8929; *Apache* 885-2276. Sheepshead Bay: *Betty W. II* (1-718) 769-9815; *Dorothy B.* (1-718) 646-4057; *Flamingo III* (1-718) 891-3980; *Helen H.* (1-718) 646-7030; *Tampa 6* (1-718) 835-2812; *New Avenger* (1-718) 258-7070.

Flying

In order to fly a plane in the New York City area, you must have a single- or multi-engine license.

Academics of Flight
43-49 45 Street, Sunnyside, Queens. (1-718) 937-5716. FAA-approved ground school; will also arrange for flying lessons.

DeAngelo Aviation
MacArthur Airport, Islip, Long Island. (1-516) 588-2344. Learn both single- and multi-engine flying for licenses.

Safair Flying Service
Teterboro Airport, Teterboro, N.J. (1-201) 288-1720. Since 1929 this school has offered single- and multi-engine training for flight. Beginners taught in single-engine planes. VA FAA-approved school.

Football

New York has 2 professional football teams: the Jets *(421-6600) and the Giants, who play across the border in New Jersey's Giants Stadium, Meadowlands, East Rutherford. (1-201) 935-3900.*
The pro-football season extends from early September through December. College football is extremely popular, culminating in the Bowl Games on New Year's Day.
For ticket and game information, check the local newspapers or call the stadiums.

—Municipal Football Fields

There are hundreds of municipal football/soccer fields in New York City. Call your borough office for fields in your area.

Golf

There are 13 public golf courses within the 5 boroughs. Call the Department of Parks for tee-off waiting times. There is a small fee; discount for senior citizens. Instruction is usually available. The golf season runs from mid-March to October.

—Municipal Golf Courses

Bronx

Mosholu Golf Course
Van Cortlandt Park, Jerome Avenue nr Holly Lane. 822-4723. 5,231 yards.

Pelham Golf Course
Pelham Bay Park, Shore Road & Split Rock Road. 885-0838. 6,405 yards.

Split Rock Golf Course
Pelham Bay Park, Split Rock Road north of Bartow Circle. 885-0838. 6,462 yards.

Van Cortlandt Golf Course
Van Cortlandt Park, Park South and Bailey Avenue. 543-4595. 5,702 yards.

Brooklyn

Dyker Beach Park
Seventh Avenue & 86 Street. (1-718) 836-9722. 6,317 yards.

Marine Park
Flatbush Avenue bet Ave U & Belt Pkwy. (1-718) 338-7113. 6,736 yards.

Queens

Clearview Park
23rd Avenue & Willets Point Boulevard, Bayside. (1-718) 229-2570. 6,168 yards.

Douglaston Park
Commonwealth Boulevard & Marathon Parkway, Douglaston. (1-718) 224-6566. 6,314 yards.

Forest Park
Park Lane South, Forest Parkway, Main Drive & Interboro Parkway. (1-718) 296-2442. 5,492 yards.

Kissena Park
164 Booth Memorial Avenue, Flushing. (1-718) 445-3388. 4,367 yards.

Staten Island

LaTourette Park
Forest Hill & London Roads nr Richmond Hill Road. (1-718) 351-1840. 6,540 yards.

Silver Lake Park
Victory Boulevard & Park Road. (1-718) 447-5630. 5,891 yards.

South Shore Park
Huguenot Avenue & Rally Street. (1-718) 984-0108. 6,520 yards.

—Golfing Instruction

Al Lieber's World of Golf
147 East 47 Street. 242-2895 or 755-9398. Astro-turf putting green and instant-replay TV camera.

Galvano Golf Academy
Southgate Towers, 371 Seventh Avenue at West 31 Street (sub-basement). 736-4435, 458-0189. Group and private lessons from a pro who taught for the Italian Line.

Richard Metz's Golf Studio
35 East 50 Street. 759-6940. Practice cages, sand traps; instant-replay TV camera.

Gymnastics

Alex & Walter Physical Fitness, Inc.
30 West 56 Street, 3rd fl. 265-7270. The emphasis is on fitness through gymnastics for strength, coordination and balance.

Alzerreca's Gym
1 East 28 Street. 683-1703. Well-equipped gym. Professionally taught, grouped by ability and strength.

Kounovsky Physical Fitness Center
50 West 57 Street, 6th fl. 246-6415. Fitness through workouts on bars and rings. Classes every hour till 9pm.

McBurney YMCA
215 West 23 Street. 741-9216. Coordination, flexibility, strength taught in a coed class using Olympic regulation equipment. Year round. Free for members.

Handball
Handball is usually played on a 4-walled court. There are over 2,000 such municipal facilities throughout the boroughs. Call your local Parks Department office for one near you.

92nd Street YM-YWHA
1395 Lexington Avenue. 427-6000. Five 4-walled handball courts available on a first-come, first-served basis day and evening. Reservations accepted. Membership required.

Hockey
New York City has 2 professional hockey teams: the New York Rangers skate at Madison Square Garden, 564-4400; the Islanders at the Nassau Coliseum, Hempstead Turnpike, Uniondale, (1-516) 794-9100. The hockey season begins in October and ends in April. Catching the Rangers practicing can be fun. Call (1-914) 967-2040 for info.

Horseracing
New York's best-attended sport.

—Racetracks

Aqueduct
Rockaway Boulevard at 108 Street, Jamaica, Queens. (1-718) 641-4700. "Subway Special," a combination train and grandstand admission ticket to the "Big A." Non-stop service from 42 Street and Eighth Avenue. Mon-Fri 11am-1am; Sat 10:30am-1pm. Call (1-718) 330-1234 for exact details on travel. Thoroughbreds: race Jan-May; Oct-Dec.

Belmont Park
Hempstead Turnpike & Plainfield Avenue, Elmont, L.I. (1-718) 641-4700. Long Island Rail Road Special fare includes trip from Penn Station; Atlantic Avenue, Brooklyn; or Jamaica or Woodside, Queens; and discount admission to the park. On race days, trains leave 10:15am-1pm. For details, call (1-718) 739-4200. Thoroughbreds: race May-July, Sept-Oct. SPECIAL: Breakfast at Belmont. Trackside breakfast. Mini-train tour of paddock; watch the horses work out. *Mon-Fri 8-9:30am, Sat & Sun from 7am.* For info, call (1-718) 740-4400.

Meadowlands
Meadowlands, East Rutherford, N.J. (8 miles from Manhattan). (1-201) 935-8500.
Trotters: Jan-Aug.
Thoroughbreds: Sept-Dec.
Post time Mon-Sat 8pm.
Totally enclosed track, bleacher seats outside. The Pegasus restaurant, with lounge overlooking the races.
Transportation: Port Authority Bus Terminal, Eighth Avenue & West 41 Street, #77, Platform 233, every hour. 564-8484.

Roosevelt Raceway
Westbury, Long Island. (1-516) 222-2000.
Trotters: mid Jan-early March; mid Jun-mid Aug; mid Oct-mid Dec.
Transportation to the raceway: Long Island Rail Road Special fare includes round-trip ticket from Penn Station or Brooklyn Flatbush Ave Station, bus transportation from the station and back plus free admission to the grandstand. Weekdays bet 6:35 & 6:55pm; Sat bet 6:30 & 7:15pm. For details, call (1-718) 739-4200.

Yonkers Raceway
Yonkers, N.Y. (1-914) 968-4200.
Trotters: Mid Jan-March; mid June-July; Nov-Dec. Post time 8pm.
Transportation to the raceway: Port Authority Bus Terminal, Eighth Avenue & West 41 Street. 564-8484.

—Off-Track Betting (OTB)

Located throughout the city, OTB are convenient places to bet without going to the track. Call Customer Service, 704-5620, for details on how to bet, or stop in at any branch and pick up a pamphlet. Customer Service will also provide information on the OTB parlor nearest your location. *OPEN Mon-Fri 9am-5pm; Sat 9am-2pm.*

Dial-a-horse
Open an OTB telephone account to place bets on the phone. For information and application, call 704-5380.

Horseshoe Pitches
New York City has hundreds of horseshoe pitches throughout the boroughs. The best way to find the one closest to you is to call your borough's Parks and Recreation Department office.

Lacrosse
New York Lacrosse Club
111 West 57 Street. 247-4556. A top-notch lacrosse club that plays league games nationwide.
Membership dues required for the cost of equipment and playing fields. Call for schedule.

Lawn Bowling
*Seasonal permits are required to bowl on a muni-
cipal green. Inquire at the appropriate borough
office of the Parks Department.*

New York Lawn Bowling Club
988-3962. You must be a member in order to use
the Bowling Greens in Central Park.

Martial Arts
*(Jiu-Jitsu, judo, karate, Tai Chi Chuan.) Martial
Arts is an Eastern mix of physical training and
philosophy for self-defense and mental discipline.*

Eastern Karate Center, Inc.
1487 First Avenue nr East 77 St. 628-0661, 650-
1585. Good exhibition karate. Top qualified black-
belt teachers. Call for class or observation times.
McBurney YMCA
215 West 23 Street. 741-9210. Judo, karate, Iaido
for men and women.
Seido Karate
61 West 23 Street, 2nd fl. 924-0511. Self defense,
physical fitness, zen meditation. Classes early
am-evening 7 days a week.
Tai Chi Chuan Center of New York
1117 Sixth Avenue nr West 43 St. 221-6110. You
are welcome to come in and observe. Call for
class times.

Paddleball
*Paddleball can be played on 1 wall and requires
very little expense to play, which is one reason for
its popularity. There are over 400 paddleball
courts in the city. Call your borough Parks Department office for one nearest you.*

92nd Street YM-YWHA
1395 Lexington Avenue. 427-6000. Five 4-walled
courts are available for paddleball and are also
used to play handball. Call for details.
YMCA Central Queens
89-25 Parsons Blvd, Jamaica. (1-718) 739-6600.
Two 4-walled handball courts can be used to play
paddleball. Must be a member of the Y to play
here.

Polo
*Polo, long known as "the rich man's sport," is still
just that. There is only one polo club in the New
York area.*

Meadowbrook Polo Club
c/o Braunstein & Chernin, 50 East 42 Street, New
York, N.Y. 10017. 687-3939. The oldest polo club
in the United States. It operates out of Hicock's
Field, south of Route 25a, off Whitney Lane, Old
Westbury, Long Island. Practice sessions are
held every Tues & Thurs evenings at 5:30pm, Sat
at noon. Free to watch. Formal games are held

from the last Sun in May to mid-Oct, at Bethpage
State Park Polo Fields. Admission charge to park
and game; children under 12, free. To become a
member, call (1-516) 626-9790.

Racquetball
*One of the hottest sports in the United States.
Easier than tennis or squash to learn; requires
more skill than force.*

BQE Racquetball Club
26-50 Brooklyn-Queens Expressway West,
Woodside, Queens. (1-718) 726-4343. Seven-
teen racquetball courts, pro instruction, shop. Bar/
lounge; free nursery. Exercise room, complete
aerobic conditioning program; Nautilus. Membership only.
Courts of Appeal
300 West Service Road, Staten Island. (1-718)
698-4500. Fifteen racquetball courts; 5 Hartru
tennis courts. Daily round robbins; league play.
Manhattan Plaza Racquet Club
450 West 43 Street. 594-0554. This private club
offers 2 racquetball courts, lessons, a pro shop
and pool; 5 Elastoturf tennis courts. Open to the
public by appointment in advance without
membership.

Riding
—Riding Instruction
Claremont Riding Academy
175 West 89 Street. 724-5100. Manhattan's only
remaining riding academy for expert private &
group instruction, Western and English on indoor
ring. Annual show. Central Park's 6 miles of bridle
paths are 1½ blocks away for those qualified to
ride. Street-smart horses.
Clove Lake Stables, Inc.
1025 Clove Road, Staten Island. (1-718) 448-
1414. One of the oldest and most reputable
stables in New York. Good selection of horses and
English and Western instruction for children and
adults.
Cullmitt Stables
51 Caton Place, Brooklyn. (1-718) 438-8849. Lessons, outdoor ring; Prospect Park trails.
Cy's Pelham Parkway Riding Academy, Inc.
1680 Pelham Parkway, Bronx. 822-8510. Instruction for beginners and those who need a brushup.
Western only. Good riding facilities.
Jamaica Bay Riding Academy
7000 Shore Parkway, Brooklyn. (1-718) 531-
8949. Western and English lessons, indoors and
out. Rentals and trails (300 acres of riding land,
including some on the beach).
Lynn's Riding School
88-03 70th Road, Forest Hills, Queens. (1-718)
261-7679. Specializes in English riding. Forest
Park bridal paths. Indoors in winter. Lessons,
rental, boarding.
Pelham Bit Stables
9 Shore Road, Bronx. 885-9848. English and
Western riding. Trails along the waterfront.
Van Cortlandt Park Riding Academy
Broadway & West 254 Street, Bronx. 549-6200.

Specializes in English instruction. Lounge with fireplace.

West Shore Stables, Inc.
52 Hughes Avenue, Staten Island. (1-718) 698-0634. Western and English riding lessons. No rental.

Rugby

The Mad Hatter Pub
1485 Second Avenue nr East 77 St. 628-4917. Unofficial "headquarters" for New York rugby players.

New York Rugby Club
501 Fifth Avenue. 953-9054. Call for information.

Randalls Island .
Playing fields 100 yards to the right of ramp off the Triborough Bridge. *Games every Sat am, spring-late Fall.*

Running & Jogging

Call the Parks and Recreation Department office in your borough for the municipal running track nearest you.

McBurney YMCA
215 West 23 Street. 741-9216. This Y has many programs for the runner. Physical-fitness evaluation is given to test the amount of stress your heart can take. The best running track in New York (indoors); 20 laps equal a mile. Runners' clinic and a 100-, 250- and 500-mile jogging program for those who want to keep a record on their mileage.

Road Runners Club of New York
9 East 89 Street. 860-4455. The largest runners' club in the world; the sponsor of the New York City Marathon. Open to all who have run or wish to run the marathon. Runners' clinic, classes and "roadways" maps provided. Group runs in summer every Sat at 10am; Mon & Wed at 6:30pm. Club house *OPEN Mon-Fri 10am-8pm; Sat till 5pm; Sun till 3pm.*

Sailing

Bring Sailing Back, Inc.
Battery Park. 825-1976. Sail on the *Petrel,* a 70-ft yawl, the fastest sailboard in New York Harbor. Classes are given on a group basis in the spring and fall. Call for details.

Matterhorn Sports Club
3 West 57 Street. 486-0500. Club organizes weekend tours, parties, sailing trips, scuba diving and tennis days. Basically for singles.

New York Sailing School
340 Riverside Drive. 864-4472. Learn to sail, cruise or race on Long Island Sound.

Offshore Sailing School, Ltd.
190 East Schofield Street, City Island, Bronx. 885-0477. Offers sailing instruction to beginner, intermediate, and advanced students of the sea.

Skating

—Ice Skating
Allowed on natural-ice park lakes and ponds in all boroughs if we have a "hard freeze;" call 755-4100 for round-the-clock info on safe places to skate.

—Municipal Rinks
The following rinks are operated by the City Parks

Department. OPEN Nov-April. They tend to be cheaper than the rest but more crowded, especially on weekends.

Flushing Meadows Park (Indoor)
New York City Building, Long Island Expressway & Grand Central Parkway, Queens. (1-718) 699-4215.

Lasker Memorial Rink (Outdoor)
Central Park at 107 Street. 397-3142. Large outdoor rink. A lot of racing skaters here. *CLOSED Mon & Tues.*

Abe Stark Skating Rink (Indoor)
Boardwalk & West 19 Street, Coney Island, Brooklyn. (1-718) 266-7937. *CLOSED Mon & Tues.*

Staten Island War Memorial Park (Outdoor)
Victory Boulevard & Clove Road, Staten Island. (1-718) 720-1010.

Kate Wollman Memorial Rink (Outdoor)
Prospect Park, East Drive nr Lincoln Rd & Parkside Ave, Brooklyn. (1-718) 965-6561. Speed- & figure-skating sessions nightly. *CLOSED Mon & Tues.*

Wollman Memorial Rink
Central Park, East 64 Street. This rink, which used to draw 100,000 skaters a season, has been closed for reconstruction since 1980 for what was supposed to be one season. As of this 1985 writing, no reopening has been set. When it *finally* does reopen it will be a year-round facility, functioning as a reflecting pool in spring and summer, overlooked by a glass-enclosed restaurant. For update call 408-0100.

—Other Rinks
Ice Studio
1034 Lexington Avenue nr East 74 St, 2nd fl. 535-0304. Primarily for kids. Private lessons year round; groups Sept-June. *OPEN 7 days.*

Rockefeller Skating Pond
2 Rockefeller Plaza, Fifth Avenue nr 51 St. 757-5731. Very busy, highly visible outdoor rink. Private lessons available for those who don't mind an audience. Rental and free checking. *OPEN 7 days 9am-11:30pm.*

Sky Rink
450 West 33 Street, 16th fl. 695-6556. City skating year round on Olympic-size rink in an office building. Excellent skate shop, group and private lessons, coffee shop. *Fri and Sat nights 8-10pm. Tues live organ music for over-18-year olds.*

Waterside Skating Rink
15 Waterside Plaza. 889-9180. Skating; rentals. *OPEN Mon-Fri noon-9:30pm; Sat & Sun from 10am.*

—Roller Skating
Roller skating is a year-round sport. Central Park affords 31 miles of paved walkways on which to skate.

Central Park
Mineral Springs Building, West 72 Street. 861-1818. Skate rental in the park. Two pieces of ID required, $5 deposit. *OPEN March-Nov, Mon-Fri 10am-5:30pm, Sat 10am-6:30pm.*

Lezly Dance & Skate School
622 Broadway nr Bleecker Street. 245-6033.
Roller-skating specialists—disco, jazz, figure and
free-style. Private or group lessons, outdoor and
indoor.

Village Skating
15 Waverly Place. 677-9690; for hours call 474-
9200. Indoors in Greenwich Village. Skating;
rental; available for private parties. Wed is ladies
night. *OPEN Tues-Thurs 8pm-midnight; Fri
9:30pm-1am; Sat 1-5pm, 8pm-midnight; Sun 1-
5pm.*

Skiing

—Cross-Country Skiing

*Flat-surface skiing requires untrampled snow and
more physical stamina than its more popular relative, downhill skiing. The following provide opportunities for cross-country skiing in the city.*

Bronx
Van Cortlandt Park
Jerome Ave & Holly Lane. Vast terrain, un-
trampled and smooth.

Brooklyn
Prospect Park
Flatbush Avenue & Empire Boulevard. Get there
early for smooth surface.

Queens
Alley Pond Park
Grand Central Parkway & Winchester Boulevard.
Douglaston.

—Downhill Skiing

One of the more popular winter sports.

Ski Condition Reports
Connecticut: (1-203) 307-5780.
Maine: (1-207) 289-2423.
Massachusetts: (1-800) 628-5030.
New Hampshire: (1-800) 258-3608.
New Jersey: (1-201) 827-3900.
New York: (1-800) 225-5697.
Pennsylvania: (1-717) 421-5565.
Vermont: (1-802) 229-0531.

Scandinavian
40 West 57 Street. 757-8524. Ski shop, tours and
rentals.

Skiers Express
596-4227. Regularly scheduled trips to Hunter
Mountain.

Sporthaus
1627 Second Avenue at East 85 St. 734-7677.
Instructional ski trips to Mount Killington, Hunter
and Bellaire for small groups interested in learning
how to ski, beginners, intermediate, advanced.

Soccer

*Popularized by master player-showman Pele, this
sport has caught on in New York. The New York
Cosmos draw the fans to New Jersey's Meadowlands. For details, call (1-201) 935-3900.*
*A season permit is required by the Parks and
Recreation Department if you wish to play soccer
on any of the park fields. Call 360-8100.*

—Municipal Soccer Fields

Bronx
Van Cortlandt Park Parade Field
250 Street & Broadway. 822-4599. 7 fields.

Brooklyn
Red Hook Recreation Area Center
Bay & Columbia Streets. (1-718) 965-6518. 2 soc-
cer fields, one lighted.

Manhattan
Central Park: Great Lawn
West 81 Street. 397-3110. 1 soccer field.
Central Park: North Meadow
97 Street. 3 soccer fields.

Queens
Alley Pond Park
Springfield Boulevard & Union Turnpike, Queens
Village. (1-718) 520-5328. 1 soccer field.

Softball

*Softball can be played on the baseball diamonds
in the city. A permit is required. (See Baseball.)
Call your borough Parks and Recreation office for
fields near you. There are 656 softball fields in the
city. For a permit to use the ball fields in Central
Park, call 408-0213.*

Squash

Fifth Avenue Racquet Club
404 Fifth Avenue nr 37 St. 594-3120. Complete
squash facilities and lessons for men and women.
Nautilus center. *Membership only.*

New York Health & Racquet Club
20 East 50 Street. 593-1500. Good facilities and
extras like a sauna, steam room and exercise
room. *Membership only.*

Park Avenue Squash & Racquet Club
3 Park Avenue nr East 34 St. 686-1085. Good
facilities. 10 courts. Lessons for men and women.
Open to non-members on an hourly basis.

Park Place Squash Club
25 Park Place nr Church Street. 964-2677.
Squash instruction and games on 5 courts. Men
and women. *Open to the public on an hourly basis.*

Uptown Racquet Club & Fitness Center
151 East 86 Street. 860-8630. Fourteen squash
courts. Lessons by professionals. Restaurant,
sauna, lockers, pro shop. Nautilus and exercise.
Members only.

West Side YMCA
5 West 63 Street. 787-4400. 2 squash courts,
lessons available. Also, racquetball court and 3
handball courts.

Swimming

—Municipal Swimming Pools

*Outdoor pools are open Memorial Day through to
Labor Day. Indoor pools are open year round.*

Bronx
Outdoor
Claremont Park
170 Street & Clay Avenue. 822-4834. 75 by 60 ft.
Crotona Park
173 Street & Fulton Avenue. 822-4440. 120 by
330 ft.

Haffen Park
Ely & Hammersley Avenues. 822-4834. 75 by 60 ft.
John Mullay Park
164 Street at Jerome & River Avenues. 822-4834. 75 by 60 ft.
Van Cortlandt Park
244 Street east of Broadway. 549-6494. 164 by 104 ft.
Indoor
St. Mary's Recreation Center
St. Ann's Avenue & East 145 Street. 822-4681. 75 by 40 ft.

Brooklyn
Outdoor
Betsy Head Pool
Betsy Head Memorial Playground. Hopkinson & Dumont Avenues. (1-718) 965-6581. 165 by 330 ft.
Kosciusko Street Pool
Marcy & DeKalb Avenues. (1-718) 965-6585. 75 by 60 ft.
McCarren Pool
McCarren Park, Driggs Avenue & Lorimer Street. (1-718) 965-6580. 165 by 330 ft.
Red Hook Recreation Area Pool
Bay & Henry Streets. (1-718) 965-6579. 160 by 330 ft.
Sunset Park Pool
Seventh Avenue & 43 Street. (1-718) 965-6578. 165 by 256 ft.
Indoor
Brownsville Playground Recreation Center
Linden Boulevard & Stone Avenue. (1-718) 965-6583. 75 by 30 ft.
Metropolitan Avenue Pool
Metropolitan & Bedford Avenues. (1-718) 965-6576. 75 by 30 ft.
St. John's Park
1251 Prospect Place nr Troy & Schenectady Aves. (1-718) 965-6574. 75 by 42 ft.

Manhattan
Outdoor
Carmine Street Pool
Clarkson Street & Seventh Avenue South. 397-3147. 50 by 100 ft.
East 23rd Street Pool
Playground at Asser Levy Place. 397-3184. 47 by 115 ft.
Highbridge Park Pool
Amsterdam Avenue & West 173 Street. 397-3187. 165 by 228 ft.
Jackie Robinson Pool
Bradhurst Avenue & West 145 Street. 397-3147. 81 by 235 ft.
John Jay Park Pool
East 77 Street nr York Avenue. 397-3159. 50 by 145 ft.
Loula D. Lasker Memorial Pool
Harlem Meer, West 106 Street in Central Park. 397-3142. 225 by 106 ft.
Marcus Garvey Park
Madison Avenue & East 124 Street. 397-3142. 75 by 60 ft.

Sheltering Arms Park
West 129 Street & Amsterdam Avenue. 397-3172. 75 by 60 ft.
Sen. Robert F. Wagner Houses Playground
East 124 Street bet First & Second Aves. 397-3141. 75 by 60 ft.
Thomas Jefferson Park Pool
East 111 Street & First Avenue. 397-3140. 100 by 246 ft.
West 59th Street Pool
West 59 Street & West End Avenue. 397-3170. 75 by 100 ft.
Indoor
Carmine Street Gymnasium & Pool
Clarkson Street & Seventh Avenue South. 397-3147. 70 by 20 ft.
East 23rd Street Pool
East 23 Street & Asser Levy Place. 397-3184. 60 by 30 ft.
Gymnasium & Pool
342 East 54 Street at First Avenue. 397-3148. 54 by 50 ft. Diving permitted. Free Aquatics program, call 507-2123 for details.
Gymnasium & Pool
West 59 Street bet 10 & 11 Avenues. 397-3170. 60 by 34 ft.
Gymnasium & Pool
35 West 134 Street. 397-3193. 75 by 45 ft.

Queens
Outdoor
Astoria Park Pool
19 Street & 23 Drive, Astoria. (1-718) 520-5360. 165 by 330 ft.
Flushing Meadows-Corona Park Amphitheater
Long Island Expressway & Grand Central Parkway. (1-718) 699-4228. 70 by 145 ft.
Liberty Park
172 Street south of Liberty Avenue, Jamaica. (1-718) 520-5324. 75 by 60 ft.

Staten Island
Outdoor
Faber Park Pool
Faber Street & Richmond Terrace, Port Richmond. (1-718) 442-1524. 75 by 140 ft.
Hylan Boulevard Pool
Hylan Boulevard & Joline Avenue, Tottenville. (1-718) 442-7640. 75 by 60 ft.
Lyons Pool
Victory Boulevard & Murray Hulbert Avenue, Tompkinsville. (1-718) 442-8981. 100 by 165 ft.
West Brighton Pool
Broadway & Henderson Avenue, West Brighton. (1-718) 448-9848. 75 by 60 ft.

—Other Swimming Pools
Parc Swim & Health Club
363 West 56 Street. 586-3675. Co-ed, for members only, a 60-foot pool; free classes. Nautilus, steam room, sauna. *OPEN 24 hours.*
Sheraton City Squire
790 Seventh Avenue nr West 51 St. 581-3300. 48 by 24 ft. Dressing rooms. Indoor pool, outdoor sundeck. Admission charge; children half price. *OPEN year round 7 days 7:30am-8pm.*

Tennis
New York is the scene of the US Open Championships (early Sept) at the National Tennis Center at Flushing Meadows Park, Flushing, Queens. (1-718) 271-5100.

In order to play tennis on a municipal court during the season (early April-end Nov), you must get a season's permit from the Arsenal, 830 Fifth Avenue at 64 Street, 360-8204, Mon-Fri, 9am-4pm. You must register a week in advance and bring a passport or similar-type photo with you.

—Municipal Tennis Courts

Bronx

Bronx Park
Bronx Park East & Brady Avenue. 822-4624. 6 hard courts.

Crotona Park
East 173 Street & Crotona Avenue. 822-4502. Lockers, 5 hard and 20 clay courts.

Mullaly Park
164 Street & Jerome Avenue. 822-4382. Lockers, 8 bubbled hard courts, 7 clay courts.

Pelham Bay Park: Rice Stadium
Bruckner Boulevard & Middletown Road. 822-4834. 10 hard courts. No permit necessary weekdays.

St. James Park
Jerome Avenue & 193 Street. 822-4271. 8 clay courts.

Van Cortlandt Park-Woodlawn
233 Street & Jerome Avenue. 8 clay courts, lockers.

Williamsbridge Oval
208 Street & Bainbridge Avenue. 822-4508. 8 hard courts.

Brooklyn

Bensonhurst Park
Cropsey Avenue & Bay Parkway. (1-718) 965-6525. 8 hard courts.

Fort Hamilton Parkway
Ft. Hamilton Parkway & 95 Street. (1-718) 965-6528. 10 hard courts.

Gravesend Playground
18 Avenue & 56 Street. (1-718) 965-6575. 8 hard courts.

Kaiser Playground
Neptune Avenue & 25 Street. (1-718) 965-6548. 12 hard courts.

Kelly Memorial Playground
Avenue S & 14 Street. (1-718) 965-6589. 7 hard courts.

Leif Ericson Park
Eighth Avenue & 66 Street. (1-718) 965-6528. 9 hard courts.

Marine Park
Filmore Avenue & Stuart Street. (1-718) 965-6551. 12 hard courts.

McCarren Park
Driggs Avenue & Lorimer Street. (1-718) 965-6580. 7 hard courts.

McKinley Park
Seventh Avenue & 75 Street. (1-718) 965-6528. 9 clay courts.

Parade Ground
Coney Island & Caton Avenues. (1-718) 438-3435. 10 bubble-topped courts.

Playground
Bay 8 Street & Cropsey Avenue. (1-718) 965-6528. 9 hard courts.

Playground
Linden Boulevard & Vermont Street. (1-718) 257-9678. 8 clay courts.

Manhattan

Central Park
West 94 Street & West Drive. 397-3138. Locker facilities. 30 courts, 4 all weather, 26 clay.

East River Park
Broome Street. 397-3175. 12 hard courts.

Fort Washington Park
Riverside Drive & West 172 Street. 397-3188. 10 hard courts.

Inwood Park
West 207 Street & Seaman Avenue. 567-5000. 9 hard courts.

Playground
West 151 Street nr Seventh Avenue. 868-3330. 8 hard courts.

Randalls Island
860-1827. 4 bubble-topped hard courts, 11 clay courts.

Riverside Park
Riverside Park & West 96 Street. 397-3150. 10 hard courts.

Riverside Park
Riverside Park & West 119 Street. 397-3150. 10 clay courts.

Queens

Alley Pond Park
Grand Central Parkway & Winchester Blvd, Queens Village. (1-718) 465-9706. Lockers, 15 hard courts.

Astoria Park
21 Street & Hoyt Avenue, Astoria. (1-718) 520-5378. 14 hard courts.

Crocheron Park
215 Place & 33 Road, Bayside. (1-718) 520-5367. 10 hard courts.

Cunningham Park
Union Turnpike & 196 Street, Hollis. (1-718) 520-5319. Lockers, 20 hard courts.

Edgemere
Alameda Avenue nr Beach 51-54 Streets, Rockaway. (1-718) 634-7065. 8 clay courts.

Flushing Memorial Park
149 Street & 25 Avenue, Flushing. (1-718) 520-5367. 8 clay courts.

Forest Park
Park Lane South & 89 Street, Woodhaven. (1-718) 520-5350. Lockers, 7 hard and 7 clay courts.

Highland Park Lower Playground
Jamaica Avenue & Elton Street. Cypress Hills. (1-718) 520-5355. 13 hard and 13 clay courts.

Juniper Valley Park
62 Avenue & 180 Street, Middle Village. (1-718) 520-5362. 8 hard courts.

Kissena Park
Rose & Oak Avenues, Flushing. (1-718) 520-5359. 4 hard and 8 fast-dry courts.

Liberty Park
Liberty Avenue & 173 Street, Jamaica. (1-718) 520-5357. 10 hard courts.

Staten Island

Silver Lake Park
Hart Boulevard & Revere Street. (1-718) 447-9720. 4 clay courts.

Walker Park
Bard Avenue & Delafield Place. (1-718) 442-9696. 6 hard courts.

—Other Tennis Courts

NOTE: *Tennis is the most expensive racquet sport.*

Alley Pond Indoor Tennis
Winchester Boulevard, Grand Central Parkway, Queens Village. (1-718) 468-4420. 6 indoor hard courts; 16 outdoor courts. *OPEN end Oct-early April 24 hours (winter season).*

Boulevard Gardens Tennis
51-26 Broadway, Woodside, Queens. (1-718) 545-7774. 6 clay courts. Lessons available. *OPEN 7 days 7am-11pm.*

Brooklyn Racquet Club
2781 Shell Road, Brooklyn. (1-718) 769-5167. 11 indoor Hartru and 3 outdoor courts. *OPEN 7am-midnight.*

Crosstown Tennis Development Clinics
14 West 31 Street. 947-5780. 4 Elasturf courts. *OPEN 6am-midnight.* Book in advance.

East River Tennis Club
44-02 Vernon Boulevard, Long Island City, Queens. (1-718) 937-2381. Largest tennis facility in the city. 22 Hartru and Omni courts. Sauna, whirlpool, Nautilus. Minibus service to Manhattan.

East Side Tennis, Ltd.
177 East 84 Street. 472-9114. Professional teachers, instructional courts with ball machine for continuous swing practice. Pride themselves as a developmental facility with very good results. *OPEN 7 days 9am-10pm.*

Midtown Tennis Club
341 Eighth Avenue at West 27 St. 989-8572. 8 Hartru courts. *OPEN 7 days 7am-midnight.*

Paerdegat Racquet Club
1500 Paerdegat Avenue North, Brooklyn. (1-718) 531-1111. 8 Elasturf courts. Lessons. Daily junior program. *OPEN 7 days 7am-midnight.*

Richmond Tennis Club
2282 Forest Avenue, Staten Island. (1-718) 727-6787. 5 Plexi-cushioned, 4 Hartru courts.

Stadium Tennis Center
11 East 162 Street nr Jerome Ave, Bronx. 293-2386. 8 indoor Elasturf courts. *OPEN 7 days a week. 24 hours a day. Oct-early May.*

Sterling Tennis
40-15 126 Street, Corona, Queens. (1-718) 446-5419. 8 Hartru courts. Lessons. *OPEN 7 days 9am-10pm.*

Sutton East Tennis Club
488 East 60 Street. 751-3452. 8 clay courts, 1 bubble. Has Manhattan's largest junior development program. *OPEN 7 days 7am-midnight.*

Tennis Club of Staten Island
261 Graham Avenue, New Springville, Staten Island. (1-718) 698-6474. 7 clay courts. Lessons. *OPEN 7 days, 8am-11pm.*

Tennis Club
15 Vanderbilt Avenue over Grand Central Station. 687-3841. Oldest indoor facility. 2 Elasturf courts. *OPEN 7 days 8am-10pm.*

Tennisport, Inc.
51-24 Second Street nr Borden Avenue, Long Island City, Queens. (1-718) 392-1880. There are 16 indoor courts and 14 outdoor courts of mixed surfaces. Lessons. *OPEN Mon-Fri 8am-10pm; Sat & Sun till 8pm.*

Wall Street Racquet Club
Piers 13-14, East River. 952-0760. 9 Hartru tennis courts. *OPEN 7 days 6am-1am.*

Volleyball

The 1984 Olympics gave this sport new life. There are more than 330 volleyball courts in New York City. Call your borough Parks Department office for one nearest you.

Windsurfing

Offshore Sailing Center
190 East Schofield Street, City Island, Bronx. 885-0477. Windsurfing lessons and a shop for all the equipment you may need.

Sunshine Sailboarding Center
1516 Outlook Avenue, Bronx. 823-3847. Sail-rider certified instruction. Lessons, rentals, sales.

Wrestling

Madison Square Garden has championship, professional and exhibition wrestling matches one weekend a month. Call 564-4400 for further details.

McBurney YM-YWCA
215 West 23 Street. 741-9216. Classes for beginners and better wrestlers. Free-style wrestling taught by National YMCA Wrestling Champ.

92nd Street YM-YWHA
1395 Lexington Avenue. 427-6000. Free-style wrestling taught. Coed classes.

Yoga

Integral Yoga Institute
500 West End Avenue nr West 84 Street; 227 West 13 Street. 929-0585. Beginners, intermediate, advanced; relaxation, posture, meditation, breathing.

Sivananda Yoga Vedanta, Inc.
243 West 24 Street. 255-4560. Small instructional groups. From breathing exercises to the yoga postures. Meditation as well. Two-hour sessions.

Yoga Society of New York
94 Fulton Street, 4th fl. 233-3887. Relaxation, breathing exercises and yoga taught as an alternate lifestyle along with meditation and philosophy.

Yoga Studios of New York
351 East 84 Street. 988-9474. Basic Hatha (physical) yoga. Must be in good condition to appreciate this course. Call for class information.

Entertainment

Carnegie Hall

Tickets

Tickets can be bought in advance by mail or in person at the box office. Most theaters will take telephone orders and charge to a major credit card. The New York Times', Friday Weekend section lists ticket availability for Broadway shows Fri, Sat, Sun. Below are four discount ticket booths which sell half-price tickets for Broadway and Off-Broadway shows as well as music and dance performances, same day only. Be prepared to line up and have alternate selections as shows may be sold out as the line progresses. (There are two transactions a minute at TKTS!)

Times Square Theater Center (TKTS)
West 47 Street & Broadway. Recorded info about the booth only 354-5800. Same-day evening performances: *Mon-Sat 11am-5:30pm*. Matinee performances: *Wed & Sat noon-2pm*. Sun matinee & evening performances: *noon-8pm*.

Lower Manhattan Theater Center
#2 World Trade Center mezzanine. Taped info 354-5800. Same day evening performances: *Mon-Sat 11am-5:30pm*. Matinee & Sun performances: *sold one day prior to performance*.

Fulton Mall Theater Center
Albee Square Mall, Fulton Street & DeKalb Avenue, Brooklyn. Taped info (1-718) 625-5015. Same day evening performances: *Mon-Sat 11am-5:30pm*. Matinee & Sun performances: *sold one day prior to performance date* (also sold here, full price advance tickets to Brooklyn music, theater and dance).

Music & Dance Booth
Bryant Park, West 42 Street bet Fifth & Sixth Avenues. Taped info on availability (after 12:30pm) 382-2323. Same day evening performances for music and dance throughout the city; *Tues, Thurs & Fri noon-2pm, 3-7pm; Wed & Sat 11am-2pm, 3-7pm; Sun noon-6pm. Mon tickets are sold on Sun.*

Ticketron Outlets
977-9020. Tickets for Broadway shows, special events and concerts. Service charge per ticket. There are over 100 locations including:
Grand Central Station, East 42 Street & Lexington Avenue.
J&R Music World, 33 Park Row, opp. City Hall. 732-8600.
Macy's Herald Square, enter West 34 Street & Seventh Avenue.

Chargit
944-9300. Order tickets by phone for many Broadway and Off-Broadway shows, and charge to major credit cards. Service charge per ticket. *Mon-Fri 9am-10pm, Sat 10am-8pm, Sun 10am-pm.*

Broadway

Theater in New York has traditionally referred to Broadway, the "Great White Way," but in recent years Off-Broadway theater has come of age. Often thought of as more experimental, adventurous and independent. Many of Broadway's brightest lights in recent years were kindled Off Broadway.

Even more avant-garde is the emerging Off-Off-Broadway scene: unconventional in setting—church basements, coffeehouses, converted lofts—and in performance structure. Often actors work for free, and admission is a donation. For info call the Off-Off-Broadway Alliance, 757-4473, Mon-Fri 10am-6pm.

For current theater and movie information available see The New Yorker, New York *magazine,* The New York Times, Friday Weekend *section, and Sunday* Times, Arts and Leisure *section. For Off-Broadway, the* Village Voice *is best.*
NOTE: Stubs, $3.95, *has the seating plans for all of New York's theaters, stadiums and music halls.*

Ambassador Theater
219 West 49 Street. 541-6490.
Ethel Barrymore Theater
243 West 47 Street. 239-6200.
Belasco Theater
111 West 44 Street. 239–6200.
Bijou Theater
209 West 45 Street. 221-8500.
Biltmore Theater
261 West 47 Street. 582-5340.
Booth Theater
222 West 45 Street. 239-6200.
Broadhurst Theater
235 West 44 Street. 239-6200.
Broadway Theater
1681 Broadway nr West 53 St. 239-6200.

Brooks Atkinson Theater
256 West 47 Street. 245-3430.
Century Theater
235 West 46 Street. 354-6644.
Circle in the Square
1633 Broadway, enter West 50 St. 581-0720.
Cort Theater
138 West 48 Street. 239-6200.
Edison Theater
240 West 47 Street. 757-7164.
Eugene O'Neill Theater
230 West 49 Street. 246-0220.
46th Street Theater
226 West 46 Street. 221-1211.
Gershwin
222 West 51 Street. 586-6510.
Golden Theater
252 West 45 Street. 239-6200.
Helen Hayes Theater
240 West 44 St. 944-9450.

Helen Hayes Theater
(formerly the Little Theater)

Imperial Theater
249 West 45 Street. 239-6200.
Longacre Theater
220 West 48 Street. 239-6200.
Lunt-Fontanne Theater
205 West 46 Street. 575-9200.
Lyceum Theater
152 West 46 Street. 664-9708.
Majestic Theater
247 West 44 Street. 239-6200.
Mark Hellinger Theater
237 West 51 Street. 757-7064.
Martin Beck Theater
302 West 45 Street. 246-6363.
Minskoff Theater
200 West 45 Street. 869-0550.
Music Box Theater
239 West 45 Street. 246-4636.
Neil Simon Theater
250 West 52 Street. 757-8646.
New Apollo Theater
234 West 43 Street. 921-8558.

Newhouse Theater
Lincoln Center, 150 West 65 Street. 799-9100.
Palace Theater
1564 Broadway nr West 47 St. 757-2626.
Playhouse Theater
359 West 48 Street. 541-9820.
Plymouth Theater
236 West 45 Street. 730-1760.
Princess Theater
200 West 48 Street. 586-3903.
Royale Theater
242 West 45 Street. 239-6200.
St. James Theater
246 West 44 Street. 398-0280.
Shubert Theater
225 West 44 Street. 239-6200.
Trafalgar Theater
209 West 41 Street. 921-8000.
Uris Theater
1633 Broadway, enter West 50 St. 586-6510.
Virginia Theater
245 West 52 Street. 977-9370.
Vivian Beaumont Theater
Lincoln Center, 150 West 65 Street. 874-6770.
Winter Garden Theater
1634 Broadway nr West 51 St. 239-6200.

Off Broadway

Abbey Theater
136 East 13 Street. 677-4120.
American Place Theater
111 West 46 Street. 279-4200.
Astor Place Theater
434 Lafayette Street. 254-4370.
Ballroom Theater
253 West 28 Street. 594-0326.
Beacon Theater
Broadway & West 74 Street. 724-9500.
Samuel Beckett
410 West 42 Street. 594-2826.
Bouwerie Lane Theater
330 Bowery at Bond Street. 677-0060.
John Cazale Theater
2162 Broadway at West 76 Street. 580-1313.
Circle in the Square Downtown
159 Bleecker Street nr Thompson Street. 254-6330.
Circle Repertory
99 Seventh Avenue South nr West 4 Street. 924-7100.
Cherry Lane Theater
38 Commerce Street nr Bleecker Street. 989-2020.
Harold Clurman Theater
412 West 42 Street. 594-2370.
Downstairs City Center
135 West 55 Street. 246-8997.
Duplex
55 Grove Street. 255-5438.
Eastside Playhouse/Light Opera
334 East 74 Street. 861-2288.
Ensemble Studio
549 West 52 Street. 247-4982.

Entermedia Theater
189 Second Avenue nr East 11 Street. 475-4191.
Douglas Fairbanks
432 West 42 Street. 239-4321.
Folksbeine
123 East 55 Street. 755-2231.
Greene Street Café
101 Greene Street. 925-2415.
Hartley House Theater
413 West 46 Street. 246-9872.
Hudson Guild Theater
441 West 26 Street. 760-9810.
Inter Art
549 West 52 Street. 279-4200.
Lambs Theater
130 West 44 Street. 997-1780.
Lucille Lortel
121 Christopher Street nr Hudson St. 924-8782.
Manhattan Theater Club
321 East 73 Street. 472-0600.
Mirror Theater
St. Peters Church, East 54 Street & Lexington Avenue. 223-6440.
Ohio Theater
54 Greene Street. 226-7341.
Park Royal Theater
23 West 73 Street. 787-3980.
Perry Street Theater
31 Perry Street. 255-9186.
Phoenix Theater
221 East 71 Street. 730-0794.
Players
115 MacDougal Street. 254-5076.
Playwrights Horizons Main Stage
416 West 42 Street. 279-4200.
Promenade Theater
2162 Broadway at West 76 St. 580-1313.
Provincetown Playhouse
133 MacDougal Street. 777-2571.
Public Theater
425 Lafayette Street nr Astor Pl. 598-7150. Quiktix: For all Joseph Papp's Shakespeare Festival Public Theater attractions, reduced-price tickets on sale at *1pm for matinees, 6pm for evening performances.*

Public Theater

Quaigh Theater
108 West 43 Street. 221-9088.
Roundabout Theater
100 East 17 Street. 420-1360.
South Street
424 West 42 Street. 279-4200.

Sullivan Street Playhouse
181 Sullivan Street nr Bleecker St. 674-3838. For *The Fantasticks,* world's longest-running musical play (26 years).
Theater East
211 East 60 Street. 838-0177.
Theater Four
424 West 55 Street. 246-8545.
Top of the Gate
160 Bleecker Street nr Thompson Street. 982-9292.
Westbeth Theater Center
151 Bank Street. 691-2272.
West Side Arts Theater
407 West 43 Street. 541-8394.

Dance

Dance flourishes in New York year round. Check the papers for current programs.

Brooklyn Academy of Music
30 Lafayette Avenue, Brooklyn. (1-718) 636-4100. The Pennsylvania Dance Company in residence spring and fall. Many other American companies appear during the year.
Brooklyn Center for the Performing Arts
Brooklyn College, Campus Road off Flatbush Avenue, Brooklyn. (1-718) 434-1900. Gaining recognition as important dance theater. Emphasis on American dance. *Sept-May.*
City Center
131 West 55 Street. 246-8989. Busy ballet theater. The following appear on a regular basis: the Joffrey Ballet, *March & Oct;* Paul Taylor Dance Company, *April;* Alvin Ailey American Dance Theater, *early May & end of Nov.*
Danspace
St. Marks Church, Second Avenue & East 10 Street. 674-8112. Where Isadora Duncan and Martha Graham once danced. Presents some of the most adventurous dance today.
Dance Theater Workshop (DTW)
Bessie Schoenberg Theater, 219 West 19 Street. 924-0077. In Chelsea; the country's most active dance theater.
The Joyce Theater
175 Eighth Avenue at West 18 Street. 242-0800. Home of the Eliot Feld Ballet and other modern companies.
Metropolitan Opera House
Lincoln Center, Broadway & West 64 Street. 799-3100. American Ballet Theater: *new season every spring.* Also Summer Dance features visiting national ballet companies.
New York State Theater
Lincoln Center, Broadway & West 64 Street. 870-5570. New York City Ballet: *May-July, mid Nov-mid Feb.*

Opera

After Dinner Opera Company
A movable feast of American opera only. Call for program and place. 477-6212.

Amato Opera
319 Bowery nr East 4 St. 228-8200. Since 1947.
Season: *Sept-June*.

Bel Canto Opera
220 East 76 Street. 535-5231. Victor Herbert revival *every June*.

Light Opera of Manhattan
334 East 74 Street. 861-2288. Light opera all *year round*.

Metropolitan Opera Company
Metropolitan Opera House, Lincoln Center, Broadway & West 64 Street. 799-3100. New Season: *Sept-May*.

New York City Opera
New York State Theater, Lincoln Center, Broadway & West 64 Street. 870-5570. A 20-week opera season *July-Nov;* musical theater for 5 weeks *Feb-March*.

Concert Halls

Alice Tully Hall
Broadway at West 65 Street. 362-1911.

Amato Opera Theater
319 Bowery nr East 2 Street. 228-8200.

The Apollo
253 West 125 Street. 749-5838.

Avery Fisher Hall
Broadway at West 65 Street. 874-2424.

Bargemusic Ltd.
Fulton Ferry Landing, Brooklyn. (1-718) 624-4061.

Beacon Theater
Broadway at West 74 Street. 874-1717.

Bloomingdale House of Music
323 West 108 Street. 663-6021.

Brooklyn Academy of Music (BAM)
30 Lafayette Avenue, Brooklyn. (1-718) 636-4100. Bus Express to and from Brooklyn from Manhattan. Call for details.

Carnegie Hall & Carnegie Recital Hall
154 West 57 Street. 247-7459.

Greenwich House Music School
46 Barrow Street nr Seventh Ave. South. 242-4770.

Juilliard School Theater
144 West 66 Street. 799-5000.

Kaufman Concert Hall
92 Street Y, 1395 Lexington Avenue. 427-4410.

Lehman College Center for the Performing Arts
Bedford Park Boulevard West, Bronx. 960-8833.

Madison Square Garden
Seventh Avenue & West 33 St. 563-8000.

Merkin Concert Hall
Abraham Goodman House, 129 West 67 Street. 362-8719.

Metropolitan Museum
Fifth Avenue & 82 St. 879-5512.

Metropolitan Opera House
Lincoln Center, Broadway & West 64 St. 580-9830.

New York City Center
131 West 55 Street. 246-8989.

Queensborough Community College Theater
56 Avenue off Springfield Blvd, Bayside, Queens. (1-718) 631-6284.

Radio City Entertainment Center
Avenue of the Americas at West 50 Street. 757-3100.

Symphony Space
2537 Broadway at West 95 St. 864-1414.

Third Street Music School
235 East 11 Street. 777-3240.

Town Hall
123 West 43 Street. 840-2824.

Triangle Theater of L.I.U.
385 Flatbush Avenue, Brooklyn. (1-718) 628-4120.

Movie Theaters: First-Run

Below 42 Street

Art
36 East 8 Street. 473-7014.

Bay Cinema
East 32 Street & Second Avenue. 679-0160.

8th Street Playhouse
52 West 8 Street. 674-6515.

Essex
Essex at Grand Street. 982-4455.

Film Forum
57 Watts Street. 431-1590.

Gramercy
23 Street nr Lexington Ave. 475-1660.

Greenwich Twin
West 12 Street nr Greenwich Ave. 929-3350.

Loews 34 Street Showplace
East 34 Street nr Second Ave. 532-5544.

Murray Hill
East 34 Street nr Third Ave. 685-7652.

Quad Cinemas (I, II, III, IV)
34 West 13 Street. 255-8802.

23rd Street West Triplex
333 West 23 Street. 989-0060.

34th Street East
East 34 Street nr Second Avenue. 683-0255.

Waverly
Avenue of the Americas at West 3 Street. 929-8037.

43-60 Street

Baronet
Third Avenue nr East 59 St. 355-1663.

Bombay Cinema
225 West 57 Street. 581-4740.

Cine 42 Twin I, II
West 42 Street nr Seventh Ave. 221-1992.

Cine I & II
West 47 Street nr Seventh Ave. 489-7690.

Cinema I
Third Avenue nr East 60 St. 753-6022.

Cinema II
Third Avenue nr East 60 St. 753-0774.

Cinema 3
Plaza Hotel, West 59 Street. 752-5959.

Cinerama I
Broadway & West 47 Street. 975-8366.

Cinerama II
Broadway & West 47 Street. 975-8369.
Coronet
East 59 Street & Third Avenue. 355-1663.
Criterion Center
West 45 Street & Broadway. 354-0900.
D.W. Griffith Cinema
East 59 Street off Second Avenue. 759-4630.
Eastside Cinema
East 55 Street & Third Avenue. 755-3020.
Embassy 5
Broadway & 46 Street. 354-5636.
Embassy 46th Street
Broadway & West 46 Street. 757-2408.
Embassy II, III, IV
Broadway & West 47 Street. 730-7262.
Festival
West 57 Street nr Sixth Ave. 757-2715.
59th Street East
East 59 Street bet Second & Third Avenues. 755-2770.
57th Street Playhouse
West 57 Street nr Sixth Ave. 581-7360.
Forum
West 47 Street & Broadway. 757-8320.
Guild
33 West 50 Street. 757-2406.
Harris
West 42 Street & Seventh Avenue. 221-9662.
Little Carnegie
136 West 57 Street. 246-5123.
Loew's Astor Plaza
West 44 Street & Broadway. 869-8340.
Loew's State I & II
Broadway & West 45 Street. 582-5060.
Manhattan 1 & 2
East 59 Street nr Third Avenue. 935-6420.
Paris
4 West 58 Street. 688-2013.
Playboy
West 57 Street nr Sixth Ave. 586-6448.
Plaza
East 58 Street nr Madison Ave. 355-3320.
Rivoli
Broadway & West 49 Street. 247-1633.
RKO National
Broadway & West 44 Street. 869-0950.
Selwyn 42nd Street
229 West 42 Street. 730-0307.
Sutton
East 57 Street & Third Avenue. 759-1411.
Times Square Theater
219 West 42 Street. 730-0321.
Trans-Lux East
East 58 Street & Third Avenue. 759-2262.
Victoria
West 46 Street & Broadway. 354-5636.
Ziegfeld
141 West 54 Street. 765-7600.

Upper East Side
Beekman
Second Avenue nr East 65 St. 737-2622.
Gemini 1
East 64 Street & Second Avenue. 832-1670.

Gemini 2
East 64 Street & Second Avenue. 832-2720.
86th Street East
East 86 Street nr Third Ave. 249-1144.
Loew's Cine
Third Avenue nr East 86 St. 427-1332.
Loew's New York Twin I, II
East 66 Street & Second Avenue. 744-7339.
Loew's Orpheum 1 & 2
East 86 Street nr Third Ave. 289-4607.
Loew's Tower East
Third Avenue nr East 71 St. 879-1313.
RKO 86th Street Twin
East 86 Street at Lexington Avenue. 289-8900.
72nd Street East
East 72 Street nr First Ave. 288-9304.
68th Street Playhouse
East 68 Street at Third Avenue. 734-0302.
Trans Lux 85th Street
Madison Ave nr East 85 St. 288-3180.
UA East
East 84 Street nr First Ave. 249-5100.

Upper West Side
Cinema Studio, I, II
Broadway & West 66 Street. 877-4040.
Embassy 72nd Street
West 72 Street & Broadway. 724-6745.
Loew's 83rd Street Quad
Broadway & West 83 Street. 877-3190.
New Yorker 1 & 2
Broadway & West 88 Street. 580-7900.
Olympia
Broadway & West 107 Street. 865-8128.
Paramount
West 61 Street & Broadway. 247-5070.
RKO Coliseum I, II
Broadway & West 181 Street. 927-7200.
RKO Coliseum III
Broadway & West 181 Street. 927-7240.

Movie Theaters: Revival

Bleecker Street Cinema
144 Bleecker Street nr LaGuardia Pl. 674-2560.
Carnegie Hall Cinema
Seventh Avenue at West 57 Street. 757-2131.
Cinema Village
22 East 12 Street. 924-3363.
Hollywood Twin Cinema
777 Eighth Avenue nr West 47 St. 246-0717.
Mini Cinema
1234 Second Avenue at East 65 Street. 650-1813.
Public Theater
425 Lafayette Street nr Astor Pl. 598-7150.
Regency
Broadway & West 67 Street. 724-3700.
Squat
256 West 23 Street. 206-0945.
Thalia
250 West 95 Street. 222-3370.
Theater 80 St. Marks
80 St. Marks Place nr First Ave. 254-7400.

Free Entertainment

Call 755-4100 *daily for a listing of free cultural events on that day. In addition check* ANNUAL EVENTS *for listings of many very special happenings, especially during the summer months, most of which are FREE.*

Church Music

See The New York Times *Saturday edition for current church musical programs.*

Television Shows

For free tickets to TV programs go to the Convention & Visitors' Bureau, 2 Columbus Circle, 397-8222 or call or write the appropriate station:

WABC (Channel 7)
1330 Avenue of the Americas nr West 54 St. 10019. 581-7777.
WCBS (Channel 2)
51 West 52 Street, 10019. 975-2476.
WNBC (Channel 4)
30 Rockefeller Plaza nr Fifth Ave. 10020. 664-4444. *David Letterman Show, Phil Donahue Show, Bill Cosby Show.*
WNET (Channel 13)
356 West 58 Street, 10019. 560-2000.
WNEW (Channel 5)
205 East 67 Street, 10021. 535-1000.
WOR (Channel 9)
1440 Broadway nr West 40 St. 10036. 764-6683.
WPIX (Channel 11)
220 East 42 Street, 10017. 949-1100.

Radio Stations

In radio jargon: MOR = "middle of the road." AOR = "all over the road."

AM-Radio

WABC-AM: 770. News/Talk
WADO-AM: 1280. Spanish.
WALK-AM: 1370. MOR (Long Island).
WBNX-AM: 1380. Ethnic (New Jersey).
WCBS-AM: 880. All News.
WEVD-AM: 1330. Talk.
WFAS-AM: 1230. MOR (Westchester).
WGBB-AM: 1240. MOR (Long Island).
WGLI-AM: 1290. MOR/Information (Long Island).
WGRC-AM: 1300. Oldies (Rockland).
WGSM-AM: 740. MOR (Long Island).

WHLI-AM: 1100. Contemporary (Long Island).
WHN-AM: 1050. Contemporary/Country. Mets Baseball.
WINS-AM: 1010. All News.
WJIT-AM: 1480. Latin.
WLIB-AM: 1190. Black/West Indian/Reggae.
WLIX-AM: 540. MOR/Contemporary (Long Island).
WLNA-AM: 1420. MOR (Westchester).
WMCA-AM: 570. Telephone/Talk/News. Islander hockey/Notre Dame football.
WNBC-AM: 660. Adult Contemporary.
WNEW-AM: 1130. MOR/Contemporary. NY Giants, Rangers, Knicks.
WNYC-AM: 830. Information/Talk. NYC Public Radio
WNYG-AM: 1440. Gospel (Long Island).
WOR-AM: 710. Talk.
WPAT-AM: 930. Beautiful music.
WQXR-AM: 1560. Classical.
WRKL-AM: 910. MOR (Rockland).
WVIP-AM: 1310. MOR (Westchester).
WVOX-AM: 1460. MOR (Westchester).
WWRL-AM: 1600. Contemporary Black. NY Nets Basketball

FM-Radio

WALK-FM: 97.5. MOR (Long Island).
WAPP-FM: 103.5. Rock.
WBAB-FM: 102.3. Contemporary (Long Island).
WBAI-FM: 99.5. Listener sponsored, non commercial.
WBGO-FM: 88.3. Jazz (Newark).
WBLS-FM: 107.5. Black/Disco/R&B
WCBS-FM: 101.1. Golden Oldies '50s & '60s.
WEVD-FM: 97.9. Diversified/Talk.
WFUV-FM: 90.7. Classical/Rock/Talk (College).
WHTZ-FM: 100.3. Top 40.
WIOK-FM: 98.3. Show Music (Long Island).
WKCR-FM: 89.9. Classical/Jazz (College).
WKRC-FM: 92.3. Rock.
WLTW-FM: 106.7. MOR.
WNCN-FM: 104.3. Classical.
WNEW-FM: 102.7. Progressive.
WNYC-FM: 93.9. Classical/Talk. NYC Public Radio
WNYE-FM: 91.5. Educational/Talk.
WNYU-FM: 89.1. Classical/Jazz.
WPAT-FM: 93.1. Beautiful Music.
WPIX-FM: 101.9. Soft Contemporary.
WPLJ-FM: 95.5 Top 40.
WQXR-FM: 96.3. Classical.
WRFM-FM: 105.1 Easy Listening.
WRKS-FM: 98.7. Urban Contemporary.
WTFM-FM: 103.5. Beautiful Music.
WXLO-FM: 98.7. Top 40/Contemporary.
WYNY-FM: 97.1. MOR/Soft Contemporary.

Nightlife

Limelight

Nightspots Index

The following is an index of the clubs you will find in this section. The categories are as follows: Blues; Cabarets; Dinner/Dancing; Nightclubs; Comedy Clubs; Country/Western; Jazz; Blues; Rock; Dance Clubs; Roller Discos. You will find a particular club in the category which appears in parentheses following the name of the club. Full descriptions of the nightspots follow this index.

Lush Life (Jazz)
Michael's Pub (Jazz)
Mikell's (Jazz)
Mostly Magic (Nightclubs)
O'Lunney's (Country/Western)
Other End (Rock)
Palladium (Dance Clubs)
Palsson's (Cabarets)
Panache (Cabarets)
Paradise Garage (Dance Clubs)
Peppermint Lounge (Rock)
Pip's Cafe (Comedy Clubs)
Playboy Club (Nightclubs)
Private Eyes (Rock)
Pyramid (Dance Clubs)
Rainbow Grill (Nightclubs)
Rainbow Room (Dinner/Dancing)
Red Parrot (Dance Clubs)
Reggae Lounge (Dance Clubs)
Regine's (Dance Clubs)
Ritz (Rock)
Roma di Notte (Dinner/Dancing)
Roseland (Dance Clubs)
Roxy (Dance Clubs)
Saint (Dance Clubs)
Seventh Avenue South (Jazz)
Sirocco (Nightclubs)
S.N.A.F.U. (Rock)
S.O.B.'s (Sounds of Brazil) (Nightclubs)
. . . .Something Different (Cabarets)
Surf Club (Dance Clubs)
Surfmaid (Jazz)
Sweet Basil (Jazz)
Sweetwater's (Cabarets)
Tavern on the Green (Dinner/Dancing)
Top of the Gate (Cabarets)
Tramps (Blues)
Trax (Rock)
Upstairs at Greene Street (Cabarets)
Village Corner (Jazz)
Village Gate (Jazz)
Village Skating (Roller Disco)
Village Vanguard (Jazz)
Visage (Dance Clubs)
West Bank Café (Cabarets)
West Boondock (Jazz)
West End Café (Jazz)
Who's on First (Comedy Clubs)

Cabarets

Algonquin Oak Room
59 West 44 Street. 840-6800. Sophisticated setting and New York crowd. The attraction is the
gifted pianist and song stylist, Steve Ross. Tues-
Sat from 9pm; Sun from 5pm. Reserve. Cover &
minimum. *OPEN 7 days 5pm-2am.*
Applause
360 Lexington Avenue nr East 40 Street. 687-
7267. Singing waiters and waitresses perform
nightly from 7:30pm in a Broadwaylike setting.
American menu. Minimum Sat only. AE, DC, MC,
V. *OPEN Mon-Thurs 11:30am-midnight; Fri & Sat
till 2am.*

The Ballroom
253 West 28 Street. 244-3005. Famed SoHo
cabaret alive and well in Chelsea. Cabaret/
theater/restaurant (*see* RESTAURANTS, Spanish: Topas Rojas Lombardi at the Ballroom). Call
for current program. AE, MC, V. *OPEN Tues-Sun.*
Cover charge.
Café Carlyle
Carlyle Hotel, Madison Avenue & East 76 Street.
744-1600. Bar/supper club home of urbane entertainer Bobby Short Sept-Dec and April-June each
year. A New York tradition. Tues-Sat at 10pm &
midnight. Sun-Mon 9pm-1am, dancing to Big
Band Sounds. Cover charge. AE, CB, DC, MC, V.
OPEN 7 days.
Duplex
55 Grove Street nr Sheridan Sq. 255-5438.
Casual upstairs Village cabaret/piano bar with the
accent on comedy. Shows Sun-Thur at 8 & 10pm,
Fri & Sat at 9 & 11pm. Drinks only. Cover and
minimum. Piano bar downstairs, no cover. *OPEN
7 days 4pm-4am.*
Freddy's Supper Club
308 East 49 Street. 888-1633. Restaurant/
cabaret for top names and up and comers in music
and comedy. Lovely supper club setting. Cover &
minimum. AE, MC, V. *OPEN Mon-Sat 6pm-2am.*
Palsson's
157 West 72 Street. 595-7400. Long running "For-
bidden Broadway," a satirical musical comedy-
parody of some of Broadway's top shows and their
stars. Great fun. Cover & minimum. AE, MC, V.
Shows Sun & Tues-Thurs at 8:30pm; Fri & Sat at
8:30 & 11pm. *OPEN Tues-Sun.*
Panache
1409 Sixth Avenue nr West 57 St. 765-5080.
Cabaret and musical talent showcase at this intimate supper club above the Magic Pan Creperie.
Shows Sun-Thurs at 8pm; Fri & Sat at 8 & 11pm.
Cover charge. AE, MC, V. *OPEN 7 days.*
. . . .Something Different
1488 First Avenue nr East 77 St. 570-6666. Dessert nightclub. Soda-sipping showcase for professional waiters and waitresses who sing as well
as serve. Sets are 25 mins. each with a 15-min.
break. Entertainment: Mon-Thurs 8pm-2am, Fri &
Sat till 3am, Sun till 1am. *OPEN 7 days.*
Sweetwater's
170 Amsterdam Avenue at West 68 St. 873-4100.
Good food and entertainment in the Lincoln Center area. Tues-Thurs at 9 & 11pm; Fri & Sat 10pm
& midnight. AE, DC, MC, V.
Top of the Gate
160 Bleeker Street nr Thompson St. 982-9292.
Theater cabaret with wide range of acts from comedy to live theater. Drinks only. Admission charge,
plus minimum (except for theater shows). Call for
current attraction.
Upstairs at Greene Street.
101 Greene Street nr Prince St, upstairs. 925-
2415, A SoHo showplace for music and comedy.
Light menu, cocktails, or desserts. Cover charge.
OPEN Wed-Sat from 8pm.
West Bank Café
407 West 42 Street. 695-6909. At the Downstairs

Theatre Bar, plays, musical revues at 8:30pm & 10:30pm, and a free midnight comedy show on Sat. Very friendly and casual. Admission charge. AE, V, MC. *OPEN Tues-Sat noon till.*

Dinner/Dancing

Atrium Club
174 Montague Street nr Court Street, Brooklyn. (1-718) 875-7900. Très romantic. Upstairs, continental food by the fireplace or on the balcony, weather dictating. Live music Fri & Sat, D.J. Wed & Thurs. Small but adequate dance floor. Downstairs they serve an irresistible menu of desserts daily. Minimum. AE, CB, DC, MC, V. *OPEN Mon-Thurs 5pm-midnight, Fri & Sat till 2 am. CLOSED Sat & Sun in summer.*

Café Pierre
Pierre Hotel, 2 East 61 Street. 838-8000. Sophisticated Continental dining in an elegant room. Dancing to a trio Tues-Sat 8pm-midnight, piano music Sun and Mon. Jacket and tie. AE, CB, DC, MC, V. *OPEN 7 days noon-2am.*

Circle Line
Circle Line Plaza, West 42 Street & the Hudson River. 563-3202. Music, dancing and hors d'oeuvres while cruising around Manhattan. June-Oct; Tues & Wed, leaves promptly at 7:30pm, returns 9:30pm. Cash bar. Fee includes tax and tip. AE, MC, V.

Copacabana New York
10 East 60 Street. 755-6010. Dance to disco or just listen. Shows at 10pm & midnight. Cover and minimum unless dining à la carte. *OPEN Tues-Sat 9pm-2am.*

Edwardian Room
Plaza Hotel, Fifth Avenue & 59 Street. 759-3000. Elegant dining and dancing to a trio in candlelit setting with Central Park view. Fri & Sat 10:30pm-1:30am. Piano music Sun-Thur 6-11pm; Fri & Sat till 10:30pm. Minimum after 10pm. AE, CB, DC, MC, V. *OPEN 7 days 5:30pm-1am.*

Empress/Riveranda
See RESTAURANTS, Rooms with a view.

King Cole Room
St. Regis Sheraton Hotel, 2 East 55 Street. 753-4500. Regal Art Deco room. Showcase for established performers. Continental and American cuisine. Cover charge. Jacket and tie required. AE, CB, DC, MC, V. *OPEN 7 days 6pm-4am.*

Rainbow Room
30 Rockefeller Plaza, 65th fl. 757-9090. Fifty years old and every bit as stylish as the day it opened. French/Italian cuisine and cheek-to-cheek dancing to a Big Band high above Manhattan. Tues-Thurs 7pm-1am; Fri & Sat 8pm-2am; Sun 6pm-midnight. Sophisticated, elegant dining room, exquisite views. Music charge. Jacket and tie required. *Sun Brunch 11:30am-3pm.* AE, CB, DC, MC, V. *OPEN 7 days.*

Roma di Notte
137 East 55 Street. 832-1128. Marble dance floor amid Roman artifacts. Strolling singers; Italian and Continental cuisine and music. Mon-Sat

7:30pm-1am. Minimum. AE, CB, DC. *OPEN Mon-Sat 5:30pm-2am.*

Tavern on the Green
Central Park West at 67 St. 873-3200. On warm summer nights, in the Terrace Garden, dance under the stars in a fairyland setting in Central Park. Cocktails and dinner. No cover or minimum. No reservations for the garden. *OPEN Tues-Sun 9pm-1am.* (*See also* RESTAURANTS, Rooms with a View.)

Nightclubs

Amazonas
492 Broome Street. 966-3371. Authentic regional Brazilian cuisine and music nightly 6:30-11:30pm. AE, CB, DC, *OPEN 7 days.*

Café Feenjon
115 MacDougal Street nr West 3 Street. 254-3630. Continuous Middle Eastern and Israeli music and food. Inexpensive, unpretentious good fun. *OPEN Wed, Thurs & Sun 8:30pm-2am; Fri & Sat till 4am.*

Café Versailles
151 East 50 Street. 753-3471. Continental food with spicy revues in an elegant atmosphere. Floor shows at 9pm & 11:30pm. Piano music Mon-Fri 5-8pm; midnight-4am. No cover with dinner. AE, CB, DC, MC, V. *OPEN 7 days 5pm-4am.*

Chippendale's
1110 First Avenue at East 61 St. 935-6060. To the Big Apple via LA (where else?) comes this unsophisticated—albeit popular—good fun. An all-male revue and strip show "For Ladies only." The audience is split between the embarrassed and the bold. Shows Wed-Sat at 8:30pm. From 10:15pm there is dancing (men allowed) till 4am. Cover charge. AE only. *OPEN Wed-Sat 6pm-4am.*

Club Ibis
151 East 50 Street, upstairs. 753-3884. Egyptian decor. Mid-Eastern music and belly dancing from 10pm-4am. Continental and Middle Eastern cuisine. AE, CB, DC, MC, V. *OPEN 7 days 7:30pm-4am.*

Hawaii Kai
1638 Broadway nr West 50 Street. 757-0900. Hawaiian Revue, plus contemporary music for dancing. Two shows a night Mon-Thurs 8 & 11pm; Fri & Sat. 9 & 11pm & 1am; Sun 7, 9 & 11pm. Chinese-American, and Polynesian food in South Seas setting. Cover charge. AE, CB, DC, MC, V. *OPEN Mon-Thurs 5pm-midnight; Fri & Sat till 3am.*

Mostly Magic
55 Carmine Street. 924-1472. Some comedy is thrown in for good measure, so call ahead for information. Shows Tues-Thurs 9:30pm. Fri & Sat 9pm, 11:30pm. Tues is showcase night. Drinks only. Admission. AE, MC, V. *OPEN Tues-Sat from 1 hour before first show.*

Playboy Club
5 East 59 Street. 752-3100. Live entertainment will resume in what once was the Cabaret Room

when renovation is completed sometime before 1986. Membership fee. No denim; jacket required. Reserve. AE, CB, DC, MC, V. *OPEN 7 days.*

Rainbow Grill
30 Rockefeller Plaza, 65th fl. 757-8970. Extravagant glittering musical revues nightly 9:15pm & 11:30pm. Dinner, disco dancing and a romantic sky-high view of Manhattan. Cover charge. Jacket required. AE, CB, DC, MC, V. *OPEN Mon-Sat 5pm-2am.*

Sirocco
29 East 29 Street. 683-9409. Israeli-Greek supper club. Two bands for dancing, plus belly-dance entertainment, singers and dancing waiters. Shows at 10pm & 1am. Minimum. AE, DC. *OPEN Tues-Sun 7pm-3am.*

S.O.B.'s (Sounds of Brazil)
204 Varick Street at West Houston. 243-4940. It's like a night out in Rio. Delicious Brazilian food served from 6pm-10:30pm. Live samba bands and dancing from 10pm till dawn. Cover & minimum. AE, MC, V. Reserve. *OPEN Tues-Sat 6pm-dawn.*

Sex Clubs & Shows

New York offers a wide variety of strip and burlesque shows as well as numerous topless bars, "massage parlors" and adult movies. Over the last several years a number of open-to-the-public swingers' clubs have flourished. Understandably the erotic business tends to be somewhat erratic. For what is current in this particular segment of nightlife we refer you to the best guide of its nature—the weekly newspaper *Screw*, available at many newsstands throughout the city.

Comedy Clubs

Other clubs offer one or two nights to showcase new talent, but at the following every night is amateur night. You don't know what you'll get for the price of a drink, but you will have fun. This is where some of today's top stars got their start, and lightning keeps striking. Top alumni occasionally drop by to try out new material. They are all popular, and reservations are highly recommended.

Caroline's
332 Eighth Avenue nr West 27 St. 924-3499. Plush, professional Chelsea comedy/nightclub where established funny people (like Robert Klein, Elayne Boosler, Father Guido Sarducci, and Sandra Bernhard) try new material before taking it on TV. American-continental food, popular bar. Shows Tues-Thurs 8:30pm; Fri & Sat 9pm & 11:30pm; Sun at 9pm. Minimum. AE, MC, V. *OPEN Tues-Sun.*

Catch a Rising Star
1487 First Avenue nr East 77 St. 794-1906. East Side ambiance in this improvisation club known for its consistent good humor. Hosts of comics

onstage, talent scouts and producers in the audience. Sun-Thurs at 9pm, Fri & Sat 8:30pm & midnight. Cover and minimum. AE, MC. *OPEN 7 days.*

Comedy Celler
117 MacDougal Street nr Bleecker St. 254-3630. Informal Village comedy club for fledgling comics and singers. Cover & minimum. Shows Sun-Thurs at 9pm; Fri & Sat at 9 & 11:30pm. No credit cards. *OPEN 7 days.*

Comedy U
86 University Place nr East 11 St. 206-1296. Graduates of this club may go on to the big time. Thurs night, female comics only; open mike on Sun. No credit cards. Shows Wed-Sun at 9 pm. *OPEN Wed-Sun.*

Comic Strip
1568 Second Avenue nr East 81 St. 861-9386. Comedy improvisation club, where Eddie Murphy made them laugh a few years ago. Merriment Sun-Thurs from 9:30pm; Fri 9pm & midnight. Sat 8:30pm & midnight. Cover and minimum. AE, MC, V. *OPEN 7 days.*

Dangerfield's
1118 First Avenue nr East 61 St. 593-1650. Comedian Rodney "I don't get no respect" Dangerfield's popular club. Specializes, of course, in good comedy, often by Rodney Dangerfield; American food. Shows Sun-Thurs at 9 & 11:15pm; Fri 9pm & midnight; Sat 8:30pm & midnight. New talent Sun from 9pm. Cover and minimum. AE, CB, DC, MC, V. *OPEN 7 days 8pm-4am.*

Improvisation
358 West 44 Street. 765-8268. Oldest and most famed of the comedy showcase spots. Very crowded on weekends and very informal. Fri & Sat at 8pm & midnight; Sun-Thurs 7pm-4am. Food available. Cover and minimum. No credit cards. *OPEN 7 days.*

Pip's Café
2005 Emmons Avenue nr Ocean Ave. Brooklyn. (1-718) 646-9433. Tues & Thurs for showcase talent, Wed for auditions at 9:30pm. Comedians featured Fri & Sat at 9:30pm and 11:30pm No credit cards.

Who's On First
1205 First Avenue at East 65 St. 737-2772. Full menu, drinks and comedy. Shows Thurs at 10pm; Fri & Sat 10pm & at midnight, the resident improv group. Cover & minimum. AE only. *OPEN Sun-Thurs 4pm-midnight; Fri & Sat till 1:30am.*

Country/Western

Eagle Tavern
355 West 14 Street. 924-0275. Live country and Bluegrass music every Sat 8:15pm-midnight. British and Irish music, Wed 9pm-1am. Irish Jam, Mon & Fri 9pm-4am. Bar only. Cover charge. No credit cards. *OPEN 7 days 8am-4am.*

Lone Star Cafe
Fifth Avenue at 13 Street. 242-1664. The official Texas embassy in N.Y. Great country, rhythm and

blues and rockabilly after 9pm nightly, plus 1-, 2-, or 3-alarm chili make this a hot spot. Texas beers. Admission charge and minimum at tables. AE, CB, DC, MC, V. *OPEN Mon-Thurs 11:30am-3am; Fri till 4am; Sat 7:30pm-4am; Sun 7:30pm-3am.*

O'Lunney's
915 Second Avenue nr East 48 St. 751-5470. Folksy hangout for displaced Texans. Good country and Bluegrass music, crowded bar and plenty of foot stompin'. Music from 9pm. Cover and minimum at tables. AE, DC, MC, V. *OPEN Mon-Fri 11:30am-4am; Sat & Sun 5:30pm-3am.*

Jazz

Jazzline: (1-718) 463-0200. A 24-hour information service. When and where info on New York jazz.

Ali Baba East
400 East 59 Street. 688-4710. Traditional jazz from 10:30pm. Large piano bar. Minimum at tables. *OPEN 7 days 8pm-4am.*

Angry Squire
216 Seventh Avenue at West 23 Street. 242-9066. Jazz in pub atmosphere. Tues, Fri & Sat 10pm-2:30am. English-style food. Sun Brunch with music, noon-4pm. Minimum Fri & Sat. *OPEN Sun-Thurs noon-2am; Fri & Sat till 4am.*

Arthur's Tavern
57 Grove Street nr Seventh Avenue South. 675-6879. Dixieland on Mon, blues by Mabel Godwin on Thurs, Fri & Sat 9:30pm-3:30am. *OPEN 7 days 9pm-4am.*

Blue Note
131 West 3 Street nr Sixth Ave. 475-8592. Respected jazz club/restaurant presenting many well-known artists. Shows at 9 & 11pm; Fri & Sat 1am as well. There's a nightly jam session after the late show till 4am. Full breakfast menu till closing. Admission and minimum. AE, MC, V. *OPEN 7 days from 5pm.*

Brown's
8727 Fourth Avenue, Brooklyn. (1-718) 745-8528. Well attended by true jazz enthusiasts. Live shows nightly in a pleasant atmosphere. Limited menu, reasonable prices. Minimum at tables. *OPEN 7 days from 7pm-4am.*

Bradley's
70 University Place nr East 11 St. 228-6440. Noisy, casual, wood-paneled Village bar/restaurant features topflight jazz artists nightly from 9:45pm. Minimum at the tables (if you can get one). AE, CB, DC, MC, V. *OPEN 7 days 11:30am-3pm; 6pm-4am.*

Café Ziegfeld
218 West 45 Street nr Eighth Ave. 840-2964. Theatrical motif. Good jazz, some greats on occasion. Food and drink. Music Mon-Sat 6:15pm & 10:45pm. *OPEN 7 days 12:30pm-1am.*

Cajun
See RESTAURANTS, Soul & Creole.

Carnegie Tavern
165 West 56 Street. 757-9522. Cozy supper club

for traditional jazz. Music 9pm-midnight. Minimum. AE, DC, MC, V. *OPEN Mon-Sat 11:30am-midnight. CLOSED Mon.*

Cousins
160 Court Street, Brooklyn. (1-718) 596-3514. Classy yet casual bar/restaurant serving American and Italian food. Jazz and blues Wed, Thurs, Sun 8:30pm-midnight; Sat from 10pm-2am. Piano brunch on Sun. Minimum at tables. AE, CB, DC. *OPEN 7 days from noon Wed-Sun; from 4pm Mon & Tues.*

Eric
1700 Second Avenue nr East 88 St. 534-8500. Good vibes at this showcase jazz club, restaurant and bar from 9pm. Kitchen open till 3:30am. Cover and minimum. AE, MC, V. *OPEN 7 days noon-4am.*

Fat Tuesday's
190 Third Avenue nr East 17 St. 533-7902. Good food and drink in this mirrored mainstream jazz club, downstairs at Tuesday's restaurant. Two sets Tues-Thurs & Sun at 9:30 & 11:30pm; Fri & Sat at 1am as well. Cover and minimum. AE, MC, V. *OPEN Tues-Sun 8:30pm-2am.*

Five Oaks
49 Grove Street nr Seventh Avenue South. 243-8885. Longtime casual Village cellar club features Marie Blake at the piano 9:30pm-4am and lots of impromptu entertainment. Dinner available till 1am. AE, MC, V. *OPEN Tues-Sun 7pm-4am.*

Greene Street Café
101 Greene Street nr Prince St. 925-2415. Wicker chairs and trees appoint this beautiful 3-story-high former truck warehouse; bar, lounge with tables, sunken dining area with small stage and, literally topping it all, a balcony. Easy-listening jazz and pop artists. Expensive à la carte menu. Piano music 6pm-2am, Fri & Sat till 3am. Shows Tues-Sat 11pm. Cover (except at bar) and minimum AE, MC, V. *OPEN 7 days.*

Gregory's
1149 First Avenue nr East 63 St. 371-2220. Modern jazz 7pm-3am in small, cozy New York bar. Snacks available. Cover. AE, CB, DC, MC, V. *OPEN Sun-Fri 6pm-4am; Sat from 9pm.*

Jazz Center of New York
380 Lafayette Street nr East 4 St. 3rd fl. 505-5660. Home of the Universal Jazz Coalition. Call for schedule of performances and exhibitions, better yet, get on their mailing list.

Jimmy Weston's
131 East 54 Street. 838-8384. Extremely popular restaurant with good jazz. Dancing from 9pm. Cover. AE, CB, DC, MC, V. *OPEN Mon-Sat noon until 3am. CLOSED Sun.*

Kenny's Castaways
157 Bleecker Street nr Thompson St. 473-9870. Magical Irish bar in Greenwich Village. Shows nightly at 9:30 & midnight. Jazz, rock, folk music. Gaelic specialties in the restaurant. Minimum. *OPEN 7 days noon-4am.*

Little Kitchen
See RESTAURANTS, Soul & Creole

Lush Life
184 Thompson Street at Bleecker St. 228-3788.

Attractive, relatively new club (same owners as Sweet Basil) serves up good Continental food and an eclectic range of jazz. Three sets starting at 8:30pm Sun-Thurs; from 9pm Fri & Sat. Minimum and cover. AE, MC, V. *OPEN 7 days 6pm-2am.*

Michael's Pub
211 East 55 Street. 758-2272. Good food and traditional jazz in comfortable surroundings. Shows at 9:30 & 11:30pm. If you're lucky, Woody Allen on clarinet with the New Orleans Funeral & Ragtime Band Mon nights. Minimum in restaurant. AE, DC, MC, V. *OPEN Mon-Sat noon-1am.*

Mikell's
760 Columbus Avenue at West 97 Street. 864-8832. Intimate and softly lit longtime jazz enclave. Limited menu, great jazz and R&B. Shows from 10pm-2am. Call for information. Minimum and cover varies. AE, CB, DC, MC. *OPEN Mon-Sat from 4pm.*

Seventh Avenue South
21 Seventh Avenue South at Leroy St. 242-4694. Good New York jazz spot. Two sets Tues-Thurs & Sun at 10pm & midnight; Fri & Sat at 10pm, midnight, & 1:30am. Light snacks available. Cover and minimum. MC, V. *OPEN Tues-Sun 4pm-4am.*

Surfmaid
151 Bleecker Street nr Thompson St. 473-8845. Surf and turf, plus jazz piano from 9pm. Minimum on weekends. AE, DC, MC, V. *OPEN 7 days 1pm-4am.*

Sweet Basil
88 Seventh Avenue South nr Bleecker St. 242-1785. Popular Greenwich Village eatery and bar with good menu and mainstream jazz in comfortable, natural wood-and-brick surroundings. Three shows nightly at 10 & 11:30pm & 1am. Sat & Sun brunch (no cover) and live music. Cover and minimum. AE, MC, V. *OPEN 7 days noon-3am.*

Village Corner
142 Bleecker Street at LaGuardia Place. 473-9762. Jazz piano Tues-Thurs from 8pm; Fri, Sat & Sun from 9:30pm. Special Sun jazz brunch 2:30-6pm. *OPEN Tues-Fri 4pm-4am; Sat & Sun from noon.*

Village Gate
160 Bleecker Street at Thompson St. 475-5120. Most-recorded jazz room in the world. Mon 9pm-3am jazz meets Salsa. Nightly from 9:30pm jazz in the Terrace. No music charge. No credit cards. *OPEN Tues-Sun.*

Village Vanguard
178 Seventh Avenue South nr West 11 St. 255-4037. Since 1935, a renowned New York jazz institution. This quintessential noisy, smoky Greenwich Village basement club has featured all the greats. Three shows nightly 10pm, 11:30pm & 1am. No food. Minimum and admission charge. No credit cards. *OPEN 7 days till 2am.*

West Boondock
114 Tenth Avenue at West 17 St. 929-9645. For nearly 20 years, contemporary jazz in old-fashioned setting 8:30pm-1am. Good soul food, especially the fried chicken and sweet potato pie. AE, MC, V. *OPEN 7 days till 2am.*

West End Café
2911 Broadway nr West 114 St. 666-9160. Popular jazz bar and restaurant serves over fifty brands of beer. Swing along with some of the greats from the Basie and Ellington bands, and other top-flight jazz musicians. From 9pm. Minimum, occasional cover but still inexpensive. MC, V. *OPEN 7 days 10am-4pm, kitchen till 3am.*

Zinno
See RESTAURANTS, Italian.

Blues

Dan Lynch
221 Second Avenue nr East 14 St. 677-0911. Old neighborhood bar for low-priced drinks and some of the best blues in the city. During the week the music starts at 10pm till 2am; Sat till 3am. Sun matinee music starts at 4pm till 3am. No cover. No credit cards. *OPEN Mon-Fri 8am-2am; Sat till 3am; Sun noon-3am.*

Tramps
125 East 15 Street nr Irving Pl. 777-5077. Restaurant/bar features wide range of musical talent in pub atmosphere. Shows Thurs-Sat 9pm & midnight. Showcase Sun-Wed 9pm. Blues featured on weekends. Cover; minimum weekends only. AE, MC, V. *OPEN 7 days till 4am.*

Rock

Back Fence
155 Bleecker Street at Thompson Street. 475-9221. Folk and rock music nightly 8:30pm. Friendly Greenwich Village atmosphere. No cover. *OPEN 7 days noon-4am.*

Bitter End
147 Bleecker Street nr LaGuardia Pl. 673-7030. Once upon a time Bob Dylan showcased here—now it offers rock, jazz and comedy (Mon & Tues). Also food and dancing. Shows Wed-Sat 10pm & 12:30am; Sun at 9pm. Admission and minimum. *OPEN 7 days from 8:30.*

Bottom Line
15 West 4 Street at Mercer St. 228-7880. Still a good club for name acts and showcase performers. Food and drink available. Admission charge for table seats and standing room. Two shows nightly. Tickets sold in advance. *OPEN 7 days 6:30pm till 2am.*

CBGB
315 Bowery at Bleecker Street. 982-4052. The birth place of punk still showcases up-and-coming bands (no dancing). *Great* sound system. Admission charge. *OPEN 8:30pm-3am.* Fri & Sat till 4am. Sat & Sun "hardcore matinees" 3:30-7pm.

8 BC
337 East 8 Street (bet Avenues B and C). Ultrametro club amid the decay for the adventurous. A showcase for local musicians, dancers and artists who perform at irregular intervals. Gritty downtown art and crowd. Admission. *OPEN 7 days 4pm-4am.*

Folk City
130 West 3 Street. 254-8449. Durable survivor. Features folk, rock, jazz, blues, new wave and country. Hootenanny Mon, comedy Sun. Tues & Wed shows at 9pm & 11pm. Fri & Sat at 8pm & 11pm. Admission charge. *OPEN 7 days.*

Irving Plaza
17 Irving Place at East 15 St. 477-3728. Old Polish-American meeting hall turned rock'n'roll theater. Great live dance bands and rock concerts with dancing between acts. Large stage, dance floor, balcony for viewing and a bar. Admission charge. *OPEN Thurs-Sat only 9pm-4am.*

Other End
147 Bleecker Street nr LaGuardia Place. 673-7030. Features headline jazz, rock, folk and blues. Dabbling in New Wave. Shows at 9pm & midnight. Food available. *OPEN Mon-Fri 3pm-4am; Sat & Sun from noon.*

Peppermint Lounge
100 Fifth Avenue at 15 St. 989-9505. The legend lives on in new quarters. Two rock bands nightly from 11:30pm. Dancing, video and a trio of dynamite D.J.'s. Admission charge. *OPEN Tues-Sun 10pm-4am.*

Private Eyes
12 West 21 Street. 206-7770. What you see is what you get, at this, the ultimate video club. At last count, there were 34 screens showing an eclectic selection of music videos, old film-clips, etc. There's a "vee-jay." Free admission Mon-Wed. *OPEN 7 days from 10pm-4am.*

Ritz
119 East 11 Street. 228-8888. An old Deco dance palace is the top club for rock. Features New Wave bands and young energetic crowds. Enormous video screen; loud sound, both live and recorded; mezzanine for viewing. Dress, retro chic; special theme events. You'll think you died and went to teen heaven. Admission charge. Minimum at tables sometimes. *OPEN Mon-Sat 10pm-6am. Occasionally Sun.*

S.N.A.F.U.
676 Sixth Avenue at West 21 St. 691-3535. Small rock club/cabaret in Chelsea. Live rock shows; some space for dancing. Bar and tables. Music starts 9pm. Admission charge. *OPEN Wed-Sun 8:30pm-4am.*

Trax
100 West 72 Street. 799-1448. Features live rock bands. Showcase for up-and-coming bands to be seen by record-label talent scouts. Dancing after midnight to music of the 50s and 80s. Admission charge. AE, DC, MC. *OPEN Mon-Sat 9pm-4am.*

Dance Clubs

Area
157 Hudson Street. 226-8423. The hot "in" spot; more of an event than a club. Periodically redecorated to reflect a new theme. Mixed crowd includes celebs, yuppies, gays, and the avant garde. Selective door policy leads to curb-side chaos in the late pm/early am. Admission charge. *OPEN Wed-Mon 11pm-4am.*

Club A
333 East 60 Street. 308-2333. Stylish glitzy international set in a dimly lit elegant setting. Sophisticated clientele includes some offspring of exiled royalty. Cover charge. AE, V. *OPEN Mon-Sat 10pm-4am.*

Danceteria
30 West 21 Street. 620-0790. Intense spot, progressive, taking up four floors—one each for live progressive music, dancing, video and parties. Admission charge. *OPEN 7 days 9pm-5am.*

Fun House
526 West 26 Street. 691-0621. Carnival-theme disco with game room; sometimes live bands; serves light snacks. Admission charge. *OPEN Wed, Fri & Sat 10pm until.*

Heartbreak
179 Varick Street at Charlton St. 691-2388. Not the fashionable spot it once was but the cafeteria setting and the 50s and 60s rock and r & b are still a draw. Live bands on Mon nights. Admission charge. No credit cards. *OPEN 7 days 10pm-4:30am.*

Ipanema
240 West 52 Street. 765-8025. Two-story disco, lit from beneath dance floor; neon lights, viewing balcony. Two bars on weekends. Admission charge. Ladies free before 11pm Thurs & Fri. Sat reduced admission after 11pm. Free admission for all on Sun. Live Latin bands Thurs-Sat. *OPEN Thurs-Sun 9pm until.*

Kamikaze Klub
531 West 19 Street. 807-0838. Neighborhood punk place for dancing (downstairs) and lounging (upstairs). Thursday it's a gallery for local artists, serving free wine until 11pm, when the dancing resumes. Admission charge. *OPEN Wed-Sat 10pm-4am.*

Leviticus
45 West 33 Street. 564-0408. Pleasant disco. Admission charge. No denim, jacket required. AE, DC, MC, V. *OPEN Thurs-Sun 10pm until.*

The Library
Barbizon Plaza Hotel, Avenue of the Americas nr West 58 Street. 247-7000. Disco dancing in book-lined library setting. Reading permitted. Complementary buffet Mon-Fri 5pm-7pm. Minimum Wed, Fri, Sat only. No denim; jacket required. AE. *OPEN Mon-Fri 4:30pm-3am; Sat 9pm-4am; Sun 9-3am.*

Limelight
660 Sixth Avenue at West 20 St. 807-7850. Landmark (1846) church converted to accommodate dance floor, bar and VIP lounge, leaving stained-glass windows intact. Middle of the new-wave road, popular with music and movie people. Admission charge. *OPEN 7 days 10pm-4am.*

Palladium
126 East 14 Street. 473-7171. Weep no more for the refugees of the old Studio 54—Calvin, Bianca, Halston, Grace and Andy—for Steve Rubell has opened his Studio 54 of the 80s. The former Academy of Music's 104,000 sq. ft. have been transformed into a multimedia club. The main dance space is overlooked by a 800-seat balcony and mezzanine. There are suspended staircases;

50 video monitors; art by some of today's top downtown artists and loads of theatrical dazzle. There are also quiet spaces, pillows and platforms and conversation nooks with soft music. Don't be put off by the seedy exterior—it's part of the effect. Holds 3,500. AE, MC, V. *OPEN Tues-Sun; (in summer) Wed-Sat 10pm-4am.*

Paradise Garage
84 King Street at Varick St. 989-2975. One of the best sound systems in the city may be found in this renovated parking garage. The crowd is a street tough one made up of an interesting mix of Blacks, Latinos and gays. Boy George has been known to drop by. (Note: One must go through a metal detector before entering the club.) Cover. No credit cards. *OPEN Fri & Sat midnight till 10am.*

Pyramid
101 Avenue A nr East 6 St. 420-1590. Lots of attitude on the "Gloria Vanderbilt Memorial Dance Floor" downstairs and in the Pasadena Safari Lounge upstairs. Kitsch art shows, theme parties and an unpredictable assortment of live performances. Sunday is the *hot* night for this quintessential East Village club. Admission. *OPEN 7 days 4pm-4am.*

The Red Parrot
617 West 57 Street. 247-1843. A glamorous high-tech haunt, boasting a motorized stage and staircase, elaborate laser displays, tremendous dancefloor and, of course, real live parrots. Live music runs the gamut from c/w to jazz; on Fri & Sat Big Band, 40s and 50s sounds. Admission. *OPEN Wed-Sat 10pm-4am.*

Reggae Lounge
285 West Broadway at Canal St. 226-4598. Live grassroots reggae in a no-frills atmosphere. Colorful crowd and dancing. Drinks only. Cover charge. Tues & Fri ladies free. *OPEN Tues-Sat 10pm till.* Admission.

Regine's
502 Park Avenue at East 59 St. 826-0990. Cafe society's restaurant-discotheque. Appropriately expensive to boogie with the jet set. Disco from 10:30pm. Cover charge. Jacket and tie required; "evening elegant" for women. AE, CB, DC, MC, V. *OPEN Mon-Sat 6pm-midnight.*

Roseland
239 West 52 Street. 247-0200. No longer 10¢ a dance, but you can still see the best ballroom dancing here, where they're serious about it. Also, disco Wed & Thurs, from 11pm, Fri & Sat from midnight. Wed special: dance lessons and all-

you-can-eat-and-drink buffet 6:30-10pm. Two orchestras, restaurant and bar. Admission charge. *OPEN Wed 6:30pm-2am; Thurs 2:30pm-midnight; Fri 6:30-4am; Sat & Sun 2:30pm-4am.*

Roxy
515 West 18 Street. 691-3113. Sun-Wed this is a roller skating palace, but on Fri and Sat it becomes one of the city's hottest spots for serious "Hip Hop"—break dancing, rapping and graffiti art. Large dance floor, capacity 1000. Thurs, there's salsa music. *OPEN 7 days.*

The Saint
105 Second Avenue at East 6 Street. 674-8369. Rising on the ashes of the old Filmore East. Space-age video and audio effects like no others. All-black high-tech décor. No booze. For male members only, but exceptions are made. Live entertainment and disco. Light snacks and refreshments. *OPEN Sat & Sun only, midnight until.*

Surf Club
415 East 91 Street. 410-1360. Striped umbrellas, bartenders in shades, dancing to Motown and old-wave surfing tunes—all part of the beach motif here. Preppy crowd. Jacket & tie required. No cover Tues & Wed. *OPEN Tues-Sat 9pm-4am.*

Visage
610 West 56 Street. 247-0612. Stylish spot for hearing rock music, dancing and watching skaters and mere people perform in an indoor rink and pool. All in plush, overwhelmingly pink surroundings. Admission charge. AE, DC. *OPEN Wed-Sun 10pm-4am.*

Roller Discos

Empire Roller Disco Skating Rink
200 Empire Boulevard nr Bedford Avenue, Brooklyn. (1-718) 462-1570. Birthplace of roller disco. Easily holds 1,000. Neon, strobes, excellent sound. Snack bar; viewing area. Showtime Wed 11pm. Admission charge, plus skate rental. *OPEN Tues-Wed 8pm-1am; Fri 11pm-5am; Sat 11pm-4am.*

Roxy
See Dance Clubs

Village Skating
15 Waverly Place nr Washington Sq. 677-9690. For a freewheeling evening. Skate rental. Admission charge. Call for hours. *OPEN 7 days.*

Restaurants

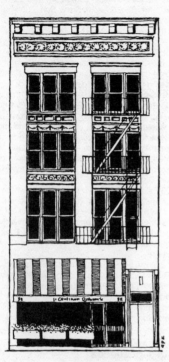

Il Cantinori

Reservations

Telephone to make a reservation, since this will determine that the particular restaurant is still in business and that a table will be available. If reservations are not accepted you can determine whether to expect a long wait prior to being seated.

Tipping

The rule of thumb is approximately 15% of the total (exclusive of tax), easily calculated by doubling the amount of the 8¼% city sales tax. Generally, New York restaurants do not add a service charge.

Key

The price of dinner at these restaurants has been classified on the basis of a complete dinner for two, excluding wine, tax and tip, as follows:
$ $35 or less

$$ $35 to $50
$$$ $50 to $65
$$$$ More than $65
$$$$+ More than $100
The key used for meals served is:
B Breakfast
L Lunch
D Dinner

Restaurants: Alphabetical Index

New York has nearly 30,000 restaurants! The following represent a good cross section of every type of food and price range. Restaurant categories appear in parentheses.

In addition to the usual ethnic categories, I have included the following special listings for your convenience and pleasure: Afternoon Tea; Bars & Burgers; Breakfast/Brunch; Cafés; Deluxe; Fireplaces; Garden/Outdoor Dining; Inexpensive; Late Night/24 Hours; No Smoking Areas; Omelettes & Crepes; Outdoor Dining; Pizza; Rooms with a View; Sidewalk Cafés; Soup & Salad; Steak Houses. A complete description of a particular restaurant can be found in the category that appears in parentheses. Following the Alphabetical Index is a listing of restaurants by geographic area.

Barnabus Rex (Bars & Burgers)
Barney Greenglass (Jewish)
Bayamo (Latin American)
Beach House (Mexican)
Beatrice Inn (Italian)
Beijing Duck House (Chinese)
Benihana of Tokyo (Japanese)
Bergdorf Goodman (Department Store Restaurants)
Bernstein-on-Essex Street (Delicatessen)
Berry's (Continental)
Bienvenue (French)
Black Sheep (French)
Blue Plate (Inexpensive)
Bloomingdale's (Department Store Restaurants)
BoBo's (Chinese)
Bombay Palace (Indian & Pakastani)
Bon Temps Rouler (Soul & Creole)
Box Tree (French)
Brasserie (Late Night/24 Hours)
Brazilian Coffee Restaurant (Latin American)
Brazilian Pavilion (Latin American)
Bridge Café (Continental)
Brittany du Soir (French)
Broadway Joe (Steak Houses)
Broome Street Bar (Bars & Burgers)
Brownie's (Health & Vegetarian)
Buffalo Roadhouse (Sidewalke Cafés)
Cabana Carioca (Latin American)
Café Argenteuil (French)
Café Central (Late Night/24 Hours)
Café de la Paix (Sidewalk Cafés)
Café des Artistes (Continental)
Café des Bruxelles (Belgian)
Café in the Cradle (Middle Eastern)
Café Loup (French)
Café Luxembourg (Late Night/24 Hours)
Café Marigold (Continental)
Café Marimba (Mexican)
Café Orlin (Breakfast/Brunch)
Café Seiyoken (Japanese)
Café Un Deux Trois (Stargazers)
Café Vivaldi (Cafés)
Caffè Biondo (Cafés)
Caffè Regglo (Cafés)
Caffè Roma (Cafés)
Cajun (Soul & Creole)
Cam Fung (Breakfast/Brunch: Dim Sum)
Capsouto Frères (French)
Caramba! & !! & !!! (Mexican)
Carlyle Restaurant (Continental)
Carnegie Delicatessen (Delicatessen)
Carolina (American)
Casa Brasil (Latin American)
Castillian (Spanish)
The Cattleman (Steak Houses)
Cedars of Lebanon (Middle Eastern)
Cellar in the Sky (Deluxe)
Cent'Anni (Italian)
Chalet Suisse (Swiss)
Chanterelle (French)
Charley O's Bar & Grill (Bars & Burgers)
Chatfield's (Continental)

Chelsea Place (Continental)
Chez Brigitte (Inexpensive)
Chez Napoléon (French)
Chi Mer (Chinese)
Chinese Chance (Bars & Burgers)
Christ Cella (Steak House)
Chumley's (Bars & Burgers)
Cinco de Mayo (Mexican)
City Lights Bar & Hors D'Oeuvrerie (Bars & Burgers)
Claire (Fish & Seafood)
Cloister Cafe (Cafés)
Coach House (American)
Contrapunto (Italian)
Cornelia Street Café (Cafés)
Crawdaddy (Soul & Creole)
Csarda (Hungarian)
Cupping Room Café (Breakfast/Brunch)
Curtain Up! (Bars & Burgers)
Darbar (Indian & Pakistani)
Da Silvano (Italian)
Délices La Cote Basque (Breakfast/Brunch)
De Robertis (Cafés)
Dézaley (Swiss)
Eclair Shop (Hungarian)
Elaine's (Stargazers)
El Coyote (Mexican)
Elephant & Castle (Omelettes & Crepes)
El Faro (Spanish)
El Gaucho (Latin American)
El Internacionale (Spanish: Tapas)
El Parador Café (Mexican)
El Rincón de España (Spanish)
El Tenampa (Mexican)
Empire Diner (Late Night/24 Hours)
Empress/Riveranda (Rooms with a View)
Erminia (Italian)
Evelyne's (Continental)
Fanelli's Café (Bars & Burgers)
Farnie's 2nd Avenue Steak Parlour (Steak Houses)
Felidia (Italian)
Ferrara's (Cafés)
Figaro Café (Sidewalk Cafés)
Fine & Shapiro (Delicatessen)
Fiorello's Roman Café (Sidewalk Cafés)
Fonda La Paloma (Mexican)
Food (Soup & Salad)
Forlini's (Italian)
Fountain Café (Sidewalk Cafés)
Four Seasons (Deluxe)
Francesca's (Italian)
Frank's (Steak Houses)
Fraunces Tavern Restaurant (American)
Frère Jacques (French)
Friday's (Bars & Burgers)
Front Porch (Soup & Salad)
Fulton Fish Market (Fish & Seafood)
Gage & Tollner (Fish & Seafood)
Gallagher's (Steak Houses)
Gargiulo's (Italian)
Garvins (American)
Gaylord (Indian & Pakistani)
Giambelli 50th Ristorante (Italian)

Serendipidy (American)
Shagorika (Indian & Pakistani)
Shezan (Indian & Pakistani)
Shun Lee Palace (Chinese)
Sign of the Dove (Continental)
65 Irving Place (Continental)
Smokey's (Soul & Creole)
SoHo Charcuterie (French)
SoHo Kitchen and Bar (Wine Bars)
Soom Thai (Thai)
Spark's Steak House (Steak Houses)
The Stage (Inexpensive)
Stage Deli (Delicatessens)
Suerken's Restaurant (German & Austrian)
Summerhouse (Continental)
Sumptuary Restaurant (Continental)
Sushiko (Japanese)
Sushi Zen (Japanese)
Sweet's (Fish & Seafood)
Swiss Inn (Swiss)
Sylvia's (Soul & Creole)
Taj Mahal (Indian & Pakastani)
Takesushi (Japanese)
Tavern on the Green (Rooms with a View)
Tavola Calda de Alfredo (Italian)
Teacher's (American)
Tennessee Mountain (American)
The Terrace (Rooms with a View)
Terrace Cafe (Sidewalk Cafés)
Texarkana (American)
Thailand Restaurant (Thai)
Thwaite's Inn (Fish & Seafood)
Tino's (Italian)
Tio Pepe (Spanish)
Top of the Park (Rooms with a View)
Top of the Sixes (Rooms with a View)
Top of the Tower (Rooms with a View)
Tout Va Bien (French)
Trader Vic's (Polynesian)
Trastevere & Trastevere 84 (Italian)
Trattoria da Alfredo (Italian)
Tres Carabelas (Spanish)
Tuesday's (Breakfast/Brunch)
24 Fifth (French)
"21" Club (Stargazers)
Ukrainian Restaurant (Inexpensive)
Umbert's Clam House (Fish & Seafood)
Uncle Tai's Hunan Yuan (Chinese)
Vanessa (American)
Vasata (Czechoslovakian)
Veselka (Breakfast/Brunch)
Victor's Café (Latin American)
Vienna '79 (German & Austrian)
Village Green (French)
Vivolo (Italian)
The Water Club (Rooms with a View)
Water's Edge Restaurant (Rooms with a View)
White Horse Tavern (Bars & Burgers)
Whole Wheat 'n' Wild Berries (Health & Vegetarian)
Windows on the World (Afternoon Tea; Rooms with a View)
Wine Bar (Wine Bars)
Woods (Continental)
Wylie's (Soul & Creole)

Wynn's Ba-Nam (Vietnamese)
Yellowfingers (Bars & Burgers)
Ye Olde Chop House (American)
Ye Waverly Inn (American)
Yonah Schimmel's (Jewish)
Yun Luck Rice Shoppe (Chinese)
Z (Greek)
Zinno (Italian)
Zucchini (Health & Vegetarian)

Restaurants: Geographic Index

—Downtown (Financial District, Seaport Area, Lower East Side)

American Harvest Restaurant (American)
Bernstein-on-Essex Street (Delicatessen)
Bridge Café (Continental)
Cellar in the Sky (Deluxe)
City Lights Bar (Rooms with a View)
El Rincón de España (Spanish)
Fraunces Tavern Restaurant (American)
Fulton Fish Market (Fish & Seafood)
Greenhouse (Soul & Creole)
Grand Dairy Restaurant (Jewish)
Hors D'Oeuvrerie (Breakfast/Brunch)
Jeremy's Ale House (Bars & Burgers)
Katz's Delicatessen (Delicatessen)
Nature's Kitchen (Health & Vegetarian)
Ratner's Dairy Restaurant (Jewish)
Sammy's Roumainian (Jewish)
Suerken's Restaurant (German & Austrian)
Sweets (Fish & Seafood)
Ye Olde Chop House (American)
Yonah Schimmel's (Jewish)
Windows on the World (Afternoon Tea; Rooms with a View)
Wynn's Ba Nam (Vietnamese)

—Chinatown

Bobo's (Chinese)
Cam Fung (Brunch: Dim Sum)
Chi Mer (Chinese)
Hee Seung Fung HSF (Brunch: Dim Sum)
Home Village (Chinese)
Hong Fat (Chinese)
Hwa Yuan Szechuan Inn (Chinese)
Little Shanghai (Chinese)
Nom Wah Tea Parlor (Brunch: Dim Sum)
Phoenix Garden (Chinese)
Say Eng Look (Chinese)
Thailand Restaurant (Thai)
Yun Luck Rice Shoppe (Chinese)

—Little Italy

Angelo's (Italian)
Ballato (Italian)
Caffè Biondo (Cafés)
Caffè Roma (Cafés)
Ferrara's (Cafés)
Forlini's (Italian)
Grotta Azzurra (Italian)
Osteria Romana (Italian)
Paolucci's (Italian)

Patrissey's (Italian)
Peacock (Italian)
Puglia's (Italian)
Umberto's Clam House (Fish & Seafood)

—TriBeCa

Barnabus Rex (Bars & Burgers)
Beach House (Mexican)
Bon Temps Rouler (Soul & Creole)
Capsouto Frères (French)
El Internacionale (Spanish: Tapas)
Laughing Mountain (Continental)
Le Saint Jean de Pres (Belgian)
Le Zinc (French)
Montrachet (French)
Odeon (French)

—SoHo

Abyssinia Restaurant (Ethiopian)
Berry's (Continental)
Broome Street Bar (Bars & Burgers)
Chanterelle (French)
Cinco de Mayo (Mexican)
Cupping Room Café (Breakfast/Brunch)
Elephant & Castle (Omlettes & Crepes)
Fanelli's Cafe (Bars & Burgers)
Food (Soup & Salad)
G. Lombardi (Italian)
La Gamelle (French)
Moondance Diner (Inexpensive)
Raoul's (French)
SoHo Charcuterie (French)
SoHo Kitchen Bar (Wine Bars)
Tennessee Mountain (American)
Wine Bar (Wine Bars)

—Greenwich Village

Amy's (Inexpensive)
Arnold's Turtle (Health & Vegetarian)
Asti (Italian)
Beatrice Inn (Italian)
Black Sheep (French)
Buffalo Roadhouse (Sidewalk Cafés)
Café des Bruxelles (Belgian)
Café Loup (French)
Café Vivaldi (Cafés)
Caffè Reggio (Cafés)
Cent'Anni (Italian)
Chez Brigitte (Inexpensive)
Chinese Chance (Bars & Burgers)
Chumley's (Bars & Burgers)
Coach House (American)
Cornelia Street Cafe (Cafés)
Da Silvano (Italian)
Elephant & Castle (Omelettes & Crepes)
El Faro (Spanish)
El Gaucho (Latin American)
El Rincón de España (Spanish)
Figaro Café (Sidewalk Cafés)
Front Porch (Soup & Salad)
Garvins (Continental)
Gordon (Italian)
Gotham Bar & Grill (Continental)
Gulf Coast (Soul & Creole)
Harbour House (Fish & Seafood)

Horn of Plenty (Soul & Creole)
Il Cantinori (Italian)
Il Mulino (Italian)
Il Ponte Vecchio (Italian)
Jane Street Seafood Cafe (Fish & Seafood)
Janice's Fish Place (Fish & Seafood)
Jimmy Day's (Bars & Burgers)
John Clancy's (Fish & Seafood)
John's Pizzeria (Pizza)
La Chaumière (French)
La Gauloise (French)
La Grande Corniche (Rooms with a View)
La Tulipe (French)
Le Café de la Gare (French)
Le Canard Englouti (French)
Le Métairie (French)
Le Petit Robert (French)
Lion's Head (Bars & Burgers)
Marylou's (Late Night/24 Hours)
Mary's (Italian)
Montana Eve (Bars & Burgers)
One Fifth (American)
One If By Land (American)
Peacock (Cafés)
Pink Tea Cup (Breakfast/Brunch)
Pirandello (Italian)
Ray's Pizza (Pizza)
Riviera Cafe (Sidewalk Cafés)
Rumbuls (Inexpensive)
Sabor (Latin American)
Sazerac House (Soul & Creole)
Tavola Calda da Alfredo (Italian)
Texarkana (American)
Trattoria da Alfredo (Italian)
24 Fifth (French)
Vanessa (American)
Village Green (French)
White House Tavern (Bars & Burgers)
Whole Wheat 'n' Wild Berries (Health & Vegetarian)
Ye Waverly Inn (American)
Zinno (Italian)

—East Village/NoHo

B & H Dairy (Jewish)
Bayamo (Latin American)
Café Orlin (Breakfast/Brunch)
Caramba!! (Mexican)
Cloister Cafe (Cafés)
De Robertis (Cafés)
El Coyote (Mexican)
Evelyne's (French)
Great Jones Café (Late Night/24 Hours)
Indochine (Vietnamese)
Little Kitchen (Soul & Creole)
Kiev International (Late Night/24 Hours)
McSorley's Old Ale House (Bars & Burgers)
Mie (Japanese)
103 Second Avenue (Late Night/24 Hours)
Paul's Restaurant & Lounge (Bars & Burgers)
Phebe's Place (Bars & Burgers)
Pier Nine (Fish & Seafood)
Pizza Piazza (Breakfast/Brunch)

Second Avenue Kosher Delicatessen (Delicatessen)
Shagorika (Indian & Pakistani)
The Stage (Inexpensive)
Ukrainian Restaurant (Inexpensive)
Veselka (Breakfast/Brunch)

—East 14th–23rd Streets

America (American)
Brownie's (Health & Vegetarian)
Farnie's 2nd Avenue Steak Parlour (Steak Houses)
Front Porch (Soup & Salad)
Hubert's (American)
Joanna (Continental)
Pesca (Fish & Seafood)
Pete's Tavern (Bars & Burgers)
Positano (Italian)
65 Irving Place (Continental)
Smokey's (Soul & Creole)
Tuesday's (Bars & Burgers)
Woods (Continental)
Z (Greek)

—East 24th–42nd Streets

Akasaka (Japanese)
Ararat (Middle Eastern)
Balkan Armenian (Middle Eastern)
B. Altman (Department Store Restaurants)
Bienvenue (French)
Cedars of Lebanon (Middle Eastern)
El Parador (Mexican)
Francesca's (Italian)
Horn and Hordart Automat (Inexpensive)
Jackson Hole Wyoming (Bars & Burgers)
Josephine (Italian)
Kitty Hawk (Breakfast/Brunch)
La Bonne Bouffe (French)
La Colombe d'Or (French)
La Louisiana (Soul & Creole)
Marchi's (Italian)
Mary Elizabeth (Afternoon Tea)
Mexico Lindo (Mexican)
Mimosa (Omelettes & Crepes)
Mon Paris (French)
Nicola Paone (Italian)
Orchid (American)
Oyster Bar & Restaurant (Fish & Seafood)
Sumptuary Restaurant (Continental)
Tres Carabelas (Mexican)
The Water Club (Rooms with a View)

—East 43rd–59th Streets

Alexander's (Department Store Restaurants)
Ambassador Grill (Breakfast/Brunch)
Auberge Suisse (Swiss)
Beijing Duck House (Chinese)
Benihana of Tokyo (Japanese)
Bloomingdale's (Department Store Restaurants)
Box Tree (French)
Brasserie (Late Night/24 Hours)
Brazilian Pavilion (Latin American)
Café Argenteuil (French)
Castillian (Spanish)
The Cattleman (Steak Houses)

Chalet Suisse (Swiss)
Christ Cella (Steak Houses)
Crawdaddy (Soul & Creole)
Dézaley (Swiss)
Felidia (Italian)
Fonda La Paloma (Mexican)
Four Seasons (Deluxe)
Gaylord (Indian & Pakistani)
Giambelli 50th Ristorante (Italian)
Goldberg's Pizzeria (Pizza)
Healthworks (Soup & Salad)
Helmsley Palace (Afternoon Tea)
Hunam (Chinese)
Il Menestrello (Italian)
Il Nido (Italian)
India Pavilion (Indian & Pakistani)
Jake's (Steak Houses)
Kaplan's at the Delmonico (Delicatessen)
Kenny's Steak Pub (Steak Houses)
Kitcho (Japanese)
La Bibliothèque (French)
La Bonne Soup (Soup & Salad)
La Cave Henri IV (French)
La Côte Basque (Deluxe)
La Grenouille (Deluxe)
La Mangeoire (French)
La Petite Marmite (French)
Laurent (French)
Le Bistro (French)
Le Chantilly (French)
Le CherchéMidi (French)
Le Cygne (Deluxe)
Le Steak (French)
Les Tournebroches (French)
Louise Junior (Italian)
Lutèce (Deluxe)
Magic Pan Creperie (Omelettes & Crepes)
Mimosa (Omelettes & Crepes)
Mr. Chow (Chinese)
Nanni's (Italian)
Nippon (Japanese)
Nyborg Nelson (Inexpensive)
Oliver's (American)
Palm (Steak Houses)
Pen & Pencil (Steak Houses)
P.J. Clarke's (Bars & Burgers)
Quilted Giraffe (French)
Saito (Japanese)
Shun Lee Palace (Chinese)
Spark's Steak House (Steak House)
Swiss Inn (Swiss)
Takesushi (Japanese)
Tino's (Italian)
Top of the Tower (Rooms with a View)
Wylie's (Soul & Creole)
Yellowfingers (Bars & Burgers)

—East 60th–79th Streets

Adam's Apple (Bars & Burgers)
Adam's Rib (American)
Alo Alo (Italian)
American Place (American)
Aunti Yuan (Chinese)
Cafe Marimba (Mexican)
Café Marigold (Continental)
Carlyle Restaurant (Continental)

Chatfield's (Continental)
Contrapunto (Italian)
Csarda (Hungarian)
Délices La Côte Basque (Breakfast/Brunch)
Friday's (Bars & Burgers)
Il Caminetto (Italian)
Il Monello (Italian)
Il Vagabondo (Italian)
Jackson Hole Wyoming (Bars & Burgers)
Jams (American)
J.G. Melon (Bars & Burgers)
Jim McMullen (Bars & Burgers)
John's Pizzeria (Pizza)
La Goulue (French)
La Petite Ferme (French)
Le Cirque (Stargazers)
Le Lavendou (French)
Le Perigord Park (French)
Le Relais (French)
Le Veau d'Or (French)
Lion's Rock (Continental)
Madame Romaine de Lyon (Omelettes & Crepes)
Mayfair Regent (Afternoon Tea)
Maxwell's Plum (Continental)
Mezzaluna (Italian)
Mortimer's (Continental)
Nanni al Valetto (Italian)
Oscar's Salt of the Sea (Fish & Seafood)
Parma (Italian)
Petaluma (Late Night/24 Hours)
The Polo (French)
The Post House (Steak Houses)
Ravelled Sleave (Continental)
Regency Hotel (Breakfast/Brunch)
Ruc (Czechoslovakian)
Safari Grill (American)
Serendipity (American)
Sign of the Dove (Continental)
Soomthai (Thai)
Taj Mahal (Indian & Pakistani)
Uncle Tai's Hunan Yuan (Chinese)
Vasata (Czechoslovakian)
Vienna '79 (German & Austrian)
Vivolo (Italian)
Woods (Continental)
Zucchini (Health & Vegetarian)

—East 80th–96th Streets

Casa Brazil (Latin American)
Elaine's (Italian)
Erminia (Italian)
Gibbon (Japanese)
Gimbels East (Department Store Restaurants)
Jackson Hole Wyoming (Bars & Burgers)
Kleine Konditorei (German & Austrian)
Le Boeuf a la Mode (French)
Martell's (Bars & Burgers)
Parioli Romanissimo (Italian)
Pig Heaven (Chinese)
Pinocchio (Italian)
Sarabeth's Kitchen (Breakfast/Brunch)
Summerhouse (Continental)
Terrace Cafe (Sidewalk Cafés)
Trastevere & Trastevere 84 (Italian)

—Above East 97th Street

Rao's (Italian)

—West 14th–23rd Streets

Blue Plate (Inexpensive)
Café Seiyoken (Japanese)
Cajun (Soul & Creole)
Chelsea Place (Continental)
Claire (Fish & Seafood)
Empire Diner (Late Night/24 Hours)
Empress/Riveranda (Rooms with a View)
Frank's (Steak Houses)
La Colonna (Italian)
Moran's (Bars & Burgers)
Old Homestead Restaurant (Steak Houses)
Quatorze (French)
Roxanne's (American)

—West 24th–34th Streets

Gimbels (Department Store Restaurants)
Hershey Dairy Restaurant (Jewish)
Macy's (Department Store Restaurants)
Market Diner (Late Night/24 Hours)
Ohrbach's (Department Store Restaurants)
P.J. Clarke's, Macy's Celler (Bars & Burgers)
Rojas Lombardi at the Ballroom (Spanish: Tapas)
Smokey's (Soul & Creole)

—West 35th–49th Streets
(Theater District)

Algonquin Rose Room (Late Night/24 Hours)
Amy's (Inexpensive)
Barbetta (Italian)
Barking Fish Cafe (Soul & Creole)
Benihana of Tokyo (Japanese)
Brazilian Coffee Restaurant (Latin American)
Broadway Joe (Steak Houses)
Cabana Carioca (Latin American)
Café in the Cradle (Middle Eastern)
Café Un Deux Trois (Stargazers)
Carolina (American)
Charley O's Bar & Grill (Bars & Burgers)
Curtain Up! (Bars & Burgers)
El Tenempa (Mexican)
Frère Jacques (French)
Giordano (Italian)
Jezebel (Soul & Creole)
Joe Allen's (Stargazers)
Kashmir (Indian & Pakistan)
Kitcho (Japanese)
La Crepe (Omelettes & Crepes)
Landmark Tavern (Bars & Burgers)
Lattanzi (Italian)
Lavin's (French)
Le Chambertain (French)
Lord & Taylor (Department Store Restaurants)
Lou Siegel's (Jewish)
Mama Leone's (Italian)
Manganero's Grosseria Italiana (Italian)
Market Diner (Late Night/24 Hours)
Molfeta's (Greek)
Moshe Peking (Jewish)
Myong Dong (Korean)
Nick & Guido (Italiana)
Nirvana Club One (Rooms with a View)

Orso (Italian)
Pantheon (Greek)
Pearl's Chinese Restaurant (Chinese)
Raga (Indian & Pakastan)
Rose Room (Late Night/24 Hours)
Sardi's (Stargazers)
Sea Grill (Fish & Seafood)
Sushi Zen (Japanese
Woods (Continental)

—West 50th–57th Streets

Amy's (Inexpensive)
Aperitivo (Italian)
Arirang House (Korean)
Assembly Steak House (Steak Houses)
Bangkok Cuisine (Thai)
Benihana of Tokyo (Japanese)
Bombay Palace (Indian & Pakistani)
Britanny du Soir (French)
Cabana Carioca (Latin American)
Caramba! (Mexican)
Carnegie Delicatessen (Delicatessen)
Chez Napoleon (French)
Darbar (Indian & Pakistani)
Gallagher's (Steak Houses)
Great American Health Bar (Health & Vegetarian)
Hard Rock Cafe (Late Night/24 Hours)
Joe's Pier 52 (Fish & Seafood)
King Crab (Fish & Seafood)
La Bonne Soup (Soup & Salad)
La Caravelle (Deluxe)
La Crêpe (Omelettes & Crepes)
La Fondue (Inexpensive)
Le Quercy (French)
Les Pyrénées (French)
Luchows on Broadway (German & Austrian)
Manhattan Ocean Club (Fish & Seafood)
Orsini's (Italian)
René Pujol (French)
Restaurant Raphael (French)
Richoux of London (Late Night/24 Hours)
Rio de Janeiro/Boat 57 Seafood House (Latin American)
Romeo Salta (Italian)
Russian Tea Room (Stargazers)
Sea Fare of the Aegean (Fish & Seafood)
Seeda Thai (Thai)
Sushiko (Japanese)
Stage Deli (Delicatessen)
Top of the Sixes (Rooms with a View)
Tout Va Bien (French)
"21" Club (Stargazers)
Victor's Cafe (Latin American)
Wylie's (Soul & Creole)

—West 58th–72nd Streets

Alfredo (Italian)
Amy's (Inexpensive)
Bergdorf Goodman (Department Store Restaurants)
Café de la Paix (Sidewalk Cafés)
Café des Artistes (Continental)
Café Luxembourg (Late Night/24 Hours)
Eclair Shop (Hungarian)

Fine & Shapiro (Delicatessen)
Fiorello's Roman Café (Sidewalk Cafés)
Fountain Café (Sidewalk Cafés)
Ginger Man (American)
Jean Lafitte (French)
La Crépe (Omelettes & Crepes)
Nirvana (Rooms with a View)
Oak Bar (Bars & Burgers)
O'Neal's Baloon (Bars & Burgers)
Petrossian (French)
The Plaza (Afternoon Tea)
The Saloon (Sidewalk Cafés)
Shezan (Indian & Pakistani)
Tavern on the Green (Rooms with a View)
Top of the Park (Rooms with a View)
Trader Vic's (Polynesian)
Victor's Café (Latin American)

—West 73rd–96th Streets

Amsterdam's Bar & Rotisserie (Late Night/24 Hours)
Barnery Greenglass (Jewish)
Café Central (Late Night/24 Hours)
Caramba!!! (Mexican)
Front Porch (Soup & Salads)
Hunam Taste (Chinese)
J.G. Melon (Bars & Burgers)
Julia (Continental)
Memphis (Soul & Creole)
Museum Café (Bars & Burgers)
Oenophilia (Continental)
Rúelles (Continental)
Sarabeth's Kitchen (Breakfast/Brunch)
Smokey's (Soul & Creole)
Teacher's (American)
Victor's Café (Latin American)

—Above West 97 Street

Amy's (Inexpensive)
Green Tree (Inexpensive)
Sylvia's (Soul & Creole)
The Terrace (Rooms with a View)

—Brooklyn

Abraham & Straus (Department Store Restaurants)
Gage & Tollner (Fish & Seafood)
Gargiulio's (Italian)
Hamilton House (Steak Houses)
Junior's (Inexpensive)
Lisanne (French)
Nathan's (Inexpensive)
Old Mexico (Mexico)
Peter Lugar (Steak House)
River Café (Rooms with a View)

—Bronx

Anna's Harbor Restaurant (Rooms with a View)
Thwaite's Inn (Fish & Seafood)

—Queens

Water's Edge Restaurant (Rooms with a View)

Restaurants by Specialty

Afternoon Tea
Perhaps part of the Europeanization of America, afternoon tea is catching on and it's oh so civi-

lized. In addition to the hotels described below, afternoon tea is served at the Algonquin, the American Stanhope, Berkshire Place, the Carlyle, the Inter-Continental, and the Pierre, all in extremely attractive settings.

Helmsley Palace
455 Madison Avenue at East 51 St. In the opulent 19th-century Gold Room a choice of Fortnum & Mason teas, tea sandwiches, scones with Devonshire cream and jam, miniature pastries, fruit tarts. The stiffest prix fixe but worth the view. Harpist as well. *Served 7 days 2:30-5:30pm.* $

Mary Elizabeth
6 East 37 Street. 683-3018. A lovely anachronism: tearoom, cruller bar and bakery. Old fashioned spot to have a different soup daily but most of all tasty homemade desserts with your tea. A la carte. *Served Mon-Sat 11am-3pm.* $

Mayfair Regent
610 Park Avenue at East 65 St. 288-0800. In the intimate and elegant lobby lounge a wide choice of teas including herbal. Tea sandwiches, pastries, scones, cream and jam. Also, espresso and cappuccino. Prix fixe. *Served 7 days 3-6pm.* $

The Plaza
Fifth Avenue & 59 Street. 759-3000. Tea in the Old World Palm Court is a New York tradition. Choice of several teas, open-face sandwiches and pastries. In a palm-bedecked enclave, serenaded by violins. A la carte. *Served Mon-Fri 3:30-8pm; Sat & Sun 4-8pm.* $

Windows on the World
1 World Trade Center, 107th fl. 938-1111. In the Hors D'Oeuvrerie, tea (coffee, too) is served in time to watch the day turn to night and in winter view the most spectacular sunsets from this ¼-mile-high perch. Fine selection of teas offered; open-face tea sandwiches and pastries, too. Piano music from 4:30pm; dancing on Sun from 4pm. No cover before 7:30pm, so this is one of the town's best bargains. Jacket required; no denim. Free parking. A la carte. *Served 7 days 3-6pm.* $

American

This list includes the traditional as well as the latest food rage, "new" American or "regional" American cooking.
See also Soul/Creole and Steak.

Adam's Rib
23 East 74 Street. 535-2112. Traditional restaurant specializes in prime ribs of beef on or off the bone. Burgers and omelettes at lunch. Reserve. DC, MC, V. *OPEN Mon-Fri noon-11pm; Sat & Sun from 4:30pm.* $$

America
9-13 East 18 Street. 505-2110. Restaurant as theater, and a noisy one at that. Huge is the key word here—the place (seats 400), the plates, and the portions. The copious menu features such all-American treats as macaroni and cheese, chili, sweet potato pancakes, Buffalo chicken wings; even fluffernutters! Just don't take any of it

seriously. Reserve! AE, DC, MC, V. *OPEN 7 days 11:30am-1am. Bar till 2 or 3am.* $

American Harvest Restaurant
Vista International, 3 World Trade Center. 938-9100, ext 7231. Seasonal American fare in a traditional setting. Menu changes monthly. Smithfield ham with ripe fruit garnishes, broiled salmon, Caesar Salad. Reserve. AE, CB, DC, MC, V. *L Mon-Fri noon-2:30pm. D Mon-Sat 6-10pm. CLOSED Sun.* $$$

American Place
969 Lexington Avenue nr East 70 St. 517-7660. Larry Forgione's own place—an intimate space in which to enjoy artfully presented American grown foodstuff. New Orleans blackened fish, barbequed mallard, Key West shrimp with mustard sauce. Tops of its genre. American wines only. Jacket & tie. Prix fixe. Reserve! AE, CB, DC, MC, V. *L Mon-Fri noon-2pm. D Mon-Sat 6-11pm. CLOSED Sun.* $$$$

Carolina
355 West 46 Street. 245-0058. Smart Theater Row newcomer serves beautifully-prepared regional American dishes. Much of the meat is smoked over a wood-fired barbecue process called "hot smoke." Eclectic menu offers crab cakes, rich and spicy beanless chili, beef brisket, red pepper shrimp. The Mudd Cake is a must! Quieter front and upstairs dining rooms; glitzy mirrored skylit backroom. American wines & champagnes. Reserve. MC, V. *L Mon-Fri noon-3pm. D Mon-Sat 5:30-midnight; Sun 5-10pm.* $$$

Coach House
110 Waverly Place nr Sixth Ave. 777-0303. A former coach house (circa 1843) provides a handsome setting for American/Continental dishes. Famed crab cakes, black bean soup; wonderful desserts. Jacket & tie. Reserve. AE, CB, DC, MC, V. *OPEN Tues-Sat 5:30-10:30pm; Sun 4:30-10pm. CLOSED Mon & major holidays.* $$$$

Fraunces Tavern Restaurant
54 Pearl Street nr Broad St. 269-0144. Mainly of historic value. Reconstructed on the site of Washington's farewell to his troops in 1783. There is a museum upstairs. (*See* MUSEUMS & GALLERIES, Historic Museums.) Colonial dining room, with fireplace, serves yankee pot roast, steak, burgers, baked chicken á la Washington. Jacket & tie. Reserve. AE, CB, DC, MC, V. *OPEN Mon-Fri 11:45am-9pm. CLOSED Sat & Sun.* $$

Ginger Man
51 West 64 Street. 724-7272, 399-2358. For over 20 years this attractive, fashionable Lincoln Center-vicinity restaurant has drawn crowds, especially before and after performances. Steaks, fish, burgers, omelettes, great spinach-bacon-mushroom salads and tasty onion soup. Enclosed sidewalk café. Reserve. AE, CB, DC, MC, V. *OPEN 7 days 11:30am-midnight. Sun Brunch 11:30am-4pm.* $$

Hubert's
102 East 22 Street. 673-3711. Famed Brooklyn restaurant crosses the Bridge, bringing their new American cuisine to new, sophisticated, albeit spare, surroundings. Traditional dishes using the

freshest native ingredients, all cooked to order. Superb desserts. Reserve. AE only. *L Mon-Fri noon-3pm. D Mon-Sat 6-10:30pm. CLOSED Sun (except Sun, holidays).* $$

Jams
154 East 79 Street. 772-6800. Jonathan Waxman's famed "California minimalist" cooking; nouvelle meets LA and the results are very successful. Fish and fowl, beef and lamb, grilled over mesquite, vegetables poached or steamed; all on oversized plates from the exposed kitchen. Menu changes daily. As expected the California wine selection is quite good. Downstairs is quieter. Reserve! AE only. *L Tues-Fri noon-2:15pm. D Mon-Sat 6-11:15pm.* $$$$

Oliver's
141 East 57 Street. 753-9180. Congenial spot for American food, burgers, prime ribs, lobsters, salads. Piano music 7pm-midnight and a fireplace. Reserve. AE, CB, DC, MC, V. *OPEN 7 days 11:30am-1am.* $$

One Fifth
1 Fifth Avenue at 8 St. 260-3434. The décor: authentic salvage from the *S.S. Caronia*. Classy, extremely relaxed setting for wonderful food and wine. Double chicken breast with two mustards, roquefort beignets, grilled veal chop and one of the best-valued wine lists in the city. Suffer the service. Reserve. AE, CB, DC, MC, V. *L Mon-Fri noon-3pm. D Mon-Thurs 6pm-12:30am; Fri 6pm-1:30am; Sat 6:30pm-1:30am; Sun 6:30pm-12:30am. Brunch: Sat noon-3pm; Sun 11am-4:30pm.* $$

One If by Land, Two If by Sea
17 Barrow Street nr Sheridan Sq. 255-8649. Beautiful romantic dining in Aaron Burr's former carriage house. Emphasis is on American dishes; some Continental entrées. Two working fireplaces in winter. Reserve. AE, CB, DC, MC, V. *OPEN 7 days 5:30pm-midnight.* $$$

Orchid
81 Lexington Avenue at East 26 St. 889-0960. A modest restaurant, done up in down-market Deco. Offers an imaginative eclectic menu. Chicken Kiev, fettucine, spare ribs. Good burgers, friendly bar. Jazz Sat at 10pm. Reserve. AE, DC, MC, V. *OPEN Sun-Fri noon-11:30pm; Sat till 12:30am; Sun noon-11:30pm. Brunch: Sat noon-4pm; Sun noon-6pm.* $

Roxanne's
158 Eighth Avenue at West 18 St. 741-2455. Romantic blossom-bedecked Chelsea bistro for well-prepared new American cooking. On the lower level a small special umbrella-shaded garden. Reserve. AE, MC, V. *L Mon-Fri noon-2:30pm. D Mon-Sat 6-11pm.* $$

Safari Grill
1115 Third Avenue nr East 65 St. 371-9090. A stylish brasserie-inspired creation where uptown trendies dine on quite good American cuisine. In-view grill separates the two dining areas. AE, DC. Reserve. *L Mon-Fri 11:30am-3pm. D 7 nights 6pm-midnight. Sun Brunch 11:30am-3pm.* $$

Serendipity
225 East 60 Street. 838-3531. Long-time (30

years) restaurant/general store. A fun lunch spot for burgers, shepherd's pie, omelettes; or for late snacking on a frozen hot chocolate or a banana split. Up front: clothing, gifts and novelties. For the young at heart. AE, DC, MC, V. *OPEN Mon-Thurs 11:30am-12:30am; Fri till 1am; Sat till 2am; Sun noon-midnight.* $

Teacher's
2249 Broadway nr West 80 St. 787-3500. Casual Upper West Side neighborhood restaurant. Blackboard menu, seafood specials, good spinach salad. Reserve. AE, DC, MC, V. *OPEN 7 days 11am-1am.* $$

Tennessee Mountain
143 Spring Street nr Wooster St. 431-3993. Charming casual choice for fresh American food. Excellent meaty beef and baby back ribs; wonderful onion rings and vegetarian or meat chili. Apple walnut or pecan pie for dessert. Reserve. AE, MC, V. *OPEN Mon-Wed 11:30am-11pm; Thurs-Sat till midnight; Sun till 10pm.* $

Texarkana
64 West 10 Street. 254-5800. Very good specialties of the Great Southwest and Gulf Coast in an appropriately appointed setting. Everyday a suckling pig is slowly roasted over glowing charcoal in a copper-faced fireplace (reserve pig when you reserve your table). Also, pickled Gulf shrimp, crawfish pie, grilled lamb chops, black-eyed peas, cornbread, homemade ice creams. Tex & Mex beers. Reserve. AE, DC. *OPEN Sun & Mon 6pm-midnight; Tues-Sat till 3:45am.* $$

Vanessa
289 Bleecker Street at Seventh Ave So. 243-4225. Good American nouvelle in a stylish Art Deco-inspired setting. Shrimp and leek salad, calves' liver with pearl onions and bacon, sauteed salmon with sorrel sauce. Reserve. Jacket & tie preferred. AE, DC, MC, V. *D 7 days 6pm-midnight. Sun Brunch (except in winter) 11am-4pm.* $$$

Ye Olde Chop House
111 Broadway nr Wall St. 732-6119. Old mementos, Lincoln campaign posters in this financial-district eatery. Excellent grilled meats, Smithfield ham. Reserve. AE, CB, DC, MC, V. *OPEN Mon-Fri 11:30am-7pm. CLOSED Sat & Sun.* $$$

Ye Waverly Inn
16 Bank Street at Waverly Pl. 929-4377. Charming colonial-tavern feel in this original 178-year-old Greenwich Village town house. Comfortable, simple ambiance, food to match. Good pot pies and other traditional American dishes. Pleasant back garden, two working fireplaces warm in winter. AE, CB, DC, MC, V. *L Mon-Fri 11:45am-2pm; D Mon-Thurs 5:15-10pm; Fri & Sat till 11pm; Sun 4:30-9pm. (Lower priced early bird dinner Mon-Thurs 5:15-6:15pm.) Sun Brunch noon-3:30pm.* $

Bars & Burgers

Adam's Apple
1117 First Avenue nr East 61 St. 371-8651. Singles spot for drinks, burgers, steaks, lobster and salads. Enclosed sidewalk café. Reserve on weekends. AE, CB, DC, MC, V. *OPEN 7 days 4pm till 4am.* $

Barnabus Rex
155 Duane Street nr West Broadway. 962-9692.
Good untrendy bar with jukebox and pool table in
TriBeCa. Spills out onto the street in good weath-
er. Burgers only. No reservations. No credit cards.
OPEN 7 days 11am-4am. $

Broome Street Bar
363 West Broadway at Broome St. 925-2086.
Comfortable busy bar/restaurant reputed to have
the best burgers in SoHo. Homemade soup and
desserts. The drinks are big. Popular with artists.
No reservations. No credit cards. *OPEN Sun-
Thurs noon-1:30am; Fri & Sat till 2:30am. Bar till
2am weekdays, 4am Fri & Sat. Weekend Brunch
11am-4pm.* $

Charley O's Bar & Grill
33 West 48 Street. 582-7141. Busy Irish-pub-style
restaurant. Self-service sandwich-and-oyster/
clam/shrimp bar and dining room specialties:
corned beef and cabbage, fish and chips. Reserve for lunch. AE, CB, DC, MC, V. Free parking
at Rockefeller Center Garage. *L Mon-Fri
11:30am-3pm. D 7 days 5-11:30pm. Weekend
Brunch noon-3pm.* $

Chinese Chance
1 University Place at Washington St. 677-4440.
The late great Mickey Ruskin of the late great
Max's (amen) founded this one. Called "One U" by
those in the know. Not bad food, but the bar is for
serious drinking downtowners who find each
other here. *OPEN 7 days noon-4am.* $

Chumley's
86 Bedford Street nr Barrow St. 243-9729. Colorful old Greenwich Village literary landmark. No
sign to indicate its presence, but once you find it
comfort, good inexpensive food and drink are
yours. Fireplace ablaze in winter. AE, CB, DC,
MC, V. *OPEN Sun-Thurs 5pm-midnight; Fri & Sat
till 1am. Weekend Brunch noon-4pm.* $

Curtain Up!
402 West 43 Street. 564-7272. Broadway-theater
theme; youthful showbiz feel. Burgers, salads,
chili, omelettes, steak, home-baked desserts.
Sidewalk café in summer. Reserve. AE, CB, DC,
MC, V. *OPEN Sun & Mon noon-midnight; Tues,
Wed & Thurs till 1am; Fri & Sat till 2am.* $$

Fanelli's Café
94 Prince Street nr Mercer St. 226-9412. A 125-
year-old neighborhood bar that serves daily
specials. The food is basic, the atmosphere au-
thentic. No credit cards. *OPEN 7 days noon-
1am.* $

Friday's
1152 First Avenue nr East 63 St. 832-8512.
Famed popular singles spot. Crowd is young and
lively. Food is the usual pub fare: burgers, steaks,
ribs, salads. Brunch is value for volume. AE, DC,
MC, V. *OPEN Sun-Thurs 11:30am-1am; Fri & Sat
till 3am. Weekend Brunch 11:30am-4pm.* $

Jackson Hole Wyoming
232 East 64 Street (371-7187); 1633 Second Ave-
nue at East 85 St (737-8788); 531 Third Avenue nr
East 34 St (679-3264). Hamburger connoisseurs
consider this the best in town. Twelve versions of
burger; if you can resist them, there are omelettes

too. Beer & wine only. *OPEN Mon-Sat 11am-1am;
Sun noon-midnight.* $

Jeremy's Ale House
259 Front Street at Dover St. 964-3537. A few
blocks north of the restored Seaport is a ram-
shackle 1806 landmark building housing this long
narrow restaurant with a 60-foot bar. Bare bones
decor, beer by the quart (styrofoam "buckets"),
chalkboard menu for sandwiches, fish and chips,
clam chowder and chili. Atmospheric and con-
vivial. No credit cards. *OPEN Mon-Sat 7am-
9:30pm. CLOSED Sun.* $

J. G. Melon
1291 Third Avenue at East 74 St. 744-0585; *349
Amsterdam Avenue at West 81 St. 874-8291. For
years the best bar-burger (dripping onto a paper
plate) on the Upper East Side; now on the West
Side too. No reservations. MC, V. ($20 minimum)
*OPEN 7 days 11:30am-2:30am for food; bar till
4am. *Food till 1am; bar till 2:30am.* $

Jim McMullen
1341 Third Avenue nr East 76 St. 861-4700.
Handsome bar and dining room with Art Deco
motif. OK steaks, chops, seafood; daily specials.
Glass-enclosed garden. The bar where "pretty
people" find one another is crowded. Reserva-
tions not accepted. No credit cards. *OPEN 7 days
11:30am-1:45am.* $

Jimmy Day's
186 West 4 Street at Barrow St. 929-8942. Busy
Village Irish saloon with outdoor café, cable TV. The
cocktails are the cheapest in town. No credit cards.
OPEN Mon-Sat 10am-3:30am; Sun from noon. $

Landmark Tavern
626 Eleventh Avenue at West 46 St. 757-8595.
The Tavern, which dates back to 1868, features
traditional fare, including steak-and-kidney pie,
fish and chips, shepherd's pie. Upstairs dining
room has two fireplaces; the back room, a potbelly
stove to warm you in winter. Reserve. *L Mon-Sat
noon-4pm. D Sun-Thurs 5pm-midnight, Fri & Sat
till 1am. Sun Brunch noon-4pm.* $

Lion's Head
59 Christopher Street nr Sheridan Square. 929-
0670. Popular Greenwich Village literary gather-
ing place. Burgers, quiche, shepherd's pie, steak.
Wide selection of ales and beers on tap. *L Mon-Fri
noon-3pm. D Sun-Thurs 5pm-2am; Fri & Sat till
2:30am. Weekend Brunch noon-4pm.* $

Martell's
1469 Third Avenue at East 83 St. 861-6110.
Casual Upper East Side bar/restaurant; a la carte
Continental menu; good burgers on pita bread,
fried onions. In winter two woodburning fire-
places; in summer a wraparound sidewalk café.
AE, DC, MC, V. *OPEN Mon-Fri 4pm-2am; Sat &
Sun from noon.* $

McSorley's Old Ale House
15 East 7 Street. 473-8800. Operating con-
tinuously (even through Prohibition) since 1854.
Colorful, no-nonsense, formerly males-only East
Village ale house. Pub grub and a collegiate clien-
tele. Potbelly stove in winter. No reservations. No
credit cards. *OPEN Mon-Sat 10:30am-midnight;
Sun from 1pm.* $

Montana Eve
140 Seventh Avenue South nr West 10 St. 242-
1200. Appealing Greenwich Village eatery for
casual dining on burgers, salads, quiches. Two
fireplaces in winter, enclosed and open-air sidewalk cafés in summer. No credit cards. *OPEN 7
days noon-2am. Bar till 4am.* $

Moran's
146 Tenth Avenue at West 19 St. 989-9225. No
less than three fireplaces cozy up this old neighborhood Irish bar. Specialty: seafood. Fresh
clams and oysters and, of course, *great* Irish coffee. Enclosed sidewalk café. Reserve. AE, DC,
MC, V. *OPEN 7 days 11am-1am.* $

Museum Café
366 Columbus Avenue nr West 77 St. 799-0150.
Bright, popular glassed-in outdoor café, bar and
restaurant. Good burgers, omelettes, and Columbus Avenue view. Reserve. AE, DC, MC, V.
OPEN 7 days 11:30am-1am. $

Oak Bar
Plaza Hotel, Fifth Avenue & 59 Street. 759-3000.
Traditional, wood-paneled bar in famed hotel.
Attractive, friendly ambiance. Jacket required.
AE, CB, DC, MC, V. *OPEN Mon-Sat 11am-2am;
Sun noon-1am.* $

O'Neal's Baloon
48 West 63 Street. 399-2353. Popular Lincoln
Center-area saloon/restaurant. Enclosed sidewalk café. Great burgers, chili, salads, fried chick-
en. Reserve for large parties only. AE, CB, DC,
MC, V. *OPEN 7 days 11:30am-midnight. Bar till
2am.* $$

Paul's Restaurant & Lounge
46 Third Avenue at East 10 St. 473-8821. This
friendly neighborhood bar will surprise you with its
fine Italian specialties. Great burgers too. AE.
OPEN 7 days 11:30am-3:30am. $

Pete's Tavern
129 East 18 Street at Irving Pl. 473-7676. Atmo-
spheric 1864 tavern where O. Henry, who lived
across the street, wrote "The Gift of the Magi." The
original bar is quite popular. Mainly Italian food;
outdoor café in summer. AE, CB, DC, MC, V.
*OPEN Mon-Thurs & Sun noon-11:30pm; Fri & Sat
till 12:30am. Weekend Brunch noon-5pm.* $

Phebe's Place
361 Bowery at East 4 St. 473-9008. Extremely
casual gathering spot for Off-Broadway actors
and audience. Great burgers, fried chicken, spin-
ach salad. Wide menu available. Good bar; en-
closed sidewalk café. AE, CB, DC, MC, V. *OPEN
7 days 11:30am-4am.* Nightowl low-priced special
Sun-Wed midnight-4am. Weekend & Holiday
Brunch 11:30am-4:30pm. $

P. J. Clarke's
915 Third Avenue at East 55 St. 759-1650. Also at
Macy's Cellar. 564-5690. It's a classic: white-
haired bartenders. European beers, sawdust on
the floor. Literally rub shoulders with New Yorkers
at the extremely popular front-room bar at noon
and 5pm. Atmospheric dark back-room dining
room. Best bites: the burgers and spinach salad.
Reserve. No credit cards. *OPEN 7 days noon till
4am.* $

White Horse Tavern
560 Hudson Street at West 11 St. 243-9260.
Famed and friendly old Greenwich Village literary
watering hole; Dylan Thomas and Norman Mailer
are among the many who have imbibed here.
Great burgers, fish and chips, and chili, to go with
the booze. In season, the largest outdoor cafe in
the Village. No credit cards. *OPEN Sun-Thurs
11am-2:30am; Fri till 4am; Sat till 3am. Weekend
Brunch 11am-4pm.* $

Yellowfingers
1009 Third Avenue at East 60 St. 751-8615.
Where the pretty people have burgers and salads
and a good view of Bloomingdale's. AE, DC, MC,
V. *OPEN Mon-Sat 11:30am-midnight; Sun 2-
10pm.* $

Belgian

Café des Bruxelles
118 Greenwich Avenue at West 13 St. 206-1830.
The hearty cuisine of Belgium in a handsome
Greenwich Village setting. Waterzooi de poulet
carbonnade flamanade, boudin blanc et frites.
Belgian chocolate mousse. Good inexpensive
wine selection. Reserve. AE, MC, V. *L Mon-Fri
noon-3:30pm. D Mon-Thurs 6-11pm; Fri & Sat till
midnight; Sun till 10pm. Weekend Brunch noon-
3:30pm.* $$

Le Saint Jean de Prés
112 Duane Street nr Church St. 608-2332. Vast
TriBeCa venue (a former shoe warehouse) for
classic Belgian cuisine. Smoked fish, cheese cro-
quettes, chicken waterzooi. Good desserts flown
from Belgium. Duvel beer. Reserve. AE, CB, DC,
MC, V. *L Mon-Fri noon-3pm; D Mon-Sat 6-
12:30am.* $$

Breakfast/Brunch

Ambassador Grill
United Nations Plaza Hotel, First Avenue at East
44 St. 355-3400. Sophisticated dining in a beauti-
ful, prism-mirrored room. Sumptuous Sunday
brunch buffet with unlimited champagne. Piano
music. Prix fixe. *Sun Brunch: 2 sittings—noon &
2pm.* Reserve. AE, CB, DC, MC, V. *OPEN 7
days.* $

Angry Squire
See NIGHTLIFE, Jazz.

Café Orlin
41 St. Marks Place nr Second Ave. 777-1447.
Brunch is a treat in this, the very best café in the
East Village. Egg dishes accompanied by cap-
puccino and fresh-squeezed oj. Food and service
are wonderful and in good weather the Europe-
an-style outdoor café for the best bizarre-people
watching. *Weekend Brunch 9am-4pm. OPEN 7
days 9am-2am.* $

Cupping Room Café
359 West Broadway at Broome St. 925-2898.
SoHo locals breakfast in this skylit brick and wood
setting. Go for the wonderful omelettes, muffins
and the café au lait. A la carte. Reserve for dinner
only. AE, DC, MC, V. *OPEN 7 days 8am-
11:30pm.* $

Délices La Cote Basque
1032 Lexington Avenue at East 73 St. 535-3311.

Le petit déjeuner in this aromatic bakery or at one of tables set outside in summer. *Breakfast served 7 days from 7:30am.* $

Hors D'Oeuvrerie
Windows on the World, #1 World Trade Center, 107th fl. 938-1111. There is no more spectacular breakfast/brunch venue in the city. The room, ¼ mile high, overlooks New York Harbor and Lady Liberty. Mon-Fri there is a lovely a la carte breakfast menu; on Sun a choice of an international brunch—Mexico, China or Scandinavia are featured—or one of several lovely egg dishes. Jacket required; no denim. Reserve for Brunch. AE, CB, DC, MC, V. *Breakfast Mon-Fri 7:30-10:30am. Sun Brunch noon-3pm.* $

Kitty Hawk
565 Third Avenue nr East 37 St. 661-7406. Dim pub atmosphere but best value brunch in town. Unlimited champagne and lots of food for one low price. Burgers, steaks, etc., rest of the time. *Brunch Sat noon-3:45pm; Sun 11:30-3:45pm.* AE, CB, DC, MC, V. *OPEN 7 days till 3am.* $

Pink Tea Cup
42 Grove Street nr Bleecker St. 807-6755. Long-time unpretentious soul-food eatery in new surroundings still serves a satisfying breakfast of eggs, grits, homemade corn muffins. Followed by apple pie if you can handle it. No credit cards. *OPEN 7 days 8am-1am.* $

PizzaPiazza
785 Broadway at East 10 St. 505-0977. Fine fun alternative to traditional brunch—a deep dish brunch pizza! *The Broadway* with eggs, cottage cheese, scallions and Nova; *The Great Western* with tomato, onion, eggs, jalapeño and sausage, or *The Florentine*, a garlicky spinach and cheese pizza topped with two poached eggs. Bloody Mary or Mimosa, and coffee. All in a Milton Glaser-designed interior. Piano music Fri & Sat pm, Sun brunch. Reserve for 6 or more. AE, MC, V. *Brunch Sat & Sun noon-4pm. OPEN Sun-Thurs 11:30am-1am; Fri & Sat till 3am.* $

Regency Hotel
540 Park Avenue at East 61 St. 759-4100. The movers and shakers breakfast here while their chauffeurs bide their time outside. AE, DC, MC, V. *Breakfast 7 days 7-11am.* $

Sarabeth's Kitchen
1295 Madison Avenue nr East 92 St. 410-7335. Also, 412 Amsterdam Avenue nr West 79 St. 496-6280. Like eating in the kitchen of a friend's country house. Brunch all day, every day. Omelettes, homemade muffins, potato and cheese blintzes and pumpkin waffles. Wonderful marmalades, Linzer tortes and short breads. *Breakfast/Brunch menu 7 days 9am-4:30pm. AE, DC, MC, V. OPEN 7 days 9am-10pm.* $

Tuesday's
190 Third Avenue nr East 17 St. 533-7900. Former speakeasy. Serves steaks, salads, burgers and very good value brunch. *Weekend Brunch 11:30am-3:30pm. AE, MC, V. OPEN 7 days till 1am.* $

Veselka
144 Second Avenue at East 9 St. 228-9682.

Where East Village natives (and that's quite a mix) eat breakfast. Those in the know head for the formerly private back room of this Polish luncheonette and order the blueberry wheatcakes; also great are the apple or blueberry wholewheat muffins. Breakfast specials are served *Mon-Sat 7am-noon; Sun till 5pm* (they know their clientele sleeps late!) P.S. The rest of the menu is satisfying *and* inexpensive too. No credit cards. *OPEN 7 days 7am-1am.* $

—Dim Sum

Literally meaning "to take your heart's desire," it's the Chinese version of brunch. A tea lunch (tea is the beverage traditionally consumed with Dim Sum) consisting of dumplings, rolls, and buns filled with varieties of chicken, meat, fish and vegetables; rice and noodle dishes; and sweet cakes. The food comes from the kitchen in a continuous stream, you beckon the server, and at the end of the meal the number of empty plates on your table are totaled to produce your bill. Listed are four Chinatown restaurants serving authentic Dim Sum. NOTE: *This is one of the few times a seat near the kitchen is desirable.*

Cam Fung
20 Elizabeth Street nr Bowery. 964-5256. Dim Sum served *7 days a week, 8am-4pm.* $

Hee Seung Fung (HSF)
46 Bowery nr Canal St. 374-1319. Dim Sum is served *7 days a week, 7:30am-5pm.* $

Nom Wah Tea Parlor
13 Doyers Street nr Pell St. 962-6047. Only Dim Sum. *OPEN 7 days 10:30am-6pm, Sat & Sun till 8pm.* $

*The following also serve Breakfast or Brunch. The asterisk * indicates highly recommended:*

Arnold's Turtle (Health & Vegetarian)
Barking Fish Cafe (Soul & Creole)
***Berry's** (Continental)
Black Sheep (French)
***Brasserie** (Late Night/24 Hours)
Broome Street Bar (Bars & Burgers)
Café de la Paix (Sidewalk Cafés)
***Café des Artistes** (Continental)
Café des Bruxelles (Belgian)
Café Loup (French)
Caffè Reggio (Cafés)
***Cajun** (Soul/Creole)
Capsouto Freres (French)
Carlyle Hotel (Continental)
Charley O's Bar & Grill (Bars & Burgers)
Chatfield's (Continental)
Elephant & Castle (Omelettes & Crepes)
***Evelyne's** (Continental)
Food (Soup & Salad)
Friday's (Bars & Burgers)
Garvin's (Continental)
Ginger Man (American)
Gordon (Italian)
Gotham Bar & Grill (Continental)
Great Jones Café (Late Night/24 Hours)
Greene Street Kitchen & Bar (Wine Bars)
Janice's Fish Place (Fish & Seafood)

La Colonna (Italian)
La Gauloise (French)
Landmark Tavern (Bars & Burgers)
Le Petit Marmite (French)
Magic Pan Creperie (Omelettes & Crepes)
Marylou's (Late Night/24 Hours)
Memphis (Soul & Creole)
Odeon (French)
*__One Fifth__ (American)
Orchid (American)
Oenophilia (Continental)
Raoul's (Continental)
Ravelled Sleave (Continental)
River Café (Rooms with a View)
Ruelles (Continental)
Sazerac House (Soul & Creole)
Sign of the Dove (Continental)
*__SoHo Charcuterie__ (French)
*__Sylvia's__ (Soul & Creole)
24 Fifth (French)
*__Vanessa__ (American)
Village Green (French)
Water's Edge (Rooms with a View)
Whole Wheat 'n' Wild Berries (Health & Vegetarian)
Wine Bar (Wine Bars)
*__Ye Waverly Inn__ (American)

Cafés

See also Sidewalk Cafés.

Café Vivaldi
32 Jones Street nr Bleecker St. 929-9384. Charming café on a quiet Greenwich Village side street. For quiche, tostini, coffees, teas and desserts. Outside tables in fair weather. No credit cards. *OPEN 7 days 10am-2am.* $

Caffè Biondo
141 Mulberry Street nr Hester St. 226-9285. Pretty Little Italy newcomer for snacks, desserts, coffees. Outdoors in summer. No credit cards. *OPEN Mon-Fri noon-midnight; Sat & Sun noon-2am.* $

Caffè Reggio
119 MacDougal Street nr West 3 St. 475-9557. Authentic old-time Village coffeehouse: crowded, cramped and cozy. Good ambiance, espresso, cappuccino and pastry. Sidewalk tables in summer to watch an interesting street scene. No credit cards. *OPEN 10am-2am; Fri & Sat till 3am.* $

Caffè Roma
385 Broome Street at Mulberry St. 226-8413. Little Italy's best old *pasticceria*, tastefully redecorated. Cappuccino, cannoli, Sicilian cassata and more. Busy, be prepared to wait on weekends. No credit cards. *OPEN 7 days 8am-midnight.* $

Cloister Cafe
238 East 9 Street. 777-9128. In the East Village; a mirage of a garden (late April-Oct) is the very special feature of this café. Stick to the salads or just linger over a wonderful café au lait (served in a bowl that requires two hands to lift) and a pastry. Day or evening it's a treat. In winter inside there's a potbelly stove. In or out you must suffer the service. No reservations, no credit cards. *OPEN Sun-Thurs noon-12:30am (kitchen till 9:45pm); Fri & Sat till 1:30am (kitchen till 11pm).* $

Cornelia Street Café
29 Cornelia Street nr Bleecker St. 929-9869. An oasis of calm in the Village for coffee and croissants; cheese, fruit, wine and other light fare. Outdoor tables in summer. Poetry spoken here (Wed). Blues and jazz played (Tues & Sun) too. *OPEN 7 days 8am-2am.* $

De Robertis
176 First Avenue nr East 11 St. 674-7137. Wonderful, no longer secret, 80-year-old *pasticceria* much as you would find in Rome. For espresso, cappuccino, and homemade Italian pastries. Weekends you'll wait. *OPEN Mon-Thurs 9am-11pm; Fri-Sun till 1am.* $

Ferrara's
195 Grand Street nr Mulberry St. 226-6150. Famed Little Italy café is the granddaddy of them all and it spills into the street in summer. Espresso, cappuccino, delicious pastries and gelati. Very bright and lively. Be prepared to wait in the pm. *OPEN 7 days 7:30am-midnight.* $

Peacock
24 Greenwich Avenue nr West 10 St. 242-9395. Antique tables, chairs, paintings and opera music lend a Renaissance air to this longtime Village coffeehouse. Be patient for good cappuccino and cannoli; food too. *OPEN Tues-Thurs 1pm-1am; Fri & Sat till 2am. CLOSED Mon.* $

Chinese

See also Breakfast/Brunch: Dim Sum.

Auntie Yuan
1191A First Avenue at East 64 St. 744-4040. Sophisticated Chinese cookery in a setting to match. Some fascinating dishes in addition to the standards. There's a 7-course "tasting dinner" and Cruvinet dispenses wine by the glass. AE only. Reserve. *OPEN 7 days noon-midnight.* $$$

Beijing Duck House
144 East 52 Street. 759-8260. For those who can't anticipate a craving for Peking duck 24 hours in advance. Always available (20 minute wait) and always perfectly crisp. Also good, the fried spareribs with honey, barbecued beef on a stick. Reserve. AE, MC, V. *OPEN Sun-Thurs noon-11pm; Fri & Sat till midnight.* $

BoBo's
20½ Pell Street nr Mott St. 267-8373. One of Chinatown's most popular spots for Cantonese food. Daily menu. Bring your own wine. Reserve. AE, MC, V. *OPEN 7 days 11:30am-11pm.* $

Chi Mer
11-12 Chatham Square nr Mott St. 267-4565. Excellent Chinese cookery, predominantly that of Peking and Shanghai. Reserve. AE, CB, DC, MC, V. *OPEN 7 days 11:30am-11:30pm.* $

Home Village
20 Mott Street nr Park St. 964-0381. Two-story clamourous Chinatown restaurant. Exhaustive menu (over 200 dishes) serves the food of the Hakka people of Canton; unusual specialties. Bring your own wine or beer. Reserve on weekends. No credit cards. *OPEN Sun-Thurs 11am-1am; Fri & Sat till 2am.* $

Hong Fat
63 Mott Street nr Canal St. 962-9588. Tiny utilitari-

an restaurant; its specialty is noodles. Other Cantonese dishes too. No credit cards. *OPEN 7 days 9:30am-5am.* $

Hunam
45 Second Avenue nr East 45 St. 687-7471. First New York restaurant to serve the spicy dishes of the Hunan province. Highly recommended still. Hunam beef, sauteed smoked chicken, crisp fried boneless duck. Reserve for lunch. AE, CB, DC. *OPEN Sun-Thurs noon-midnight; Fri & Sat till 1am.* $

Hunam Taste
2270 Broadway nr West 81 St. 724-9449. Large informal West Side restaurant for very good Szechuan and Hunan province cooking. Enclosed outdoor café. Reserve. MC, V. *OPEN 7 days 11am-11pm.* $

Hwa Yuan Szechuan Inn
40 East Broadway nr Market St. 966-5534. Cavernous Chinatown restaurant. Excellent spicy Szechuan dishes the specialty. Shredded chicken with pepper sauce, whole carp with hot sauce, cold noodles in sesame paste a must. Crowded on weekends. Serves beer, bring your own wine. Reserve for 6 or more only. AE, DC, MC, V. *OPEN Sun-Thurs noon-10pm; Fri & Sat till 11pm.* $

Little Shanghai
26 East Broadway nr Chatham Sq. 925-4238. Small pleasant find for wonderful, subtly spiced Shanghai-style cooking: dumplings, seafood specials, bean curd dishes. For dessert, exotic sherbets in season. Bring your own wine or beer. No credit cards. *OPEN 7 days 10am-10:30pm.* $

Mr. Chow
324 East 57 Street. 751-9030. Via London and Beverly Hills. Through the Lalique doors, a sleek setting and crowd, noisy, busy ambiance, good but not very Chinese food. Reserve. AE, DC, MC, V. *L Mon-Fri 12:30pm-2:30pm. D 7 days 6:30-11:55pm.* $$$

Moshe Peking
See Jewish

Pearl's Chinese Restaurant
38 West 48 Street. 586-1060. Sophisticated, sleek ambiance. Beautifully prepared and served Chinese food. Specialty, lemon chicken. Popular with fashion crowd. (But will they come when Pearl leaves?) Reserve for dinner only. No credit cards. *L Mon-Fri noon-2:30pm. D Sun-Fri 5-10pm. CLOSED Sat & major holidays.* $$

Phoenix Garden
46 Bowery (in the arcade) nr Canal St. 233-6017. Cantonese as it's meant to be. (Not for chow mein aficionados.) Shark fin soup, roast pigeon, fried milk with crab. No frills, no bar, no dessert, no reservation. Yes, a wait. *OPEN Tues-Sun 11:30am-10:30pm. CLOSED Mon.* $

Pig Heaven
1540 Second Avenue nr East 80 St. PIG-4333. One more from David Keh (Auntie Yuan and Uncle Tai's); this is his ode to the pig. Delicious and authentic food; silly decor. Though much of the menu features pork, there's a great deal for nonpig fanciers. Don't miss the dumplings—fried, steamed or boiled. Reserve. AE, DC. *OPEN Sun-Thurs noon-midnight; Fri & Sat till 1am.* $$

Say Eng Look
5 East Broadway nr Catherine St. 732-0796. Excellent Chinatown restaurant features mainly Shanghai specialties. Pork loin, aromatic duck (24 hour notice), bean curd in hot sauce. Bring your own wine or beer. Reserve for more than 5 only. MC only. *OPEN Sun-Thurs 11:15am-10:30pm; Fri & Sat till 11:30pm.* $

Shun Lee Palace
155 East 55 Street. 371-8844. Plush setting in which to enjoy excellent Hunan, Szechuan and Cantonese dishes. There's a low-calorie meal for dieters, but the temptations of the regular menu are too strong. Vegetable duck pie, hacked chicken, shrimp puffs, Hunan duckling with smoke flavor. Very popular, it bustles. Reserve. AE, CB, DC. *OPEN Sun-Thurs noon-11pm; Fri & Sat till midnight.* $$

Uncle Tai's Hunan Yuan
1059 Third Avenue nr East 63 St. 838-0850. Large, bright and modern. Serves some of the most original Hunan and Szechuan dishes in the city. Reserve. AE, DC. *OPEN Sun-Thurs noon-11pm; Fri & Sat till 11:30pm.* $$

Yun Luck Rice Shoppe
17 Doyers Street nr Pell St. 571-1375. Outstanding authentic Cantonese food in noisy no frills Chinatown favorite. Bring your own wine. Reserve for 5 or more. No credit cards. *OPEN Sun-Fri 11:30am-midnight; Sat till 1am.* $

Continental

Berry's
180 Spring Street at Thompson St. 226-4394. Beautiful cozy SoHo pub/restaurant. Imaginative, frequently changing menu. Excellent brunch choice. Reserve. AE, MC, V. *L Tues-Fri noon-3pm. D Tues-Thurs 6-11:30pm; Fri & Sat 6-midnight; Sun 5-10:30pm. Brunch: Sat noon-3:30pm; Sun 11am-4pm. CLOSED Mon.* $$

Bridge Café
279 Water Street at Dover St. 227-3344. The kitchen of this early 19th-century neighborhood saloon turns out some of the best and least expensive food in the newly sanitized Seaport area. No reservations, no credit cards. *L Mon-Fri 11:45am-3pm; Sat & Sun noon-3:30pm. D Mon-Sat 6pm-midnight; Sun 5-11pm.* $

Café des Artistes
1 West 67 Street. 877-3500. Beautiful, nostalgic ambiance; the famed sweetly naughty murals by Howard Chandler Christy and an imaginative Continental menu that changes frequently: rough country paté, cassoulet caviar omelette, curried mussels. Jacket required at dinner. Reserve. AE, CB, DC, MC, V. *L Mon-Fri noon-3pm. D Mon-Sat 5:30pm-12:30am; Sun 5-11pm. Brunch: Sat noon-3pm; Sun 10am-4pm.* $$

Café Marigold
746 Madison Avenue nr East 64 St. 861-8820. Popular and attractive café for a respite from Mad Ave shopping and gallery hopping. A nice selection of uncomplicated entrees; good light lunch choices. Outdoor tables in summer. AE, DC, MC, V. Reserve. *L Mon-Sat 11am-5pm. D Mon-Sat 5-11:30pm; Sun till 10pm. Sun Brunch 11am-4pm.* $

Carlyle Restaurant
Madison Avenue at East 76 St. 744-1600. Attractive, spacious dining room serves very good Continental dishes, pleasantly served. Jacket required. Reserve for dinner. AE, CB, DC, MC, V. *B 7-11am. Buffet L Mon-Sat noon-6pm. D Mon-Sat 6-11pm; Sun 7-11pm. Sun Brunch noon-6pm.* $$$

Chatfield's
208 East 60 Street. 753-5070. A credit card's toss from Bloomies is this casual yet polished pub/restaurant. Limited but fine a la carte menu includes excellent pasta choices, steamed mussels, lamb chops with Roquefort sauce, and several grilled daily specials. Real wood fire in the hearth and a friendly bar make this an inviting place. Reserve. AE, MC, V. *L Mon-Sat noon-3pm. D 7 days 6-11pm. Sun Brunch noon-3:45pm.* (Note: CLOSED weekends July 4-Labor Day.) $$

Chelsea Place
147 Eighth Avenue nr West 17 St. 924-8413. Walk through an antique shop to get to this small popular restaurant. Continental dishes, Italian are featured; good fish choices too. Reserve. AE, DC, MC, V. *L Mon-Fri noon-2:30pm. D Mon-Sat 5-11:30pm; Sun till 11pm.* $$

Evelyne's
87 East 4 Street. 254-2550. Good East Village choice for very fine albeit expensive-for-the-neighborhood Continental food. Calves liver with raspberry sauce, grilled rabbit, LI duckling with fresh spearmint sauce. Lovely mirrored bar, charming garden in summer. Reserve. AE, CB, DC, MC, V. *D Tues-Sat 6:30-midnight; Sun till 11pm. Sun Brunch noon-3pm. CLOSED Mon.* $$

Garvins
19 Waverly Place nr Mercer St. 473-5261. Beautifully decorated, spacious restaurant-café-bar for steak, seafood, veal and duck. Friendly bar till 2am, piano music nightly. Reserve. AE, DC, V. *L Mon-Fri 11:30am-3:30pm. D Mon 5-11pm; Tues-Fri till 11:30pm; Sat till midnight. Weekend Brunch 11am-4pm.* $

Gotham Bar & Grill
12 East 12 Street. 620-4020. Yet another gorgeous trendy brasserie, this one with 17-foot-high ceilings, soft lighting and cast-stone ledges that give the sense of an outdoor garden courtyard. The eclectic menu runs the gamut from a $10 (at this writing) hamburger to sophisticated offerings. The kitchen's recent turnaround is nothing short of miraculous. Now you can go for the food too. Reserve. AE, DC, MC, V. *L Mon-Fri noon-3pm. D 7 days 5:30-midnight. Sun Brunch 11:30am-3:30pm.* $$$

Joanna
18 East 18 Street. 675-7900. A beauty in an 1875 landmark building. Interesting eclectic menu, casual café ambiance. A favorite of photographers and their models. Dancing till the wee hours downstairs. Reserve. AE. *OPEN 7 days. L noon-3pm; D 6pm-1am. Bar till 4am.* $$

Julia
226 West 79 Street nr Broadway. 787-1511.

Small, extremely pleasant Upper West Side spot for tasty grilled food, reasonably priced wine and a choice of over 20 beers. Glass-enclosed garden with a movable glass roof. Reserve. AE, DC, MC, V. *OPEN 7 days 11am-2am.* $

Laughing Mountain
148 Chambers Street nr West Broadway. 233-4434. Skylit, plant-filled TriBeCa spot for very good fish dishes, beef bourguignonne. Less buttoned down in the pm. Reserve. AE, DC, MC, V. *OPEN 7 days 11:30am-midnight. Weekend Brunch 11:30am-4pm.* $

Lion's Rock
316 East 77 Street. 988-3610. Good little Continental restaurant with a wonderful open-to-the-sky garden. (There resides the "lion's rock," a glacial remnant.) Reserve. AE, DC, MC, V. *L Mon-Fri 11:30am-3pm. D 7 days 5-midnight. Weekend Brunch 11:30am-4pm.* $$

Maxwell's Plum
1181 First Avenue at East 64 St. 628-2100. Art deco palace popular with New Yorkers and visitors. Famed Tiffany stained glass ceiling and lamps make it one of New York's most stunning watering holes. Intriguing à la carte menu in Café and Back Room ranging from steamed rock shrimp, veal piccata, salads, hamburgers to tempting desserts. Pre-Theatre Menu Mon-Sat 5-7pm is an incredible bargain. Reserve. AE, CB, DC, MC, V. *OPEN 7 days noon-1:30am. Brunch: Sat noon-5pm; Sun from 11am.* $$

Mortimer's
1057 Lexington Avenue at East 75 St. 861-2481. Fashionably clubby brick-walled Upper East Side pub/restaurant. Features Continental fare: rack of lamb, chicken paillard, twin burgers. Reserve for 5 or more only. AE, DC, MC, V. *L Mon-Fri noon-3:30pm; Sat & Sun 12:15-4:30pm. D 7 days 6pm-midnight. Late supper Tues-Sat midnight-2:30am.* $$

Oenophilia
473 Columbus Avenue nr West 83 St. 580-8127. Good Upper West Side spot for well-prepared Continental food, casual, pleasant ambiance but service can be slow. Reserve. AE, DC, MC, V. *D Mon-Sat 6-11pm; Sun 4-10pm. Sun Brunch 11:30am-4pm.* $

Ravelled Sleave
1387 Third Avenue nr East 79 St. 628-8814. Romantic setting—fireplace and piano music for fine Continental dining. Reserve. AE, DC, MC, V. *D Mon-Fri 5:30pm-midnight; Sat till 12:30am; Sun 5-11pm. Weekend Brunch noon-3:30pm.* $$

Rúelles
321 Columbus Avenue at West 75 St. 799-5100. Popular West Side eating and meeting place that spills out on the street in good weather. Eclectic menu. DC, MC, V. *OPEN 7 days 11am-midnight. Bar till 3am. Sun Brunch 11am-4pm.* $$

Sign of the Dove
1110 Third Avenue at East 65 St. 861-8080. Extremely pretty restaurant with the look of an indoor garden. Stay with the simpler fare. Jacket & tie required in the dining room. Reserve. AE, CB, DC, MC, V. *L Tues-Sat noon-3pm. D Tues-Sat 6pm-*

midnight; Sun & Mon till 1am. Sun Brunch 11am-4pm. $$$

65 Irving Place
65 Irving Place at East 18 St. 673-3939. Near Gramercy Park, pleasantly stylish surroundings and food. Good pasta specials. Visible kitchen, terrific sunny sidewalk café in good weather. Reserve. AE, CB, DC, MC, V. *L Mon-Fri noon-3pm. D Sun-Thurs 6-11pm; Fri & Sat till 11:30pm.* $$

Summerhouse
1269 Madison Avenue at East 91 St. 289-8062. Charming Carnegie Hill restaurant for simple fare. There's a pasta of the day and a wonderful apple tart for dessert. You may bring your own wine. AE, MC, V. *OPEN Tues-Sat 11:30am-10pm; Sun noon-10pm. CLOSED Mon.* $

Sumptuary Restaurant
400 Third Avenue nr East 28 St, upstairs. 889-6056. Imaginative dishes and a very pretty setting provide an extremely pleasant dining experience. Open to the sky dining terrace in summer; fireplace in one of the cozy dining rooms on chilly nights. AE, MC, V. *L Tues-Fri noon-3pm. D Tues-Sat 6-10pm. CLOSED Sun & Mon.* $$

Woods
718 Madison Avenue nr East 64 St. 688-1126; *148 West 37 Street. 564-7340; **24 East 21 Street. 505-5252. Very popular trendy spots. Beautiful décor, consistently fine Continental food. Dessert here is a must, specifically the roulade. Reserve. AE, MC, V. *OPEN Mon-Sat L noon-3pm. D 6-10:30pm. CLOSED Sun. *L Mon-Fri noon-3pm. D 5:15-9:30pm. CLOSED Sat & Sun. **L Mon-Fri noon-3pm. D 7 days 6pm-1am. Weekend Brunch noon-4pm.* $$$

Czechoslovakian

Ruc
312 East 72 Street. 650-1611. Long-established informal Czech restaurant. Very good hearty food. Roast duck, goose, veal shank, goulash, and, for dessert, apricot dumplings or palacinky crepes. Try the divovitz, prune brandy if you dare. Lovely large outdoor garden in summer. Reserve. AE, DC, MC, V. *OPEN Mon-Fri 5-11pm; Sat & Sun noon-11pm.* $

Vašata
339 East 75 Street. 650-1686. Lovely, comfortable Czech restaurant, serves the national specialties. Famed for its schnitzels, its dumplings, its European atmosphere. Reserve. AE, MC, V. *OPEN Tues-Sat 5-11pm; Sun noon-10pm. CLOSED Mon.* $$

Delicatessen

Bernstein-on-Essex Street
135 Essex Street nr Delancey St. 473-3900. Long-established Lower East Side eatery. Strictly kosher Jewish-style food. Unique feature: kosher Chinese food. Excellent deli sandwiches, especially the pastrami. AE, MC. *OPEN Sun-Thurs 8am-1am; Fri till 4pm; Sat 9pm-3am.* $

Carnegie Delicatessen
854 Seventh Avenue nr West 55 St. 757-2245. Good, Jewish-style (not kosher) dishes (dairy and meat). The delicious pastrami and corned beef

are made on premises. Generous-sized sandwiches. Friendly, informal. Beer only. No credit cards. *OPEN 7 days 6am-4am.* $

Fine & Shapiro
138 West 72 Street. 877-2874. Since 1920, famed kosher delicatessen/restaurant serves very good, inexpensive sandwiches; wonderful chicken soup. Reserve for more than 6 people. AE only. *OPEN Sat-Thurs 11am-11:30pm; Fri till 9pm.* $

Kaplan's at the Delmonico
59 East 59 Street. 755-5959. Hearty Jewish-style food. Excellent delicatessen sandwiches. AE, CB, DC, MC, V. *OPEN Mon-Sat 8am-11pm; Sun 9am-9pm.* $

Katz's Delicatessen
205 East Houston Street at Ludlow St. 254-2246. A Lower East Side institution. Terrific hot dogs, inexpensive pastrami and corned-beef sandwiches (not kosher). On Sunday unbeatable for local color and informality, especially on the part of the waiters. Self-service too. No credit cards. *OPEN Sun-Thurs 7am-11:30pm; Fri & Sat till 1:30am.* $

Second Avenue Kosher Delicatessen
156 Second Avenue at East 10 St. 677-0606. The best kosher deli restaurant in the city. Delicious hot meals vie with traditional deli delights. Great chopped liver, and, oh, the pastrami sandwiches. Take out and catering. No reservations so lineups are usual on weekends. No credit cards. *OPEN 7 days 6:30am-11:30pm.* $

Stage Deli
834 Seventh Avenue nr West 53 St. 245-7850. Show-biz hangout named for the stars who did and do eat here. Home-style cooking and delicious deli sandwiches. Bustling NY experience. No credit cards. *OPEN 7 days 6:30am-2am.* $

Deluxe

NOTE: *They require men to wear jacket, and in most cases a tie.*

Cellar in the Sky
1 World Trade Center, 107th fl. 938-1111. A cloistered, viewless enclave in the famed Windows on the World. Seats only 36 for an exquisite 7-course meal accompanied by 5 different wines and a classical guitarist. Menu changes every 2 weeks. Prix fixe. Reserve! (A $20 deposit is required to reserve the table.) AE, CB, DC, MC, V. *One sitting only, at 7:30pm. CLOSED Sun.* $$$$

Four Seasons
99 East 52 Street. 754-9494. Large, beautiful modern restaurant of some repute. Bar-Grill area for lunch, dinner and late snacks, dining room with center marble pool for pre-theater 5-6:30pm as well as after-theater dining 10-11:30pm. Menu changes with the seasons. Special spa menu for dieters. Favored by publishing execs. Reserve. AE, CB, DC, MC. Jacket required. Reduced rate parking. *Mon-Sat L noon-2:30pm; D 5-11:30pm. CLOSED Sun.* $$$$

La Caravelle
33 West 55 Street. 586-4252. One of the city's most fashionable *haute cuisine* French restaurants. Prix-fixe lunch, à la carte dinner. Reserve! AE, DC, MC, V. *Mon-Sat L 12:15-2:30pm; D 6-10:15pm. CLOSED Sun & holidays.* $$$$+

La Côte Basque
5 East 55 Street. 688-6525. New owners, but still a NY institution. Elegantly beautiful. Lovely French menu. Reserve! AE, CB, DC, MC, V. *L Mon-Sat noon-2:30pm. D Mon-Fri 6-10:30pm; Sat till 11pm. CLOSED Sun.* $$$$+

La Grenouille
3 East 52 Street. 752-1495. At the very top. Attractive setting, impeccable service. Excellent French cuisine beautifully prepared. Reserve! AE, DC. *Mon-Sat L noon-2pm; D 6-10pm. CLOSED Sun & August.* $$$$+

Le Cygne
53 East 54 Street. 759-5941. French *haute cuisine.* Elaborate, imaginative menu offers exquisitely prepared dishes. Sky-high wine prices, beware. Reserve! AE, DC. *L Mon-Fri noon-2:30pm. D Mon-Fri 6-10pm; Sat till 11pm. CLOSED Sun.* $$$$+

Lutèce
249 East 50 Street. 752-2225. The word is *best;* the excellent traditional French food, the town house setting, the service. Nightly *menu de dégustation* must be ordered by all in your party. Prix-fixe lunch. Reserve very well ahead! AE, CB, DC. *L Tues-Fri noon-2pm. D Mon-Sat 6-10pm. CLOSED Sun.* $$$$+

Department Store Restaurants
A sampling of restaurants and snack bars where shoppers can eat and relax without leaving the store. There is a great variety of foods, décor, and prices available.

Abraham & Straus
420 Fulton Street nr Hoyt St, Brooklyn. (1-718) 875-7200. *Garden Room,* 4th fl. Burgers, soup and sandwich combos or a full meal. No-smoking section. A&S charge. *Snack Bar,* lst fl. Burgers, pizza, franks on the run, or sit down and have breakfast, soup, or quiche. $

Alexander's
East 58 Street & Lexington Ave. 593-0880. *Cafe A'Lex,* 5th fl. Counter or table service in this chic café, which includes a champagne (N.Y. State) bar. Serves crepes, espresso, pastries, and an all-day brunch. AE, MC, V. $

B. Altman
361 Fifth Avenue at 34 St. 679-7800. *Charleston Gardens,* 8th fl. Since 1947 an old-fashioned treat with a Southern accent. Roast chicken, filet of cod, and homemade blueberry muffins are some of what makes this an extremely popular place. Afternoon tea 3:30-5pm. No-smoking section. AE, Altman charge. $

Bergdorf Goodman
754 Fifth Avenue at 58 St. 753-7300. *Pasta & Cheese,* 6th fl. Daily pasta specials to stay or go. AE, Bergdorf, Neiman Marcus charge. $

Bloomingdale's
1000 Third Avenue at East 59 St. 355-5900. *Espresso Bar,* subway level. A chic spot for Saturday's Generation to have pâté, quiche, or a fruit plate accompanied by a glass of champagne. Perrier, beer, espresso, or cappuccino. Bloomie's charge. $

40 Carrots, lower level. Frozen yogurt topped with fruit du jour and other healthy delights. No smoking allowed at this busy counter restaurant. Bloomie's charge. $

The Green House. 7th fl. Sandwiches, salads, quiche, and crepes at an ivy-bedecked counter. No-smoking section. Bloomie's charge. $

Le Train Bleu, 6th fl. Old European-train ambiance: overlooks Queensborough Bridge. Continental menu; alcohol served. Featured specials are demonstrated in Main Course. Bloomie's charge. $

Gimbels
1275 Broadway at West 33 St. 564-3300. *Hot Diggity,* ground fl. Snack bar for a bargain-priced fish sandwich, burgers, and franks. Cash only.

The Roost, main fl. Complete inexpensive meals at a counter. No-smoking section. Gimbels charge. $

Gimbels East
126 East 86 Street. 348-2300. *Penthouse Restaurant,* 11th fl. A salad bar to accompany full hot meals. Sun Brunch: Surf 'n' Turf, lox 'n' bagels, steak 'n' eggs with champagne.

Penthouse Coffee Shop, 11th fl. $

Lord & Taylor
424 Fifth Avenue at 38 St. 391-3344. *Lord & Taylor Café,* 5th fl. A la carte menu, hot specials or quiche in a comfortable contemporary setting. Popular, so be prepared to wait. No-smoking section. AE, Lord & Taylor charge. $

Intermission, 6th fl. Sandwiches, cheese and fruit, salads and yogurt in an efficient yet pleasant ambiance. AE, Lord & Taylor charge. $

Soup Bar, 10th fl. Generous helpings of soup: Scotch broth plus vichyssoise in summer; and great apple pie. A traditional Early American setting in existence for over 40 years and still a secret to most who shop here. AE, Lord & Taylor charge.   · $

Macy's
West 34 Street & Broadway. 695-4400. *Carving Board,* 8th fl. Hearty meat sandwiches, unlimited salad, and wine and beer for lunch only. AE, Macy's charge. $

Fountain, 5th fl. Fresh foods and wonderful desserts, including Sedutto ice cream and fresh-ground coffee in an attractive gardenlike setting. Features a special children's lunch. AE, Macy's charge. $

Café L'Etoile, Balcony. Light French food: quiche, salads, onion soup. Afternoon tea 3-5 daily. AE, Macy's charge. $

Patio, 8th fl. French onion soup, salads, hearty omelettes, burgers and deep-fried shrimp at a counter. Wine & beer. AE, Macy's charge. $

Le Petit Café, 3rd fl. Lovely pastries, cappuccino, and espresso: pâté, cheese, and fruit too at this chic counter eatery. $

P J Clarke's in the Cellar. Entrance, 135 West 34 Street. 564-5690. The East Side saloon uncannily re-created down to the smallest detail. Same blackboard menu and prices, good burgers. Remain long after store closing. Reserve for lunch: noon, 1 & 1:30pm. AE, Macy's charge. $

Self-Treat, 4th fl. Health food bar for frozen yogurt, fresh juices and fruit, pita bread sandwiches. AE, Macy's charge. $

Ohrbach's
5 West 34 Street. 695-4000. *Coffee Café and Wine Cellar,* lower level. Some comforting items at the counter, such as egg creams and sangria with fresh fruit. Cash only. $

Ethiopian

Abyssinia Restaurant
35 Grand Street at Thompson St. 226-5959. In a SoHo storefront, a cheerful unique dining experience awaits. Hearty spicy Ethiopian beef or chicken stew—*wot*—eaten in the traditional manner *sans* silverware. The thin crepe-like bread called *injera,* is used to scoop the food. It's family-style dining and the helpful staff will aid the uninitiated. For dessert, refreshing melon or papaya. Bring your own wine. Reserve. No credit cards. *OPEN 7 days 6-10:30pm.* $

Fireplaces

The following have working fireplaces:

Beatrice Inn (Italian)
Chatfield's (Continental)
Chumley's (Bars & Burgers)
El Gaucho (Latin American)
Fraunces Tavern Restaurant(American)
Gibbon (Japanese)
Il Caminetto (Italian)
Jane Street Seafood Café (Fish & Seafood)
Landmark Tavern (Bars & Burgers)
Martell's (Bars & Burgers)
Marylou's (Late Night/24 Hours)
Mary's (Italian)
McSorley's (Bars & Burgers)
Montana Eve (American)
Moran's (Bars & Burgers)
Oliver's (American)
Ravelled Sleave (Continental)
Restaurant Raphael (French)
Riviera Café (Sidewalk Cafés)
Rumbuls (Inexpensive)
Sazerac House (Soul & Creole)
"21" Club (Stargazers)
Village Green (French)
Vivolo (Italian)
Water Club (Rooms with a View)
Ye Waverly Inn (American)

Fish & Seafood

Claire
156 Seventh Avenue nr West 19 Street. 255-1955. High-ceilinged cool cousin of the Key West original. A good choice for mussels, squid salad, bay scallops. For carnivores: a lovely filet mignon with bacon. For dessert, Mississippi Mud pie and, of course, Key Lime pie. Busy and rightly so. Reserve. AE, MC, V. *OPEN Mon-Sat noon-1am; Sun till 12:30am.* $$

Fulton Fish Market
11 Fulton Street nr Front St, 2nd fl. 608-2920. You can't get much closer to the source than the fish market's retail outlet. No-frills spot for the very best clams and oysters. Eat on the run or at the counter. Cash only. *OPEN 7 days 8am-10pm.* $

Gage & Tollner
372 Fulton Street nr Jay St, Brooklyn. (1-718) 875-5181. Casual Brooklyn Heights seafood restaurant established in 1879. The handsome original gaslit dining room provides a charming atmosphere for fish, and steaks too. Piano music Fri & Sat. Reserve. AE, DC, MC, V. *OPEN Mon-Fri 11:30am-9pm; Sat 4-11pm; Sun 3-9pm.* $$

Harbour House
410 Sixth Avenue nr West 8 St. 473-0670. Fresh fish in a tasteful Greenwich Village location. Good Italian-accented seafood pastas, a zesty bouillabaisse on the menu daily. Reserve. AE, CB, DC, MC, V. *OPEN 7 days noon-midnight.* $$

Jane Street Seafood Cafe
31 Eighth Avenue at Jane St. 243-9237. A Village favorite for fresh seafood in a snug, authentically rustic New England-like setting. Wonderful steamed mussels, deep-fried oysters and soft-shelled clams. Fireplace in winter. No reservations. AE, MC, V. *OPEN Sun-Thurs 5:30-11pm; Fri & Sat till midnight.* $

Janice's Fish Place
570 Hudson Street at West 11 St. 243-4212. Casual Greenwich Village bar/restaurant for fish with an Oriental twist. Whole fish is served here with scallions, garlic and soy. Wonderful vegetarian dishes. A la carte. Reserve. AE, MC, V. *OPEN Mon-Thurs 6-11pm; Fri till midnight; Sat 5pm-midnight; Sun noon-11pm. Sun Brunch noon-4pm.* $

Joe's Pier 52
163 West 52 Street. 245-6652. Busy place serves 30 varieties of fish, 10 meat dishes, bouillabaisse every day. Cocktail lounge, music nightly from 7pm. Reserve. AE, DC, MC, V. *OPEN 7 days 11:30-1am.* $$

John Clancy's
181 West 10 Street at Seventh Ave So. 242-7350. The specialty of this delightful, very special Village restaurant is grilled fish scented with the smoke of mesquite branches. Also recommended: poached CoHo salmon, lobster a l'Américaine, scallops en brochette, shrimps sauteed with jalapeño peppers. Bitter chocolate velvet in whipped cream for dessert. Reserve! AE, CB, DC, MC, V. *OPEN Mon-Sat 6-11:30pm; Sun 5-10:30pm.* $$$$

King Crab
871 Eighth Avenue at West 52 St. 765-4393. Homey and extremely popular. Reported to have the best and cheapest lobsters in town. AE, DC. *L Mon-Fri noon-3:30pm. D 7 days 5-11:30pm.* $$

Manhattan Ocean Club
57 West 58 Street. 371-7777. Spiffy setting for good, albeit pricey, fish dishes. Service often very slow. Request not to sit on the 2nd-floor balcony (this is the old Thursday's). Good crab cakes, swordfish en brochette, blackened red fish. Steaks, chops and chicken too. Very good wine list. Reserve. AE, CB, DC, MC, V. *OPEN Mon-Fri noon-midnight; Sat & Sun from 5pm.* $$$$

Marylou's
See Late Night/24 Hour

Oscar's Salt of the Sea

1155 Third Avenue nr East 67 St. 879-1199. Large East Side fish restaurant that draws crowds. Very good fresh fish prepared in a variety of ways. Reserve. AE, DC, MC, V. *OPEN Sun-Thurs noon-11pm; Fri & Sat till midnight.* $$

Oyster Bar & Restaurant

Grand Central Terminal, 42 Street & Vanderbilt Avenue, lower level. 490-6650. Interesting, comfortable landmark locale for very good oysters. Six versions of clam chowder and grilled fresh fish. Wide variety, including the unusual. Dining room, oyster bar, counter. Reserve. AE, CB, DC, MC, V. *OPEN Mon-Fri 11:30am-9:30pm. CLOSED Sat & Sun.* $$

Pesca

25 East 22 Street. 533-2293. Large, comfortable fish restaurant in what is now being referred to as "the Flatiron" area. Broiled Norwegian salmon steak, cold poached Louisiana shrimp, a hearty satisfying cioppino; pastas of the day. Piano music in the pm. Reserve. AE only. *L Sun-Fri noon-3pm. D 7 days Mon-Sat 6-11:30pm; Sat till 10pm.* $$

Pier Nine

149 Second Avenue nr East 9 St. 673-9263. Very pretty antique bedecked and gaslit East Village spot for food and drink. Popular for the nicely prepared seafood, accompanied by hot garlic bread and salad. Well-priced early bird special (Mon-Sat at 5pm; Sun at 4pm). AE, MC, V. *OPEN Mon-Thurs 5-11pm; Fri & Sat till 11:30pm; Sun 4-10pm.* $

Sea Fare of the Aegean

25 West 56 Street. 581-0540. Large, elegant fish restaurant on three levels. The specialties have Greek leanings, the plainer dishes are most successful. Reserve. AE, CB, DC, MC, V. *OPEN Mon-Sat noon-11pm; Sun 1-3pm.* $$

Sea Grill

Rockefeller Center, 19 West 49 Street. 246-9201. One of the new Rockefeller Center restaurants designed to draw the sophisticated New Yorker as well as the tourist. Stunning decor. Good are the Sea Grill chowder, mussels, lobster salad. The glass-enclosed kitchen turns out fine nonfish dishes too. Outdoors in the Summer Garden in spring and summer. Complimentary park Mon-Sat after 5:30pm; Sun after 10am. Reserve. AE, CB, DC, MC, V. *OPEN 7 days. L 11:30am-3pm; D 5-11pm.* $$$

Sweet's

2 Fulton Street nr South St, upstairs. 344-9189. Where does one eat fish at the sparkling new Seaport? The same place one ate it before the sparkle—the famous fine fish and seafood restaurant housed in an 1842 building now gussied up to match the Seaport. Go but be prepared to wait; note the early closing. Reserve. AE, MC, V. *OPEN Mon-Fri 11:30am-8:30pm. CLOSED Sat & Sun.* $$

Thwaite's Inn

536 City Island Avenue, City Island, Bronx. 885-1023. Since 1870 this City Island restaurant has specialized in shellfish. Steak and roast beef too. Reserve. AE, CB, DC, MC, V. *OPEN Tues-Sun noon-10pm. CLOSED Mon.* $$$

Umberto's Clam House

129 Mulberry Street nr Hester St. 431-7545. Good seafood and sweet Italian pastries are the specialties. No credit cards. *OPEN 7 days 11am-6am.* $$

French

Bienvenue

21 East 36 Street. 684-0215. Small, charming, very busy at noon. French specialties include crepes, quiches, sausage en croute. Wine only. AE, MC, V. *L Mon-Fri 11:30am-2:30pm. D Mon-Sat 5:30-10pm. CLOSED Sun.* $$

Black Sheep

342 West 11 Street at Washington St. 741-9772. Far West Village restaurant for good value country French food. Six-course prix fixe dinner includes crudités, soup and pâté, salad and dessert with your choice of main course. Roast duck with grapes, venison with chestnuts, Provençal fish stew. Impressive wine list. Reserve. AE, MC, V. *OPEN Sun-Thurs 6-11pm; Fri & Sat till midnight. Sun Brunch noon-4pm.* $$

Box Tree

242 East 49 Street. 758-8320. Small romantic town house setting. Lovely French food, very attentive service. A rose accompanies your rather steep bill. Jacket & tie required. Reserve! No credit cards. *L Sun-Fri noon-2pm. D 7 days, two seatings 6:30 & 9:30pm.* $$$$

Brittany du Soir

800 Ninth Avenue at West 53 St. 265-4820. Longtime comfortable and friendly country French restaurant. Specialties: duck à l'orange, foie de veau au bacon. Very good value. Reserve on weekend. AE. *L Mon-Thurs noon-2:45pm. D Mon-Thurs 5-10pm; Fri & Sat till 11pm. CLOSED Sun.* $$

Café Argenteuil

253 East 52 Street. 753-9273. Small, very French bistro offers quite good classical French food. Popular with publishing people. Jacket required. Reserve. AE, CB, DC, MC, V. *L Mon-Fri noon-3pm. D Mon-Fri 6-10:15pm; Sat 6-10:45pm. CLOSED Sun.* $$$

Café Loup

18 East 13 Street. 255-4746. Small neighborhood French restaurant. Casual ambiance, good food, Mushrooms à la Grecque, duck Montmorency, sautéed calves' liver. Tiny garden in summer. Reserve. AE, DC, MC, V. *L Mon-Fri noon-3pm; D Mon-Sat 6-11pm. CLOSED Sun.* $$

Capsouto Frères

451 Washington Street at Watts St. 966-4900. Remote French bistro in 1891 landmark TriBeCa building. Simple country French fare: sauteed calves' liver, blanquette de veau, coq au vin, ratatouille, mussels ravigote. Handsome surroundings and crowd. Umbrella-shaded terrace in summer. *OPEN Mon 5pm-1am; Tues-Thurs & Sun noon-1am; Fri & Sat till 2am; Bar till 4am. Weekend Brunch noon-5pm.* $$

Chanterelle

89 Grand Street at Greene St. 966-6960. Beautifully spare elegance SoHo style. Ambitious *nouvelle cuisine*, à la carte or prix-fixe 7-course "tasting dinner." Menu changes weekly. Reserve.

AE, MC, V. *OPEN Tues-Sat 6:30-10:30pm. CLOSED Sun & Mon.* $$$

Chez Napoléon
365 West 50 Street. 265-6980. Consistently good, unpretentious bourgeois French fare in a friendly setting. Cassoulet on Thurs; bouillabaisse Fri. Reserve. AE, MC, V. *L Mon-Fri noon-2:30pm. D Mon-Thurs 5-10:30pm; Fri & Sat till 11pm. CLOSED Sun.* $

Frère Jacques
151 West 48 Street. 575-1866. Friendly, small French restaurant in the Theater District. Pre-theater special *5-6:30pm.* Reserve. AE, V. *L Mon-Fri noon-3pm. D Tues-Sat 5-9pm. CLOSED Sun.* $$

Jean Lafitte
68 West 58 Street. 751-2323. Art Nouveau-inspired decor, tasty bourgeois bistro fare. Steak tartare, boiled short ribs, scallops poached in lobster sauce. Reserve. AE, CB, DC, MC, V. *L Mon-Fri noon-3pm. D 7 days 6pm-12:30am.* $$

La Bibliothèque
341 East 43 Street, overlooking First Ave. 661-5757. Attractive book-lined interior. Glass-enclosed terrace. Wide windows face the United Nations. Good basic French dishes, noisy convivial crowd. Reserve for lunch. AE, CB, DC, MC, V. *L Mon-Fri noon-3pm. D Mon-Fri 6-11pm; Sat 5:30-11pm. CLOSED Sun.* $$

La Bonne Bouffe
127 East 34 Street. 679-9309. Small, unpretentious bistro offers lovely French specialties. Grilled lamb brochette with mustard sauce a standout. Everything homemade from the pâtés to the desserts. Dinner reservations only. AE only. *L Mon-Fri 11:30am-2:30pm. D Mon-Sat 6-10pm. CLOSED Sun.* $

La Cave Henri IV
227 East 50 Street. 755-6566. Intimate below-street-level French restaurant. Traditional simple fare. Piano music Tues-Sat eve. Reserve. AE, DC, MC, V. *Mon-Sat L noon-3pm; D 6-11:30pm; CLOSED Sun.* $

La Chaumière
310 West 4 Street nr Bank St. 741-3374. French country-inn pretty—flowers everywhere. Lovely satisfying food. Reserve. AE, MC, V. *OPEN Sun-Thurs 5pm-midnight; Fri & Sat till 1am.* $$

La Colombe d'Or
134 East 26 Street. 689-0666. A small, charming, pretty Provençal restaurant. Imaginative offerings all beautifully prepared and served. Bouillabaisse every day. Reserve. AE, DC, MC, V. *L Mon-Fri noon-2:30pm. D Mon-Sat 6-11pm. CLOSED Sun.* $$

La Gamelle
59 Grand Street nr West Broadway. 431-6695. Stylish SoHo eatery for flavorful Provençal dishes. Popular up-front bar. Reserve. AE, MC, V. *OPEN 7 days 4:30pm-4am (kitchen till 3:30am).* $$

La Gauloise
502 Sixth Avenue nr West 13 St. 691-1363. Handsome Art Nouveau bistro. Features very good French food and ambiance. Excellent onion soup, omelet fines herbs, cassoulet on Sun. Lovely daily specials. Reserve. AE, MC, V. *L Mon-Fri noon-3pm. D 7 days 5:45-11:30pm. Brunch: Sat noon-3pm; Sun noon-4pm.* $$

La Goulue
28 East 70 Street. 988-8169. Beautiful antique Art Nouveau décor. Chic art world crowd, nice French food. Outdoor café in summer. Reserve. AE, DC, MC, V. *OPEN Mon-Sat: L noon-3pm; D 6-11pm. CLOSED Sun & holidays.* $$$

La Mangeoire
1008 Second Avenue nr East 53 St. 759-7086. Exquisite French country restaurant with food to match. Filet of sole, sautéed calves' liver, wonderful omelettes. Reserve. AE, MC, V. *OPEN 7 days. L noon-3pm; D 6-10:30pm.* $$

La Métairie
189 West 10 Street nr Bleecker St. 989-0343. A handful of tables in a rustic, country-French setting. Delicious food including couscous, duck with calvados; tempting desserts. Menu changes daily. Reserve. MC, V. *OPEN Sun-Thurs 6-10:30pm; Fri & Sat till 11:30pm.* $$$

La Petite Ferme
973 Lexington Avenue at East 70 St. 249-3272. Excellent *cuisine bourgeoise* in a rustic setting. Small menu, tiny room, memorable dining experience. Recommended: the poached fish moules vinaigrette, beef paillard. Reserve. AE, CB, DC, MC, V. *OPEN Mon-Sat: L noon-2:30pm; D at 7 & 9pm. CLOSED Sun.* $$$

La Petite Marmite
5 Mitchell Place, First Ave & East 49 St. 826-1084. Successful East Side French restaurant with UN clientele. Serves consistently good food in a pleasant atmosphere. Reserve. AE, CB, DC, MC, V. *L Mon-Fri noon-2:30pm. D Mon-Sat 6-10:30pm. Sat Brunch noon-4pm. CLOSED Sun & holidays.* $$$

La Tulipe
104 West 13 Street. 691-8860. Handsome, romantic town house setting for impeccably prepared seasonal foods. Stylish all around. Unforgettable desserts, especially the apricot soufflé. Prix fixe. (Watch the sky-high wine prices.) Reserve! AE, DC, MC, V. *OPEN Tues-Sun 6:30-10pm. CLOSED Mon.* $$$$

Laurent
111 East 56 Street. 753-2729. Elegantly handsome. Serves fine French cuisine; excellent game in season. Try the pancakes Laurent: seafood and spinach served in thin pancakes with cream. Exceptional wine list. Reserve. AE, CB, DC. *L Mon-Fri noon-3pm. D Mon-Fri 6-10:30pm; Sat 5-11pm; Sun 5-10:30pm.* $$$

Lavin's
23 West 39 Street. 921-1288. Handsome room draws fashion industry execs at noon, wine buffs in the pm. Wonderful artfully presented food, Cruvinet dispenser (America's first) for excellent wines by the glass. Good California selection, too. Wine bar up front; wine-tasting courses available. *OPEN Mon-Fri L noon-2:30pm; D 6pm-midnight. CLOSED Sat & Sun.* $$$

Le Bistro
827 Third Avenue nr East 50 St. 759-8439. Small, casual French-style setting features good hearty

food: bouillabaisse, boeuf Bordelaise, pieds de porc grillés. Busy for lunch. Reserve. AE, DC, MC, V. *L Mon-Fri noon-3pm. D Mon-Fri 6-10pm; Sat 5:30-10:30pm. CLOSED Sun & holidays.* $$

Le Boeuf à la Mode
539 East 81 Street. 650-9664. Unpretentious neighborhood French restaurant. Friendly atmosphere, good food. Daily specials. Reserve. AE, DC, MC. *OPEN Tues-Sun 5:30-11pm. CLOSED Mon.* $$

Le Café de la Gare
143 Perry Street nr Washington St. 242-3553. Small, inviting and unpretentious Village bistro for delicious hearty French "home" cooking. Cassoulet, pot au feu, blanquette de veau. Draws crowds. Reserve! No alcohol (bring your own wine). No credit cards. *OPEN Tues-Sat 6-10:30pm; Sun 5:30-9pm. CLOSED Mon.* $

Le Canard Englouti
72 Bedford Street at Commerce St. 243-8593. Stylish Greenwich Village restaurant for lovely artfully presented French food. Snails sauteed in tarragon in puff pastry, salmon filets in onion butter, rack of lamb for two. For dessert the inventive "fettucine" au chocolat. Reserve. AE, DC, MC, V. *OPEN Tues-Sat 6:15-10:30pm. CLOSED Sun & Mon.* $$$$

Le Chambertin
348 West 46 Street. 757-2154. Good French Theater District restaurant. Excellent onion soup. Reserve. AE, DC, MC, V. *OPEN Mon-Sat 11:30am-9:30pm. CLOSED Sun.* $$

Le Chantilly
106 East 57 Street. 751-2931. Popular with the international set. Pretty, plush and spacious. Very good French cooking. Reserve. AE, DC, MC, V. *OPEN Mon-Sat: L noon-3pm; D 6-10:30pm. CLOSED Sun.* $$$$

Le Cherche-Midi
936 First Avenue nr East 51 St. 355-4499. Spare Provençal decor and Provençal-inspired specialties. Small open-to-the-sky backyard. Reserve. AE, MC, V. *L Mon-Fri noon-2:30pm. D Mon-Sat 6-11pm.* $$

Le Lavandou
134 East 61 Street. 838-7987. Popular, small, formal East Side French restaurant: imaginative, well-prepared food. Jacket required. Reserve. AE. *OPEN Mon-Sat: L noon-2:30; D 6-10pm. CLOSED Sun.* $$$$

Le Périgord Park
575 Park Avenue nr East 63 St. 752-0050. Elegant French dining from a very fine wide-ranging menu. Reserve. AE, DC, MC, V. *L Mon-Fri noon-3pm. D Mon-Sat 6-10:30pm. CLOSED Sun.* $$$$

Le Petit Robert
314 West 11 Street. 691-5311. One of the best in the Village and charming, too. Reserve. AE only. *OPEN Tues-Sat 6-11pm; Sun till 10pm. CLOSED Mon.* $$

Le Quercy
52 West 55 Street. 265-8141. Smart yet inexpensive French restaurant. Small complimentary appetizers, delicious entrées change daily. Attentive service. Reserve. AE, CB, DC, MC, V. *OPEN Mon-Sat: L noon-3pm; D 5-10:30pm. CLOSED Sun.* $

Le Relais
712 Madison Avenue nr East 63 St. 751-5108. Chic, beautifully appointed bistro-style restaurant. Features OK French food in a European ambiance. Trendy international crowd at the bar. Open to the street in summer for Mad Ave people watching. Reserve. AE. *L Mon-Sat noon-3pm; Sun 12:30-3:30pm. D Mon-Fri 6:30-11pm; Sat & Sun 7-11pm.* $$$

Les Pyrénées
251 West 51 Street. 246-0044. One of the better Theater District French restaurants. Good country French cooking, excellent wine cellar. Jacket requested. Reserve. AE, DC, MC, V. *Mon-Sat L noon-3pm; D 5-11pm. CLOSED Sun.* $$

Les Tournebroches
Citicorp Market, 153 East 53 Street. 935-6029. Very good simple French cookery-grilling and roasting done within your view. Lovely hors d'oeuvres. Reserve. AE, CB, DC, MC, V. *Mon-Sat L 11:30am-3pm; D 5-10pm. CLOSED Sun.* $

Le Veau d'Or
129 East 60 Street. 838-8133. Consistent excellence from this well-established, popular French restaurant. Tends to be extremely crowded. Reserve. AE. *L Mon-Fri noon-2:30pm; D Mon-Sat 6-10:15pm. CLOSED Sun & holidays.* $$$

Le Zinc
139 Duane Street nr West Broadway. 732-1226. Former shoe factory now bustles with the trendy (and those who aspire to be) of TriBeCa (same owners of Café Un, Deux, Trois). The French bistro fare is quite good: lamb stew, boudins noir, salmon steak, roast duck. Sidewalk tables in summer. Reserve. AE only. *OPEN Mon-Thurs 6:30pm-12:30am; Fri & Sat till 1am; Sun till 11:30pm.*

Lisanne
448 Atlantic Avenue nr Nevins St. (1-718) 237-2271. Casual tin-ceilinged, skylit Brooklyn restaurant serves a very fine French menu. Duck with cassis and figs, a selection of fish and beef grilled over mesquite. AE, DC, MC, V. *L Tues-Fri noon-2:30pm. D Tues-Sat 6-10pm. Sun Brunch 11:30am-8pm. CLOSED Mon.* $$

Mon Paris
111 East 29 Street. 683-4255. Long-established, very popular, very good French restaurant. Duck à l'orange, steak au poivre, shrimp Provençal, chicken in red wine. Bouillabaisse Fri & Sat. Jacket required. Reserve. AE, MC, V. *L Mon-Fri noon-3pm. D Mon-Fri 5:30-10:30pm; Sat till 11pm. CLOSED Sun.* $$$

Montrachet
239 West Broadway nr White St. 219-2777. Lovely highly recommended TriBeCa choice for fine French food in an appealing high-ceilinged setting. Prix fixe dinners; good wine list. AE. Reserve. *OPEN Tues-Sun 6-11:30pm. CLOSED Mon.* $$

The Odeon
145 West Broadway at Thomas St. 233-0507. Large, remodeled, 40s-style cafeteria is a trendy TriBeCa "in" spot. Very fine French food, low-key ambiance and an interesting cast of characters. Reserve. AE, MC, V. *L Mon-Fri noon-3pm. D Mon-*

at 7pm-12:30am; Sun 7:30pm-12:30am. Late supper 7 days till 2:30am. Sun Brunch noon-3:30pm. $$

Petrossian
182 West 58 Street. 245-2214. Elegant Belle Epoque decor (leather-and-mink-trimmed banquets, Limoges china) provide the proper setting for the city's first caviar café. Owned by the famed Parisian caviar firm of the same name. In addition to the specialty, caviar, there is foie gras served with warm truffles, smoked salmon and a small choice of dinner specials. In all an indulgent—and expensive—experience. Champagne by the glass; fine vodka. Reserve. AE, DC, MC, V. OPEN Mon-Sat: L noon-3pm; D 6pm-midnight. Caviar Bar 3-6pm. CLOSED Sun. $$$

The Polo
Westbury Hotel, Madison Avenue at East 69 Street. 535-9141. Revamped, reopened and resplendent. In an attractive, clubby atmosphere, lovely elegant French food. Salmon fillet in beurre blanc, medaillions of veal with poached pears, rack of lamb in tarragon sauce with couscous for two. A la carte. Reserve. AE, CB, DC, MC, V. OPEN 7 days: L noon-2:30pm; D 6:30-10pm. $$$$

Quatorze
240 West 14 Street. 206-7006. An off-the-beaten-track charmer for reasonably priced French fare in a casual bistro setting. AE only. Reserve. L Mon-Fri noon-2:30pm. D 7 days 6pm-midnight. $

Quilted Giraffe
955 Second Avenue nr East 51 St. 753-5355. Attractive setting for highly adventuresome, almost always successful nouvelle cuisine. Menu dégustation. Impressive wine list. (P.S. The washrooms draw raves, have a look.) Prix fixe. Reserve. AE, MC, V. OPEN Mon-Fri 6-10:30pm. CLOSED Sat & Sun. $$$

Raoul's
180 Prince Street nr Sullivan St. 966-3518. Extremely hectic crowded SoHo saloon updated to bistro status. Features good country French cooking and a wait. Reserve. AE, MC, V. OPEN Sun-Thurs 6:30-midnight; Fri & Sat till 12:30am. Sun Brunch noon-3:30pm. $$$

René Pujol
321 West 51 Street. 246-3023. Cozy French country-inn setting. Serves good traditional French fare close to the Theater District. Reserve. AE, DC, MC, V. L Mon-Fri noon-3pm; D Mon-Sat 5-11:30pm. CLOSED Sun. $$

Restaurant Raphael
33 West 54 Street. 582-8993. Small, sophisticated setting for very good French food. Fireplace in winter, garden in summer. Carefully planned menu with choices of fish, veal, lamb, chicken and beef, all beautifully prepared. (Service charge added to bill.) Reserve. AE, CB, DC. OPEN Mon-Fri: L noon-2pm. D 6-9:30pm. CLOSED Sat & Sun. $$$$

SoHo Charcuterie
195 Spring Street at Sullivan St. 226-3545. Bright, modern charcuterie/restaurant. Simple, light dishes to elaborately cooked entrées. Prix fixe or à la carte. Inexpensive wine list. Homemade cakes

and pastries. Reserve for brunch. AE, V. L Tues-Fri noon-3:30pm; Sat 11:30am-4:30pm. D Tues-Fri 6-11pm; Sat 6-11:30pm. Sun Brunch 11am-4:30pm. CLOSED Mon. $$$$

Tout Va Bien
311 West 51 Street. 265-0190. Theater District reliable. French café, simple country food, small courtyard with umbrella-shaded tables. Steak au poivre, bouillabaisse, onion soup. Reserve. AE, DC, MC, V. OPEN Mon-Sat: L noon-2:30pm; D 5-11:15pm. CLOSED Sun. $

24 Fifth
24 Fifth Avenue at 9 St. 475-0880. Posh setting for Michel Fitoussi (the former chef at the Palace) and his inventive culinary talents. Filet mignon with juniper berry sauce; paupiette of chicken; game in season. Incredible desserts. Nicest spot to sit—the enclosed café. Reserve. AE, CB, DC, MC, V. L Mon-Fri noon-4pm. D Mon-Sat 5:30pm-11pm. Weekend Brunch 11am-4pm. $$$

Village Green
531 Hudson Street nr Charles St. 255-1650. Very beautiful, small split-level Greenwich Village restaurant. Two fireplaces add a charming, romantic glow. Very good limited menu features French Creole dishes. Bananas Foster for dessert. Piano music Tues-Sat. Reserve. AE, MC, V. OPEN Tues-Sat 4-11:30pm; Sun 5-10pm. Sun Brunch (winter only) noon-4pm. CLOSED Mon. $$

Garden/Outdoor Dining

The following have outdoor dining facilities in the form of a garden or a café. In season, usually May-Oct, weather permitting.
See also Sidewalk Cafés.

Barbetta (Italian)
Café Marigold (Continental)
Café Orlin (Breakfast/Brunch)
Caffè Biondo (Cafés)
Caffè Reggio (Cafés)
Capsouto Freres (French)
Cloister Cafe (Cafés)
Curtain Up! (American)
Da Silvano (Italian)
El Internacional (Spanish: Taps)
Empire Diner (Late Night/24 Hours)
Evelyn's (Continental)
Giordano (Italian)
Gordon (Italian)
Horn of Plenty (Soul & Creole)
Jimmy Day's (Bars & Burgers)
La Goulou (French)
Le Relais (French)
Le Zinc (French)
Lion's Rock (Continental)
Martell's (Bars & Burgers)
Montana Eve (American)
Pete's Tavern (Bars & Burgers)
Roxanne's (American)
Ruc (Czechoslovakian)
Ruelles (Continental)
Sea Grill (Fish & Seafood)
65 Irving Place (Continental)
Sumptuary (Continental)
Tavern on the Green (Rooms with a View)
Tout Va Bien (French)

Water Club (Rooms with a View)
White House Tavern (Bars & Burgers)
Ye Waverly Inn (American)

German & Austrian
Kleine Konditorei
234 East 86 Street. 737-7130. Friendly, informal
Yorkville restaurant for simple, hearty fare. Spicy
sauerbraten, wursts; German beer. Homemade
cakes and tortes tempt you in entry bake shop.
Reserve weekends. AE, DC. *OPEN Sun-Thurs
11am-11:15pm; Fri & Sat till midnight.* $
Luchow's on Broadway
1633 Broadway at West 51 St. 582-4697. A vast
below-ground-level substitution for the venerable
old 14 Street original building. Not worth the tariff,
which is steep. AE, DC, MC, V. *L Wed 11:30am-
3pm; Sat & Sun noon-3pm. D Mon, Tues, Thurs &
Fri 5pm-midnight; Wed & Sat 4:30pm till midnight;
Sun till 10pm.* $$$
Suerken's Restaurant
27 Park Place nr Church St. 267-6389. Large
107-year-old downtown restaurant. Fresh fish,
schnitzels, wursts, dumplings, sauerbraten and
Löwenbräu. Great fresh apple strudel. Reserve.
AE, CB, DC, MC, V. *OPEN Mon-Thurs 11:30am-
11:30pm; Fri till 12:30am. CLOSED Sat & Sun.*$
Vienna '79
320 East 79 Street. 734-4700. Authentic Austro-
German food in an elegant, sophisticated setting.
The boiled beef, calves' liver with onions and ap-
ples, veal goulash—all standouts. Leave room for
cream strudel. Jacket required. Reserve. AE, DC,
MC, V. *OPEN Mon-Thurs 5:30-11pm; Fri & Sat till
11:30pm. CLOSED Sun.* $$$

Greek
Molfeta's
307 West 47 Street. 840-9537. Well-known informal Greek cafeteria restaurant features a wide
variety of good food, the fish dishes especially. No
credit cards. *OPEN 7 days 11:30am-12:30am.* $
Pantheon
689 Eighth Avenue nr West 44 St. 664-8294. Well-
respected, well-priced Theater District restaurant.
Exceptional broiled fish; Greek specialties. Daily
lamb specials. Retsina wines only. No reservations. AE, DC, MC, V. *OPEN Mon-Sat 11:30am-
11pm. CLOSED Sun.* $
Z
117 East 15 Street. 254-0960. Extremely
pleasant, inviting restaurant serving excellent
hearty Greek fare. Small outdoor garden in summer. A little gem. AE only. *OPEN Mon-Fri
11:30am-11pm; Sat & Sun from 1pm.* $

Health & Vegetarian
See also Jewish for several dairy restaurants.
Arnold's Turtle
51 Bank Street at West 4 St. 242-5623. Popular
informal Village vegetarian café. Inventive daily
specials, great salads, homemade soups, lovely
desserts. Wine, beer, saki. No reservations. MC,
V. *OPEN 7 days noon-midnight. Weekend Brunch
noon-4pm.* $
Brownie's
21 East 16 Street. 255-2838. Long-established

casual vegetarian restaurant serves fish as well
as salads. Very popular with health faddists and
dieters. Counter (no smoking) and table service.
No reservations. No credit cards. *OPEN Mon-Fri
11am-8pm; Sat noon-4pm. CLOSED Sun.* $
Great American Health Bar
35 West 57 Street. 355-5177. Counter and table
service. Specializes in vegetarian salads and
sandwiches. No alcohol. No smoking at counter.
*OPEN Mon-Fri 7:30am-8:30pm; Sat & Sun from
9:30am.* $
Nature's Kitchen
150 Fulton Street nr Broadway. 233-6102. Good
Lower Manhattan cafeteria-style restaurant spot
for salads, hot vegetarian dishes, soups, juices,
honey, goat's-milk ice cream. No alcohol. Smoking discouraged. No reservations. No credit
cards. *OPEN Mon-Fri 10am-6pm. CLOSED Sat &
Sun.* $
Whole Wheat 'n' Wild Berries
57 West 10 Street. 677-3410. Omelettes, daily hot
specials, fresh bread, salads and great desserts.
No credit cards. *L Tues-Sat 11:30am-4:30pm. D 7
nights 5-11pm. Sun Brunch 11:30am-4:30pm.* $
Zucchini
1336 First Avenue at East 72 St. 249-0559. Attractive location for quite good sandwiches on pita
bread, salads, and soups. Delicious desserts. A la
carte. No alcohol, you may bring your own wine.
Reserve. AE, DC, MC, V. *OPEN 7 days 11am-
10:30pm. Weekend Brunch 11:30am-4pm.* $

Hungarian
Csarda
1477 Second Avenue at East 77 St. 472-2892.
Women own and run this very good, very cheerful
Hungarian restaurant. Stuffed cabbage, stuffed
peppers, spicy sausage. Homemade pastries, in-
cluding apricot palacsinta and apple strudel.
Hungarian wines. Reserve. AE only. *OPEN Mon-
Fri 5-11pm; Sat & Sun noon-10pm.* $$
Eclair Shop
141 West 72 Street. 873-7700. Informal West
Side spot for Viennese/Hungarian dishes. Steaks
and burgers too. Best known for its pastries, sold
retail as well. No credit cards. *OPEN 7 days 8am-
midnight.* $
Green Tree
See Inexpensive.

Indian & Pakistani
*Sixth Street between Second and First Avenues
has been dubbed "Little India," for the number of
Indian restaurants it boasts. They are all cheap
and cheerful.*

Bombay Palace
30 West 52 Street. 541-7777. Expansive, hand-
somely decorated restaurant for the mildly spiced
cuisine of northern India. Good Muligatawny, gost
patiala, nan. Reserve. AE, DC, MC, V. *L 7 days
noon-3pm. D Mon-Sat 5:30-11:30pm; Sun till
11pm.*
Darbar
44 West 56 Street. 432-7227. Quite beautiful du-
plex setting for the authentic Mogul cookery of

Northern India. Recommended: the soups, the lamb stew, tandoori dishes, the carrot or rice pudding for dessert. Prix fixe pre- and after-theater dinners. Buffet lunch. Reserve. AE, DC, MC, V. *OPEN 365 days of the year. L 7 days noon-3pm. D Mon-Thurs & Sun 5:30-10:30; Fri & Sat till 11pm.* $

Gaylord
50 East 58 Street. 759-1710. Good classic Indian cuisine. Tandoori is the specialty, prepared in glass-enclosed kitchen. Reserve. AE, CB, DC, MC, V. *L Mon-Fri 11:30am-3pm. D 7 days 5:30-11pm.* $$

India Pavilion
325 East 54 Street. 223-9740. Small, informal and pleasant. Serves very good Indian food: curry, vindaloo, and tandoori. Bring your own wine. Reserve. AE, MC, V. *L Mon-Fri noon-2:30pm. D 7 days 5-10:30pm.* $

Kashmir
10 West 46 Street. 730-9201. Very spicy authentic Pakistani cuisine. Reserve. AE, DC, MC, V. *OPEN Mon-Sat noon-midnight; Sun till 10pm.* $

Raga
57 West 48 Street. 757-3450. One of the consistent bests. Excellent food in elegant digs. Specifications as to how hot are followed. AE, CB, DC, MC, V. *L Mon-Fri noon-3pm. D 7 days 5:30-11:15pm.* $$

Shagorika
100 Second Avenue nr East 6 St. 982-0533. A consistently good East Village Indian establishment. The curries are seasoned to your instructions; good mulligatawny, chicken tandoor. Service is efficient, the surroundings dark; live sitar music every Fri and Sat. AE, MC, V. *OPEN 7 days 2pm-midnight.* $

Shezan
8 West 58 Street. 371-1414. Good Pakistani and Indian cuisine in a lovely subterranean modern-mirrored, candle-lit setting. Speak up if you like it hot. Reserve. AE, DC, MC, V. *L Mon-Fri noon-2:30pm. D Mon-Sat 6-10:45pm. CLOSED Sun & holidays.* $$

Taj Mahal
1154 First Avenue nr East 63 St. 755-3017. Small, pleasant Indian restaurant serves delicious and satisfying entrées, including very good tandoori chicken, lamb biryani and chicken makhanala. Complete bar. Reserve. AE, DC, MC, V. *OPEN Mon-Fri noon-midnight; Sat & Sun 3pm-1am.* $

Inexpensive
Good meals at less than $10 per person.

Amy's
108 University Place nr East 13 St. 741-2170; 28 West 40 Street. 944-0195; 147 West 57 Street. 246-5445; 1877 Broadway at West 62 St. 265-5191; 2067 Broadway at West 72 St. 595-3708; 2888 Broadway at West 112 St. 666-1100. Attractive self-service chain. Falafel, the tasty Israeli vegetarian snack, as well as hamburger, steak and codfish come in pita—a thin, rounded, hollow flat bread. Inexpensive meal in a sandwich. *OPEN 7 days 8am-midnight. CLOSED Sun.*

Blue Plate
150 Eighth Avenue nr West 17 St. 255-8516. Cheap and more cheerful than most—if not all—fast-food emporiums. Self-serve, plastic utensils and plates; zippy black-and-turquoise decor. Soups, sandwiches and salads. No credit cards. *OPEN Mon-Thurs 7am-11pm; Fri till midnight; Sat & Sun 10:30am-midnight.*

Chez Brigitte
77 Greenwich Avenue nr West 11 St. 929-6736. Luncheonette, with only 11 seats, serves delicious inexpensive Provençal homemade specialties. No reservations. No credit cards. *OPEN Mon-Fri 11am-9pm.*

Green Tree
1034 Amsterdam Avenue at West 111 St. 864-9106. Longtime informal favorite with Columbia University and Barnard College students. Serves hearty Hungarian dishes, including excellent goulash, chicken paprikash, potato pirogen. No reservations. No credit cards. *OPEN Mon-Sat noon-9pm. CLOSED Sun.*

Horn and Hardart Automat
200 East 42 Street. 599-1665. The last of the coin-operated Automat food-dispensing sites. More a nostalgic than culinary treat. No-smoking section. No credit cards. *OPEN 7 days 6:30am-10pm.*

Junior's Restaurant
386 Flatbush Avenue Extension at DeKalb Ave, Brooklyn. (1-718) 852-5257. Famous Brooklyn restaurant for good sandwiches and snacks and great cheesecake. Pianist 5-11pm. AE, DC. *OPEN Sun-Thurs 6:30am-1:30am; Fri & Sat till 3am.*

La Fondue
43 West 55 Street. 581-0820. Popular and casual, features Swiss fondue and light meals of fruit, cheese, bread and wine. A really nice spot! No reservations. No credit cards. *OPEN Mon-Thurs 11:45am-midnight; Fri & Sat till 12:30am; Sun till 11pm.*

Manganaro's Grosseria Italiana
488 Ninth Avenue nr West 37 St. 563-5331. Famous Italian grocery since 1893. Tables in rear and upstairs. The offerings are tasty homemade pasta dishes and a wide range of hero sandwiches. Beer & wine, excellent cappuccino. AE only. *OPEN Mon-Sat 10am-7pm. CLOSED Sun.*

Moondance Diner
80 Avenue of the Americas at Grand St. 226-1191. The old Tunnel Diner resurrected for the 80s. Quality food at good prices: fresh-fruit buttermilk pancakes, potato skins and onion rings, spinach and swiss omelettes. Some good New York specialties too, like challah french toast and egg creams. Beer & wine. No reservations. No credit cards. *OPEN Mon-Fri 8:30am-midnight; Sat from 9am; Sun 9am-6pm.*

Nathan's
Surf Avenue at Stillwell Ave, Coney Island, Brooklyn. (1-718) 266-3161. The neighborhood isn't what it used to be but the famed hot dogs are. Also, still one of the best places for fresh oysters and clams. Dining room and counter ser-

vice. *OPEN Sun-Thurs 8am-2am; Fri & Sat till 4am.*

Nyborg Nelson
Citicorp Market, 153 East 53 Street. 223-0700. The smorgasbord plates, open-face sandwiches and hot daily specials are a treat. AE, CB, DC, MC, V. *OPEN Mon-Fri 11:30am-9pm; Sat noon-7pm; Sun noon-6pm.*

Rumbuls
20 Christopher Street nr Greenwich Ave. 924-8900. Full meals as well as coffee and sweets in charming informal setting. Two working fireplaces, card reader by appointment. You may bring your own wine. *OPEN 7 days 1:30pm-midnight.*

The Stage
Second Avenue nr St. Marks Place. 473-8614. Friendly Ukrainian luncheonette serves the best chicken soup in the East Village (daily). Good too are the pierogi, blintzes, kielbasy omelette, beef goulash and heaping portions of vegetables including kasha and wonderful mashed potatoes topped with fried onions. Counter only seats 16. No credit cards. *OPEN Mon-Sat 7am-9:30pm. CLOSED Sun.*

Ukrainian Restaurant
123 Second Avenue at St. Marks Pl. 533-6765. A new, less charming, setting for the still hearty and inexpensive Eastern European specialties. Crispy cheese blintzes, pierogi, stuffed cabbage and more. Wrap around sidewalk café in summer. No credit cards. Full bar. *OPEN Mon-Fri 11am-midnight; Sat & Sun till 2am. Weekend brunch 11am-5pm.* $

Italian

Alfredo
240 Central Park South nr Broadway. 246-7050. Good, albeit expensive, Italian dishes in a comfortable setting. Some of the pasta classics are exceptional. Reserve. AE, DC, MC, V. *L Mon-Fri noon-3pm. D Mon-Sat 5-11pm. CLOSED Sun.* $$$$

Alo Alo
Trump Plaza, 1030 Third Avenue at East 61 St. 838-4343. Dino De Laurentis finally has a culinary hit. The fashionable are flocking to this new sophisticated grand café for the excellent pastas and the scene. AE, DC, MC, V. Reserve. *OPEN 7 days 11:30am-2am.* $$

Angelo's
146 Mulberry Street nr Grand St. 966-1277. In Little Italy, a hectic but good Italian restaurant. Try the special *antipasto di mare*, a foot-long platter of squid, shrimp, scallops and celery for two. Reserve for more than 2. AE, DC, MC, V. *OPEN Tues-Sun noon-11:30pm. CLOSED Mon.* $$

Aperitivo
29 West 56 Street. 765-5155. Attractive décor, friendly atmosphere and service. Exceptionally good Italian food. Jacket required. Reserve. AE, DC, V. *L Mon-Fri noon-3pm. D Mon-Fri 5:30-10:30pm; Sat till 11pm. CLOSED Sun.* $$

Asti
13 East 12 Street. 741-9105. Large Italian restaurant where enthusiastic customers and waiters, hosts and performers sing opera with your supper. Good fun for groups. No reservations. AE, CB, DC, MC, V. *OPEN Tues-Sun 5pm-1am. CLOSED Mon & July & Aug.* $$

Ballato
55 East Houston Street nr Mott St. 226-9683. Very good Italian restaurant, popular, though off the beaten path. Excellent pasta, half portions of which are available as a starter. No credit cards. *Mon-Sat L noon-2:30pm; D 5:30-8:45pm. CLOSED Sun.* $$

Barbetta
321 West 46 Street. 246-9171. Distinguished Italian restaurant on Theater Row. The dishes are mainly Northern Italian Piedmontese specialties. Luxurious outdoor dining garden is a true oasis. Reserve. AE, CB, DC, MC, V. *OPEN Mon-Sat: L noon-2pm; D 5pm-midnight. Pre-theater 5:30-7pm. CLOSED Sun.* $$$

Beatrice Inn
285 West 12 Street nr Eighth Ave. 929-6165. Convivial Greenwich Village basement restaurant serves very good Northern Italian dishes, notably the pastas. Casual cozy smaller dining room has a fireplace; lingering in the pm is encouraged. Reserve for 4 or more. AE, CB, DC, MC, V. *L Mon-Fri noon-2:30pm. D Mon-Sat 5-10pm. CLOSED Sun.* $$

Cent'Anni
50 Carmine Street nr Bleecker St. 989-9494. Small, casual West Village trattoria for very good simple Florentine cooking. Wonderful seafood salad, grilled meats and fish. Finish with the zabaglione. Reserve. AE. *OPEN Mon-Sat 5:30-11:30pm; Sun 5-11pm.* $$

Contrapunto
200 East 60 Street (above Yellowfingers). 751-8616. Cheerful busy Bloomies neighbor for an interesting variety of pasta preparations, *vino,* and *gelati.* No reservations. AE, DC, MC, V. *OPEN Mon-Fri noon-11:30pm; Sat noon-4pm & 5-11:30pm; Sun 5-9:30pm.* $

Da Silvano
260 Sixth Avenue nr Houston St. 982-0090. Stylishly attractive storefront restaurant, outdoor sidewalk dining in summer. Excellent Northern Italian food, notably the pastas, the osso buco and the fileto Carpaccio. Reserve. No credit cards. *L Mon-Fri noon-3pm. D Mon-Sat 6-11:30pm; Sun 5-11pm.* $$

Erminia
250 East 83 Street. 879-4284. Informal and cozy (40 seats) family-run (same owners have the two Trasteveres and Lattanzi) restaurant for foods grilled over a Tuscan wood fire. Also, tasty pastas and bruschetta, olive oil and garlic drenched toasted bread. Reserve. No credit cards. *OPEN Mon-Sat 5-11pm; Sun till 10pm.* $$

Felidia
243 East 58 Street. 758-1479. Handsome sparkling restaurant for wonderfully original Italian creations. Tasty antipasti, homemade pastas with seasonal ingredients; polenta; risotto; game. Jacket required. Reserve. AE, CB, DC, MC, V.

OPEN Mon-Fri noon-midnight; Sat from 5pm. CLOSED Sun. $$$

Forlini's
93 Baxter Street nr Canal St. 349-6779. Popular casual spot for Northern Italian cooking. Be prepared to wait on weekends. Reserve for 6 or more. AE, CB, DC, MC, V. Reduced rate parking. *L Mon-Sat 11:30am-3pm. D Tues-Sat 5pm-2am; Sun & Mon till 11:30pm.* $$

Francesca's
129 East 28 Street. 685-0256. Cozy below-street-level restaurant for home-style Italian cooking: pastas, chicken, fish, veal and eggplant dishes. Bring your own wine. D, AE, MC, V. *L Mon-Fri noon-3pm. D Mon-Sat 6-11pm. CLOSED Sun.* $$

Gargiulo's
2911 West 15 Street, Brooklyn. (1-718)266-0906. In Coney Island, a huge boisterous family-run restaurant renowned for its home-style Neapolitan cooking. Mozzarella en carozza, baked clams, fettucine Gargiulo, tortellini Michaelangelo, risotto with mushrooms. Worth a trip for the food and the local color. Reserve. AE, DC, MC, V. Free parking. *OPEN Tues-Fri & Sun 11:30am-10pm; Sat till 11:30pm. CLOSED Mon.* $

Giambelli 50th Ristorante
46 East 50 Street. 688-2760. Good midtown Northern Italian restaurant. Elegant ambiance and clientele. Reserve. AE, CB, DC, MC, V. *OPEN Mon-Sat noon-midnight. CLOSED Sun.* $$$

Giordano
409 West 39 Street. 947-9811. Out-of-the-way Italian favorite of those who know it. Atrium garden beneath the stars. Reserve. AE, CB, DC, MC, V. *OPEN Mon-Thurs noon-11pm; Fri & Sat till midnight. CLOSED Sun.* $$

G. Lombardi
53 Spring Street nr Broadway. 226-9866. Good pasta, sausage and peppers in this tidy Art Deco-styled dining room on the edge of SoHo. Reserve. AE, MC, V. *OPEN Tues-Fri noon-11pm; Sat 4pm-midnight; Sun 1-11pm. CLOSED Mon.* $

Gordon
138 MacDougal Street nr Prince St. 475-7500. Informal Italian-accented bistro with a charming, romantic trellised garden. Good bruschetta, fettucine with shrimp, scottata, cheese torta. Reserve. AE, CB, DC, MC, V. *L Mon-Fri 11:30am-4pm. D Mon-Sun 6-11pm. Brunch Sat & Sun noon-5pm.* $

Grotta Azzurra
387 Broome Street at Mulberry St. 226-9283. Well-known subterranean restaurant in Little Italy. Lobster fra diavolo, cacciatore, ravioli. No credit cards. *OPEN Tues-Thurs noon-11:30pm; Fri till midnight; Sat till 12:30am. CLOSED Mon.* $$

Il Caminetto
1226 Second Avenue nr East 64 St. 758-1775. Small East Side Italian restaurant serves very good pastas. Reserve. AE, DC, MC, V. *L Mon-Fri noon-3pm. D Mon-Sat 5-midnight. CLOSED Sun.* $$

Il Cantinori
32 East 10 Street. 673-6044. Lovely uncomplicated Tuscan specialties in a low-key

country dining room, the front of which spills out onto the street in good weather. Wonderful daily specials. Penne with veal and sage, stracotto, Tuscan braised beef; donzellini toscana are fritters that *must* be tasted. Reserve for dinner. *L Mon-Fri noon-3pm. D Mon-Fri 6pm-11:30pm; Sat till midnight; Sun till 11pm.* $$

Il Menestrello
14 East 52 Street. 421-7588. The French décor is from a previous tenant, the food is very good Northern Italian: Bresaola, zuppa di spinaci, spaghetti carbonara. Jacket required. Reserve. AE, DC, MC, V. *OPEN Mon-Sat: L noon-3pm; D 5pm-11pm. CLOSED Sun.* $$$

Il Monello
1460 Second Avenue nr East 76 St. 535-9310. Plush Upper East Side Northern Italian restaurant. Carpaccio, crostacei marinara; excellent wine list. Reserve. AE, CB, DC, MC, V. *OPEN Mon-Sat: L noon-3pm; D 5pm-midnight. CLOSED Sun.* $$$

Il Mulino
86 West 3 Street. 673-3783. Another very good Greenwich Village Italian restaurant. Fried zucchine to start with; stuffed mushrooms; breaded clams; carpaccio; good pastas, especially the carbonara. For dessert, the zabaglione, hot or cold! Reserve. AE only. *OPEN Mon-Sat noon-11:30pm. CLOSED Sun.* $$

Il Nido
251 East 53 Street. 753-8450. Good Tuscan regional dishes in an elegant, softly lit, rather formal setting. *Great* wine list. Jacket & tie required. Reserve. AE, CB, DC, MC, V. *OPEN Mon-Sat: L noon-2:30pm; D 5:30-10pm. CLOSED Sun.* $$$

Il Ponte Vecchio
206 Thompson Street nr Bleecker St. 228-7701. Low-priced tasty food draws the locals to this neighborhood Italian restaurant. Good mussels, clams, shrimps oreganati and simply divine pastas. Reserve for more than 2. AE only. *L Mon-Fri noon-3:30pm. D Mon-Sat 5-11pm; Sun 3-10pm.* $

Il Vagabondo
351 East 62 Street. 832-9221. Popular and boisterous neighborhood Italian restaurant. Unique feature: a well-used earth-floor boccie court. No reservations. AE, CB, DC, MC, V. *L Mon-Fri noon-3pm. D Mon-Sat 5:30-midnight; Sun till 11pm.* $

Josephine
229 Lexington Avenue nr East 34 St. 532-6375. Small, friendly restaurant serves very satisfying Neapolitan home-style cooking. Informal. Daily specials on a blackboard menu. Reserve. MC, V. *L Mon-Fri noon-2:30pm; D Mon-Fri 5-9pm; Sat till 10pm. CLOSED Sun.* $

La Colonna
17 West 19 Street. 206-8660. Former warehouse expensively and expansively transformed into a beautiful people watering station. This trendy brasserie has Corinthian columns, Pompeiian frescoes and a casual yet elegant crowd. The food plays a decided supporting role and the tariff is steep. Reserve. AE, DC, MC, V. *L Mon-Fri noon-3pm. D 7 days 6:30-12:30am. Bar till 2am. Sun Brunch 1-4pm.* $$$$

Lattanzi
361 West 46 Street. 315-0980. In the Theater District. Rustic, informal setting for hearty Italian dining. Vegetable fritto misto, calamari, stuffed veal chop. Reserve. AE only. *L Mon-Fri noon-3pm. D Mon-Thurs 5-10:30pm; Fri & Sat till midnight.* $$$

Louise Junior
317 East 53 Street. 752-7832. Congenial Italian restaurant with a standout antipasto that includes shrimp and crabmeat. Jacket appreciated. Reserve for lunch. AE, CB, DC. *L Mon-Sat noon-3pm. D Mon-Fri 5-10:30pm; Sat till 11pm. CLOSED Sun.* $$

Mamma Leone's
239 West 48 Street. 586-5151. Festive Italian *carnivale* from the décor to the waiters to the enormous quantities of food served. Everyone should go—at least once. Reserve. AE, CB, DC, MC, V. *OPEN Mon-Fri 3:30-11:30pm; Sat 2:30-11:30pm; Sun 2-10pm.* $$

Marchi's
251 East 31 Street. 679-2494. Durable old Northern Italian restaurant in a brownstone. Several attractive dining rooms. An OK fixed meal consisting of antipasto, lasagna, fish, vegetables, chicken, roast beef, salad, cheese, fruit, ristoli, espresso is proffered to all. *Buon apetito!* Jacket required. Reserve only Mon-Thurs. AE. *OPEN Mon-Fri 5-10pm; Sat & Sun till 11pm.* $$

Mary's
42 Bedford Street nr Seventh Ave So. 741-3387. Atmospheric old Village restaurant with two fireplaces. Home-style Italian cooking; Abruzzi specialties. Very good pastas. Reserve weekends. AE, CB, DC, MC. *OPEN Mon-Thurs 5pm-midnight; Fri till 1am; Sat 4pm-1am; Sun 4pm-11pm.* $

Mezzaluna
1295 Third Avenue nr East 74 St. 535-9600. In with the in crowd—and crowd is the operative word here. Elegant, celestial decor—cloud-painted ceiling, half moon (mezzaluna) theme; shoulder to shoulder seating; ear-blasting music. Limited menu: beef carpaccio with a choice of fixings; pasta main courses, change daily; vegetable and herb pizzas from wood-burning ovens (at lunch and after 10:30pm only). Cheese, fruit and sorbets for dessert. All-Italian wine list. All-Italian experience. No reservations, *expect* a long wait and you won't be disappointed. No credit cards. *OPEN 7 days: L noon-3pm; D 6pm-1am.* $$

Nanni al Valletto
133 East 61 Street. 838-3939. Many Italians considered this the tops for osso buco, spinach and ricotta ravioli, baked clams and pasta, especially the carbonara. Reserve. AE, CB, DC, MC, V. *L Mon-Fri noon-3:30pm. D Mon-Sat 5:30-midnight. CLOSED Sun.* $$$

Nanni's
146 East 46 Street. 697-4161. Long-established Italian restaurant with a clubby feel. Classic Northern dishes beautifully prepared. Convivial and *very* highly recommended. Reserve for lunch and dinner. AE, DC, MC, V. *L Mon-Fri noon-3pm. D Mon-Sat 5:30-11pm. CLOSED Sun.* $$

Nick & Guido
334 West 46 Street. 974-9895. Popular with Alitalia Airlines personnel, this no-frills restaurant serves very good simple Italian food, especially pastas. Reserve. AE, CB, DC, MC, V. *L Mon-Fri noon-2:30pm. D Mon & Tues 4:30-8:30pm; Wed-Sat till 11:30pm. CLOSED Mon.* $

Nicola Paone
207 East 34 Street. 889-3239. Comfortable, friendly skylit restaurant. Serves quite good Italian specialties. Leisurely service. Enclosed garden. Reserve. AE, DC. *OPEN Mon-Sat: L noon-1:30pm; D 5-9:30pm. CLOSED Sun.* $$$

Orsini's
41 West 56 Street. 757-1698. Famed Italian restaurant draws a *haute* fashion crowd. Intimate and calm. Very good scampi, mozzarella in carrozza, osso bucco, calves' liver Veneziana, penne with vodka. Jacket & tie required. Reserve. AE, CB, DC, MC, V. *L Mon-Fri noon-3pm. D Mon-Sat 5:30pm-1am. CLOSED Sun.* $$$

Orso
322 West 46 Street. 489-7212. For theater-goers, a charming casual Italian bistro for pre- or post-theater pasta, pizza and grilled entrees. Attracts a show-biz crowd to its vaulted skylit back room. Reserve. MC, V. *OPEN 7 days noon-11:30.* $

Osteria Romana
174 Grand Street nr Mulberry St. 925-8540. A Little Italy landmark for good food and atmosphere. AE, DC, MC, V. *OPEN Tues-Sun 5pm-midnight. CLOSED Mon.* $

Paolucci's
149 Mulberry Street nr Grand St. 226-9653. Dine Italian in a homey two-story 1816 landmark Federal building. Reserve. AE, DC, MC, V. *OPEN Thurs & Fri; Sun-Tues noon-10:30pm; Sat till 11:30pm. CLOSED Wed.* $$

Parioli Romanissimo
24 East 81 Street. 288-2391. This restaurant located in a turn-of-the century brownstone serves some of the city's very best Northern Italian dishes. Unequaled veal and pasta dishes. Reserve. Jacket & tie. AE, CB, DC. *OPEN Tues-Sat 6-11pm. CLOSED Sun & Mon.* $$$$

Parma
1404 Third Avenue nr East 79 St. 535-3520. Noisy informal East Side bistro. Serves very good Italian food to a fashionable East Side crowd. Highly recommended: the pastas. Reserve for 4 or more. AE only. *OPEN 7 days 5pm-12:30am.* $$

Patrissey's
98 Kenmare Street nr Mulberry St. 226-8509. Substantial Little Italy fixture since the 1930s serves good Neapolitan specialties. Reserve. AE, CB, DC, V. *OPEN 7 days noon-11:30pm.* $$

Pinocchio
168 East 81 Street. 650-1513. Tiny family-run storefront restaurant serves well-prepared Northern Italian food. Carpaccio, fegato Veneziano, paglia and fieno. Reserve. No credit cards. *OPEN Tues-Sat 5:30-10:30pm; Sun 4:30-9:30pm. CLOSED Mon.* $$

Pirandello
7 Washington Place East at Mercer Street. 260-

066. High-ceilinged sophisticated slice of Italy in the Village. Consistently good Northern specialties, impeccable service. Reserve. AE only. *OPEN Mon-Thurs 5:30-11pm; Fri & Sat till 11:30pm. CLOSED Sun.* $$

Positano
250 Park Avenue South at East 20 St. 777-6211. Hot commercial (Miller Lite) and video (Michael Jackson's "Beat It") director Bob Giraldi's ode to the Amalfi Coast. Daily specials, very good pastas and fish dishes. Crostini dei Monti Lattari, linguine alla giudea, and the dessert of the moment, tiramisu. Best view: from the "summit" tables. As you would expect the crowd is young and chic. No smoking section. Reserve! AE, CB, DC, MC, V. *L Mon-Fri noon-3pm; D Mon-Sat 5:30-11:30pm. CLOSED Sun.* $$

Puglia's
189 Hester Street at Mulberry St. 226-8912. Little Italy's most festive restaurant. Peasant-style home cooking, shared tables, lots of camaraderie and singing. The food may be better elsewhere but not the fun. No reservations. No credit cards. *OPEN Tues-Sun noon-1am. CLOSED Mon.*

Rao's
455 East 114 Street at Pleasant Ave. 534-9625. Way uptown, but worth the trip (if you can get in) to savor Neapolitan seafood dishes and pasta the way the Raos make it. All dishes are cooked to order and for dessert: a platter of seasonal fresh fruit. Only 6 tables; reserve months in advance! No credit cards. *OPEN Mon-Fri 6-11pm. CLOSED Sat & Sun.* $

Romeo Salta
30 West 56 Street. 246-5772. Housed in a former mansion, attractive Italian restaurant with an open kitchen. Excellent food, especially the pastas. Jacket required. Reserve. AE, CB, DC, MC, V. *OPEN Mon-Sat noon-11pm. CLOSED Sun.* $$$

Tavola Calda da Alfredo
285 Bleecker Street nr Seventh Ave So. 924-4789. Attractive, airy restaurant serves lovely Italian food. Special pastas daily. Take-out as well. No reservations. No credit cards. *OPEN Thurs-Tues noon-10:30pm. CLOSED Wed.* $

Tino's
235 East 58 Street. 751-0311. Lovely beamed-and-brick-walled skylit room. Extensive choice of pasta, risotto dishes. Jacket required. Reserve. AE, CB, DC, MC, V. *OPEN 7 days noon-3pm; 5pm-midnight.* $$$

Trastevere & Trastevere 84
309 East 89 Street. 734-6343; *155 East 84 Street. 744-0210. Tiny candlelit settings for Roman specialties. Spiedino alla romana, pasta primavera, pollo gaetano. Wine only. AE only. Reserve. *D Mon-Sat two seatings only at 7 & 9pm. *D Mon-Sat 5:30-11pm.* $$

Trattoria da Alfredo
90 Bank Street at Hudson St. 929-4400. Tiny (9-table) bustling storefront Greenwich Village restaurant. Popular for its very good Italian cooking. Bring your own wine. Reserve *well* in advance. No credit cards. *L Wed-Mon noon-2pm. D Mon & Wed-Sat 6-10:30pm; Sun 5-9:30pm. CLOSED Tues.* $

Vivolo
140 East 74 Street. 628-4671. Simple and satisfying Neapolitan food and a fireplace draws crowds. Enclosed sidewalk café. Jacket required. Reserve. AE. *L Mon-Fri noon-3pm. D Mon-Sat 5:30-11:30pm. CLOSED Sun.* $$

Zinno
126 West 13 Street. 924-5182. Comfortable, convivial replacement for the old Reno's. Simple Neapolitan dishes. Best are the linguine with vodka, fried zucchine, pork chop alla pizzaiuola, calves' liver alla nonna. Jazz in the pm. Reserve. AE, V. *L Mon-Fri noon-2:30pm. D Mon-Thurs 5:30-11:15pm; Fri & Sat till 11:45pm. CLOSED Sun.* $$

Japanese

Akasaka
715 Second Avenue nr East 38 St. 867-6410. Large, busy Japanese restaurant and sushi bar offers good traditional raw fish dishes and tempura. No credit cards. *Mon-Sat L noon-2:30pm; D 5-10pm. CLOSED Sun.* $

Benihana of Tokyo
47 West 56 Street. 581-0930; 15 West 44 Street. 682-7120; 120 East 56 Street. 593-1627. Chicken or steak, accompanied by shrimp and vegetables, is prepared and cooked at the table shared with others (unless there are 8 people in your party). Fun for all. Warm saki & Japanese beer available. Reserve. AE, CB, DC, MC, V. *L Mon-Thurs noon-2:30pm. D Mon-Thurs 5:30-10:30pm; Fri & Sat till 11:30pm; Sun 5-10:30pm.* $

Café Seiyoken
18 West 18 Street. 620-9010. Brightly lit, vast (seats 180) but stylish dining room for Continental food with Japanese overtones. Sushi bar for purists. Quieter for lunch. Reserve for dinner. AE, CB, DC, MC, V. *L Mon-Fri noon-3pm. D Mon-Thurs 6-midnight; Fri & Sat till 1am; Sun till 11pm.* $$

Gibbon
24 East 80 Street. 861-4001. In a tranquil and spacious clubby town-house setting. French-influenced Japanese: mussels with garlic, cucumber stuffed with lobster, wonderful tataki (sliced filet mignon), negima (thin sliced beef with onions and zucchini), prawns à la Kyoto, rack of lamb and wonderful appetizers. Sushi, sashimi for the purists. Homemade banana ice cream for dessert. Extremely popular with the art crowd. Working fireplace in the bar. Jacket preferred. Reserve. AE, DC, MC, V. *L Mon-Fri noon-2pm. D Mon-Sat 6-10pm. CLOSED Sun.* $$

Hatsuhana
17 East 48 Street. 355-3345. Sushi connoisseurs know this is the very best and they wait in line for their conviction. Japanese beers. No reservations for lunch. AE, DC, MC, V. *L Mon-Fri 11:45am-2:30pm. D Mon-Fri 5:30-9:30pm; Sat & Sun from 5pm.* $

Kitcho
22 West 46 Street. 575-8880. A longtime standout for wonderfully fresh, imaginatively prepared gril

led meats and fish. Traditional tatami or modern dining room. For the initiated and the wealthy an unusual sky's-the-limit 10-course chef's choice dinner. Japanese nationals predominate. Reserve. AE, DC. *L Mon-Fri. L noon-2:30pm; D Mon-Fri. 6-10:30pm; Sun 5-10pm. CLOSED Sat.* $$

Mie
196 Second Avenue nr East 12 St. 674-7060. Below-street-level East Village sushi bar and restaurant. Very popular because it serves some of the best sushi, sashimi, at the bar; also some original dishes including deep-fried oysters, hot pot of clams, oya ko-don chicken, scallion omelet, fried chicken. AE only. *OPEN 7 days 5pm-midnight.* $

Nippon
155 East 52 Street. 355-9020. Large well-known Japanese restaurant serves well-prepared tempura dishes. The à la carte menu has some interesting choices. Tatami or regular dining rooms. Reserve. AE, CB, DC, MC, V. *L Mon-Fri noon-2:30pm. D Mon-Thurs 5:30-10pm; Fri & Sat till 10:30. CLOSED Sun.* $$$

Saito
305 East 46 Street. 759-8897. Well-regarded Japanese restaurant for Western-style or tatami dining. Sushi and tempura bars. Very good food and service. Reserve. AE, DC, MC, V. *L Mon-Fri noon-3pm. D Mon-Fri 5:30-10pm; Sat till 10:30pm. CLOSED Sun.* $$

Sushiko
251 West 55 Street. 974-9721. Sushi bar and dining room for very fresh sashimi and sushi. Popular with theater folk and Japanese nationals. Also good, teh katsu don (breaded pork), gyudon (steamed beef). Selection varies with the day's catch. Reserve. AE, CB, DC, MC, V. *L Mon-Fri noon-2:30pm. D Mon-Sat 5-11:30pm.* $$

Sushi Zen
57 West 46 Street. 302-0707. Sushi bar for beautiful to look at and taste sushi and sashimi. Limited menu for non-raw-fish lovers. A la carte or a 4-course prix fixe. Reserve. AE, DC. *L Mon-Fri noon-2:30pm. D Mon-Fri 5:30-10:30pm; Sat 3-9pm.* $$

Takesushi
71 Vanderbilt Avenue at 45 St. 867-5120. Good midtown sushi choice. Counter, tables plus two private tatami suites. Reserve. AE, DC, MC, V. *L Mon-Fri noon-3pm. D Mon-Fri 5-10pm; Sat 1-8pm.* $$

(*See also* Delicatessen)

B & H Dairy
127 Second Avenue nr St. Marks Pl. 777-4707. Jewish Eastern-European dairy luncheonette with a few small tables draw East Village-neighborhood types for the good homemade soups and challah, pirogen and hearty sandwiches. Cash only. *OPEN 7 days 6am-11pm.* $

Barney Greenglass
541 Amsterdam Avenue nr West 86 St. 724-4707. Over 53 years of serving wonderful borscht, lox, sturgeon and white fish to Upper West Siders. Best bite: the omelettes of Nova, onions and eggs.

No credit cards. *OPEN Tues-Fri & Sun 9am-4pm; Sat till 5pm. CLOSED Mon.* $

Grand Dairy Restaurant
341 Grand Street at Ludlow St. 673-1904. Informal dairy restaurant for Jewish-style foods. Potato pirogen, fried herring, crisp apple blintzes, good rice pudding. *OPEN Sun-Thurs 6am-4pm; Fri till 3pm. CLOSED Sat.* $

Hershey Dairy Restaurant
167 West 29 Street. 868-6988. Old-time fur-district dairy restaurant serves very good fish dishes, blintzes, pirogen and *kibbitzing.* AE, DC. *OPEN Mon-Thurs 6am-7:30pm; Fri till 2:30pm. CLOSED Sat & Sun.* $

Lou Siegel's
209 West 38 Street. 921-4433. Large, informal kosher restaurant featuring Jewish home-style cooking. Lunchtime crowded with garment manufacturers. No dairy. No smoking section. Reserve. AE, DC, MC, V. *OPEN Sun-Thurs 11:30am-9pm; Fri till 3pm. CLOSED Sat.* $

Moshe Peking
40 West 37 Street. 594-6500. Complete kosher-Chinese restaurant features non-spicy Cantonese-style dishes. Reserve. AE, DC, MC, V. *OPEN Sun-Thurs noon-10pm; Sat from 1 hour past sunset till 1am. CLOSED Fri & Sat until sunset.* $

Ratner's Dairy Restaurant
138 Delancey Street nr Norfolk St. 677-5588. Famous Lower East Side Jewish dairy restaurant offers an extensive range of well-prepared dishes. Vegetable goulash, stuffed cabbage, blintzes, baked stuffed fish. No credit cards. *OPEN Sun-Fri 6am-11pm; Sat till 2am.* $

Sammy's Roumanian
157 Chrystie Street nr Delancy St. 673-0330. Rumanian tenderloin "with or without garlic." A NY institution; it's terribly entertaining and filling. Not for dieters. Reserve. AE, CB, DC. *OPEN Sun-Fri 4-10pm; Sat till 11:30pm.* $$

Yonah Schimmel's
137 East Houston Street nr Eldridge St. 477-2858. Also*, 1275 Lexington Avenue & East 86 St. 722-4849. The place (here since 1895) and food are remnants of the old Jewish East Side. Authentic knishes—the best are still potato and kasha, though good updates include cherry cheese. Other age-old treats: clabbered milk, borscht and a glass of tea. No credit cards. *OPEN 7 days 8am-6pm. Till 8pm.* $

Arirang House
28 West 56 Street. 581-9698. Bar and restaurant popular with Korean nationals. Unusual and tasty foods on the spicy side. Yauk hae (steak tartar), pul koki (marinated beef) and tui kim (fried chicken). Reserve. AE, CB, DC, MC, V. *L Mon-Fri noon-2:30pm. D Mon-Wed 5-10:30pm; Thurs-Sat till 11pm; Sun 4-10pm.* $$

Myong Dong
42 West 35 Street. 695-6622. Though the décor of this Korean restaurant leaves something to be desired, the good food does not. AE, MC, V. *OPEN 7 days noon-3pm; 5-11pm.* $

Late Night/24 Hours

Amsterdam's Bar & Rotisserie
428 Amsterdam Avenue nr West 80 St. 874-1377. Also, 454 Broadway nr Grand St. 925-6166.Stylish Upper West Side neighborhood meeting place serves simple rotisserie cooking. Good food and service; extremely casual air. Bar with juke box. As the crowds outside should tell you, no reservations. So successful, they have moved the formula downtown. *OPEN 7 days noon-2am.* $

Brasserie
100 East 53 Street. 751-4840. Huge, informal yet sophisticated French brasserie for good onion soup, burgers, quiches, salads. Also, a nice breakfast spot. Counter & table service. Reserve for dinner only. AE, CB, DC, MC, V. *NEVER CLOSES!* $

Café Central
384 Columbus Avenue nr West 79 St. 724-9187. The Upper West pretty people who come here find decent "American eclectic" food, crayons on the table and one another. Reserve. AE, MC, V. *OPEN Mon-Thurs noon-1:30am; Fri & Sat till 2:30am; Sun till 1am. Bar till 4am.* $

Café Luxembourg
200 West 70 Street. 873-7411. Bright, noisy Art Deco-ish interior, evocative of 1930s Paris. "The Luxembourg" is one of the most popular see and be seen late-night trendy spots and there are plenty of star-gazing opportunities—best of all you will also get a wonderful meal. Imaginative seasonal menu: seafood wrapped in sausage, duck with fresh figs, lamb chops grilled over mesquite. Great burger on the simple late menu. Suffer the service. Book well in advance and you'll wait anyway. AE, MC, V. *OPEN Mon-Thurs 5:30pm-12:30am; Fri, Sat & Sun from 6pm. Late light supper Mon-Thurs 1-2:30am; Fri & Sat till 3am. Sun Brunch: 11am-3pm.* $$$

Empire Diner
210 Tenth Avenue nr West 22 St. 243-2736. Unlike any other diner anywhere. Attractive Art Deco design. Interesting menu, some unusual choices. Best for late-night snacking. Outdoor café in summer. Live music. No reservations. AE only. *OPEN 7 days, 24 hours.* $

Great Jones Café
54 Great Jones Street nr the Bowery. 674-9304. Informal and crowded Bowery-area spot for flavorful burgers, chili, red- or bluefish filets. The house drink—a jalapeño martini! To top it all off—a great juke box. The noise is deafening but the young crowd doesn't mind. No reservations, no credit cards. *D Mon-Thurs & Sun 5pm-1am; Fri & Sat till 2am. Weekend Brunch noon-4pm. Bar till 4am.* $

Hard Rock Café
221 West 57 Street. 489-6565. Tennessee to New York via London; the famed Hard Rock provides down-home cooking and rock nostalgia—and for that 15,000 people a week line up outside to gain access. Burgers, chili, guacomole, but most of all "the scene"; backed up by the loudest music this side of a rock concert. (Membership cards are held by "special" customers—no waiting.) The

1960 Cadillac on the façade has drawn protests and gasps. AE, MC, V. *OPEN 7 days 11:30am-3 or 4am.* $

Kiev International
117 Second Avenue at East 7 St. 674-4040. Queue up with the denizens of the East Village who know a good inexpensive meal when they can still find one. Pierogi, blintzes (the cheese are NY's best), homemade soups at any hour. No reservations. No credit cards. *OPEN 7 days, 24 hours.* $

Market Diner
Ninth Avenue at West 33 Street. 695-6844; Eleventh Avenue at West 43 Street. 244-6033; 256 West Street nr Laight Street. 925-0856. In less-than-attractive locales, these good-American-food diners have extensive menu choices at all times. No credit cards. *OPEN 7 days, 24 hours.* $

Marylou's
21 West 9 Street. 533-0012. Unbeatable combination: attractive brownstone setting and crowd—including some names and faces you'd recognize—and, best of all, excellent seafood served weekdays till the wee hours. Two working fireplaces. Save room for NY's best rice pudding. Reserve! AE, CB, DC, MC, V. *L Mon-Fri 11:30am-3pm. D Mon-Thurs 5:30pm-1am; Fri & Sat till 2am; Sun 5:30-10:45pm. Sun Brunch noon-4pm.* $$

103 Second Avenue
103 Second Avenue at East 6 St. 533-0769. Light- and music-filled East Village 'round the clock spot for good burgers, chili, fish specials, salads. Good breakfast choices, too. Full bar. Counter and table service. No reservations, no credit cards. *OPEN 7 days, 24 hours.* $

Petaluma
1354 First Avenue nr East 73 St. 772-8800. They come in droves to this convivial cafe for thin crust pizza from wood burning ovens and good pasta specials. There's the *de rigueur* open kitchen and the elevated front dining room for the best "view." As good an example of restaurant-as-theater as you may find. No credit cards. Reservation taken for 5 or more only. *OPEN 7 days 11:30am-2am.*$

Richoux of London
Avenue of the Americas nr West 55 Street. 265-3090. Casual atmosphere for English and Continental dishes. AE, CB, DC, MC, V. *OPEN 7 days, 24 hours.* $$

Rose Room
Algonquin Hotel, 59 West 44 Street. 840-6800. A sumptuous after-theater supper buffet. AE, CB, DC, MC, V. *OPEN Mon-Sat 9:30pm-12:15am. CLOSED Sun.* $$

The following serve food at least until midnight every night of the week. For other late night spots see also Bars & Burgers.

Alo Alo (Italian)
America (American)
Amy's (Inexpensive)
Anna's Harbor Restaurant (Rooms with a View)
Asti (Italian)
Auntie Yuan (Chinese)

Bayamo (Latin American)
Beach House (Mexican)
Café Figaro (Sidewalk Cafés)
Café Marimba (Mexican)
Café Orlin (Breakfast/Brunch)
Café Seiyoken (Japanese)
Café Un Deux Trois (Stargazers)
Caffè Biondo (Cafés)
Caffè Reggio (Cafés)
Caffè Roma (Cafés)
Caffè Vivaldi (Cafés)
Capsouto Fréres (French)
Caramba!, !! & !!! (Mexican)
Carolina (American)
Castillian (Spanish)
Chaumiére (French)
Cinco de Mayo (Mexican)
City Lights Bar & Hors d'Oeuvrerie (Rooms
with a View)
Claire (Fish & Seafood)
Cornelia Street Café (Cafés)
Eclair (Hungarian)
Elaine's (Stargazers)
El Faro (Spanish)
El Internacional (Spanish: Tapas)
Farnie's (Steak)
Felidia (Italian)
Ferrara's (Cafés)
Fiorello's (Sidewalk Cafés)
Fonda La Paloma (Mexican)
Food (Soup & Salad)
Forlini's (Italian)
Fountain Café (Sidewalk Cafés)
Gallagher's (Steak)
Giambelli 50th Ristorante (Italian)
Ginger Man (American)
Gotham Bar & Grill (Continental)
Grotta Azzura (Italian)
Harbour House (Fish & Seafood)
Home Village (Chinese)
Hong Fat (Chinese)
Hunam (Chinese)
Il Caminetto (Italian)
Il Monello (Italian)
Il Vagabondo (Italian)
Indochine (Vietnamese)
Jake's (Steak)
Jean Lafitte (French)
Joanna (Continental)
Julia (Continental)
Junior's (Inexpensive)
Kenny's Steak Pub (Steak)
Kitty Hawk (Breakfast/Brunch)
La Colonna (Italian)
La Gamelle (French)
La Fondue (Inexpensive)
Le Saint Jean de Pres (Belgian)
Luchows on Broadway (German & Austrian)
Manhattan Ocean Club (Fish & Seafood)
Mary's (Italian)
Memphis (Soul & Creole)
Mezzaluna (Italian)
Mie (Japanese)
Molfeta's (Inexpensive)
Moondance Diner (Inexpensive)
Mortimer's (Continental)

Nanni al Valletto (Italian)
Nathan's (Inexpensive)
Odeon (French)
One Fifth (American)
One if by Land (American)
Osteria Romana (Italian)
Parma (Italian)
Pig Heaven (Chinese)
Pink Tea Cup (Breakfast/Brunch)
PizzaPiazza (Breakfast/Brunch)
Puglia's (Italian)
Quatorze (French)
Ray's Pizza (Pizza)
Riveranda/Empress (Rooms with a View)
Riviera Café (Sidewalk Cafés)
Rojas Lombardi at the Ballroom (Spanish:
Tapas)
Rùelles (Continental)
Rumbuls (Inexpensive)
Russian Tea Room (Stargazers)
Sabor (Latin American)
Safari Grill (American)
Sardi's (Stargazers)
Serendipity (American)
Sign of the Dove (Continental)
SoHo Kitchen & Bar (Wine Bars)
Soom Thai (Thai)
Taj Mahal (Indian)
Tavern on the Green (Rooms with a View)
Teacher's (American)
Tennessee Mountain (American)
Texarkana (American)
Tino's (Italian)
Tio Pepe (Spanish)
Top of the Sixes (Rooms with a View)
Tuesday's (Bars & Burgers)
"21" Club (Stargazers)
Ukrainian Restaurant (Inexpensive)
Umberto's (Fish & Seafood)
Vanessa (American)
Veselka (Breakfast/Brunch)
Victor's Cafe (Latin American)
Wylie's (Soul & Creole)
Yun Luck Rice Shoppe (Chinese)

Latin American

Amazonas
See NIGHTLIFE, Nightclubs.
Bayamo
704 Broadway nr East 4 St. 475-5151. Chino-
Latino goes Post-Modern on Lower Broadway (it
seats close to 300). Stick to the Latino dishes or
the light corn crust pizzas and you will be nicely
fed. There are also classic Cuban sandwiches
and some interesting egg dishes. Frozen mar-
gheritas draw the youngish bar crowd. AE, MC, V.
OPEN 7 days 11:30am-2am. Bar till 4am. $$
Brazilian Coffee Restaurant
45 West 46 Street. 719-2105. The pioneer on this
block now known as "Little Brazil." A mecca for
Brazilian nationals away from home who are
drawn by the authentic regional cooking, relaxed
atmosphere. Feijoada Wed & Sat. Reserve for
lunch. AE, CB, DC, MC, V. *OPEN Mon-Sat noon-
10pm. CLOSED Sun.* $

Brazilian Pavilion
316 East 53 Street. 758-8129. More posh than its West Side "Little Brazil" counterparts. Popular for the unusual Brazilian cocktails; broiled lobster with garlic butter; feijoada every night. Reserve. AE, DC, MC, V. *OPEN Mon-Thurs noon-11pm; Fri & Sat till midnight. CLOSED Sun.* $$

Cabana Carioca
123 West 45 Street. 581-8088. Also, Cabana Carioca II at 133 West 45 St. 730-8375. Huge portions of simple hearty Brazilian food. Predominately Brazilian national crowd. Convivial; on two floors (a counter on 2nd fl). Reserve. AE, CB, DC, MC, V. *OPEN Mon-Thurs noon-11pm; Fri till 1am; Sat 4pm-1am. CLOSED Sun.* $

Casa Brasil
406 East 85 Street. 288-5284. Beautifully appointed town-house dining rooms. Each evening an elaborate set menu of five courses. Choices include Beef Wellington, veal scallops, roast duck, on Wed only, fejoada is served. Good Brazilian coffee. Bring your own wine. Jacket & tie required. Reserve. *OPEN Mon-Sat two sittings: 6:30 & 9:30pm. CLOSED Sun.* $$$

El Gaucho
95 MacDougal Street nr Bleecker St. 260-5350. Congenial spot for Argentinian mixed grill, the good-value specialty. Working fireplace, Latin American clientele. Reserve. AE, CB, DC, MC, V. *OPEN Sun-Fri 4pm-midnight; Sat till 1am.* $

Rio de Janeiro/Boat 57 Seafood House
41 West 57 Street. 935-1232. Delicious authentic Brazilian and Portuguese food in an informal setting. Clams in garlic sauce, Portuguese sausage, feijoada Wed & Sat. Brazilian beer, Portuguese wines. Reserve. AE, MC, V. *OPEN Mon-Thurs noon-11:30pm; Fri & Sat till midnight; Sun noon-10pm.* $$

Sabor
20 Cornelia Street nr West 4 St. 243-9579. This small, attractive, lively Cuban restaurant is the city's best for that island's food. Interesting menu; fresh-fruit daiquiris. Reserve. AE, MC. *OPEN Sun-Thurs 6-11pm; Fri & Sat till midnight.* $$

S.O.B.'s *See* NIGHTLIFE, Nightclubs

Victor's Café
240 Columbus Avenue at West 71 St. 595-8599. Also, 236 West 52 Street. 586-7714. Long-established Upper West Side Cuban restaurant. Roast suckling pig, black beans and rice, hearty paella, black bean soup, fried bananas, strong Cuban coffee. Enclosed sidewalk café. AE, DC, MC, V. *OPEN 7 days 9:30am-1:15am.* $$

Mexican

Beach House
399 Greenwich Street at Beach St. 226-7800. One of the city's best Tex/Mex in a relaxed, inviting atmosphere. Beautiful Victorian bar, high ceilings, and banquettes from the late, lamented Belmore Cafeteria. Hearty, robust dishes: quite good burritos, nachos, chimichangas, and fine regional specialties. Good TriBeCa choice. Reserve. AE, MC, V. *OPEN Mon-Thurs & Sun noon-midnight; Fri & Sat till 1:30am.* $

Café Marímba
1115 Third Avenue at East 65 St. 935-1161. Delicious authentic Mexican "home cooking." Pollo borracho (chicken cooked in tequilla); camerones al ajillo (shrimp, garlic and raw chili pepper) and butterflied filet mignon filled with poblano and cheese. Like no other Mexican food you've had. (A non-Chinese eatery from David Keh.) Reserve. AE, DC. *OPEN Mon-Thurs 6pm-midnight; Fri & Sat till 1am; Sun 5-11pm.* $$

Caramba! & !! & !!!
918 Eighth Avenue nr West 54 St. 245-7910; 684 Broadway at East 3 St. 420-9817; Broadway at West 96 St. Lively mob scene for Tex/Mex food and slush margaritas (famed for the latter). Downtown is airier and lighter. Good huevos rancheros at weekend Brunch noon-4pm. Buñelo is the gluttonous dessert. Reserve! AE, DC, MC, V. *OPEN 7 days noon-midnight.* $

Cinco de Mayo
349 West Broadway nr Broome St. 226-5255. Attractive SoHo spot for authentic regional Mexican dishes. Good seafood, grilled meats; dangerous margaritas. Kahluá-based mousse for dessert. Well-populated bar. Reserve. AE, MC, V. *OPEN Tues-Sun noon-midnight. CLOSED Mon.* $$

El Coyote
774 Broadway nr East 9 St. 677-4291. The best and most inviting Mexican restaurant in the East Village. Chalupa, chicken en mole, chimichangas, shrimp in salsa verde, enchiladas suizas. Always packed. No reservations. AE, MC, V. *OPEN Mon-Thurs 11:30am-11:30pm; Fri & Sat till 12:30am. CLOSED Sun.* $

El Parador Café
325 East 34 Street. 679-6812. Attractive and very popular. Serves good Mexican food and *great* margaritas. Legions of loyal followers; be prepared to wait. No reservations. No credit cards. *OPEN Mon-Sat 5-11pm. CLOSED Sun.* $

El Tenampa
304 West 46 Street. 664-8519. Many nonstandard, fiery hot Mexican dishes. Convenient-to-theater Restaurant Row locale. Bring your own wine or have one of their margaritas. Reserve. DC only. *L Mon-Fri noon-3pm. D Mon-Fri 5-11pm; Sat 4:30-11:30pm; Sun 5-10pm.* $

Fonda La Paloma
256 East 49 Street. 421-5495. One of the city's best Mexican restaurants features regional cuisine. Pleasant ambiance, strolling guitarists. Cocktail lounge, Mexican hors d'oeuvres. Reserve. AE, CB, DC, MC, V. *L Mon-Fri noon-3pm. D Mon-Thurs 5pm-midnight; Fri & Sat till 1am; Sun 5-10:30pm.* $$

Mexico Lindo
459 Second Avenue at East 26 St. 679-3665. One of the best. Extremely good Mexican food in a pleasant, airy setting. Spanish wine and Mexican and domestic beer. Strolling guitarist. AE, V. *OPEN Mon-Fri noon-11pm; Sat 3pm-midnight; Sun 3-11pm.* $

Old Mexico
115 Montague Street nr Henry St, Brooklyn. (1-718)624-9774. Popular, long-standing Brooklyn

Heights restaurant. Serves well-prepared Mexican dishes. AE, CB. *OPEN Mon-Thurs noon-10:30pm; Fri & Sat till 11pm; Sun 4-10pm.* $

Middle Eastern
(*See also* NIGHTLIFE, Nightclubs.)
Ararat
4 East 36 Street. 686-4622. Garish decor but if you like Armenian food, some of the dishes here are unusual. Armenian tartar steak: ground raw lamb and seasoned cracked wheat garnished with fresh onion and parsley. Reserve. AE, DC, MC, V. *OPEN Mon-Sat 4-10pm; Sun till 9pm.*$$
Balkan Armenian
129 East 27 Street. 689-7925. This small neighborhood dining spot is the city's oldest Armenian restaurant (over 70 years) and still serves wonderfully satisfying authentic food. Reserve. AE, DC, MC, V. *L Mon-Fri noon-2:30pm. D Mon-Thurs 4:30-9pm; Fri & Sat till 10pm. CLOSED Sun.* $
Café in the Cradle
27 West 38 Street. 221-6466. Interesting Middle Eastern vegetarian eatery. Excellent homemade soups, salads, and pies. Comfortable spot. Reserve for lunch. AE, DC, MC, V. *OPEN Mon-Fri noon-8:30pm. CLOSED Sat & Sun.* $
Cedars of Lebanon
39 East 30 Street. 725-9251. Long-established Lebanese restaurant. Shish-kebab, falafel and a belly dancer Fri & Sat at 9pm. Reserve. AE, DC, MC, V. *L Mon-Fri noon-3pm. D 7 days 5-11pm.*$

No-Smoking Areas
B. Altman, Charlston Gardens (Department Store Restaurants)
Bloomingdale's, Forty Carrots (Department Store Restaurants)
Brownie's (Health & Vegetarian)
Great American Health Bar (Health & Vegetarian)
Horn and Hardart Automat (Inexpensive)
Lord & Taylor, The Café (Department Store Restaurants)
Lou G. Siegel (Jewish)
Magic Pan Creperie (Omelettes & Crepes)
Pen & Pencil Restaurant (Steak)
Positano (Italian)
Top of the Park (Rooms with a View)

Omelettes & Crepes
Elephant & Castle
68 Greenwich Avenue nr West 11 St. 243-1400; also *183 Prince Street at Sullivan St. 260-3600. Pleasant Village and SoHo restaurants feature 24 variations of omelette. Good choices of burgers and homemade desserts as well. Bring your own wine. No reservations. AE, CB, V. *OPEN Mon-Thurs 9am-midnight; Fri & Sat 10am-1am; Sun 11am-midnight. Brunch: Sat 10am-5pm; Sun 11am-5pm. *OPEN Mon-Thurs 8am-midnight; Fri from 8am; Sat 10am-1am; Sun 10am-midnight. Weekend Brunch 10am-5pm.* $
La Crêpe
158 West 44 Street. 246-5388; 57 West 56 Street. 247-1136; 1974 Broadway nr West 67 St. 874-6900. An attractive chain restaurant; features thin

French wheat or buckwheat crepes as appetizers, main course or dessert. A choice of over 50 fillings. Now also features Mexican food, obviously the fashionable thing to do. AE, DC. *OPEN 7 days.* $
Madame Romaine de Lyon
29 East 61 Street. 758-2422. In a new location (the tearoom setting is gone courtesy of the wrecker's ball) and there is now a French-Continental menu at dinner, but for lunch, the 40 year-old tradition continues: exquisite omelettes from a choice of over 600, filled with caviar or ham or spinach or chestnuts or. . . . Brioches, croissants, green salad, lovely desserts and wine available. All a la carte, and it adds up. Reserve for 3 or more. AE ($30 minimum). *OPEN 7 days 11am-3pm.* $
Magic Pan Creperie
149 East 57 Street. 371-3266. Also, *1409 Avenue of the Americas nr West 57 Street. 765-5080. A friendly place for a wide variety of delicious crepe entrées, soups, salads, desserts. No smoking sections. AE, MC, V. *OPEN Mon & Tues 11:30am-11pm; Wed-Sat till midnight; Sun till 10pm. Sun Brunch 11:30am-3:30pm. *OPEN Mon-Sat 11:30-midnight; Sun till 10pm. Brunch: Sat 11am-5pm; Sun till 4pm.* $
Mimosa
153 East 33 Street. 685-2595; *233 East 43 Street. 697-0049. Charming café/restaurant offers basic menu of delicious omelettes, eggs mimosa, quiches, crepes, salads and accompaniments; specials too. Reserve for 3 or more. AE, DC, MC, V. *OPEN Mon-Sat 11:30am-10pm. CLOSED Sun. *CLOSED Sat & Sun.* $

Pizza
Goldberg's Pizzeria
996 Second Avenue nr East 52 St. 593-2172. The place for unique New York pizza. Table service. Reserve for 8 or more. No credit cards. *OPEN 7 days noon-11pm.* $
John's Pizzeria
278 Bleecker Street nr Cornelia St. 243-1680. *Also, 408 East 64 Street. 935-2895. For purists this is the city's best and only really authentic pizza, baked in stone floor ovens. Pies only, no slices, in the old-fashioned booths; celebrity photos line the walls. Also recommended, the calzone. Beer & wine. No credit cards. *OPEN Mon-Thurs 11:30am-midnight; Fri & Sat till 1am; Sun noon-11:30pm. *OPEN Sun-Thurs 11:30am-11:30pm; Fri & Sat till 12:30am.*
Mezzaluna
See Italian.
PizzaPiazza
See Breakfast/Brunch.
Ray's Pizza
465 Sixth Avenue at West 11 St. 243-2253. When you hear some people say that Ray's Pizza is the best *this* is the Ray's they mean. The line moves quickly. *OPEN 7 days 11am-2am.* $

Polynesian
Trader Vic's
Plaza Hotel, Fifth Avenue & 59 Street. 355-5185.

Famed Polynesian restaurant with South Seas décor. Beautiful alcoholic fruit drinks decorated with fresh flowers, and wonderful appetizers: butterfly shrimp, ribs, good fish dishes. Reserve. AE, CB, DC, MC, V. *L Mon-Fri 11:30am-2:30pm. D Mon-Fri 5pm-midnight; Sat 4pm-12:30am; Sun 4pm-1am.* $$$

Rooms with a View

Anna's Harbor Restaurant
565 City Island Avenue, City Island, Bronx. 885-1373. Glass-enclosed dining room affords views of New York's own salty little seaport. Very good Italian seafood specialties and bouillabaisse served daily. Reserve on weekends. AE, MC, V. *OPEN 7 days 11:30am-midnight.* $$

City Lights Bar & Hors D'Oeuvrerie
Windows on the World, 1 World Trade Center. 938-1111. From 3pm each day, enjoy a cocktail and hors d'oeuvres (a la carte) and one of the world's most exciting views ¼ mile in the sky! Piano music from 3pm; trio for dancing 7:30pm-1am. Jacket required, no denim. AE, CB, DC, MC, V. Cover charge after 7:30pm. *OPEN Mon-Fri 3pm-1am; Sat noon-1am; Sun noon-9pm.* $

Empress/Riveranda
World Yacht Enterprises, Pier 62 at West 23 St. 929-7090. For years Paris has had the Bateaux Mouches and New Yorkers have wondered why not here. Well now we have our own version of the floating restaurant with a view. Dine and enjoy the dazzle of the skyline, as your yacht (the Empress seats 400, the Riveranda, 300) glides around the tip of Lower Manhattan. Lunch is served, dinner and brunch is buffet-style, and there's dancing in the pm. Believe me fellow natives this is not for tourists only. You must reserve with a credit card (cancellations within 48 hours or you forfeit the cost). AE, DC, MC, V. You may board one hour before sailing for cocktails. Jacket required. Parking available. *Year round, 7 days. L 12:30-2:30pm. D 7-10pm. Midnight cruise with a la carte menu midnight-2am.* $$

La Grande Corniche
River Hotel, 180 Christopher Street at West St, 6th fl. 206-0727. A duplex penthouse restaurant with a greenhouse lounge and Hudson River-filled views. Especially lovely at sunset. Imaginative menu: fusilli with tomato, herbs and goat cheese, rabbit terrine with cranberry apple chutney, filet of sole with pears and white wine. Cabaret Fri & Sat 11:30pm-2am. Reserve. AE, MC, V. *OPEN Sun-Thurs 6-11:30pm; Fri & Sat till midnight. Sun Brunch noon-3:30pm.* $$

Nirvana
30 Central Park South, 15th fl. 486-5700. Fine authentically spiced Indo-Bengali cuisine in a romantic setting overlooking Central Park. Spectacular view. Interesting regional dishes. Live sitar music. Reserve. AE, CB, DC, MC, V. *OPEN 365 days a year noon-1am.* $$

Nirvana Club One
1 Times Square, West 42 Street bet Broadway & Seventh Ave, 16th fl. 486-6868. Spacious two-story dining room with breathtaking city-filled views. Excellent Theater District choice for Mogul dishes of Northern India. Good vegetarian dishes, excellent biryanis, tandoori specialties and wonderful breads. Good pre-theater dinner spot. Reserve. AE, CB, DC, MC, V. *OPEN 365 days a year noon-1am.* $$

Rainbow Room
See NIGHTLIFE, Dining & Dancing.

River Café
1 Water Street (beside the Brooklyn Bridge), Brooklyn. (1-718) 522-5200. Constructed on a permanently moored barge adjacent to the Brooklyn Bridge. The view of Lower Manhattan's towers is postcard-perfect, the food is interesting *nouvelle* American. Fair weather offers light dining opportunities outdoors. (May-Oct, noon-4pm, there is a free round trip motor trip from Pier 11, South & Wall Streets for brunch patrons.) Piano music till 1am. Be prepared to wait. Jacket required. Reserve well in advance. Prix fixe. AE, CB, DC. *L Mon-Fri noon-2:30pm. D Sun-Thurs 6:30-11pm; Fri-Sat 7-11:30pm. (In summer D 7 days 7-11:30pm; Brunch Sat & Sun noon-2:30.)* $$$

Tavern on the Green
Central Park West at West 67 St. 873-3200. The Central Park setting and the dazzling Crystal Room make this restaurant a *must*. The menu offers a wide variety of choice and price. (It's hard to believe that this opulent building was once a sheepfold housing 200 sheep and a shepherd—from 1870-1934.) In winter a snow-making machine turns the Terrace Garden into a white wonderland; in summer it's one of the city's most bucolic settings for dining and dancing to a live orchestra (April-Oct, Tues-Sun 9pm-1am). Anytime, it's a joyful place. Reserve (especially for the Crystal Room but not taken for the Garden). AE, DC, MC, V. *L Mon-Fri noon-4pm. D Mon-Fri 5:30pm-1am; Sat & Sun from 5pm. Pre-theater menu Mon-Sat 5-7pm* (one of the city's great values). *Weekend Brunch 10am-4pm.* $$

The Terrace
Butler Hall, 400 West 119 Street at Morningside Dr. 666-9490. Only 16 stories up but offers a panoramic view of the city. *Very* good Continental food in a beautifully romantic skylight penthouse setting, outdoor terrace in summer. Reserve. Jacket required. AE, DC, MC, V. *L Tues-Fri noon-2:30pm. D Tues-Thurs 6-10pm; Fri & Sat till 10:30pm. CLOSED Sun & Mon.* $$$

Top of the Park
Gulf & Western Building, West 60 Street & Central Park West, 43rd fl. 333-3800. The view of the Hudson from the lounge is the city's best. No smoking section. Reserve. AE, CB, DC, MC, V. *D Mon-Sat 5-10pm. Bar 4:30pm-midnight. CLOSED Sun.* $$

Top of the Sixes
666 Fifth Avenue at 53 St. 757-6662. A spacious clubby restaurant/lounge on the 39th floor for great city viewing. Best for cocktails and the wonderful finger food hors d'oeuvres 5-7pm. Also, some inexpensive lunch choices. Reserve for dining. AE, DC, MC, V. *OPEN Mon-Sat 11:30am-1am (kitchen till midnight). CLOSED Sun.* $$$

Top of the Tower
Beekman Tower, 3 Mitchell Place, East 49 St &
First Ave, 26th fl. 355-7300. Lovely views in all
directions of midtown and the river. Glass-
enclosed wraparound roof terrace, romantic cock-
tail-lounge ambiance. Piano music from 9pm.
Jacket required; no denim. AE, CB, DC. No cover
or minimum. L Mon-Fri noon-2pm. Cocktails 7
days 5pm-2am. $

The Water Club
East River at East 30 Street. (From FDR Drive
enter service road at East 23 Street.) 683-3333.
Simple, albeit expensive, dining on the East River
on a permanently moored barge (same owner as
the River Café). Enhanced by fireplaces, skylights, a view of the river traffic and the topside
open-air for drinks in good weather. Jacket requested. Reserve. Valet parking. AE, CB, DC,
MC, V. L Mon-Fri noon-2:30pm. D Mon-Sat 5:30-
11:15pm; Sun till 10pm. Brunch: Sat noon-
2:15pm; Sun 11:30am-3pm. $$$

Water's Edge Restaurant
East River & 44 Drive, Long Island City, Queens.
(1-718)392-8890. Lovely restaurant close by the
59 Street Bridge offers a wonderful East River/
Midtown Manhattan view and an eclectic menu
with a seafood emphasis. Open-air deck; glass-
enclosed dining room. Jacket required. Reserve.
AE, DC, MC, V. L Mon-Fri noon-3pm. D Mon-
Thurs 5-11pm; Fri & Sat till midnight; Sun till 9pm.
Sun Brunch noon-3pm. $$

Windows on the World
1 World Trade Center, 107th fl. 938-1111. Quite
simply one of the world's most spectacular restaurants. The food, though secondary to the view—
which is unsurpassed—is quite good, with a nice
variety of entrées, prix fixe or à la carte. The
wonderful service is a plus; the wine list is exceptional and affordable. Reserve well in advance
and pray for a clear night. Jacket and tie required;
no denim. AE, CB, DC, MC, V. D Mon-Sat 5-
10pm. Buffet Sat noon-3pm; Sun till 7:30pm. (See
also Cellar in the Sky, City Lights Bar & the Hors
D'Oeuvrerie). $$$

Sidewalk Cafés
Columbia Avenue and the South Street Seaport
offer a variety of opportunities to sup outdoors.
See also Garden/Outdoor Dining

Buffalo Roadhouse
87 Seventh Avenue South at Barrow St. 243-
8000. Stylish casual ambiance, interesting crowd,
Waldorf salad, good burgers, hearty steak and
eggs and simple specials with a flair nightly. In
summer sip banana daiquiris and dine outdoors
'neath a weeping willow in one of the Village's
most popular people watching cafés. No reserva-
tions. No credit cards. OPEN Mon-Sat 11am-
3am; Sun till 2am. $

Café de la Paix
St. Moritz Hotel, Central Park South at Sixth Ave
755-5800. Cosmopolitan café and crowd across
from Central Park. Continental restaurant and
bar. AE, CB, DC, MC, V. L Mon-Fri noon-4pm. D 7
days 5:30-11pm. Sun Brunch 11:30am-4pm. $

Figaro Café
186 Bleecker Street at MacDougal St. 677-1100.
Reincarnation of long-established Village coffee
house. Outdoor sidewalk café in good weather at
this Greenwich Village crossroad for great
people-watching. Good burgers, cheese and fruit
board, cappuccino. Music on weekends. OPEN
Mon-Thurs 11am-2am; Fri till 4am; Sat & Sun
10am-4am. $

Fiorello's Roman Café
1900 Broadway nr West 63 St. 595-5330. Bright,
bustling café for salads and pasta. Very good
pizza in a pan. (It gets expensive if you go beyond
these.) Outdoor café in summer for Lincoln Center
crowd watching. AE, MC, V. OPEN 7 days noon-
midnight. $

Fountain Café
Lincoln Center Plaza, Broadway & West 64
Street. 874-7000. As close to a Roman piazza as
you can find in NY. A special spot for a light lunch,
dinner or just drinks, while the ballet and opera
buffs head for the performances. OPEN 7 days
11:30am-midnight.

Riviera Café
225 West 4 Street at Seventh Ave So. 242-8732.
Indoor/outdoor café known as the best spot to
see, and be seen by, Greenwich Village. In winter
two fireplaces make up for the sidewalk café's
closing. OPEN 7 days noon-4am. $

The Saloon
1920 Broadway at West 64 St. 874-1500. Best
when you can sit at the sidewalk terrace and
watch the West Side crowds go by. Waiters on
roller skates and fun food—crayfish tails, rata-
touille niçoise, tortellini salad. AE, CB, DC, MC, V.
OPEN 365 days of the year, 11:30am-2am. Bar
until 4am. $

The Terrace
American Stanhope Hotel, Fifth Avenue & 81
Street. 288-5800. Perhaps the most civilized side-
walk café in NY, with a view of the Metropolitan
Museum with its nearly resident street perform-
ers. AE, MC, V. OPEN 7 days noon-10pm (food till
3pm only).

Soul & Creole
Barking Fish Cafe
705 Eighth Avenue nr West 44 St. 757-0186.
Louisiana Creole comes to Eighth Avenue. Rib-
sticking and lip-smacking good pork ribs, gumbo,
Cajun jambalaya, crackly barbecued chicken, and
po-boys. Bread pudding in bourbon for dessert.
Informal and a bit frenetic. Take-out too. Jazz
Brunch on Sun. Reserve. AE, CB, MC, V. L Mon-
Fri 11:30am-4pm. D Mon-Fri 5:30-11pm; Sat
4:30-11:30pm; Sun 5-10pm. Sun Brunch noon-
5pm. $

Bon Temps Rouler
59 Reade Street nr Broadway. 513-1333. The
good times roll right out of the kitchen at this very
good Cajun Creole outpost in TriBeCa. Crayfish,
seafood gumbo, voodoo stew and for the adven-
turesome—alligator sausage. Bread pudding for
dessert. Lovely 50-foot Art Deco bar and dining

room. AE. *L Mon-Fri 11:30am-2:45pm. D Mon-Sat 6-11:30pm. CLOSED Sun.* $$

Cajun
129 Eighth Avenue at West 16 St. 691-6174. Tangy Cajun food: gumbo, jambalaya, shrimp Creole, crab cakes in a convivial Chelsea bar/restaurant. Live Dixieland jazz Wed-Fri from 8:30pm; Jazz Brunch Sun noon-4pm is great fun. Reserve for 6 or more. AE, DC, MC. *L Mon-Sat noon-3pm. D Sun-Thurs 6-11pm; Fri & Sat till 11:30pm.* $

Crawdaddy
45 East 45 Street. 687-1860. New Orleans motif and Creole cooking. Also a stand-up oyster bar. Reserve. AE, CB, DC, MC, V. *OPEN Mon-Fri: L noon-3pm; D 5:30-10:15pm. CLOSED Sat & Sun.* $

Greenhouse
Vista International, 3 World Trade Center. 938-9100. Every Friday evening a Cajun Buffet under the consulting auspices of New Orleans' chef Paul Prudhomme. Gumbo, jambalaya, fresh shrimp and crawfish. Reserve. AE, CB, DC, MC, V. *Served Fri only 6:30-11:30pm.* $$

Gulf Coast
489 West 12 Street at the West Side Highway. 206-8790. Down-market, extremely casual Louisiana-style restaurant in the far West Village. Features a changing menu of Cajun-Creole dishes. Shrimp grilled over mesquite, crawfish étouffé, deep-fried catfish. Bread pudding for dessert. No reservations. No credit cards. *OPEN 7 days 5-11:30pm.* $

Horn of Plenty
91 Charles Street at Bleecker St. 242-0636. Long-time duo-level Village restaurant with romantic outdoor garden and indoor greenhouse. Southern-style cooking, some international dishes too. Spare ribs in a hot pepper and vinegar sauce, stuffed pork chops, cornbread, pecan pie and apple cobbler. Reserve for 6 or more. AE, CB, DC, MC, V. *OPEN Mon-Thurs 6-11:45pm; Fri & Sat 6-12:45pm; Sun 5-11pm.* $$

Jezebel
630 Ninth Avenue at West 45 St. 582-1045. Vintage clothing aficionados who miss that wonderful mood-piece of a shop called Jezebel can come to this mood-piece of a restaurant where the clothes (not for sale) are a nostalgic backdrop for the satisfying Southern cooking. Corn bread, honey chicken, shrimp Creole, grits, yams, sweet potato pie and bread pudding. A well-priced choice. Reserve. AE. *OPEN Mon-Sat 5:30-11:30pm. CLOSED Sun.* $

La Louisiana
132 Lexington Avenue nr East 29 St. 686-3959. Elegant little storefront restaurant serving Cajun French food. (They also own Texarkana.) Crudité de boeuf (thin raw sirloin), Spanish shrimp with garlic, boudin of pork, red beans and rice, rum pecan pie. Excellent food, gracious service. Reserve. No credit cards. *OPEN Mon-Sat 6-11:45pm. CLOSED Sun.* $$

Little Kitchen
243 East 10 Street, upstairs. 477-4460. East Village institution. Informal restaurant for good homestyle Southern cooking. Jazz nightly at 9. Reserve. *CLOSED Mon.* $

Memphis
329 Columbus Avenue nr West 75 St. 496-1840. Handsome setting; wonderful down-home Southern cooking; star-studded crowd (the owners are actors). Belle River crayfish plate; baby back ribs; crispy duck; jambalaya. Noisy; joyful. Reserve. AE, MC, V. *D Mon-Sat 6pm-midnight; Sun till 10:30pm. Weekend Brunch noon-3:30pm.* $$

Sazerac House
533 Hudson Street at Charles St. 989-0313. Greenwich Village eatery with enclosed sidewalk café and fireplace. Serves American food, emphasis on New Orleans specialties: jambalaya, crab chops. AE, DC, MC, V. *OPEN 7 days 11:30am-1am. Sun brunch 11:30am-3:45pm.* $

Smokey's
Ninth Avenue & West 24 Street. 924-8181; Third Avenue & East 23 Street. 674-3000; Amsterdam Avenue & West 93 Street. 865-2900. Smoked pork ribs with a 5-alarm hot sauce for asbestos palates. Good chili, too. Beer only. Cafeteria style. No credit cards. *OPEN Mon-Fri 11am-11pm; Sat & Sun from noon.* $

Sylvia's
328 Lenox Avenue at West 127 Street. 534-9414. Known as the "Queen of Soul Food," and a Harlem institution for over 25 years. Southern specialties include her famed barbecued prime ribs, fried chicken with black-eyed peas, salmon croquettes, sweet potato pie, fresh-baked cornbread. Counter and tables; jukebox. No reservations, No credit cards. *OPEN Mon-Sat 7:30am-10pm. Sun Brunch with live music 1-7pm.* $

West Boondock
See NIGHTLIFE, Jazz.

Wylie's
891 First Avenue nr East 50 St. 751-0700. Also, 59 West 56 Street. 757-7910. Terrific baby back ribs; fried onion loaf in a stylish East Side setting. No reservations. AE, DC, MC, V. *OPEN 7 days 11:30am-1am.* $

Soup & Salad

Food
127 Prince Street at Wooster St. 473-8790. Unpretentious serve-yourself cafeteria-style. Simple homemade soups, specials, great salads and desserts. Good wholesome SoHo choice. No reservations. No credit cards. *OPEN Mon-Sat noon-midnight. Sun Brunch 11:30am-4:30pm.* $

Front Porch
253 West 11 Street. 675-8083; 2272 Broadway nr West 81 St. 877-5220; 119 East 18 Street 473-7940. Simple and charming soup-and-sandwich restaurants. Choices are imaginative and delicious, desserts irresistible. No reservations. No credit cards. *OPEN 7 days noon-11pm.* $

Healthworks
Citicorp Market, 153 East 53 Street. 838-6221. Pioneer in the clean healthy look in food and surroundings. Salads, hot casseroles, quiches in modern, cafeteria-style setting. They deliver too. *OPEN Mon-Fri 7am-9pm; Sat & Sun 11am-8pm.* $

La Bonne Soupe
48 West 55 Street. 586-7650. Also 987 Third Avenue nr East 59 Street. 759-2500. Soups, salads, quiches, omelettes, wine by the carafe add up to a simple French-accented dining experience. *Les* hamburgers available too. Reserve for 5 or more. AE only. *OPEN Mon-Sat 11:30am-midnight; Sun till 11pm.* $

Spanish

Castillian
303 East 56 Street. 688-6435. Excellent Spanish restaurant with a wide variety of choice. Seafood casserole, paella Valenciana, veal riojana. Reserve for more than 4. AE, CB, DC, MC, V. *OPEN 7 days noon-midnight.* $

El Faro
823 Greenwich Street at Horatio St. 929-8210. *Extremely* popular, small Spanish restaurant in the West Village. Noted for its paella. Also the mariscado ajillo. Be prepared to wait, but it's worth it. *OPEN Mon-Thurs 11am-midnight; Fri & Sat till 1am; Sun 1pm-midnight.* $

El Rincón de España
226 Thompson Street nr Bleecker St. 260-4950. *Also, 82 Beaver Street nr Pearl St. 344-5228. Busy, congenial Greenwich Village Spanish restaurant. Excellent authentic dishes recommended: paella, all shellfish dishes, arroz con pollo, and the octopus. Guitarist in the pm. Reserve. AE, CB, DC, MC, V. *L Mon-Fri noon-3pm. D Mon-Thurs 5-11pm; Fri till midnight; Sat noon-midnight; Sun 1-11pm. *OPEN Mon-Fri noon-9:30; Sat 1-10pm. CLOSED Sun.* $$

Tío Pepe
168 West 4 Street. 242-9338. Pleasant, dimly lit Greenwich Village restaurant. Offers good Spanish food, with emphasis on seafood. Enclosed sidewalk café. Reserve. AE, DC, MC. *OPEN Mon-Thurs noon-1am; Fri & Sat till 2am. Sun Brunch noon-4pm.* $$

Tres Carabelas
314 East 39 Street. 689-6388. In the Spanish cultural mission. Large, attractive restaurant. Serves authentic Iberian-style food. Gazpacho, tripe, paella. Reserve. AE. *OPEN Tues-Sun 5:30-11pm. CLOSED Mon.* $

—Tapas
Literally meaning lid, the term derives from the habit of Spaniards to put a slice of bread over an open bottle of wine to keep the flies out. Putting a piece of sausage on the bread was a logical next step. In any case, a new dining experience was born. Like dim sum, the saucers containing the finger foods—tapas—are tallied to produce the tariff.

El Internacional
219 West Broadway nr White St. 226-8131. The former home of Teddy's is now a Catalan tapas bar. Authentic and delicious food; the kitschy décor is a giggle. Dining rooms on several levels; best fun is the bar. Deep-fried squid, grilled eggs, chicken croquette, baby eels, and more. Outdoor tables in summer. Reserve. AE only. *OPEN Mon-Sat noon-1am; Sun from 5pm-midnight.* $

Rojas Lombardi at the Ballroom
253 West 28 Street. 244-3005. Tapas, a Spanish tradition transplanted to a charming Chelsea setting by Barcelona chef. Exotic, mouth-watering selection of hors d'oeuvres. The cooking is authentic; priced by the plate like dim sum—it *can* add up. Well prepared entrees and specials as well. Reserve. AE, CB, DC, MC, V. *OPEN Tues-Sat 4:30pm-1am. CLOSED Sun.* $

Stargazers
The following are some places where the "stars" are almost certain to be seen—especially late pm or early am.

Café Un Deux Trois
123 West 44 Street. 354-4148. French brasserie-style eatery. Leftover Corinthian columns, Crayolas (for doodling), and a chalk-board menu offering very basic French fare. But the crowd's the thing. No reservations. AE, DC, MC, V. *OPEN Mon-Fri noon-midnight; Sat & Sun 4:30pm-midnight.* $

Elaine's
1703 Second Avenue nr East 88 Street. 534-8114. Successful "literary and theatrical watering hole." Small, crowded, informal, good—mainly Italian—specialties. Treatment depends on what best-selling author is ahead or behind you in line. Woody Allen is a virtual fixture here. Reserve. AE only. *OPEN Mon-Fri noon-2am; Sat & Sun from 6pm.*$$

Joe Allen's
326 West 46 Street. 581-6464. Late-night bar and restaurant for theater crowd—both the actors and the audience. Skylight dining room offers steaks, chili burgers, daily specials. Bass Ale on tap. Reserve. MC, V. *OPEN Mon, Tues, Thurs, Fri & Sun noon-1am; Wed & Sat from 11:30am.* $$

Le Cirque
58 East 65 Street. 794-9292. Spaghetti primavera and a chance to see Nancy Reagan when she's in town; if not there is usually Diana Vreeland, Kirk Douglas or Gloria Vanderbilt. The powerful come for the classic French cuisine and for each other. Reserve! AE, CB, DC. *Mon-Sat L noon-2:45pm, D 6-10:30pm.* $$$

Russian Tea Room
150 West 57 Street. 265-0947. One of the best for remarkably authentic Russian food and a colorful New York crowd—dancers, musicians, impresarios, you and me. Very lively possibly because there's a vodka menu! Jacket required. Note: OPEN on holidays—festive times to go. Reserve. AE, CB, DC, MC, V. *OPEN Sun-Fri 11:30am-midnight; Sat from 11am.* $$$

Sardi's
234 West 44 Street. 221-8440. Traditional site for Broadway-opening parties to await reviews. Celebrity caricatures line the wall, and one or two stars grace the premises nightly. Fair Continental food with an Italian emphasis. Jacket & tie required. Reserve. AE, CB, DC, MC, V. *OPEN Mon-Thurs 11:30am-12:30am; Fri & Sat till 1am; Sun till 11pm. Sun Brunch 11:30am-3pm.* $$$

"21" Club
21 West 52 Street. 582-7200. Triple-parked limos

mark the spot for this de facto club in turn-of-the-century setting. Where the "power" people lunch and sup. Good simple food. Jacket & tie required. Reserve. AE, CB, DC, MC, "21" charge. *OPEN 7 days noon-midnight. CLOSED Sun & Sat in summer.* $$$$

Steak Houses

Assembly Steak House
16 West 51 Street. 581-3580. Popular, very busy and noisy at lunchtime. Known for good-quality steaks, done to your specification, and tasty lobster. Reserve. AE, CB, DC, MC, V. *OPEN Mon-Fri 11:30am-3pm; 4:30-10pm. CLOSED Sat & Sun.* $$$$

Broadway Joe
315 West 46 Street. 246-6513. Nondescript décor but this Theater District restaurant has excellent high-quality sirloin and chopped steak, lamb chops and chicken. Reserve. AE, DC, MC, V. *OPEN Mon-Sat noon-12:30am. CLOSED Sun.* $$$

The Cattleman
5 East 45 Street. 661-1200. Turn-of-the-century posh saloon-style décor. Features prime sirloin steaks. Good family food and fun. Free parking for dinner patrons. Reserve. AE, DC, MC, V. *OPEN Mon-Fri 11:30am-11pm; Sat 4-11:30pm; Sun 3-10pm.* $$

Christ Cella
160 East 46 Street. 697-2479. Justly renowned for excellent steaks, chops and lobsters. Conservative, almost Spartan environment. Jacket & tie required. Reserve. AE, CB, DC, MC, V. *OPEN Mon-Thurs 11:45am-10:30pm; Fri till 10:45; Sat 5-10:45pm. CLOSED Sun.* $$$$

Farnie's 2nd Avenue Steak Parlour
311 Second Avenue at East 18 St. 228-9280. Old-time New York décor. Popular for steak, chops and lobster tails. Reserve. AE, CB, DC, MC, V. *OPEN Mon-Thurs 11:30am-midnight; Fri & Sat 3pm-1am; Sun 3pm-midnight.* $

Frank's
431 West 14 Street. 243-1349; 243-9641. This old Italian steak house has been around for 75 years—in the Gansevort Market District. The sawdust on the floor and the tin ceiling are authentic; the welcome is warm; the prime beef very fine. The wholesale meat market workers come here for breakfast (at 2am!). Office workers come for lunch and uptowners tend to come for dinner. AE, CB, DC, MC, V. *OPEN Mon-Fri (for breakfast, lunch) 4am-3pm; Mon-Thurs 5-10pm; Fri & Sat till 11pm. CLOSED Sun.* $$

Gallagher's
228 West 52 Street. 245-5336. Popular Broadway-area sports hangout for steaks, good seafood as well. Glass refrigerator to view the steaks aging. Charcoal and hickory-cooked. Reserve. AE, CB, DC, MC, V. *OPEN 7 days noon-midnight.* $$$

Hamilton House
101 Street and Fourth Avenue off Belt Parkway, Ft. Hamilton, Brooklyn. (1-718)745-6359. Old-fashioned steaks, chops and seafood restaurant

overlooking the Verrazano Narrows Bridge. Parking facilities. Reserve for large groups only. AE, DC, MC, V. *OPEN Mon-Thurs 11:30am-11pm; Fri & Sat till midnight; Sun noon-11pm.* $$

Jake's
801 Second Avenue at East 43 St. 687-5320. Beef eaters rejoice—a sophisticated steak house for sirloin, filet mignon, roast prime rib, sauteed calves' liver, rack of lamb chops. Lobster, too. Cruvinet for a good choice of wine by the glass. Suffer the service. Reserve for dinner. AE, DC, MC, V. *L Mon-Fri noon-3pm. D 7 days 5pm-1am.* $$

Kenny's Steak Pub
565 Lexington Avenue nr East 50 St. 355-0666. Popular steak house. Comfortable, friendly, attracts a sports crowd. Very good steaks. For the hardy, steak and eggs breakfast 7am-noon. Reserve. AE, CB, DC, MC, V. *OPEN 7 days 7am-11:45pm.* $$

Le Steak
1089 Second Avenue nr East 57 St. 421-9072. Sophisticated candle-lit ambiance, serves only French-style steak, great pommes frites and accompaniments. Decisions kept to a minimum. Good value. Reserve. AE, DC, MC, V. *OPEN Mon-Sat 5:30-10:45pm; Sun till 9:45pm.* $$

Old Homestead Restaurant
56 Ninth Avenue at West 14 St. 242-9040. Oldest New York steak house, it's been open since 1868. Steaks, shrimp, lobster, roast beef. Reserve. AE, CB, DC, MC, V. *L Mon-Fri noon-2:45pm. D Mon-Fri 4-10:45pm; Sat 1-11:45pm; Sun 1-9:45pm.* $$$

Palm Restaurant
837 Second Avenue nr East 45 St. 687-2953. Sawdusted floors, caricature-covered walls create the backdrop for the friendly, very noisy steak and lobster house, considered the best by many. Excellent steaks and enormous lobsters, good cottage fries. Watch the bill add up, it's *all* a la carte. Reserve. AE, CB, DC, MC, V. *OPEN Mon-Fri 11:30am-10:45pm; Sat 5-11pm. CLOSED Sun.* $$$$

Pen & Pencil
205 East 45 Street. 682-8660. Large popular steak house. Pre-theater dinner 4-7pm. No smoking section. Reserve. AE, CB, DC, MC, V. *OPEN Mon-Fri 11:45am-11:30pm; Sat & Sun from 4:30pm.* $$$

Peter Luger's
178 Broadway at Driggs Ave, Brooklyn. (1-718)387-7400. Located in a depressed edge of Brooklyn just across the Williamsburg Bridge: one of the legendary bests, according to steak lovers. Bare-essential décor and no-frills accompaniments to the delicious porterhouse steaks and double lamb chops. Reserve. No credit cards. *OPEN Mon-Fri 11:45am-10:45pm; Sat noon-11:15pm; Sun 1-9:45pm.* $$$

The Post House
28 East 63 Street. 935-2888. Attractive new place for steak, less macho than the rest. Good steak, chops and lobster too. Reserve. Jacket requested. AE, DC, MC, V. *OPEN Mon-Thurs*

noon-11pm; Fri & Sat till midnight; Sun 5:30-
11pm.　　　　　　　　　　　　　　　　　　$$
Spark's Steak House
210 East 46 Street. 687-4855. Informal restau-
rant, well known for fine steaks and lobsters and
the excellent extensive wine list. Reserve.
AE, DC, MC, V. L Mon-Fri noon-3pm. D Mon-
Thurs 5-11pm; Fri & Sat till 11:30pm. CLOSED
Sun.　　　　　　　　　　　　　　　　　　$$

Swiss
Auberge Suisse
Citicorp Market, 153 East 53 Street. 421-1420.
Handsome, modern setting for flavorful Swiss
food beautifully served. Highly recommended:
éminćé de veau, supreme de volaille en croute, so
too is the fondue vaudoise. Reserve for lunch
during the week. AE, CB, DC, MC, V. L Mon-Sat
noon-2:30pm. D Mon-Sat 5-10pm; Sun 4:30-9pm.
CLOSED Sun July & Aug.　　　　　　　　$$$
Chalet Suisse
6 East 48 Street. 355-0855. City's oldest, most
authentic, most charming Swiss restaurant.
Bündnerfleisch, veal à la Suisse, cheese and on-
ion pie, fondue. Reserve. Jacket & tie required.
AE, DC, MC. OPEN Mon-Fri: L noon-2:30pm; D
5-9:30pm. CLOSED Sat & Sun.　　　　　$$$
Dézaley
54 East 58 Street. 755-8546. Very good non-
fondue Swiss foods in a modern setting. Oxtail
soup, calves' liver with bananas and bacon, fillet
of herring, raclette; white Dézaley wine and Swiss
beer. Reserve especially for lunch. AE, CB, DC,
MC, V. L Mon-Fri noon-2:30pm. D Mon-Sat 5-
10pm.　　　　　　　　　　　　　　　　　$$
La Fondue
See Inexpensive.
Swiss Inn
882 First Avenue nr East 49 St. 758-3258. Com-
fort and good filling food at affordable prices.
Cheese fondue for two, mixed grill, smoked pork
chops. Reserve. AE, CB, DC, MC, V. L Mon-Fri
noon-3pm. D Mon-Sat 5-9:30pm. CLOSED Sun.$

Thai
Bangkok Cuisine
885 Eighth Avenue nr West 52 St. 581-6370. Also,
1470 First Avenue nr East 76 St. 744-9891. Au-
thentic Thai cuisine. Interesting eating, courteous
service, colorful setting. Reserve. AE, DC, MC, V.
OPEN Mon-Sat: L 11:30am-3pm; D 4pm-3am.
CLOSED Sun.　　　　　　　　　　　　　　$
Seeda Thai
204 West 50 Street. 586-4513. Tiny and ex-
tremely popular for wonderful soups, curries, sa-
tays and shrimp rolls. Reserve. AE, MC, V. OPEN
Mon-Fri 11:30am-11pm; Sat & Sun 5-11:30pm.$

Soomthai
1490 Second Avenue nr East 77 St. 570-6994.
Atmospheric native décor, large servings of savo-
ry Thai specialties. Pork satay, pad Thai, shrimp
soup, spicy chicken. Full bar. Reserve. AE, MC, V.
OPEN 7 days 5pm-midnight.　　　　　　　$
Thailand Restaurant
106 Bayard Street nr Mulberry St. 349-3132.
Everyone in the know recommends this small,
no-frills non-Chinese luncheonette in Chinatown
for the best-tasting and lowest-priced spicy
Thai specialties in the city. Reserve for more than
two. No credit cards. OPEN 7 days 11:30am-
11:30pm.　　　　　　　　　　　　　　　　$

Vietnamese
Indochine
430 Lafayette Street nr Astor Pl. 505-5111. Mourn
not for Lady Astor (great bar, terrible food) for
Indochine is here now. Authentic Vietnamese/
Cambodian cuisine in a clamorous Hollywoody-
glamorous setting. A hot spot for wonderful food;
fun to order several salads and appetizers and
share. Vietnamese ravioli, stuffed boneless chick-
en wings, frogs' legs in coconut milk, scampi be-
ignet. Drawback: the noise. Reserve. No credit
cards. OPEN 7 days 6pm-12:30am.　　　　$$
Wynn's Ba-Nam
3 Pike Street nr East Broadway. 227-4784.
Owned by a lovely Vietnamese family. Everything
is authentic—but don't miss the cha gio, the traditional spring rolls. You may bring your own wine.
Reserve. No credit cards. OPEN Tues-Sun 10am-
10:30pm. CLOSED Mon.　　　　　　　　　$

Wine Bars
Lavin's
See French
SoHo Kitchen & Bar
103 Greene Street nr Prince St. 226-9130. High-
ceilinged SoHo newcomer with a 60-foot bar. Cruvinet dispenses wine by the glass—over 100
choices including champagnes; nibbles and full
meals available at the bar and tables. No reservations except for large parties. AE, DC, CB, MC, V.
OPEN Mon-Fri 4pm-1am (kitchen till midnight);
Sat noon-midnight. Sat Brunch noon-5pm.
CLOSED Sun.　　　　　　　　　　　　　　$
Wine Bar
422 West Broadway nr Prince St. 431-4790. New
York's first wine bar serving over 45 wines by the
glass, demi, or full bottles from a list of over 100 is
featured. Light accompaniments: pâtés, cold cuts,
cheeses, and desserts. A pleasant SoHo-casual
place. AE only. OPEN Mon-Fri noon-1am; Sat &
Sun till 3am. Sun Brunch 11am-4pm.　　　　$

Shopping

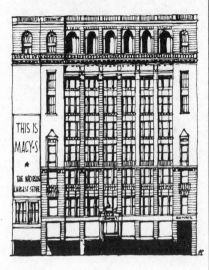

Macy's

Shopping Information

New York is an international center of art, food, fashion, antiques, and furnishings. This is only a selection of some of the best, unique, or inexpensive shops in each category. Good general shopping areas are West 34 Street, SoHo, Greenwich Village, 57 Street, Upper Madison Avenue, Columbus Avenue and the Lower East Side. Unless otherwise noted, all these shops are OPEN Mon-Sat. CLOSED Sun, approximately 9am-6pm.

Uptown late-night shopping is usually Mon & Thurs. Downtown shops, such as those in Greenwich Village, the East Village and SoHo have a different rhythm, reflecting those areas' slower pace: later openings but later closings; sometimes open Sunday, other times not; many Monday closings, often only a 5-day schedule. In summer many shops are closed on Saturday, and often for all of August. It's therefore best to call ahead if you are coming any distance to a particular shop. Price tags do not reflect the 8¼% city sales tax, which will be added by the salesperson or cashier upon purchase. NOTE: Street vendors selling anything from $2 umbrellas to $80 designer handbags have become a common sight, especially near the larger stores in popular shopping areas, much to the chagrin of the store managers. Bargains can be had; after all, the overhead is low. But check the merchandise carefully;

remember, these are migratory merchants and there are no returns or exchanges.

Consumer Protection

The New York City Department of Consumer Affairs, 80 Lafayette Street, New York 10013 (577-0111), mediates and arbitrates disputes, and can fine a merchant, when warranted. If you have any problems with a merchant, call *Mon-Fri 9am-5pm.* The Better Business Bureau, 257 Park Avenue South, 10010 (533-6200), has no legal power but can inform you of any complaints of past instances of poor performance and does arbitrate some disputes. *Mon-Fri 9am-4:30pm.* As a general rule, always find out what a particular store's policy is regarding return of a purchased item. Is it a final sale or is it returnable for credit or cash? *Always* keep receipts.

Department Stores

Abraham & Straus
420 Fulton Street nr Hoyt St, Brooklyn. (1-718) 875-7200. Since 1908 this large, unpretentious store has flourished in Brooklyn. Short on hype, long on stock: the variety of styles and prices is most impressive. A & S charge only. *OPEN Mon 9:45am-7pm; Tues, Wed, Fri, & Sat till 6pm; Thurs till 9pm; Sun noon-5pm.*

Alexander's
East 58 Street & Lexington Ave. 593-0880. A patient bargain-hunter's paradise. Designer clothes without the labels and good accessory-copy shopping. AE, MC, V. *OPEN Mon-Sat 10am-9pm; Sun noon-5pm.*

Alexander's
4 World Trade Center Plaza nr Church St. 466-1414. Billed as an "adult" fashion store; moderate prices. AE, MC, V. *OPEN Mon-Fri 8am-5:45pm; Sat 10am-5pm.*

B. Altman & Co.
Fifth Avenue at 34 St. 679-7800. Since 1865, a fine, traditional department store with clothes ranging from the moderately priced to expensive. Emphasis is on quality and service. AE, DC, MC, V, Altman charge. *OPEN Mon, Tues, Wed, Fri & Sat 10am-6pm; Thurs till 8pm.*

Bergdorf Goodman
754 Fifth Avenue at 58 St. 753-7300. The lush surroundings give this store an affluent feel, though the prices range from moderate to—on the 2nd fl—some of New York's highest. A $15 million renovation has given the store and its image a lift. Bergdorf, Neiman Marcus charge. *OPEN Mon, Tues, Wed, Fri & Sat 10am-6pm; Thurs till 8pm.*

Bloomingdale's
1000 Third Avenue at East 59 St. 355-5900. A New York phenomenon and above all a trendsetter. Do it justice, floor by floor. AE, Bloomingdale's charge. *OPEN Mon & Thurs 10am-9pm; Tues, Wed, Fri & Sat till 6:30pm; Sun noon-5pm.*

Bonwit Teller at Trump Tower
4 East 57 Street (also accessible through the Trump Tower Atrium). 593-3333. Bonwit is back—albeit a classy abbreviation of its former self. Women's fashions (there's a small men's furnishings department on the lower level of Trump Tower) in a serene and easy setting. Great for US and European ready-to-wear. AE, CB, DC, MC, V, Bonwit Charge. *OPEN Mon, Tues, Wed & Fri 10am-7pm; Thurs till 8pm; Sat till 6pm; Sun noon-5pm.*

Gimbels
1275 Broadway at West 33 St. 564-3300. *OPEN Mon, Thurs & Fri 9:45am-8:30pm; Tues & Wed till 6:45; Sat till 6:30; Sun noon-6pm.*

Gimbels East
125 East 86 Street. 348-2300. Each has bargain and designer merchandise under one roof. The newer uptown store has a more modern feel and look than the longstanding downtown store. AE, MC, V, Gimbels charge. *OPEN Mon-Sat 10am-9pm; Sun noon-6pm.*

Henri Bendel
10 West 57 Street. 247-1100. More a series of trendy boutiques than a department store. It's a beautiful place to shop or browse; luxurious and fashion-conscious. Innovative new 3rd and 4th floors. Remember, up to size 10 *only!* AE, MC, V, Bendel charge. *OPEN Mon, Tues, Wed, Fri & Sat 10am-5:30pm; Thurs till 8pm.*

Lord & Taylor
424 Fifth Avenue at 38 St. 391-3344. A fine stable store for classic designer sportswear leaning heavily toward contemporary American designers. Excellent sales Jan and July. AE, Lord & Taylor charge. *OPEN Mon, Tues, Wed, Fri & Sat 10am-6pm; Thurs till 8pm.* (If you arrive early you are treated to free coffee and "The Star Spangled Banner.")

Macy's
West 34 Street & Broadway. 695-4400. Orders: 971-6000. This huge (2.2 million feet of floor space!) full-service (post office, pharmacy . . .) department store, excellent in so many areas, is

Size Comparison Chart for Clothing

Ladies' dresses, coats & skirts

American -	3	5	7	9	11	12	13	14	15	16	18
Continental -	36	38	38	40	40	42	42	44	44	46	48
British -	8	10	11	12	13	14	15	16	17	18	20

Ladies' blouses & sweaters

American -	10	12	14	16	18	20
Continental -	38	40	42	44	46	48
British -	32	34	36	38	40	42

Ladies' stockings

American -	8	8½	9	9½	10	10½
Continental -	1	2	3	4	5	6
British -	8	8½	9	9½	10	10½

Ladies' shoes

American -	5	6	7	8	3	10
Continental -	36	37	38	39	40	41
British -	3½	4½	5½	6½	7½	8½

Children's clothing

American -	3	4	5	6	6X
Continental -	98	104	110	116	122
British -	18	20	22	24	26

Children's shoes

American -	8	9	10	11	12	13	1	2	3
Continental -	24	25	27	28	29	30	32	33	34
British -	7	8	9	10	11	12	13	1	2

Men's suits

American -	34	36	38	40	42	44	46	48
Continental -	44	46	48	50	52	54	56	58
British -	34	36	38	40	42	44	46	48

Men's shirts

American -	14	15	15½	16	16½	17	17½	18
Continental -	37	38	39	41	42	43	44	45
British -	14	15	15½	16	16½	17	17½	18

Men's shoes

American -	7	8	9	10	11	12	13
Continental -	39½	41	42	43	44½	46	47
British -	6	7	8	9	10	11	12

Men's hats

American -	6⅞	7⅛	7¼	7⅜	7½	7⅝
Continental -	55	56	58	59	60	61
British -	6¾	6⅞	7⅛	7¼	7⅜	7½

now a fashion force to be compared to Bloomies, and the Cellar is pure joy. Cheap to expensive. The recently restored Art Deco elegance of the main floor and the new Balcony shops are worth a visit. AE, Macy's charge. *OPEN Mon, Thurs, Fri 9:45am-8:30pm; Tues & Wed till 6:45pm; Sat till 6pm; Sun noon-6pm.*

Ohrbach's
5 West 34 Street. 695-4000. Good for inexpensive basics, especially accessories. There's little fashion image. AE, Ohrbach's charge. *OPEN Mon, Tues, Wed, Fri 10am-6:45pm; Thurs till 8:30pm; Sat till 6pm; Sun noon-6pm.*

Saks Fifth Avenue
611 Fifth Avenue at 50 St. 753-4000. A quality store for wide selections of elegant designer clothes or young sportswear in a conservative setting. The range is moderate to expensive (on the newly redecorated 3rd fl). AE, DC, Saks charge. *OPEN Mon, Tues, Wed, Fri & Sat 10am-6pm; Thurs till 8pm.*

Shopping Centers

This concept is new to Manhattan. See also SIGHTSEEING, On Your Own: Atriums.

Herald Center
1 Herald Square at West 34 St. Newcomer to the Herald Square area (Macy's country); a 10-level retail center with Manhattan locale themes on every floor. There are 140 shops featuring American and European retailers. *OPEN Mon, Thurs & Fri 9:45am-8:30pm; Tues & Wed till 6:45pm; Sat till 6pm; Sun noon-6pm.*

Itokin Plaza
520 Madison Avenue nr East 54 St. 319-0520. Under one roof, over 25 European and Japanese designers including Carolina Herrera, Courrèges, Tokio Kumagai, Takako Kozai. 10:30am-6:30pm.

South Street Seaport Marketplace
Fulton & South Streets. In the old Seaport District: over 75 shops and restaurants and more on the glass-enclosed Pier 17 pavilion. Shops *OPEN Mon-Sat 10am-10pm; Sun noon-6pm.*

Trump Tower
Fifth Avenue & 56 Street. (Enter also through Bonwit Teller on East 57 Street.) The lavish atrium is a vertical shopping plaza devoted to high-style and high prices (Harry Winston, Cartier, Lina Lee, Charles Jourdan.) *OPEN Mon-Sat 9am-6pm.*

Children's Clothes

(*See* KIDS' NEW YORK.)

Women's Clothes

Shopping Services
B. Altman, Bergdorf Goodman, Bloomingdale's, Lord & Taylor, Macy's and Saks Fifth Avenue offer the services of a personal shopper. Set up an appointment; make your needs, taste and budget known, and sit back while someone else does the legwork and brings the selections back for you to try on. There is no obligation and it's free.

Boutiques

—Contemporary

Agnès B.
*116 Prince Street nr Greene St. 925-4649; Also, 1063 Madison Avenue nr East 81 St. 570-9333. In a comfortable environment, unpretentious, very French and *very* affordable, simple separates in suede, linen, leather, cotton and silk. Sexy tees and sweaters her forte. AE, MC, V. *OPEN Tues-Sun.*

American High
717 Madison Avenue nr East 63 St. 319-0350. Also, 410 West Broadway. 925-6730. Camp shirts, tees and more youthful—"typically American"—casualwear. Catalog available. AE, MC, V. *OPEN 7 days.*

Ann Taylor
3 East 57 Street. 832-2010; Also, 805 Third Avenue. 308-5333; Seaport Marketplace, 25 Fulton Street 608-5600. and *Herald Center, 1 Herald Square at West 34 St. 695-4474. Well-organized and well-stocked mini "department" store for moderate to expensive contemporary clothes and footwear for work and play. AE, MC, V, Ann Taylor charge. *OPEN 7 days.*

Barney's
Seventh Avenue & West 17 St. 929-9000. Now, the skylit women's duplex features the *newest* fashions for women from Armani, Lauren, Chloè, Miyake. Shoes by Maud, Manolo Blahnik. But come next year, there will be a unique new women's store located in a series of brownstones on 17th Street. Free alterations, delivery, parking. AE, MC. Barney's charge. *OPEN Mon-Fri 10am-9pm; Sat till 8pm.*

Basha &
908 Madison Avenue nr East 73 St. 794-8877. All clothes designed and manufactured on the premises. Elegant yet affordable; size 4-12. AE, MC, V ($75 minimum).

Benetton
475 Fifth Avenue nr 41 St. 685-2727; 601 Madison Avenue nr East 57 St. 751-3155; 705 Lexington at East 57 St. 832-0810; and additional branches. (They cover the town.) Mass merchandiser of stylish Italian sportswear separates; strong on sweater dressing. Colorful, affordable, classic. AE, MC, V.

Betsey, Bunky & Nini
746 Madison Avenue nr East 65 St. 744-6716. A lovely shop with expensive, imaginative separates by Claude Montana, Complice, Byblos. Unique handmade sweaters from Great Britain. AE, MC, V.

Betsey Johnson
130 Thompson Street nr Prince St. 420-0169. Also, 248 Columbus Avenue nr West 72 St. 362-3364; 251 East 60 Street. 319-7699. Colorful body-conscious clothes from a pro; first on

SoHo's other good-shopping street, now uptown on the East and West side. Price range $25-130. AE, MC, V. *OPEN 7 days.*

Black Market
307 East 9 Street. 677-6266. Unique shop in a unique area. One-of-a kind fashions by some of today's best avant-garde designers (Pedro and Alejandro, Patti Pomerantz, Prudence Moriarity); high-tech jewelry and objects—and it's all in black! AE, MC, V. *OPEN Tues-Sun.*

Blades
1452 Second Avenue nr East 76 St. 734-6666. Really three shops in one, all gems, featuring beautifully tailored French and Italian sportswear at moderate prices. AE, DC, MC, V. *OPEN 7 days.*

Capezio in the Village
177 MacDougal Street nr West 8 St. 477-5634. The dancer's store for everyone. Fluid, fanciful and colorful clothes for men (upstairs) and women; great shoe selection. The best windows. AE, MC, V. *OPEN 7 days.*

Carioca
312 East 9 Street. 475-3124. Well-designed and sewn-on-the-premises colorful contemporary fashions by owner-designer Carolyn Dwyer. Pretty and feminine, clean and simple lines. Range $19-90. MC, V.

Charivari
2307 Broadway nr West 83 St. 873-1424; Sport, 2345 Broadway nr West 85 St. 799-8650; **72,** 58 West 72 Street. 787-7272; Workshop, 441 Columbus Avenue nr West 81 St. 496-8700; **57,** 16-18 West 57 Street. 333-4040. High-priced designer merchandise, 70% of which is imported, in this clutch of West Side shops well-known for innovative retailing and forward-looking fashions. Armani, Basile, Byblos, Castelbajac, Issey Miyake, Claude Montana, Katherine Hamnett, Kenzo. At **57** & 19,000 sq. ft. Yohji Yamamoto boutique, his first in NY. *The Workshop:* the most avant-garde. *OPEN 7 days (except* **57).**

Clovelly
430 West Broadway nr Spring St. 966-7254. Trendy yet feminine imports and new American and European designer separates with a lot of style. Prices: $40-200. AE, MC, V. *OPEN 7 days.*

Dianne B.
729 Madison Avenue nr East 64 St. 759-0988. Also in SoHo, *426 West Broadway. 226-6400. Wonderful up-to-the-minute boutique for Japanese and French sportswear and accessories, ranging from moderate to very expensive. Great selection of Issey Miyake, Dorothée Bis, Cygne, Castalbajac. AE, DC, MC, V. *OPEN 7 days.*

Diddingtons
143 Prince Street at West Broadway. 228-1748. Good SoHo spot for very attractive imported sportswear, separates and amusing accessories. Shoes, downstairs. AE, MC, V. *OPEN 7 days.*

Enz
5 St. Marks Place nr Third Ave. 420-1857. Decadent dress-up on the punkiest street in town. AE, MC, V. *OPEN 7 days till 8pm.*

Fiorucci
125 East 59 Street. 751-5638. Offbeat and upbeat shop features Italian, colorful, and mostly whimsical clothes and accessories. Don't miss the experience even if the clothes are not for you. Free espresso bar. AE, MC, V. *Mon & Thurs till 8pm.*

Fonda's
209 East 60 Street. 759-3260. American and European designer clothes and their own exclusive designs (their own fabrics too). A staple: new-out-of-old-fabric, one-of-a-kind dresses and skirts, plus mint antique clothes (strong on beaded dresses and Victorian) and accessories. AE, MC, V.

Forza
269 Columbus Avenue nr West 72 St. 877-2070. Well-designed Italian imports. Simple and stylish for both men and women. AE, MC, V. *OPEN 7 days.*

Gallery of Wearable Art
480 West Broadway at Houston St. 425-5379. A boutique/gallery of one-of-a-kind fantasy clothing and accessories by talented craftspeople. MC, V. *OPEN 7 days.*

Henry Lehr
464 West Broadway nr Houston St. 460-5500. Also, 1070 Third Avenue nr East 63 St. 753-2721; 410 Columbus Avenue nr West 79 St. 580-0533. Vast SoHo shop for trendy casual "seasonless" sportswear separates for women, men (kids too). Lehr's own designs plus the likes of Paul Smith and Katherine Hamnett. AE, MC, V. *OPEN 7 days.*

Honeybee
7 East 53 Street. 752-8851. Very popular midtown shop. Excellent stock of well-priced sportswear, dresses and accessories on 2 levels. AE, CB, DC, MC, V, Honeybee charge.

IAN'S
1151 Second Avenue nr East 60 St. 838-3969: 49 Grove Street nr Seventh Ave South. 675-1062. Pioneer punker. For the adventurous woman who wants to stop traffic. AE, MC, V.

Ibiza
46 University Place nr East 10 St. 533-4614. In new larger quarters. Gorgeous colorful now fashions. Great feminine style and pulled together looks; terrific accessories and the prettiest windows in the Village. Moderate to expensive. AE, MC, V.

In Wear/Matinique
394 West Broadway nr Broome St. 219-8187. Two shops in one: Danish sportswear separates in coordinated colors for men and women; and their own designs in shoes, socks, hats, scarves, and belts. AE, MC. *OPEN 7 days.*

Jimmy's
1226 Kings Highway nr 12 St, Brooklyn. (1-718) 645-9685. Where high fashion lives in Brooklyn; the best of Milan and Paris. Claude Montana, Alaïa, Basile, Biagotti, Byblos, Complice, Ferre, Missoni, Yamamoto, Soprani, etc. For men and women. AE, CB, DC, MC, V. *OPEN Mon, Tues & Thurs till 8:30pm.*

Johnny Ward
194 Columbus Avenue nr West 69 St. 595-7918.

Tiny, funky, stocks an avant-garde breed of NY designers. AE, MC, V. *OPEN 7 days.*

Laura Ashley
21 East 57 Street. 735-1010. 398 Columbus Avenue nr West 79 St. 496-5151; South Street Seaport, 4 Fulton Street. 809-3555. Also at Macy's. A floral oasis straight from London. Inexpensive and charming mainly cotton and corduroy print fashions for the young-at-heart woman. Children's fashions and home furnishings, including fabric and wallpaper. AE, MC, V.

Le Grand Hotel/Tales of Hoffman
471 West Broadway nr Houston St. 475-7625. Longtime SoHo showcase for young designers, known and not so. Sophisticated individuality. Day and evening wear, accessories and elegant shoes and boots. AE, MC, V. *OPEN Tues-Sun.*

Marimekko
7 West 56 Street. 581-9616. Large store for the Finnish designer's complete line, from ready-to-wear to paper products. AE, MC, V.

Ménage à Trois
760 Madison Avenue nr East 65 St. 249-0500. Exclusive designs of soft feminine clothing, some imports, some vintage. Very expensive. AE, MC, V.

Miso Clothes, Inc.
416 West Broadway nr Spring St. 226-4955. This SoHo shop has the latest from the newest young designers at realistic prices. AE, MC, V. *OPEN 7 days.*

Modern Girls at Play
169 Thompson Street nr Houston St. 533-1022. Young avant-garde fashions: silver lamé stirrup pants, neon topcoats, and appropriate accessories for such "modern girls'" fashions. AE only. *OPEN Tues-Sun 1:30pm-7pm.*

Monahan Ross
341 West Broadway nr Grand St. 219-2266. Distinctive sportswear for men and women. Calla, Jennifer George, Seelars, Liancarlo. One of a kind knits; unique accessories. AE, DC, MC, V. *OPEN Tues-Sun noon-7pm.*

Nancy & Co.
1242 Madison Avenue nr East 89 St. 427-0770; 1051 Third Avenue nr East 62 St. 980-4884. High-fashion designer imports. AE, MC, V. *OPEN 7 days.*

Nicole Handknit Sweaters
South Street Seaport, 19 Fulton Street. 608-1237. Hand-knit, hand-loomed and hand-crocheted sweaters, shawls; hats. Some of the fanciest sweaters in town. Pricey too. AE, MC, V. *OPEN 7 days.*

Off Broadway
139 West 72 Street. 724-6713. Incredible selection of American and imported separates, swimsuits, shoes, bags; free alterations too. AE, CB, DC, MC, V. Off Broadway charge. *OPEN 7 days.*

Parachute
121 Wooster Street nr Prince St. 925-8630. Also, 309 Columbus Avenue nr West 74 St. 799-1444. Airplane-hangar-sized shop for high-tech, functional, colorful unisex clothes. Inexpensive but "not for everyone." AE, MC, V. *OPEN 7 days.*

Patricia Field
10 East 8 Street. 254-1699. Innovative trendsetter on the cutting edge of fashion. Unusual, whimsical, colorful, practical, affordable. Avant-garde makeup and jewelry, too. AE, MC, V. *OPEN 7 days.*

Phenomena
40½ St. Marks Place nr Third Ave. 674-3067. Sophisticated young designers; turn out simple unconstructed clothing for men and women; high-tech accessories. AE, DC, MC, V. *OPEN Tues-Sun 1-9pm.*

Plenda
208 Third Avenue nr East 18 St. 982-8640. Casual simplicity in separates and dresses with easy lines. Lots of one-size-fits-all. Finity, Sermoneta, Bis, Carol Horn. Jacques Cohen espadrilles and wonderful accessories including jewelry. Moderate prices. AE, MC, V. *OPEN Tues-Sat.*

Riding High
1147 First Avenue at East 63 St. 832-7927. Elegant, highly distinctive separates and shoes. Individuality worth the price. AE, CB, DC, MC, V.

Rodier Paris
715 Madison Avenue nr East 64 St. 751-7506. Classic, well-tailored French contemporary wear. Specializes in a coordinated color range of separates. Fabulous windows. AE, MC, V.

San Francisco
975 Lexington Avenue nr East 71 St. 472-8740. "Tweedy" all natural fabric tailoring for men and women, much of it interchangeable, in an attractive, unique setting. Wonderful robes and night shirts. Moderately expensive. AE, MC, V.

Sunday in New York
347 West Broadway. 966-6366. Casual to formal wear by young designers. Exclusive, handmade sweaters & knits, wide price range; will make to order. Classy accessories. AE, DC, MC, V. *OPEN 7 days.*

Tous les Caleçons
72 Thompson Street nr Spring St. 219-3465. Unique. Direct from France: men's cotton underwear—bottoms and tops in beautifully patterned cotton—being snatched up by women for outer and under wear. Men buy them too. AE, MC, V.

Traffico
722 Broadway nr Astor Pl. 477-2722. Low-priced colorful Italian sporty clothes including Fiorucci and Americano. Very youthful and affordable. AE, MC, V. *OPEN 7 days.*

Unique Clothing Warehouse
726 Broadway at Washington Pl. 674-1767. The new shop is a "specialty department store" for street chic styles, as well as New Wave fashions. Not quite as cheap as the original—except for the accessories. The trends are here first—for the lowest prices. MC, V. *OPEN 7 days till 9pm.*

Urban Outfitters
20 University Place at East 8 St. 475-0009. The old Brentano's bookstore now a cheap chic outpost for clothing and accessories for the entire family. Kids' toys, too. MC, V. *OPEN Mon-Sat till 10pm; Sun noon-6pm.*

Veneziano
819 Madison Avenue nr East 68 St. 988-0211. For over 25 years beautifully simple Italian clothing from t-shirts to evening wear at exhorbitant prices. Jackie O. turf. AE, MC, V.

Vermont Classics
284 Columbus Avenue nr West 73 St. 874-0480. Classic yet feminine New England-conservative apparel for women; hand knits and other hand-made items. AE, MC, V. *OPEN 7 days.*

Wild Game
222 Third Avenue at East 19 St. 777-3337. Chock full of attractive contemporary sportswear by established and new young designers. AE, MC, V. *OPEN 7 days.*

Yves St. Tropez
4 West 57 Street. 765-5790. For the slim and rich. Elegant silks, extravagant furs, plus shoes, boots, slacks, suits all made in Paris. AE, MC, V.

—Conservative

Alcott & Andrews
335 Madison Avenue at East 44 St. 818-0606. Totally devoted to the executive woman—no more, no less. *OPEN 7 days.*

Brooks Brothers
346 Madison Avenue nr East 44 St. 682-8800. Since 1818 the consummate men's tailor—now for women on four.

Jaeger
818 Madison Avenue at East 69 St. 628-3350; 19 East 57 Street. 753-0370. The classics in beautiful fabrics for both men and women. No surprises but great quality. AE, DC, MC, V.

La Cabine
48 East 57 Street, Suite 400. 826-1111. Separates for the working woman, and advice on how to put it all together. MC, V.

Paul Stuart
Madison Avenue at East 45 St. 682-0320. Clones of the men's classics for women. Dresses too. AE, DC, MC, V.

Sport & Travel
511 Madison Avenue at East 53 St. 758-0881. Tailored sports and outerwear for the conservative woman. AE, CB, DC, MC, V.

Streets & Co.
2030 Broadway nr West 69 St. 787-2626; *916 Lexington Avenue nr East 69 St. 517-9000; 14 East 44 Street. 697-2566. Caters to the business and professional woman: conservative clothes and accessories, on-the-premises tailor, delivery service, evening hours, wardrobe planning. AE, DC, MC, V. *OPEN 7 days.*

T. Jones
1050 Third Avenue at East 62 St. 838-5990. Expensive classics. AE, MC, V.

—Designer

Comme des Garçons
116 Wooster Street nr Prince St. 219-0661. Stark bunkerlike setting in SoHo for Rei Kawakubo's intriguing fashions. For women, men, homewear, accessories and shoes. AE, DC, MC, V. *OPEN 7 days.*

Diane von Furstenberg
783 Fifth Avenue nr 58 St. 753-1111. A dramatic post-modern salon for the couture collection for the thin and rich—presumably like the Princess herself. AC, MC, V.

Emanuel Ungaro
803 Madison Avenue at East 68 St. 249-4090. Ungaro's exquisite fabrics, simple styling. AE, DC, MC, V.

Emilio Pucci
24 East 64 Street. 752-8957. *Emilio Pucci, Emilio Pucci, Emilio Pucci* all over his colorful print clothing and accessories. AE, DC, MC, V.

Gianni Versace Boutique
816 Madison Avenue nr East 68 St. 744-5572. Modern shop for Versace's entire luxurious collection for women and men; shoes, leather goods, accessories, jewelry, perfume. AE, MC, DC, V.

Giorgio Armani
815 Madison Avenue nr East 68 St. 988-9191. Armani's perfectly executed tailoring on 3 floors: street level for women and accessories; second for men, and third for Emporio Armani, a less expensive sportswear line. AE, MC, V.

Givenchy
954 Madison Avenue at East 75 St. 772-1040. Audrey Hepburn's long-time favorite; his clothes and accessories. For the gentleman, ties only. AE, MC, V.

Gucci
685 Fifth Avenue at 54 St. 826-2600. Four levels of Gs around a central atrium. Accessories and apparel for men and women. On four, the Galleria, accessible only to those with an 18kt gold key or accompanied by the manager. AE, DC, MC, V.

Hanae Mori
27 East 79 Street. 472-2352. Beautiful, sophisticated Japanese-inspired fashions. AE, MC, V.

Joseph Tricot
804 Madison Avenue nr East 68 St. 570-0077. *Also, 326 Columbus Avenue nr West 75 St. 787-0036. Via London's South Molton Street, Joseph Ettedgui's knits designed to mix and match and layer. Simple shapes, interesting textures, inventive accessories, including shoes. AE, MC, V. *OPEN Tues-Sun.*

Kenzo Boutique
824 Madison Avenue at East 69 St. 737-8640. All of Kenzo's stylish and colorful clothes and accessories. AE, MC, V

Koos van den Akker Couture
795 Madison Avenue nr East 67 St, 2nd fl. 249-5432. Elaborate fabric collages to wear. Imaginative and expensive. AE, MC, V.

Lina Lee
Trump Tower, 725 Fifth Avenue at 56 St. 556-2678. Synonymous with California high-style. Mary McFadder Thierry Mugler, Bob Mackie, Laura Biagiotti. Great evening looks; trendy accessories. For men: Mario Valentino, Ferre. AE, MC, V.

Martha
475 Park Avenue at East 58 St. 753-1511; Also, at Trump Tower, 725 Fifth Avenue at 56 St, 3rd and 4th levels. 826-8855. The best: Beene, Blass,

Trigere, Halston, Mary McFadden, Oscar de la Renta, Valentino, in elegant settings. AE, DC, MC, V.

Matsuda
854 Madison Avenue nr East 70 St. 988-9514; 465 Park Avenue at East 57 St. 935-6969. Mitsuhiro Matsuda's Japanese New Wave fashions for men and women. More classics on Park Ave. AE, DC, MC, V.

Missoni
Westbury Hotel, 836 Madison Avenue at East 69 St. 517-9339. Sleek, modern all-black setting, the better to appreciate the fabulous distinctively hued, imaginatively patterned knits. Their entire masterful collection for women and men is here. AE, MC, V.

OMO Kamali
11 West 56 Street. 957-9797. New digs in a 100-year-old building. To the delight of Kamali fans (legions) it has 6 levels for her imaginative clothes, hats, shoes, socks, bathing suits, evening clothes and kidswear. AE, MC, V. *Thurs till 8pm.*

Saint Laurent Rive Gauche Boutique Femme
855 Madison Avenue at East 71 St. 988-3821. Ready-to-wear from the influential master of fanciful dressing. AE, DC, MC, V.

Sonia Rykiel Boutique
792 Madison Avenue at East 67 St. 744-0880. Famed French designer finally has her own showcase for her easy-to-wear knits, accessories, too. AE, DC, MC, V.

Ted Lapidus
1010 Third Avenue at East 60 St. 751-7251. Very expensive classic French clothes in exquisite fabrics for men and women. AE, CB, DC, MC, V.

Valentino
677 Fifth Avenue nr 53 St. 421-7550. Lavish high fashion at high prices. AE, DC, MC, V.

Zoran
214 Sullivan Street, 6th fl. 674-6087. The Yugoslavian designer's expensive minimalist creations in the finest fabrics. Famed for his "tees." *By appointment.*

—Discount

Though discount designerwear can now be found all over town, the traditional bargain-hunting area is the Lower East Side. Orchard Street has the highest concentration of shops selling from chic to schlock and everything in between. Sunday is a hectic but very NY experience not to be missed. Orchard Street itself becomes a pedestrian mall closed to cars on that day. If you can, leave your car at home.

A. Altman
182 Orchard Street nr Houston St. 982-7722; also, 204 Fifth Avenue at 25 St. 889-0782. The Lower East Side's "in" shop for *very* well-discounted European designer sportswear, dresses and coats. An especially fine silk shirt selection. Some amenities at Fifth Ave Store, none downtown. Be prepared to line up for admittance. MC, V. *OPEN Sun-Fri.*

Berent & Smith
94 Rivington Street nr Orchard St. 254-0900. Large, chaotic Lower East Side shop for discounted dresses, sportswear and raincoats, sizes 3-24½. MC, V. *OPEN Sun-Fri.*

Bolton's
43 East 8 Street. 475-6626; 53 West 23 Street. 924-6860; 1180 Madison Avenue at East 86 St. 722-4419; 225 East 57 Street. 755-2527; 27 West 57 Street. 935-4431; 2251 Broadway nr West 81 St. 873-8545; 59 Liberty Street. Well-known no-nonsense discount chain store with many high-quality designer labels, including Halston V, Ralph Lauren and Ann Klein, at 20-50% off. Sizes 4-16. MC, V. *OPEN 7 days (ex 23 Street).*

Castañada
1298 Third Avenue nr East 74 St. 736-6960. European, American and Japanese designer shirts, blouses, pants, sweaters, day and evening dresses; all at discount. Sizes 2-22. AE, MC, V. *OPEN 7 days.*

Emotional Outlet
91 Seventh Avenue at West 16 St. 206-7750; 242 East 51 Street. 838-0707; 435 East 86 Street. 534-4825; *135 West 50 Street. 957-9340. Friendly offers of free coffee or wine along with contemporary sportswear and shoes at 20% off make this an attractive shopping spot. AE, DC, MC, V. *OPEN 7 days. CLOSED Sun.*

Filene's Basement
Fresh Meadows Shopping Center, 187-04 Horace Harding Expressway, Fresh Meadows, Queens. (1-718) 479-7711. A long-time Boston tradition comes to NY. Nearly perfect merchandise from some of the country's top retailers including Neiman Marcus, I. Magnin and Sakowitz. Clothes for the entire family; also, shoes, giftware, housewares. Automatic markdown policy on items that linger. *OPEN Mon-Sat 10am-9:30pm; Sun noon-5pm.*

First Class
117 Orchard Street nr Delancey St. 475-8147. American and European designer sportswear, including Kasper and Dior. Discounted 20-60%. AE, MC, V. *OPEN Sun-Fri.*

Fishkin
314 Grand Street at Allen St. 226-6538. Also, 318 Grand Street and 63 Orchard Street. European and American dresses and sportswear, designer boots and shoes, 20% below list price. Norma Kamali, Harvé Bernard, Calvin Klein, Regina Potter, La Belle France. Lineups are usual on Sun. AE, DC, MC, V. *OPEN Sun-Fri.*

Friedlich, Inc.
196 Orchard Street nr Houston St. 254-8899. Discounted famous-name Seventh Avenue designer and French and Italian sportswear sizes 5-15, 4-16. Hectic, few amenities and sometimes rude, but good Lower East Side bargains make it all worthwhile. AE, MC, V. *OPEN 7 days. CLOSED Tues in summer.*

Gabay's
225 First Avenue nr East 13 St. 254-3180. This secret bargain source sells overstock, end-of-season, flawed, or returned merchandise from the

best name uptown department stores. Cacharel blouses, Ralph Lauren sweaters, Jourdan shoes, *all thrown on a table!* Prices depend on whether damaged and how badly. Smart, careful shoppers do well here. New merchandise daily. Best to go with a veteran shopper. MC. *OPEN 7 days.*

Gucci on Seven
2 East 54 Street, 7th fl. 826-2675. A floor of specially priced—in other words, on sale—Gucci fashions, shoes, luggage, bags and accessories for men and women. *Very* good buys can be found here. AE, DC, MC, V.

Harris
275 Seventh Avenue nr West 25 St. 989-9765. Fine designer dresses, suits, and separates at up to 50% off. MC, V. *OPEN 7 days.*

Hit or Miss
417 Fifth Avenue nr 38 St. 889-8703. Harvé Bernard, Crazy Horse, Fenn Wright Mason, Calvin Klein, Evan Picone, Cathy Hardwick, Regina Porter, Wayne Rogers, WilliWear, French Connection; all at 20-50% off. New shipments 2-3 times a week. AE, MC, V. *Thurs till 8pm.*

House of Fashion
317 Grand Street nr Orchard St. 226-6106. Up to 50% off Adolfo, Bill Blass, Oscar de la Renta, Ann Klein, Calvin Klein, Harvé Bernard. Menswear, too. MC, V. *OPEN Sun-Fri. (CLOSES early on Fri.)*

Labels for Less
639 Third Avenue at East 41 St. 682-3330; *130 East 34 Street. 689-3455; *1116 Third Avenue at East 65 St. 628-1100; 130 West 48 Street. 997-1032. Good spots for discounted junior and misses' sportswear. MC, V. *OPEN 7 days.*

L & N Fashions
81 Delancy Street nr Orchard St. 431-6081. French and Italian imports: dresses and separates, suits and coats, sizes 4-14, from 30-50% off. *Parlons française ici.* AE, MC, V. *OPEN Sun-Thurs. (CLOSES early on Fri.)*

The Little Shop
63 East 9 Street. 473-4096. This closet of a shop is a veritable WilliWear discount outlet. Great prices for this season's pieces. Also, Clickpoint. AE, MC, V. *OPEN Mon-Sat noon-7pm.*

Loehmann's
The original: 9 West Fordham Road at Jerome Ave, Bronx. 295-4100; also, 19 Duryea Place nr Beverly Rd, Brooklyn. (1-718) 469-9800; 60-06 99 Street nr Horace Harding Expressway, Rego Park, Queens. (1-718) 271-4000. Legendary Loehmann's is more than a store, it's a tradition handed down from one generation of New York women to another. Everything a bargain-hunter could want and put up with: outrageously low prices, uneven selections, communal dressing rooms and hints of designer labels still attached. Some women go daily (2,400 new garments arrive each day). *Beware.* No refunds, no exchanges. *OPEN 7 days.*

Mr. Ephram
235 East 42 Street. 697-0086; 1796 Broadway nr West 59 St. 247-7640; 730 Third Avenue nr East 46 St. 986-2638. Good selection of quality mod-

erate junior sportswear, dresses, suits and coats, at 15-30% discount. MC, V.

Ms., Miss, or Mrs.
462 Seventh Avenue at West 35 St, 8th fl. 736-0557. Well-known wholesaler for moderate to expensive name-designer separates and coats. Huge stock, excellent discounts, sizes 2-22½. *Sat only till 4pm.*

New Store
289 Seventh Avenue nr West 26 St. 741-1077. Some of the best buys north of Orchard Street. Kasper, Givenchy Sport, Carol Horn and European imports at 40-50% off! Seasonal sales too. Great for silk blouses and cashmere sweaters. Sizes 4-14. AE, MC, V. *OPEN 7 days.*

S&W
165 West 26 Street. 924-6656; 287 Seventh Avenue. 924-6656; 291 Seventh Avenue. 924-6656; 283 Seventh Avenue. 924-6505. A top discount store for the best American designer sportswear. The prices are 30-50% off, but there are always sales to accommodate the seasonal flows of merchandise. Up-to-the-minute Albert Nippon, Kasper and many others. At 283 Seventh Avenue, designer boots, shoes, and handbags; at 287, designer coats; and at 291 a range of more moderate merchandise. AE, MC, V. *OPEN Sun-Fri.*

Secaucus Outlet Center
Lincoln Tunnel to Rte 3 West to Meadowlands Parkway. (1-201) 330-1030. Ten minutes from Manhattan (by car) to this New Jersey bargain shoppers' paradise. (Would I tell you to leave NY for anything but a bargain?) Over 60 famous names including Anne Klein, Ralph Lauren, Norma Kamali, Bill Blass; also, housewares, furniture, lighting, gifts, luggage, linens. Savings 20-80%. Extra bonus: no sales tax on clothing.

Spitzer's Corner Store
101 Rivington Street at Ludlow St. 477-4088; 156 Orchard Street at Rivington St. 473-1515 Large selection of velvet blazers, junior suits, coats and casual dresses well below retail price. MC, V. *OPEN Sun-Fri.*

Unlimited Pret à Porter
121 Orchard Street nr Delancey St. 473-8550. Top American and French designer sportswear at 30-60% off. AE, DC, MC, V. *OPEN 7 days.*

Yves St. Tropez
247 East 60 Street. 751-2222. No-longer-secret outlet for markdowns of their other shops' women's (and men's) French and Italian ready-to-wear. AE, MC, V.

—Ethnic

Azuma
*666 Lexington Avenue nr East 56 St. 752-0599; *251 East 86 Street. 369-4928; 415 Fifth Avenue nr 38 St. 889-4310; *25 East 8 Street. 673-2900; *387 Sixth Avenue nr Waverly Pl. 989-8690. Inexpensive Chinese, Indian and Mexican clothes and accessories for peasant dressing on a shoestring budget. AE, DC, MC, V. *OPEN 7 days.*

Back from Guatemala
306 East 6 Street. 228-9496. A most unusual

stock of fashions, jewelry and artifacts, not only from Guatemala but from China, Bali, Afghanistan, South America and Tibet as well. AE, MC, V. OPEN 7 days.

Buen Dia
108 West Houston Street at Thompson St. 673-1910; 201 West 11 Street nr Seventh Ave. 929-1512. Colorful, well-priced Central and South American clothes and accessories; beautiful Mexican gowns. At West Houston store, the city's largest selection of handmade hammocks and textiles by the yard. AE, CB, DC, MC, V.

Butik Stockholm
928 Madison Avenue at East 74 St. 988-9441. Attractive, moderately priced Scandinavian clothing, including Marimekko prints. No credit cards.

Chor Bazaar
801 Lexington Avenue at East 62 St. 838-2581. Antique and new Afghanistan, Indian, Mexican and Chinese fashions in a wide variety of styles, colors and prices. All natural fabrics. AE, MC, V.

Craft Caravan
127 Spring Street at Greene St. 966-1338. From East and West Africa, clothing, jewelry, sculpture, baskets and hand-loomed fabrics fill this SoHo shop. No credit cards. OPEN Sun-Fri.

Handloom Batiks
214 Mulberry Street nr Spring St. 925-9542. Indian, Indonesian and Malaysian batiks. No credit cards. OPEN Wed-Sun.

Ozymandias
32 St. Marks Place nr Second Ave. 254-6206. Colorful artifacts and clothing from Afghanistan, Bali, Java, Tibet. Large selection of Chinese cloisonné jewelry and magnificent Chinese opera puppets. AE, MC, V. OPEN 7 days.

Paracelso
432 West Broadway nr Prince St. 966-4232. Everything in this exotic SoHo bazaar is unusual, including the owner. You'll find contemporary and antique European and Asian clothes, jewelry, and curios not found anywhere else. No credit cards. OPEN 7 days.

Putumayo
857 Lexington Avenue at East 65 St. 734-3111; *339 Columbus Avenue nr West 76 St. 595-3441; *147 Spring Street nr Wooster St. 966-4458. Welcoming shops for inexpensive handmade imports from Bolivia, Chile, Iceland, Tibet and Afghanistan. Wonderful accessories. Folk art and textiles. MC, V. *OPEN 7 days.

Seaport Landing
50 Fulton Street nr Pearl St. 619-5050. Fine apparel from around the world—ethnic but high style at very good prices. AE, MC, V.

Sermoneta
740 Madison Avenue nr East 64 St. 744-6551. Good-value pretty imports from Peru, Ecuador and India. MC, V.

Surma
11 East 7 Street. 477-0729. Exquisite albeit expensive hand-embroidered Rumanian peasant blouses among beautiful traditional Ukrainian handicrafts in the Little Ukraine section of the East Village. OPEN 7 days (Sun 11am-2pm only).

Swing Low
1181 Second Avenue nr East 63 St. 838-3314. Natural and colorful South American imports at moderate prices. AE, MC, V. OPEN 7 days.

—Resale Clothing

Encore Resale Dress Shop
1132 Madison Avenue nr East 84 St. 879-2850. Excellent-condition name-label, including Calvin Klein, used clothing at moderate prices. Sophisticated recycling. OPEN 7 days.

Exchange Unlimited
563 Second Avenue at East 31 St. 889-3229. Secondhand contemporary clothing, including designer, on consignment.

Michael's Resale Dress Shop
1041 Madison Avenue nr East 79 St, upstairs. 737-7273. Pragmatic snob appeal! Nothing older than a year, meticulous condition. OPEN Tues-Sat.

Revivals Unlimited, Inc.
240 East 81 Street. 744-0519. Moderately priced used clothes. MC, V.

—Vintage

(See also Men's Clothes: Secondhand.) Most "antique" clothing shops have a final-sale policy, so purchase carefully and wisely. The East Village and Lower Broadway are the best areas for vintage values. See also Specialty Shops & Services: Antique & Flea Markets.

Antique Boutique
712-714 Broadway nr Washington Pl. 460-8830. A top spot on Lower Broadway (a hot new place to shop) for a trip through a fashion time-capsule in this, the city's largest used-clothing store. Over 30,000 items, including kimonos, tuxedo shirts, 40s gab shirts, 50s capris, 60s minis; for men and women. Range $1-800. AE, CB, DC, MC, V. OPEN Mon-Sat 10:30am-midnight; Sun noon-9pm.

Best of Everything
307 East 77 Street. 734-2492. Good variety of antique clothes, jewelry and accessories. A selection of Victorian and wicker furniture too. Will layaway. Annoyance: no price tags on the clothing. OPEN 7 days.

Bogie's Antique Furs & Clothing
201 East 10 Street. 260-1199. The uptown shops buy here on Tues at noon. The rest of the time, the rest of the world needs patience and diligence to find quite incredible vintage buys culled mainly from clothes literally piled floor to ceiling. Be prepared to clean, press and possibly mend.

Brascomb & Schwab
148 Second Avenue nr East 9 St. 777-5363. Also, 247 East 10 Street. 254-3168. One of the city's best-selected and best-priced collections of 20s, 30s, and 40s mint-condition clothing for women and men. Customers include rock star Prince and English actress Maggie Smith. The weekly window display is a visual-seasonal-fashion treat and temptation. AE, MC, V. OPEN 7 days.

Canal Jean Company
304 Canal Street nr Broadway. 431-8439; 504

Broadway nr Spring St. 431-4765. A supermarket of cheap chic from underwear to actionwear to eveningwear. A fun place. AE, DC, MC, V. *OPEN 7 days.*

Cheap Jack's Antique Clothes
167 First Avenue nr East 10 St. 473-9599. Also, 841 Broadway nr East 14 St. Full to the rafters with 30s, 40s, 50s and 60s vintage clothes for women and men. Coats, suits, jackets, dresses. Wide range of quality and price. Good updates include the cashmere jackets—from old coats for men and women. Some imaginative current youth trends concocted on-premises, including hand-painted tees and jackets by East Village artist Michael Roman. MC, V. Personal checks. *OPEN 7 days.*

Cherchez
864 Lexington Avenue nr East 65 St. 737-8215. A very personal shop full of fragrant potpourri and exquisite antique clothes for women and children. From 19th-century Chinese silk robes to Victoriana. A treat. AE, MC, V.

Diane Love
851 Madison Avenue nr East 71 St. 879-6997. A very special selection of expensive vintage Japanese kimonos, scarves, fabric, silk flowers and accessories for the home. MC, V.

Double Image
305 East 9 Street. 533-8736. Stylish and interesting mix of vintage and contemporary clothing for women. Fabulous accessories, jewelry too. No credit cards. *OPEN Tues-Sun.*

East East
230 East 80 Street. 861-3692. Exquisite collection of antique kimonos, Ikat bags and shawls and decorative objects from the Orient: silks, robes, embroideries, decorative accents. Lovely. AE, MC, V.

East Side Story
227 East 59 Street. 888-6310. Uptown store for "downtown" fashions. Beaded sweaters, tweed coats, pleated pants, fatigues, gab shirts. AE, MC, V. *OPEN 7 days.*

Ellen O'Neill's Supply Store
242 East 77 Street. 879-7330. Genuine old-fashioned general store is a delight. Some clothes, 1800s-1920s antique bed and kitchen linens, old buttons, bows, ribbons, and lace for the creative. Discoveries abound. Fast turnover. No credit cards.

F.D.R. Drive
109 Thompson Street nr Spring St. 966-4827. A handsome stock of dresses, blouses, accessories, jewelry, Victorian–40s. The whites and 20s beaded dresses are outstanding. So too are the 40s and 50s men's collarless shirts (many never worn). AE, MC, V. *OPEN 7 days.*

Harriet Love
412 West Broadway nr Spring St. 966-2280. One of the prettiest and best vintage-clothes and accessory shops. All mint condition, 1920-1950, moderate to very expensive. MC, V. *OPEN Tues-Sun.*

Jean Hoffman-Jana Starr Antiques
236 East 80 Street. 861-8256. Antique clothing

and beautiful vintage table and bed linens, plus jewelry, furniture and collectibles. All obviously gathered with care. Rental of period props. MC, V.

Joia
1151 Second Avenue nr East 60 St. 754-9017. Lovely Deco shop with large selection of 20s, 30s, & 40s clothes at not-bad (for the location) prices. AE, MC, V.

Liza's Place
32 Thompson Street nr Prince St. 966-1662. Aficionados will appreciate the quality and range—if not the prices. The 1880s-1940s are represented. *Exquisite* beaded dresses. High-priced accessories, too. No credit cards. *OPEN 7 days 11am-8:30pm.*

Love Saves the Day
119 Second Avenue at East 7 St. 228-3802. An entire shop dressed like Cyndi Lauper! Much funk from the 50s and 60s. Best older stuff hangs from the ceiling. Windows look like a traffic jam. MC, V. *OPEN Mon-Thurs noon-9pm; Fri & Sat till midnight; Sun 2-8pm.*

Marlene
185 East 79 Street. 737-7671. An extremely fine selection of clothes from the Victorian era through the 40s. Accessories, jewelry, bibelots; some linens and quilts. Stratospheric prices. AE, MC, V.

New Republic
15 Greene Street nr Canal St. 219-3005. A mixture of good-condition antique clothing and one of a kind new designs. AE, MC, V. *OPEN 7 days noon-7pm.*

Opal White
131 Thompson Street nr Prince St. 677-8215. A *perfect* collection of very fine antique clothing and accessories for women. A treat for lovers of the fine fabrics and styles of the past. Moderate to expensive. AE only. *OPEN Tues-Sun from noon.*

Panache
525 Hudson Street nr West 10 St. 242-5115. Good quality, well-organized, well-priced selection of antique clothing for men and women. AE, MC, V. *OPEN 7 days noon-7pm.*

Pentimenti
126 Prince Street nr Wooster St. 226-4354. Longtime SoHo source for pretty vintage clothes in a tight setting. You must ask for the prices. *OPEN Tues-Sun.*

Random Harvest
60 West 75 Street. 799-0134. Specializes in Victorian whites and 20s dresses; also, 30s and 40s day dresses; lace, iron beds, antique quilts and linens. AE only. *OPEN 7 days noon-7pm.*

Reminiscence
74 Fifth Avenue nr 13 St. 243-2292. Very busy big-business operation. From frilly prom dresses to colorfully dyed military surplus; a pioneer in street chic. Follows fashion trends, manufactures updates of old favorites for men and women. Best: the Hawaiian shirts, linen jackets and pleated trousers for both sexes. MC, V. *OPEN 7 days.*

Richard Utilla
112 Christopher Street nr Bleecker St. For the nostalgic man or woman: 1930s-50s clothing, including socks, shoes and hats, 98% of which has

never been used! In an authentic albeit depressing setting. AE, DC, MC, V. *OPEN 7 days.*

Smitty's
184 West 4 Street. 929-6892. Village vintage—40s through early 60s. Hats and jewelry, too. Good value for some good looks. MC, V. *OPEN 7 days.*

Trash & Vaudeville
4 St. Marks Place nr Third Ave, upstairs. 982-3590; also, 170 Spring Street. 226-0590. Large eclectic East Village shop with some 40s dresses (upstairs) but mainly inexpensive knockoffs of New Wave fashions. Downstairs 50s and 60s alternative fashions—lots of black leather, spandex, and leopard spots. Inexpensive. MC, V. *OPEN 7 days.*

Victoria Falls
147 Spring Street nr West Broadway. 226-5099. Beautiful mint Victoriana and modern interpretations. Twenties beaded dresses and chinoiserie. Expensive. AE, DC, MC, V. *OPEN 7 days.*

Zoot
734 Broadway at Waverly Pl. 505-5411. Add this to your list of Lower Broadway stops (on your way to I. Buss, Unique and the Antique Boutique). Vintage and Next Wave fashions from this former wholesaler, who decided to eliminate the middle man and sell direct to *you*. On 2 levels, good selection and prices for women and men. AE, DC, CB, MC, V. *OPEN 7 days.*

Furs
New York's wholesale, and to some extent retail, fur district is centered around Seventh Avenue and West 30 Street. On weekdays the area bustles with activity as merchandise is carted or carried through the streets.

Antonovich
333 Seventh Avenue nr West 28 St, 2nd fl. 244-5875. New York's largest fur factory and showroom for savings up to 50%. Thousands of furs for both men and women. AE, CB, DC, MC, V. *OPEN Sun-Fri.*

Bergdorf Goodman
754 Fifth Avenue at 58 St, 2nd fl. 753-7300. The colorful, offbeat Fendi furs, among others. AE, Bergdorf and Neiman-Marcus charge.

Fur & Sport by Albert Gompertz
333 Seventh Avenue nr West 28 St, 6th fl. 594-8873. Manufacturer of contemporary furs for men and women, with all the services of a fine retail shop. Storage, cleaning, repairs. AE, MC, V. *Mon-Sat by appointment.*

Fred the Furrier
581 Fifth Avenue nr 47 St. 765-3877. Yes, there is a "Fred the furrier," the man who brought furs within the reach of "Carole" and "Susan," the working woman. He offers some of the lowest prices in town for furs from 60 manufacturers in 30 countries. Incredible variety and value, watch for monthly sales. AE, MC, V. *OPEN 7 days.*

Hy Fisherman's Fur Fantastic
305 Seventh Avenue nr West 27 St, 6th fl. 244-4948. Fashionable furs direct from this designer-manufacturer at huge savings. Thousands of coats, sizes 3-18 in stock. AE, DC, MC, V. *OPEN 7 days. CLOSED Sun in summer.*

Maximillian Fur Company
20 West 57 Street, 3rd fl, 247-1388. Also at Bonwit Teller. Famed as New York's most expensive and prestigious furrier.

Revillon Fur Salon
Saks Fifth Avenue, 611 Fifth Avenue at 50 St, 5th fl. 753-4000. The ultimate luxury furs, be it a sable parka or a skunk trench coat. Casual styling, costly pricing. Good Feb sales. AE, Saks charge.

—Resale Furs

Mem'ries
34½ St. Marks Place nr Second Ave. 673-9640. "Antique" furs from the 30s, 40s, 50s. Silver fox, red fox, mink, mouton, more. Buy with knowledge and care. AE, MC, V.

New Yorker
822 Third Avenue nr East 50 St. 355-5090. Since 1935. Buy, sell, or trade new and used furs. Remodeling, cleaning, glazing. Knowledgeable, helpful. AE, CB, DC, MC, V.

Ritz Thrift Shop
107 West 57 Street. 265-4559. Respected source for good used furs at affordable prices. Everything has been cleaned and glazed, and there are free alterations. Men's furs too. AE, MC, V.

Gloves
The department stores have the largest and best selections of gloves. Alexander's is a good source for inexpensive imported leather gloves.

Handbags
The department stores have large selections of handbags in all price ranges. Bloomingdale's and Saks have excellent handbag sales. Alexander's has a good range of lower-priced yet stylish leather bags, many of which are designer copies. See also Specialty Shops & Services, Leather Goods.

Artbag
See Handbag Repairs.

Barbara Shaum
13 East 7 Street. 473-8132. Longtime East Village craftswoman turns out elegant, fashionable and very affordable handbags; sandals, too. No credit cards. *OPEN Wed-Sat. 1-7pm.*

Bottega Veneta
635 Madison Avenue nr East 59 St. 371-5511; Also, at Bergdorf Goodman. Fine Italian leather bags and shoes and accessories, "when your own initials are enough." AE, MC, V.

Cachet
1159 Second Avenue at East 61 St. 753-1650. Current handbag styles for day, for evening; belts and scarves too. AE, MC, V.

The Coach Store
754 Madison Avenue nr East 65 St. 594-1581. The familiar American-classic Coach-brand leather bags and belts. AE, MC, V.

Fine & Klein
119 Orchard Street nr Delancey St. 674-6720. Lower East Side institution for expensive, well-known day and evening bags at great discounts.

They will often special-order what you want. Sunday is madness, try for a weekday. No credit cards. *OPEN Sun-Fri.*

Gucci
685 Fifth Avenue at 54 St. 826-2600. The famed signature *G*s on a wide variety of handbags and accessories. Luggage, jewelry, scarves and gifts too. AE, DC, MC, V.

La Bagagerie
727 Madison Avenue nr East 64 St. 758-6570. Every color, style and fabric of fashion bags. AE, MC, V.

Lederer
613 Madison Avenue nr East 58 St. 355-5515. Long-established shop for fashionable leather handbags, accessories and luggage from France and Italy. Expensive. AE, MC, V.

Louis Vuitton
51 East 57 Street. 371-6111. Also at Saks Fifth Avenue, entrance 11 East 49 Street. 753-4000. Leather and luggage maker since 1896. The ultimate albeit overexposed status "LV" initials on well-made bags, belts, accessories and luggage. New line for the secure—no LVs! AE.

Madler Park Avenue
450 Park Avenue at East 57 St. 688-5045. Large selection of very expensive handbags from Germany and Italy. AE, CB, DC, MC, V.

Robins Bags
141 Orchard Street nr Rivington St. 475-9280. Pleasant Lower East Side shop for first-quality name-brand handbags, including better Italian imports at ⅓ off. No credit cards. *OPEN Sun-Fri.*

Suarez
67 East 56 Street. 759-9443. Longtime source for fine bags, wide selection at *very* good prices.

Tony Bryant Design
339 Lafayette Street nr Bleecker St. 254-5743. Smart selection of handcrafted leather and canvas bags. Vibrant colors, original designs. Sandals and accessories too. AE, MC, V. *OPEN 7 days.*

—Handbag Repairs

Art Bag
735 Madison Avenue nr East 64 St. 744-2720. Expert, albeit expensive, handbag repairers. Also finely crafted low-priced copies of expensive bags.

Leather

Design Studio
216 Third Avenue nr East 18 St. 254-8880. Very good prices on custom-made leather fashions: skirts, jackets, trousers; fine alterations, as well. AE, MC, V.

Hermès
11 East 57 Street. 751-3181. Spacious shop for the leather and silk luxuries synonymous with the 146-year-old saddlery. In addition to the saddles, there's sportclothes for men and women, perfume, and the famed equestrian-theme scarves and of course, the legendary kelly bag. AE, DC, MC, V.

Loewe
126 East 56 Street. 308-7700. Exquisitely-crafted and luxurious ladies' and men's leather clothing, shoes, handbags, luggage and accessories from this leading Spanish firm. AE, DC, MC, V.

Manuel Herrero
Herald Center, 1 Herald Square at West 34 St. 868-3317. The Madrid designer's all-season leathers apparel and accessories. AE, DC, MC, V. *OPEN 7 days.*

North Beach Leather
772 Madison Avenue at East 66 St. 772-0707. For men and women: eye-catching, distinctively styled, buttery soft, leather and suede clothing and accessories for all seasons. AE, MC, V.

San Michel
396 Fifth Avenue at 37 St, 2nd fl. 736-2000. Suede and sheepskin coats, leather and leather-trimmed fashions. Jackets and accessories, leather blazers, vests and pants. Manufacturer, so prices are low. Layaway. AE, MC, V. *OPEN 7 days.*

Tannery West
*South Street Seaport Marketplace. 608-1310. Also, Trump Plaza, 725 Fifth Avenue, 319-5112. *Herald Center, 1 Herald Square at West 34 St. 760-9010. A glamorous collection of year-round suedes and leathers in high styles and hot colors; for men and women. AE, CB, DC, MC, V. *OPEN 7 days.*

—Leather Cleaning

Leathercraft Process
62 West 37 Street. 586-3737. Since 1938, specialists in cleaning shearlings, sheepskins, suede and leather garments. MC, V.

Lingerie & Nightwear
The department stores have lovely lingerie departments now that pretty underthings have made a comeback. Bloomingdale's, Altman's, Bergdorf Goodman and Macy's Private Lives are standouts.
See also Vintage Clothing, *for antique undies.*

A. W. Kaufman
73 Orchard Street nr Grand St. 226-1629. Carries every major designer's lingerie, loungewear and sleepwear at big discounts. AE, MC, V. *OPEN Sun-Fri.*

Enelra Lingerie & Cosmetics
48½ East 7 Street. 473-2454. A first for this Ukrainian neighborhood (which has seen almost everything)—high-price, high-style, sexy and sensuous European and American lingerie. Also, silk tees and boxer shorts for men! *OPEN Mon & Wed 1-9pm; Thurs & Fri till 11pm; Sat till 8pm; Sun till 7pm.*

Goldman & Cohen
54 Orchard Street nr Hester St. 966-0737. Brand-name and designer lingerie, loungewear and swimsuits at 20-70% below usual retail prices. MC. *OPEN Sun-Fri.*

L'Affaire
226 Third Avenue nr East 19 St. 254-1922. Fanci-

ful undies and nighties from France, England, Italy and Switzerland, in luxurious styles and fabrics. AE, MC, V. *OPEN 7 days.*

La Lingerie
792 Madison Avenue nr East 67 St. 772-9797. Also, Trump Tower, 725 Fifth Avenue at 56 St. 980-8811. Sheer indulgences fit for a princess and requiring a dowry. Luxurious silk, lace, satin, much from Italy and France, exquisite hand-embroidery. Silk stockings. Trousseau-oriented (there's a registry). AE, MC, V.

La Petite Coquette
52 University Place nr East 10 St. 473-2478. Charming little Greenwich Village shop for luxurious cotton and fine-silk designer lingerie from around the world. AE, MC, V. *OPEN Mon-Sat noon-7pm.*

Lee Baumann Specialty Shop
38 East 8 Street. 473-3548. This well-stocked neighborhood Village shop has all the latest in lingerie from the routine to the risqué. AE, CB, MC, V.

Mendel Weiss, Inc.
91 Orchard Street at Broome St. 925-6815. Famous-name brands at 25% off. MC, V. *OPEN Sun-Fri.*

Montenapoleone
789 Madison Avenue at East 67 St. 535-2660. Very expensive and luxuriously seductive Italian lingerie, including pure silk. Custom orders as well. Now, swimsuits, too. AE, MC, V. *CLOSED Sat in July & Aug.*

Roberta
1252 Madison Avenue nr East 90 St. 860-8366. Exquisite lingerie in a wide price range. Silk pantyhose! MC, V.

Rosenthal
92 Orchard Street nr Delancey St. 473-5428. In business for 35 years, this pleasant Lower East Side shop sells high-style John Kloss, Dior, Pucci, and Vassarette lingerie at 25-50% off. Carries over 50 brands of bras. No try-ons. MC, V. *OPEN Sun-Fri.*

Ultima
18 East 53 Street. 688-8273. Famous-name, very pretty and feminine French and Italian underthings. AE, MC, V.

Wife/Mistress
1042 Lexington Avenue nr East 74 St. 570-9529. The name speaks volumes. Sensual underthings for either or both. Lounge and leisurewear, too.

Mastectomy Boutiques
Regenesis
18 East 53 Street, 14th fl. 593-2782. A mastectomy boutique; bras and a full line of swimsuits. *OPEN Tues-Sat.*

Maternity Wear
All the large stores have maternity departments.
Jonal
17 East 67 Street. 628-5820. Custom-made, well-designed maternity clothes in sumptuous fabrics. MC, V.

Lady Madonna
793 Madison Avenue at East 67 St. 988-7173; 107-12 71 Road nr Queens Boulevard, Forest Hills, Queens (1-718) 544-3432. The pioneer in the well-dressed-though-pregnant idea. Everything everyone else wears for the mother-to-be. Tasteful, yet imaginative. AE, MC, V.

Mothers Work NY
50 West 57 Street, 4th fl. 399-9840. Dress-for-success-though-pregnant. Business-like maternity wear. Wonderful idea! MC, V. *Thurs till 7:30pm.*

Reborn Maternity
1449 Third Avenue at East 82 St. 737-8817. Everything a pregnant woman might want to wear, including Sasson maternity jeans, at discount prices. Catalog available. AE, MC, V. *OPEN 7 days.*

Raincoats
All the major department stores have a wide selection of raincoats.
(*See also* Men's Clothes: Rainwear.)

Shoes & Boots
Anbar's
93 Reade Street nr Church St. 227-0253. Discontinued styles from the large stores can be found at this downtown discount shoe house. Name brands include Charles Jourdan, Margaret Jerrold, Garrolini, Andrew Geller, Allure, Beverly Feldman, Miguel Hernandez at 20-30% off retail.

Bally of Switzerland
689 Madison Avenue nr East 62 St. 751-2163. The famed import for women. Also, Magli, Pancaldi, Adriano Fosi and Figli. AE, DC, MC, V.

Botticelli
612 Fifth Avenue nr 50 St. 582-6313. Also, 416 Columbus Avenue at West 80 St. 496-2222. Fine, handmade Italian women's shoes and boots. Luggage and accessories. AE, MC, V.

Carrano
677 Fifth Avenue at 53 St. 752-6111; 750 Madison Avenue nr East 65 St. 570-9020; also Trump Tower. Moderate to expensive high-fashion Italian shoes, boots and handbags. AE, CB, DC, MC, V.

Chandlers
695 Fifth Avenue nr 54 St. 688-2140. Reasonably priced shoes in fashionable styles. MC, V.

Charles Jourdan
Trump Tower, 725 Fifth Avenue at 56 St. 541-8440; 769 Madison Avenue nr East 66 St. 628-0133; also at Macy's. A fashion pace-setter. Fabulous French imports, accessories, women's apparel, too, at Trump Tower. AE, DC, MC, V.

Ferragamo
717 Fifth Avenue at 56 St. 759-3822. Top-quality fashionable shoes from Florence for men and women. No heel higher than 3½ inches. Clothes and accessories too. AE, DC, MC.

Fiorentina Shoes
482 Park Avenue nr East 58 St. 838-9098. Understated and expensive shoes and boots. AE, MC, V.

Giordano's
1118 First Avenue nr East 61 St. 688-7195. Spe-

cializes in ladies shoe sizes 6½-3½B; 6½-5½AA *only*. Ann Klein, Andrew Geller, YSL, Julianelli, L'Idea, Petra, Mignani, Liz Claiborne. AE, MC, V.

Grand Street Bootery
65 Orchard Street nr Grand St. Inter shoe, Caressa, Freye, Timberland, Capezio, 20-30% off. MC, V. *OPEN Sun-Fri.*

Hélène Arpels
470 Park Avenue nr East 57 St. 755-1623. Wives of Presidents have bought their flats here. AE, MC, V.

I. Miller Shoes
734 Fifth Avenue at 57 St. 581-0062. Casual and elegant designer shoes. Well known for quality and style. David Evins, Ann Klein, Halston, Ferragamo. AE, CB, DC, MC, V.

Lace-Up Shoe Shop
110 Orchard Street at Delancey St. 475-8040. Top name fashionable designer shoes and boots well discounted. Joan & David, Liz Claiborne, Evan Picone, Jourdan. MC, V. *OPEN Sun-Fri.*

La Marca
43 East 57 Street. 759-8588. Exquisite, expensive avant-garde Italian footwear. AE, MC, V.

Le Shu
421 East 65 Street. 580-4601. The latest styles in shoes for women, direct from the factory in Spain which means savings. Sizes 5-10, AA, B, and C widths. AE, DC,. MC, V.

Leslie's Bootery & Designer Shoes
36 Orchard Street nr Canal St. 431-9196. High-fashion imports, including Jacques Cohen, Bally, Joan & David, at discount prices. MC, V. *OPEN Sun-Fri.*

Manolo Blahnik
15 West 55 Street. 582-3007. Innovative pricey shoe fashions straight from London's Chelsea. AE, MC, V.

Mario Valentino
5 East 57 Street. 486-0322. Via Milano. An elegant shoe store for women and men. AE, DC, MC, V.

Maud Frizon
49 East 57 Street. 980-1460. Very expensive, imaginative, beautifully detailed creations. Special orders in special cases. Men's and a new collection of costly children's shoes too. AE, MC, V.

Monique
47 West 8 Street. 260-1830; 811 Madison Avenue nr East 68 St. 535-9553. Stylish Italian imported shoes and boots. Medium priced. AE, DC, MC, V.

New Store for Shoes
293 Seventh Avenue nr West 26 St. 255-1070. Off-price designer footwear. *OPEN 7 days.*

Perry Ellis
680 Madison Avenue nr East 61 St. 980-7012. Small shop for the designer's fashion conscious footwear for women only. Moderately expensive. AE, MC, V.

S & T
1405 Second Avenue nr East 73 St. 861-9470; 1043 Lexington Avenue nr East 75 St. 988-0722. Good discounts on famous-name shoes and boots, including Rosina Farragamo, Hanna Mackler, B. Mez. Kids shoes, too. AE, DC, MC, V.

Santini e Domenici
697 Madison Avenue nr East 62 St. 838-1835. Also, at Macy's. Energetic, youthful and modern shop offering great looking Italian shoes and boots at affordable prices. Limited but near perfect selections; for men, too. Range $25-200 and best of all the window display, uniquely positioned, is fully priced. AE, MC, V.

Shoecraft
603 Fifth Avenue nr 48 St. 755-5871. Tall gals' headquarters for sizes 10-13. MC, V.

Shoe Steal
116 Duane Street nr Church St. 964-4017. Dress and sport shoes, sandals and boots at a discount of 40-60%. Sizes 5-10. AAA-E widths. Naturalizer, Caressa, Bandolino, Nickels, Beene Bag. *OPEN Mon-Fri.*

Susan Bennis/Warren Edwards
440 Park Avenue at East 56 St. 755-4197. Beautifully designed, unusual, extravagant and appropriately expensive ($250-1,250) shoes and boots for women and men. Luggage and clothes, too. AE, MC, V.

Tree-mark
27 West 35 Street. 594-0720. New York's largest selection of wide-calf boots. AE, DC, MC, V.

Vigevano
969 Third Avenue at East 58 St. 755-9090. Truly vast selection of superior Italian footwear. Custom services, too. For women and men. Good sales. AE, DC, ·MC, V.

Village Cobbler
60 West 8 Street. 673-8530. Small shop with a huge stock of all the very latest fashions in casual and high-fashion shoes and boots. Lower prices than uptown. CB, DC, MC, V. *OPEN 7 days.*

Vittorio Ricci
645 Madison Avenue nr East 60 St. 688-9044. Feminine, exclusive, expensive. Belts and bags. Men's shoes, too. AE, DC, MC, V.

Walter Steiger
739 Madison Avenue at East 65 St. 570-1212. Elegant, unusual and (of course) expensive shoes for women and men. The patterned fabric shoes are very fine. AE, MC, V.

Wendy's Footwear
46 West 39 Street. 391-2926; 123 Nassau Street nr Beekman St. 285-2120. Osvaldo, Bandolino, Boutique Marco, Unisa, Hanna Mackler, at discount. Good seasonal sales as well. AE, MC, V.

Swimsuits
The department stores have year-round swim and cruisewear departments as well as swimwear in the lingerie department.

Unusual Sizes
Saks Fifth Avenue has a petite shop and a "12 plus" shop; Bloomingdale's, Gimbels and Bergdorf all have large-size departments.

Ashanti
872 Lexington Avenue at East 65 St. 535-0740. High-quality stylish elegance in large (12-26) sizes. More individual than most for the larger woman. Natural handwoven and hand-dyed fab-

rics, imports; jewelry and accessories. AE, DC, MC, V. *Thurs till 8pm.*

Brief Encounter
1594 Second Avenue nr East 83 St. 628-2663. Specializes in contemporary women's clothing in sizes 4-12. MC, V.

Forgotten Woman
880 Lexington Avenue at East 66 St. 535-8848. Fashionable clothes for the large woman, sizes 14-24. Day or evening dresses, sportswear, sweaters, swimsuits. AE, MC, V.

Greater N.Y. Woman
215 East 23 Street. 725-0505. For day and evening, sizes 14-24. AE, DC, MC, V.

Lane Bryant
465 Fifth Avenue at 40 St. 532-0200. Sizes 16½-24½. AE, MC, V. Lane Bryant charge.

Le Piccoli
877-1633. For the petite and small-boned woman, 5'4" and under, sophisticated, innovative designs. Emphasis on separates. Custom orders filled. *By appointment only.*

Minishop Boutique
38 West 56 Street, 2nd fl. 247-0697. Carries the largest stock of size 0-6 sportswear in the country. A wide variety of dresses, suits, slacks, coats and jackets. Free alterations. AE, MC, V.

Piaffe
830 & 841 Madison Avenue at East 69 St. 744-9911. Sophisticated European and American clothes, including lingerie for the very thin, sizes 2-6 and the true petite, 5'2" or under, sizes 2-10. Free alterations. AE, DC, MC, V. *OPEN 7 days.*

Shelley's Tall Girl Shop
13 East 41 Street. 697-8433. Contemporary dresses and sportswear for tall gals 5'7"-6'4", sizes 7-22. Belts, bags, jewelry, too. MC, V.

Smart Size
20 West 39 Street. 398-0580; 111 East Fordham Road nr Morris Ave, Bronx. 367-5404. Discounts on overstock first-quality or irregulars from Lane Bryant. Complete wardrobe in women's sizes 38-52, 16½-32½; for tall gals sizes 12-20. Shoes, hats, accessories and an excellent lingerie selection. MC, V. *OPEN 7 days.*

Men's Clothes

Large Stores
(*See also* Department Stores.)

Barney's
Seventh Avenue & West 17 St. 929-9000. The world's largest men's store (60,000 suits, 600 employees!) and a men's fashion institution. Excellent range for men of every taste, size, and lifestyle. Hats to shoes; toiletries too. But there are no bargains here—except at the once-a-year big sale that gets the most jaded New Yorker to stand in line. Free alterations, delivery, parking. AE, MC, Barney's charge. *OPEN Mon-Fri 10am-9pm; Sat till 8pm.*

Boutiques

André Oliver
34 East 57 Street. 758-2233. Only natural fabrics beautifully styled. The colorful cashmere sweaters are classics. Expensive. AE, DC, MC, V.

A. Peter Pushbottom
1157 Second Avenue nr East 61 St. 879-2600. Updated classic sweaters only of cotton and Shetland. Also, cashmere, worsted. Excellent value. Pushbottom for kids, too. AE, MC, V.

Arbiter
830 Lexington Avenue nr East 63 St. 371-5641. Excellent shop for distinctive European clothing. Moderate to expensive. AE, DC, MC, V.

Battaglia
473 Park Avenue nr East 57 St. 755-1358. Superb quality Italian clothing, shoes and accessories. AE, DC, MC, V.

Bellocchio Uomo
827 Madison Avenue at East 69 St. 472-1112. Superlative collection of elegant, expensive Italian men's fashions and accessories. AE.

Bijan
699 Fifth Avenue nr 54 St. 758-7500. Straight to you from Rodeo Drive in Beverly Hills *if* you have extravagant taste and a bank roll to match, not to mention *an appointment.*. Shirts start at $240; ties $110!

Blue & White Men's Shop
50 East 58 Street. 421-8424. A small elegant shop with expensive, unusual European imports. AE, CB, DC, MC, V.

Bobby Dazzler
1450 Second Avenue nr East 76 St. 628-2287. Men's forward fashions from Milan, Paris and London. Casual, stylish clothes. Lovely collection of cotton shirts. AE, DC, MC, V.

Camouflage
141 Eighth Avenue at West 17 St. 741-9118, 929-7237. Top Chelsea specialty shop for expensive American-made sportswear with an upbeat, imaginative feel. Perry Ellis, Alexander Julian, Jeffrey Banks. For women, too. AE, MC, V.

Charivari for Men
2339 Broadway at West 85 St. 873-7242; also at 18 West 57 St. European and American *now* fashions for men, including Giorgio Armani, Gianni Versace, Perry Ellis Ferre and Kenzo. Well-stocked, well-run. AE, MC, V.

Clothes to Boot
256 Columbus Avenue at West 72 St. 877-7572; Also, Bergdorf Goodman. New York and Texas merge. Traditional sportswear for men, and, of course, Western gear, including Stetsons. AE, MC, V. *OPEN 7 days.*

Copperfield
220 East 60 Street. 371-1584. Good selection of classic fabrics, Italian styling in jackets, suits, sweaters and shirts. AE, DC, MC, V.

Daniel Hechter
625 Madison Avenue nr East 58 St. 223-3950. Spacious shop for the French designer's sophisticated yet easy-going and well-tailored sportswear for men and women. Everything of his is here:

accessories (street level); children's wear, home furnishings, bath linens and stationery (lower level). AE, MC, V.

DeNoyer, Inc.
219 East 60 Street. 838-8680. Fine, expensive European boutique. Excellent quality and service. Women's, too. AE, DC, MC, V.

Ferragamo Uomo
730 Fifth Avenue nr 57 St. 246-6211. Two floors of high quality Florentine ready-to-wear for men. Wonderful fabrics. AE, MC, V. *Thurs till 7pm.*

Frank Stella
440 Columbus Avenue nr West 81 St. 877-5566. Super men's fashions. Silk shirts in solids and stripes; 100% cotton too. Sweaters, hundreds of ties, accessories, too. AE, MC, V. *OPEN 7 days.*

Giorgio Armani
815 Madison Avenue nr East 68 St. 988-9191. Armani's tailoring perfection for men and women.

High Gear
133 Eighth Avenue nr West 16 St. 243-1747. American-designed, active-sportswear-inspired fashions. AE, MC, V.

Koos in SoHo
72 Thompson Street nr Spring St. 219-2645. Unconstructed yet elegant men's clothing in sizes small, medium and large from Koos Van den Akker. They work for women, too. AE, DC, V. *OPEN Tues-Sun noon-7pm.*

Madonna
223 East 60 Street. 832-0268. Exclusive European trendsetter. Large swimwear collection. AE, DC, MC, V.

Mano A Mano
421 West Broadway nr Prince St. 925-6066. Large, elegant SoHo boutique for casual and dress clothes by European designers. *OPEN 7 days.*

Napoleon
Trump Tower, 725 Fifth Avenue at 56 St. 759-1110; 1048 Third Avenue nr East 62 St. 688-3156. *Very* expensive, stylish European tailoring. Suits, sports jackets; fine shirts and ties. AE, DC, MC, V.

N.Y. Jock
220 Tenth Avenue nr West 22 St. 924-7942. Also, 164 Christopher nr West St. 206-0707. Gymnasium décor (shower-stall changing rooms!) for *very* active sportswear. AE, MC, V. *OPEN 7 days.*

New York Man
13 Christopher Street at Gay St. 255-2809. High-tech fittings—"hot men's clothes." For those unafraid to wear fuschia, purple and red. AE, MC, V. *OPEN 7 days.*

Saint Laurent Rive Gauche for Men
543 Madison Avenue at East 55 St. 371-7912. High-priced high fashion. AE, DC, MC, V.

Steve
97 Wooster Street nr Prince St. 925-0585. One of the city's best men's boutiques (some things for women) for moderate to expensive, very stylish, mostly sporty clothes. AE, MC, V. *OPEN 7 days.*

Stewart Ross/Stone Free
754 Madison Avenue nr East 65 St. 744-3870; 105 West 72 Street. 362-9620; 150 Spring Street

nr West Broadway. 966-1024. Excellent shops for a pulled-together, now look. Subtle styles and colors. Handknits a specialty. AE, MC, V.

Ted Lapidus
1010 Third Avenue at East 60 St. 751-7251. Luxurious fabrics and impeccable design. One of the best, albeit *very* expensive. AE, CB, DC, MC, V.

Custom Tailoring
See also Shirts: Custom.

A. Sulka
711 Fifth Avenue at 55 St. 980-5200. Also, at the Waldorf Astoria. Custom-made shirts, silk pajamas, and the like. Rich tastes and pockets. Off-the-peg range also. AE, DC, MC, V.

Chipp
14 East 44 Street. 687-0850. Custom tailoring, including riding clothes. High-quality, bespoke suits, plus ready-to-wear. Very expensive. AE, MC, V.

Dunhill Tailors
65 East 57 Street. 355-0050. Tailoring perfection. Both custom and ready-to-wear. Very expensive. AE, MC, V.

Discount

BFO and BFO Plus
149 Fifth Avenue nr 21 St, 2nd & 6th fls. 254-0059, -0060. Prices below wholesale for jackets, suits, coats, raincoats, trousers. From 36 regular to 48 extra large, YSL, Cerutti, Ralph Lauren, Cardin. AE, MC, V. *OPEN 7 days.*

Dollar Bills
99 East 42 Street. 867-0212. Well-located, nicely stocked, well-priced menswear. AE, MC, V.

Eisenberg & Eisenberg
149 Fifth Avenue at 21 St, 11th fl. 674-0300. Men's clothing direct from the manufacturer at discount prices. MC, V. *OPEN 7 days.*

Gorsart
9 Murray Street nr Broadway, 2nd fl. 962-0024. Classic traditional "natural shoulder" clothing. No frills, low prices, free alterations. MC, V.

Harry Rothman
111 Fifth Avenue nr 18 St. 777-7400. Since 1926, a wide range of style and size. Discounted quality suits and sport coats: 25-50% savings. MC, V.

Hertling & Pollack
85 Fifth Avenue nr 16 St. 243-2420. Wide range of famous-maker fashion clothing at direct-from-the-on-premises-factory prices. AE, MC, V.

L & S Men's Clothing
23 West 45 Street, 2nd fl. 575-0933. Natural shoulder and designer-styled suits, sportscoats, outerwear and slacks, 45-65% off retail. AE, MC, V. *OPEN Sun-Fri. (CLOSES early Fri).*

Merns Mart
*525 Madison Avenue nr East 54 St. 371-9175. Also, 75 Church Street nr World Trade Center. 227-5471. Large selection of French, English and American suits, sportswear, accessories and shoes. Discounted up to 50%. Women's also. MC, V. *Thurs till 8pm.*

Moe Ginsburg
162 Fifth Avenue at 21 St, 7th fl. 242-3482. De-

signer clothing at less than you would pay at fine department stores. Large selection. MC, V. *OPEN 7 days.*

NBO
1965 Broadway at West 67 St. 595-1550. European and American designer clothes up to 65% off list. This classy discount store has everything (except shoes) for the well-dressed man. AE, MC, V. *OPEN Mon-Sat 10am-9pm; Sun 11am-6pm.*

Saint Laurie, Ltd.
897 Broadway at East 20 St. 242-2530. Specialty: well-tailored business suits (for men and women) in fine fabrics. Discounted. Now located in the old Lord & Taylor building; the ground floor remembers Ladies' Mile, what Fifth Avenue was once called. AE, DC, MC, V. *OPEN 7 days.*

Syms
45 Park Place nr Church St. 791-1199. Three floors of well-discounted (30-50%) men's apparel from shoes and socks to hats and coats. Specialty: shirts (original retail-price tags on). Women's wear as well. Note: under age 18 not admitted without an adult.

Furs

(*See also* Women's Clothes: Furs.)

Brother's II
333 Seventh Avenue nr West 28 St; 3rd fl. 695-8469. A large selection of furs for men. AE, MC, V. *OPEN 7 days.*

Hats

JJ Hat Center, Inc.
1276 Broadway at West 33 St. 244-8860. Large Stetson hat collection. AE, MC, V.

Van Dyke Hatters
848 Avenue of the Americas nr West 29 St. 683-6266. Wide variety, including Borsalino, Stetson and their own brand, plus cleaning and blocking. DC, MC, V.

Worth & Worth Ltd.
331 Madison Avenue at East 43 St. 867-6058. The complete hatter for men (women, too): fedoras by Borsalino, Cavanagh, Stetson, Christy's of London. Caps and walking hats in cashmere, shetland, viyella and Harris tweed. AE, MC, V.

Leather

(*See also* Women's Clothes: Leather.)

Bridge Merchandise Corporation
74 Orchard Street nr Grand St. 674-6320. Large selection of leatherwear substantially discounted. AE, MC, V. *OPEN Sun-Fri.*

Leather Man
111 Christopher Street nr Bleecker St. 243-5339. Custom-designed black leather jackets, pants, vests, tees, briefs too. Moderately expensive. AE, CB, DC, MC, V. *OPEN Tues & Wed till 7pm; Thurs-Sat till 11pm. CLOSED Sun & Mon.*

Lee Shop
43 Greenwich Avenue nr Charles St. 989-7215. Moderately expensive lightweight leather jackets and vests all handmade in U.S. Footwear, accessories, jewelry. All for men and women. AE, DC, MC, V. *OPEN 7 days.*

—Leather Outerwear

David Muller
1168 First Avenue at East 64 St. 737-3443. Sheepskin and wool quality fashions for men and women imported from Great Britain. AE, MC, V.

Ice Age Fashions
555 Eighth Avenue at West 38 St, 4th fl. 695-7382. Everything for a cold winter's day. Well-priced shearling coats, hats and gloves for men and women at this factory outlet. MC, V.

Rainwear

Aquascutum
680 Fifth Avenue at 54 St. 975-0250. English clothing firm famed for its trench coats and the luxurious tailoring of its cashmere coats for men and women. Sweaters, blouses, too. AE, DC, MC, V. *Thurs till 7pm.*

British American House
488 Madison Avenue nr East 51 St. 752-5880. Specializes in English rainwear, overcoats, Burberry and Aquascutum labels. AE, MC, V.

Burberry's
9 East 57 Street. 371-5010. The famed raincoats as well as men's wear and women's country clothes. Five floors to sell the English look. AE, DC, MC, V.

Charlie's Place
61 Orchard Street nr Grand St. 431-8880. Large selection of discounted rainwear, outerwear, too. London Fog, Aquascutum, Misty Harbor. Name-brand shirts and slacks also. MC, V. *OPEN Sun-Fri.*

Rentals

Herman's
1190 Avenue of the Americas nr West 46 St. 245-2277. Latest styles: After Six, Adolfo. Same-day service. AE, CB, DC, MC, V.

Hollywood Legend
112 Fulton Street nr Nassau St, 2nd fl. 349-1561. Interesting alternative: buy a set of vintage evening clothes. AE, MC, V.

Lordae Formal Wear
597-5100. Eighteen branches in Manhattan, Bronx, Queens. Call for nearest one.

Zeller Tuxedos
201 East 56 Street, 2nd fl. 355-0707. Traditional to trendy formalwear. Formal accessories, too. Alterations, delivery. AE, MC, V. *Thurs & Fri till 8pm.*

Secondhand & Surplus

(*See also* Women's Clothes: Boutiques, Vintage.)

Academy
1703 Broadway at West 54 St. 765-1440. Clutterful. Never-been-worn vintage men's wear. Special orders, free alterations. Women's too. (Call first.) AE, MC, V.

Avirex
627 Broadway nr Houston St, 7th fl. 420-1600. Loft space for nylon or leather sheepskin-lined air force jackets, flight jumpsuits; authentic aviator sunglasses, accessories, military insignias. MC, V. *OPEN Mon-Fri 11am-4pm; Sat call first.*

Brascomb & Schwab
247 East 10 Street. 254-3168. Go East, young

man, for great fashion flashbacks in a calm setting: pleated front trousers, gab and Pendleton shirts, raglan-sleeved tweed overcoats, Harris tweed sports jackets and more. Clothes for her, too. AE, MC, V. OPEN 7 days.

Broadway Army-Navy
2576 Broadway nr West 97 St. 662-2626. Military fashions: sailor blouses. field jackets. paratrooper jumpsuits. MC, V.

Chameleon
270 Bleecker Street at Charles St. 924-8574. Specialty of this vintage emporium: military and aviator leather jackets; other good oldies sometimes. Stiff staff for where and what they purvey. MC, V. OPEN 7 days noon-8pm.

Church Street Surplus
327 Church Street nr Canal St. 226-5280. Army, navy and civilian surplus clothing fill the store and the overflowing bins on the street. Dusty bargains.

Good Old Days
351 Bleecker Street nr West 10 St. 242-0554. Inexpensive vintage clothes of the 40s & 50s. Good sweaters, gab and Hawaiian shirts. AE, CB, DC, MC, V. OPEN 7 days.

Hollywood Legend
178 Spring Street nr West Broadway. 925-5799. Thirties, 40s, 50s, 60s suits, coats, shoes and hats. AE, MC, V. OPEN Tues-Sun.

I. Buss & Company
738 Broadway nr Astor Pl. 242-3338. Great long-time source for European and American army surplus: leather jackets, sweaters, pea jackets and British greatcoats. AE, MC, V.

Reminiscence
75 Fifth Avenue nr 13 St. 243-2292. Best here for men, the modern translations of vintage vests, pleated trousers, Hawaiian and silk collarless shirts. MC, V. OPEN 7 days.

Unique Clothing Warehouse
718 Broadway at Washington Pl. 674-1767. Don't miss this one—its street-chic headquarters. War surplus, new and renewed: athletic wear, industrial uniforms, colorfully dyed duds. Good prices. MC, V. OPEN 7 days.

Weiss & Mahoney
142 Fifth Avenue at 19 St. 675-1915. An army/navy surplus-clothing shop from the pre-cheap chic era (1924). Good buys. AE, MC, V.

Shirts

Addison on Madison
698 Madison Avenue nr East 62 St. 308-2660. Also, Trump Tower, 725 Fifth Avenue at 56 St. 752-2300. Small shop sells shirts only (pure cotton, French made).

Bancroft Haberdashers
363 Madison Avenue nr East 45 St. 687-8650. Branches. Largest selection of ready-to-wear men's shirts and neckwear in New York. AE, CB, DC, MC, V.

Lew Magram
830 Seventh Avenue nr West 53 St. 586-4828. Ready-to-wear shirts, suits and sportswear. AE, CB, DC, MC, V.

Turnbull & Asser
Bergdorf Goodman, 754 Fifth Avenue at 58 St.

753-7300. London's legendary haberdasher. Bergdorf, Neiman-Marcus charge.

Victory Shirt Company
345 Madison Avenue at East 44 St. 687-6375; 96 Orchard Street nr Delancey St. 677-2020; 10 Maiden Lane nr Broadway. 349-7111. These 100% cotton and permanent-press shirts that sell under department stores' private labels. Here they are 25% less costly. AE, DC, MC, V. OPEN Sun-Fri.

—Shirts: Custom

(See also Custom Tailoring.)

Chris-Arto Custom Shirt Company, Inc.
39 West 32 Street. 563-4455. Choose from nearly 500 natural fabrics. Six-shirt minimum order. Four-week delivery.

Custom Shop
555 Lexington Avenue nr East 50 St. 759-7480; 716 Fifth Avenue nr East 56 St. 582-4366. Branches. Custom-made shirts at no extra charge (minimum of 4). Six-week delivery. Choose from over 300 cotton and cotton-blend fabrics. Ready-to-wear as well. AE, DC, MC, V.

Duhamell, Inc.
944 Madison Avenue nr East 74 St. 737-1525. Fine imported cotton and silks only. Six-shirt minimum. Expensive. Three-week delivery. Custom suits and fine leather clothing also. MC, V.

Pec & Company
45 West 57 Street. 755-0758. Shirts made from a selection of fine cottons and silks or from your own material. Minimum, 3 shirts. Delivery up to 8 weeks.

Shoes & Boots

(See also Western Wear.)

Bally of Switzerland
645 Madison Avenue nr East 59 St. 832-7267; 22 East 43 Street. 986-0872; 553 Seventh Avenue at West 39 St. 279-7259. Stylish, high-quality shoes imported from Switzerland, Italy and France. AE, DC, MC, V.

Benedetti Custom Shoes, Inc.
530 Seventh Avenue nr West 39 St. 221-9830. Expensive men's footwear, including special made-to-orders. AE, CB, DC, MC, V.

Bloom's Shoe Gallery
311 Sixth Avenue nr West 3 St. 243-8749. After 85 years this well-known shop is a Greenwich Village institution. Rugged shoes, boots, sandals and moccasins for men and women. DC, MC, V. OPEN 7 days.

Botticelli
666 Fifth Avenue nr 53 St. 582-2984. Fine expensive Italian shoes in elegant surroundings. AE, DC, MC, V.

Carina Nucci Uomo
1071 Third Avenue nr East 63 St. 888-1033. High-style Italian shoes and boots. AE, DC, MC, V.

Church's English Shoes
428 Madison Avenue nr East 49 St. 755-4313. Classic fine-quality English shoes, good sales. AE, CB, DC, MC, V.

Del Pino, Ltd.
1871 Broadway nr West 61 St. 757-6853. De-

signer shoes and Western boots at impressive savings. AE, CB, DC, MC, V.

Eliot
1597 Second Avenue nr East 83 St. 628-3922. Imported Italian shoes. AE, CB, DC, MC, V.

Gucci
689 Fifth Avenue at 54 St. 826-2600. The statusy shoes for men and women; fashions and accessories too. AE, DC, MC, V.

Lord John Bootery
428 Third Avenue nr East 30 St. 532-2579. This store runs a wide fashion gamut of discounted shoes and boots. MC, V.

McCreedy & Schreiber
47 & 55 West 46 Street. 582-1552; *213 East 59 Street. 759-9241. One of the best selections of boots (including Lucchese) and shoes for casual and dress wear in this excellent emporium. AE, DC, MC, V. *OPEN Sun.

Nino Gabriele
1022 Third Avenue nr East 60 St. Also, 169 East 60 Street. 421-3250. For high-priced, luxurious, au courrant men's shoes. AE, DC, MC, V. Mon & Thurs till 9pm.

St. Marks Leather Company, Ltd.
17 St. Marks Place nr Third Ave. 982-3444; 1490 First Avenue nr East 78 St. 628-1727. Terrific selection of trendy footwear. Boots and shoes by Dan Post, Frye, Tony Lama, Acme. Discounts on all boots. Handmade sandals. MC, V.

To Boot
256 Columbus Avenue at West 72 St. 724-8249. The Western boots have been joined by casual, business and formal footwear for men. English, Italian and American; high quality. AE, DC, MC, V. OPEN Mon-Fri noon-8pm; Sat 11am-7pm; Sun 1-6pm.

Sports Clothes & Shoes

Abercrombie & Fitch
South Street Seaport, 199 Water Street at Fulton St. 809-9000. The sporting goods specialist—established in 1892—returns to NY. For serious sports gear and wear for the man (or woman) who has it all. The famed safari jackets, pith helmets; the huge expensive stuffed animals are still here. Clothes by Jeff Banks, Alan Flusser and Polo, too. AE, DC, MC, V. OPEN 7 days.

Ar-Bee Men's Wear, Inc.
1598-1601 Second Avenue at East 83 St. 737-4661. Inexpensive outdoor clothes and equipment for active people. MC, V.

Athlete's Foot
16 West 57 Street. 586-1936; 739 Third Avenue nr East 46 St. 697-7870; *34 East 8 Street. 260-0750. Other branches. Incredible selection of moderately priced athletic shoes. AE, MC, V. *OPEN 7 days.

Athletic Attic
1170 Third Avenue at East 68 St. 249-2133; *464 Sixth Avenue nr West 11 St. 255-5890. Well stocked with running gear primarily. Knowledgeable staff. MC, V. *OPEN 7 days.

Ben's Clothes Shop
1149 Second Avenue nr East 60 St. 753-4792. Good-value jeans and other dress-down items and accessories. AE, MC, V.

Billy Martin's Western Wear
812 Madison Avenue at East 68 St. 988-3622. Unique custom-made shirts, jackets, hats, boots, buckles, and belts. AE, DC, MC, V.

The Gap
354 Sixth Avenue at Washington Pl. 777-2420; 145 East 42 Street. 286-9490; 734 Lexington Avenue nr East 58 St. 751-1543; 1535 Third Avenue nr East 86 St. 427-2155; 22 West 34 Street. 695-2521; *545 Madison Avenue nr East 55 St. 421-7610; 113 East 23 Street. 533-6670; 2109 Broadway nr West 73 St. 787-6698. The Levi's jean store (other brands, too) now emphasizes youthful, color-coordinated, moderately priced casual sportswear; "sweats" are now center stage. MC, V. *OPEN 7 days.

Herman's
110 Nassau Street. 233-0733; 845 Third Avenue nr East 51 St. 688-4603; *39 West 34 Street. 279-8900; 135 West 42 Street. 730-7400. Huge selection of athletic shoes, clothes and equipment. Good sales. AE, DC, MC, V. *OPEN 7 days.

Hudson's Camping Supplies
105 Third Avenue at East 13 St. 475-9568. Great outdoor-clothing store, its NY's oldest. Huge selection, very popular. MC, V.

Kreeger & Sons
16 West 46 Street. 575-7825. Also, 150 West 72 Street. 799-6200. Well-known outfitters for the outdoors. For both men and women. AE, MC, V.

Modell's
243 West 42 Street. 962-6200. Branches. Bargain store for casual clothes; jeans, workshirts and shoes. MC, V.

The Playing Field
Herald Center, 1 Herald Square at West 34 St., 5th fl. 244-3200. For the avid sports fan: authentic pro jerseys, satin sports jackets and embroidered caps. Sportswear of the major teams including a complete line for infants and toddlers. MC, AE, DC. OPEN 7 days.

Robbins Men's-Boys' Wear
1265 Broadway nr West 32 St. 684-5429; 1717 Broadway nr West 55 St. 581-7033; 146 East 14 Street. 260-0456. Other branches. Real buys on active clothes, much that's fashionable, some name brands. Patience!

Wrangler Wranch
2150 Broadway nr West 76 St. 873-9645; *9 West 8 Street. 228-0890; 1074 Third Avenue nr East 63 St. 371-0838. Mostly American—some French—jeans, shirts and Western-style accessories. MC, V. OPEN 7 days.

Ties

Allen Street between Delancey & Houston Streets on the Lower East Side has 9 necktie stores featuring nice, low-priced ties.

Countess Mara
110 East 57 Street. 751-5322. Well known for expensive ties ($25-$5,000). Casual shirts, too. AE, DC, MC, V.

Tie City
591 Lexington Avenue. 421-5327. Choose from 10,000 different ties. MC, V.

Wind-Schaper
39 East 46 Street. 355-1260. Specialty: high-quality, low-priced neckwear. AE, MC, V.

World Trade Center Tie Company
118 Liberty Street nr Greenwich St. 964-9742. Good value and selection. MC, V. *OPEN Mon-Fri 7:45am-4:30pm.*

—Tie cleaning

Tiecrafters
116 East 27 Street, 4th fl. 867-7676. Ties only. Will remove even the most difficult stains. *CLOSED Sat & Sun.*

Traditional Clothing

Alexander Shields
198 East 58 Street. 832-1616. Men's clothing designed by Mr. Shields. Expensive. AE, DC, MC, V.

Brooks Brothers
346 Madison Avenue nr East 44 St. 682-8800; 1 Liberty Plaza nr Wall St. 682-8595. The consummate classic men's store—America's oldest—established 1818. Moderate to expensive. AE, DC, Brooks charge.

Burton
475 Fifth Avenue nr 41 St, 2nd fl. 685-3760. Well-made, well-priced traditional styling in suits, shirts, jackets, coats, robes and shoes. MC, V.

F. R. Tripler & Company
366 Madison Avenue at East 46 St. 922-1090. Long-established store for fine quality men's apparel and shoes. Largest selection of Hickey-Freeman in US. Custom suits and shirts, too. Women's department. AE, MC, V, Tripler Charge.

H. Herzfeld, Inc.
509 Madison Avenue nr East 53 St. 753-6756. High-quality traditional clothing in fine fabrics. AE, MC, V.

Jaeger
818 Madison Avenue nr East 69 St. 628-3350; 19 East 57 Street. 753-0370. The classics beautifully made. AE, DC, MC, V.

J. Press
16 East 44 Street. 687-7642. For 78 years quintessential Ivy League clothes. Ready-to-wear and bespoke. AE, MC, V.

Paul Stuart
Madison Avenue at East 45 St. 682-0320. British tweedy image. Natural fabrics, custom-made shirts. Expensive. AE, DC, MC, V, Paul Stuart charge. *OPENS at 8am, Mon-Fri* for before work shopping.

Wallach's
555 Fifth Avenue nr 46 St. 687-0106. Branches. Famous-label suits (the largest selection of Hart Schaffner & Marx in the world), imported sportswear, free alterations. Moderate to expensive. AE, DC, MC, V, Wallach's charge.

Underwear

Under Wares
1098 Third Avenue nr East St. 535-6006. Solely devoted to men's underwear. Custom made and hand-painted briefs and boxers. Note: 80% of their customers are women.

Unusual Sizes

Imperial Wear
48 West 48 Street. 541-8220. Large selection of quality clothing and accessories for the big or tall man including Lauren, Givenchy, Cardin, Dior and Adolf. Free alterations. AE, DC, MC, V. *Thurs till 8pm.*

London Majesty
1211 Sixth Avenue at West 48 St. 221-1860. Expensive European and English fashions for men of royal—read, very large—proportions. Also over 6'3" tall. Free alterations. AE, DC, MC, V. *Thurs till 8pm.*

Beauty

Beauty Specialists
Many of the following have half- and whole-day beauty packages available. Call for details.

Anushka
241 East 60 Street. 355-6404. Every aspect of beauty and body care, including diet, cellulite treatments, body sluffs, acupressure facial, shiatsu massage. MC, V.

Christine Valmy
767 Fifth Avenue at 58 St. 752-0303; 153 West 57 Street. 581-9488; 107-27 71 Avenue, Forrest Hills, Queens. (1-718) 793-0222. Skin-care expert. Uses Swiss fresh-cell therapy. Two-hour facials for men and women. Special post-plastic surgery care; makeup and foot massage, too. At the Valmy school for aestheticians, lower-priced facials done by supervised students, are available 4 times a day, Mon-Fri; call 581-1520 for an appointment. AE, DC, MC, V. (except at school).

Diane Young
243 East 60 Street. 753-1200. Holistic skin care: treatments, herbal aromatherapy facials, expert nutritional advice, evaluations by a professional dermatologist.

Elizabeth Arden
691 Fifth Avenue nr 54 St. 486-7900. Behind the red door, a Manhattan mini-spa for head-to-toenail pampering. Appointment necessary for a Miracle Morning or a Maine Chance Day. AE, MC, V.

Elisabeth Unger Skin Care
20 East 69 Street. 772-6422. Anti-wrinkle treatment as well as facials, body treatments and pedicures. Call for appointment.

Georgette Klinger Skin Care
501 Madison Avenue nr East 52 St. 838-3200. Expert skin treatment including surface peeling, deep-pore cleansing and scalp care for men and women. New "intensive curriculum" at 978 Madison. AE, MC, V.

Ilona of Hungary Institute of Skin Care
629 Park Avenue nr East 65 St. 288-5155. Well-trained estheticians give facials, body skin treatments. Climate-keyed products.

Janet Sartin
480 Park Avenue at East 58 St. 751-5858. Consultation and product/treatment prescription. A stellar social clientele.

Judith Lontosh
20 East 68 Street, Suite 214. 988-8364. European facials, peeling, waxing, makeup and eyelash tinting. *OPEN Mon-Fri.*

Mario Badescu Skin Care, Inc.
320 East 52 Street. 759-8485. Expert analysis and skin care. His methods and products have a loyal following. MC, V. *OPEN Tues-Sat.*

Moi Cosmetology, Ltd.
38 East 63 Street. 752-4447. Expert skin treatments, facials, waxing. Nail specialist as well. Mon is reserved for men.

Orlane Institut de Beauté
Bloomingdales mezzanine, 1000 Third Avenue at East 59 St. 705-2828. Facials, cleansing, exfoliating, purifying masks. The latest products from France.

Richard Stein Beauty Services
768 Madison Avenue nr East 65 St. 879-3663. Expert hair care plus customized herbal facials; massage. Aromatherapy products to alleviate skin problems, stress and fatigue.

Stephanie of Vienna
326 East 86 Street. 737-2616. Cellulite body treatments, as well as facials. *OPEN Tues-Sat.*

Fragrance
Major department stores carry a full line of fragrances for both men and women on their main floor. (See also Pharmacies*).*

The Bath House
215 Thompson Street nr Bleecker St. 533-0690. Custom blending of scents—bath oils, bubble bath and body lotion. Specializes in hair and skin products with natural ingredients. AE, MC, V ($15 minimum). *OPEN 7 days noon-8pm.*

Caswell-Massey Co., Ltd.
518 Lexington Avenue nr East 48 St. 755-2254. In business since 1752! This is the oldest apothecary in the US. The cologne, specially blended for George and Martha Washington and Lafayette, the cold cream made for Sarah Bernhardt, and the world's largest collection of imported soaps are for sale in this pretty and fragrant shop. *Now also at the Seaport Marketplace, 608-5401. AE, CB, DC, MC, V. *OPEN 7 days.*

Crabtree & Evelyn
30 East 67 Street. 734-1108. Also, *1310 Madison Avenue nr East 92 St. 289-3923, and at *Citicorp. England's famed all-natural toiletries and comestibles—beautifully presented and packed. AE, MC, V. *OPEN 7 days.*

Giorgio
47 East 57 Street. 319-5660. A fragrance and a phenomenon—direct from Rodeo Drive at $150 an ounce and selling like crazy. Lavish gifts. AE, CB, DC, MC, V.

Jean Laporte Perfumers
870 Madison Avenue nr East 70 St. Enchanting scents; enchanting shop. AE, MC, V.

Penhaligon's
Bergdorf Goodman, 745 Fifth Avenue at 58 St. 753-7300. The famed English toilet water, shampoo and bath oils. Lovely accessories. Bergdorf charge.

Soap Opera
*51 Grove Street nr Christopher St. 929-7756; Also, 30 Rockefeller Plaza, lower concourse. 245-5090. More than 200 varieties of soap: bath oil and bubble baths; potpourri. AE, MC, V. *OPEN 7 days noon-7pm.*

Hair
—Hairdressers for Men & Women

Act II Haircutters
117 East 60 Street, upstairs. 838-5320. Low-priced haircuts for men and women. Many locations. No appointment necessary.

Astor Place Barber Stylist
2 Astor Place nr Broadway. 475-9854. Success story: 1940s family-owned barber shop finds new life as the "in" place to have your tresses trimmed—that is if you're young and/or adventuresome. Choose the Guido, Detroit, Little Tony, Punk, Mohawk, James Dean, Fort Dix, Sparkle Cut, What-the-Hell, Spike, Spina di Pesce, or. . . . Cheap but expect a wait of up to 2 hours. The street scene is interesting in and of itself. P.S. They still give shaves. *OPEN Mon-Sat 8am-8pm; Sun 9am-6pm.*

Clive Summers, Inc.
Olympic Tower, 645 Fifth Avenue at 51 St, 2nd fl. 751-7501. Elegant high-quality full-service salon for both men and women. Custom designed conditioning for individual problems. MC, V.

Configero
245 East 60 Street, 2nd fl. 688-3894. Haircuts to suit your facial structure. *OPEN Tues-Sat.*

Davian
833 Madison Avenue nr East 69 St. 535-1563. Easy-to-care-for "now" hairstyles. Full-service salon.

Bruno Dessange
760 Madison Avenue nr East 66 St, 2nd fl. 517-9660. Well-regarded French stylist renowned for his hair cutting skills. Clips to suit *your* face—highly individual.

Hair Power
27 St. Marks Place nr Second Ave. 982-6300. For East Village-creative cuts and colors. *OPEN 7 days till 10pm.*

Industrial Hair
124 Second Avenue nr East 7 St. 228-6808. In the East Village, stylist Diane Ries' creative high-tech, no-nonsense salon for creative—yes—avant-garde *now* hair. Don't let the whip (on the ceiling) scare you. *OPEN Tues-Sat.*

Julius Caruso
72 East 55 Street. 759-7574. Wash-and-wear cuts for all types and lengths of hair styled to suit one's life style. AE, MC, V.

Kenneth
19 East 54 Street. 752-1800. The lovely townhouse salon of the famed hair stylist, a favorite of Jackie O. Appointment necessary well in advance for haircut only by the master himself. Complete makeover days available. *OPEN Mon-Fri.*

La Coupe
694 Madison Avenue nr East 62 St. 371-9230. Many models (and their mentor Eileen Ford) take

their tresses to this dynamic savvy salon. Expert colorist; facials, manicures, waxing, too. Boon for the working woman: *OPENS at 7am!*

Larry Mathews
536 Madison Avenue nr East 54 St, upstairs. 246-6100. Reasonably priced salon special for its hours—very early to late. MC, V. *OPEN Mon-Sat 7am-10pm; Sun 9am-5pm.*

Le Salon
16 West 57 Street. 581-2760. Easy-to-maintain natural looks dominate.

Louis Guy D.
41 East 57 Street. 753-6077. Expert staff to deal with both curly and straight hair. Superior coloring.

Michel Kazan
16 East 55 Street. 688-1400. Hair cut to fit one's lifestyle. Longtime full-service salon including electrolysis and eyelash tints. AE, MC, V.

Nardi Salon
143 East 57 Street. 421-4810. Top haircutting salon in a brownstone. Gives free haircutting lessons Tues & Wed eves.

Onstage Hairstylists
127 East 60 Street, 2nd fl. 753-7722. Wash, cut, and blow-dry for one low price. Men and women.

Pierre Michel
Trump Tower, Fifth Avenue & 56 St. 593-1460. Longtime specialist in treatment and styling of long hair. Full-service salon for men and women.

Private World of Leslie Blanchard
19 East 62 Street. 421-4564. Hair-coloring expert, consultant to Clairol. Results are natural, and the *price* is right. Consultations Tues-Thurs. MC, V.

Raymond & Nasser
747 Madison Avenue nr East 64 St. 737-7330. Experts in wash-and-wear haircuts. Full-service salon dedicated to educated beauty. Will dispatch staff to home or office. Also, massage, makeup, henna body treatment.

Robert Renn
260 West Broadway nr Canal St. 966-4335. The inventor of color highlighting, shading and weaving.

Rose Reti
673 Madison Avenue nr East 61 St. 355-3152. Long-time coloring specialist. Blondes in the know go here.

Suga
115 East 57 Street. 421-4400. New York's best—the top salon for easy-to-keep classic hairstyles. *OPEN Wed till 8pm.*

Vidal Sassoon
GM Plaza, 767 Fifth Avenue at 59 St. 535-9200. The man who liberated hair, 32 stylists, popular, good service spot for men and women. AE, V.

—Hair Removal

Alise Spiwak
20 East 68 Street. 535-6878. Waxing here or at your place. *By appointment.*

Allana of New York
160 East 56 Street. 980-0216. Electrolysis salon very highly recommended.

Edith Imre
8 West 56 Street. 247-4022. Longtime waxing specialist, plus a full line of other services.

Individually Yours
14 East 60 Street, Room 509. 593-2240. America's largest waxing salon. Full body waxing, electrolysis, too. Pedicures, manicures, facials available.

Lucy Peters
150 East 58 Street. 486-9740. Also, 95-20 63rd Road, Rego Park, Queens. Relatively painless, no scarring, permanent.

—Hair Treatment

Philip Kingsley
Damaged hair revitalized by *the* expert in hair and scalp care. Consultation and treatment. Candice Bergen sings his praises.

Makeup

Each of the department stores devotes most of its main floor to cosmetics. All of the major names are represented, and often there are sample demonstrations and promotional gifts available.

Barone
414 West Broadway nr Prince St. 431-9460. Whimsical boutique for avant-garde cosmetics and accessories. AE, MC, V. *OPEN 7 days 11:30-7:30pm.*

Beauty Checkers, Inc.
At Henri Bendel, 10 West 57 Street, 4th fl. 247-1100. Step-by-step lessons in how to use makeup—your own or theirs—to achieve a natural look. AE, MC, V. *By appointment. Thurs till 8pm.*

Boyd Chemists
655 Madison Avenue nr East 60 St. 838-6558. Dazzling array of European makeup and treatment products, their own line as well. Experts in residence give beauty advice, makeup demonstrations, lessons and encouragement. A mecca for the beautiful people and those who aspire to be. Private consultation by appointment. AE, CB, DC, MC, V. *CLOSED Sat in summer.*

Cosmetics Plus
518 Fifth Avenue nr 43 St. 221-6560; 275 Seventh Avenue nr West 26 St. 924-3493. Largest selection of cosmetics and fragrances in the city, at discount.

Favia Cosmetics
832 Lexington Avenue nr East 63 St. 751-1505. Fragrance-free cosmetics and skin-care products. AE, MC, V.

G-Method
Patricia Field, 10 East 8 Street. 254-1699. Raw materials for the avant-garde look—practical nonsmudge liners; metallic eyeshadow pastes; day-glo nail polishes.

Il Makiage
107 East 60 Street. 371-3992. Upper East Side trendsetter. Over 200 eye and cheek colors, updated seasonally. Makeover programs from an elementary eye primer to a full makeup consultation. *OPEN 7 days.*

"I" Natural Cosmetics
737 Madison Avenue nr East 64 St. 734-0664. Cosmetics, treatment preparations, and perfumes made of only natural things. Makeup styl-

ing, consultation and lessons. Manicures, too. AE, MC, V. *OPEN 7 days.*

Makeup Center, Ltd.
150 West 55 Street. 977-9494. A professional does your face and answers all your questions along the way. Learn techniques of contouring and shading, all for a reasonable fee. Great makeup selection; custom blending if you can't find your shade.

Merle Norman Cosmetic Studio
640 Lexington Avenue nr East 54 St. 752-7985. Make an appointment for a free makeup consultation and lesson. AE, DC, MC, V.

Paint
175 Bleecker Street nr MacDougal St. 420-0557. Low-priced cosmetics and beauty tools. Makeup application free with minimum purchase. *OPEN Mon-Thurs noon-midnight; Fri and Sat till 1am.*

Stan Place
877-7045. The makeup director of the Miss Universe Pageant can make a beauty out of you. Soft makeup techniques; available *by appointment.*

Nail Care

(*See also* Beauty Specialists *and* Hair, Hairdressers for Men & Women.)

Ame
29 East 61 Street, 2nd fl. 371-1266. Specialty: paper nail wrapping to impede breakage. Pedicures too.

Irene
47 East 77 Street, 2nd fl. 861-7314. The expert whose services include manicure, pedicure, nail wrapping, facials, eyebrow shaping and leg waxing. All done with a smile. *OPEN Mon-Thurs.*

Nail House
134 East 60 Street, 2nd fl. 838-7844. Nail problems solved. Wrapping done.

Nina's Pattinail Salon
178 East 70 Street. 249-7995; 650-1696. Full manicuring services including paper wrapping, pedicures.

Sculpt-Nail
1174 Second Avenue nr East 61 St. 759-1165. Will create a new set of nails for you.

Ursula
16 East 79 Street. 744-5992. Specialty: healing unhealthy nails. All natural products—no acrylics.

Food

Appetizing Stores
Very special New York institutions originating on the Lower East Side at the turn of the century, when the pushcarts became stores that carried the staple foods the Middle European Jewish residents craved. Yesteryears' version of a gourmet shop; some are still going strong.

Russ & Daughters
179 East Houston Street nr Orchard St. 475-4880. Grandfather Russ started it in 1909, and the 3rd generation carries on. Appetite-teasing aromas from the many barrels (in bygone days they were outside) filled with herrings and sour pickles. The

lox, smoked cod, carp, whitefish and lake sturgeon are all traditional; the Nova Scotia and Scotch salmon, modern additions. A nostalgic and taste treat, the best of the genre, due in part to its locale. *OPEN Mon-Fri 9am-6:30pm; Sat & Sun 8am-6:30pm.*
The following represent three more fine examples of the tradition:

Barney Greengrass
541 Amsterdam Avenue nr West 86 St. 724-4707. Take out or eat in. Over 50 years on the Upper West side. Tops for the double-smoked Nova; herring cured and pickled on premises. *OPEN Tues-Sat 8:30am-5:45pm; Sun 8am-4:30pm.*

Murray's Sturgeon Shop
2429 Broadway nr West 89 St. 724-2650. *OPEN Tues-Fri & Sun 8am-7pm; Sat till 8pm. CLOSES Sun at 2pm, July-Aug.*

Schacht
99 Second Avenue nr East 6 St. 475-1232. Great for its selection, its friendly atmosphere and its hours—great for late-night noshing. AE, DC, MC, V. *OPEN Mon-Fri and Sun 8am-11:30pm; Sat till 1:30am.*

Baked Goods: Breads, Cakes, Cookies, & Rolls

Betsy's Place
236 West 26 Street. 691-5775. Betsy's loaf, cookies, and brownies are very special. Giftwrapping and mailing service. Café for light lunch, pastries, cappuccino. MC, V.

Black Forest
177 First Avenue at East 11 St. 254-8181. Wonderful European confections. The rum truffle and Black Forest cakes are delicious.

Bonté Patisserie
1316 Third Avenue nr East 75 St. 535-2360. Delicious French pastries. Seasonal specialties.

Colette
1136 Third Avenue nr East 66 St. 988-2605. Croissants, quiches, brioches, plus petit fours, chocolate cakes and fresh fruit tarts. *OPEN Tues & Sat.*

Creative Cakes
400 East 74 Street. 794-9811. A "portrait-likeness" cake (chocolate only) of a person, pet, house, car, or anything else that you can think of. Expensive but delicious, as well as fabulously creative. *OPEN Tues-Sat.*

David's Cookie Kitchen
1098 Second Avenue nr East 54 St. 888-1610. Also at Macy's and *everywhere* else. Made with Lindt chocolate, they are the tops for many. In danger of over-exposure. *OPEN 7 days.*

Dumas Patisserie
1042 Madison Avenue nr East 88 St. 744-4804. Excellent French patisserie. Great croissants.

Encore & Encore II
141 Second Avenue nr East 9 St. 505-1188; 952 Lexington Avenue nr East 69 St. 628-1377. Buttery Parisian pastries baked on the Second Ave premises. Served in many fine restaurants. Lovely fruit mousses.

Erotic Baker
73 West 83 Street. 362-7557; 246 East 51 Street.

752-9790; 117 Christopher Street nr Hudson St. 989-8846. X-rated baked goodies, good for a giggle. Custom orders. MC, V. *OPEN Tues-Sun.*

Just Desserts
443 East 75 Street. 535-4964. Small, homey blue-and-white store filled with cakes and pastries. Watch the cakes come out of the oven. *OPEN Tues-Sun.*

Kramer's
1643 Second Avenue nr East 86 St. 535-5955. There are those who travel uptown *just* for their butter and chocolate cookies, not to mention the fruit pies.

La Boulange
712 Third Avenue nr East 45 St. 949-7454. A French bakery plus. Old-fashioned breads (made with natural yeast), delicious croissants, brioches, pastries. Quiches, soups, salads, gratins and other French-accented daily deli specials. They deliver and cater breakfast, cold lunches and teas.

Les Delices Guy Pascal
1231 Madison Avenue at East 89 St. 289-5300; 939 First Avenue nr East 51 St. 371-4144. Lemon tarts, mocha butter cream cake and fudge roulade—yum. Also, for lunch, simple pâtés, salads, sandwiches.

Miss Grimble
305 Columbus Avenue nr West 74 St. 362-5531. Most connoisseurs' favorite cheesecake; have here or take home. *OPEN Tues-Sun.*

Mr. Philip's Pastry Box
12 Park Avenue nr East 35 St. 686-4331. Specialty of the house: rich and dark black velvet mousse cake. Orders for special occasion cakes. *OPEN 7 days.*

Moishe's Homemade Kosher Bakery
181 East Houston Street nr Orchard St. 475-9624; 115 Second Avenue nr East 7 St. 505-8555. One of the oldest and finest Jewish bakeries and newer branch. Very special cornbread, egg challah, homemade bagels (Some call them the only authentic ones in the city) and ruggelah. *OPEN Sun-Fri (closes early on Fri).*

Ninth St. Bakery
350 East 9 Street. 777-0667. An eccentric little place for lovers of Russian black, sourdough pumpernickel, raisin challah and cheese babka. *OPEN 7 days.*

Orwasher
308 East 78 Street. 288-6569. Since 1916, baking done on premises in hearth oven. Specializes in Hungarian potato bread, Vienna twists. The originators of raisin pumpernickel and marble bread. Over 35 varities of bread and rolls. Cheeses, coffees, teas, too.

Patisserie Lanciani
271 West 4 Street nr Perry St. 929-0739. Also, 177 Prince Street nr Thompson St. 477-2788. Beautiful baked goods (great sacher torte). To take out or eat in the café. AE. *OPEN Tues-Fri 8am-11pm; Fri & Sat till midnight; Sun till 9pm.*

Poseidon Confectionery Company
629 Ninth Avenue nr West 44 St. 757-6173. The best in Greek pastries. *OPEN Sun; CLOSED Mon.*

Sutter's
2512 Grand Concourse nr Fordham Rd, Bronx. 295-4664. French confection perfection for over 50 years. *OPEN Mon-Fri 7am-8pm; Sat & Sun 9am-6pm.*

Veniero's
342 East 11 Street. 674-7264. Well-known (since 1894) Italian sweets as tasty as they are beautiful. Cappuccino, and espresso café. *OPEN Sun-Thurs 8am-midnight; Fri & Sat till 1am.*

Vesuvio Bakery
160 Prince Street nr West Broadway. 925-8248. White, whole wheat, and seeded bread baked in the coal-fired ovens in the basement, without sugar, fat or preservatives. Just follow your nose.

Well-Bred Loaf
1612 Third Avenue nr East 90 St. 534-6951. Fabulous—*and* all natural—fudge brownies: banana nut, carrot raisin and cranberry loaf cakes; layer cakes and danish. All made with unbleached or whole-grain flours and no preservatives, additives or colorings. No credit cards.

William Greenberg, Jr., Bakery
*1100 Madison Avenue nr East 82 St. 744-0304; 1377 Third Avenue nr East 78 St. 876-2255. The best brownies, honey buns and cookies in the city. Spectacular custom-designed cakes at Third Ave store. *OPEN 7 days.*

Zito & Sons
259 Bleecker Street nr Cornelia St. 929-6139. The bestseller is the delicious whole-wheat loaf. Frank Sinatra has it delivered fresh to the Waldorf when he's in town. *OPEN 7 days.*

Candy/Chocolate
Macy's Marketplace in the Cellar has the largest—2,000 square feet—candy department in New York.

Au Chocolat
Bloomingdale's, East 59 Street entrance. 705-2953. The best of the boxed, plus loose filled confections including Godiva. AE, Bloomie's charge. *OPEN 7 days.*

Basket Shop
21 Barclay Street nr Broadway. 349-3895. Candies by the handful or pound. Extensive seasonal and holiday selection. Elegant gift baskets are their specialty. AE, MC, V. *OPEN Mon-Sat.*

Candy Kisses
58 Greenwich Avenue nr Perry St. 929-7133. Homemade, hand-dipped nut patties, cashew raisin clusters and creams. Downtown source for Godiva. *OPEN 7 days.*

Chez Chocolat
Citicorp Market, 153 East 53 Street. 935-6495. Hand-dipped fresh fruits, strawberries, banana, orange, pineapple. *OPEN 7 days.*

Chocolate Photos
200 West 57 Street, N.Y. 10019. 977-4340. (1-800) 262-0024. Twenty-four pieces of sweet or semisweet chocolate impressed with the likeness of your favorite person or your company logo. Gift boxed. After they receive the snapshot, allow 2-4 weeks. Call for specifics. AE, MC, V.

Chocolaterie Corné Toison d'Or
Trump Tower, garden level, 725 Fifth Avenue at

56 St. 308-4060. Lovely chocolate shop. Arriving on Thursday from Belgium: cocoanuggets, hazelnut pralines, sugar-glazed truffles, coffee butter creams. AE, MC, V.

Davies Candies
101-07 Jamaica Avenue, Richmond Hill, Queens. (1-718) 849-7750. Homemade and hand-dipped. Over 60 varieties, all in dark and milk chocolate. Creams, marshmallows, nut and fruit, caramels, small peppermint patties and combinations of all of the above. An old-fashioned best. Mails everywhere. *OPEN Tues-Sat 2-6pm.*

Elk Candy
240 East 86 Street. 650-1177. Specialty of this storefront: delicious homemade marzipan, flavored or chocolate-coated. *OPEN 7 days.*

Evelyn Chocolates
4 John Street nr Broadway. 267-5170. Handmade chocolate sculptures. *OPEN Mon-Fri.*

Godiva Chocolatier, Inc.
701 Fifth Avenue nr 55 St. 593-2845; 560 Lexington Avenue at East 50 St; 85 Broad Street. The famed elaborately boxed sweets. AE, MC, V.

Le Chocolatier Manon
872 Madison Avenue at East 71 St. 288-8088. Exquisite shop for exquisite caramels, marzipan, chocolate praline, truffle glacée and—yes—even more. High priced, beautifully packaged. AE, MC, V.

Li-Lac Chocolates
120 Christopher Street nr Bleecker St. 242-7374. Also, 987 Lexington Avenue nr East 71 St. 734-5219. Exquisite milk and dark chocolates. Great mint patties, fudge, peanut butter bark and extremely edible Empire State Buildings. Made on premises since 1923. AE, MC, V. *OPEN 7 days.*

Macy's Marketplace
Herald Square, The Cellar. 695-4400. A dream (or nightmare, depending upon your waistline). Every imaginable boxed chocolate plus the likes of Michel Guérard, Godiva, Neuhaus, Perugina—loose. Over 2,000 square feet of candy! AE, Macy's charge. *OPEN 7 days.*

Mondel Chocolates
2913 Broadway at West 114 St. 864-2111. For over 40 years, homemade chocolates, natural flavored—rum, orange, coffee and chocolate with a very low fat content. *OPEN on Sun close to major holidays.*

Perugina
637 Lexington Avenue at East 54 St. 688-2490. Italian chocolate *baci* and lovely gift-packaged candies. Loose at Zabar's and Macy's Cellar. AE, MC, V.

Plumbridge Confections & Gifts
30 East 67 Street. 744-6640. Beautifully packaged edibles and gifts. Since 1883, "confections for the carriage trade." AE. *CLOSED Sat in summer.*

St. Moritz
506 Madison Avenue nr East 52 St. 486-0265. The name has changed but the unique tasty Kron chocolate specialties (wooden boxed) handmade from only natural ingredients are the same. Female torsos, yard sticks, computers and golf balls—all in chocolate! Fresh fruit dipped daily. AE, MC, V.

Sweet Temptations
128 West 57 Street. 757-5318; 1070 Madison Avenue nr East 81 St. 734-6082; 414 Amsterdam Avenue nr West 79 St. 877-1402. Old-fashioned candy store re-created for buttons on paper, wax bottles, spider chocolates, Mary Janes, and nostalgia. Hand-dipped fresh and preserved fruits as well. *OPEN 7 days.*

Teuscher Chocolates of Switzerland
25 East 61 Street. 751-8482; Also, 620 Fifth Avenue at 50 St. 246-4416. The *ultimate* Swiss chocolate treats, including champagne truffles (you can buy just one). Flown in weekly. The best! AE, MC, V.

Caterers

(Also check Gourmet Shops and RESTAURANTS most of which will prepare foods for a gathering for a price.)

Breadline
22 East 13 Street. 777-3565. Full-service outside catering: specializes in lavish corporate and private parties.

Cooking for Company
101 West 12 Street. 206-8313. Imaginative buffets; all natural ingredients; special diets accommodated. Call and discuss your needs.

Donald Bruce White
159 East 64 Street. 988-8410. The establishment. Superb food and service for dinner (25 or more) or cocktail party (30 or more).

Glorious Food
172 East 75 Street. 628-2320. The hottest caterer in town right now. Known for innovative creations. Cocktails (35 or more), buffets (20 or more), dinner (16 or more). Beautiful food, beautifully presented.

Manganero Hero Boy
492 Ninth Avenue nr West 38 St. 947-7325. Heros from 2 to 6 ft long! Simple but fun way to cater your own party. The 6-footer serves 40 hungry folks. Delivered with breadboard and knife; other fixings. They require 24 hours notice.

Mr. Babbington
1454 First Avenue nr East 75 St. 737-0786. Well-known gourmet caterer extraordinaire. AE.

Modern Food
821 Second Avenue nr East 44 St. Their forte: exquisite finger food. Cocktails for 25 to 500; buffet or sit down dinner, 25 to 200.

Paplisky Caterers
305 West End Avenue nr West 74 St. 724-3761. Glatt kosher on an elegant scale for large affairs.

William Poll
1051 Lexington Avenue nr East 61 St. 288-0501. This caterer is a fine food take-out gourmet pioneer. Known for the smoked salmon, caviar, hors d'oeuvres, handmade truffles; their own aged cheeses. AE, DC.

Cheese

Macy's Cellar carries a nice selection of imported cheeses, so too Zabar's, Dean & DeLuca and Balducci; see also Gourmet Shops.

Alleva Latticini
188 Grand Street nr Mulberry St. 226-7990. Family-run cheese dairy in Little Italy (established in

1892) that specializes in mozzarella, both plain and smoked, fresh ricotta and *formaggio fresco*, a white cheese formed in baskets. Made fresh daily. Imported cheeses, too. *OPEN 7 days (Sun till 2pm only).*

Cheese of All Nations
153 Chambers Street nr West Broadway. 964-0024. Famed for its variety and stock (over 1,000) of fine cheese. Also has breads, crackers and hors d'oeuvres. Will ship anywhere. AE, MC, V.

Cheese Please
158 East 39 Street. 689-5929. Cheese, pâté, meats, breads and Italian cold cuts.

Cheese Unlimited, Inc.
1529 Second Avenue nr East 79 St. 861-1306. Over 400 varieties from all over the world. *OPEN 7 days.*

Di Palo's Dairy Store
206 Grand Street at Mott St. 226-1033. Fresh-ground Parmesan cheese and smoked mozzarella. Homemade ricotta-cheese-filled ravioli. Take a number and join the crowd, it's well worth it. *OPEN 7 days (Sun till 2pm only).*

East Village Cheese Store
239 East 9 Street. 477-2601. For a neighborhood shop the owners should be more pleasant, *but* their prices can't be beat. Weekly specials abound, so do lineups; ¼ lb. minimum purchase. *OPEN 7 days.*

Fairway
2127 Broadway nr West 75 St. 595-1888. Along with the freshest fruits and vegetables, Fairway stocks one of the best selection of cheeses in the city, including an extensive goat cheese selection. *OPEN 7 days.*

Ideal Cheese
1205 Second Avenue nr East 63 St. 688-7579. Top-rated cheese shop for imported and domestic cheeses. Over 300 varieties. Also, pâté and crème fraîche.

La Marca Cheese Shop
161 East 22 Street. 673-7920. Wide variety of cheeses cut to order; fresh-baked farmer cheese with various fruit fillings, good croissants. They will keep a file for you re purchases you've made.

Mad for Cheese
1064 First Avenue nr East 58 St. 759-8615. Fine store for cheese, pâté, quiches and breads.

Coffees
(*See* Teas & Coffee.)

Ethnic Foods: Markets & Stores
New York's markets, whether a concentration of outdoor stalls or small stores, reflect the diversity of its population and are unmatched for color, vitality, variety and friendliness.

Atlantic Avenue
Atlantic Avenue from Henry to Court Street, Brooklyn. Exotic delights of the Middle East such as Turkish coffees, Lebanese pita breads, chumus, stuffed grape leaves, halvah, baklava.

Belmont
Arthur Avenue & East 187 Street, Bronx. Large Italian area for baked goods, homemade pasta and pepperoni; pastry shops and cafes.

Bensonhurst
Eighteenth Avenue from 61 to 86 Street, Brooklyn. A thriving Italian shopping area for salamis, sausage, cheeses, prosciutto, pizza *rustica*.

Chinatown
South of Canal Street, west of the Bowery. A wealth of Chinese restaurants, tea parlors, bakeries and gift shops. Main street is Mott Street.

Indian Area
Lexington Avenue nr East 28 Street. Indian spices, condiments, sweets and saris.

La Marqueta
Park Avenue from East 110 to East 116 Street. An aromatic Latin-American market with over 250 stalls displaying colorful exotic fruits and vegetables; grains, spices, hot sauces, smoked meats and fish.

Little Athens
Ditmars Avenue from 31 to 38 Street, Astoria, Queens. The largest Greek community outside of Greece. Greek tavernas, coffee houses (raffenion), restaurants and churches bouzouki music; baklava, and thick, rich Greek coffee.

Little Italy
West of Bowery, north of Canal Street, all along Mulberry Street. Restaurants, pastry and espresso *caffès*, cheese and pasta shops, outdoor food and a fun festival yearly in Sept (*see* ANNUAL EVENTS).

Lower East Side
East Houston Street to Delancey Street. Food shops purveying the specialties that Jews from various Eastern European countries called their own. Knishes, schmaltz herring from a barrel, pastrami, corned beef, pickles and bagels share the spotlight with the discount clothing stores.

Paddy's Market
Ninth Avenue from West 37 to West 42 Street. Stores with sidewalk stands have replaced the pushcarts. Once predominantly Italian and Greek, it is now a United Nations of food. The scene of an annual food fair in May (*see* ANNUAL EVENTS).

Ukrainian & Polish Area
First Avenue at East 7 Street. For wonderful pierogi, blintzes, kielbasa, headcheese, babka and black bread. Ukrainian Fair every May (*see* ANNUAL EVENTS).

Yorkville
Lexington Avenue to York Avenue from East 72 to East 90 Street. The German area features restaurants serving home-style hearty foods and bock beer, *Konditorei* serving exquisite pastries, and shops for specialty foods. A small Hungarian enclave exists within this district.

Fish
Balducci's
424 Sixth Avenue at West 9 St. 673-2600. More interesting than most purveyors. High quality.

Central Fish Company
527 Ninth Avenue nr West 39 St. 279-2317. Paddy's Market area fish-monger known for its enormous variety of fresh fish.

Fulton Retail Fish Market
South Street Seaport, 11 Fulton Street nr Front St. 483-8391. One of the best sources for freshness and variety.

Leonard's
1213 Third Avenue nr East 70 St. 744-2600. Exquisite selection.

Lobster Place
487 Amsterdam Avenue nr West 84 St. 595-7605. Specialists for lobsters—great variety of sizes.

Pisacane
940 First Avenue nr East 52 St. 355-1850. Good selection, high quality.

Ruggiero
253 Bleecker Street nr Sixth Ave. 929-8789. In the old Italian section of the Village: high quality and variety. Italian specialties.

Gourmet Shops

B. Altman, Bloomingdale's and Macy's have very fine gourmet departments.

As You Like It
120 Hudson Street at No. Moore St. 226-6654. In TriBeCa, tasty main dishes, salads and soups to go, desserts and homemade ice cream too. AE.

Balducci's
422 Sixth Avenue nr West 9 St. 673-2600. Greenwich Village gourmet giant. Renowned for quantity, variety and atmosphere. Hard-to-find items, fresh breads and pastries, meats, exquisite in- and out-of-season produce and an amazing assortment of cheeses. AE. *OPEN Mon-Sat 7am-8:30pm; Sat till 6:30pm.*

Big Kitchen
1 World Trade Center, concourse level. 938-1153; 938-1197 (bakery). The Rotisserie, the Delicatessen and the Bakery sell some of the dishes featured at the Windows on the World restaurant. *OPEN 7 days.*

Call Cuisine
1032 First Avenue nr East 58 St. 752-7070. Quality entrées (over a dozen daily) and accompaniments to be reheated. Party catering. *OPEN Mon-Sat till 8pm.*

Casa Moneo
210 West 14 Street. 929-1644. Fixings for festive Mexican and Spanish dishes for over 51 years.

Catering à la Russie
315 West 54 Street. 246-6341. Regional Russian specialties: beet borscht, eggplant caviar, cabbage rolls; homebaked bread. Carryout and catering. No credit cards.

Caviarteria
29 East 60 Street. 759-7410. Caviar specialist, stocks 8 varieties of fresh, 6 preserved. Importers of Scotch salmon; Nova Scotia sold as well. They ship anywhere. AE, MC, V.

Chelsea Foods
198 Eighth Avenue at West 20 St. 691-3948. Great Chelsea takeout charcuterie and café. *OPEN Mon-Fri 9am-9pm; Sat & Sun till 6pm.*

Dean & DeLuca
121 Prince Street nr Wooster St. 431-1691. SoHo's gorgeous gourmet grocery. Everything is state of the art: the 175 cheeses, the olives, the oils, the vinegars, the herbs and spices; in short, the best of everything, beautifully presented, knowledgeably purveyed. *OPEN Mon-Sat 10am-7pm; Sun 6pm.*

Délices La Côte Basque
1032 Lexington Avenue nr East 74 St. 535-3311. Daily specials, excellent quiches; beautiful French pastries, brioches and croissants. Café. AE, DC. *OPEN Mon-Sat 7:30am-7:30pm; Sun till 3pm.*

E.A.T.
867 Madison Avenue at East 72 St; 1064 Madison Avenue nr East 80 St. 879-4017; also at Bergdorf Goodman. Handsome food shop for high-priced, lovely imported food items. Also, daily specials, good assortment of pâtés, cheeses, breads, coffees. Magnificent chocolate truffle cake. AE. *OPEN Mon-Fri 7:30am-7:30pm; Sat till 7pm; Sun till 6pm.*

Fortnum & Mason
B. Altman, Fifth Avenue & 34 St, 5th fl. 679-7800. The famed English comestibles. AE, DC, MC, V, Altman charge.

Maison Glass
52 East 58 Street. 755-3316. Smoked Scotch and Nova Scotia salmon, Smithfield ham, *foie gras*, cheeses, canned and packaged gourmet items. AE, CB, DC, MC, V.

Old Denmark
133 East 65 Street. 744-2533. Danish delicacies: meatballs, cold cuts, meat or fish salads, cheeses, and fresh breads. *OPEN Mon-Sat 9am-5:30pm.*

Out of the Woods
24 East 21 Street. 505-7868. The carryout wing of Woods restaurant. Goodies include their famed chocolate roulade. AE, MC, V. *OPEN Mon-Fri.*

Silver Palate
274 Columbus Avenue nr West 73 St. 799-6340. In this tiny but famed jewel of a food emporium everything for a gourmet feast, imaginative, daily entrées, hors d'oeuvres and their own bottled condiments. AE, MC, V. *OPEN Mon-Fri 10:30am-9:30pm; Sat & Sun till 7:30pm.*

Todaro Brothers
555 Second Avenue nr East 31 St. 532-0633. Complete gourmet line, 20 varieties of fresh bread, 300 cheeses, Italian cold cuts, pastas, coffees, confections, catering. *OPEN Mon-Sat 8:30am-9pm; Sun till 6pm.*

Word of Mouth
1012 Lexington Avenue nr East 72 St. 734-9483. International array of main courses daily. Tasty vegetable dishes, beautifully prepared entrées, consistently high quality. AE. *OPEN Mon-Fri 10am-7pm; Sat 11:30am-6pm; Sun 11:30am-5:30pm.*

Zabar's
2245 Broadway nr West 80 St. 787-2000. Humbly begun as a deli/cheese store it's now the Champ! A mind-boggling array of cheeses, meats, smoked fish, coffees, teas and entrées; plus a wide array of kitchenwares and gourmet gadgetry. Go for the sight, smells, the fun of it all. AE, DC, MC, V. *OPEN Mon-Fri 8am-7:30pm; Sat till midnight; Sun 9am-6pm.*

Health Food

Brownies Foods, Inc.
91 Fifth Avenue nr 16 St. 242-2199. Since 1936,

renowned health food store/restaurant. Stocks over 5,000 natural organic-diet foods including vitamins, nuts, grains, herbs, teas, breads, dried fruit. MC.

Commodities
117 Hudson Street at No. Moore St. 334-8330. A super supermarket. Over 5,000 square feet of variety and quantity. 125 tea choices, 24 types of granola, 30 bins of grains, 50 kinds of honey. Fresh organically raised produce. *OPEN 7 days 10am-9pm.*

Gramercy Natural Food Center
387 Second Avenue nr East 23 St. 725-1651. Fresh daily special sandwiches to go and natural grains, herbs, spices, nuts, natural cheeses and dairy products, some organic produce. MC. *OPEN 7 days.*

Natural Source
258 Columbus Avenue at West 72 St. 874-4678. Natural-foods store and snack spot for fresh salads and breads, juices, yogurts. AE, MC, V. *OPEN 7 days till midnight.*

New Era
12 St. Marks Place nr Third Ave. 477-6056. A health food haven. Vitamins, fitness equipment, too. Counter to eat in or take out. AE, CB.

Nutrition Centre
247 East 50 Street. 753-5363. Herbs and organic produce, packaged foods, natural cosmetics and vitamins. Lunch and juice bar. AE, MC, V.

Pete's Spice Shop
174 First Avenue nr East 10 St. 254-8773. A 4th-generation East Village establishment for basic foods. Burlap sacks full of grains, coffees, nuts, flour, dried fruit. Fresh breads, natural vitamins.

Vim & Vigor Health Food Shop
157 West 57 Street. 247-8059. Health snack bar with fresh-daily natural meals, snacks, drinks. Vitamins and natural cosmetics. *OPEN 7 days.*

Whole Foods in SoHo
117 Prince Street nr Wooster St. 673-5388. Complete natural-food market, organic grains, produce, gourmet takeout and herb selection. Natural cosmetics and vitamins. MC, V. *OPEN 7 days 10am-9pm.*

Herbs & Spices
(See also Health Food)

Aphrodisia Products, Inc.
282 Bleecker Street nr Seventh Ave So. 989-6440. Over 450 herbs and spices and a good selection of essential oils. Loose herbal teas without caffeine. MC, V.

Horticulture House
217 East 83 Street. 752-1559. Fresh potted herb garden in the store year round.

Kalustyan's
123 Lexington Avenue nr East 28 St. 685-3416. New York's oldest Indian store. Grains, nuts and spices in bulk. *OPEN 7 days.*

Kiehl's
109 Third Avenue nr East 13 St. 475-3400. Since 1852. Over 800 varieties of herbs and an impressive selection of their own herbal products.

Lekvar by the Barrel/H. Roth & Son
1577 First Avenue at East 82 St. 734-1110. Fa-

mous old (1926) Yorkville firm carries over 170 spices and herbs; dried and candied fruits, nuts. Specialties are imported Hungarian sweet paprika and lekvar (prune butter). AE, MC, V. *OPEN Tues-Sat.*

Meadowsweet Herbal Apothecary
77 East 4 Street. 254-2870. Herbs, herbal medicines, oils, ointments, liniments. Bach flower remedies. Free advice from a nutritionist every Sat 1-4pm.

Paprikás Weiss Importer
1546 Second Avenue nr East 80 St. 288-6903. It started with paprika (they have hot, half-sweet and sweet) and other Hungarian food and cooking products from "home," now there are hundreds of imported herbs and spices, foie gras, and so much more. Good housewares selection. MC, V.

St. Remy
818 Lexington Avenue nr East 62 St. 759-8240. Enchanting shop with fragrant naturally grown herbs from St. Remy, France, purveyed from open sacks. Over 320 varieties of herbs and spices, dried flowers for potpourris, virgin olive oil, herbal teas, pure fruit preserves. Natural non-detergent vegetarian soaps. AE, MC, V.

Meat & Fowl

Kurowycky Meats
124 First Avenue nr East 7 St. 477-0344. Prepares and purveys some of the city's finest smoked and cured meats. Baked hams, unusual sausage (all ham, with carraway seeds, or the spicy Ukrainian *kobasy*).

Lobel Brothers Prime Meats
1096 Madison Avenue nr East 82 St. 737-1372. Buffalo, rabbit, venison, grouse, quail, wild turkey and guinea hen among more traditional fare.

Nevada Meat Market
2012 Broadway nr West 68 St. 362-0443. Smoked pheasant, duck, goose, wild turkey, quail and guinea hens; fresh in season, frozen all year.

Ottomanelli Brothers
1549 York Avenue nr East 82 St. 355-4413. Prime cuts and fresh game in season. They deliver in the area. *OPEN Tues-Sat.*

Regent Foods
1593 Second Avenue at East 82 St. 734-5436. Meat specialists. Fresh quail, partridge and pheasant in season, as well as hard-to-find meats. *CLOSES Mon at 1pm.*

Store 48 for Steak
48 Ninth Avenue nr West 14 St. 924-3043. Gourmet shop for shell steaks, filets, brochettes, lamb and pork chops, cutlets and roasts. Chicken Kiev and Cordon Bleu, lobster tails and jumbo shrimp, ready to heat and serve. Gift-boxed; telephone orders taken. AE, DC, MC, V. *OPEN Mon-Sat 6am-6pm; Sun till 1pm.*

—Washington Market

Washington Market, from Gansevoort Street to West 14 Street between Ninth and Tenth Avenues, is the city's wholesale meat district servicing hotels and restaurants. But many of the outlets do sell retail. For the adventuresome non-vegetarian it's a hectic, colorful experience, and the selection and savings are incomparable.

Basior Schwartz Meat Products
421 West 14 Street. 929-5368. The most retail-oriented outlet in the wholesale meat district. Fresh meats as well as cheese, fish, imported canned goods, dried fruit and nuts. Excellent prices on all. *OPEN Mon-Fri 5am-noon only.*

Cut Well Beef
426 West 13 Street. 989-8240. In the heart of the wholesale meat district. Sells only prime and choice cuts of beef. Bulk purchase may be required for some items but the savings are substantial. Call ahead to order; they're very accommodating. *OPEN Mon-Fri 6am-3pm.*

Nuts & Seeds
(*See also* Candy/Chocolate; Gourmet Shops; Health Food.)

Broadway Nut Shoppe
2246 Broadway nr West 81 St. 874-5214. Georgia pecans, English walnuts. Roasted on the premises. Mails anywhere. *OPEN 7 days; CLOSED Sun in summer.*

Nat's Nut Shop
1324 Lexington Avenue nr East 88 St. 369-3811. Pecans, filberts, walnuts. Roasted on the premises.

Sahadi Importing Company
187 & 189 Atlantic Avenue nr Court St, Brooklyn. (1-718) 624-5762. Purveyors of nuts and dried fruit since 1895. The selection is impressive and worth a trip to this Middle Eastern area of Brooklyn.

Treat Boutique
840 Seventh Avenue nr West 54 St. 757-2515. Nice specialty shop. Stocked with candies, nuts, dried fruit and assorted gourmet items. Ambrosia consisting of cashews, walnuts, almonds, pecans and sunflower seeds mixed with dried apricot, pineapple, raisins and currants. AE, CB, DC, MC, V. *OPEN 7 days 9:30am-11pm.*

Pasta

Borgatti's Ravioli
632 East 187 Street nr Arthur Ave, Bronx. 367-3799. Wonderful family business. Every thickness of fresh egg and spinach noodle available daily. Pastas lightly flavored with whole wheat, tomato and carrot are interesting. Stuffed pastas too. *OPEN Tues-Sun (CLOSES Sun at 1pm).*

Bruno Ravioli Co.
653 Ninth Avenue nr West 45 St. 246-8456. Fresh specialties: manicotti, tortellini, lasagna, egg fettucine.

Green Noodle
313 Columbus Avenue nr West 75 St. 874-2892. Homemade egg, spinach and whole-wheat noodles; various shapes of macaroni, filled noodles like canneloni, manicotti and lasagna. AE, MC, V. *OPEN 7 days.*

Pasta & Cheese, Inc.
1375 Third Avenue nr East 78 St. 988-0997; 1312 Second Avenue nr East 69 St. 628-1313; 1198 Madison Avenue nr East 88 St. 369-2980; 31 East 72 Street. 249-2466. Also at Macy's Cellar and Zabar's. Egg and spinach noodles; cheese-and-meat-filled pastas and sauces all prepared. Ready for you to heat and mix. Uptown atmosphere and prices. *OPEN 7 days.*

Piemonte Homemade Ravioli Company
190 Grand Street nr Mulberry St. 226-0475. In the heart of Little Italy, a variety of fresh pastas made daily, including gluten macaroni for those allergic to wheat. *OPEN Tues-Sun (CLOSES at 3pm).*

Raffetto's Corporation
144 West Houston Street nr Sullivan St. 777-1261. Long-established Village shop for fresh pasta, egg and spinach noodles cut to your specifications as you watch. Ravioli stuffed with cheese or meat are prepared daily. Nobody does it better. *OPEN Tues-Sat.*

Supreme Ravioli Company
2317 86 Street, Brooklyn. (1-718) 372-6132. Fresh daily, spinach, egg, semolina and wheat noodles. *OPEN 7 days.*

Picnics
City picnic baskets, like city picnic sites, tend to be sophisticated and unusual. Also see Gourmet Shops for where to buy do-it-yourself fixings.

Balducci's
424 Sixth Avenue at West 9 St. 673-2600. Two different size "lap buffets" include a potpourri of treats. Order 24 hours in advance. AE, Balducci's charge. *Available year round.*

Brasserie
100 East 53 Street. 751-4840. Offers a choice of 6 French Picnique boxes, order three hours in advance. They deliver for 10 or more. *Available year round.* AE, CB, DC, MC, V.

Gaylord
50 East 58 Street. 759-1710. Boxed lunch of tandoori chicken, lamb, or vegetables from famed Indian restaurant. No notice necessary. *Available 7 days 11:30am-3pm.*

In a Basket
250 East 83 Street. 472-9787. Country-feel gourmet shop offers a standard picnic for 2, from a choice of 2, packed in a mushroom basket. One day's notice. *Available year round.*

Macy's Cellar
Herald Square, 34 Street & Broadway. 695-4400, ext. 2027. Five moveable feasts for 2, including "Garden Delight" for vegetarians; "NY Picnic" with lox, bagels, onions and cream cheese: "Parisian" with Perrier. AE, Macy's charge. *Available year round.*

Silver Palate
274 Columbus Avenue nr West 72 St. 799-6340. Picnics including a "decadent box," from a choice of 6; or they will make up one of your choosing. One day's notice. AE, MC, V. *Summer only.*

Seltzer
Before Perrier there was seltzer—filtered water and CO_2 gas. Delivered to your door like the old days.

Gimme Seltzer
226-6079.

Marty the Seltzerman
966-6892.

Teas & Coffees
Zabar's, Bloomingdale's, B. Altman and Macy's Cellar have shops that sell a variety of fresh and packaged teas and coffees. (See also Gourmet Shops.)

Gillies 1840
160 Bleecker Street nr Sullivan St. 260-2130. America's oldest coffee merchants (1840). Eighteen varieties of coffee bean, including decaffeinated espresso. Rare and exotic teas and botanicals. Plus soup to nuts. MC, V. *OPEN 7 days. CLOSED Sun in July & Aug.*

McNulty's Tea & Coffee Company
109 Christopher Street nr Bleecker St. 242-5351. Well-known Village shop established in 1895. Offers rare teas and over 200 choice imported coffees, sold straight or custom blended for you. Imported jams and jellies. AE, MC, V. *OPEN 7 days.*

Porto Rico Importing Co.
201 Bleecker Street nr Sixth Ave. 477-5421. Since 1907, high-grade teas and coffees. Custom blends; Jamaican Blue Mountain; decaffeinated espresso. Mail order. MC, V ($15 minimum.) *OPEN 7 days.*

Schapira Coffee Company
117 West 10 Street. 675-3733. Good coffee source including the coveted and expensive Jamaica Blue Mountain.

Sensuous Bean
228 Columbus Avenue nr West 70 St. 724-7725. Will blend from a wide variety of coffees. MC, V. *OPEN 7 days. CLOSED Sun in summer.*

Home

Bath, Bathrooms
(See also Linens *for discount towels)*

Elegant John
812 Lexington Avenue nr East 62 St. 725-5770. In an elegant setting, a superior selection of everything for the bath, including wallpapers; striped and printed toilet tissue, as well. MC, V.

Sherle Wagner International
60 East 57 Street. 758-3300. The world's most elegant and expensive bathroom fixtures. *OPEN Mon-Fri.*

Brass

A Parable's Tale, Ltd.
172 Ninth Avenue nr West 20 St. 255-1457. Contemporary brass furniture: cocktail tables, headboards, etageres. MC, V. *OPEN Tues-Sun.*

Brass Antique Shoppe
32 Allen Street nr Canal St. 925-6660. Treasure hunt for 19th-century American brass fixtures. Old Russian candlesticks, silver Judaica. Good bargains. MC, V. *OPEN Sun-Fri 10am-4pm.*

Brass Bed Factory
3 West 35 Street. 594-8777. High-quality solid-brass beds manufactured on the premises and sold directly to the public at 20-30% below retail. *OPEN 7 days.*

Brass Loft
20 Greene Street at Canal St, 3rd fl. 226-5467. Factory outlet specializes in brass and copper fireplace equipment, candlesticks, planters, chandeliers at substantial discounts. MC, V. *OPEN Tues-Sun.*

Isabel Brass
120 East 32 Street. 689-3307. Handmade solid brass beds and other furnishings. Expensive.

Carpets & Rugs
Macy's, B. Altman, and Bloomingdale's carry a selection of Oriental rugs.

ABC Carpet Company
881 & 888 Broadway at East 19 St. 677-6970. Since 1897. Oriental, designer, area, scatter or rag rugs. Over 5,000 rolls of national brands plus a large selection of remnants in a variety of fibers, colors and sizes. Immediate delivery and installation. AE, MC, V. *OPEN 7 days.*

Aronson's
135 West 17 Street. 243-4993. A floor-covering supermarket for all your flooring needs: carpeting remnant, close-out or custom-cut, tile, linoleum. MC, V.

Berdj Abadjian
1015 Madison Avenue nr East 79 St. 737-1114. Persian, Turkish and Caucasian antique rugs. Four generations of experience. Restoration and cleaning.

Beshar & Co.
49 East 53 Street, 2nd fl. 758-1400. Since 1898, handsome Oriental rugs plus cleaning and repair service. *CLOSED Sat in summer.*

Central Carpet
426 Columbus Avenue nr West 81 St. 787-8813. Great source for low-priced antique and semi-antique Oriental and Chinese rugs, modern Belgian rugs. Large collection of Art Deco Chinese rugs and flat weave Indian Dhurries. Huge selections. MC, V. *OPEN 7 days.*

Doris Leslie Blau
15 East 57 Street, 5th fl. 759-3715. Antique and exemplary Oriental and European rugs. *OPEN Mon-Fri by appointment only.*

Dildarian, Inc.
595 Madison Avenue nr East 57 St, 3rd fl. 288-4948. Since 1916. Antique and decorative rugs and tapestries. The largest retailer of fine rugs in New York. *OPEN Mon-Fri.*

Einstein Moomjy
150 East 58 Street. 758-0900. A carpet department store: Orientals, broadlooms, area rugs. MC, V.

Kaufman Carpet
26 West 40 Street. 921-5353. Large selection of indoor and outdoor carpeting. Good value. MC, V. *OPEN 7 days.*

Pottery Barn Warehouse
231 Tenth Avenue nr West 23 St. 741-9120. Unique, colorful, hand-loomed cotton Indian dhurries. AE, MC, V. *OPEN 7 days.*

Rug Warehouse
2222 Broadway at West 79 St. 787-6665. For over 50 years, a best price guarantee—for Caucasians, Persians, Art Deco Chinese, dhurries, kilims, both antique and modern. MC, V. *OPEN 7 days.*

Ceramic Tiles
(*See also* Paint *and* Hardware.)

Country Floors
300 East 61 Street. 758-7414. Specializes in fine hand-painted tiles—antique and modern—mainly imported from Italy, France, Holland, Peru, Finland, Spain and Portugal. MC, V. *CLOSED Sat in summer.*

The Quarry
183 Lexington Avenue nr East 31 St. 679-2559. New York's largest stock of reasonably priced Spanish, Dutch, Portuguese and Mexican tiles in bright colors and patterns. Installation or do-it-yourself guidance and tool rental. Bathroom accessories, too.

China, Glassware, Porcelain, Pottery
Fine china can be found in the large department stores. Even finer: Tiffany's and Cartier.

Baccarat, Inc.
55 East 57 Street. 826-4100. The famed, expensive imported crystal. Limoges stemware china by Ceralene, porcelain by A. Raynaud, pewter by Etains du Manoir, silver by Ercills Christofle.

Cache-Cache
758 Madison Avenue nr East 65 St. 744-6886. Italian ceramics, cabbage ware, linens and fine table settings. Gift accessories. AE, MC, V.

Crystal Clear
55 Delancey Street nr Allen St. 925-8783. Large collection of crystal and china at discount prices. *OPEN Sun-Fri.*

Finkelstein's
95 Delancey Street nr Orchard St. 475-1420. For over 60 years, up to 50% off retail price on imported crystal from Poland, Germany, France. *OPEN Sun-Fri.*

Ginori Fifth Avenue
711 Fifth Avenue nr 55 St. 752-8790. Elegant Italian china and porcelain giftware. Lalique, St. Louis, Duam crystal and glassware specialists. AE, CB, DC, MC, V.

Lanac Sales Company
73 Canal Street at Allen St. 226-8925. Imported and domestic china and crystal at discount. Sterling flatware; clocks. *OPEN Sun-Fri.*

Mad Monk
500 Sixth Avenue nr West 13 St. 242-6678. Interesting handmade pottery and mirrors. *OPEN 7 days.*

Plummer McCutcheon
Hammacher Schlemmer, 145 East 57 Street, 2nd fl. 421-1600. Royal Crown, Derby, Spode and Herend china specialists. AE, DC, MC, V.

Pottery Barn
117 East 59 Street. 741-9132; 231 Tenth Avenue nr West 23 St. 741-9120; 1292 Lexington Avenue nr East 87 St. 741-9134; 49 Greenwich Avenue nr

Charles St. 741-9140; 2109 Broadway nr West 73 St. 741-9123; 1451 Second Avenue nr East 76 St. 741-9142; 700 Broadway at East 4 St. 741-9147. *The* source for great-value glasses, dishes, cutlery. *Excellent* sales several times a year. AE, MC, V. *OPEN 7 days.*

Rogers & Rosenthal
105 Canal Street nr Forsyth St. 925-7557. Substantial discounts on fine china and crystal. *OPEN Mon-Fri.*

Royal Copenhagen Porcelain
683 Madison Avenue nr East 61 St. 759-6457. Danish china, Orrefors crystal, Boda-Kosta, plus Georg Jensen silver. AE, MC, V. *OPEN Mon-Fri.*

Steuben Glass
715 Fifth Avenue at 56 St. 752-1441. Unique glass sculpture. Browse—it's like a museum. AE, DC, MC, V.

Wolfman-Gold & Good
484 Broome Street at Wooster St. 431-1888; 142 East 72 Street, 288-0404; South Street Seaport, 422-8688. A French country look for the table. Very appealing. AE, MC, V. *OPEN 7 days.*

—China: Restorers, Repairers, Searchers

Fix-It Master
1160 Fifth Avenue nr 97 St. 289-5211. Will fix crockery, pottery, china, porcelain or glass. *CLOSED Sat & Sun.*

Hess Repairs
200 Park Avenue South nr East 17 St. 260-2255. "Repairers of the irreparable"—china, glass, ivory, mother-of-pearl, silver combs, brushes. Blue glass liners for salt and mustard holders.

Mr. Fixit
1300 Madison Avenue nr East 92 St. 369-7775. China, glass, quartz, jade; chipped glasses polished. Also, refinishes iron.

Pattern Finders
P.O. Box 206, Port Jefferson Station, NY 11776. (1-516) 928-5158. They seek matching china and stemware patterns. They stock many or they will trace for a reasonable fee.

Clocks

Clock Hutt, Ltd.
1050 Second Avenue nr East 55 St. 759-2395. Antique clocks from France, England, Germany. Some cuckoos. Watches 1920s–40s. Repair work also done. *OPEN 7 days.*

Joseph Fanelli Clocks & Things
1001 Second Avenue at East 53 St. 755-8766. Specialty: Antique carriage clocks in cases from England and France. Also, appraisals. Repairs, too. *By appointment.*

Cutlery & Gadgetry
(*See also* Hardware *and* Housewares.)

Delbon Cutlery
121 West 30 Street. 244-2297. Since 1840. Every type of knife, scissors and shears. *OPEN Mon-Fri; Sat by chance.*

Hammacher Schlemmer
147 East 57 Street. 421-9000. Six floors devoted to gadgets, conveniences and indulgences for the home (every room), the car, the sauna, or your

airplane. Phone orders: 937-8181. AE, CB, DC, MC, V.

Hoffritz
331 Madison Avenue nr East 43 St. 697-7344. Branches. The most impressive selection of cutlery and gadgetry to be found under one roof. AE.

—Cutlery: Knife & Scissors Sharpener

Fred de Carlo
(1-201) 945-7609. A knife- and scissors-sharpener who walks his territory—East 52 to East 92 Street. Fifth Avenue to the East River. To be sure to catch him, call in PM for appointment.

Furniture

Lord & Taylor, Bloomingdale's, Altman's and Macy's have a large variety of home furnishings, contemporary and traditional as well as antique. Bloomingdale's model rooms are always special. (See also Antiques; Brass; Plastic; Wicker and Specialty Shops & Services, Antiques.)

—Furniture: Antique & Collectible

Better Times Antiques
500 Amsterdam Avenue at West 84 St. 496-9001; 201 West 84 Street. 424-2286. Always an interesting selection of 19th-century pine furnishings and accessories. Also, oak and when they can find it, Lloyd Loom Wicker. Knowledgeably purveyed. MC, V. *OPEN Thurs-Tues. CLOSED Wed..*

Eastbourne Galleries
130 West 26 Street. 929-3042. Art Deco furniture, carpets, lamps and accessories. MC. *OPEN Mon-Fri.*

Eileen Lane Antiques
150 Thompson Street nr Houston. 475-2988. Spacious quarters for a lovely well-priced selection of French Art Deco, French Country and Scandinavian-Modern furnishings and art objects. AE, DC, MC, V. *OPEN Wed-Sun from noon.*

Fifty/50
793 Broadway nr East 10 St. 777-3208. Designer furniture and objects of the 30s, 40s, and 50s. Eames, Nelson, Noguchi, Miller, Knoll and the master himself, Wright. Scandinavian and Italian, including Vennini, glass.

Florian Papp, Inc.
962 Madison Avenue nr East 76 St. 288-6770. Since 1900, a source for William and Mary, Sheraton, and other periods of fine English furniture.

French & Company, Inc.
17 East 65 Street. 535-3330. Museum-quality French and English 18th-century furniture. *By appointment only.*

Howard Kaplan's French Country Store
35 East 10 Street. 674-1000. French country furnishings embellished with contemporary accessories. A beautiful shop. AE, MC, V.

Hyde Park Antiques, Ltd.
836 Broadway nr East 12 St. 477-0033. Eighteenth- and 19th-century English furniture.

Incurable Collector
42 East 57 Street. 755-0140. (Part of Stair & Company.) Eighteenth- and 19th-century English and Oriental furniture and paintings.

Iris S. Layne
1384 Second Avenue nr East 71 St. 988-5357. Mint-condition Victorian oak furniture. *OPEN Tues-Sun.*

Israel Sack, Inc.
15 East 57 Street, 3rd fl. 753-6562. Established in 1905. Specialists in fine 17th- and 18th-century American furniture.

Macklowe Gallery, Ltd.
982 Madison Avenue nr East 76 St. 288-1124. Specializes in Art Nouveau furniture, vases, bronzes, lamps. AE, CB, DC, MC, V.

Newel Art Galleries
425 East 53 Street. 758-1970. Six stories of the most extensive collection of antique furnishings from Renaissance to Deco. Accommodates people in the trade and those who know *exactly* what they want. *OPEN Mon-Fri.*

Philip Colleck of London, Ltd.
122 East 57 Street. 753-1544. Fine English antique furniture and accessories. *OPEN 7 days.*

Pierre Deux Antiques
369 Bleecker Street at Charles St. 243-7740. Exquisite 18th- and 19th-century country French furniture and accessories. AE, MC, V.

Retro Modern Studio
214 East 10 Street. 674-0530. Modernist interior specialists Art Deco–1960s. Designer furniture, decorative and fine arts. MC, V. *Sun. by appointment.*

Salvage Barn
525 Hudson Street nr West 10 St. 929-5787. Often a good source for well-priced used and antique furniture. No credit cards. *OPEN 7 days.*

Second Hand Rose
573 Hudson Street nr West 11 St. 989-9776; 131 Perry Street nr Greenwich Ave. 243-9522. Deco furniture through to 50s. American pieces only. Also wallpaper and fabrics. A splendid collection—*if* it's your cup of tea.

Second Helping
2768 Broadway nr West 106 St. 866-0658. Large selection of pine and oak furniture from the turn of the century. *OPEN 7 days.*

Stair & Company, Inc.
59 East 57 Street. 355-7620. Top-quality antiques, especially 18th-century English furniture.

Things Antique
250 West 77 Street. 799-0755. Good source for moderately priced oak and walnut furniture. *OPEN 7 days.*

Vaughn Antiques
630 Hudson Street nr Jane St. 243-0440. Victorian walnut furniture, including rolltop desks. MC, V. *OPEN Tues-Sun.*

Vernay & Jussei, Inc.
825 Madison Avenue nr East 69 St. 879-3344. America's oldest established art dealer. Fine 17th- and 18th-century English furniture and clocks.

—Furniture: Contemporary

Bon Marché
*55 West 13 Street 6th Fl. 620-5550; 1060 Third Avenue nr East 63 St. 620-5592. Wall units, con-

temporary furniture and accessories. Good value.
MC, V. *Thurs till 9pm.*

Brancusi
938 First Avenue nr East 51 St. 688-7980. Large
selection of modern tables in glass, chrome,
brass, stainless steel and forged iron. MC, V.

Brazil Contempo
42 East 20 Street, 2nd fl. 505-2277. Branches.
Contemporary, imported Brazilian leather furniture in more than 1000 styles and colors. Moderate prices. AE, DC, MC, V. *OPEN 7 days.*

Castro Convertibles
43 West 23 Street. 255-7000. Branches. One of
NY's largest selections of convertible sofas,
recliners, wall units. MC, V. *OPEN 7 days.*

Conran's
Citicorp Center. 160 East 54 Street. 371-2225;
also 2 Astor Place. 505-1515. A complete home
furnishings store featuring affordable "lifestyle"
home furnishings much of which you can carry
out. AE, MC, V. *OPEN 7 days.*

Decorators Warehouse
665 Eleventh Avenue nr West 48 St. 489-7575.
On 5 floors, discontinued, overruns, canceled orders, showroom samples from fine manufacturers, at 20-60% off. Retail and trade. Special orders at similar discount. MC, V. *OPEN 7 days.*

Devon Shop
111 East 27 Street. 686-1760. Formerly just for
decorators, now offering custom hand-carved formal and country French and Italian furniture
frames with your choice of custom upholstery and
finishing. Complete design service available. MC,
V. *OPEN 7 days.*

Door Store
210 East 51 Street. 753-2280; 1 Park Avenue at
East 33 St. 679-9700. Low-priced no-frills contemporary furniture design. Very extensive chair
selection. MC, V. *OPEN 7 days.*

The Futon Shop
178 West Houston Street. 620-9015. The traditional sleep mat from the Far East now popular in
NY. Natural cotton; wide selections of coverings.
MC, V. *OPEN 7 days.*

Gothic Cabinet Craft
104 Third Avenue at East 13 St. 674-1090.
Branches. Unpainted stock and custom-built furniture. Fast, reliable, reasonable. MC, V. *OPEN 7
days.*

J & D Brauner Butcher Block
298 Bowery nr Houston St. 477-2830; 316 East 59
Street. 421-1143. The solid, sturdy butcher block
translated into contemporary furnishings. AE,
MC, V. *OPEN 7 days.*

Jensen-Lewis
89 Seventh Avenue at West 15 St. 929-4880.
Delightful store features the director's chair in every shape, height and color imaginable. Personalized if desired. Other canvas furniture,
accessories and contemporary canvas in 34 colors by-the-yard. AE, MC, V. *OPEN 7 days.*

Maurice Villency
200 Madison Avenue nr East 35 St. 725-4840.
High-quality contemporary furniture. Excellent
design. MC, V. *OPEN 7 days.*

OOPS
530 LaGuardia Place nr Bleecker St. 982-0586.
Originals On Permanent Sale. The originals are
designer samples of contemporary furnishings.
OPEN Tues-Sun from noon.

Raimundo Antiques
125 Christopher Street at Hudson St. 691-4035.
Beautiful country furniture custom made, antique
accessories. *CLOSED Sun & Mon.*

Scandinavian Gallery
Broadway & West 63 Street. 307-5360; 185 Madison Avenue at East 34 St. 689-6890. World's
largest importer of Scandinavian furniture. AE.

Space Makers for Living
33 West 21 Street. 242-6619. Quality pillow-
furniture at discount. Sofas, ottomans; Murphy-
style beds. Oversize pillows without the coach as
well.

This End Up Furniture Company
*461 West Broadway nr Prince St. 673-0705;
1139 Second Avenue nr East 59 St. 755-6065.
"Packing crate" furniture for an inexpensive, modern look. MC, V. *OPEN 7 days.*

Workbench
470 Park Avenue South nr East 32 St. 481-5454.
Branches. Attractive contemporary furniture at
reasonable prices. Excellent sales. MC, V. *OPEN
7 days.*

—Furniture: Rental

A.F.R. The Furniture Rental People
986 Third Avenue nr East 59 St, 2nd fl. 751-1530.
Rents groups or single pieces of furniture. Long or
short term. AE, MC, V.

—Furniture: Restoration

Antique Furniture Restorations
1103 First Avenue nr East 60 St. 737-6270. Total
restoration of antique furniture for over 40 years at
affordable prices. French, English, Italian; gilding,
caning, doweling. Free estimates. *OPEN Mon-Fri
8am-6pm.*

House- & Kitchenwares

*The large department stores have good selec-
tions of kitchenware.
The Bowery, near Cooper Square and below
Grand Street, is where the restaurant-equipment
suppliers are located. Find good buys on practical, no-frills professional cooking implements.*

AAA Restaurant Equipment Company
280-284 Bowery at East Houston St. 966-1891.
Discount butcher-block tops and cutting boards,
gourmetware, copperware, cutlery, tableware,
commercial stoves, espresso and cappuccino
machines. No credit cards. *Sat till 2pm only.*

Bazaar Française
33 Union Square West nr East 16 St. 243-6660.
Well known to serious cooks for its definitive stock
of professional cooking utensils. Mostly copperware and stainless steel. AE, MC, V. *OPEN Mon-
Fri.*

Bridge Kitchenware
214 East 52 Street. 688-4220. No-nonsense shop
for great-priced professional equipment for the

home: copperware, earthenware, woodware, French porcelain baking supplies, restaurant-size stockpots and more. Know what you want before you go—they have over 40,000 items. But do go. Julia Child does. MC, V.

Broadway Panhandler
520 Broadway nr Spring St. 966-3434. Extensive collection of first-quality gourmet cookware, bakeware, cutlery and gadgets at low prices. Special orders taken. *CLOSED Sat in summer.*

The Cellar at Macy's
West 34 Street & Broadway, downstairs. 971-6000. A cook's tour de force. Beautifully stocked series of "shops" dedicated to housewares and food. There are gourmet foods and baked goods, coffees and teas, as well as the utensils and equipment for creative cookery. Cooking demonstrations, free food samples and special events all through the year. *OPEN 7 days.*

D. F. Sanders
386 West Broadway nr Broome St. 925-9040. *Also, 952 Madison Avenue nr East 83 St. 628-6415. Industrial high-tech housewares, gadgets in a spacious SoHo setting. Well-stocked. AE, MC, V. *OPEN 7 days. *CLOSED Sun.*

Empire Food Service
114 Bowery nr Grand St. 226-4447. Discounts on professional and restaurant cookware: Vulcan stoves, Buffalo china and Hall. *OPEN Mon-Fri.*

La Cuisinière, Inc.
867 Madison Avenue nr East 72 St. 861-4475. Caters to the gourmet cook. Distinctive, many imports. AE, MC, V.

Main Course
Bloomingdale's. Third Avenue & East 59 St, 6th fl. 355-5900. A total environment of 16 shops feature all the accoutrements for gourmet cooking, serving, dining and entertaining from heavy-duty cookware to the dining-table candles. Demonstrations, special events. AE, Bloomie's charge.

Manhattan Ad Hoc
842 Lexington Avenue at East 64 St. 752-5488. Stocked with beautifully displayed professional cooking supplies and well-designed contemporary housewares and accessories: industrial organizers. AE, MC, V.

Pottery Barn Warehouse
231 Tenth Avenue nr West 24 St. 741-9120. Huge selection, on 3 floors, of gourmet cookware and gadgets: glassware, pottery, utensils, flatware, stoneware and copperware at very reasonable prices. Seconds, closeouts and 4 very special sales during the year. AE, MC, V. *OPEN 7 days.*

Spice Market
265 Canal Street nr Broadway. 966-1310. Discount Cuisinarts, copper and aluminum kitchenware. Farberware, espresso machines, gourmet accessories and gadgets. In addition to the spices, herbs, teas and health foods. AE, MC, V. *OPEN 7 days.*

Zabar's
2245 Broadway nr West 80 St. 787-2000. The gourmet giant's housewares-browsing branch. Everything is for sale in the main store. AE, DC, MC, V. *OPEN 7 days.*

—Kitchenware Repair

Retinning & Copper Repair
525 West 26 Street, 4th Fl. 244-4896. City's oldest tinsmithery; since 1916. Repairs cookware; restores copper, tin, steel, cast iron and brass. *OPEN Mon-Fri.*

Lamps/Lighting

Department stores stock modern and traditional lamps. Inexpensive, modern light fixtures can be found at many neighborhood houseware hardware stores.
The Bowery from Delancey to Grand Street is the cash-and-carry discount lamp and light fixture district. Shop after shop offers what's new and modern in most cases, tacky and tasteless in others, all at below-list prices. All are OPEN Sun.

Apartment Dweller
604A Second Avenue nr East 33 St. 532-1706. Track lighting systems and modern-design lighting fixtures. AE, MC, V. *OPEN Tues-Sun.*

Bon Marché
1060 Third Avenue nr East 63 St. 620-5592; *55 West 13 Street, 7th fl. 620-5550. Contemporary lamps, good value. MC, V. *Thurs till 9pm.*

Bowery Lighting
132 Bowery nr Grand St. 966-4034. Also, 1144 Second Avenue nr East 60 St. 832-0990. Large selection of track lighting units. Emphasis on *very* contemporary lighting; Italian designs. All at 20-40% off list price. AE, MC, V. *OPEN 7 days.*

George Kovacs Lighting, Inc.
300 East 59 Street. 838-3400. Showroom: 230 Fifth Avenue nr 27 St. 683-5744. Class contemporary design in a wide price range. AE, MC, V. *OPEN 7 days.*

Just Bulbs
938 Broadway at West 22 St. 228-7820. Just that—over 2,500 bulbs of every description for every need. Great for the hard-to-find.

Just Shades
188 Bowery at Spring St. 966-2757. New York's largest selection of just shades. Every size and material at 20-30% discount. Or recover your old one. *CLOSED Wed.*

Light, Inc.
1162 Second Avenue nr East 61 St. 838-1130. Best contemporary designs in lamps and lighting. Full line of track lighting, some traditional lamps. AE, MC, V.

Thunder 'N Light
171 Bowery nr Delancey St. 219-0180. Track lighting and modern Italian and Venetian glass and fixtures. MC, V. *OPEN 7 days.*

Uplift
506 Hudson Street nr Christopher St. 929-3632. Specialty: turn-of-the-century and Deco lighting fixtures; all rewired. Some repros, most originals. AE, MC, V. *OPEN 7 days.*

Linens

Bergdorf, Bloomies, Macy's and Saks have good linen departments, and the time to shop in them for bargains is during the Jan & Aug white sales. Year-round bargains can be found on the Lower

East Side: Grand Street from Allen to Forsyth Streets for first-quality seconds and discontinued designer lines. Though CLOSED on Saturday, all are OPEN Sunday, but be prepared for crowds. For shops selling antique linens, see Women's Clothing, —Vintage and Specialty Shops & Services, Antiques.

Ad Hoc Softwares
410 West Broadway at Spring St. 925-2652. Terrific modern SoHo shop for the finest in contemporary accessories for bed and bath. Distinctive European and American bedding in cotton and linen.

Descamps
723 Madison Avenue nr East 64 St. 355-2522. French sheet-and-towel chain arrives in NY: 100% cotton, pastel, delicate prints. Table linens too. Expensive. AE, MC, DC, V.

Ezra Cohen
307 Grand Street at Allen St. 925-7800. Famed far and wide for its splendid selection of discount merchandise on 2 floors. Every brand-name sheet in current styles is represented, plus famous-maker bedspreads. Everything for the bed and bath, at 15-20% off retail. MC, V. *OPEN Sun-Fri.*

Frette
787 Madison Avenue at East 67 St. 988-5221. Sleek shop for Italian bed and table linens: cotton, piqué, damask, silk. For the well-dressed bed. AE, MC, V.

Harris Levy
278 Grand Street nr Eldridge St. 226-3102. Hectic-but-worth-it spot for discounts (25-40%) on name-brand bed linens, imported tablecloths and anything you might need for the bathroom. Second floor: custom and ready-made curtains, bedspreads, dust ruffles, lamp shades, and draperies. MC, V. *OPEN Sun-Fri.*

Porthault
57 East 57 Street. 688-1660; also at Macy's Herald Square, 6th fl. The Rolls-Royce of sheets. Exclusive and extravagantly expensive line of 100% cotton floral and print bed linens. Choose from 600 prints in a variety of colors. AE, DC, MC, V. *CLOSED Sat in summer.*

Pratesi Shop
829 Madison Avenue nr East 69 St. 288-2315. Their own fine bed linens manufactured in Italy (in Florence, since the turn of the century). Very expensive. AE, MC, V.

Paint & Wallpaper
Hardware stores carry basic paints and supplies; the extent of stock usually depends on the size of the shop. The stores below are specialists.

Janovic Plaza
Third Avenue at East 67 St. 772-1400; 159 West 72 Street. 595-2500; 213 Seventh Avenue nr West 23 St. 243-2186; *96-36 Queens Boulevard, Rego Park, Queens. (1-718) 897-1600. Wholesale and retail paint and wallpaper center; 15,000 wallpaper patterns available and they will mix paint to match any of them. Bath and fabric departments, too. Expert professional staff. Free delivery. MC, V. *OPEN 7 days.*

Pintchik
478 Bergen Street at Flatbush Ave, Brooklyn. (1-718) 783-3333; Also, 278 Third Avenue nr East 22 St. 982-6600. *Enormous* selection of major-brand paints at discount prices. NY's most extensive wallpaper stock. All at great prices. Great sales during inventory. Also, accessories. AE, MC, V. *OPEN 7 days.*

Sheila's Wall Styles
273 Grand Street nr Eldridge St. 966-1663. Up to 70% discount on large selection of decorator wallpapers, overruns, discontinued and close-outs. Manufactures draperies, blinds and fabrics to match. Half-price Levelors, woven-wood blinds. AE, MC, V. *OPEN Sun-Fri (Fri till 2pm only).*

Stief Paint & Wallpaper Company
196 Allen Street nr Houston St. 473-5181. Discount wall coverings and a truly amazing selection of contact paper. *OPEN Sun-Fri.*

Wallpaper Hangup Design Gallery
443 Third Avenue nr East 30 St. 532-3610. Carries designer wall coverings, plus matching fabrics. Custom linens, draperies. Full interior design services. Very good selection. MC, V.

Wallpaper Mart
187 Lexington Avenue nr East 31 St. 889-4900. Paints, wall coverings including vinyl and cloth, graphics and accessories. Reasonable. MC, V.

Wolf's
771 Ninth Avenue at West 52 St. 245-7777. The city's oldest paint store (1869) and likely the most knowledgeable regarding anything to do with paint and color. Supplier of the exterior latex used to repaint the Empire State Building in 1962. MC, V.

Pillows
The major department stores have good selections of decorative pillows.

Economy Foam Center
173 East Houston Street at First Ave. 473-4463. Foam cut to size while you wait or shredded by the pound for "piller filler." Polyester fiber fill, too. Ready-made sleep and decorative pillows; foam mattresses, designer sheets, spreads, all closeout at 30-50% off retail. Wall covering and upholstery fabric and vinyl. *OPEN Sun-Fri.*

I. Itzkowitz
161 Allen Street nr Rivington St. 477-1788. Seat cushions, decorative and sleeping pillows in every size and shape; choice of fillings. (*See also* Quilts: Modern.) *OPEN Sun-Fri 8am-4pm.*

The Pillowry
1034A Lexington Avenue nr East 73 St, 2nd fl. 628-3844. Pillows made of pure wool, kilims from Persia, Afghanistan, Turkey. Also, textiles— needlepoint, old silk, damask and lace. *OPEN Mon-Fri; Sat by appointment.*

The Pillow Salon
238 East 60 Street. 755-6154. Beautiful sculptured pillows in Oriental silks, brocades and Southwestern American Indian weaving. Handwoven textiles, objects and pottery too. AE, MC, V. *OPEN Mon-Fri.*

Plastic

Abacus
135 West 26 Street. 807-7966. Complete collection of Lucite furniture and accessories. AE, MC, V. OPEN 7 days.

Ain Plastics, Inc.
300 Park Avenue South nr East 22 St. 473-2100. Acrylic in sheets and giftware items: napkin holders, salt shakers, magazine racks. MC, V.

Canal Plastic Center
345 Canal Street nr Church St. 925-1032. Small bits and pieces in plastic. Will cut to size Lucite sheets. MC, V.

Lucidity
775 Madison Avenue nr East 66 St. 861-7000. Lucite chairs, tables, carts, accessories, imported from France and Italy. Plastic housewares and giftware. Sales in Jan and July. AE, DC, MC, V.

Perplexity Lucite Discount Center
237 East 53 Street. 688-3571. Custom-made Lucite furnishings. AE. OPEN 7 days.

Plastic Supermarket
309 Canal Street at Mercer St. 226-2010. Huge stock of plastics in every form. Custom designs (yours or theirs) for plastic home furnishings.

Plexi-craft
514 West 24 Street. 924-3244. Factory with showroom sells plexiglas furnishings and accessories retail. Carry out or custom made or to your design. MC, V.

Quilts

—Quilts: Antique

Most antique stores have a few quilts in stock. The following have outstanding collections in terms of quality, originality and quantity.

America Hurrah
766 Madison Avenue at East 66 St. 535-1930. American textile folk art: hooked rugs, samplers, embroidered blankets, crewel spreads, figural table rugs, and the largest, most impressive selection of quilts anywhere. OPEN Tues-Sat.

Gazebo
660 Madison Avenue nr East 61 St. 832-7077. A beautiful must. American quilts mainly from the 1920s and 1930s; and new ones in traditional patterns. Vintage wicker furnishings and accessories, old and new baskets, silk flowers and other pretty accessories. AE, MC, V. OPEN 7 days. CLOSED Sun in July & Aug.

Kelter Malcé Antiques
361 Bleecker Street nr Charles St. 989-6760. Very large, very fine collection of antique American quilts. Folk art, rag rugs, American primitives. AE, MC. OPEN Tues-Sat.

Spirit of America
269 West 4 Street nr Perry St. 255-3255. Lovely selection of pretty quilts, original 18th- & 19th-century painted country American furniture, and accessories. Knowledgeable and caring owner. AE, MC, V. OPEN Tues-Sat.

Thos. K. Woodard
835 Madison Avenue nr East 73 St, 2nd fl. 988-2906. Well-known source for antique American quilts from the 1850s on. AE, MC, V. CLOSED Sat in summer.

—Quilts: Modern

The linen department of the major stores carry ready-made quilts in a wide range of fillings and price.

The Down Shop
673 Madison Avenue at East 61 St. 759-3500. Large selection of ready-made down-filled all-cotton Continental quilts in all sizes and colors. AE, MC, V.

European Feather Importing Company
85 Allen Street nr Broome St. 226-2282. Buy white goose down by the pound and ticking by the yard—they do the rest. OPEN Sun-Fri.

I. Itzkowitz
161 Allen Street nr Rivington St. 477-1788. The best quilt man in America. You pick the filling and the covering. He's the last of a breed. OPEN Sun-Fri 8am-4pm.

Schachter
115 Allen Street at Delancey St. 533-1150. Long-time source for custom-made comforters and quilts; choose the filling, the design, the covering. Or have your favorite patchwork made into a comforter. Upstairs for closeout or discontinued; all at discount. MC, V. OPEN Sun-Fri. (Closes early on Fri.)

Splendid Linen Company
4915 Thirteenth Avenue nr 49 St, Brooklyn. (1-718) 438-0160. Custom duvets of Polish goose down. They make covers and curtains from current sheets. OPEN Sun-Fri.

Wicker

—Wicker: Antique

Rosycheeks
101 Atlantic Avenue nr Hicks St, Brooklyn. (1-718) 625-0396. Early-20th-century antique wicker furnishings and accessories in a beautiful setting. Wicker repair too. AE. OPEN 7 days.

Wicker Garden
1318 Madison Avenue nr East 93 St. 348-1166. Lovely Carnegie Hill shop specializes in expensive 19th- and early 20th-century wicker furnishings, quilts, stuffed toys and potpourri too. MC, V.
See also, Children's Shopping: Wicker Garden's Baby. KIDS' NEW YORK.

—Wicker: Contemporary

Azuma and similar import shops all carry inexpensive contemporary wicker furnishings and accessories.

Bazaar
125 West 3 Street nr Sixth Ave. 673-4138; 1453 First Avenue nr East 75 St. 737-2003; 501 Second Avenue nr East 28 St. 683-2293; 1362 Third Avenue nr East 77 St. 861-5999; 1145 Third Avenue nr East 66 St. 988-7600; 1037 Lexington Avenue nr East 74 St. 734-8119; *1186 Madison Avenue nr East 86 St. 348-3786; 2025 Broadway nr West 69 St. 873-9153; 540 Columbus Avenue nr West

86 St. 362-7335; 107-25 Continental Avenue.
Forest Hills. Queens (1-718) 263-2310. Large
selection of quality wicker furnishings at reasonable prices. AE, MC, V. *OPEN 7 days. *CLOSED
Sun.*
Deutsch, Inc.
196 Lexington Avenue at East 32 St. 683-8746.
Lovely and unusual collection of new wicker and
rattan furnishings. *OPEN Mon-Fri.*

Specialty Shops & Services

Acting Schools
American Academy of Dramatic Arts
120 Madison Avenue nr East 30 St. 686-9244.
Acting, voice, movement, mime.
Herbert Berghof Studio
120 Bank Street nr Hudson St. 675-2370. Founded by actors Uta Hagen and Herbert Berghof. For
beginners and advanced students.
Lee Strasberg Theater Institute, Inc.
115 East 15 Street. 533-5500. Founded by creative genius Lee Strasberg, Pacino and De Niro
are alumni.

Adult Education
*The following offer an extensive selection of
courses, in a wide variety of fields, geared to adult
interests and lifestyles.*

**Columbia University School of General
Studies**
Lewisohn Hall, West 116 Street & Broadway. 280-
2752. Day, some evening credit and non-credit
courses.
Fordham University at Lincoln Center
113 West 60 Street. 841-5210. Their "Excel" program offers the opportunity to use life experience
for credit toward a degree.
New School
66 West 12 Street. 741-5620. America's first university for adults. Over 1700 courses in the most
amazing array of subjects, given 7:30am-10pm
daily, Sat & Sun too. For intellectual stimulation,
career advancement, degree credit (or not).
**New York University School of Continuing
Education**
25 West 4 Street. 598-3591. Most classes are
evening and not for credit. New "life experience"
program.
YMCA of Greater New York
582-2000. Daytime and evening classes at over
30 co-ed YMCAs in the NY area, in fine arts,
fitness, sports, dance, photography, crafts, or languages.

Adult Stores
Eve's Garden
119 West 57 Street, 14th fl. 757-8651. "Know your
body." A store for women by women. Men welcome. Catalog available. MC, V. *OPEN Tues-Sat.*
Pink Pussycat
161 West 4 Street nr Sixth Ave. 243-0077. Items
for the body and a kinky imagination. *OPEN 7
days.*

Pleasure Chest
156 Seventh Avenue South nr West 10 St. 242-
2158; 302 East 52 St. 371-4465. Pioneer shop for
a complete range of sexual aids, lotions, potions
and underwear. MC, V. *OPEN 7 days noon-
midnight.*

Air Cargo
Door-to-door service for a price.

—Domestic
Emery Air Freight
995-6400.
Federal Express
777-6500.

—International
Air Express International
632-3500.
DHL Worldwide Courier Express
917-8000.
Purolator
392-6150.

Antiques
*New York has hundreds of antique shops, only
some of which sell antiques; others sell nostalgia,
memorabilia, collectibles, bric-a-brac. This list is
representative of the best, brightest, wittiest, most
highly rated, or just plain funky.*
*Throughout this shopping section, antiques are
also listed under specific categories (e.g., Furniture, Silver).*
*Several areas are particularly rich in antique
shops: Bleecker Street west of Sixth Avenue;
Second Avenue in the East 50s; Madison Avenue
in the East 60s to 80s; University Place to Broadway, East 11 to 13 Streets (the highest concentration in the city, both retail and to the trade); East 57
Street. In Brooklyn, Atlantic Avenue from Court to
Clinton Street; Coney Island Avenue from Beverly
Road to Avenue M.*

—Antique Shops
A la Vieille Russie, Inc.
781 Fifth Avenue at 59 St. 752-1727. Exquisite
antiques, clocks, art objects—especially
Fabergé, Russian silver and porcelain. *OPEN
Mon-Fri.*
Added Treasures
577 Second Avenue nr East 32 St. 889-1776. An
incredible collection of collectibles from the best
collector of them all—Lynn the "merch queen."
OPEN Mon-Sat.
America Hurrah
766 Madison Avenue at East 66 St. 535-1930.
Americana source: weather vanes, advertising
tins and magnificent quilts. Folk art, primitive paintings; early photography. *OPEN Tues-Sat.*
Back Pages
125 Greene Street nr Prince St. 460-5998. Antique amusement and slot machines, plus ju-
keboxes, player pianos and other large items.
OPEN Tues-Sun.
Bernard & S. Dean Levy, Inc.
Carlyle Hotel, 981 Madison Avenue nr East 76 St,

2nd fl. 628-7088. Top-quality late 17th- early 19th-century American antiques, furniture, silver, paintings and English pottery and porcelain. *OPEN Tues-Sat.*

Black Bird Antiques
374 Second Avenue nr East 22 St. 982-2074. Interesting and well-priced selection of antiques and collectibles: quilts, Black Americana, Oceanliner memorabilia, oak and pine furniture all 1850–1950. AE, MC, V.

Carol Alderman
353 Third Avenue nr East 26 St. 532-7242. A hodgepodge, but interesting. Strong on costume jewelry, 1940–1960. Large stained-glass-panel collection. *OPEN Mon-Sat 1-8pm.*

Darrow's Fun Antiques
1164 Second Avenue nr East 61 St. 838-0730. Antique toys of every description for the Peter Pans among us. Automobiliana, wind-ups, mechanical banks, carousel animals, toy soldiers, gambling devices, arcade machines. Range $2–5,000.

D. Leonard & Gary Trent
950 Madison Avenue nr East 75 St. 737-9511. Art Nouveau and Art Deco: Tiffany lamps, glass, posters, bronzes, and mirrors: English and French cameo glass. AE, MC, V. *CLOSED Sat in summer.*

D. M. & P. Manheim
305 East 61 Street. 758-2986. Old English pottery, porcelain, and enamels. *OPEN Mon-Fri by appointment.*

Dworkin & Daughter
1214 Lexington Avenue nr East 82 St. 988-3584. A dream for the collector of the small and beautiful. A vast array of antiques and collectibles; silver, jewelry; ephemera; political memorabilia; enamels. AE, MC, V. *OPENS at 1pm.*

Eclectiques
483 Broome Street at Wooster St. 966-0650. Aptly named. Deco, Nouveau, Mission furniture, 20th-century oils, illustrations. Some vintage clothes, jewelry. AE, MC, V. *OPEN 7 days, 1-6pm.*

Elizabeth Danielle Antiques
464 Broome Street. 226-0400. Cross the threshold and step back in time into this huge shop with a eclectic collection of Deco, French, Victorian and early American furniture, quilts, vintage clothes, shoes, accessories and a fabulous selection of antique linens is a mini-department store of antique treasures. AE *OPEN 7 days from noon.*

The English Way
115 East 60 Street, 2nd fl. 308-6119. Antique lace and dressing table accessories; linens from England for the bed; European large square pillow shams. Lloyd Loom chairs. AE, MC, V. *OPEN Tues-Sat.*

Great American Salvage Company
34 Cooper Square. 505-0070. A splendid collection of the past in the form of old Carousel horses, paneled frontdoors, vintage lighting fixtures, pedestal sinks, large mirrors and so much more. MC, V. *OPEN Tues-Sat.*

Ibiza Home
42 University Place nr East 9 St. 533-0875. Ex-

tremely romantic look for the home. Drapery panels from the 20s, 30s, 40s; fine lace for the bed, table and windows. Accessories like chintz-wrapped hat boxes made by them. AE, MC, V. *OPEN Mon-Sat noon-7:30pm; Sun 12:30-6pm.*

Irreplaceable Artifacts
14 Second Avenue at Houston St. 777-2900; *259 Bowery nr Houston St. 982-5000; Also at Trump Plaza, Third Avenue at East 61 St. 223-4411. Original spectacular architectural ornamentation for interior and exterior use—stained glass, mantel pieces, wrought iron, paneling and much, much more. *OPEN Mon-Fri; Sat & Sun by appointment.*

Jenny Bailey Antiques
24 East 93 Street. 410-6210. Nice selection of antique furniture and accessories, fairly priced.

Irving Barber Shop Antiques
210 East 21 Street. (no phone) Cramped quarters overflowing with glassware, costume jewelry, beaded evening bags, prints and some pieces of antique linens, quilts and vintage cloths. Browsable. *OPEN Mon-Fri.*

Leo Kaplan Antiques
910 Madison Avenue nr East 73 St. 249-6766. Extensive selection of French and American modern and antique paperweights. Russian enamels. 18th-century English pottery and porcelains. English and French art glass. AE, MC, V.

Lillian Nassau
220 East 57 Street. 759-6062. *The* place and *the* person for Art Nouveau and Deco, especially Tiffany glass, rare art glass, furniture and sculpture. AE.

M. Glueckselig & Son
1232 Madison Avenue nr East 88 St. 427-0527. Antiques, drawings, furniture, china, sculpture, silver and art objects.

M.H. Stockroom, Ltd.
654 Madison Avenue nr East 61 St, 21st fl. 752-6696. "Small" treasures from England and the Continent are the specialty of this charmer. Match strikers, Majolica, framed botanicals, antique boxes and more. *OPEN Tues & Wed 10am-5pm; rest of the week by appointment.*

Miss Liz
143 East 13 Street. (no phone) A charming collection of the best of this and that from the turn of the century-1950s: furniture, clothing, jewelry, bric-a-brac, toys, ephemera, linens, china, lamps. Drawers full of buttons and bows, lace, trimmings and notions. *OPEN Tues-Sun. CLOSED Sun in summer.*

Moriah
699 Madison Avenue nr East 62 St, 2nd fl. 751-7090. Filled with antique Judaica, prints, engravings, curios. *OPEN Mon-Fri.*

Norman Crider Antiques
Trump Tower, 725 Fifth Avenue, level 5. 832-6958. Jewelry and art objects 17th-20th century including Fabergé, Tiffany. Autographs, too. AE, DC, MC, V.

Old Versailles, Inc.
315 East 62 Street. 421-3663. French and Con-

tinental antiques and furniture. *OPEN Mon-Fri.*

Phases
163 Eighth Avenue nr West 18 St. 675-7861. Decorative arts of the 20th century: Deco furniture, art and depression glass. MC, V.

Philip Suval, Inc.
17 East 64 Street. 517-8293. Antique English porcelain and pottery, paintings. China trade porcelain, English furniture and glass from the 19th century. *OPEN Mon-Fri; Sat by appt.*

Philip W. Pfeifer
900 Madison Avenue nr East 72 St. 249-4889. Specializes in 18th- and 19th-century pharmaceutical and medical instruments; seals, snuffboxes too. *OPEN Mon-Fri.*

The Place Off Second Avenue
993 Second Avenue nr East 52 St. 308-4066. Photographica, eclectic decorator furnishings. Rental of props. AE, DC, MC, V. *OPEN 7 days.*

Pony Circus Antiques, Ltd.
381 Second Avenue at East 22 St. 679-9637. Full of fascinating finds from the past. Loads of furniture, lamps, accessories (and 2 wonderful dogs). Prop rental, too. No credit cards. *OPEN 7 days.*

Price Glover, Inc.
817½ Madison Avenue nr East 68 St, 2nd fl. 772-1740. Eighteenth-century English pewter and pottery, furniture, paintings and decorative objects. *OPEN Mon-Fri.*

Primavera Gallery
808 Madison Avenue nr East 68 St. 288-1569. Art Deco, Art Nouveau, jewelry and Viennese furniture and collectibles from the 1900s. AE, MC, V.

R. Brooke
138½ East 80 Street. 535-0707. An impeccable collection of English furniture, export porcelain, antique silver and more. *OPEN Mon-Fri 10am-4:30pm.*

Sideshow
184 Ninth Avenue nr West 21 St. 675-2212. Fun antiques and memorabilia, old kitchen utensils, and advertising tins. A browser's, not to mention collector's, delight. MC, V. *OPEN Tues-Sat.*

Thos. K. Woodard
835 Madison Avenue nr East 73 St. 2nd fl. 988-2906. Extensive and prime selection of American antiques and quilts, folk art, rag rugs, both old and wood-and-weave reproductions. AE, MC, V.

Urban Archaeology
137 Spring Street nr Wooster St. 431-6969. Gargoyles and other grand bygone architectural embellishments, all saved from the wrecker's ball. Americana from 1880s to 1925, focus mainly on NYC. Major dealer in Art Deco interiors and exteriors. Also, antique slot and arcade machines. AE, MC, V. *OPEN 7 days.*

Vitto Giallo
966 Madison Avenue nr East 75 St. 535-9885. Tastefully chosen items fill this small shop: quilts, paisleys, Staffordshire, objects and small treasures from the past. Fast turnover. AE, MC, V.

Waves
32 East 13 Street. 989-9284. Vintage radios, phonographs, sold, repaired, rented. Also, 78 records and advertising memorabilia owned by

famed deejay "Cousin Brucie" Morrow. *OPEN Tues-Sat.*

—Antique & Flea Markets

With escalating rents forcing out many small businesses, flea markets are becoming the last bastion of affordable goods.

Annex Flea Market
West 25 Street & Sixth Avenue. 243-5343. Outdoors, weather permitting. A serious dealers' market: good antiques and collectibles, little junk. Strong on silver, jewelry, vintage clothes. Varies from week to week, since most of the dealers are itinerant and go where the action is. Free parking: $1 admission charge. *OPEN Apr-mid Nov every Sun 9am-6pm.*

Antiques Market
137 Ludlow Street nr Rivington St. 674-9805, 475-5496. Oldest indoor market in NYC. Antiques, but mostly bric-a-brac; 15 dealers in a one-floor market. Free admission. *OPEN Tues-Fri noon-5pm; Sun 11am-5pm.*

Avenue I Flea Market
Avenue I & McDonald Avenue, Brooklyn. (1-718) 338-4660. The world's largest indoor flea market for all things new. Clothes, furniture, appliances. Free parking and admission. *OPEN Fri 5-10pm; Sat 10am-9pm; Sun 10am-7pm.*

Canal Street Flea Market
Canal & Greene Streets. 226-7541. Over 70 dealers sell antiques, used goods, second-hand clothes, junk. Colorful hurly burly, especially in the winter when it's only for the hardy. On clamorous, unglamorous Canal Street. Outdoors. *March-Dec Sat & Sun 9am-6pm.*

East Side Antiques, Flea & Green Market
P.S. 183, East 67 Street & First Avenue. 737-8888. A friendly spot for antiques, linens, new goods, fresh produce. Indoors & outdoors. Free admission. *Year round Sat 9am-5pm.*

Manhattan Art & Antique Center
1050 Second Avenue nr East 56 St. 355-4400. This is a class act. Over 70 shops and galleries featuring antiques and fine art objects from around the world. Prices range from $10-300,000. Indoors. Free admission. *Year round Mon-Sat 10:30am-6:15pm; Sun noon-6pm.*

Market I.S. 44
Columbus Avenue & West 76 Street. 724-8580. Antiques, collectibles, old clothes, jewelry and new merchandise too. Rivaling 26th Street as the Sunday flea to go to. Indoors & outdoors. Free admission. *Year round Sun 9am-6pm.*

New Essex Street Flea Market
140 Essex Street nr Delancey St. 673-5934. Old warehouse now a second-hand furniture mart. Wide selection of old oak. Free admission. *OPEN 7 days 10am-6pm.*

110 West Antiques
110 West Houston Street nr Thompson St. 505-0508. A unique antique collective of 5 women who sell vintage fur, clothes for men and women, kimonos, antique wristwatches and jewelry. "They span the ages." DC, MC, V. *OPEN Wed-Sun noon-7pm.*

—Antiques: Shows

Check the New York Times *Weekend section on Fri for current calendar. For major shows, see* ANNUAL EVENTS.

Aquariums
Crystal Aquarium
1659 Third Avenue at East 93 St. 534-9003. Specializes in selling and servicing imported tropical fish, aquatic plants and aquariums up to 300 gallons. *OPEN 7 days.*

Art Reproductions
The major museums have shops that sell reproductions from their permanent collections as well as from special exhibits. See also Posters.

Nelson Rockefeller Collection
63 East 57 Street. 753-7624. Exclusive reproductions of Mr. Rockefeller's personal collection. Picassos, Rodin sculpture, African artifacts, English and French china as well as original contemporary paintings and sculpture. AE, MC, V.

Art Schools
Art Students' League
215 West 57 Street. 247-4510. Founded in 1875. Learn to draw, paint, or sculpt. No entrance exam or prerequisites. Sat classes.

Brooklyn Museum Art School
188 Eastern Parkway nr Washington Ave, Brooklyn. (1-718) 638-4486. Courses in painting, drawing, sculpture, printmaking. *Wed-Sun.*

Pratt Graphics Center
160 Lexington Avenue nr East 30 St. 685-3169. Classes and workshops; silk-screening, lithography, photoprinting, etching. MC, V.

School of Visual Arts
209 East 23 Street. 683-0600. Drawing, painting, graphic design, illustration. Check for requirements. Eves & weekends. MC, V.

Art Stores
Arthur Brown & Bro., Inc.
2 West 46 Street. 575-5555. Long-established, superior art supply store, the largest in America. AE, MC, V. *OPEN Mon-Fri.*

Eastern Artists
352 Park Avenue South nr East 25 St, 11 fl. 725-5555. Large selection of art supplies discounted 20-50%. Fine custom framing, too. *CLOSED Sat in summer.*

New York Central
62 Third Avenue nr East 11 St. 473-7705. Superior shop carries everything for the artist, including handmade papers, parchment. AE, DC, MC, V.

Pearl Paint Company
308 Canal Street nr Broadway. 431-7932. Wonderful source for artists' and crafts materials, as well as house and industrial paints at discounts of 20% or more. Five floors. MC, V. *OPEN 7 days. CLOSED Sun in summer.*

Sam Flax, Inc.
25 East 28 Street. 620-3040; 15 Park Row nr Broadway. 620-3030; 55 East 55 Street. 620-

3060; *747 Third Avenue at East 46 St. 620-3050; 12 West 20 Street. 620-3038. *Very* complete art supply store. School and office too. AE, MC, V.

Auction Houses
Astor Galleries
1 West 39 Street. 473-1658. Antique furniture and works of art. Sale every 3rd week on Thurs. Viewing Mon-Wed. Check their ads.

Christie's
502 Park Avenue nr East 59 St. 546-1000. *219 East 67 Street. 570-4141. New York branch of famed London house. Auctions fine art, furnishings, tapestries, books and manuscripts. Mid Sept-May. Viewings Tues-Sat; *Mon, too.

Greenwich Auction Room
110 East 13 Street. 533-5930. American, English, European furniture. Art Deco, American folk art and quilts. Art moderne, decorative arts and glass; Victorian clothing.

Harmer Rooke & Company, Inc.
3 East 57 Street, 6th fl. 751-1900. Coin and antiquities auctions, 3 or 4 a year.

Lubin Galleries
30 West 26 Street. 254-1080. Auctions of estates of varying quality. Good buys on holiday weekends especially. They sell items from as little as $5 to $5,000. Sale every other Sat year round.

Phillips
406 East 79 Street. 570-4830. Founded in London in 1796. Fine-art and estate sales. Exhibition days 2-3 days prior to actual auction. Check their ads.

Plaza Fine Art Auctioneers
406 East 79 Street. 472-1000. Jewelry, art, furniture. Auction every Thurs.

Sotheby Parke Bernet, Inc.
1334 York Avenue at East 72 St. 472-3400. World-famous auctioneer and appraiser since 1744. Exciting to visit even if you are not buying. Paintings, jewelry, furniture, silver, books, porcelain, Orientalia, rugs and more.

Tepper Galleries
110 East 25 Street. 677-5300. Furniture, paintings, rugs, accessories, jewelry. Auction every other Sat year round. Viewing on Fri.

William Doyle Galleries
175 East 87 Street. 427-2730. Eighteenth- and 20th-century decorative and fine arts, including furniture, paintings, rugs and accessories. Auction every other Wed year round. Viewing Sat-Tues.

Baskets
Azuma
415 Fifth Avenue nr 37 St. 889-4310; 666 Lexington Avenue nr East 56 St. 752-0599; 25 East 8 Street. 673-2900; *387 Sixth Avenue nr Waverly Pl. 989-8690; 251 East 86 Street. 369-4928. Excellent source for wide selection of inexpensive imported baskets. *OPEN 7 days.*

Be Seated
66 Greenwich Avenue nr Seventh Ave So. 924-8444. For over 25 years, a place for inexpensive and unusual baskets in all sizes and shapes, antique and new.

Meunier's
140 Montague Street nr Henry St, Brooklyn. (1-718) 855-7835. Heights shop, for picnic, pie, flower, apple and lunch baskets; kitchen knickknacks and a wide variety of domestic and imported housewares. MC, V.

Potcovers
101 West 28 Street, 2nd fl. 594-5075. Full of beautiful, pricey baskets. AE. *OPEN Mon-Fri.*

Bicycles

Bicycles Plus
1400 Third Avenue nr East 79 St. 794-2929; 204 East 85 Street. 794-2201. A complete bike store. Sells, rents, repairs every speed bike. Will beat any price in town. AE, DC, MC, V. *OPEN 7 days.*

14th Street Bicycles
332 East 14 Street. 228-4344. Three-, 5-, and 10-speed bikes; sale, rental, repair. MC, V. *OPEN 7 days.*

Gene's Bicycle Shop
242 East 79 Street. 249-9218. Low prices on major brands and a vast stock makes this a top spot for bikes. Sales, rentals, trades. Reliable repairs. Lessons, too. *OPEN 7 days.*

Pedal Pusher Bike Shop
328 East 66 Street. 879-0740. Rental 3- and 10-speed bikes; repair. Private lessons available. MC, V. *CLOSED Tues.*

Books

Fifth Avenue has the largest concentration of bookstores in the city.

—Books: Chain Stores

Barnes & Noble, Inc.
105 Fifth Avenue at 18 St. 807-0099. The most comprehensive store for new and used textbooks. *OPEN 7 days.*

Barnes & Noble Discount Bookstores
38 Park Row at Beekman St. Broadway & 45 Street; Penn Station, Concourse Level; Seventh Avenue at West 33 St; Seventh Avenue at West 57 St; West 57 Street nr Sixth Ave; 56 West 8 Street; Third Avenue nr East 47 St; 120 East 86 Street; 107-24 Continental Avenue, Forest Hills, Queens.

Barnes & Noble Sale Annexes
*126 Fifth Avenue at 18 St. 255-8100; 600 Fifth Avenue nr East 48 St. 765-0590. Up to 35% discount on current fiction and non-fiction. The *best* bargains. Good art books, remainders, classical records, too. Shopping carts provided! *OPEN 7 days.*

B. Dalton
666 Fifth Avenue nr 52 St. 247-1740; Also, 369 Avenue of the Americas & West 8 St. 674-8780; 109 East 42 Street. 490-7501. Well-designed store has 300,000 books arranged by author on 2 floors. Personalized, helpful service. AE, MC, V. *OPEN 7 days.*

Doubleday
724 Fifth Avenue nr 57 St. 397-0550; 673 Fifth Avenue at 53 St. 953-4805. Other branches. The Fifth Avenue shops have books galore, classical and show records. Excels in performing-arts

books. Each store adapts to its local market. AE, CB, DC, MC, V. *OPEN 7 days.*

Waldenbooks
57 Broadway nr Rector St. 269-1139. Branches. Large general bookstore with current titles. AE, MC, V. *OPEN Mon-Fri.*

—Books: General

Books & Co.
939 Madison Avenue nr East 74 St. 737-1450. More interested in literature than in best-sellers. Stocks an author's complete works; autographed volumes too. Many special literary events. Also, strong on philosophy. AE, MC, V. *OPEN 7 days.*

Classic Bookshop
1212 Sixth Avenue nr West 48 St. 221-2252; 133 World Trade Center Concourse. 466-0668. Good source for paperbacks, current and otherwise. Excellent sales of remaindered books. AE, MC, V. *OPEN 7 days.*

Coliseum Books, Inc.
1771 Broadway at West 57 St. 757-8381. Huge, well-stocked store for current and remainder books. AE, DC, MC, V. *OPEN 7 days.*

Endicott Booksellers
450 Columbus Avenue at West 81 St. 787-6300. Books in a charming setting. Literature, good paperback backlists, small press. A children's room. Author readings. AE, MC, V. *OPEN Sun & Mon 11am-9pm; Tues-Sat 10am-10pm.*

Gotham Book Mart and Gallery
41 West 47 Street. 719-4448. Once a literary mecca, it endures. Strong on theater, general literature; the city's largest poetry collection; 250 literary and small press magazines. Wise men do fish here. AE, MC, V.

St. Marks Bookshop
13 St. Marks Place nr Third Ave. 260-7853. One of the finest bookstores in the city. Upstairs, for the new, avant garde, fiction, poetry, drama, criticism. Downstairs, for Latin American, women's studies, foreign, and small press. Mail order. AE, MC, V. *OPEN Mon-Thurs 10:30am-11pm; Fri & Sat noon-midnight; Sun noon-11pm.*

Scribner Book Store
597 Fifth Avenue nr East 48 St. 486-4070. The city's most beautiful book store. Personalized service; strong travel and juvenile departments. Hard cover mainly. DC, MC, V.

Three Lives & Co.
154 West 10 Street. 741-2069. Three women run this lovely book shop named for the Gertrude Stein work. Dedicated to literature. Salon readings by noted authors are a special feature. AE ($15 minimum), MC, V ($10 minimum). *OPEN 7 days.*

Womrath Trinity Bookshop
74 Trinity Place nr Rector St. 349-0376. Branches. Financial books and best-sellers. *OPEN Mon-Fri.*

—Books: Antiquarian, Old & Used

See also —Books: Special Interest

Antiquarian Booksellers Center
50 Rockefeller Plaza. 246-2564. First editions,

rare European and American books. *OPEN Mon-Fri.*

B. Altman & Company
Fifth Avenue & 34 Street, 8th fl. 679-7800. Antiquarian books, original autographs and antique maps. AE, Altman charge.

Books & Things
64 East 7 Street. 533-2320. Longtime well-regarded bookseller for used, out-of-print, rare. Strong on modern poetry, the performing arts—film, dance and theater; good art and photography sections. Antique postcards, valentines, and WW II posters.

Gryphon Book Shop
2244 Broadway nr West 80 St. 362-0706. Used and rare paperbacks; special interest in the theater, music, drama, film. Search service. MC, V.

Pageant Book & Print Shop
109 East 9 Street. 674-5296. Good used book store; extensive selection of old prints, engravings. AE, MC, V.

Strand
828 Broadway at East 12 St. 473-1452. Also, at 159 John Street. 809-0875. Eight miles of books (2 million books) in America's largest second-hand book store. Review copies of new books 50% off. Excellent new and used history, art and Americana. Warning, you'll spend more time and money than you intended. AE, MC, V. *OPEN 7 days.*

—Books: Kiosks
Fifth Avenue & 60 Street on the park side: Bookstalls from Strand and Barnes & Noble. Also in Bryant Park.

—Books: Special-Interest

Argosy Book Store
116 East 59 Street. 753-4455. Out-of-print history. European and American biographies. Search service.

Brunner/Mazel, Inc.
19 Union Square West nr East 15 St. 924-3344. Psychiatry and psychotherapy texts. MC, V.

Books of Wonder
See KIDS' NEW YORK, Children's Shopping: Books.

Cinemabilia Inc.
10 West 13 Street. 989-8519. Books, posters, autographs and memorabilia from theater and movies. Current and backlist periodicals. AE, DC, MC, V. *OPEN Tues-Sat.*

The Complete Traveller
199 Madison Avenue at East 35 St. 679-4339. A shop completely devoted to travel: guides, maps, foreign-language dictionaries for near and far afield. Some posters—art books too. Current and used, too. Will order.

Drama Book Shop
723 Seventh Avenue nr West 48 St, 2nd fl. 944-0595. Books on the theater, films, TV, published plays. Strong on criticism; well organized. MC, V.

Eeyore's Books for Children
See KIDS' NEW YORK, Children's Shopping: Books.

East West Books
78 Fifth Avenue nr 14 St. 243-5994. Alternative-

lifestyle bookshop: Eastern religion and philosophy; mental and physical well-being.

General Medical Book Company
310 East 26 Street. 532-0756. Dental, medical, nursing and veterinarian books.

Gordon's
12 East 55 Street. 759-7443. Books concerning cars, aircraft, military, fashion and decorating. AE, DC, MC, V.

Hacker Art Books
54 West 57 Street, 2nd fl. 757-1450. Large bookstore with art; architecture; crafts books, both old and rare. Reprints of important art books.

Jaap Rietman
167 Spring Street nr West Broadway, 2nd fl. 966-7044. Art, architectural, photography. Art periodicals, exhibition catalogs in a SoHo loft.

Kew Books
667 Madison Avenue nr East 61 St, suite 704. 308-4014. Over 7,000 books on gardening including the rare. *By appointment.*

Kitchen Arts & Letters
1435 Lexington Avenue nr East 93 St. 876-5550. Cookbooks from everywhere; food and wine guides; food ephemera; original art and photography related to food; kitchen-related stationery goods. Mail and phone orders. MC, V. *Thurs till 8pm.*

Maritime Book Shop
24 Beaver Street nr Broadway. 425-0123. Nautical technical books. AE, MC, V. *OPEN Mon-Fri.*

Maxwell M.M. Einhorn
80 East 11 Street, Room 404. 228-6767. Used, out-of-print and antiquarian books on food and wine; cookbooks, gastronomy and oenology. Large selection of regional American cookbooks. *By appointment.*

Military Bookman
29 East 93 Street. 348-1280. Used and out-of-print books; prints and posters regarding military, naval and aviation history. *OPEN Mon-Fri.*

Morton Books
989 Third Avenue nr East 59 St. 421-9025. Current books and periodicals on design, decorating and architecture. AE, MC, V ($25 min.).

Murder Ink®M
271 West 87 Street. 362-8905. Mystery and suspense novels, new, used and out-of-print.

Mysterious Bookshop
129 West 56 Street. 765-0900. Mystery, murder, mayhem. New, used, out-of-print. Will order. AE, MC, V ($20 min.).

New York Astrology Center
63 West 38 Street. 719-2919. Complete astrology book line. Also acupuncture and healing arts. MC, V.

New York Bound Bookshop
43 West 54 Street, 4th fl. 245-8503. This shop sells new, used, old, rare and out-of-print books, maps and graphics related to New York City. *OPEN Tues-Sat.*

Oscar Wilde Memorial Bookshop
15 Christopher Street nr Greenwich Ave. 255-8097. Specializes in Gay Liberation books. MC, V. *OPEN 7 days.*

Paraclete Book Center
146 East 74 Street. 535-4050. Theological bookstore. All faiths represented.
Richard Stoddard Performing Arts Books
See Memorabilia.
Rivendell Bookshop
109 St. Marks Place nr First Ave. 533-2501. British, Scottish and Irish books. Myth, lore and legend; fantasy and faerie. Search service.
Rizzoli
31 West 57 Street. 397-3700; newly located in the Sohmer building. Strong on art, architecture, photography and university press. French, Italian and German books, translations, foreign magazines and newspapers; classical records and a small art gallery. AE, DC, MC, V. *OPEN Mon-Sat till 11pm.*
Samuel Weiser, Inc.
132 East 24 Street. 777-6363. The bookstore for the metaphysical, occult, Eastern philosophy. Current and out-of-print. MC, V.
Science Fiction Shop
56 Eighth Avenue nr Horatio St. 741-0270. Small shop with walls of books on science fiction, fact and fantasy, new and old, rare, too. MC, V. *OPEN 7 days.*
Sky Books International
48 East 50 Street, 2nd fl. 688-5086. Aviation, military, naval books, magazines, prints and records. AE, V.
South Street Seaport Book & Chart Store
209 Water Street. 669-9453. Charming shop for nautical and New York books. Also, maritime periodicals, posters, prints and charts. MC, V. *OPEN 7 days.*
Supersnipe Comic Book & Art Euphorium
222 East 85 Street. 879-9628. Rare first-edition comics, sets of comics for the collector and works of famous comic-book artists. AE, MC, V.
Theater Arts Book Shop
405 West 42 Street. 564-0402. Theater books, memorabilia; the "acting editions" of current and popular plays. *OPEN 7 days.*
Traveller's Bookstore
22 West 52 Street lobby. 664-0995. An intelligently organized bookshop for the best in travel guides as well as books about every country under the sun. AE, MC, V. *OPEN Mon-Fri.*
Urban Center Books
457 Madison Avenue nr East 51 St. 935-3595. Operated by the Municipal Art Society. Specializes in architecture, urban design and planning, and historic preservation. AE, MC, V.
Weyhe Art Books
794 Lexington Avenue nr East 61 St. 838-5466. Art books, especially 20th-century, out-of-print, used, new.
Wittenborn Art Books, Inc.
1018 Madison Avenue nr East 78 St, upstairs. 288-1558. Large selection of art and architectural books, scholarly works. Forte: the Renaissance. MC, V.
Womanbooks
201 West 92 Street. 873-4121. Just as the name implies, books by, for, and about women plus nonracist, nonsexist children's books. *OPEN Tues-Sat.*

—Book Binding & Restoration
The following are specialists:
ffolio
888 Madison Avenue nr East 71 St. 879-0675.
Froelich
18 West 18 Street, 4th fl. 243-1585. *OPEN Mon-Fri.*
Sidney Perl
405 East 70 Street. 879-5080. *OPEN Mon-Fri.*

Buttons
Becoming harder to find in New York, Macy's, Gimbels and Altman's have a small supply in their Notions department. See also Notions.

Gordon Button Co.
142 West 38 Street. 921-1684. Ten million buttons, 5,000 varieties. Classic to novelty—3¢ to $3. Trimmings too. *OPEN Mon-Fri.*
Reliable
65 West 37 Street, 2nd fl. 869-0560. Factory for leather- or fabric-covered buttons—by the dozen. Same-day service. Rhinestones, nail heads, belt buckles too. *OPEN Mon-Fri.*
Tender Buttons
143 East 62 Street. 758-7004. On display, every kind of button imaginable, including sets of the old and rare in this very special shop.

Calligraphy
Bergdorf, Cartier, Saks and Tiffany have their own calligraphy services.

Calligraphy Workshop
17 West 17 Street, 7th fl. 741-1198. Well-known calligraphers teach all styles. Beginners, intermediate and advanced. Spring, summer and fall. Affiliated with the New School.
Jan Bryant
532-6029. Talented perfectionist specializes in announcements, invitations, envelopes and personalized gift items.

Candles
Azuma shops and most large greeting-card stores have a good selection of candles.

Candle Shop
118 Christopher Street nr Bleecker St. 989-0148. The best. Every color, shape, and for every occasion. AE, MC, V. *OPEN 7 days.*

Coins
Gimbels
West 33 Street & Broadway, 6th fl. 564-3300. American and foreign coins both old and new. Good selection of gold coins. AE, MC, V, Gimbels charge. *OPEN 7 days.*
Macy's
Herald Square, Broadway & West 34 Street, 7th fl. 736-1045. Rare coins bought and sold. AE, MC, V, Macy's charge. *OPEN 7 days.*
Perera
630 Fifth Avenue nr 51 St. 757-0100. Since 1928, basically stocks modern coins from United States: gold and limited editions. Also carries some antique coins. "Gold line": for recorded current quotations, call 586-2175.

Stack's
123 West 57 Street. 582-2580. America's oldest and largest coin dealers. Coins, medals, paper money; appraisal.

Cooking Schools

A la Bonne Cocotte
23 Eighth Avenue nr West 12 St. 675-7736. Classical and bourgeois French cooking. Full participation.

China Institute in America
125 East 65 Street. 744-8181. Participation and demonstration of the cooking of all regions of China.

Cooking with Class
226 East 54 Street. 355-5021. French and Continental cookery taught in a 6-week course. Participation and demonstration. Full-participation baking course.

Epicurean Gallery, Ltd.
443 East 75 Street. 861-0453. Excellent baking and French and Northern Italian; slimming cuisine cooking courses; full participation. *Mon-Fri.*

Karen Lee Chinese Cooking Classes
142 West End Avenue. 787-2227. Basic, intermediate and advanced Chinese cooking. Full participation. *Mon-Thurs.*

La Cuisine Sans Peur
216 West 89 Street. 362-0638. Emphasis on Provençal and Alsatian dishes. Participation and demonstration.

Le Cordon Bleu de Paris
Richard Grausman, 155 West 68 Street. 873-2434 (inquiries). Only authorized representative of the school in this country. Demonstration and participation classes. Spring & fall. *Mon-Fri.*

Solar Yoga & Arts Center
373 Ninth Street, Park Slope, Brooklyn. (1-718) 499-3669. Vegetarian-cooking workshops based on a natural diet. Demonstration and participation.

Costume Rental

(*See also* Women's Clothes: —Vintage Clothing.)

Eaves Brooks Costume Co.
21-07 41 Avenue Long Island City, Queens. (1-718) 729-1010. Thousands of theatrical costumes in very good condition. MC, V. *OPEN Mon-Fri.*

Gene London's Million $ Costume Collection
106 East 19 Street, 9th fl. 533-4105. *Magnificent* collection of vintage duds. *OPEN Mon-Fri by appointment.*

Crafts

(*See also* Needlework.)

Adventures in Crafts
1321 Madison Avenue nr East 93 St. 410-9793. Courses in basic and advanced decoupage, gold-leafing and under-glass decoupage. Supplies. MC, V.

Clay Crafts
222 West 79 Street. 595-2222. Courses, demonstrations and workshops in stoneware and earthenware. MC, V.

Coulter Studios, Inc.
118 East 59 Street, upstairs. 421-8085. Learn knitting all levels. Largest selection of high-quality yarns in the city.

Elder Craftsmen
850 Lexington Avenue nr East 64 St. 861-5260. Skilled craftsmen over age 60, who can do anything that can be done by hand, including finishing something you've started.

Erica Wilson, Needleworks
717 Madison Avenue nr East 63 St, 2nd fl. 832-7290. All needle arts and supplies. Crocheting, knitting, embroidery, needlepoint, crewel, patchwork. Custom canvases.

Glassmasters Guild
27 West 23 Street, 4th fl. 924-2868. Stained glass: instruction, tools, supplies, how-to books and demonstrations every Sat 11am. AE, MC, V.

Greenwich House Pottery
16 Jones Street nr West 4 St. 242-4106. Courses and weekend workshops in ceramics year round.

Hired Hand
1324 Lexington Avenue nr East 88 St. 722-1355. Fabrics for quilting, patchwork and applique: all supplies. MC, V.

Know How Workshops
The New School, 66 West 12 Street. 741-5600. Over 40 workshops in which to learn useful and pleasurable skills. MC, V.

The Lighthouse Craft Shop
111 East 59 Street. 355-2200. Features over 300 handmade, mainly hand-knit, items created by blind craftspeople. MC, V. *OPEN Mon-Fri.*

Medieval Crafts
The Cloisters, Fort Tryon Park. 927-3700. Medieval crafts, such as tapestry weaving, illumination of manuscripts and stained glass, using techniques similar to those used in medieval workshops. *Sat & Sun only.*

Woodsmith's Studio, Inc.
525 West 26 Street, 3rd fl. 563-9317. Woodworking classes: carving, turning, finishing, cabinetry and frame-making year round.

Dance Schools

(*See also* Exercise: Health Clubs.)

Fred Astaire Dance Studios
2 West 55 Street, 2nd fl. 541-5440. Branches. Every type of social and ballroom dancing taught, including disco. AE, MC, V. *Mon-Fri.*

Henry Le Tang
1595 Broadway nr West 48 St. 974-9332. Tap, ballet, jazz. Dancercise and acrobatics too. *Mon-Fri.*

Joffrey Ballet School
434 Avenue of the Americas nr East 10 St. 254-8520. Teaching arm of the famed company.

Martha Graham
316 East 63 Street. 838-5886. Beginning modern. Sat teen and kids program.

New York Academy of Ballet and Dance Arts
667 Madison Avenue nr East 61 St. 838-0822. Ballet or jazz for the beginner too. *Mon-Sat.*

Serena Studios
201 West 54 Street. 247-1051. Group belly-dancing classes, beginners to professional levels. *Mon-Sat.*

Diet

(*See also* Exercise *and* Health Clubs.)

Nutrition Counseling Service
Strang Clinic, 55 East 34 Street. 683-1000. Individual and group counseling programs. Medical supervision.

Thin Forever! Inc.
60 East 42 Street. 867-3466. Free consultation for medically approved weight-loss method. Custom-tailored diet to fit requirements. Approved by the Department of Health.

Weight Watchers
896-9800. Popular group method for weight loss. 300 classes in the Manhattan area. Call for location of class nearest you.

Discount Merchandise

These stores make it easy to go broke saving money. See also Women's Clothes: Discount.

Century 21
12 Cortlandt Street nr Church St. 227-9092. Three floors of discounted merchandise: clothing, electronics, toys and more. AE, MC, V. *OPEN Mon-Fri from 7:45am.*

City Dump
332 Canal Street nr Broadway. 226-1636. Stereo equipment, floor tiles, hardware or iced-tea mix. Anything they can get they seem to be able to sell. MC, V. *OPEN 7 days.*

Demitzer Bros.
5 Essex Street at Canal St. 254-1310. Small appliances at small prices. MC, V. Hectic; know what you want. *OPEN Sun-Fri.*

Job Lot Trading Company
140 Church Street nr Chambers St. 962-4142. Also, 412 Fifth Avenue nr 37 St. 398-9320. Two floors of unbelievable buys on whatever they can acquire: from salamis to greeting cards; discount jeans to hardware; perfume to pool cues. *Very busy* at noontime.

Odd Job Trading Corp
*3 East 40 Street. 686-6825; 66 West 48 Street. 575-0477. Best buys for sports gear and small appliances. *OPEN Sun-Fri.*

Ethnic Shops

(*See also* Women's Clothes: —Ethnic Clothing; Food: Ethnic Foods.)

Folklorica
89 Fifth Avenue nr 17 St. 255-2525. Unusual high-quality handicrafts imported from faraway places, including Ethiopia, Ecuador, Peru, Botswana and China. MC, V. *OPEN 7 days.*

In the Spirit
460 East 79 Street, suite 9B. 861-5222. Lovely selection of Judaica by a number of talented artists and craftspeople. *By appointment Sun-Fri.*

Irish Pavilion
130 East 57 Street. 759-9041. Irish linen, hand-knits, jewelry. Shanagarry pottery and Irish whiskey close by. AE, CB, DC, MC, V.

Norsk
114 East 57 Street. 752-3111. Scandinavian Rya rugs, furniture, crystal, porcelain, silver and jewelry. AE, CB, DC, MC, V. *OPEN 7 days.*

Tianguis Folk Art
284 Columbus Avenue nr West 73 St. 799-7343. Colorful Latin-American folk art. AE, MC, V. *OPEN 7 days.*

United Nations Gift Center
United Nations, First Avenue & East 46 Street, downstairs. 754-7700. Handicrafts, jewelry, gifts from most of the member nations. Wide price range. Bonus: *no sales tax* on purchases. AE, MC, V. Traveler's checks very welcome. *OPEN 7 days.*

Exercise

(*See also* Health Clubs.)

Alex & Walter Physical Fitness, Inc.
30 West 56 Street, 3rd fl. 265-7270. Fitness and fun: combination gymnastics, floor exercises, stretching for strength, coordination and balance. Co-ed.

Barbara Pearlman Slendercises
628-3682. Call for one-on-one consultation with the well-known fitness expert. Program worked out to fit your lifestyle. Call for appointment.

Body Designs by Gilda
139 East 57 Street, 2nd fl. 759-7966; 187 East 79 Street. 737-8440; 65 West 70 Street. 799-8540. Designed by fitness expert, Gilda Marx. Light aerobics for flexibility, toning, balance and coordination. Pro aerobics, a more challenging series. Done to music. Classes AM, lunchtime & PM. Co-ed.

Elizabeth Arden Exercise Program
Elizabeth Arden Salon, 691 Fifth Avenue nr 54 St, 9th fl. 407-7908. Under the auspices of fitness expert Barbara Pearlman; small group and private classes throughout the day. Emphasis on figure firming and proper body alignment. Truly custom care. Women only. AE, DC, MC, V.

Integral Yoga Institute
227 West 13 Street. 929-0586; 500 West End Avenue nr West 84 St. 874-7500. Open classes in Hatha yoga for beginners, advanced and very advanced. Four classes daily. Co-ed.

Jon Devlin's Dancercise
157 East 86 Street, 3rd fl. 831-2713; 1845 Broadway nr West 60 St. 245-5200. Total exercise system, aerobics, muscle toning, stretch, jazz, eurhythmics, stress release. Taught by professional dancers. Co-ed.

Kounovsky Physical Fitness Center, Inc.
25 West 56 Street, 4th fl. 246-6415. Calisthenics, floor work, gymnastics. For men, builds strength; for women, flexibility.

Lotte Berk Method
23 East 67 Street, 2nd fl. 288-6613. Rigorous combination of dance and yoga, abdominal and pelvic muscle toning for shape-up or slim-down. Women only.

Nickolaus Exercise Centers
*509 Fifth Avenue nr 43 St. 986-9100; 308 East 73 Street. 472-3030; 250 Third Avenue nr East 20 St. 673-6265; *767 Lexington Avenue nr East 60 St. 355-2693; *160 Broadway nr Maiden Ln. 425-3915; 237 West 72 Street. 877-0755. The technique consists of 30 exercises for a stronger, slim-

mer body. Co-ed. AE, MC,V.
*Schedules geared to the working person. Free
baby-sitting at the others.
Pineapple Dance Studio
599 West Houston Street & Broadway. 219-8860.
City's largest dance studio - a 4-story SoHo complex with shop, canteen, rehearsal rooms, dance
studios. Classes in jazz, modern, yoga, ballet,
belly dancing. Membership fee. *OPEN 7 days
9am-10pm.*
Pretty Body
681 Fifth Avenue nr 53 St, 6th fl. 752-2106. Based
on classical ballet principles taught by professional dancers. Sauna, steam and sun rooms.
Women only. AE, MC, V.

—Exercises for pregnant women:

Exercise Plus, 30 West 57 Street. 586-1742.
Family Fours, 1370 Lexington Avenue nr East 91
St. 410-0035.
Sports Training Institute, 239 East 49 Street. 752-
7111.
Suzy Prudden Studios, 2291 Broadway nr West
82 St. 595-7100.

—They make house calls:

Aly Hower, 799-1588.
Laurie Weiss, 724-5728.
Rebecca Sager. 673-8921.

Fabric
Macy's has an excellent large fabric department.
Ashil Fabrics, Inc.
101 West 34 Street (enter 1313 Broadway). 560-
9049. Domestic fabrics in a wide variety of knits
and blends at great prices.
Beckenstein
Women's: 130 Orchard Street nr Delancey St.
Men's: 125 Orchard Street. Bargains: 118
Orchard Street. 475-4525. These 3 stores cover
the widest variety of fabrics on the Lower East
Side. Bridal materials to upholstery velvets and
imported cashmere and mohair. AE, MC, V. Good
prices. *OPEN Sun-Fri.*
China Seas
979 Third Avenue nr East 58 St. 752-5555. Lush,
deep-hued fabrics and matching wallpaper for
home decorating. *OPEN Mon-Fri.*
Conran's
Citicorp Center, 160 East 54 Street. 371-2225;
Also, 2 Astor Place nr Broadway. 505-1515. Good
selection of crisp modern fabrics. AE, MC, V.
OPEN 7 days.
Diamond Fabric Discount Center
165 First Avenue nr East 10 St. 228-8189. Stocks of
spandex and leopard distinguish this East Village
fabric emporium, but there are all the usuals, too. All
at discount prices. No credit cards. OPEN 7 days.
Fabric Alternative
78 Seventh Avenue, Brooklyn. (1-718) 857-5482.
High-quality fabrics at a discount. Excellent silk
prices. MC, V. *OPEN Tues-Sun.*
Fabric Warehouse
406 Broadway nr Canal St. 431-9510. Three
floors of every type of fabric imaginable. Designer,
upholstery and some imported fabrics. Also a

good selection of notions. Fantastic savings. Custom service, too. MC, V. *OPEN 7 days.*
Fabric World
283 Grand Street nr Eldridge St. 925-0412. Lovely
line of fabrics at discount prices. The bonus: they
will convert your fabric into wallpaper. *OPEN Sun-
Fri.*
Laura Ashley, Inc.
714 Madison Avenue nr East 63 St. 371-0606.
The finest purveyor of the English country-house
look. Delicate floral and geometric prints on natu-
ral-cotton fabrics with wallpapers and home furnishings to match. AE, MC, V.
Liberty of London
229 East 60 Street. 888-1057. The famed English
prints by the yard. Wide range of upholstery, drapery and dress fabrics, including glazed chintz. AE,
MC, V.
New Frontier Fabrics
144 Chambers Street nr West Broadway. 925-
3000. Sample and closeout fabrics, solids and
prints in a variety of fibers. Way below wholesale.
OPEN Mon-Fri.
Pierre Deux Fabrics
381 Bleecker Street nr Charles St. 675-4054; 870
Madison Avenue at East 71 St. 570-9343. Exclusive American outlets for Souleiado hand-
screened Provençal print fabric and beautiful
accessories. AE, MC, V.
Silk Surplus, Inc.
223 East 58 Street. 753-6511. Designer silk, velvet and brocades for draperies, upholstery and
slipcovers. Scalamandre closeouts and seconds;
popular with the trade. *OPEN Mon-Fri.*

Flowers (real & otherwise)
*The wholesale flower market, a 4-block area at the
intersection of Avenue of the Americas and West
28 Street, with 25 outlets. Almost everyone will
sell retail. Go early to find a wide variety.*

Bouquets à la Carte
419 East 77 Street. 535-3720. Delightful fresh and
or paper-flower creations for special occasions.
Imaginative specialty is giant balloon decorated
with streamers and flowers.
Diane Love
851 Madison Avenue nr East 70 St. 879-6997.
Delicate stems or arrangements of fabric flowers—silk, linen, velvet, cotton. They won't wilt.
Classes in flower arranging. MC, V.
Ethel Rogers
192 East 72 Street. 737-5522. Beautiful and clev-
er floral arrangements by a skillful lady. AE, CB,
DC, MC, V.
Flower Cart
Grand Central Station, concourse level. 599-
1492. To apologize for your train being late. AE.
Madderläke
25 East 73 Street. 879-8400. Flowers from California, Holland, South America and Israel—
creatively used for every occasion. The top party
florist.
Rialto Florist
707 Lexington Avenue nr East 57 St. 688-3234.
Full-service florist and the only one with round-

the-clock service. AE, CB, DC, MC, V. *OPEN 24 hours, 7 days a week.*

Ronaldo Maia Flowers
27 East 67 Street. 288-1049. Expensive and inventive floral creations in natural cachepots or baskets. Elegant simple centerpieces; wonderful potpourri. AE. *CLOSED Sat in summer.*

South Flower Market
Second Avenue & East 55 Street. 355-6800; *181 Columbus Avenue at West 68 St. 496-7100. Also Macy's Cellar. Fresh-cut flowers sold by the stem. Over 75 varieties from which to choose. Creative fun. AE, DC, MC, V ($15 minimum). *OPEN Mon-Fri 8am-10pm; Sat till 9pm; Sun noon-9pm; *Mon-Thurs till 11pm; Fri & Sat till midnight; Sun noon-10pm.*

Un Jardin . . . en Plus
24 West 57 Street. 489-9760. Fake flowers, trees, and plants. Flower bedecked everything . . . china, fabrics, wicker furnishings, bedding. AE, MC, V.

Framing

A.P.F., Inc.
783 Madison nr East 66 St. 988-1090. Their own factory supplies a variety of custom frames, museum-quality reproductions as well as contemporary styles.

Frame-It-Yourself
220 East 23 Street. 689-2908. Low-cost framing you do yourself. Individual instruction takes approximately 2 hours. Also, a huge collection of fine-art posters.

Frames Unlimited
1069 Madison Avenue nr East 81 St. 535-1566. Framemaker to museums and art galleries. *OPEN Mon-Fri.*

Jerry Josef
113 Prince Street nr Greene St. 475-3815. Custom framing by an expert. Museum-quality conservation framing. Natural wood, contemporary. *OPEN Tues-Sat.*

Make a Frame, Ltd.
406 Third Avenue nr East 29 St. 684-1215; 180 Atlantic Avenue nr Court St., Brooklyn. (1-718) 875-6150. Low-cost frames you can assemble yourself in approximately 1½ hours. Custom-work, too. MC, V. *OPEN Tues-Sun.*

Natural Wood Frames
53 Third Avenue nr East 10 St. 475-1636. Beautiful natural-wood frames sanded very smooth with rounded corners. Ash, oak, walnut, mahogany.

Ready Frames
14 West 45 Street. 719-2720. Ready-made wood, plexi, metal frames. Over 2,000 styles at 20-50% off list. AE, MC, V.

Yale Picture Frame and Moulding
770 Fifth Avenue at 28 St, Brooklyn. (1-718) 777-0840. Over 400 moldings for custom-made frames at 25% below retail. Over 20,000 ready-made frames. *OPEN Sun-Fri.*

Games & Game Rooms
Alexander's and Macy's have a large selection of adult as well as children's games.

Backgammon Headquarters
669 Madison Avenue at East 61 St. 838-5671. Every type of set imaginable. Custom orders taken. Instruction given. AE, DC, MC, V.

Bridge & Games East
227 East 56 Street. 838-0780. Duplicate bridge is the staple. *OPEN 7 days noon-dawn.*

Chess Backgammon Club
212 West 72 Street, mezzanine. 874-8299. All board games played, but mainly chess and backgammon. *OPEN 7 days till the last player leaves.*

Chess Mart
240 Sullivan Street nr West 3 St. 473-9564. Lovely chess and backgammon sets for sale. Homey game room. Books and lessons too. *OPEN 7 days noon-midnight.*

Game Room
2130 Broadway at West 75 St, downstairs. 595-0923. Mecca for good Scrabble, chess and backgammon players. Pinball machine and a bar. Chess, backgammon and bridge computers for sale. *Never closes.*

Manhattan Chess Club
154 West 57 Street, 10th fl. 333-5888. The oldest chess club in the Western Hemisphere—since 1877. Boasts Bobby Fischer as a member. All levels from beginner to grand master. Welcomes new members. *OPEN 7 days 3pm-last member leaves.*

Olive Tree Café
117 MacDougal Street nr West 3 St. 254-3630. Middle Eastern restaurant where chess, backgammon and Scrabble are played. Silent movies are shown, too! *OPEN 7 days noon-4am.*

Village Chess Shop
230 Thompson Street nr West 3 St. 475-9580. Relaxed chess parlor/shop. Pick-up games for serious devotees. Four chess computer opponents available. Lessons too. MC, V. *OPEN 7 days noon to midnight.*

Gems & Minerals

Astro Minerals, Ltd.
155 East 34 Street. 889-9000. World's largest gallery of gems and minerals. Beautiful collection of exotic jewelry. AE, CB, DC, MC, V. *OPEN 7 days.*

Collector's Cabinet
153 East 57 Street. 355-2033. Natural treasures in the form of minerals, seashells, butterflies, fossils. Egyptian, Roman, Greek antiquities. AE, MC, V.

Gifts
Azuma shops are good for inexpensive gift items. See also Ethnic Shops for some interesting gift choices.

Any Occasion
209 Amsterdam Avenue nr West 69 St. 580-1049. Gift shop for crystal, cards, stationery and home accessories. AE, MC, V.

Aris & Mixon
381 Amsterdam Avenue nr West 79 St. 724-6904. Beautiful shop for old, new and renewed treasures. MC, V. *OPEN 7 days.*

Balloonacy
784-2172. Balloon gift surprises delivered any-where in NYC. *Available 7 days.*

Hubert des Forges
1193 Lexington Avenue nr East 81 St. 744-1857. Lovely house-gift shops with a French accent. AE, MC, V.

Jenny B. Goode
1194 Lexington Avenue nr East 81 St. 794-2492. 11 East 10 Street. 505-7666. Pace-setting, trendy gift boutique. AE, DC, MC, V.

Johnny Jupiter
884 Madison Avenue nr East 71 St. 744-0818. A unique, old-time general store, literally brimming over with the small, the witty, the old, the colorful. For kids of *all* ages. *OPEN Tues-Sun.*

Matt McGhee
18 & 22 Christopher Street nr Greenwich Ave. 741-3138. Old and new, tiny and not so, trea-sures. Mainly from China, including porcelains, baskets, miniatures, fans. Also, hand-blown Ger-man glass. Seasonal specialties; wonderful at Xmas. AE, MC, V. *OPEN 7 days.*

Mythology
370 Columbus Avenue nr West 77 St. 874-0774. A treat for eye and heart. Eclectic mix of unusual, colorful objects—old, new, rare. AE, MC, V. *OPEN 7 days.*

Only Hearts
281 Columbus Avenue nr West 73 St. 724-5608. For shameless romantics. If you "gotta have heart," this is where to find it. On everything from small collector's items, cards, balloons and party favors, to sportswear, accessories and un-derwear (hand-painted). AE, MC, V.

Paris-New York
120 Thompson Street nr Prince St. 925-0073. If you love Paris you'll love this shop full of little things *Parisienne.* Miniature Eiffel Towers, key chains, games, blow up plastic pillows, tee shirts, purses and jewelry. It's all highly whimsical and affordable. MC, V. *OPEN Tues-Sun.*

Sointu Modern Design Store
20 East 69 Street. 570-9449. A gallery-like shop for things chosen for their functional and aesthetic excellence—sleek housewares, glassware, clocks, stainless-steel pens, etc. AE, MC, V.

Star Magic
743 Broadway nr East 8 St. 228-7770. A celestial supermarket via California (where else?) for prisms; telescopes, space maps and books; electronic music and crystals to meditate by.

Think Big
390 West Broadway nr Spring St. 925-7300. You'll feel like a Lilliputian in this shop filled with outsized versions of everyday objects—a 1½-ft paper clip or a 6-ft pencil! AE, MC, V. *OPEN 7 days.*

—Gifts: Personalized

Frank Bara
246-5908 or 787-7515. Commissioned, highly personalized wooden jigsaw puzzles. Intricate, witty, tells someone's life story. *By appointment.*

Jill Gill
841-2342 or 362-8440. Your brownstone facade or interior or New York street painted in ink and/or watercolor. *By appointment.*

Spectacolor, Inc.
1 Times Square, Broadway & West 42 Street. 221-6938. A 20-by-40 ft "personalized message" in multicolored lights in Times Square. *Call Mon-Fri 9am-5pm.*

Hardware
For true hardware buffs, Canal Street from Lafayette Street to West Broadway offers a mindboggling array of nuts, bolts, screws, wiring, widgets and gadgets.

Albert Constantine & Son
2050 Eastchester Road nr Pelham Parkway, Bronx. 792-1600. Specializes in woodworking materials and tools; furniture-building kits, plans and books. AE, MC, V. *OPEN Thurs till 8pm; Sat till 3pm only.*

Brookstone
Schermerhorn Row, 18 Fulton Street. 344-8108. Also, Herald Center, 1 Herald Square at West 34 St. 564-7661. Famed New Hampshire purveyor of the hard-to-find tool and gadget. Everything is on display; you pick up a clipboard upon entering—it's your order form. Goods quickly appear. AE, MC, V. *OPEN 7 days.*

Canal Hardware
305 Canal Street nr Mercer St. 226-0825. If you need it, they have it. MC, V. *OPEN 7 days.*

Reliable Hardware
303 Canal Street nr Broadway. 966-4166. Experts in many trades. Reasonable prices, free advice. MC, V. *OPEN 7 days.*

Simon's Hardware
421 Third Avenue nr East 30 St. 532-9220. Busy well-stocked source for decorative hardware for the home plus tools and supplies. *OPEN Mon-Fri.*

Health Clubs
See also Exercise.

Apple Health Spa, Ltd.
88 Fulton Street nr Gold St. 227-7450; 211 Thompson Street nr Bleecker St. 777-4890; 321 East 22 Street. 673-3730. Small swimming pool, sundeck, whirlpool, sauna: Nautilus training center; aerobics, yoga, modern dance, calisthen-ics, karate classes. Co-ed. AE, CB, DC, MC, V. *OPEN 7 days.*

Elaine Powers Figure Salons
130 East 57 Street. 486-9094; 153 Third Avenue. 876-7600; 170 West 72 Street. 595-1772. In-dividualized exercise and diet programs. Spot-reducing equipment. No frills. Women only. MC, V.

European Health Spas
505 Park Avenue nr East 59 St. 688-5330; 401 East 55 Street. 688-1620. Swimming pool, sauna, steam room, whirlpool, massage and Universal figure equipment. Alternating days for men and women. AE, MC, V. *OPEN 7 days.*

Hudson Health Club East
Henry Hudson Hotel, 353 West 57 Street. 586-

8630. A 60-ft pool, 3 gyms, yoga, calisthenics daily, dance classes daily; sauna, steam and sun deck, private dressing facilities. Swedish body massage available. Jog track. Co-ed. AE, MC, V. *OPEN 7 days.*

Jack LaLanne
45 East 55 Street. 688-6630; 233 Broadway nr Park Pl. 227-5977; *677 Fifth Avenue nr 53 St. 759-6404; 144 East 86 Street. 722-7371. Most branches have swimming pool. Nautilus equipment, exercise classes, steam, sauna and sun rooms, whirlpool. Co-ed. *Women only. AE, DC, MC, V.

Manhattan Plaza Swim & Health Club
484 West 42 Street, 2nd fl. 971-0892. A 75-ft swimming pool; weight room; Nautilus, aerobics. Co-ed. MC, V. *OPEN 7 days.*

New York Health & Racquet Club
1433 York Avenue nr East 76 St. 737-6666; *24 East 13 Street. 924-4600; *20 East 50 Street. 593-1500; 132 East 45 Street. 986-3100; 110 West 56 Street. 541-7200. Swimming pool, whirlpool, sauna, steam room; Nautilus equipment, dance classes, yoga, calisthenics, karate. Co-ed. *Facilities for racquet sports. AE, DC, MC, V. *OPEN 7 days from 7:30am.*

Profile Health Spa for Women
11 East 44 Street. 697-7177. Nautilus and Universal equipment, dance and yoga classes, cellulite program, massage, full-service salon for hair and facials. Women only. AE, DC, MC, V. *OPEN 7 days.*

Sports Training Institute
239 East 49 Street. 752-7111. Exercise with a trainer. Staff nutritionist. Nautilus equipment. Work on spots or the whole body. Co-ed.

Tenth Street Baths
268 East 10 Street. 674-9250. And now for something different; this is the last of the old traditional Russian-Turkish baths that served the immigrant population on the lower East Side at the turn of the century. This *schvitz* (Yiddish slang for steam bath) is not glamorous but it is authentic. Spring for the *platzka,* a vigorous scrub with an oak-leave brush. Cool off then with a shot of Stolichnaya in the bar. The clientele runs the gamut from rabbis to rock stars. There are lockers and a sundeck. Mon & Wed are reserved for ladies. *OPEN 7 days.*

Vertical Club
330 East 61 Street. 355-5100. The Studio 54 of health clubs; on 7 floors with neon lighting, contemporary music. Classes all day; a 40-foot pool; 3 racquet and 6 squash courts; free weights, Nautilus; 1/10-mile indoor running track; rooftop sun deck; restaurant and bar for the affluent crowd to meet one another. Co-ed. Membership only.

Y's
YMCA: McBurney, 215 West 23 Street. 741-9210; Vanderbilt, 224 East 47 Street. 755-2410; West Side, 5 West 63 Street. 787-4400.
YM/YWHA: 1395 Lexington Avenue at East 92 St. 427-6000. Though details vary, these all have good swimming pools, tracks, gymnasiums, classes and sports facilities. Co-ed.

Horsedrawn Carriages

Chateau Stables
608 West 48 Street. 246-0520. For a romantic evening, party event, or gas saver. 200 varieties of horsedrawn carriages available: pony cart, hayride wagon, stagecoach, hearse, vintage ice, bread or milk wagon, or a fancy open or glass-enclosed carriage. The choice is yours. *OPEN 7 days.*

Hansom Cabs
Fifth Avenue & Central Park South. The limousines of a former era. A wide variety of coaches await you; some drivers even sport top hats. The traditional and most humane (for the horse) ride is through Central Park—*don't take it anywhere else.* Agree on the fare beforehand (they're meant to be set, but enforcement is difficult), then sit back and enjoy the ride. *Available 7 days unless the temperature is 90° or more.*

Ice

Circle Ice Company
491 Tenth Avenue nr West 37 St. 873-7469. Expert ice sculptor turns out some impressive pieces. Cubes and blocks, wet or dry ice. Order by phone; they deliver. *OPEN 7 days in summer.*

Empire Ice Cube Company
491 Tenth Avenue nr West 37 St. 594-5212. Ice: cubed, blocked, shaved, or chopped. Deliveries. *OPEN 24 hours a day, 7 days a week.*

Jewelry

New York's wholesale and retail jewelry (diamond) center, West 47 Street from Fifth Avenue to Sixth Avenue, offers a dazzling selection of gold, silver, precious stones; antique, traditional and modern designs. The concentration of shops and stalls makes comparison shopping an easy and pleasurable task and, since prices are not necessarily firm, a practical one as well.
The large department stores carry good selections of gold and silver jewelry. (See also Silver.)

—Jewelry: Antique & Estate

Antique Buff
321½ Bleecker Street nr Christopher St. 243-7144. Victorian, Georgian, Nouveau and Deco jewelry; wide selection of rings from 1800s to 1910. Silver and collectibles too. AE, MC, V.

Fred Leighton
773 Madison Avenue at East 66 St. 288-1872. Also, Trump Tower, 765 Fifth Avenue at 56 St. 751-2330. Exclusively devoted to rare antique and estate jewelry. Emphasis is on the 20s, featuring extravagant Cartier pieces, but there are pieces from the 1800s and others from the 1950s. AE, CB, MC, V.

Ilene Chazenof
19 East 69 Street, 3rd fl. 737-9668. Art Deco, Art Nouveau jewelry at *very* good prices. Also Arts and Crafts movement jewelry, metalwork and furniture; 1950s Scandinavian and Italian glass. *OPEN Mon-Sat by appointment only.*

Macklowe Gallery, Ltd.
982 Madison Avenue nr East 76 St. 288-1124. Impressive selection of Georgian, Victorian, Art

Nouveau and Art Deco jewelry. AE, CB, DC, MC, V. *CLOSED Sat July & Aug.*

Massab Brothers Jewelers
782 Lexington Avenue at East 61 St. 752-7139. Beautiful, extensive collection of Georgian, Victorian, Art Deco and Art Nouveau pieces. AE, MC, V.

Max Nass
118 East 28 Street. 679-8154. Specialty, one-of-a-kind pieces made from old beads and precious and semi-precious gemstones. Imports, antique jewelry.

Primavera Gallery
808 Madison Avenue nr East 68 St. 288-1569. Art Deco, Art Nouveau and Victorian jewelry. AE, DC, MC, V. *CLOSED Sat July & Aug.*

Ruzi
189 Second Avenue nr East 11 St. 473-0460. A designer and old-world craftsman who works in silver and gold. Wonderful creations mixing antique elements. Good selection of antique as well. *No credit cards.*

Sylvia Pines Uniquities
1102 Lexington Avenue nr East 77 St. 744-5141. An exquisite collection of antique and estate jewelry—Victorian to Deco; some Georgian pieces. Especially strong in Deco marquisite. Also, a spectacular collection of beaded and jeweled bags. *CLOSED Sat in summer.*

—Jewelry: Contemporary

Aaron Faber
666 Fifth Avenue nr 53 St. 586-8411. Imaginative designs in gold. Every 8 weeks upstairs gallery has shows of particular artists that revolve around a theme. Vintage wristwatches, too. Everything is for sale. AE, CB, DC, MC, V.

Artwear
456 West Broadway nr Prince St. 673-2000. A gallery showing unique handcrafted jewelry by contemporary artists including Robert Lee Morris. Adornments that are artworks as well: necklaces, bracelets, earrings, belt buckles, hair ornaments, all beautiful creations and all for sale. AE, MC, V. *OPEN 7 days.*

Buccellati
Trump Tower, 725 Fifth Avenue, ground and 4th level. 308-5533; 46 East 57 Street. 308-2900. Famed Milan silver- and goldsmith; each piece is unique. Specialty: antique coins beautifully set. Silver on 57th St; precious stones on street level; 4th for medium range (it's relative) and gold. AE, DC.

Bulgari
Hotel Pierre, 2 East 61 Street. 486-0086. Prestigious international name for fine precious jewels. AE. *CLOSED Sat in summer.*

Cartier
653 Fifth Avenue at 52 St. 753-0111; also, Trump Tower, 725 Fifth Avenue at 56 St. 308-0840; Westbury Hotel, Madison Avenue at East 69 St. 249-3240. Internationally famed in a beautiful former mansion traded to Cartier for two strands of Oriental pearls. Jewelry, silver, fine porcelain, picture frames, "Les Must" prestige items (modern classics) too. AE, DC, MC, V.

David Webb, Inc.
7 East 57 Street. 421-3030. The distinctive 18kt gold gem-studded jewelry most copied in costume. Large, expensive pieces, often beautiful animal images. *CLOSED Sat in summer.*

Fortunoff
681 Fifth Avenue nr 54 St. 758-6660. "The Source." Four floors of gold, silver, flatware, diamonds, watches and pewter. Antique and contemporary, all at *very* special prices. Georg Jensen, Oneida, Reed & Barton, Dansk among others. AE, DC, MC, V. *Thurs till 8pm.*

Harry Winston
718 Fifth Avenue nr 56 St. 245-2000. Also, Trump Tower. Jewelry as an investment for the wealthy. The rarest, largest and best gems in the world are behind these lovely locked doors.

Jerry Grant, Ltd.
244 East 60 Street. 371-9769. Precious and semi-precious stones in sleek modern designs. Both 14kt and 18kt gold, some silver. Will take custom orders. Unique service: diamonds reset *without* having to leave the stones. AE, MC, V.

King Fook
675 Fifth Avenue nr 54 St. 355-3636. This "expression of prosperity" via Hong Kong features jade in a variety of styles and price ranges; and 24kt (pure) gold. AE, DC, MC, V.

Michael C. Fina
580 Fifth Avenue at 47 St, 2nd fl. 869-5050. Well-known store features extensive stock of gold and silver at substantial savings. Jewelry, sterling silver flatware, tea sets, giftware, clocks and more. AE, DC, MC, V. *OPEN Mon-Fri.*

152 Prince St.
152 Prince Street nr West Broadway. 925-6496. Jewelry; silver, gold, bronze, brass, copper, ivory and ebony originals by Alex Streeter. AE. *OPEN Wed-Sun.*

Savage Jewelry
59 West 8 Street. 473-8171. Impressively stocked Greenwich Village shop for handcrafted gold and silver contemporary jewelry with a flair. AE, CB, DC, V.

Tiffany & Co.
727 Fifth Avenue at 57 St. 755-8000. The prestigious treasure house for gold and silver jewelry, including the designs of Angela Cummings, Elsa Peretti, Paloma Picasso: watches; gems; crystal; china and silver; clocks and stationery. Don't be intimidated by the name, there are some very reasonably priced items here. The windows are almost as famous as the interior. Have a look. AE, DC, MC, V. *CLOSED Sat in summer.*

Underground Jeweler
147 East 86 Street in the subway arcade. 348-7866. Extensive selection of ethnic and fine jewelry from around the world: Egypt, Israel, Rumania, Russia, France, Italy. Good value. MC, V.

Van Cleef & Arpels
744 Fifth Avenue at 57 St. 644-9500. The name is synonymous with perfection and price. World famed for a most complete Piaget watch collection. AE, DC, MC, V. *CLOSED Sat in summer.*

Wedding Rings, Inc.
50 West 8 Street. 533-2111. The original custom-

made-wedding-ring store in Greenwich Village. Handcrafted jewelry for 60 years. Will design to your specifications. AE, MC, V.

—Jewelry: Costume

Large department stores and many boutiques have wide selections of au courant costume jewelry.

Ciro's of Bond Street
711 Fifth Avenue nr 55 St. 752-0441; 6 West 57 Street. 581-0767. Fabulous fakes, though by no means cheap. AE, DC, MC, V.
Gindi
153 East 57 Street. 753-5630; 816 Madison Avenue at East 69 St. 628-4003. Extravagant-looking baubles and beads; evening bags; hair ornaments. AE, MC, V.
Jolie Gabor
699 Madison Avenue nr East 62 St. 838-3896. Expensive but high-quality costume jewelry. Copies of the best designs. AE, CB, DC, MC, V. *CLOSED Sat in summer.*
Kenneth Jay Lane
Trump Tower, 725 Fifth Avenue. 751-6166. Costume jewelry master. AE, MC, V.
Kyra's Alley
183 West 10 Street. 675-1006. Big "jewels" in a tiny shop. You'll see her things elsewhere for *much* more.
Ylang-Ylang
806 Madison Avenue nr East 67 St. 879-7028. Also, Herald Center, 1 Herald Square at West 34 St. 279-1428. Trays of faux baubles, bangles and beads. Glitz lives! AE, DC, MC, V.
Zoé
30 West 57 Street. 245-1057. Via Paris, Monte Carlo, Juan les Pins. *Fabulous* fakes for ears, neck and wrist. Range $85-250. AE, MC, V.

—Jewelry: Make-It-Yourself

Allcraft Tool & Supply Company, Inc.
64 West 48 Street, Room 1401. 246-4740. The jewelry maker's source for copper tubing, pewter ingots, mounts, clasps, screws and the tools to put it all together. Equipment for enameling, silversmithing, lapidary. MC, V. *OPEN Mon-Fri.*
Har-Man Importing Corporation
16 West 37 Street. 947-1440. Five floors of beads and rhinestones only, from all over the world, of every type, shape, description: wood, plastic, glass, crystal, semi-precious, ivory, cloisonné. From the very old to the very latest. *OPEN Mon-Fri.*
Nat Hollander
62 West 37 Street. 989-4245. Attractive supply of old African trading beads and Afghanistan silver beads. Glass, ceramic, plastic and agate chips. *OPEN Mon-Fri.*

—Jewelry: Repair & Restoration

Macy's and Gimbels do repair work on watches and antique jewelry.

B. Harris & Sons
25 East 61 Street. 755-6455. Antique-jewelry repair specialist. Sells mainly Georgian and Victo-

rian pieces; remodels, appraises and buys both contemporary and antique. *CLOSED Sat in summer.*

Kites

Go Fly a Kite
1201 Lexington Avenue nr East 81 St. 472-2623. Also, *Citicorp Market, 153 East 53 Street. 308-1666. A joyful store full of 200 varieties of colorful kites for every level of expertise and aspiration. Price range $2 to $1,000. AE, MC, V. *OPEN 7 days.*

Language Schools

Most schools with adult-education programs offer foreign-language and English courses. (See also Adult Education.)

American Italy Society
667 Madison Avenue nr East 60 St, 5th fl. 838-1561. Proven, practical method to learn Italian, for beginners, intermediate, advanced students. Conversational classes too.
Berlitz
40 West 51 Street. 765-1000; 61 Broadway nr Exchange Pl. 425-3866. World-famed language experts. Total immersion courses, private and group instruction. All spoken languages! MC.
French Institute/Alliance Française
22 East 60 Street. 355-6100. Native French teachers, small classes. Start speaking French the first day; all levels up to fluent taught in a thorough manner.
International English Language Institute of Hunter College
695 Park Avenue at East 68 St. 772-4290. English as a second language: conversation, pronunciation, grammar, business English, reading, writing. Intensive or part-time programs available. Beginner to advanced. Day, eve and Sat classes. MC, V.
Vanderbilt YMCA
224 East 47 Street. 755-2410. English for the foreign born as well as French, German, Italian and Spanish.

Leather Goods

The department stores offer a wide range of luggage, briefcases and leather accessories for pocket, purse, home, or office. (See also Women's Clothes, Handbags.)

Altman Luggage
135 Orchard Street nr Delancey St. 254-7275. Large selection of name-brand luggage at a discount; for over 30 years. AE, DC, MC, V. *OPEN 7 days.*
Bettinger's Luggage Shop
80 Rivington Street nr Allen St. 475-1690. Cluttered shop with a good selection of briefcases and leather envelopes, famous-brand luggage too, all at substantial discount prices. AE, DC, MC, V. *OPEN Sun-Fri.*
Crouch & Fitzgerald
400 Madison Avenue at East 48 St. 755-5888. Top-quality luggage and any shape or size of Louis Vuitton luggage or trunk. Anniversary sale in spring (excluding Vuitton). AE, CB, DC, MC, V.

Dinoffer Luggage Stylists
22 West 57 Street. 586-2158. Expensive, hand-crafted leather luggage and a line of smaller goods. Custom orders too. AE, CB, DC, MC, V.

Gucci
689 Fifth Avenue at 54 St. 826-2600. High quality, high price. World-renowned luggage, handbags, shoes, with or without the status initials. AE, DC, MC, V.

Innovation Luggage
World Trade Center, concourse level 432-1090; 10 East 34 Street 685-4611; 300 East 42 Street 599-2998. Huge collection of Samsonite, Ventura, Hartman and American Tourister luggage at reduced prices. OPEN 7 days.

Mark Cross
645 Fifth Avenue nr 51 St. 421-3000. Since 1845; the distinctive and expensive "MC" luggage, desk accessories, shoes, gloves and belts. AE, CB, DC, MC, V.

T. Anthony, Ltd.
480 Park Avenue nr East 58 St. 750-9797. Famed leather shop for exclusive, expensive items. Luggage made to order. AE, DC, MC, V.

Limousines

(See also TRAVEL & VACATION INFORMATION for more conventional auto rentals.)

Cooper Limousine Service
132 Perry Street nr Greenwich St. 929-0094. Rent a mint-condition vintage or new Rolls. Their oldest is a 1929 convertible with jumpseat. AE, MC, V. 24-hour phone service.

Dav-El Livery
219 West 77 Street. 406-4566. Rent a custom-built white Lincoln Continental with sun roof, stereo and bar—many rock stars do. Slightly more conservative models available. AE, CB, DC, MC, V. Available 24 hours a day 7 days a week.

Elegant Limousines
625-2600. Another favorite of the rock stars. Choose a Cadillac from an assortment of colors and lengths or perhaps a bar-equipped brown Mercedes. AE. Available 24 hours a day 7 days a week.

Manhattan Limousine, Ltd.
786-0800. Cadillac stretches, a few Lincolns. Wine and Perrier, color TV, video cassette, and bar optional (soft drinks only). AE, CB, DC, MC, V. Available 24 hours a day 7 days a week.

Style Limousine Classic Livery Service
926-0044. Vintage or modern limos, liveried chauffeurs. Luxurious extras available.

Magic

Flosso-Hornman Magic Company
304 West 34 Street, 2nd fl. 279-6079. America's oldest magic shop, established in 1856. For a time it was owned by Houdini. Every trick in the books, plus the books. Sat till 2:30pm only.

Louis Tannen, Inc.
6 West 32 Street, 4th fl. 239-8383. In business 51 years, it's the world's largest supplier of magic illusions and magic books to the trade, retail and wholesale. Full-time demonstrators, custom-made illusions. Customers include Cary Grant. MC, V.

Magical Childe
35 West 19 Street. 242-7182. Over 250 fresh imported herbs and nearly 300 oils and extracts in a specialized occult witchcraft shop. Love potions concocted to order. Lectures, classes and workshops. MC, V. OPEN Mon-Sat 11am-8pm; Sun noon-6pm.

Magic Town House
1026 Third Avenue nr East 61 St. 752-1165. Three floors devoted to magic. Shows on weekends. OPEN Tues-Fri 2:30-6pm; Sat & Sun 1-6pm.

Maps

(See also Memorabilia.)

Argosy Bookstore, Inc.
116 East 59 Street. 753-4455. Colorful and decorative original antique maps on the 2nd floor. CLOSED Sat in summer.

Hagstrom May & Travel Center
57 West 43 Street. 398-1222. Nauticals, aeronauticals, topographicals, maps, globes, charts, travel books. AE, MC, V. OPEN Mon-Fri.

Rand McNally Map Store
10 East 53 Street. 751-6300. Globes, atlases, topographical maps, domestic and foreign travel guides and maps of all publishers. Cluttered. OPEN Mon-Fri.

Memorabilia

(See also Antiques.)

Ballet Shop
1887 Broadway nr West 63 St. 581-7990. Specialty: Ballet memorabilia, including rare programs, in and out of print, signed books, records, art and sculpture. AE, MC, V.

Cinemabilia
611 Broadway nr Houston St. 533-6686. The movie buff's shop. Hollywood for sale in the form of old movie magazines, programs, sheet music, stills, autographs, posters, lobby cards, press-and scrapbooks, books on world cinema. AE, DC, MC, V.

Jerry Ohlinger's Movie Material Store
120 West 3 Street. 674-8474. Stills from every movie and TV show ever made. Movie posters, too. Great source. No credit cards. OPEN 7 days till 8pm.

Old Print Shop
150 Lexington Avenue nr East 30 St. 683-3950. Prints, advertising memorabilia, maps and cards. CLOSED Sat in summer.

Richard Stoddard Performing Arts Books
90 East 10 Street. 982-9440. Excellent selection. Rare and out-of-print books, vintage playbills and memorabilia relating to the performing arts. OPEN Wed-Sun.

Welcome to N.Y.C.
26 Carmine Street nr Sixth Ave. 242-6714. Memorabilia dealing with New York City only. Original old prints, maps, posters; postcards. MC, V. OPEN 7 days.

Miniatures

(See also Antiques and Toys: Collectible.)

Doll House Antics, Inc.
1308 Madison Avenue nr East 92 St. 876-2288. Dollhouses and all the miniature furnishings and occupants. Unique are the minuscule shopping bags from New York's posh shops. MC, V.

Lilliput
7719 Third Avenue nr 78 St, Brooklyn. (1-718) 833-3399. Specializes in personalized miniatures. MC, V. *OPEN Tues-Sun.*

Manhattan Doll Hospital
176 Ninth Avenue at West 21 St. 989-5220. Big selection of dollhouse furnishings from modern lucite to Colonial maple. All handcrafted. AE, MC, V. *OPEN Sun-Fri. (CLOSES Fri at 4:30pm.)*

Shackman
85 Fifth Avenue at 16 St. 989-5162. Extensive collection of miniature furniture and dollhouses since 1898. *CLOSED Sat in summer.*

Soldier Shop, Inc.
1222 Madison Avenue nr East 88 St. 535-6788. For the collector, old toy soldiers and military miniatures. Military books, helmets and swords. AE.

Talbert Gradisca
140 East 55 Street. 753-0468. Hand-painted miniature paintings, as small as 1 in by 1 in; florals are the mainstay. AE, CB, DC, MC, V.

Tiny Doll House
231 East 53 Street, downstairs. 752-3082. Everything conceivable in miniature for a dollhouse. AE, MC, V.

Music & Musical Instruments
West 48 Street between Fifth Avenue & Sixth Avenue is the musical-instrument district.

Buecker & Harpsichords
465 West Broadway nr Houston St. 260-3480. Expert harpsichord maker. Repairs and rentals as well. Call for hours.

Carl Fischer
62 Cooper Square at East 7 St. 677-0821. Music of all publishers: classical, jazz, choral, pop, rock, folk. MC, V.

Hansen's Music Store
1860 Broadway nr West 61 St. 246-4175. Exclusively devoted to sheet music and books on classical, jazz, rock, folk, and country music. MC, V. *OPEN 7 days.*

Jack Kahn Pianos
158 West 55 Street. 581-9420. Large selection of new and used pianos and organs. For 48 years the distributor of Bosendorfer handcrafted Viennese pianos. Boasts low prices. Tuning and rebuilding. Call about free concerts at the store.

Manny's
156 West 48 Street. 757-0576. Since 1925, 2 floors of instruments. Professionally oriented. They buy, sell, exchange. (John Lennon was a customer.) AE, DC, MC, V.

Matt Umanov Guitars
276 Bleecker Street nr Seventh Ave So. 675-2157. Large selection of new and used string instruments in a wide price range. Good repair department. MC, V.

Music Inn
169 West 4 Street nr Sixth Ave. 243-5715. New and used guitars, as well as banjos, mandolins, dubros, dulcimers, sitars, balalaikas, flutes, tabla drums and zithers and more. Expert guitar repairs. AE, DC, MC, V.

Sam Ash
160 West 48 Street. 245-4778. Since 1924. Popular with professional musicians. Wide inventory of brass instruments, guitars and amplifiers and reed instruments, horns and drums. Good prices. Rentals too. Books on music; musical scores. MC, V.

Music Boxes
(See also Antiques.)

Nathanial's Music Box
At Last Wound Up, 290 Columbus Avenue nr West 74 St. 787-3388. In this west side outpost of whimsy: antique, restored and new music boxes. AE, MC, V. *OPEN 7 days.*

Rita Ford Music Boxes
19 East 65 Street. 535-6717. The best collection of working antique music boxes in the world; 1830-1910. Contemporary boxes too. Some can be made up with a song of your choosing. Wide price range. Restores and repairs.

Music Schools
Greenwich House Music School
46 Barrow Street nr Seventh Ave So. 242-4770. A variety of instrumental classes and music appreciation too.

Guitar Study Center
The New School, 60 West 12 Street. 688-7452. Classical, jazz, country, folk, rock and blues guitar lessons. Piano, bass, voice and songwriting too. MC, V.

School of Music
The 92nd Street YM/YWHA, 1395 Lexington Avenue. 427-6000. Well-respected school. Private and group instruction, wide range of subjects relating to musical theory and practice. MC, V.

Third Street Music School Settlement
233 East 11 Street. 777-3240. Since 1894. Private, group instruction: music, art, dance. Age 3-adult. Concert series. MC, V.

Needlework
(See also Crafts.)

Alice Maynard
133 East 65 Street, upstairs. 535-6107. Lessons for beginners in needlepoint. Canvas by the yard to design your own, or artists will create a design to your specifications. *CLOSED Sat in summer.*

B&M Yarn Company
151 Essex Street nr Rivington St. 475-6380. Great selection of needlepoint, crewel, rug-hooking kits and yarn. Free instruction. *OPEN Sun-Fri.*

Bell Yarn Company
75 Essex Street nr Broome St. 674-1030. Also, 96-16 63 Road, Flushing, Queens. (1-718) 459-1134. Huge longtime (1917) discount store for knitting wools. Free instruction with purchase. Also hundreds of needlepoint, crewel and rug-hooking kits; embroidery materials such as tablecloths, aprons, pillowcases. *OPEN Sun-Fri.*

Erica Wilson Needleworks
717 Madison Avenue nr East 63 St. 832-7290.
Knitting, needlepoint, embroidery wools, patterns,
custom canvases and kits.

Sunray Yarn Company, Inc.
349 Grand Street nr Essex St. 475-0062. Reasonably priced supplies and yarns for needlepoint,
knitting, rug-hooking. *OPEN Sun-Fri.*

Two Needles
1266 Madison Avenue nr East 91 St. 348-6510.
Unique Carnegie Hill shop. Magnificent hand-
painted needlepoint canvases; will custom design. Also very special knitting patterns, mainly
interpretations of current fashions. The European
yarns are all natural fibers: silk chenille, wool,
cotton, linen. Will hand-knit to measure for you.
MC, V.

Yarn Center
61 West 37 Street, 2nd fl. 921-9293. Good discount yarn store in midtown. MC, V.

**Newspapers and Magazines: Foreign &
Out-of-Town**

Eastern Newsstand
Pan Am Building, 200 Park Avenue at East 45 St.
Magazines—2,500-3,000 different titles including
foreign language.

Hotaling's: Foreign & Domestic
142 West 42 Street. 840-1868. Over 200 out-of-
town newspapers; over 35 foreign language
newspapers, large selection of magazines. Language books and maps. *OPEN Mon-Sat 7:30am-
9:30pm; Sun till 8pm.*

Idle Hour
59 Greenwich Avenue nr Seventh Ave. So. 924-
6517. Some newspapers, many magazines.
Open Mon-Thurs till midnight, Fri & Sat till 1am.

—Magazines: Backlist

Jay Bee Magazines
134 West 26 Street. 675-1600. Over 2 million
backdate magazines and periodicals; some go
back as far as 1910. Cultured setting, helpful service. Good research source.

Notions
*The large stores have small notions departments,
but this city has a notions street! On West 38
Street between Fifth Avenue and Avenue of the
Americas there are 20 stores that carry trimmings.*

Hyman Hendler & Sons
67 West 38 Street. 840-8393. Full to the brim with
ribbons of every variety: satin, grosgrain, velvet,
silk in every color, size, width. *OPEN Mon-Fri.*

M&J Trimming
1008 Sixth Avenue nr West 37 St. 391-9072. All
the makings of any day's fashion accessories.
Satin ribbons, lace, eyelet, embroidered trim, silk
ropes, large feather boas. You supply the imagination. AE, CB, DC, MC, V.

Tinsel Trading Company
47 West 38 Street. 730-1030. Metallic yarns,
threads, lamés, gauzes, rosebud trimmings, antique ribbons, embroideries and more. *CLOSED
Sat in summer.*

Office Furnishings
*On West 23 Street between Ninth and Tenth Ave-
nues there are many suppliers of new and used
office furniture.*

Abie's Baby, Inc.
524 West 23 Street. 741-1920. Also, 290 Madison
Avenue at East 41 St. 686-1717. Four floors of
office furniture at discount prices. Great values:
go here first.

Office Supplies

Airline Stationery Company, Inc.
284 Madison Avenue at East 40 St. 532-6525.
Long-established reputable firm. Will supply
everything from a paper clip to a filing system. AE.

All Languages Typewriter Company
119 West 23 Street. 243-8086. Need a Hebrew,
Greek or Russian typewriter? Or perhaps one with
mathematical or astrological symbols? This is the
place.

Goldsmith Brothers, Inc.
347-1611. Long-established firm. Call for the
catalog. Wholesale and retail.

Kroll Stationers, Inc.
145 East 54 Street. 541-5000. Fine stationery and
office-supply store. Chairs, desks too. AE, MC, V.

Paper/Paper Products
(*See also* Art Stores *and* Stationery.)

80 Papers
80 Thompson Street nr Spring St. 966-1491. Specializes in paper: American handmade, Japanese
rice or lace, Italian marble and so much more.
OPEN 7 days.

Engelhard Bag & Paper Company
2358 Nostrand Avenue nr Avenue J, Brooklyn.
(1-718) 338-4680. Discounts on paper products
for party, picnic or home use. Napkins, cups,
plates, items for seasonal paper needs, some
stationery. *OPEN Mon-Fri.*

Hallmark Card & Party Basket
464 Madison Avenue nr East 51 St. 838-0880.
Wide selection of paper party products. MC, V.

Il Papiro
1021 Lexington Avenue nr East 73 St. 288-9330.
Also, Hearld Center, 1 Herald Square, at West 34
St. 563-1555. The full line of fine handmade
Florentine papers. Wonderful photo albums. AE,
DC, MC, V.

Paper East Party Goods
866 Lexington Avenue at East 65 St. 249-0129.
Well-stocked party store. Piñatas, napkins,
plates, hats and handmade cards.

Paper House
18 Greenwich Avenue at West 10 St. 741-1569;
1370 Third Avenue at East 78 St. 879-2937.
Everything for a party in paper: hats, plates, napkins, favors, invitations. RSVP and thank-you
cards. Toys, favors, masks, gift wraps and holiday
specialty items. MC, V. *OPEN 7 days.*

Party Bazaar Dennison
390 Fifth Avenue nr 36 St. 695-6820; 30 Rockefeller Center, concourse and upstairs 581-0310.
The original party store. Plates, favors, napkins,
hats, cards, settings, wrapping paper and stationery items. Party consultants, too. AE, MC, V.

Pineider
Trump Tower, 725 Fifth Avenue at 56 St, 5th level.
688-5554. Handsome Florentine papers in glorious
colors, from the famed 200-year-old Italian firm.
Leather desk accessories, too. AE, MC, V.

Party

For children's party information, see KIDS' NEW
YORK. See Caterers for party foods, also Paper/
Paper Products for decorations and party suppl-
ies.

—Party Help

Columbia Student Bartending Agency
280-4535. Undergraduates trained in tending bar.
Reasonable rates.

Great Performances
219-2800. Waitresses and waiters, male and
female bartenders, all with theatrical aspirations.
Catering, too, from cocktail parties to full dinners.
Professional performers produce a perfect party.

Lend-a-Hand
362-8200. Aspiring actors and actresses who
have bartending, waitressing and baby-sitting experience. Also available: clowns, Santas, belly
dancers, piano players. Four-hour minimum.

Linda Kaye
195 East 76 Street. 288-7112. Party-planner extraordinaire. Rent a hollow 3-tiered cake for a real
surprise party. Other imaginative services.

Manhattan Party Package
Barbara Gillen. 741-0567. Capable lady, will create a party from invitations and flowers to rental of
her own Greenwich Village town house with garden for special occasions.

Places
737-7536. Free information to those who need
special-events location advice.

Renta Yenta
759-1131. Will do "anything that is legal and kind."
Executes amazing feats: dinner in a treehouse,
transportation via rickshaw or stagecoach, party
invites delivered by carrier pigeon, and more. Call
Mon-Fri.

World Yacht Enterprises Ltd.
14 West 55 Street. 246-4811. Caters private parties on yachts for 2-250 people.

—Party Invitations

(See also Calligraphy and Telegrams: Unusual.)

ffolio 72
888 Madison Avenue nr East 72 St. 879-0675.
Stunning, creative invitations custom designed.

—Party Music

Fiddlers Two
478-2982. A concert performance of show tunes
and romantic Continental songs set the mood for
gracious dining and intimate conversation. A gracious touch.

Juilliard School
144 West 66 Street. 799-5000, ext 313. Will send
student musicians who can play Bach, Bee-
thoven, or Beatles.

Manhattan School of Music
120 Claremont Avenue nr West 122 St. 749-2802.
School acts as mini concert bureau.

Michael Carney
200 East 71 Street. 628-4447. Middle-of-the-road
music by a full-size orchestra or one musician.
Book a year in advance for maestro Carney himself.

Robert Psotto
288-5226. Has bagpipes, will travel in full traditional dress.

Stoy Mobile Discotheque
211 East 43 Street. 557-1588. For a disco evening: a disc jockey. 5,000 of the most recent and
oldie discs, and lights too.

—Party Paraphernalia

(See also Paper/Paper Products and Ice.)

**Famous Party Suppliers & Broadway Party
Tent Service**
868 Kent Avenue, Brooklyn. (1-718) 783-2700. All
boroughs. Can fill orders on a day's notice for
china, glassware, silverware, tables and cloths,
napkins, chairs, coat racks, and bars.

Jamaica Tent Company, Inc.
94 East Industry Court, Deer Park, Long Island.
(1-516) 242-0399. Will rent tents, caravans, or
dance floors, for outside affairs.

New York Fair & Rental Company
961 East 51 Street, Brooklyn. (1-718) 467-4512.
Las Vegas bazaar booths, cotton-candy
machines. OPEN 7 days.

Party Time
82-33 Queens Boulevard, Elmhurst. Queens. (1-
718) 457-1122; 429-7852. Services all 5
boroughs. Rents china (Ginori if you wish, or
kosher), glassware, tablecloths and napkins,
chairs, coat racks, bars, hot dog or ice cream
wagons. Free pickup and delivery.

Service Party Rental
521 East 72 Street. 288-7361. Services Manhattan only. Silverware, china, tablecloths, napkins, chairs (plain or ballroom) and bars. Needs a
week's notice in the holiday season. OPEN Mon-
Fri.

Toy Balloon Corporation
204 East 38 Street. 682-3803. Will imprint balloons of all shapes and sizes. Minimum 2 dozen.
Order must be in person or prepaid in the mail.
OPEN Mon-Fri.

Pens

(See also Art Stores; Office Supplies; Stationery.)

Arthur Brown & Bro., Inc.
2 West 46 Street. 575-5555. The International
Pen Shop carries every brand you can name from
Anson to Waterman, including Mont Blanc,
Staedtler, Garland, etc., in a wide variety of styles.
Authorized Parker repair spot. AE, DC, MC, V.
OPEN Mon-Fri.

Stanton's Quills
924 West Beach Street, Long Beach. 327-7000.
Also at Bloomingdale's and the South Street
Museum Shop. Unique, inexpensive, old-
fashioned and functional hand-cut goose quill
pens. Non-spill inkwells and sepia ink. AE, MC, V.
By appointment only.

Writing Shop
Sam Flax. 55 East 55 Street. 620-3050. Pens from

$2.95 to $4,500. Antique desk accessories too. AE, MC, V. *CLOSED Sat in summer.*

Pets

(*See also* Aquariums. *For animals in transit, see* TRAVEL & VACATION INFORMATION.)

—Pets: Adoption

Bulletin boards in veterinarians' offices and the classified sections of the New York Times *and* Village Voice *offer pets free to someone who can provide a good home.*

A.S.P.C.A.
441 East 92 Street. 876-7700. To adopt a cat or dog you must have ID and be over age 18. Will spay or neuter your pet for a small fee. *OPEN 7 days.*

Bide-a-Wee Home Association
410 East 38 Street. 532-4457; recording, 532-4455. To adopt, you must be over 18 and have 2 pieces of ID. *OPEN 7 days.*

Humane Society of New York City
306 East 59 Street. 752-4840. There is a small fee to adopt a cat or dog, but it's well worth it. *OPEN 7 days.*

Pet Rescue
P.O. Box 393; Larchmont, NY 10538. (1-914) 834-6770. Nonprofit agency will match a pet to your needs and requirements. Appointment necessary; fee is a tax deductible contribution.

—Pets: Burial

Hartsdale Canine Cemetery, Inc.
75 North Central Avenue, Hartsdale, NY. (1-914) 949-2583. Established in 1896 for all pets. Interment.

—Pets: Grooming

The larger pet stores offer grooming services.
Karen's
1220 Lexington Avenue nr East 82 St. 472-9440. Specializes in plucking.
New York School of Dog Grooming
248 East 34 Street. 685-3777. All breeds groomed at low prices by supervised students. *By appointment.*

—Pets: Lost & Found

Petfinders
609 Columbus Avenue nr West 90 St. 877-5191. Nonprofit organization. Clearinghouse for lost-and-found pet information. *OPEN Mon-Fri 9am-2pm.* At other times recorded info.

—Pets: Stores

American Kennels
55 West 8 Street. 260-6230; 786 Lexington Avenue nr East 61 St. 838-8460. Wide selection of AKC-registered purebred pups, CFC purebred kittens. AE, DC, MC, V. *OPEN 7 days.*
Fabulous Felines, Inc.
133 Lexington Avenue nr East 29 St. 889-9865. For over 20 years. Good source for exotic cats. MC, V.
Fang & Claw
304 West 14 Street. 675-2669. Best selection of

reptiles and snakes outside of the Amazon. *OPEN Mon-Fri 3-7pm.*
Felines of Distinction, Ltd.
552 Hudson Street nr Perry St. 675-9023. Large variety of pedigree cats: supplies, grooming, boarding. AE, MC, V.

—Pets: Supplies

Animal Feeds, Inc.
3255 Park Avenue nr 163 St, Bronx. 293-7750. Over 300 varieties of pet food available.
Beasty Feast
605 Hudson Street nr East 10 St; 237 Bleecker Street nr Sixth Ave. 243-3261. Good discounts on food. Delivery available. Natural dog food and accessories too.
Karen's
1220 Lexington Avenue nr East 82 St. 472-9440. Carries King Mutt fashions: doggie T-shirts, raincoats, boots, and accessories. Grooming; small selection of puppies and kittens. AE, MC, V.

—Pets: Training

City Dog
158 West 23 Street. 255-3618. Basic obedience classes to solve housebreaking and chewing problems. For puppies, dogs of all ages. Observe a lesson free.
New York Academy of Dog Training
655-0700. Highly recommended for its caring training techniques. *In your home.* Takes 4-6 weeks.

—Pets: Treatment

Animal Ambulance Service
New York City. 233-3300. Payment in advance; someone has to accompany animal to hospital. *On call 24 hours a day. 7 days a week.*
Animal Medical Care Center
510 East 62 Street. 838-8100. *24 hours a day. 7 days a week.*
A.S.P.C.A.
441 East 92 Street. Emergency information: day 876-7701; evening 876-7711.
Friends of Animals
11 West 60 Street. 247-8077. Private agency dedicated to humane animal treatment. Free info regarding spaying, neutering and declawing.
Mobile Veterinary Unit
2441 Bath Avenue, Brooklyn. (1-718) 373-0240. House calls for basic exams or emergency. The van is equipped for surgery. Services Brooklyn, Lower Manhattan, Staten Island and Queens. On the road: *Mon-Fri 11am-7pm.* Emergencies only *Sat 9am-2pm.* AE, MC, V.

Pharmacies

Alexander's has a low-priced pharmacy department. (*See also* Bath)

Bigelow Pharmacy
414 Sixth Avenue nr West 8 St. 533-2700. Lovely chemist shop in business since 1838. For prescriptions, surgical supplies, cosmetics and perfumes. MC, V. *OPEN 7 days; holidays too.*
Cambridge Chemists
21 East 65 Street. 734-5678. Exclusive purveyor of Cyclax of London, Queen Elizabeth's favorite

beauty products, as well as Floris of London soaps and a wide variety of toiletries, treatment preparations and cosmetics from Europe. Such a civilized place. MC, V.

Duane Reade
*40 Beaver Street nr Broad St. 943-3690; *19 Park Place nr Broadway. 349-5175; 50 Pine Street nr Water St. 425-3720; *90 John Street nr Gold St. 349-1285; 300 Park Avenue South nr East 22 St. 533-7580; *360 Park Avenue South nr East 26 St. 685-6717; *1412 Broadway nr West 39 St. 354-2553; 370 Lexington Avenue nr East 41 St. 683-9704; 20 East 46 Street. 682-2448; 485 Lexington Avenue nr East 47 St. 682-5338; 1150 Sixth Avenue nr West 44 St. 221-3588. Excellent chain for good values on prescriptions, cosmetics, vitamins, perfumes and beauty-care products. Windows display current good buys. NY trivia: the name is a meeting of 2 downtown streets. *CLOSED Sat & Sun.

Freeda Pharmacy
36 East 41 Street. 685-4980. The highest quality nutritional supplements including Freeda© vegetarian "born free"; no sugar, nor artifical color or flavor. OPEN Mon-Fri.CLOSED Sat & Sun.

Kaufman Pharmacy
557 Lexington Avenue at East 50 St. 755-2266. Make a note of this one; it never closes! Good for emergency prescriptions; delivers too. AE, MC, OPEN 7 days a week 24 hours a day.

Kiehl's Pharmacy
109 Third Avenue nr East 13 St. 475-3400. Since 1851 this fascinating pharmacy has carried a large selection of herbs, roots, dried flowers, berries and spices, all natural ingredients for remedies to cure what ails you. They make all their own products including age retardent cream. Alas, they no longer carry leeches. P.S. Have a peek at the Lamborgines—in the shop! AE, CB, DC, MC, V.

Photographic Equipment
If you are shopping for the best price, check the Sunday Times Arts and Leisure section, where camera stores advertise their weekly specials.

Alkit Camera Shop
866 Third Avenue nr East 53 St. 832-2101. Knowledgeable staff takes care of your camera needs. Rentals, repairs and processing too. AE, MC, V.

Camera Discount Center
89A Worth Street nr Broadway. 226-1014. Discounts on name-brand cameras. Meet or beat any price advertised. MC, V. OPEN Sun-Fri.

Forty-Seventh St. Photo, Inc.
67 West 47 Street, 2nd fl. 260-4410. Perhaps the lowest prices in the city. Good value and selection, weekly specials. Also TVs, typewriters, video games and recorders. MC, V. OPEN Sun-Fri (only till 2pm on Fri).

Hirsch Photo
699 Third Avenue at East 44 St. 557-1150. Excellent well stocked discount store. Very personal, helpful service. MC, V. OPEN Mon-Fri.

Nikon House
620 Fifth Avenue nr 50 St. 586-3907. Hold and handle Nikon cameras, lenses and accessories. Nothing is for sale, and the expert knowledge and info to be found here are free. OPEN Tues-Sat.

Willoughby's
110 West 32 Street. 564-1600. Large camera department store with complete range of cameras, lighting and darkroom equipment, and second-hand department. AE, DC, MC, V. OPEN 7 days.

Plants
The wholesale plant district, Avenue of the Americas from West 25 to West 30 Street, is a good place to shop for plants, especially on Sunday. Most new shipments arrive on Monday and many times room is needed—which means even lower prices.

—Plants: Stores

Farm & Garden Nursery
2 Sixth Avenue at White St. 431-3577. Established 1939. Large indoor and outdoor garden center open year round. Sells trees, bushes, potted plants and trays of flowering plants. Service uneven, sometimes rushed. MC, V. OPEN 7 days.

Grass Roots Garden
75 University Place nr East 11 St. 533-0380. Very complete source of plants, materials and services. AE, MC, V. OPEN Tues-Sun; CLOSED Sun in summer.

Terrestris
409 East 60 Street. 758-8181. Unique rooftop greenhouse—"specialists in plants that survive." Written 1-year guarantee on plants and trees. Low prices. AE, MC. OPEN 7 days (Mon & Thurs till 9pm.)

—Plants: Care
Many of the larger plant stores have people who maintain and doctor plants.

Rain-dears, Ltd.
129 West 56 Street. 265-2629. Horticultural consultants dispense very personal care: design, maintain, install, or plant-sit while you're on holiday.

—Plants: Planters
(See also Baskets.)

Pottery World/Clay Craft
807 Sixth Avenue nr West 27 St. 242-2903. If you've got the plant, they've got the pot. Specialists in terracotta. Many imports. MC, V. OPEN 7 days.

Postcards
(See also Memorabilia.)

Untitled
159 Prince Street nr West Broadway. 982-2068. This small SoHo store stocks the world's largest collection of museum art postcards and more. A small delight. Now also in larger quarters at 680 Broadway, 982-1145.

Posters
(See also MUSEUMS & GALLERIES, Prints & Posters)

—Posters: Original

Belgis Freidel Gallery
90 Thompson Street nr Spring St. 431-9270. Art
Deco and Art Nouveau original posters: Cheret,
Paul Colin, Grasset, Lautrec, Mucha, Steinlen.
MC, V. OPEN Tues-Sun.

L'Affiche Galerie
145 Spring Street nr Wooster St. 966-4620. Contemporary posters and prints, both American and
European. AE, MC, V. OPEN Tues-Sun.

Motion Picture Arts Gallery
133 East 58 Street, 10th fl. 223-1009. Original
vintage movie posters, silent era through the
present, with the emphasis on older material.
Price range $20-50,000. MC, V. OPEN Tues-Sat.

Poster America
174 Ninth Avenue nr West 21 St. 691-1615. Old
movie, war, theatrical posters. Friendly,
knowledgeable people. AE, DC, MC, V.

Poster Originals Ltd.
924 Madison Avenue nr East 73 St. 861-0422;
*158 Spring Street. 226-7720. American and Eu-
ropean contemporary art posters. AE, MC, V.
*OPEN Tues-Sun.

Reinhold-Brown Gallery
26 East 78 Street. 734-7999. Fine posters: Bayer,
Beggarstaffs, Bradley, Cassandre, Hohlwein,
Klimt, Lautrec, Lissitzky, Macintosh, Mucha,
Tschichold, Van de Velde. OPEN Tues-Sat.

Triton Gallery
323 West 45 Street. 765-2472. Broadway theatrical posters. Mostly new, some old. AE, MC, V.

—Posters: Reproduction

Azuma is a good source for popular posters, including show-business personalities and reproductions of Art Nouveau classics. Most museum
gift shops carry posters of artworks in their permanent collections. (See also Memorabilia.)

Postermat
37 West 8 Street. 982-2946. Huge selection of art
print, film and personality posters. T-shirts with
popular sayings and images. MC, V. OPEN 7
days.

Records & Tapes

Colony Records
1619 Broadway nr West 49 St. 265-2050. A
Broadway institution; carries the new, but specializes in hard-to-get items. AE, CB, DC, MC, V.
OPEN Mon-Fri 9:30am-2:30am; Sat & Sun till
3am.

Disc-O-Mat
*1518 Broadway nr West 44 St. 575-0686; 581
Fifth Avenue nr 47 St. 751-7778; 714 Lexington
Avenue nr East 57 St. 759-3777; 474 Seventh
Avenue at West 36 St. 736-1150; 101 East 42
Street. 682-2151. Good prices on current records
and tapes. *OPEN 7 days.

J & R Music
23 Park Row. 732-8600. Large, comprehensive
record store.

King Karol
*126 West 42 Street. 354-6880; *1500 Broadway
nr West 43 St. 869-0230; *1521 Third Avenue nr

East 86 St. 472-2922. Large comprehensive
stores deal exclusively in records and tapes.
Good selections all categories. Will take special
orders. AE, DC, MC, V. *OPEN 7 days.

Record Hunter
507 Fifth Avenue nr 42 St. 697-8970. An independent discount store established in 1945.
Well-stocked in spoken-word, international and
children's records, but carries a full line. AE, CB,
DC, MC, V.

Sam Goody
*666 Third Avenue nr East 43 St. 986-8480; *1290
Sixth Avenue nr West 51 St. 246-8730; 235 West
49 Street. 246-1708; *5309 Kings Plaza Mall,
Brooklyn. (1-718) 253-6701; *91-21 Queens
Boulevard, Elmhurst, Queens. (1-718) 779-5020.
Large record and tape selections, including some
hard-to-find. Video and audio equipment too.
Great weekly sales on current albums. Full label-
line sales as well; check Sunday Times, Arts and
Leisure section, for listings. AE, MC, V. *OPEN 7
days.

Tower Records
*Broadway & East 4 Street. 505-1500. Also, 1965
Broadway & West 68 Street. 799-2500. Mammoth
record emporium—more than 400,000 titles!
From the current hot rock to the obscure import.
Well-stocked in all areas including jazz and classical. Video rental, too. *Classical annex around
the corner for bargains. OPEN 365 days a year
9am-midnight.

—Records: Specialized

Bleecker Bob's Golden Oldies
118 West 3 Street. 475-9677. Specializes in New
Wave music, independent labels, British imports.
Very knowledgeable re "what's happening" in
music today. OPEN 7 days till 3am.

Dayton's
824 Broadway at East 12 St. 254-5084. Specializes in out-of-print records. Huge selection of
movie sound tracks, original-cast shows and
spoken-word records. Used rock, jazz, classical.
Perfect-condition review copies of albums at half
price.

Discophile, Inc.
26 West 8 Street. 473-1902. Specializes in classical music. Large selection of imported records.
Hard-to-find classics and "private" recordings.
MC, V.

Golden Disc
239 Bleecker Street nr Sixth Ave. 255-7899.
"World's largest oldies shop." Rock, sound tracks
and jazz LPs and 45s. Color and photo discs
available, too. MC, V. OPEN 7 days.

Gryphon Record Shop
606 Amsterdam Avenue nr West 88 St. 874-1588.
Over 30,000 rare and out-of-print LPs—excellent
classical stock. Also, Broadway, jazz, spoken arts
and more. Good prices. Welcome want lists. MC,
V. OPEN 7 days.

Jazz Record Center
133 West 72 Street. 877-1836. Old, rare, out-of-
print jazz.

Music Inn
169 West 4 Street nr Sixth Ave. 243-5715.

Obscure international and ethnic records, including English, Irish and Celtic folk music. Strong on African music. Also, jazz, blues and folk. AE, DC, MC, V.

Music Masters
25 West 43 Street. 840-1958. The opera buff's store. Private-label recordings of operas and shows, rare works and performances on disc or tape. Will actually let you play a record. AE, MC, V.

Record Exchange
842 Seventh Avenue nr West 54 St. 247-3878. Mainly for collectors looking for specific nostalgic out-of-print items. Radio shows, movie sound tracks, non-rock recordings. Expensive.

SoHo Music Gallery
26 Wooster Street at Grand St. 966-1637. New rock, electronic, modern classical. Jazz and ethnic music. AE, MC, V. *OPEN 7 days.*

Venus Records
61 West 8 Street, 2nd fl. 598-4459. Current and 1960s British rock. MC, V. *OPEN 7 days.*

Vinylmania
52 Carmine Street nr Bleecker St. 691-1720. Used records but the specialty is the 12" disco single. At 30 Carmine Street is the rock outlet. *OPEN 7 days.*

Rubber Stamps
For conventional functional stamps, see Art Stores *or* Office Supplies. *These are of a more "artsy," whimsical nature.*

Mythology
370 Columbus Avenue nr West 77 St. 874-0774. Largest retail rubber-stamp collection in the world. Hundreds of images ready made. AE, MC, V. *OPEN 7 days.*

Silver
(*See also* Antiques: Jewelry.)

Asprey & Co., Ltd.
Trump Tower, 725 Fifth Avenue at 56 St. 688-1811. The prestigious London establishment known for its exclusive silver patterns; antique and modern silver, crystal, china. Luxurious gift items such as 18kt beard combs, and custom-made leather goods. AE, MC, V.

B. Altman & Company
Fifth Avenue & 34 Street. 689-7000. Good silver department: flatware, coffee & tea sets by the leading manufacturers. AE, Altman charge.

Eastern Silver Co.
54 Canal Street nr Orchard St, 2nd fl. 226-5708. Large selection of silver articles. In addition your own design can be reproduced. Repairs, too. *OPEN Sun-Fri (till 2pm on Fri).*

James Robinson
15 East 57 Street. 752-6166. For over 70 years the premier purveyor of fine 17th- to 19th-century English hallmark silver, rare porcelain dinner sets and antique jewelry. Known, too, for their own hand-forged silver flatware. Upstairs: James II for 19th-century bibelots.

Jean's Silversmiths
16 West 45 Street. 575-0723. Largest selection of discontinued silver patterns (over 900), plus new ones at lower prices than most other shops (flat and holloware). Replating. MC, V. *OPEN Mon-Fri.*

S. J. Shrubsole
104 East 57 Street. 753-8920. Antique English and American silver, jewelry and early American silver. The best selection of silver in New York. AE, MC, V. *CLOSED Sat in summer.*

S. Wyler, Inc.
713 Madison Avenue at East 63 St. 838-1910. Antique and modern silver and fine porcelain. Repairs.

—Silver: Repairs
Brandt & Opis Silversmiths
145 West 45 Street, Rm 1209. 245-9237. Silver and gold replating; removal of dents, bruises and monograms. *OPEN Mon-Fri 8am-3:30pm.*

Columbia Lighting & Silversmiths
499 Third Avenue at East 33 St. 725-5250. Since 1935, silver replating and repair; 24kt gold replating, too. AE, MC, V. *OPEN Mon-Fri; Thurs till 8pm.*

Mr. Fixit
1300 Madison Avenue at East 92 St. 369-7775. You bring it; they'll try to repair, replate, repolish, or rework it.

Thome Silversmith
328 East 59 Street. 758-0655. Established 1931. They repair, polish, replate silver and gold; remove monograms. Copper and brass work too. Buys and sells silverware. *OPEN Mon-Fri from 8:30am.*

Sports Equipment
—Sports Equipment: General
Alexander's and Macy's have large departments for sporting and exercise equipment.

Herman's World of Sporting Goods
135 West 42 Street. 730-7400; 845 Third Avenue nr East 51 St. 688-4603; 110 Nassau Street nr Fulton St. 233-0733; *39 West 34 Street. 279-8900. Leading merchandiser of discount sporting goods and apparel from running shoes to boxing equipment. Large selection for men, women and kids. AE, DC, MC, V. **OPEN 7 days.*

Modell's
243 West 42 Street. 525-8111. Branches. Well-known sporting-goods store for the serious athlete. Also carries blue-jeans and shirts. MC, V.

Morsan's
747 Third Avenue nr East 46 St. 758-2855. Caters to outdoor activities. Camping and exercise equipment. AE, MC, V. *OPEN 7 days.*

Paragon Sporting Goods
867 Broadway at East 18 St. 255-8036. Since 1908. Impressive selection of sporting clothes and equipment from down jackets, track shoes and shorts to baseball equipment, football gear, skates & skis, lacrosse and hockey. Good roller-skate department. *Great* values. Mail and phone orders. AE, DC, MC, V.

—Sports Equipment: Boating
Goldberg's Marine
12 West 46 Street. 840-8280. *The* source for marine supplies—at discount. The necessities plus fowl weather apparel. AE, MC, V.

Hans Klepper Corporation
35 Union Square West nr West 16 St. 243-3428.
Inflatable boats, easy to carry, fast to assemble. MC,
V.

—Sports Equipment: Camping &
Mountaineering

Greenman's Down East Service Center
93 Spring Street nr Broadway. 925-2632. Down
jackets, knapsacks, tents, hiking publications. Expert cleaning and repair of down vests and jackets. *

Hudson's
Third Avenue at East 13 St. 473-7321. Cots, cool-
ers, canvas tarp, and tents. Back packs for rent.
AE, MC, V. *OPEN 7 days.*

—Sports Equipment: Fishing

Capitol Fishing Tackle Co.
218 West 23 Street. 929-6132. Since 1897. The
fisherman's friend. Equipment for fresh, salt-
water, deep-sea and big-game fishing. Big discounts. *OPENS at 8am.*

Louis' Fishing Tackle
139 Orchard Street nr Delancey St. 475-0174.
Large selection of discount fishing equipment for
the sport fisherman.

Orvis New York
355 Madison Avenue at East 45 St. 697-3133.
Complete line of fly rods, reels and accessories.

—Sports Equipment: Golf

Richard Metz Golf Studio
36 East 50 Street. 759-6940. Golf clubs for men
and women. Instruction. MC, V.

—Sports Equipment: Hunting

Hunting World
16 East 53 Street. 755-3400. For the big-game
hunter or the poser. Clothes and equipment (except guns) for a mini-safari. AE.

—Sports Equipment: Riding

H. Kaufman & Son
139 East 24 Street. 684-6060. Longtime saddler
housed in a former horse auction gallery. Mostly
Western-, some English-style, riding paraphernalia. Fine selection of *authentic* western duds.
AE, DC, MC, V.

Miller Harness Company
123 East 24 Street. 673-1400. Western-tradition
riding equipment, clothes, hats and accessories.
AE, DC, MC, V.

M. J. Knoud
716 Madison Avenue nr East 63 St. 838-1434. In
the English riding tradition, britches, hats, boots,
jackets, crops, blouses. AE, V.

—Sports Equipment: Running

Athlete's Foot
170 West 72 Street. 874-1003. (Ten Manhattan
locations.) For the serious runner. Every type of
running shoe available for men and women. Also a
line of active sports basics. AE, MC, V. *OPEN 7
days.*

Runner's World, Inc.
275 Seventh Avenue nr West 26 St. 691-2565.

Large choice of track and running shoes; jogging
outfits. Hiking and work boots, too. MC, V.

—Sports Equipment: Skating

Dream Wheels
295 Mercer Street nr East 8 St. 677-0005. A none-
too-serious spot for rentals, sales of pre-
assembled or custom, service, instruction,
accessories. Spring and summer flashlight skate
parties. Skateboards and aerobic equipment too.
MC, V. *OPEN Tues-Sat.*

Paragon Sporting Goods Company
867 Broadway at East 18 St. 255-8036. Excellent
stock and custom indoor and outdoor skates plus
paraphernalia, including safety gear. Knowledgeable staff. AE, DC, MC, V. *OPEN 7 days.*

Peck & Goodie
919 Eighth Avenue nr West 54 St. 246-6123. Well-
known skate shop. Large variety of ice and roller
skates for men and women.

—Sports Equipment: Skiing

Bogner
655 Madison Avenue at East 60 St. 752-2282.
The people who revolutionized the slopes—with
stretch pants (in the 1950s). Ski fashions and
Bogner ready-to-wear from Germany.

Olympic Ski Shops, Inc.
1106 Cortelyou Road, Brooklyn. (1-718) 284-
3155. Ski outfits, boots, goggles, and skis. AE,
DC, MC, V.

Princeton Skate & Ski Chalet
379 Fifth Avenue nr 36 St. 684-0100. Figure and
roller skates, skis, down jackets and outfits. A
good selection. Expert advice. AE, DC, MC, V.

—Sports Equipment: Tennis

Feron's Racquet & Tennis Shop
55 East 44 Street. 867-6350. Good values on
racquets and outfits for men and women. AE, MC,
V. *CLOSED Sat in summer.*

Stationery
*Each of the major department stores, plus Tif-
fany's and Cartier's, has a line of stationery. (See
also* Office Supplies; Paper/Paper Products.)

Brown & Co., Stationers
South Street Seaport. 211 Water Street. 669-
9419. A restored 1836 stationer complete with an
antique hand printing press that works! Antique
and modern merchandise for sale. *OPEN 7 days.*

ffolio 72
888 Madison Avenue nr East 72 St. 879-0675.
Lovely stationery boutique. Imprinting done. AE.

Henri Bendel
10 West 57 Street. 247-1110. The Paper Shop
carries the trendiest in non-traditional stationery
and invitations. AE, MC, V.

Paper by the Pound
Macy's Cellar, Broadway & West 34 Street. 971-
6000. Stationery, sizes 4½ by 6 in. 6 by 9. 8½ by
10¼, in a huge assortment of colors, sold by the
pound (you can buy ¼ or ½ lb if you wish). Wrapping and tissue paper too. AE, Macy's charge.
OPEN 7 days.

Stereo & Sound Systems

ABC Trading Company
31 Canal Street nr Essex St. 228-5080. Stocks most major brands and will order what they don't have. Good discounts. *OPEN Sun-Fri.*

Central Electronics
37 Essex Street nr Grand St. 673-3220. Substantial discounts available on Sony, Panasonic, KLH, Fisher and Garrard. Call with model number. MC, V. *OPEN Sun-Fri.*

Crazy Eddie's
405 Sixth Avenue nr West 8 St. 645-1196; 2067 Coney Island Avenue nr Kings Highway, Brooklyn. (1-718) 645-1196; 300 East Fordham Road, Bronx. 645-1196. Popular sound-equipment and record store. Claims it won't be undersold. Go *in spite of* the commercials. MC, V. *OPEN 7 days.*

Grand Central Radio
155 East 45 Street. 599-2630. Established in 1925, this friendly shop sells Awig, Bang & Olufsen, Proton, KLH, and Nakamichi, plus many other famous makers stocked at this audio showroom. Available for overseas: 220 volt equipment. AE, DC, MC, V.

Radio Shack
350 Fifth Avenue nr 32 St. 244-0444; 1616 First Avenue nr East 84 St. 737-2151; 120 East 59 Street. 838-5745; 308 East 23 Street. 673-8548; 469 Seventh Avenue nr West 36 St. 947-6820; 31 Park Row. 349-8533; 250 West 57 Street. 581-7731; 925 Lexington Avenue nr East 68 St. 249-3028. The supermarket of sound. Good value.

Uncle Steve
343 Canal Street nr Church St. 226-4010. Low prices on stereo equipment (Technics, Akai, JVC, Teac) plus TV and video recorders. Sound room every day but Sun. *OPEN 7 days.*

—Stereo Repair

Analogique Systems Laboratories
17 West 17 Street, 10th fl. 989-4240. Very professional servicing and repair, plus custom designing of sound systems. *OPEN Mon-Fri.*

Telegrams: Unusual
Western Union has resumed its national singing-telegram service, either by telephone (4-hours' notice) or in person (14-hours' notice). For details, call 962-7111. For more traditional telegrams see BASIC INFORMATION.

Balloons to You™
895-3717, (1-516) 868-2325. For a lighthearted greeting, two mylar balloons, imprinted with your message sent anywhere in the US via UPS (3 days). In addition to solicitations, invitations, centerpieces, too.

National Singing Telegram
(1-800) 227-4702. Musical telegrams for any occasion. Either in person or via telephone, they will get your message across.

Yenta-gram
475-0566. For a little gelt—a lot of guilt.

Theatrical
(*See also* Costumes *and* Memorabilia.)

One Shubert Alley
1 Shubert Alley, 311 West 43 Street. 944-4133. Posters, buttons, T-shirts, sweatshirts, theatrical theme jewelry, duffles, recordings of current B'way and Off-B'way productions. Plus souvenirs of past hits. Mail order, nationwide and overseas. AE, MC, V. *OPEN 7 days.*

Performer's Outlet
222 East 85 Street. 249-8435. First class crafts shop. Sells crafts and art done by theater people. One-of-a-kind items. Complimentary sherry or tea. AE, MC, V.

Thrift Shops
There's a heavy concentration of thrift shops from East 75 Street and Second Avenue/Third Avenue to East 89 Street and Third Avenue. They all offer secondhand and some unused merchandise of varying quality. Some bargains can be found, and the proceeds do go to charity. Caveat: not all shops with thrift in their names are charity stores.

Tobacconists

Alfred Dunhill of London
620 Fifth Avenue at 50 St. 481-6950. Also at Bloomingdale's. Famed tobacconist. Custom-blended tobaccos, pipes, humidors, cigars and gifts, including their famed expensive lighters. AE, MC, V.

Connoisseur Pipe Shop
51 West 46 Street. 247-6054. Established in 1917. Unique pipes custom made: Briars, Meerschaums. Tobacco mixtures. Skillful pipe repairs. AE, MC, V.

Don-Lou Pipe Shop
2058 Bath Avenue nr 21 Ave, Brooklyn. (1-718) 372-9032. Custom shop for handmade pipes and house blends of tobacco.

Gilbert's Pipeline, Ltd.
122 East 42 Street. 687-6907. Hand-carved and aged briarwood pipes. Wide selection of domestic and imported tobacco and accessories. AE, MC, V. *OPEN Mon-Fri.*

J. R. Tobacco Corporation
11 East 45 Street. 869-8777; *219 Broadway nr Barclay St. 233-6620. Cigars: a stock over 2,800 different sizes, shapes and colors, nickel cigars and rare expensive ones. Discount. *OPEN Mon-Fri.*

Nat Sherman Cigars
711 Fifth Avenue at 55 St. 751-9100. Pipe tobacco, cigars and 30 blends of cigarette tobacco to be wrapped in choice of paper color, with your name imprinted if you wish. Large choice of pipes, cigarette lighters. Huge walk-in humidor. AE, CB, DC, MC, V.

Tobacco Center
130 St. Marks Place nr Ave A. 674-2208. Established in 1902; offers a wide assortment of loose tobaccos.

Wally Frank, Ltd., Pipes
344 Madison Avenue nr East 44 St. 349-3366. Carries its own line of pipes and accessories, plus distinctive blends of tobacco. AE, DC, MC, V.

Toys: Collectible
For new, strictly children's toys, see KIDS' NEW

YORK, Children's Shopping: Toys. *These shops are mainly for collectors.* (*See also* Antiques.)

Fun Antiques
1174 Second Avenue nr East 61 St. 838-0730. Vintage toys, vending machines, character watches.

Iris Brown Antique Dolls
253 East 57 Street. 593-2882. Antique dolls bought, sold, repaired and loved. Specializes in Victorian dollhouses and miniature furniture to fill them with. MC, V.

Second Childhood
283 Bleecker Street nr Seventh Ave So. 989-6140. Charming but expensive tin and iron toys, soldiers, miniatures; 1850s-1950s. AE, MC, V.

Speakeasy
799 Broadway nr East 10 St. 533-2440. A fun shop with a little bit of everything for serious and not so serious collectors of vintage toys, games, jewelry, pens, magazines, postcards, advertising items, and Beatles memorabilia. Vintage clothes, too. MC, V. *OPEN Tues-Sat. CLOSED Sat in summer.*

Umbrellas
The large stores and many boutiques and handbag shops carry a line of umbrellas. Most rainy days someone on a busy street corner will be selling $2 umbrellas, guaranteed to get through that rainstorm at least!

Gloria Umbrella Mfg. Co.
39 Essex Street nr Hester St. 475-7388. A manufacturer of umbrellas. Famous-brand folding, even beach fashion umbrellas at substantial discount. Recovers and repairs too. Huge selection. *OPEN Sun-Fri (Fri till 2pm).*

Essex Umbrella Corp.
101 Essex Street nr Delancey St. 674-3394. Manufacture and sell their own brand at discount. Handbags, totes, imports too. Will imprint any logo, minimum of 50. DC, MC, V. Hours erratic, call first.

Salwen
45 Orchard Street nr Grand St. 226-1693. Knirps, Totes and designer umbrellas including Givenchy at a minimum of 25% off. MC, V. *OPEN Sun-Fri.*

Uncle Sam
161 West 57 Street. 247-7163; 7 East 46 Street. 687-4780. Stocks 50,000 umbrellas and 1,000 walking canes: every color, size and description, including beach and garden. Expert, reasonably priced repairs too. Since 1866. AE, DC, MC, V.

Video

Federal Rent-a-TV
1588 York Avenue nr East 84 St. 734-5777 or 535-9578. All brands, all sizes, pick up, delivery, replacement. B/W, color, Betamax and VHS. AE, CB, DC, MC, V.

New York Video
717 Lexington Avenue nr East 58 St, 2nd fl. 755-4640. A leader in projection TVs. Four- to 10-ft TV screens. Rental & sale. AE, CB, DC, MC, V.

Video Shack
1608 Broadway at West 49 St. 581-6260. Largest

video-cassette retailer and renter in New York. AE, CB, DC, MC, V. *OPEN 7 days.*

Watches: Contemporary
The large department stores stock a variety of watches in the inexpensive to moderate price range, with the accent on fashion. (*See also* Jewelry.)

Gubelin
745 Fifth Avenue nr 57 St. 755-0053. Fine, expensive watches, including Patek Philippe. AE, DC, MC, V. *CLOSED Sat in summer.*

Lyon's Bulova Accutron Center
339 Madison Avenue nr East 43 St. 661-6810. Large selection of Bulova clocks and watches. Repairs as well. AE, CB, DC, MC, V.

Swiss Time Center & Jewelry Company, Inc.
1328 Broadway nr West 35 St. 564-4968. Good Swiss watches, name brands. Repair work done.

Tourneau
500 Madison Avenue at East 52 St. 758-3265; Also, Trump Tower. 593-3333. Handsome, elegant and famous Swiss watches for the fashion-conscious. Expensive albeit there is a free lifetime battery replacement. AE, CB, DC, MC, V.

—Watches: Antique

Aaron Faber
666 Fifth Avenue at 53 St. 586-8411. Very large selection of antique and vintage wristwatches - turn of the century to the 1960s; Elgin, Hamilton, Patek Philippe, Rolex. For men and women. Catalog available. AE, CB, DC, MC, V.

Clock Doc
18 Lexington Avenue nr East 23 St. 475-9509. Antique watch and clock repair is his specialty; but there's one of the nicest 1920s and 30s watch collections. No credit cards.

Neil Isman Gallery
1100 Madison Avenue nr East 83 St. 628-3698. Speicializes in 1930s vintage watches including Hamilton, Rolex and Patek Philippe. AE, MC, V.

Time Will Tell
962 Madison Avenue nr East 76 St. 861-2663. A shop full of beautiful one-of-a-kind classic time pieces (1920s-1950s) for the wrist. Hamilton, Bulova, Rolex, Patek Philippe. AE, MC, V.

—Watch Bands

Straparama
425 Madison Avenue nr East 48 St. 753-9289. The largest selection of watch bands in the city, and the oddest hours. Lines form before opening. *OPEN Mon-Fri 7am-noon.*

Wines & Spirits

Astor Wines & Spirits
12 Astor Place at Lafayette St. 674-7500. A *must* for bargain-hunting oenophiles. The largest liquor store in NY State. Good selections, own brand label well-priced and comparable quality; good special sales several times during the year. *OPEN Mon-Sat 9am-9pm.*

Beekman Liquor Store
500 Lexington Avenue nr East 47 St. 759-5857. Largest discount liquor store in midtown. *OPEN Mon-Sat 8am-11pm.*

Morell & Company
307 East 53 Street. 688-9370. Beautiful, knowledgeably run wine shop. Large collection of port and excellent selection of California wines. *OPEN Mon-Fri 9:30am-7:30pm; Sat till 7pm.*

Sherry Lehmann, Inc.
679 Madison Avenue nr East 61 St. 838-7500. One of the best. Knowledgeable salespeople, excellent stock. *OPEN Mon-Sat 9am-6:45pm.*

67 Wines & Spirits
179 Columbus Avenue at West 68 St. 724-6767. Large selection of wines from France and Italy as well as domestic. *OPEN Mon-Thurs 10am-8pm; Fri & Sat noon-9pm.*

SoHo Wines and Spirits
461 West Broadway nr Prince St. 777-4332. Attractive, spacious, well-organized SoHo shop for wines. Large selection of champagnes. *OPEN Mon-Sat 10am-9pm.*

Wines by Wire
(1-800) 223-2660. Wire wine or champagne as a thoughtful gift. Minimum charge. Corporate charges available. AE, MC, V. *Available 24 hours a day 7 days a week.*

Woodenware

Bowl & Board
9 St. Marks Place nr Third Ave. 673-1724. *53 Christopher Street nr Seventh Ave So. 242-9512. Wooden salad bowls, chalices, cups, plates and implements, toys and butcher blocks for tabletops or counters. MC, V. *OPEN 7 days.*

Great North Woods
160 East 86 Street 369-6555; 425 Fifth Avenue nr 38 St. 889-0983. Large selection of fruitwood cheeseboards and mugs. Also butcher-block tables. MC, V. *OPEN 7 days.*

Zippers

The notions department in most large stores and tailor shops carry zippers.

A. Feibusch Zippers
109 Hester Street nr Eldridge St. 226-3964. Every length, in any color, with thread to match. Made to order, if not stocked. *OPEN Sun-Fri.*

Harry Kantrowitz, Inc.
555 Eighth Avenue nr East 38 St. 563-1610. Large selection of zippers for all purposes, heavy-duty to delicate. *OPEN Mon-Fri.*

24-Hour New York

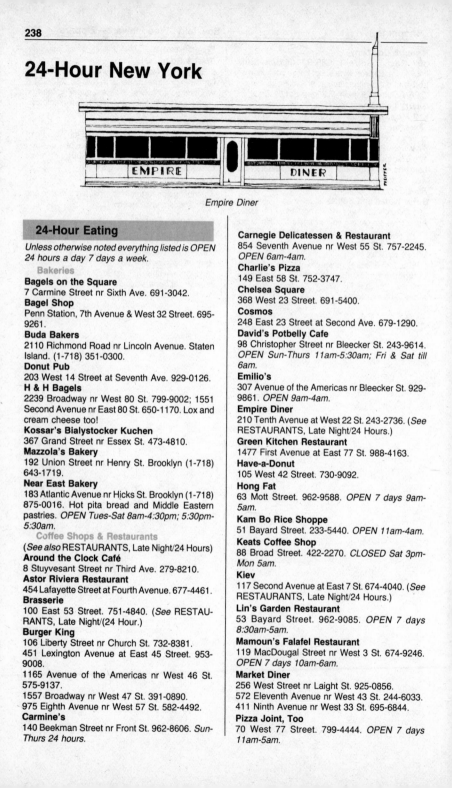

Empire Diner

24-Hour Eating

Unless otherwise noted everything listed is OPEN 24 hours a day 7 days a week.

Bakeries

Bagels on the Square
7 Carmine Street nr Sixth Ave. 691-3042.
Bagel Shop
Penn Station, 7th Avenue & West 32 Street. 695-9261.
Buda Bakers
2110 Richmond Road nr Lincoln Avenue. Staten Island. (1-718) 351-0300.
Donut Pub
203 West 14 Street at Seventh Ave. 929-0126.
H & H Bagels
2239 Broadway nr West 80 St. 799-9002; 1551 Second Avenue nr East 80 St. 650-1170. Lox and cream cheese too!
Kossar's Bialystocker Kuchen
367 Grand Street nr Essex St. 473-4810.
Mazzola's Bakery
192 Union Street nr Henry St. Brooklyn (1-718) 643-1719.
Near East Bakery
183 Atlantic Avenue nr Hicks St. Brooklyn (1-718) 875-0016. Hot pita bread and Middle Eastern pastries. *OPEN Tues-Sat 8am-4:30pm; 5:30pm-5:30am.*

Coffee Shops & Restaurants

(See also RESTAURANTS, Late Night/24 Hours)
Around the Clock Café
8 Stuyvesant Street nr Third Ave. 279-8210.
Astor Riviera Restaurant
454 Lafayette Street at Fourth Avenue. 677-4461.
Brasserie
100 East 53 Street. 751-4840. (*See* RESTAU-RANTS, Late Night/(24 Hour.)
Burger King
106 Liberty Street nr Church St. 732-8381.
451 Lexington Avenue at East 45 Street. 953-9008.
1165 Avenue of the Americas nr West 46 St. 575-9137.
1557 Broadway nr West 47 St. 391-0890.
975 Eighth Avenue nr West 57 St. 582-4492.
Carmine's
140 Beekman Street nr Front St. 962-8606. *Sun-Thurs 24 hours.*

Carnegie Delicatessen & Restaurant
854 Seventh Avenue nr West 55 St. 757-2245. *OPEN 6am-4am.*
Charlie's Pizza
149 East 58 St. 752-3747.
Chelsea Square
368 West 23 Street. 691-5400.
Cosmos
248 East 23 Street at Second Ave. 679-1290.
David's Potbelly Cafe
98 Christopher Street nr Bleecker St. 243-9614. *OPEN Sun-Thurs 11am-5:30am; Fri & Sat till 6am.*
Emilio's
307 Avenue of the Americas nr Bleecker St. 929-9861. *OPEN 9am-4am.*
Empire Diner
210 Tenth Avenue at West 22 St. 243-2736. (*See* RESTAURANTS, Late Night/24 Hours.)
Green Kitchen Restaurant
1477 First Avenue at East 77 St. 988-4163.
Have-a-Donut
105 West 42 Street. 730-9092.
Hong Fat
63 Mott Street. 962-9588. *OPEN 7 days 9am-5am.*
Kam Bo Rice Shoppe
51 Bayard Street. 233-5440. *OPEN 11am-4am.*
Keats Coffee Shop
88 Broad Street. 422-2270. *CLOSED Sat 3pm-Mon 5am.*
Kiev
117 Second Avenue at East 7 St. 674-4040. (*See* RESTAURANTS, Late Night/24 Hours.)
Lin's Garden Restaurant
53 Bayard Street. 962-9085. *OPEN 7 days 8:30am-5am.*
Mamoun's Falafel Restaurant
119 MacDougal Street nr West 3 St. 674-9246. *OPEN 7 days 10am-6am.*
Market Diner
256 West Street nr Laight St. 925-0856.
572 Eleventh Avenue nr West 43 St. 244-6033.
411 Ninth Avenue nr West 33 St. 695-6844.
Pizza Joint, Too
70 West 77 Street. 799-4444. *OPEN 7 days 11am-5am.*

Roxy Coffee Shop
20 John Street nr Broadway. 349-4704. *CLOSED Sat 3pm-Mon 6am.*
Richoux of London
1373 Avenue of the Americas nr West 55 St. 265-3090.
Silver Star
1236 Second Avenue nr East 65 St. 249-4250.
Soup Burg
1347 Second Avenue at East 71 St. 879-4814.
Tramway Coffee House
1143 Second Avenue at East 60 Street. 758-7017.
Washington Square
150 West 4 Street at Avenue of the Americas. 533-9306.

24-Hour Services

Auto Rental
Avis
217 East 43 Street. 593-8348 or (1-800) 331-1212. 30 minutes' notice. At La Guardia, JFK International and Newark International airports, available 24 hours a day.
Hertz
310 East 48 Street. 980-2002 or (1-800) 654-3131. 24-hour availability at JFK International, LaGuardia, Newark International airports.

Bank Cash Machines
Chemical Bank
Call 770-1234 for location of machine nearest you.
Citibank
Call 555-1000 for location of 24 banking centers.
Credit Cards—Lost
American Express. (1-800) 522-5500/ext 7702
Carte Blanche. Diners Club. (1-800) 525-9150.
Master Charge and Visa: Call the bank that your cards are registered with to get the appropriate phone number.

Food Stores
Manhattan
88th Street Market
1566 Third Avenue. 722-5360. *OPEN 24 hours Fri-Sat only.*
Savoy Market
940 Second Avenue nr East 50 St. 355-5132.
7-Eleven
East 22 Street & Second Avenue. 473-8613.
East 34 Street & Lexington Avenue. 684-8692.
East 69 Street & Second Avenue. 650-9551.
Sim's Deli
494 Avenue of the Americas nr West 13 St. 243-6611.
696 Third Avenue nr East 44 St. 490-7115.
Smiler's
106 Seventh Avenue South nr Sheridan Sq. 242-1889.
413 Park Avenue South nr East 28 St. 684-5175.
688 Third Avenue nr East 43 St. 682-6941.
469 Lexington Avenue nr East 45 St. 986-5120.

726 Eighth Avenue nr West 45 St. 582-2996.
637 Ninth Avenue nr West 45 St. 582-5550.
764 Eighth Avenue nr West 47 St. 581-3641.
766 Third Avenue nr East 47 St. 753-0781.
850 Seventh Avenue nr West 54 St. 757-5871.
924 Third Avenue nr East 55 St. 935-9170.
Vinnie's Market
523 Ninth Avenue nr West 39 St. 594-6045.
White Mark Delicatessen
373 Avenue of the Americas nr Waverly Pl. 473-1177.
Yorkville Delicatessen
1159 Third Avenue nr East 68 St. 535-8348.
Food Emporium
OPEN 24 hours a day Mon-Fri; Sat & Sun till midnight
316 Greenwich Street nr Duane St. 766-4598.
501 Sixth Avenue nr West 12 St.
215 Park Avenue South at East 18 St. 473-9281.
221 Lexington Avenue & East 33 St. 689-1660.
1172 Third Avenue nr East 68 St. 650-1964.
1331 First Avenue nr East 72 Street. 794-8866.
1498 York Avenue nr East 79 St. 879-9555.
1450 Third Avenue nr East 82 St. 650-9724.
2431 Broadway nr West 90 St. 874-8490.

Supermarkets
Pathmark
OPEN 24 hours a day, Mon-Fri.
Manhattan
410 West 207 Street. 569-0600.
Bronx
1851 Bruckner Boulevard. 892-0100.
1880 Bartow Avenue. 379-5001.
Brooklyn
2965 Cropsey Avenue. (1-718) 266-2705.
11110 Flatlands Avenue. (1-718) 649-8224.
Queens
31-06 Farrington Street, Whitestone. (1-718) 886-4488.
Staten Island
1351 Forest Avenue nr Crystal Ave. (1-718) 981-1900.
2875 Richmond Avenue nr Yukon Ave. (1-718) 761-8400.
2660 Hylan Boulevard. (1-718) 987-6188.

Locksmiths
All will require identification and proof of residency before they help you get into an apartment, proof of ownership with a car.
A-OK
134 East 27 Street. 431-6563.
Golden Key Locksmiths
328A Columbus Avenue nr West 76 St. 580-0066.
Liberty Locksmith, Ltd, Brooklyn
818 Flatbush Avenue nr Caton Ave. (1-718) 284-2200.
Yale Locksmiths
2314 Broadway nr West 83 St. 586-6886.

Newsstands
24-hour, Saturday only
Seventh Avenue South & Grove Street at Sheridan Square.
Hilton Hotel, 1335 Avenue of the Americas nr West 54 St.

Sheraton Center, Seventh Avenue & West 52 Street.

24-hour, 7 days a week

Avenue of the Americas at West 8 St.

Gem Spa, Second Avenue & St. Marks Place (New York's *best* egg cream!).

Third Avenue & East 23 Street.

Port Authority Bus Terminal, Eighth Avenue & West 41 Street.

Broadway & West 42 Street.

Eighth Avenue & West 46 Street.

Sixth Avenue & West 46 Street.

Second Avenue & East 53 Street.

Third Avenue & East 54 Street.

Broadway & West 72 Street.

Broadway & West 79 Street.

First Avenue & East 65 Street.

Lexington Avenue & East 65 Street.

Broadway & West 96 Street.

Broadway & West 104 Street.

Pharmacies

Kaufman Pharmacy

557 Lexington Avenue at East 50 Street. 755-2266. Deliveries within a 5-block radius. *Never closes!*

Plumbers

Sky-Way Plumbers

809 East 7 Street. 475-6233. *Available till midnight.*

Telephone Out of Order

Dial 611.

431-8100: coin-operated phones.

395-2300: telephone emergency or complaints.

Help!

Emergency

Emergency Services 24 hours a day 7 days a week.

Ambulance, Fire, Police
Dial 911.
Deaf emergency: TTY (1-800) 342-4357.
Doctor
Manhattan: 879-1000.
Bronx: 328-1000.
Brooklyn: (1-718) 771-8800.
Queens: (1-718) 268-7300.
Staten Island: (1-718) 351-3600.
Abused Child
(1-800) 342-3720.
Desperate/Suicidal
532-2400.
664-0505.
Domestic Violence Hotline
(1-800) 942-6906.
Poison
340-4494 or 764-7667 (POISONS).
Public Assistance/NYC Emergency Assistance Unit
344-5241.
Rape
732-7706.
Police Stations
Emergency: Dial 911.
Below is a listing of Manhattan police precincts and their direct numbers for questions and help.

1st Precinct
16 Ericson Place nr Canal St. 334-0611.
5th Precinct
19 Elizabeth Street nr Canal St. 334-0711.
6th Precinct
233 West 10 Street. 741-4811.
7th Precinct
19½ Pitt Street nr Broome St. 477-7311.
9th Precinct
321 East 5 Street. 477-7811.
10th Precinct
230 West 20 Street. 741-8211.
13th Precinct
230 East 21 Street. 477-7411.
Midtown Precinct South
357 West 35 Street. 239-9811.
17th Precinct
167 East 51 Street. 826-3211.
Midtown Precinct North
306 West 54 Street. 399-9311.
19th Precinct
153 East 67 Street. 472-9711.
20th Precinct
120 West 82 Street. 580-6411.
Central Park Precinct
86 Street & Transverse Road. 628-9950.
23rd Precinct
164 East 102 Street. 860-6411.

24th Precinct
151 West 100 Street. 678-1811.
25th Precinct
120 East 119 Street. 860-6511.
28th Precinct
2271 Eighth Avenue nr West 123 St. 678-1611.
30th Precinct
451 West 151 Street. 680-8811.
32nd Precinct
250 West 135 Street. 690-6311.
34th Precinct
180 Wadsworth Avenue nr West 182 St. 927-9711.

Police Services
Available 24 hours a day 7 days a week. For location of nearest precinct: 374-5000.
For general information concerning police services: 374-6700.
Ambulance
In emergency, dial 911 and a city ambulance will respond free of charge to the patient. The ambulance will take the patient to one of the 13 municipal hospitals in the city according to geographic location and hospital specialty. If a specific, non-public hospital is preferred, this list provides private 24-hour ambulance services on a fee-pay basis.
Keefe & Keefe
Covers all 5 boroughs. 988-8800.
Park Ambulance & Oxygen Service
Covers all of Manhattan and Bronx. 828-7887.
Scully-Walton
Covers all 5 boroughs. 876-6100.

Hospital Emergency Rooms
Beekman Downtown Hospital
Gold Street at Beekman Street. 233-5300. Mobile intensive care, 2 paramedic units operating 8am-8pm daily: coronary intensive-care unit.
Bellevue Hospital Center
East 29 Street at First Avenue. 561-4347. Intensive-care units include coronary, surgical (trauma), pediatric, psychiatric, neurosurgical and alcohol detoxification.
Beth Israel Medical Center
East 16 Street bet Nathan D. Perlman Pl & First Ave. 420-2840. Coronary care, neonatal intensive care, alcohol and drug detoxification.
Cabrini Medical Center
East 20 Street bet Second & Third Aves. 725-6620. Coronary-care unit, trauma-intensive-care unit, alcohol-detoxification and drug-overdose units, psychiatric facility.
Columbia Presbyterian Medical Center
622 West 168 Street. 694-2500. Metabolic, neurosurgical, pediatric intensive-care units.
Harlem Hospital
506 Lenox Avenue at East 135 Street. 491-8360. Coronary-care, neonatal and respiratory critical-care units, alcohol and drug detoxification. Crisis intervention center for battered wives and children, rape victims.
Hospital for Joint Diseases
1919 Madison Avenue at East 123 Street. 650-4000. Orthopedic problems, broken bones, arthritic pain.

Lenox Hill Hospital
100 East 77 Street bet Park & Lexington Aves.
794-4567. Coronary and neonatal intensive-care
units.
Manhattan Eye, Ear & Throat Hospital
210 East 64 Street bet Second & Third Aves. 838-
9200. Ear, eye, nose and throat emergencies.
Mount Sinai Hospital
100 Street & Fifth Avenue. 650-7171. Coronary,
trauma and medical intensive-care units, dental
emergencies; emergency pharmacy till midnight.
New York Eye & Ear Infirmary
310 East 14 Street bet First & Second Aves. 598-
1313. 24-hour emergency service for eye, ear,
nose, or throat problems.
New York Hospital
East 70 Street bet York Ave & East River. 472-
5454; 794-3200. 24-hour paramedic unit. Burn,
coronary, neurological, neonatal intensive care;
high-risk infant transport unit and treatment.
New York University Medical Center
560 First Avenue at East 33 Street. 340-7300.
Coronary care.
Roosevelt Hospital
West 58 Street off Ninth Avenue. 554-7000.
Coronary, surgical, neonatal intensive-care units;
alcohol detoxification.
St. Clare's Hospital & Health Center
West 52 Street bet Ninth & Tenth Aves. 586-1500.
Coronary, medical, surgical intensive-care units.
St. Luke's Hospital Center
West 114 Street bet Amsterdam Ave & Morning-
side Dr. 870-6661. Coronary, trauma, neonatal
intensive care; alcohol detoxification; rape in-
tervention team; 24-hour psychiatric emergency
room.
**St. Vincent's Hospital and Medical Center of
New York**
West 11 Street at Seventh Avenue. 790-7000.
Coronary, spinal-cord-trauma, psychiatric in-
tensive-care units, alcohol detoxification.

Assistance

*These organizations help and advise anyone in
need—the ill, the lonely, the victimized, the des-
perate and those people who simply need solu-
tions to problems. Remember that 24 hours a day
7 days a week, there is police assistance.*

Booklets with Useful Information
Help for Older People in New York City
A free guide for senior citizens on how to get what
you need in NYC. Send a stamped self-addressed
envelope to: The Community Council of Greater
New York, 225 Park Avenue South. New York,
N.Y. 10003. For info call 777-5000.
How to Secure Help
Free guide to social and health services in NYC.
Send a stamped, self-addressed envelope to: The
Community Council of Greater New York, 225
Park Avenue South, New York, N.Y. 10003. For
info call 777-5000.
New York Self Help Handbook
A step-by-step guide to neighborhood projects

and useful information on how to get things done
in NYC. Call or write to: The Citizens Committee
for New York City, Inc., 3 West 29 Street, New
York, N.Y. 10001. 684-6767.

General
**New York City Human Resources Administra-
tion**
250 Church Street. 553-5997. Assistance Unit:
344-5241 or -5224. *24 hours 7 days a week.* This
city agency provides public assistance in many
areas. Call for referral to appropriate divisions.
Below is a list of departments covered by HRA:
  Child Services: foster and adoption.
  Medicaid/Medicare: medical-insurance benefits.
  Family & Adult Services: home care, foster
  care for adults.
  Office of Income Support: child support from
  absent parents.
  General Social Services: referral, interced-
  ing unit, outreach center.
  Crisis Intervention Unit: Emergency housing, food, clothing.
American Red Cross Nursing Program
150 Amsterdam Avenue nr West 67 Street. 787-
1000. Free courses for expectant parents, caring
for elderly and sick, first aid. *OPEN Mon-Fri 9am-
5pm.*
Board of Education: Public Affairs
110 Livingston Street. Brooklyn. (1-718) 596-
5030. General information and special information for preschool-age children, high-school and
adult education. Handicapped-resources information as well. *OPEN Mon-Fri 9am-5pm.*
Citizen's Advice Bureau
2050 Grand Concourse nr Burnside Avenue,
Bronx. (1-718) 731-0720. An information, referral
and problem-solving center regarding housing,
welfare, Medicaid, Social Services. *OPEN Mon-
Fri 10am-4:30pm.*
Mayor's Action Center
61 Chambers Street. 566-5700. Handles and ex-
pedites complaints regarding the public's interaction with city agencies. *OPEN Mon-Fri 9am-5pm;
till 8pm by phone.*
Salvation Army of Greater New York
50 West 23 Street. Information and referral: day,
255-9400; night, 677-0270. Social worker will
counsel on family problems, foster homes, adoption, alcohol and drug rehabilitation, senior-citizen
residence problems. Thirty-three centers
throughout the city; summer camps, a general
hospital in Flushing, Queens. *OPEN Mon-Fri
9am-4:30pm.*
United Neighborhood Houses
101 East 15 Street. 677-0300. Family and individual counseling, day care, nurseries and
senior-citizens program. *OPEN Mon-Fri 8:30am-
5:30pm.*

Abortion
New York City Department of Health
Bureau of Maternity Services & Family Planning,
125 Worth Street, Room 345. 566-7076. Information and referral to clinics; sets standards for abor-

tions; surveys facilities and handles complaints. *OPEN Mon-Fri 9am-5pm.*

Alcoholism

Alcoholics Anonymous
175 Fifth Avenue. 473-6200. Support system for alcoholics who want to stop.
Alcoholism Council of Greater New York
133 East 62 Street. 935-7075. N.Y. affiliate of the National Council on Alcoholism. Information and referral hotline, 935-7070.

Crime Victims

Crime Victims Compensation Board of New York State
270 Broadway nr Chambers St, 2nd fl. 488-5080. Financial and relocation aid, out-of-pocket medical expenses reimbursed for victims of crime. *OPEN Mon-Fri 9am-5pm.*
Crime Victims Hotline
577-7777. Bi-lingual counseling, advice and referral for crime victims. *OPEN 24 hours a day 7 days a week.*

Disaster Relief

American Red Cross in Greater New York
150 Amsterdam Avenue nr West 67 St. 787-1000. Financial assistance, food, shelter, and clothing given to meet family needs caused by disaster. *OPEN 24 hours a day, 7 days a week.*

Drug Abuse

Daytop Village
54 West 40 Street. 354-6000. Rehabilitational facilities to help addicts with drug and related problems. *OPEN 24 hours a day 7 days a week.*
New York State Division of Substance Abuse Services
2 World Trade Center. 488-3954. Referrals to appropriate treatment programs, clinics and hospitals. *OPEN Mon-Fri 9am-5pm.*
Odyssey House, Inc.
309 East 6 Street. 677-3200.
47 West 20 Street. 691-8510.
210 East 18 Street. 673-4320.
Respected residential rehabilitation drug abuse centers. Vocational training, re-education and integration into society stressed. *OPEN 24 hours a day, 7 days a week.*
Phoenix House Foundation, Inc.
253 West 73 Street. 595-5810, ext 282 & 283. City's largest drug-free residential rehabilitational program. Five facilities. Encourages responsibility, self-dependence and trust. Hotline (1-718) 787-7900. *OPEN 24 hours a day, 7 days a week.*

Rape

New York Women Against Rape
477-0819. Counseling and referral service for rape victims as well as victim advocacy. Group trains hospital staff and police in the care of rape victims. Hotline: 777-4000.
Sex Crimes Analysis Unit
233-3000. Trained policewomen counselors help victim of rape with guidance, support and referral. *24 hours a day 7 days a week.* Phone is always answered by a woman.

Tenants' Rights

If you have problems in a rent-controlled or rent-stabilized apartment, call: 488-4962 or 903-9500.
Metropolitan Council on Housing
137 Fifth Avenue. 598-4900. 77 East 4 Street. 673-1000. Advises tenants in rent-controlled and rent-stabilized apartments on their rights. Organizes tenants.

Index

Fishing, 112
equipment, 234
Flea markets, 213
Flowers, 30, 220–221
Flying, 112
Folk music, 29–35, 129
Food stores, 197–198
ethnic, 200
meat and fowl, 202–203
24-hour, 239
Football, 112
Fowl, 202
Fragrance, 195
Framing, 221
Free activities, 29–35
Furniture, 206–207
antique, 206
children's, 103
contemporary, 206–207
office, 228
rental, 103, 207
restoration, 207
wicker, 210–211
Furs, 185, 191
secondhand, 185

Galleries, art, 75–84
downtown, 79–81
Eastern art, 81–82
East Village, 81
photograph, 83–84
prints and graphics at, 82–83
SoHo, 79–81
uptown, 75–79
Games, 221
Gems, 221
Gifts, 221–222
personalized, 222
Glassware, 205
Gloves, 185
Golf, 112–113
equipment, 234
Gourmet shops, 201
Graveyards, 59–61
Gymnastics, 99, 113

Hair, removal, 196
treatment, 196
Hairdressers, 195–196
children's, 104
Handbags, 185–186
repair, 186
Handball, 113
Hardware, 222
Hats, 191
Haunted sites, 67
Health clubs, 222–223
Health food, 158, 201–202
Herbs, 202
Historic sites, 37–67
buildings and areas, 37–49
churches and syn-
agogues, 52–59
graveyards, 59–61

haunted, 67
statues and monuments, 49–52
Hobbies, 104
Hockey, 35, 113
Holidays
celebrations, 29–36
legal, 4
Home, 204–211
Horsedrawn carriages, 223
Horseracing, 32, 113
Horseshoe pitches, 113
Hospitals, 241–242
Hostels, 13
Hotels, 6–14
near airports, 13–14
bed and breakfast, 14
budget, 12–13
deluxe, 6–7
expensive, 7–10
hostels, 13
moderate, 10–12
YM/YWCA's, 13
Housewares, 207–208
Housing complaints, 243
Hunting equipment, 234

Ice, 223
Ice shows, 29
Ice skates, 234
Ice skating, 29, 99, 115, 234
Information centers, 2
Inoculations, 15
Instructions. See Schools; and specific crafts or sports

Jazz
clubs, 127, 130–131
festivals, 31, 32
Jeans, 181
Jewelry, 223–225
antique, 223–224
contemporary, 224–225
costume, 225
make-it-yourself, 225
repair and restoration, 225
Jogging, 115
Judo, 114

Karate, 114
Kids' New York, 94–108
Kindergartens, 108
Kitchenwares, 207
Kites, 104, 225
Kosher food, 104, 151, 164

Lacrosse, 114
Lamps, 208
Leather
cleaning, 186
clothing, 186, 191
goods, 225–226
Libraries, 4, 43, 75
Lighting, 208
Limousine rental, 226

Linens, 208–209
Lingerie, 186–187
Liquor, 236
Locksmiths, 24-hour, 239
Lost property, 16
Luggage, 225

Magazines, 5, 228
Magic
shows, 105–107
supplies, 104, 226
Makeup, 196–197
Maps, 18, 226
Markets, food, 200–202, 239
Martial arts, 114
Mastectomy boutiques, 187
Maternity wear, 187
Meats, 202–203
Memorabilia, 226
Military surplus clothing, 191
Mime theater, 105–106
Minerals, 221
Miniatures, 226–227
Movies
festivals, 34
first-run theaters, 123–124
revival theaters, 124
Murals, outdoor, 65
Museums
art, 68–74
art-and-science, 72
for children, 95–97, 106, 107
history, 72–74, 107
libraries, 4, 43, 75
science, 72
Music
blues, 31
cabaret, 127–128
for children, 105
church, 125
classical, 32
concert halls, 123
country/Western, 129–130
dance-band, 129, 131
disco, 132–133
folk, 29–35, 129–130, 132
free, 29–35
instruments, 227
jazz, 31, 32, 130–131
for parties, 229
rock, 32, 130, 131–132
schools, 100, 227
Music boxes, 227

Nail care, 197
Nature trails, 92
Needlework, 227–228
Newspapers
foreign and out-of-town, 228
New York, 5
Newsstands, 24-hour, 239–240

624-3475

Woosley

@ ITA.Net

MGW @ APL.Com

POSTSCRIPT

I would be pleased to receive your comments, good or bad, regarding this guide or any of the establishments listed. Also, if you wish to stay current of what's new in New York restaurants, shops, and the entertainment scene, a monthly newsletter will be available by subscription. Please address your letters to Marilyn J. Appleberg, *I Love New York Guide,* c/o Macmillan Publishing Company, General Books Division, 866 Third Avenue, 5th Floor, New York, N.Y. 10022.